A Time

To Speak

by Jeanne Manning

TURNER PUBLISHING COMPANY

Publishers of America's History

By: Jeanne Manning

Editor: Bill Schiller
Designer: David Hurst
cover photo by Gene Boaz Photography
author's photo courtesy of Richard Varnes

Copyright©1999 Turner Publishing Company

All rights reserved

Publishing Rights: Turner Publishing Company

This book or any part thereof may not be reproduced without the express written consent of the publisher and/or author.

This publication was produced using available and submitted materials. The author and publisher regret they cannot assume liability for errors or omissions.

Library of Congress Catalog No. 99-67628

ISBN: 978-1-68162-303-0

LIMITED EDITION

To my grandchildren

Catherine, Sam, Anne, Alex
Rachel, Nathan, Hannah and Simon

I hope this book will help you understand what happened in World War II, the unfathomable atrocities, the unparalleled courage, and above all, my generation's solidarity of purpose. May you find that same spirit of national unity, as well as unity with other nations, so that with compassion, understanding and tolerance, you will refuse to let similar horrors happen in the future.

Contents

PUBLISHER'S MESSAGE 5
DEDICATION 6
PREFACE 7

1. ON THE EVE OF WAR 10
2. THE ANSCHULUSS, THE MUNICHAGREEMENT AND
   CZECHOSLOVAKIA 21
3. JEWISH IMMIGRANTS 29
4. ATTACK ON POLAND; THE PHONEY WAR; INVASIONS IN
   NORWAY AND DENMARK 48
5. THE BLITZKRIEG 55
6. THE FALL OF FRANCE 64
7. DAILY LIFE 69
8. GROWING UP IN HITLER'S GERMANY 79
9. FRENCH PRISONERS OF WAR 93
10. ESCAPE 101
11. BATTLE FOR BRITAIN 114
12. BRITAIN'S DARKEST HOUR 128
13. BRITAIN'S BEST KEPT SECRET 134
14. EARLY RESISTANCE MOVEMENTS, PART I 142
15. EARLY RESISTANCE MOVEMENTS, PART II 148
16. EARLY RESISTANCE MOVEMENTS, Part II 158
17. OPERATION BARBAROSSA 168
18. PEARL HARBOR, DECEMBER 7 179
19. EXECUTIVE ORDER 9066 198
20. COMBATANTS AND NONCOMBATANTS 212
21. INDUSTRIAL MOBILIZATION: WOMEN IN THE WORK FORCE 226
22. WOMEN IN THE ARMED FORCES 242
23. THE WAR ON THE HOME FRONT 258
24. SOUTHEAST ASIA 265

25. ALLIED SUCCESS IN THE PACIFIC	281
26. ALLIED SUCCESS IN EUROPE; THE GERMAN REACTION	293
27. 1943: THE MANY FACES OF RESISTANCE MOVEMENTS	302
28. CITIZENS CAUGHT BETWEEN BATTLING TROOPS	320
29. AFRICAN AMERICANS IN WORLD WAR II	331
30. BURMA AND THE SOUTH PACIFIC	348
31. THE MAQUIS IN FRANCE	360
32. D-DAY, PART I, PREPARATION	377
33. D-DAY, PART II, SAINTE-MERE-EGLISE	384
34. D-DAY, PART III, THE LONGEST DAY	396
35. WAR IN THE AIR: DESTRUCTION ON THE GROUND	425
36. INTELLIGENCE ACTIVITY	436
37. ON THE WAY TO JAPAN	448
38. LIBERATION OF PARIS	462
39. PIVOTAL BATTLES: MARKET GARDEN, BATTLE OF THE BULGE, RIVA-BELVEDERE	471
40. THE HOLOCAUST, PART I, THE VICTIMS	491
41. THE HOLOCAUST, PART II, RESCUERS AND RESCUED	508
42. THE HOLOCAUST, PART III, THE WITNESSES	521
43. IWO JIMA AND OKINAWA	528
44. APRIL, A MONTH OF DEATHS	538
45. COLLAPSE, SURRENDER, AND VICTORY IN EUROPE	543
46. OPERATION DOWNFALL-THE MANHATTAN PROJECT	557
47. THE ATOMIC BOMB	564
48. SURRENDER V-J DAY	584
49. RETRIBUTION AND RESTORATION	588
POSTSCRIPT	601
ACKNOWLEDGMENTS	604
BIBLIOGRAPHY	606

A Time to Speak

PREFACE

I wrote this book for two reasons. *First*, university students in my French classes didn't understand the allusions to words like "Vichy," except as mineral water. And what was "l'exode," they wondered. I asked our children and older grandchildren what they had learned about World War II in history classes. Their knowledge was limited to a few important dates.

They were not the only ones whose knowledge was sketchy. In London, at the time of the 50th anniversary celebration of V-E Day, I heard a teenager tell his friend, 'You know, Churchill was president of the United States during the war." A French opinion poll, conducted by the Institut Français d'Opinion in July 1995, showed that 60% of the French between the ages of 18 and 24 didn't know what Vel d'Hiv [deportation of the Jews] was. When I asked two Japanese students studying in the United States to show me what their Japanese history books said about Pearl Harbor and Japan's involvement in the war, they translating from their books, "It says, Pearl Harbor happened. I only know that Japanese armies attack Pearl Harbor. It was a good fortune."

It seems to me that the younger generation deserves to know more about World War II, especially the personal side of the war as it was lived by ordinary people in many countries.

I was also inspired by a television announcement of the Gulf War. At the time, I was with a group of French friends I'd known for twenty-five years. The conversation turned to war, particularly World War II and it was obvious that our wartime experiences differed. We had each lived according to who we were, where we were from... according to our own unique sensibilities. For myself, there was the USO at Camp Carson where I played bridge and danced with the soldiers. I also worked for the V-12 Unit stationed on my college campus. My family had a Victory Garden and we had ration stamps.

On the other hand, my friend Marie-Madeleine recalled her first anatomy lesson, learned by seeing an eviscerated corpse lying in front of her on the road. At the time, she and her family were fleeing Nancy which was under attack by German and Italian planes.

World War II was *global*. It touched the lives of men and women, soldiers and civilians around the world. Thirty-five countries sent soldiers to the armed forces; millions of people of different nationalities experienced the events of the war.

I tried to talk to as many different people as possible. I interviewed about one hundred twenty-five people over a five-year period, and received copies of letters, unpublished diaries, memoirs and out-of-print books.

To supplement the personal interviews, I relied on the Imperial War Museum Sound Archive in London, the archives of the United States Holocaust Memorial Museum and the Manuscripts Division of the J. Willard Marriott Library at the University of Utah which houses oral histories of the Navajo Code Talkers.

I placed the personal accounts in the context of the specific historical event in order to provide background information and followed the chronology of the war. All the interviews and materials in French and the letters from the German POWs in the United States were translated by me.

We need these eye-witness accounts before it is too late. For human beings however, memory works in different ways. The intervening years have given us time to distill our experiences and their impact on our lives. The memory of events may have been distorted by movies or books about the war. We remember the past selectively; storing the good moments, or eliminating the painful details. Exact dates and precise locations are often sketchy.

I talked to one French woman who had lived and worked in Paris during the Occupation. She consistently told me, "I don't remember, I've lost my memory." She remembered there was nothing to eat and she wasn't happy, but the specific details were lost. Finally, she said, "The memories of the past, they have gone with the wind. It was very disagreeable with the Germans in Paris. I was not at all agreeable. We thwarted and annoyed the Germans. It is difficult, particularly when one doesn't want to think about them."

A Bataan Death March survivor confessed, "For a long time, I kept quiet. It took me a long time to say, 'Goddammit, you were there, talk about it! Help people!'"

A Time to Speak

A former member of De Gaulle's Free French made a strong statement for talking about World War II. "It is up to our generation to pass on to the current generation our experiences of the war years and what we have learned from it. When we are gone, there will be no one to tell the story. We learned the importance of liberty, peace and tolerance." And a Polish Jew who survived Nazi concentration camps said, "I feel the time has come for me to share my experiences with more people, Jew and Gentile. I hope that by doing so the raving idealism's fanatics and religious zealots among us won't force my experiences on others ever again."

The people from many different countries, cultures, and walks of life who contributed to this book do not recount the events in the same way. This does not mean their individual stories and reminiscences of World War II events don't affirm one another. In fact, they make the war human and personal. At best, they help us appreciate the far-reaching impact World War II had on our century. Their voices combine to give us a more complete understanding on the global perspective of World War II.

> *To everything there is a season, and a time*
> *to every purpose under the heaven:*
> *...a time to keep silence,*
> *and a time to speak.*
> -Ecclesiastes 3:1,7

CHAPTER 1

ON THE EVE OF WAR

Forty-six million soldiers and civilians died during World War II. That figure is more than the combined populations of Washington, D. C., London, Paris, Tokyo, Berlin, Moscow, and Rome. The outbreak of this war came twenty years after the end of World War I which purportedly was "the war to end all wars." During that twenty-year period, what were the collective circumstances and attitudes which set in motion the events leading to the most devastating war in the 20th century?

One can identify three probable causes:

- The fear of Bolshevism or Communism.
- The Treaty of Versailles at the end of World War I.
- The Great Depression.

These factors contributed, in varying measures, to the rationale for economic and military imperialism. In the case of the United States, the rejection of the Treaty of Versailles and the Great Depression led to attitudes of isolationism.

The Fear of Bolshevism

The Bolshevik revolution of 1917 toppled the Czarist regime. Czar Nicholas II abdicated, and a Provisional Government was set up. However, Bolshevik rule in Soviet Russia was not completely established until the end of the Russian Civil War (1918-1921).

From its beginnings, the Soviet Union was a planned society. When Josef Stalin succeeded Lenin in 1924, he began a socio-economic experiment whereby the economy was tightly controlled. The Great Purge from 1934-1938 gave Stalin political control. Political trials, based on mock charges, eliminated former leading members of the Party and State administration, leaders of the Red Army, and ultimately anyone accused of sabotage or disloyalty. Figures estimate that between seven and eight million people were arrested while another one million were executed. Some eight million were sent to slave labor camps.[1]

The dictatorial methods were condemned by the World War I Allies, particularly the repudiation of all foreign debts and the seizure of foreign property without compensation. At the end of World War I, there were powerful voices, including those of Winston Churchill in Great Britain and Marshal Foch in France, who urged intervention in the Soviet Union to put an end to Bolshevism and stop "this virus" from spreading into central Europe.[2]

Containment of the vast Soviet Union and the concomitant fear of Bolshevism became convenient rationales for military imperialism against the Soviet Union.

The Treaty of Versailles

At the Peace Conference in 1919 the Allies were represented by President Woodrow Wilson of the United States, Lloyd George, the Prime Minister of Great Britain, Georges Clemenceau, the Premier of France and Orlando, the Prime Minister of Italy. Germany was not represented. The Conference established the settlements and incorporated into the Treaty the covenant of the League of Nations.

The victors of World War I dictated harsh conditions. The most severe and difficult for Germans to accept was a clause of the Treaty which stated that Germany *was* responsible for the war and should make financial reparation. The Treaty also included other provisions which were equally distasteful: disarmament and reduction in the size of the German army; demilitarization of the Rhineland between Germany and France; interdiction of a political reunion with Austria; redistribution of overseas colonies and rights in China. The defeated Germans essentially had no choice but to accept these provisions (237 voted for and 158 voted against).

Hitler, the leader of the National Socialist German Workers' Party [*Nationalsozialistische deutsche Arbeiter partei*], the abbreviated term was Nazi, came into power on 30 January 1933 when he was named Chancellor by Field Marshal von Hindenburg, the German president. Hitler's program was to restore Germany to its former grandeur, to refuse to pay reparations, to renounce the Treaty of Versailles and the League of Nations, and to establish universal military service.

Italy, after the first World War, had hoped to share the victor's spoils with its Allies. The Allied promises were ignored. Italy did not get the Adriatic islands, and their claims to Istria and part of Dalmatia on the Yugoslav coast were ignored. Fiume, also on the Yugoslav coast was denied to Italy, causing Orlando to withdraw from the Peace Conference. Instead Italy entered the post-war period feeling cheated and humiliated. The country was beset with problems: barren lands, unemployment, poverty, and strikes.

After the first World War dozens of political parties sprouted in Italy, and in 1919 Benito Mussolini founded another political faction. He called his followers *Fasci de Combattimento* or "Combat Groups." The word "Fasci" stuck and the Fascist party eventually came to mean government by dictatorship. On 28 October 1922, he took office as Prime Minister. Two of his goals were to impose social order and to restore Italy to a more prominent place in European politics.

World War I left unforgettable traces on the French population which influenced their pre-war attitudes. France suffered enormous losses from World War I. Manpower losses from death or maiming left only four men out of ten capable of working and leading useful lives. Twenty years later, those survivors were still living in France; they remembered Verdun (the most murderous battle of World War I). Although the French under Pétain were victorious at Verdun, the slogan in France was "Never again." The French wanted a peace treaty with Germany which would make Germany powerless. They counted on reassurances from the Treaty of Versailles, disarmament and the buffer zone between Germany and France.

Lloyd George, speaking for Great Britain at the meeting of the Treaty of Versailles wished for several things: to make Germany both pacific and prosperous along with a prosperous Europe; to prevent Germany from going Bolshevik; to insure that Britain should have the largest possible share in German reparation payments and to convince the British public that Germany was treated with maximum harshness.[3]

In spite of President Woodrow Wilson's pleas to Americans to endorse the Treaty of Versailles and the formation of the League of Nations, on 19 November 1919 the Treaty of Versailles was defeated in the Senate. It was brought up for reconsideration in the next session and again failed the two-thirds majority necessary to ratify the treaty. In March 1920 the Senate returned it to the President with a notice of their inability to ratify the Treaty. The referendum on the Treaty of Versailles became an issue of the presidential campaign in 1920. Wilson lost to the Republicans by an overwhelming vote. The campaign against the League of Nations argued that the United States must return to the policy of neutrality (the policy of Monroe) and stay far away from entanglements in Europe. On 25 August 1921, three years after the Armistice, Congress by joint resolution officially declared the war with Germany at an end.[4]

Post-war attitudes in the United States are best characterized by conservatism in politics and laissez-faire in business. President Harding (1921-1923) called for a "return to normalcy;" President Coolidge (1923-1929) said "The business of the United States is business;" and President Hoover (1929-1933) believed that "rugged individualism" was basic to the "American system."[5] These attitudes reinforced the prevailing American notions of isolationism and material expansion.

A Time to Speak

In 1914 Japan took over the German railway, investments and installations in Shantung. After the Versailles Treaty, Japan occupied the Marianas, Palau, Caroline and Marshall groups. The country had both the opportunity and financial resources to consolidate relations with China.[6]

Black Thursday, the Depression

It began in New York City on 24 October 1929. Headlines in the *New York Times* told the dramatic story of the stock market crash and shrinking fortunes in the United States. Americans read, *"Prices of Stocks Crash in Heavy Liquidation; Total Drop of Billions; Many Accounts Wiped Out."* By 30 October the stock market rallied. The bankers were optimistic, but the general public was less so. Millions of Americans saw their savings wiped out by 9,000 bank closings from January 1930 to March 1933. The most devastating result of the crash of 1929 was unemployment and the resulting misery.

In the United States unemployment rose from 3 percent in 1925 to 25 percent in 1933. About 25,00 families and more than 200,000 young people wandered through the country, looking for food, clothing, shelter, and a job. People stood in bread lines and went to soup kitchens, run by charitable organizations.[7]

The thirties in Great Britain had the reputation of being "the devil's decade" with images of dole queues, hunger marches and a means test, the requirement that applicants for insurance had to show they were looking for work and later to declare their resources.[8] The worst years for unemployment were 1931 through 1935, and in the winter of 1932-1933, when unemployment reached its highest point. Almost 3 million workers, or 25% of the insured population, were out of work in Great Britain.

In France, the number of unemployed rose from almost zero in 1929 to 10,000 in 1930. Salaries were reduced, factories closed each summer for two or three months with no paid vacations. These lower salaries, the terrible deflation, and the general misery among the working class, farmers and small businesses led to a dramatic rise in unemployment from 160,000 in 1931 to 440,000 in 1936.[9]

The stock market crash of 1929 had disastrous effects on Germany. The country was unable to secure loans from abroad, therefore it was unable to pay back its war reparations. With diminished world trade, Germany could not export enough material to pay for imports of raw materials and food stuffs. Industrial production fell, factories closed, small businesses failed, one of Germany's principal banks closed which resulted in the closing down temporarily all of Berlin's banks (1931). Five million Germans were out of work, and they stood in long bread lines in every city.[10]

In Italy, unemployment went from 111,000 in 1925 to 324,000 in 1928 and by 1932, over a million Italians were unemployed. The cost of living in Italy was four times the level in 1913.[11]   Roy MacGregor-Hastie paints a rosier picture of unemployment in Italy. He cites a figure for unemployment of 813,000 in April 1931, compared to 2,652,181 unemployed in Great Britain.[12]

W. G. Beasley, speaks about the big drop in Japanese exports because of the world-wide slump. Exports fell from 37 percent in 1925-1929 to 14 percent in 1935-1939. While Beasley doesn't cite unemployment statistics, he does stress the catastrophic losses for farmers producing silk for the United States and for manufacturers and merchants.[13]

Only the Soviet Union escaped unemployment because of their controlled economy. In 1920, the Bolsheviks introduced labor conscription. The government offered incentives to the workers: wage incentives, bonuses of food and money, honorific titles and awards for the sake of building Socialism.

Soviet peasants were also given incentives, loans, cattle, and agricultural equipment to encourage collectivization of farms. Most farmers resisted the movement to join collective farms or State farms.[14]   They also had a strict system of rationing. One of the Communist slogans was "Those who do not work, should not eat."[15]

Employment Lines and Bread Lines

Statistics only tell half the story. People lost their jobs and their homes at a time when social security benefits were minimal or non-existent. Looking for work was either fruitless or the job choices were very limited. In fact, many American men, unsuccessful in finding work, enlisted in the military services.

No matter what country, those who grew up during the Depression years have vivid memories of the thin, unshaven men asking for food in exchange for mowing the grass, beating the carpets, washing windows; of the well-dressed business men selling apples on 5th Avenue in New York City; of hungry children, wearing hand-me-down clothes.

Mary Mulhollen in Wisconsin remembered, *"My father had lost his business. And I can remember my father trying so hard to get a job doing anything at that time. But I remember he had to take a coaster wagon and get whatever surplus food they handed out. . . I can remember my brother crying because you had to take whatever shoes. They gave him high-top boots. We weren't dressed like the other children. . . "*.

The situation was no different in Germany. Gottfried Fährmann was seven years old during the Depression. In his interview, he remembered:

". . . My other friend's father was also out of work. He earned a little by gathering up used toothpaste tubes. We helped him to cut up the tubes and remove the remaining contents, which he then sold as chalk. . .".[16]

A Time to Speak

In June 1936, France suffered massive country-wide strikes in all of the major cities. It is estimated there were 1,830,938 strikers. Men stood in line every day at unemployment windows, hoping for a job. Many remained unemployed for as long as two years. Later in 1936 the Popular Front voted paid vacations, the adoption of the English week, that is, Saturday afternoon off, socialized insurance and a retirement plan.

The French population was badly housed, with two-thirds of the houses with no sanitary installation or running water. Antide Guesnier lived in rural Brittany during the Depression. *"I came from a family of modest means. There was no electricity, running water didn't exist, you had to go to the well with a bucket... The fire in the fireplace, it wasn't very warm. I had wooden shoes to go to school...*

"Even before the war, in a borough, you ate the fruits and vegetables that were in the garden... There was a fish-monger who came on Friday. It was primarily salt cod. It was things like that we ate. Fresh fish, we didn't have very often."

A British woman, now in her eighties, still has a vivid image of the homeless men:

"Tramps, most of them, made their way on foot across country and slept in town in 'sheltered' housing, a doss-house [crude or makeshift bed]. And a very minute sum of money secured a place where you could slap a rope across the room and create a space. Or you could go to soup kitchens and hostels where you could have a bath and a bed and a bowl of soup and bread, maximum two nights stay. I lived for a while on the great North Road, north of London. The tramps used to knock on the door and beg for food. But they didn't want that so badly as some methylated spirits to fill up their empty bottles."

Although the Soviet government controlled employment, a major problem for the Bolshevik government was lack of food. Starving workers in the cities left the factories to look for food. They were called "bagmen" and roamed from village to village trying to buy or beg for food. On 22 January 1921 the small bread ration was reduced by one-third. In the countryside, drought, dust, and locusts added to farmer's difficulties. As a result, in February there were frequent peasant uprisings.

The Russian economic recovery plan was not enough to prevent large-scale famine. In response to Maxim Gorky's plea, the United States, the Vatican and the Quakers supplied relief missions. From August 1921 to June 1923 about 180 foreign relief workers arrived in Russia and fed approximately 22 million people.[17]

Italy escaped much of the unemployment and hunger through the early efforts of Mussolini to keep workers and peasants happy. He harangued them to think of themselves as a "united labour force." There were competitions with medals and trophies, tractor rides in which he participated. He stabilized rents and ordered local authorities to fix prices so that workers and peasants lived above the subsistence level.

His list of accomplishments was the envy of European countries: he drained the Pontine Marshes, inaugurated public works programs, built a chain of cities and brought 3 million acres into cultivation. By 1932, Italy's wheat crop was 70 percent greater than it was prior to World War I.

In 1927 Mussolini managed to revalue the lira, with an improvement of 30 percent over 1922. Industrial production rose from 72.4 percent in 1932 to 100 percent in 1936. No wonder when he appeared publicly, Italians greeted him enthusiastically and cried out, "Duce, Duce."[18]

Japan's colonies, Korea, Taiwan and Karafuto, were valuable resources which provided food supplies for Japan's growing population and industrial raw materials for its industries. This lasted until 1930 when the Japanese export market diminished due to the Depression. The Japanese response was to occupy Manchuria in 1931 and add it as a part of an economic block.[19]

According to one man, this military aggression meant jobs for everyone. *"For the first time, I was able to take care of my father. War's not bad at all, I thought. As a skilled worker, I was eagerly sought after and earned my highest wages in 1938, '39 and '40. There were so many hours of overtime! I changed jobs often, each new job better than the one before. . . . New factories were being built so rapidly."* [20]

TERRITORIAL EXPANSION

Military action, together with political treaties, was the counter-action to the conditions imposed by the Treaty of Versailles, to the containment of Communism, and to economic woes. Territorial expansion through war was a way to create economic self-sufficiency, fight the Bolsheviks, and foster national pride.

Japan

Japan had been the first aggressor nation, marching into Manchuria in 1931. For most Japanese, Manchuria aided their economic recovery, providing territory for Japan's increasing population, vital resources of coal and iron, and the potential for agricultural production, and cheap labor.

Later fighting broke out between Chinese and Japanese troops in 1937. Japan captured Shanghai; then took Nanking in a brutal siege known as the "Rape of Nanking" on 12 December 1937. In January 1939, Japan occupied the island of Hainan in the Tonkin Gulf; in May the Japanese and Soviets were locked in a vicious battle in Mongolia, eventually won by the Soviets.

Ishiwara Kanji, on the staff of the Kwantung Army, planned the military operation in Manchuria. He explained that Japan, acting through the Army, was destined to save the world from Marxism, become the champion of Asia, and embody Confucian righteousness.

In August 1936 the Hirota Cabinet further outlined its principles of expansion known as the Fundamentals of National Policy which encompassed the New Order and the Co-prosperity Sphere. The justification was that they would free Asia from tyrannical Western imperialism. By 1940 Japan's Greater East Asia Co-prosperity sphere intended to include French Indo-China, Thailand, Malaya, Borneo, the Netherlands East Indies, Burma, Australia and New Zealand.[21]

It was this grandiose plan of Co-prosperity which the Japanese saw being thwarted by the United States during the American-Japan negotiations which preceded Pearl Harbor. In their reply to the American demand that Japan withdraw its military forces from China and Indo-China, the Japanese negotiators charged that the United States sought to thwart Japan's New Order in East Asia.

Italy

Mussolini was the first European aggressor, invading Ethiopia in October 1935. As Mussolini's prestige grew in Europe, he concluded he could pursue his plan of a Latin alliance, a Mediterranean confederation. He wanted to extend Italian influence in North Africa. In 1923 the British ambassador in Rome recognized Italy's interest in the "Abyssinian region" [Ethiopia]. However in secret talks with Pierre Laval of France, he was told that Italy couldn't be active west of Ethiopia without risking France's influence in Algeria, Tunis and the Sahara. In January 1935 Mussolini signed a treaty with Laval, part of which mentioned Italy's natural interests in Libya and a secret protocol giving Italy the right to do what she pleased in Abyssinia.[22]

Mussolini's armies invaded Ethiopia, at the mouth of the Red Sea, in October 1935 and entered the capital of Addis Ababa in May 1936. Mussolini proclaimed Italy's right to territorial expansion and declared that Italy had a duty to civilize backward nations.

Mussolini had often sprinkled his public speeches with references to the Rome of Caesar. Now, with success in Ethiopia, he appeared on the balcony and proclaimed "the reappearance of the Empire on the hills of Rome."[23]

His action in Ethiopia created a rapport between the two dictators, Mussolini and Hitler, and Hitler praised Mussolini as "the leading statesman in the world." Hitler suggested that together Germany and Italy could conquer Bolshevism and the West. The Rome-Berlin Axis was proclaimed in 1936, although a military pact with Italy was not signed until later in 1939. Known as the Pact of Steel, it created a military alliance in which the two parties agreed to come to one another's assistance with military forces on land, sea, and in the air.

Distrust of Bolshevism was Mussolini's pretext to justify intervention in the Spanish Civil War in 1936. He announced that his role was and always had been to contain Communism. He intended to safeguard Italy's interests and those of the Mediterranean area against Communism. This was his excuse for sending troops to Spain in the Spanish Civil War to aid Francisco Franco against the "Red Republicans."[24]

Germany

Hitler wanted to see Germany as a world economic power, and he vowed to see that everyone had a job and enough money for food. To the many people without jobs, his promises had wide appeal.

German economic success was based on the development of their transportation system, automobile, airplane and naval industries, chemical development, metallurgy, and munitions factories. The rearmament program began in 1933 and absorbed the unemployment. From February 1933 to the spring of 1937, the number of unemployed fell from six million to less than one million. National production rose 102 percent from 1932 to 1937 and the national income doubled. These economic developments masked an economy directed toward the conquest of neighboring territories which meant war.

Hitler began to form alliances with countries sympathetic to his expansionist policies. In 1936, in addition to the Rome-Berlin Axis, Germany and Japan signed the Anti-Comintern Pact in 1936 against the Communist Third International (organized for the purpose of fostering a world revolution among the working classes). In 1937 Italy joined the pact, and the three countries declared Communism to be their common danger.

A cornerstone of Hitler's foreign policy was to "secure for the German people the land and soil to which they are entitled on this earth." In *Mein Kampf*, in the chapter, "Eastern Orientation or Eastern Policy," he had made it clear he was looking at Russian territory. *"If we speak of soil in Europe today, we can primarily have in mind only 'Russia' and her vassal border states."*[25]

Hitler's second goal was the reunification of the lands, inhabited predominately by Germans, into one state. In 1936, Hitler began the reunification, going first into the Rhineland (the left bank of the Rhine which was demilitarized as part of the Versailles Treaty at the end of World War I). Further territorial expansion included the annexation of Austria, where Austrians shared a common language with Germany and the Sudetenland, home of the Sudeten Germans who occupied the northwestern and southwestern parts of Czechoslovakia.

America's Neutrality

The United States, just coming out from the Great Depression, was more concerned about its economic recovery than entanglements in foreign politics. The

American public elected Franklin D. Roosevelt president in 1932 because he promised to alleviate some of the human suffering through the creation of his New Deal in 1933. His Democratic platform was clear: unemployment relief, labor legislation, unemployment and old age insurance, relief for farmers, development of power resources in the public interest, federal regulation of holding companies, securities exchanges, and utility rates, reciprocal trade agreements, a balanced budget, sound currency, and continuous government responsibility for human welfare. The aim was to give everyone a "new deal."

Congress also passed, in August 1935, the first law of neutrality, a move to keep the United States out of any European conflict. In Europe, on the other hand, tensions increased as governments warily watched Hitler's territorial expansion.

End Notes

1. M.K. Dziewanowski, *A History of Soviet Russia*, Englewood Cliffs, New Jersey: Prentice Hall, 1989, p. 202
2. Kitchen, Martin, *Europe Between Wars*, London and New York; Longman, 1988, pp. 76-77
3. R. A. C. Parker, *Europe 1915-45*, New York: Delacorte Press, 1967, p. 2, p. 7
4. Eliot Morison and Henry Steele Commager, *The Growth of the American Republic*, New York: Oxford University Press, 1942, pp. 494-495
5. *Ibid.*, p. 515
6. W. G. Beasley, *Japanese Imperialism, 1894-1945*, Oxford: Clarendon Press, 1987, p. 102, p. 142, pp.156-158
7. *World Book Encyclopedia*, 1996, Vol. 8 p. 340
8. John Stevenson, *British Society 1914-45*, London: Allen Lane, 1984, p. 266
9. André Nouschi, Maurine Agulhon, *La France de 1914 à 1940*, Collections Nathan - Université, 1974, Chapitre 4, pp. 53-71
10. William L. Shirer, *The Rise and Fall of the Third Reich*, New York: Simon and Schuster, 1960, p. 136
11. *Europe 1919-45*, p. 160
12. Roy MacGregor-Hastie, *The Day of the Lion*, Fascism in Italy 1922-1945, New York: Coward-McCann, Inc.1963, pp. 209-210
13. *Japanese Imperialism*, p. 211
14. *A History of Soviet Russia*, p. 126-127
15. *Ibid.*, p. 99
16. Johannes Steinhoff, Peter Pechel, Dennis Showalter, *Voices from the Third Reich, An Oral History*: Washington, D. C.: Regnery Gateway, distributed to the trade by Kampman,1989, xxxiii-xxxiv.
17. *A History of Soviet Russia*, p. 126, p. 130
18. *The Day of the Lion*, p. 187, p. 191
19. *Japanese Imperialism*, p. 155, p. 188, p. 199
20. Haruko Taya Cook & Theodore F. Cook, *Japan at War, An Oral History*, New York: The New Press, 1992, p. 49
21. *Japanese Imperialism*, p. 155, p. 179, p. 182, p. 203, p. 227
22. *The Day of the Lion*, pp. 217, 223, 240
23. *Ibid*, p. 237
24. *The Day of the Lion*, pp. 241-242
25. Mein Kampf, p. 654

CHAPTER 2

THE ANSCHULUSS, THE MUNICH AGREEMENT AND CZECHOSLOVAKIA

The first page of Hitler's *Mein Kampf* states "*German-Austria must return to the great German mother country, and not because of any economic considerations. No, and again, no; even if such a union were unimportant from an economic point of view; yes, even if it were harmful, it must nevertheless take place. One blood demands one Reich. Never will the German nation possess the moral right to engage in colonial politics until, at least, it embraces its own sons within a single state. Only when the Reich borders include the very last German, but can no longer guarantee his daily bread, will the moral right to acquire foreign soil arise from the distress of our own people.*" Thus, on 11-12 March 1938 Austria ceased to exist and was named "Ostmark."

Watching the Demise of Austria

B. L. was in Austria in the summer of 1937, sharing an apartment with American friends, located within walking distance of the University of Vienna where they studied German. Everything was calm. They were innocent Americans enjoying life, the theater, the opera, winter skiing; they were making plans for summer travel in 1938.

In letters she wrote to her family, B. L. described the political changes she observed.

"*We were aware [January 1938] that there were Nazis around and we were very careful not to criticize anything. The Austrians we knew were very anti-Nazi. And I remember one of them said, 'We are Austrian and speak the same language, but that is all.'*"

By February she and her friends began to see the differences.

"*On February 15, I wrote that we had been hearing scattered rumors of a future war, but Chancellor Schuchsnigg was trying his best to keep the Nazis under control, although somehow Hitler had managed to get Nazis into his cabinet, 50-50 percent.*" [In a meeting at Berchtesgaden with Hitler, 12 February, Dr. Kurt von Schuschnigg, the Austrian Chancellor, had to accept Hitler's terms to turn over the Austrian government within a week. Schuschnigg responded that Austria had made concessions but would never voluntarily give up his independence. He suggested a plebiscite, set for 13 March, in which the Austrian people could vote *Ja oder Nein?* for a free, independent, and united Austria. Hitler, however, decided on a military take-over on 12 March.]

A card, written to her brother on 10 March, reported the situation in Vienna.

"It seems Vienna is much quieter than the rest of Austria. The Nazis are not allowed to openly demonstrate. A notice at the university forbids all Nazi colors and salutes and greetings in the building and today police are standing around everywhere inside and out to break up groups. But on the street a good number of people still greet each other with the Nazi salute and Heil Hitler. And every evening on the Kamtner Strasse groups of young people walk up and down returning their greeting. It looks at first as though everyone on the street is doing it, but it is only certain ones who are demonstrating and sometimes you could recognize the same people coming back and forth. Last night the police were closing off the street to stop it. But the police are very polite and nice about it and don't want to start any trouble. Two weeks from today, there will be a big German day. However, we also see large red and white Austrian flags, with groups singing Rot, Weiss, Rot bis zum Tode' [Red, White, Red until death, those being the colors of the Austrian flag].

"Later I wrote mother on March 12, 'Last night we were quietly standing in the opera listening to an excellent performance oblivious to everything that had happened to poor old Austria. Between acts we stood outside and watched parades that had been going on for days. And after the opera we were confronted with the news that the German Army had crossed into Austria and that Schuschnigg had resigned. What a blow! and the city was going wild, yelling, shouting and parading with torch lights, flags and trucks and motorcycles, thousands of people. There was a steady buzz of Heil Hitler all up and down the street. We stayed long enough to get a bit worried, then went home to sit and think about it. Karl and Willy, our two Austrian Jewish friends were absolutely ill. They love their Austria so much, but being both Jews, they have to leave. The paper under Nazi publication makes everything sound very quiet and natural. But right now Nazi planes are flying in big squadrons over Vienna, but I'm sure there won't be any fighting.'"

B. L. remembered seeing Hitler when he entered Vienna on 14 March.

"Two days after the opera, he [Hitler] came to Vienna himself in a big motorcade. The streets in Vienna were lined with Nazis in uniform and they had a meeting in the courtyard of the Hofburg and I saw him standing up in an open car with these mobs around him, yelling and shouting. I remember I had a little camera and I got up on a running board of a car, and I took a picture of him. This was such a blow. These dumb Austrians, letting themselves be carried away. And Vienna, the cultural center of Eastern Europe. It was amazing. On the radio, he was so convincing. We were very leery of it, but when the country had been struggling eco-

nomically, it would be hard to resist somebody who said, 'Everything is going to be wonderful and everybody will have work.' The Austrian people were charming; but they had the attitude of 'You can't do anything, so just go along.'"

With her family urging B. L. to come home, and the University closed, she and her friends left Austria in June 1938.

After his triumphant arrival in Vienna, Hitler traveled throughout Austria stirring up enthusiasm for the 10 April plebiscite. The vote was 99 percent in favor. After the plebiscite, Hitler called in General Keitel, Chief of the High Command of the Armed Forces to discuss "Case Green," the code name for the surprise attack on Czechoslovakia.

The Munich Agreement

Great Britain's policy of appeasement toward Germany was conceived as a peaceful solution to Germany's grievances over terms of the Versailles Treaty. There were some in Parliament who agreed that the Treaty of Versailles was, in some measure, unfair and that German claims to unify ethnic Germans were justified.

Neville Chamberlain, who became Prime Minister in May 1937, chose to look for negotiated solutions to Germany's grievances. He hoped to persuade Hitler to achieve his aims through peaceful methods. Chamberlain believed Britain could avoid war with Germany and was convinced of his successful ability to negotiate. In this belief, Chamberlain was encouraged and flattered by Hitler's strategy. Hitler publicly mentioned that keeping Chamberlain in office was a condition of peace.

On the other hand, Winston Churchill, the Conservative chief whip, argued, at the time of the *Anschluss*, that Hitler should be stopped from further expansion and should be warned that Britain would join in resisting further German expansion. In 1935, Churchill urged an increase in the strength of the air force and the navy to assure Britain's protection. And in 1938, he again urged the government to warn Germany that Britain would join France and the Soviet Union if Germany attacked Czechoslovakia.

The German minority of Sudeten Germans, living in the border regions of Sudetenland, were used as a ploy to enable Hitler to bring Czechoslovakia under German domination. Earlier in March 1938, Konrad Henlein, with Hitler's blessing, demanded certain concessions to Sudeten Germans, concessions which they knew would be unacceptable to the Czech government. Two months later, Hitler's May directive left no doubt about his intent. "It is my unalterable decision to smash Czechoslovakia by military action in the near future."[26]

There were stories of the Czech mobilization and Czech terror against Sudeten Germans, as well as stories of the concentration of German troops on the

Czech border. Henlein, the Sudeten leader of the Sudeten German Party broke off negotiations with the Czech government.

Neville Chamberlain called for a peaceful resolution to the crisis. On 29-30 September 1938, the Munich Conference, between Chamberlain, Mussolini of Italy, and Edouard Daladier, the French Prime Minister, and Hitler was held. Hitler got what he wanted, the territory along the northwestern and southwestern border between Czechoslovakia and Germany, in which 2,800,000 Sudeten Germans lived. There was no participation by the Czech government, and the Soviet Union was not invited in spite of the fact that they had mutual assistance treaties with both France and Czechoslovakia.

Chamberlain returned triumphant to London where he declared, "It is peace in our time." Churchill, on the other hand, criticized the Munich pact as nothing more than promises.

The Czech president, Eduard Benes, resigned and fled to Great Britain where he set up a government in exile. In October, autonomy was demanded for Slovakia. By 15 March 1939, the German army occupied the Czech lands and proclaimed the Protectorate of Moravia and Bohemia.

In fact, the Munich Agreement only put off full-scale war, something that many people knew was bound to happen later.

The Sudeten Germans
Prague in 1939

A Sudeten German woman (Mrs. A. H.) lived in Prague in 1939, and returned for her first visit since she fled the former Czechoslovakia at the end of World War II. She explained the complicated relations between the Germans and the Czechs.

"President Wilson thought he founded an ideal place, and he wanted the seven and one half million Czechs and the three and a half million Germans, Hungarians and Russians, whoever lived in that state, to have an ideal state." [A reference to the peace treaty after World War I which created Czechoslovakia from the break-up of Austria-Hungary in 1918.]

"I was in Czechoslovakia in 1938, and I lived in Prague in 1939. My father was a banker with the Kreditanstalt der Deutschen. He was one of the Direktors of the main office. The bank had eighty-four branches all over the Sudetenland. Although we lived in Sudetenland and were referred to as 'Sudeten Germans,' we called ourselves 'Deutsch-Bohmens' or Bohemian Germans, Austrian Germans.

"The history from my standpoint: we weren't happy and we felt a little bit oppressed. For centuries it went back and forth. We called it taferl politique (taferl means street signs) because sometimes the German street names were on top and

sometimes the Czech names were on top. Also the Germans thought we couldn't even speak German and thought we were some sort of gypsies. They looked down on us.

"Somehow my father was imprisoned because the Czechs had made special rules against German banks. They said the bank did something wrong according to these new rules. A Czech lawyer was able to get him out after two months, but there was no other reason but being German.

"The young people I see in the streets, they have no idea. They know what they learn in school and they probably learned that the Germans were horrible and just came in 1939 and 1940. But we were here for centuries. Many of the kings of the house of the Premyslids married German princesses. The kings called the Germans into the country in 1290 and even earlier. We were here for centuries and centuries, and the Czechs were here not much longer. There were these tribes, first there were the Markomans, then they moved to Bavaria; Boii was the other tribe. Bohemia is called after these Boii. I had Czech ancestors. There was an intermingling. I think the Czechs would have been able to live with the Sudeten Germans. We could have arranged the whole thing over the years. . .

"The Czech Sokol [sokol translates 'falcon'] and the German Deutscher Twinverein [German Sports Association] were the hotbeds of nationalism. If you were young and German, you were supposed to be a member of the German party, and if you were a Czech, you were supposed to be a Sokol."

When Czechoslovakia became part of Germany, the Nazis made no allowance for them. They were subject to the same restrictions as the Czechs and the same obligations as all Germans, participating in the German work force. Above all, tensions still existed between the Czechs and the Germans.

"I worked and finished school in Liberec (Czech), in German it was called Reichenberg, about 120 miles from Prague. I was only in Prague for visits to see my grandmother and my great-grandmother.

"There was a problem coming back and forth. You needed a certain permit to come to the 'Protectorate' as they called it. And at one time, I told somebody, my aunt, my cousin, that I went to the Petrin, that hill next to the Petschek Palais and had a date and was sitting on the park bench. Later I found out that thieves were lying under the park bench, waiting for lovers, and they stole my handbag, and I had everything in there, especially those permits and my keys. I ran to the Czech police and they told me, 'Who was the young man you were with?'

"So I had no passport and had to go to the Gestapo which was across from the theater, the big Petschek Palais. I had to go to these horrible people. To be honest, we did not like the Germans. They were Reich Germans [the Germans living within the borders of the German territories]. Nazi Germans were the ones who belonged to the Nazi party. Maybe after the war all Germans were called Nazis by the Allies. The Reich Germans had a certain attitude which we did not like and still don't like. So I had to go to these awful people, and they were very mad at me. They said, 'You gave the enemy, and they said the Czechs were the enemy, valuable papers.' And they scolded me. But what could I do, I didn't have it any more and I had to get out because I was more afraid of my mother and father than of the Gestapo. So they gave me new papers. No, it wasn't easy.

"Later, I had to go to the Arbeitsdienst, the German work force, working for a year in fields, but that was in Reich Germany, not here in Bohemia. Everybody had to work, but I could have gotten out of it, but again, this Nazi that my father went to ask if I could work on our own farm, said, 'No.' He didn't let my father sit down or anything. The Nazis were not pleasant people. I got paid twenty pfennigs a day, five cents. . .

"Then I was only on and off in Prague, and when I was here, you had the feeling it was not a desirable place for Germans anymore. I remember once I went to movies and it seemed to me that I and my boyfriend in his uniform [he was in the German army] were the only Germans all around and it was an eerie, dark feeling. It was not good.

"Another time I went swimming in the Moldau. I had a date with somebody. I was sitting there, and a young man came to me and asked me if I would have a date with him. And I said, 'You wouldn't want to have a date with me because I am German.' My accent was such that he did not recognize it. I always swallowed the endings if I wasn't sure. And he said, 'Ya, he could see that.'"

After May 1945 Germans had to wear a white arm-band and Sudeten Germans had trouble either with the Germans or with the Czechs. Mrs. A. H., armed with a pistol given her by a boyfriend, fled in a horse and wagon from Kadan to Tepla on 8 May 1945, marching toward the west with French and English prisoners of war. Eventually, she bribed some Czech officer to give her papers so she could leave Czechoslovakia. She went from Tepla to Tirschienreuth in Bavaria, then crossed the Sumava mountains in the winter of 1945.

"And I was by myself. Here of course in Prague, all these things come back to me what happened to the Germans, but I don't want to talk too much about it. It is sad enough that it happened.

"That is a big issue now [1996], that is the one issue that arouses the national feelings because the Sudeten Germans, I call myself a Sudeten German because everybody else does, the Sudeten Germans want the Czechs to apologize. We don't want anything else, we just want an apology for being sent away. In the course of the expulsion, the Sudeten Germans say 250,000 were killed. I do not know. I know a lot of people were killed.

"That we were not killed just being German, was really a miracle." [A reference to the cruel and forced expulsion at the end of the war of the German minority from inside the borders of Czechoslovakia. The Potsdam Conference on 1 August 1945 endorsed the transfer of Germans from Czechoslovakia. About 2.7 million Germans were expelled. Some estimates say there were approximately 6,500 Sudeten Germans murdered and 20,000 died as a result of exhaustion and suffering.][27]

Hitler's foreign policy of "a greater Germany for all Germans" continued to become more and more evident within German itself. The Nazi government's restrictions on Jews living in Germany which began in 1933 grew more strident and forced Jewish families to emigrate.

End Notes

26   William L. Shirer, *The Rise and Fall of the Third Reich,* New York: Simon and Schuster, 1960 p. 365

27   B. L. has retired from a long career of college teaching. Mrs. A. H. currently lives in Ohio.

CHAPTER 3

JEWISH IMMIGRANTS

Part of Hitler's vision of the new Germany was to unite all Germans, that is, those of German blood. This meant the exclusion of Jews from daily life in Germany.

To consolidate internal political authority, the Reichstag (the German imperial parliament) passed the Enabling Act, officially the "Law for Removing the Distress of People and Reich" (23 March 1933). It gave Hitler, as Chancellor, and his cabinet exclusive legislative power for four years. From then on, Hitler was the dictator of the Reich, able to rule by decree, to name members of the Nazi Party to government posts, and when president Paul von Hindenburg died, to become president. Hitler was the law, ready to mold Germany according to the ideas already expressed in *Mein Kampf*, a Germany that would become "lord of the earth" by being a community of homogeneous members of the Aryan race.

Through a series of decrees from 1933 to 1939, Hitler began to drive Jews from participation in everyday German life. Among his early actions was the 1 April 1933 announcement of the boycott of Jewish shops, forcing all of them to close. Then he eliminated all of the Jewish judges, as well as non-Jewish judges whose loyalty to Hitler and the Nazi party was questionable. He passed the Civil Service law of 7 April 1933, and later, on 26 January 1937, a new Civil Service law. Judges were no longer independent, but clearly expected to support the National Socialist State. They could be dismissed for "political unreliability" and forced to join the League of National Socialist German Jurists.

Another step taken by Hitler was the public burning of 20,000 non-German books on 10 May 1933, including books by such German authors as Thomas Mann, Albert Einstein, Erich Maria Remarque, as well as foreign authors, Jack London, Upton Sinclair, H. G. Wells, Sigmund Freud, André Gide, Emile Zola and Marcel Proust.

The Reich Press Law, 4 October 1933 forced several newspapers out of business. The first was the *Vossische Zeitung*, one of Germany's leading newspapers.

Jews had been restricted from the German school system since 1933. Hitler's decrees began to affect other aspects of German Jewish lives. In 1934 the German schools were nazified. Textbooks were rewritten and curricula changed to reflect Hitler's philosophy; teachers had to take an oath to "be loyal and obedient to Adolf Hitler."

In 1935, the Nuremberg Laws were announced and deprived the Jews of German citizenship, confining them to the status of "subjects."

Three Immigration Stories

As a result of Hitler's drastic measures, many German Jewish families prepared to immigrate to other countries, the wives to find passage on ships, temporary housing and food, the men to begin new careers.

Three women whose families emigrated from Germany tell stories that are at times painful, humorous, and always courageous. They were from families more conscious of being German citizens than being Jewish in race or religion. Sometimes as young girls, becoming adolescents, they were protected from knowing exactly what was going on politically in Germany. Yet, they were aware of a certain tension in the air, an under-current of fear, an uneasiness within their families. Grateful to escape, they eventually arrived in the United States, where life was new and strange.

1933, Berlin to England to the United States

Bine Hirsch's family left Germany in 1933 and she grew up a refugee child in Great Britain.

"My parents lived and were married in Berlin. At the end of 1933, with the rise of Hitler, my father lost his job at the Vossische Zeitung, a philosophical, scientific and political intellectual magazine, founded by Lessing, the German poet. It was the first paper that Hitler closed because it was an intellectual paper.

"My father went off to England by himself because there was a whole branch of my grandmother's Lehmann family in England. He found he could get another doctoral degree in Cambridge as there was an academic association set up for academics leaving the continent.

"All this time, my mother, my brother and myself were in Germany. I am two, and I do not have memories of that time, but I have read some of the correspondence between my parents, and between my father and his mother.

"After my father left Berlin, my mother had given up our apartment, sold the furniture, and moved in with her mother-in-law, my grandmother. It was a mutual arrangement, they liked each other. My mother would go to work when someone needed a temporary secretary because she needed the money (that came out in the correspondence)...

A Time to Speak

"My mother, my brother and I leave Berlin in September 1934, while it was still permitted: we were allowed to take household goods with us.

"I grew up in Cambridge. I was a refugee child, but in a different sense. We were living in an academic community, where people spoke lots of different languages. The children on the street spoke English. There were people who took us in, our 'sponsor' family, the Turners. It was a lovely period. This is mid-30s.

"The year before the war was definitely different. Two things were happening that I was aware of. There was more tension, there were many more people coming and going, and a different sense of alertness.

"In 1938 my father got a job at the University College at Leicester. For a while he commuted, but eventually we moved to Leicester to a house which my parents were buying.

"In the summer of 1938 I went to Wyggeston Girl's School, a public school, and my brother went to the Wyggeston Boy's School. I remember being very clear that I spoke English and I was English because that whole ambiance was different in Leicester.

"My father's oldest sister denied she was Jewish. She was a German, an educated German academic, and that has nothing to do with religion. I am very English. I go to school in England. I know how to hold my knife and fork the English way. I eat English food at school, but at home we eat continental food. The language at home is very mixed. There is some French because my parents had French friends. At that point, I am very English, wanting my parents to be English.

"When war breaks out [1939], I remember the radio broadcasts, everybody tense around a radio, everybody constantly tuning in. This was all summer long. . . The BBC had its regular broadcast and with medium wave and long wave, you could hear Germany, Holland, France and get news from lots of different places. There was a lot of discussion. There wasn't discussion at school or on the playground, 'You are German.' That comes later. The other children, at that point, weren't clued in either.

"War breaks out and this immense tension, the only thing I can think of is that sense of silence that comes with the announcement. I was not really understanding, but there was a silence because what could you say when you heard this news. I remember this silence, trying to find out why the adults are so disturbed. Something had changed. The mail still came in with all of the wonderful world stamps. And then that stops. That was a signifier. The other thing that happened almost immediately was the identification that we were German Jews that had never been there before, identified both at school and also at home. Everybody who was not British born had to turn in cameras and radios at the police station.

"We were not allowed to have short wave or regular radios; we could go to the neighbors next door. That was part of my awareness. The very first week. There is this hush and a pause. All the drills we had been through, how to put on your gas mask, how to go to the safe places, how to go to the shelters, how to listen for the sirens and to this day, I cannot bear to hear a siren. One of the things that comes to me is that sense of quiet. We didn't have a telephone. We did have music, word games, puzzles, but there was a quiet with it. Then out of this quiet comes eventually a lot of noise, planes bombing.

"I think at that time I really didn't understand what being a German Jew meant because I hadn't been brought up in any Jewish belief system. I was not put upon by the girls. I had the same uniform, I spoke very good English. One didn't go visiting to people's houses as casually as later on. We played on the street. I don't remember being jeered or taunted. Whether that is repressed or forgotten, I don't know. I do remember later knowing that I was German and Jewish.

"In the spring of 1940, anybody who is not British born is rounded up and put in internment camps until questions can be sorted out: How long have you been in England? What is your background? Who are you? Who will vouch for you? What are you doing here? Where is your family?

"I remember my father going from the house with a suitcase, it was his turn to go. I remember going to my teacher, going up the steps to the dais and telling her that my father had to leave because the police have come to get him. And I think, at that point, that I understand that the other girls, their fathers had gone to the army, the air force and the navy and my father has gone somewhere else. I think I was probably the only German descendant child in that classroom.

"My father was sent to the Isle of Man, full of residence hotels and beautiful beaches. . . The government took over the entire island and put barbed wire around the entire island and put internees inside it until things got sorted out. My father was only there for a few months.

"I remember missing my father, but life simply went on. At school, if there was a bombing raid, we went into the shelters. Everybody was the same. I wasn't treated differently in school.

"A friend, a German mathematician from Berlin (who came to England to be a maid in a household because that was the only way she could get out of Germany) and an English friend of hers have a school for young girls in Potters Bar, a suburb in northern London.

"My life changes quite dramatically when I, as a nine year old, go away to boarding school. The school had been moved from London to an empty country estate, Morcott Hall, Rutland. [1941] Mostly there were children who were sent to the country because it wasn't safe in the cities. . .

"This is where I know I am a German Jew because I do not go to church. I am not an Anglican. The first thing at school in the morning in England is Assembly, with readings from the King James Bible. I do not go to church with the other girls at school... I knew I was Jewish and Jews don't go to church. I'd go inside the church, but I didn't go to a service. I don't remember that the children said anything about the fact that I didn't go to church.

"The sense of otherness is clear at boarding school. I was different. My parents were not in the war. We never spoke German. I spoke French. German was not taught at school...

"A club of Jewish people from all over Europe was formed in Leicester, where there were lectures, skits, theater and musical evenings. For the first time in my life I met some orthodox Jews.

"Towards the end of the war in Europe, movie houses started to show newsreels of concentration camps. My parents put my head down so that I could not see the horrible pictures. That must have been in February or March of 1945. I probably saw the first pictures of a concentration camp when I was 50 years old." [29]

A Circuitous Route from Germany to the United States, 1938

Marian Kreith's family left Germany, lived in Cuba and arrived years later in the United States.

"I guess there was this constant feeling of fear and a general unease. My parents tried to protect me from the knowledge of what was going on, but it was just impossible.

"And then came the night when all of the Poles were rounded up. It was in connection with Kristallnacht or very shortly after. I don't quite remember. My grandmother used to live with us and she was from Poland. And so at seven in the morning, a policeman came, wanting to take her. She and I shared a room, and I remember being half-naked and there was this policeman walking in. The fear and the embarrassment, being totally, totally at the mercy of these forces, continuously, continuously. As it happened, she had left for Belgium a few weeks earlier. She was gone.

"I wished I could do what other kids were allowed to do. This fear of being pushed out, being left out continuously. We lived in an apartment house, kind of interesting. My parents were very, very conservative, but they had moved into this fairly modern apartment. It was on the second floor and it overlooked the low-slung house where this friend of mine was playing with a group of people. I was literally hanging out my kitchen window, watching them continue to play. I was no longer permitted to play with them. There was no contact any more. I remember asking my mother whether I looked very Jewish or whether she thought I could 'pass,' because I badly wanted to go ice skating, and Jews were not allowed in the rink.

"And another thing, when I was about six or so, we were no longer allowed to go to any public schools, so I had to go to a parochial school and the parochial school was a good thirty minute walk and that was pretty scary back and forth. Walking to school was very difficult because one was attacked verbally or with stones.

"We happened to live on one side of town and most of the Jewish community lived on the other side of town, so there was a kind of double isolation, first the isolation from the Gentile world in general and then the isolation from most of the Jewish community. So there was this double distancing, this total sense of a loneliness most of the time.

"Sometimes, I would visit Jewish friends and be greeted with tear-stained faces and worried looks; their father had been ordered to give up a practice, or forced to close a shop.

"Soon reports about smashed synagogues and physical violence against Jews became more and more frequent, so it was decided to accept my Uncle Joe's invitation to come to Belgium (late 1938) and wait for our American visa there.

"My father had already gone to Belgium. It was always scarier for the men at that point, who were more likely to be picked up than the women and children, so it was important to get him out.

"So my mother had to take care of putting everything we had together, in what was known as 'lifts' [a lift van]. They were enormously large boxes, and belongings of people were put in these boxes and then they were shipped to where the people were hoping would be their final destination. And our lift was shipped to Atlantic City because that's where we were hoping we might just end up. And my mother took care of that and just as we were leaving for Belgium, I remember she had beautiful little hand-made bags and she came home with two of these bags filled with Belgian money. She said, 'It's very heavy, but it's not worth very much.' She was given all kinds of little centime pieces. I remember her standing there with these bags. We took the train and we rejoined my father.

"We stayed in Brussels '38, '39, and '40 with my uncle, who in the summer of 1939, left for Canada.

"I went to school, French school. This little town was called St. Pieters Leeuwsteenweg, not quite a village, like a suburb of Brussels. There was the most magnificent bakery with the most magnificent cramiques (small buns with raisins). The kids were all right, the teacher was excellent, you know the European primary, very good teachers, mostly women, and I did learn French. My last year of school was in Brussels during the war from 1940 to 1941, but it was tough, tough again in terms of total isolation. I was the only Jewish kid in that class. I really don't know to what extent they knew. That year would have been equivalent to 8th or 9th grade. It was the last decent year of schooling I had.

A Time to Speak

"In May 10, 1940, Hitler invaded Belgium, and the Belgians couldn't resist that much. But what they did do, as a gesture, because they had nothing else to do, they collected all of the Germans in Brussels, and they were all Jewish refugees, but they were German, so you take these people and get rid of them. That's the one thing you can do. The government asked all men of German origin to come to the Mairie, the local courthouse to register. What was thought to be just a registration turned out to the government's attempt to isolate potential spies. The men, all of them refugees like my father, were herded into cattle cars marked Espions allemands (German spies). Whenever the cars stopped on their way to detention camps in southern France, they were pelted with stones and rotten tomatoes. All this, of course, we found out much later. All we knew at the time was that my father was not coming back from the 'Mairie,' but we had no idea of what had become of him.

"We then tried to leave Belgium in this little four-seater, a brand new car lent by my uncle's Belgian partner, nine people, six different nationalities. There was Omama Bertha, my father's mother, Tante Margot with her husband Maurice and baby Abel who was about two, my father's cousin Gerda, Boris, a nephew of Uncle Joe's, my sister Ada and I. Of course, my mother drove. Everyone was trying to get into France. There were streams and streams and streams of refugees with carts. Every so often, German airplanes would swoop down on us and there was a panicked scramble into the bushes by the side of the road. Food, I do not remember. I don't think we had that much with us. I don't know how long we were on that trip, maybe a week, two weeks. Every time we came to a border town, one of the six different nationalities in our group of nine was not permitted to pass.

"But when we finally did get to La Panne, on the Belgian side of the border, there was a small hotel away from the sea that did take us in and they were still serving food. We got there just about two days before the battle of Dunkirk and that was in June, I think. We tried to get across at two or three different frontier points, and we were stopped each time. The milling humanity of those lines trying to get across; Belgian, French and British soldiers milling around, totally demoralized by not knowing what they were supposed to do. I was roaming the streets, picking up discarded gas masks and thinking it was great fun to come back to the hotel wearing one. Since there had been an air-raid alarm while I was gone, my mother was white with anxiety and furious with me for being so playful and staying away so long.

"Another time I went around, I think Boris was with me, begging for petrol from the soldiers and we were able to collect a few gallons. The Germans were advancing and air-raids were frequent. During one of these, Tante Margot was hit in the wrist by a piece of shrapnel that came flying in through an open window. My mother managed to get her to one of the emergency hospitals that had been set up in the big hotels by the sea. That night was the battle of Dunkirk, a few miles down the coast. We were all on the floor of the dining room, with mattresses on top of us, trying to tell from the noises outside what was going on. The din continued until early morning when we soon heard the sound of the goose-stepping German infantry marching in. When a German soldier, with his coffee mug, sat down among the mattresses in the dining room, my Uncle Maurice said, with undisguised bitterness, 'Well, now we can all start speaking German again.' There was nothing to do but to return to Brussels.

"When we reached Brussels again, we found that the Germans had already occupied my uncle's house. But they had been instructed to be civil, to counteract the horrible memories the Belgians had of them from World War I, so they let us take some of our personal belongings with us, and we moved into a boarding house.

"We still had no idea what had happened to my father and even after we came back to Brussels, for months and months, we didn't know what had happened to him. And our getting together again was one of these things, a sort of a sixth sense, that pervaded much of the occupied era. You did develop a sixth sense of whom to trust. It didn't always work, but many, many a time, whom to trust and whom not to trust was a matter of life and death. And how did my father and my mother communicate? He was in a camp in southern France, in unoccupied southern France and we were in Brussels. I don't know how they communicated.

"And then she went to Antwerp on these very mysterious trips. She took her life in her hands. And by that time, the Germans were beginning to show their true colors. At the beginning, they were told, 'Hey you did a lot of mischief here, be nice.' The memory of 1914 was still strong. So back and forth between Brussels and Antwerp. I wouldn't have had the guts. She was able to make contact with this underground and she was able to get us out of Belgium.

"We tried twice. The first time the group got together, and just as we boarded the train, we were told, 'Not this week, there is a razzia, when Germans grabbed a group of refugees in a hotel. So we were told, 'Don't go this week, go back home.' The apartment was maybe still there, maybe not still there. We kind of spent this week in absolute, total limbo. And then the word, 'Next week, at such and such a day, the time, that's the meeting point.' The thing that is still so hard to understand, how communication kept up, there was no telephone, no beeper, it was all done through people. I don't know how this man, on the train between Brussels and whatever the next city, was told, 'Get your people off.' That's what I mean by the sixth sense.

"The next week when we were supposed to meet again, there was this woman, red haired, she had the most horrendous accent, the ugliest accent in French is a

Polish accent, French is beautiful, but when a Pole speaks it, you can hardly listen, and that woman had one of the most audible of accents ever. And there she was in a flowery summer dress, (this was August '41), collecting everybody's money, and she put this money in a plain handkerchief and folded it over and had the handkerchief with all of our earthly belongings in one hand and a couple of pieces of Kotex in the other, and that's how she guided us from Brussels to Abbeville [France].

"Abbeville was very tricky. It was a city where their factory was on one side of the river and the people were living on the other side. There was a bridge. At lunch, everybody went home to eat and so during the lunch hour, we were put in a little cafe.

"Again a man came and he had two passports or two identity cards. There was my sister, age four and a very old lady, who was sixty-four at that time. There were nine people in between, and the picture was changed each time, but the card was the same. Every time he was able to take two people and he came back. He kept showing the same card to the German at the bridge, and whether the German was bribed or whether he just didn't pay that much attention, I do not know. But that was about the most critical part of that illegal trip from Brussels to southern France. That went well. We were all able to cross. My little sister was put in the basket of this guy's bicycle and I was the last one. My poor mother had conniptions on the other side, waiting for me (I was fourteen).

"I don't know what happened in Paris. I have no memory of Paris whatsoever. Paris was very dangerous, exceedingly dangerous. The Germans were always on the look-out. The other thing was, you never knew what a Frenchman would do, the regular Frenchman on the street, would he or would he not turn you in.

"The next step was Paris to Bordeaux. Again, one of these mysterious inside tips. We were told, somebody whispered something to this lady, 'Bordeaux is not safe, get out one stop before Bordeaux.' in the middle of nowhere. We were all crawling through the fields, wheat, I don't remember what kind of fields. I remember my little sister, six years old, her head was barely showing over the stalks. She was our guide and I don't know how she knew whom to follow. That's the way we crossed the demarcation line between occupied and unoccupied France. And we had these visions of barricades, soldiers with machine-guns, going back and forth. It was the most peaceful countryside you can imagine. But after we had crossed, we were all terribly thirsty and we stopped at a farm house and the only thing they had was white wine. And so this old lady [the 64 year old] got a little bit tipsy on the white wine. The guide, by that time, had said good-by to us. We were on our own, that was the scariest thing, totally on our own. The guide had said, 'Something has happened, get off here, I'm going back,' took the handkerchief apart and distributed the money.

"We had to get a taxi to catch up with the train that was to take us from Bordeaux to Marseille. And in the taxi, the old lady went 'gasp, gasp,' she was totally tipsy. The memory is as sharp as anything today and maybe even sharper.

"Once in the train, my mother was absolutely exhausted and she said, 'I have all of my money in the black bag, Marian, go sleep on it.' But she had two black bags, and I slept on the wrong one. The bag with all of the money in it was up in the baggage rack. Fortunately, it was still there. Those are the small things that stay with you.

"When we got to Marseille, in terms of soldiers, no trouble, though we had been told to be very careful in the railway of Marseille because it was crowded with French soldiers and probably with whatever German officialdom that was permitted under Vichy. I remember getting out of the train and running, the station has lots and lots of stairs, running down those stairs feeling, Wonderful, I'm here, nobody caught me. The rest of the group was further back and again my mother said, 'Can't you stay with us? Stay with the group.'

"Marseille had a camp for women and children who were caught. We were lucky again, we were not caught. We were living on our own in this tiny little hotel. We had to wait a week or so before we could get permission to go and see my father in Les Milles. That's the camp where people stayed who had a chance of being allowed to leave the country pretty soon. Meeting with my father. That was really painful. Those camps, even the more benign ones, as far as they were not extermination camps, were just horrible. I don't know what my mother felt at that time, sort of pity and anger. I guess I tried not to look, to be honest, I don't remember that first visit there. I do remember walking back out of that camp, taking a bus or whatever, back to Marseille. My mother looked pretty, pretty grim.

"Then every once in a while, my father was allowed to come to Marseille and some other people were allowed to come from the camp to visit. In Marseille, I did not have any fear of being picked up. The only fear was to be sent with counterfeit ration cards to buy bread in the morning. You had regular cards and then you tried to supplement with the counterfeit stuff. I refused, so they sent my little sister. I don't know whether one was able to tell if that was counterfeit, but just the knowledge ... that was the greatest fear in Marseille.

"Fortunately, my mother had a spiritus cooker, a liquid you put a match to. And the only thing we ate was onions and tomatoes, day after day. That was the only thing there was, and with the bread. And any of my father's friends who came in from Les Milles, everybody got fed the onions and the tomatoes.

"My poor mother. The Cuban visa. You had to work on four visas simultaneously, the Cuban visa, the transit visa for Spain and Portugal and the exit visa from France. In order to get the exit visa, you first had to have the transit visa, in order to get the transit visa, you had to have the Cuban visa. And in order to get the Cuban visa, you had to have the French exit visa. It was a complete circle. Don't ask me how she broke it, but somehow she managed to get it done.

"The ship was somehow arranged. They did have some Jewish organization that was able to arrange the shipping. But there were some nasty, nasty stories of people having been sent to Barcelona, only to find that 'No, they were to leave from Balboa,' and then they went from Barcelona to Balboa, only to be told, 'Oh, no, I'm very sorry, we don't have your ticket.' People were screwed out of their means of escape at the very last minute, so there were some pretty nasty stories at that time.

"When all of the visas were together, we took the train through Spain and I think we stopped in Madrid and this was right after the Spanish Civil War, and boy that country looked awful, devastated, absolutely devastated. We stayed in Portugal for a while and then took the ship that was leaving for Cuba. We were lucky, this was in fall of '41, we could have gotten torpedoed or not gotten torpedoed.

"Havana was interesting, a very, very interesting demographic experience. There were about 10,000 refugees from the present world war. There were a great many refugees who had come at the turn of the century and before the first world war, mostly Poles. Any kind of foreigner was thus 'un Polaco.'

"We expected to be in Cuba just a few weeks; instead it took five years for our American visa to come through. But we were lucky we had escaped from Europe.

Some of the 'lifts' I told you about had come to Cuba, but the people never made it. They were exterminated. Some of these lifts were opened, because it was impossible to keep them. Space was needed for other things, and they had public sales of the contents of these lifts. I did not go, but some people I knew went and they said it was just heart-wrenching because they had photos, pictures, prayer books. Some people had been so thoughtful to even include toilet-paper. 'Think ahead, there isn't going to be any money when we get there, so we may as well take the essentials.' Anyone who went with any sense of feeling was just devastated. The pictures nobody cared about, so they were strewn about.

"At the beginning we were all dependent on the Joint Distribution Committee and surviving on what they were able to give us would have been very difficult. Fortunately, diamond people from Antwerp and the Hague had come as refugees to Havana. They talked to the authorities and were allowed to open diamond polishing factories, provided that half of the work force was Cuban and half the refugees. And it was a total win-win situation. Good money was made. They shipped diamonds from New York, diamonds to be polished as well as what is known as 'board' which is a rough diamond which is needed in order to polish the other diamonds. And the control was very keen. The fear was, of course, that one would take these rough diamonds and ship them on to Argentina for the German war effort. The weighing scales and magnifying glasses, those were the two symbols.

"I was fifteen when I was put on the wheel to polish diamonds. And that's how I helped my family survive and literally how an immigration of 10,000 people survived and survived well. You made good money. This was embarrassing because you needed identity cards and these were of different colors according to how much money you made. The people who sawed the diamonds had to stand all day and go from machine to machine and they made a lot of money and they had a red card. Then there was a blue and a gray card. You went to the authorities to have this permission to stay renewed and you came with this card which clearly indicated that you made five times as much as those officials who had to OK them. It didn't feel right. I was already socially conscious then, and this sort of disparity, this discrepancy has always bothered me, partly because of the injustice and partly because of my own embarrassment that even in a situation like Havana, Cuba, in the war, that I should have it better than the clerks, stamping these cards. And so, instead of going to school, I spent my teens polishing diamonds. But this whole diamond scene was a godsend because at least people could earn their own living again.

"When we finally came to the States in 1946, I was eighteen years old and only then did I realize how abnormal my whole life had been - abnormal and yet it was a very lucky life, I did not perish in a concentration camp.

"The most lasting effect of this unusual childhood? I think it is this: the fear of displeasing authority or anyone for that matter, is still with me. It has left a tremendously destructive imprint but I can't shake it.

"But, again, I was lucky. The wound, I can live with it, not easy because it has made relationships very difficult in all kinds of ways. But my immediate family survived and all I can say, as crazy as it sounds, with all that has happened, personally, there is an enormous sense of gratefulness." [30]

1938 in Germany

During 1938, more steps were taken to eliminate Jews from German life. They were forced to carry identification cards, their passports were stamped with a large J. Switzerland and Germany agreed to have a J for *Jude* or *Jew* stamped on the passports of German and Austrian Jews. As a result of this Swiss initiative, Germany extended this practice to all Jews. Male Jews had to add the name Israel as their middle name and women had to use the middle name Sara. Jewish doctors and lawyers were not permitted to practice. Schools and universities were closed to Jews. All streets named after Jews were renamed, and all business enterprises and property, including jewelry and art works, were confiscated by Aryans.

On 28 October 1938, Nazi Germany deported all Jews of Polish nationality

A Time to Speak

to Poland. On 7 November, a Jewish refugee in Paris killed the third secretary, Ernst vom Rath, at the German Embassy. The youth's father had been deported to Poland shortly before. What followed on 9 and 10 November was a government-organized giant pogrom, the looting and burning of Jewish houses, shops and synagogues, later known as *Kristallnacht* (Night of the Broken Glass). The German Jews were also assessed a special fine for the cleanup costs after the pogrom.

Immigration after Kristallnacht

Marianne Schwab originally described her experiences in an interview, taped in Germany in 1992.

"*I lived in Bad Homburg vor der Hohe. My family had always lived in Bad Homburg as well as my ancestors and their families since 1649. We lived in a very beautiful house, which is still standing today. I grew up there. My father was a private banker and had his office in the same house. My parents were very respected citizens in Bad Homburg. They were wonderful people who had done much for the community as well as other people. We were very happy in Bad Homburg. We had a kosher household and kept all the Jewish holidays. We felt ourselves secure as Germans. In our parents' house there was always great harmony. I have wonderful memories of this time and our being together.*

"*The Nazis came to power in January of 1933 and they quickly issued new laws designed to legitimize anti-Semitic action. I was almost fourteen years old when things were already going downhill in school. I was the only Jewish girl in the class and the other girls spoke less and less with me. Many became BDM girls (Bund Deutscher Mädel - a Nazi youth group for girls). I felt myself to be German of Jewish religion, a citizen, and I was friends with everyone and thought everyone was friends with me. The Nazi laws changed everything. It was, naturally, very depressing that one couldn't meet with one's German friends, and we felt ourselves more and more isolated. Later, it was actually illegal to have anything to do with Jews. We couldn't go to public schools anymore and instead had to look for private instruction in order to complete our education.*

"*We began to make friends with other Jewish families since fate had touched all of us. Thus we came together to exchange information and to discuss what we should do if things continued as they were. Most people tried to find relatives abroad who could provide help and support (affidavit) so that one could emigrate.*

"*My brother Eduard was interested in Zionism. He was two years younger than I and he wanted to emigrate to Palestine, as it was then called. I was more impressed by what I had heard about America, either from other people, or from the books and newsreels about the freedom, democracy and the whole lifestyle in the USA.*

"In 1938 I went to a private Jewish school in Frankfurt in order to study physical therapy, which I had always liked. As far as I remember it, my mother called me there on the 10th of November and told me our synagogue was burning and that I should come home. The Jews in Germany were assessed a special tax for whatever it took to clean up the debris of all other synagogues in Germany which were burned down during the November 1938 pogrom.

"In the afternoon around two or three, I suddenly heard a noise and saw from my window maybe ten to twelve men with axes, hatchets and clubs. The mob forcefully entered our home. I ran to my parents and told them, 'They're here, they're here.' They simply broke in the many glass doors of our apartment and immediately began to destroy everything.

"We had a red marble fireplace with old silver candlesticks on the mantel. One of the men suddenly went up to it and smashed everything within sight. Then they broke open the big Frankfurter cupboard in the dining room where my mother kept her good glassware, porcelain and dishes and smashed it all. We had an antique, valuable grandfather clock that was smashed by one of these Nazis. The man is later quoted to have said that 'It sounded beautifully gruesome when he demolished the clock in front of the Jewish madam's feet.' (My mother).

"There was a horrible racket caused by the vandalizing of all rooms. I was confused and didn't know what I should do or where I should go. As I couldn't get out of the room anymore, I then went to the window that led to the Louisen Street, opened it, let myself out and climbed down the pipes to the street below. It was rather high and I searched for a step to get down on. No one stopped me. The mob continued breaking things. It was November, the 10th of November, 1938. I ran down the Kisseleff Street. I thought about what I should do, and I decided to go to the police. I didn't know if it was a good idea or not, but in my terror I thought the police would treat me better than this band of Nazis. At the police station, I told the official there, 'My parents,' I still remember my exact words, 'are in danger of their lives.' 'Please send someone to the house.' 'No one is here at the moment,' the official answered, 'I can't do that.' I sat down and waited to see what would happen. 'Miss Rothschild, you can't stay here!' 'But I can't go home,' I replied, 'these people are breaking up everything. I can't go home now.' And then a word occurred to me: 'Protective custody'. And I asked, 'Please, couldn't you take me into protective custody?' 'But I would also like to know that I can leave at any time.' One was, in those times, in a state of mind that costs everyone's nerves.

"Then the official led me to a tiny cell. It was in a passage way behind the Louisen Street, roughly at the orphanage. They locked me in and went away. It was cold, I was alone, and after three hours, I became frightened. I wanted to knock on the window, to make myself known but there were iron bars in front so that I couldn't reach the glass panes. Finally a man came into the jail building and heard my calls. I explained to him the situation with the custody. 'Yes, that doesn't work so fast,' he said. But then he came with the key and let me out. I went home the back way through the courtyard rather than on the Louisen Street. From the outside everything looked so normal. The house doors were closed. Mrs. W. called down to me from the first floor, 'Your parents are in the back cottage.' I went to the cottage, and it was a wonderful feeling to see my father and mother again. They had fled to the house as had our relatives the Wiesenthals whose apartment had been destroyed after ours and my grandmother was also there. Later someone told me something that affected me greatly. My father was very concerned about my brother and me. We had both disappeared for a while. Father stood in the courtyard calling, 'Where are the children? Eduard?, Marianne?' He was an older gentleman, already 70, but I had never noticed because he had so touchingly cared for us when the family was still together. He was wonderful.

"My brother had gone to our relatives to warn them while our apartment was being destroyed, 'The mob is coming.' Our house had been the first that was attacked in Bad Homberg.

"Later my mother sent me to the dining room and the basement to fetch something to eat. I cut myself on my legs. Everything was broken — the dishes, the furniture, the beautiful clocks — the paintings were slashed, stabbed through with a knife. Our dining room table had become kindling. The grand piano lay turned over on the floor in the next two rooms. The next day my mother took a look at her home. Although she was a very intelligent resolute woman, she was, at this moment, as if she had been hit in the head and she said to us, 'If such a thing can happen, what can happen after that?'

"The next day I again went to the police. My uncle, Sally Wiesenthal, a very nice man, had been arrested and I brought him a toothbrush and a comb. I already knew where the little cell was. One somehow suspected that those arrested would be transported somewhere. My father was not arrested because he was an older man. My brother was also, fortunately, not taken. But in the end my parents were taken in the last transport to Theresienstadt where they both died. My brother, who left Germany for Holland to study agriculture, was arrested there when the Nazis invaded that country and was deported to Mauthausen, where he was murdered at the age of 21.

". . . Until my emigration number came up and it was my turn to leave Germany, I would have had to wait months. There was a long wait ahead, and while the situation was becoming more and more difficult, I wrote to an aunt in London, England. The sister of my mother had moved there. She invited my grandmother Emmerich and myself to live with her until I could leave for the U. S. A.

"In the meantime, letter 'J' for 'Jew' had been stamped into my passport and they added the Jewish name 'Sarah' to my name, which now became the name Marianne Sarah Rothschild. Sarah is indeed a beautiful biblical name, but at that time, it was a very demeaning one for me and for all other Jews. The name 'Israel' was added for men.

"On the 17th of March, 1939, my grandmother and I left Bad Homburg. First, we traveled to Amsterdam in order to visit for a few days with my uncle, Hugo Emmerich. My uncle, unfortunately, did not allow me to visit my brother Eduard at the Wieringwaard Sea where the emigration camp was. That was in March 1939. I would have liked to have seen my brother, but it was not to be.

"With my 80-year-old grandmother along, we crossed the border of Holland by train and finally arrived in England, a stone fell from my heart. At first, one was afraid to admit being Jewish The fear ran deep. And yet now, again, you felt that the main thing was that you were a good person. In London we lived at my aunt's. Her husband had also spent some time in a concentration camp in Germany, and while I was in London he died from mistreatment incurred in the Buchenwald concentration camp.

"Then the Second World War began. On September 3, 1939, in the evening, we had to go to the air-raid shelters. There one felt safe at night while the Germans dropped bombs on England. The entire sky was fire red. Everything was blacked out, but we could see the outlines of the houses.

"I stayed one and a half years in England and then at the age of twenty and a half, I emigrated alone to America. My grandmother stayed in England where she died.

"Finally the day came to leave for America. There were, however, such heavy bomb attacks that the ship could not set out from Liverpool. Along with other emigrants, we were sent to Scotland, to Glasgow instead. There we waited three days in port because our ship had been damaged by a German attack and needed to be repaired first. After a week of zigzagging the Atlantic in order to avoid a U-boat attack, we arrived in Canada.

"Having spent two days and nights on the train, on American soil, to my great relief, I reached my goal —New York City. A Jewish organization looked after the emigrants. The people were most helpful. They assisted us, brought food, and informed relatives. An aunt by marriage picked me up. We were dead tired and everything was new and strange. I lived for a time at my aunt's in Long Island, a suburb of Manhattan, New York. They were immigrants, just as I was, and they were supported by their daughter, Anni Klein. At the time, all I had was ten German marks. That was it, besides two suitcases of clothes. Naturally, I immediately looked for a job to get on my feet. When America entered the war, it did not help that I was

A Time to Speak

Jewish since I was still German. No one wanted to employ Germans: war is war.

"At my first job, which I got at a chocolate factory, I wrapped chocolates. After Christmas, the owner informed me that he had no orders and, unfortunately, had to let me go.

"Naturally, in the beginning, I had problems with the language. To learn better English I even went to school in the evenings which, thankfully, didn't cost anything.

"I learned from a friend that a Jewish couple, also refugees themselves, the attorneys Mr. and Mrs. Bodenheimer, in Washington, D. C., were looking for a nanny from a good home for their two small boys. I was treated very well there. The little boys were nice, and I enjoyed my job. The attorneys advised me to go to university. Since I had no money, I took out a loan and attended George Washington University. It was wonderful. Everyone was charming, and there was no difference between us. I still correspond with the girls who were in my class, even after 50 years. I majored in physical education and for my minors, I took German, French and Spanish languages.

"My parents were forced to leave their home in the Louisen St. and move into my aunt's house in the Kisseleff St. My mother is said to have had an accident. Someone deliberately ran into her with a bicycle. She fell and broke her arm. A friendly person reported that to me.

"My parents were transported to Theresienstadt concentration camp. I wrote letters to them there and received some letters via an acquaintance in Portugal. Although I received letters, I wanted very badly to get my parents out of the camp, but it was already too late.

"One was never permitted to say how bad things were going or talk about the persecution at the time. Because all mail was censored, we learned of things in a way that I can hardly describe to you. The fear that at any minute the Nazis could enter the house and do something to you was very deep.

"Before their deportation they had to move into another house a kind of ghetto in the Gorch Fock St., so I heard. But on the 28th of August, 1942, my parents were deported to the concentration camp in Theresienstadt, Czechoslovakia. Both were killed there. I never saw them again. I was nineteen years old when I had to leave them. A Mrs. Neuhaus, who survived in the same camp, told me later on that my mother did a lot of good in the camp until she perished. My father was an older man, in his late 70s, and he died very soon after arrival at the camp. The people had hardly any clothing and little to eat, if you could call what they got 'food.' To prolong her own life, my mother took father's coat off him after his death. She lived for a longer time, in fact, almost survived it all. In the conversation with Mrs. Neuhaus, I noticed that she didn't want to tell me how my mother had died. I think it is probably better that way. I don't really want to know everything, it hurts too much.

"My brother Eduard emigrated to Holland in January 1939. I still have a few letters from my brother which he had written to my uncle Hugo Emmerich in New York. Naturally, everything had to be written in a way so that the Nazis would not censor it and hold it back. He wrote: 'Please send papers. I am in a hurry.' When the Nazis invaded Holland, a very fair, well-meaning Dutch farmer wanted to hide my brother and gave him a bicycle, or at least so I have been told. Unfortunately, someone betrayed my brother and he was arrested (Jews were forbidden to have bicycles). Later I got a letter through the Red Cross in which I was told that he had died in Mauthausen concentration camp in 1942. At that time he was just 21 years old. His fate is very sad. An innocent boy, an upstanding religious person who had to lose his life in such a gruesome way.

"I had so many respectable Aryan school friends and acquaintances, but since contact with Jewish people was forbidden, the friendships fell apart. Naturally, it wasn't possible during the war to maintain contact, but after the war we again got in touch and every time we are in Germany we visit new friends and also old acquaintances. That is really wonderful. I don't harbor any hate, but I cannot forgive the people who were responsible for the injustices and atrocities that were inflicted on us." [31]

The "Final Solution"

In July 1939, Hermann Göring ordered Reinhard Heydrich to prepare a plan for the so-called "final solution concerning the Jewish Question." It wasn't until 20 January 1942 that the Wannsee Conference was held to form the "Final Solution." Heydrich and Reinrich Himmler invited the state secretaries of the most important German government ministries to attend. The Conference was significant for two reasons: it involved broad participation of the ministerial bureaucracy and it was the point at which Hitler's decision to solve the Jewish question through mass murder was transmitted. They considered options other than mass-murder by firing squad: deportation to camps which were being established with poison-gas facilities for mass-murder or use for harsh labor and worked to death. They aimed to kill every Jew in Europe.

End Notes

28	*The Rise and Fall of the Third Reich*, p. 241
29	Bine Hirsch came to the United States in 1954 and took a job as a physicist at the High Altitude Observatory in Boulder, Colorado.
30	In 1959, Marian Kreith married a young professor, also a refugee, who has since become a leading authority on heat transfer and solar energy.
31	Marianne Schwab is married toFred Schwab, whom she knew in Frankfurt. She often substitutes as a foreign language teacher in Ann Arbor, Michigan. Interview with Mrs. Schwab on 21 June, 1992. Interviewer, Angelika Rieber with Bruno Hoffman; Videotape, Gisa Hillesheimer; translation from the German, Mrs. Schwab.

CHAPTER 4

ATTACK ON POLAND; THE PHONEY WAR; INVASIONS IN NORWAY AND DENMARK

Stalin's Options

After the Munich agreement, Stalin was left with two options; maintain an alliance with France and Great Britain or form an alliance with Hitler. He attempted to do both. In June 1939, France, Great Britain and the Soviet Union began conversations on guarantees of border rights in eastern Europe.

Stalin also signed a non-aggression pact with the German government in August 1939. The treaty included a "Secret Additional Protocol," which permitted the partition of Poland between Germany and the Soviet Union and gave Stalin a free hand in the Baltic states. This allowed him to invade Poland from the east and extend the Soviet sphere of influence.

Attack on Poland

On 1 September 1939, newspaper headlines all over the world announced that Germany had attacked Poland without a declaration of war.

Hitler provided one reason for his invasion of Poland- the attack on the Gleiwitz transmitter. This was a bogus raid in which a prisoner had been dressed in a Polish uniform, taken to Gleiwitz on the German /Polish frontier, and shot by the Gestapo to fake an assault on the radio station.

Poland's army could not compete with Hitler's Blitzkrieg: air attacks, dive bombers, motorized infantry, tanks and foot soldiers. Warsaw fell on 27 September 1939. Germany and Russia signed the partition of Poland on 29 September.

Almost immediately, Poland's Secret Army was born with General Michael Tokarzewski responsible for the organization of the resistance. Polish hostility was directed against both the Germans and the Communist Russians. Their loyalty was to the government-in-exile, located first in Paris and then in London.

The Phoney War

Once Hitler invaded Poland, both France and England were obliged to declare war on Germany because of their treaty alliance with Poland.

A Time to Speak

The Tocsin Sounded

In France, the tocsin sounded in cities and villages from Paris to the provinces and 5,350,000 soldiers were mobilized, most of whom were sent to the northern and eastern fronts. Marie and Robert LeBerre from Brittany recalled the lugubrious sound of the tocsin on 3 September 1939.

"And I remember the real consternation on the faces of the people. I was only eight years old and I asked, 'Who died, what happened?' 'Oh, it's war.' I remember hearing the tocsin. It was for the war, and soon after we saw men depart for the war," said Robert.

Marie's recollection is especially poignant.

"The war caused a terrible family change. I remember the month of September when war was declared, there was all the work to be done, it was beautiful day; my parents were in the fields, my mother, my father, all the neighbors were together, my mother crying terribly; I couldn't understand what was happening. I was seven years old. My father left the day after. . . . For me it was a shock not to see my father anymore, to see my mother manage all the work of the farm by herself, and to see her often sad, pained. All of the male members of the family found themselves in the war. There was only the older brother of my father who came to help us during the harvest of '40, to help with the hoeing and plowing and things like that. So we found ourselves in a cocoon completely different than what I had known up until then." [32]

Reaction in Great Britain

In Great Britain, there had been preparations for war. In the spring, gas masks had been issued, and everyone, including children, were instructed how to use them; war production was gearing up; British Intelligence was seeking ways to obtain vital information about Hitler's intentions.

One reaction to the outbreak of war was simple acceptance, with no interruption of activity, as it was for Jean Powell, who grew up in Eastbourne on the southern coast of England.

"I remember the day war was declared. We were on our way up to see our grandparents who lived at Gravesend and we were stopped at a place called Southborough which is near Tumbridge Wells, and the police stopped us at 11 o'clock on the road and said, 'You do realize that war has now been declared and we are at war with Germany'. My father said, 'Yes, what do you want us to do?' The policeman asked us where we were going and we told him. And he said, 'No you can carry on,' and then the siren went. And everybody thought things were going to happen straight away, and of course, nothing did. And we just wended our way up and came back on a Sunday." [33]

Mobilization in France

Hitler's Blitzkrieg attack on Poland demonstrated modern war tactics of simultaneous use of air power, tanks, and field artillery. There were opposing views on France's readiness.

Historian, Auguste Le Carpentier, who was mobilized in 1938 affirmed France's readiness to wage war.

"*And the war arrived, September '39, the occupation of Poland. On September 3, France and England declared war, yes, but without doing anything for eight months. We stayed there, very tranquil, while the German troops were in the east. I think that we could have regulated the problem quickly by attacking in the west. We did not do it. That has to be added because there were certain counter truths saying that France didn't have armaments. France had sufficient armaments which they would have been able to use.*"

Others, like Louis Bedel, found that France's armies were not prepared to fight against Hitler's well-organized war machine. Bedel, a former French soldier and prisoner of war, wrote a private diary for his wife, which begins with his mobilization and concludes with his return to Brittany when he was released from a prison camp, five years later. He expressed, with complete candor, the rationale for France's entry into the war, and the subsequent inactivity of the enlisted men in the early days of the war.

"*We didn't leave in a great explosion of joy as they did in August 1914. The decision taken by our government seems to me to be logical. It is time to stop Hitler in his ambitions, only force will check the Germany military power. What I know of socialist theories seems to me completely incompatible with my ideas of liberty, democracy and the respect for all races and all beliefs. The persecution against the Jews, men from the left, socialists or communists and Christians shocks the humanitarian ideal that was nourished from my childhood and my education.*

"*Instead of staying inactive, we needed discipline and they made us march, turning to right and left. Then we had to dig trenches among the fruit trees that were already ripe and to cut the roots of the these trees seemed a sacrilege. One day I doubted the utility of our work and the propaganda that praised the inviolability of the Maginot Line. They made me understand that it was good to have a second line of defense* [referring to the trenches being dug]. *While we lost time, the Blitzkrieg, imagined by Corporal Hitler, went against Poland and our little offensive in the Warndt, taking several villages didn't really bother the German offensive. From my part, I judged that it was lamentable that our general was so timid.*

"*In October, I notice that we are going to the showers and we are going to be vaccinated against typhoid. Monday, October 16, at six o'clock in the morning, positions of combat at four kilometers, sacks filled with provisions, too heavy, and again to dig holes.*

"*What do we do Sunday, you ask. Often sleep late, get dressed, a little food, laundry, then a walk in the surrounding area. Sometimes a movie, even the general came once. At the end of the movie, music, playing the 'Marche Lorraine.'*

"*We celebrated November 11 very simply, saluting the colors, a small parade in front of the adjutant. I cannot help but think of twenty-one years ago my Father saluted this day which put an end to the nightmare of World War I.*

"*Christmas approaches and we want to celebrate it joyously and it is a success. My letter of December 25 describes the Pantagrulian feast - oysters, sausages, goose cooked to perfection and received with a cry of joy, peas, salad, plum tart, all washed down with an old Bordeaux and a Sauterne.*" [34]

Maginot Line

Even the officers stationed at the Maginot Line, which was France's first line of defense against Hitler's armies, did little to prepare against a German attack toward the west.

The Line had been constructed secretly between 1930 and 1935, along the French border, separating France from Germany, extending from Luxembourg to Switzerland. On the other side of the Maginot Line was the Siegfried line, the counteroffensive constructed by the Germans from Bâle to the Dutch border.

The Maginot Line contained forty-nine artillery fortifications and ten kilometers of underground corridors. The only thing visible from outside were the casemates and anti-tank ditches. Two hundred feet below ground, it was manned by infantry equipped with antitank guns, infantry mortars, and double-barreled machine guns. In 1939, 200,000 men were stationed there with enough food and munitions to last for three months. *On ne passe pas!* (They will not pass) was the proud motto of the Maginot Line.

Life was relaxed for the soldiers stationed there; they were able to go home on leave to stay with their families housed in near-by Nancy. René de Chambrun recalled one of the tricks played in order to break the monotony of those days underground. One day he and a friend, returning from duty at a village outpost on the Maginot Line, saw a life-size dummy in an abandoned fashion shop. She looked like a handsome girl with long, black hair. They decided she would be the first woman to visit the depths of the Maginot Line and placed the dummy, lying voluptuously on one of the officer's beds, hair spread out on the pillows with the covers pulled up to her chin. They had the pleasure of hearing him say, 'Madame, madame, what are you doing here?'[35]

No wonder this early phrase of the war was referred to as the "phoney war."

Invasion of Norway

Meanwhile, it was no phoney war for either Russia or Germany. Russian forces attacked Finland in November 1939. Unable to resist Soviet forces, Finland negotiated a peace with Russia.

Britain, hoping to deprive Germany of much needed iron ore coming from Sweden, laid mines in the Norwegian waters. Hitler was undeterred by the mines and invaded Norway on 9 April 1940.

Oddvar Solstad was seventeen years old and lived with his family in the middle of Oslo, in a large apartment building, on the top floor. He recalled the occupation:

"Suddenly in the middle of the night we heard a lot of air raid sirens going off. We hadn't expected this but we were prepared in the sense that we knew what to do and we went down into the basement. The following day we then learned on the radio what had happened and there was much confusion. We really didn't have much information about what really happened except that we had been occupied. And then there was that day and the following day, there was a suspicion that the Allies would bomb us and it resulted in panic. Everybody left town. Thousands and thousands of people were trying to get out of Oslo, including my dad's family. So we stayed at a farm outside of Oslo for the next few days. Then my dad had to go back into Oslo to his fish retail store. My family and I stayed at that farm for some time after that."

French and British troops landed in the region of Narvik, a northern port in the Norwegian sea and took the city and hoped to dislodge the German army from Norway. It was superior German air power which forced the Allies to evacuate Narvik on 28 May. On 30 May the Norwegian forces capitulated, and the pro-German government under Quisling was installed in Norway. King Haakon VII escaped to England and set up a government in exile, joining other western governments in exile.

Occupation of Denmark

The occupation of Denmark followed a surprise attack: no warning, no declaration of war, nor any complaint that Denmark had violated its neutrality.

One example of how the surprise occupation of Denmark affected individuals is the story of Aksel Schiotz, who had become a sensational tenor in London, singing over BBC radio. He had begun negotiating tours and had arranged to appear at the World Exhibit in California and to make a coast to coast tour in the

United States when the events of 1940 changed his life. His widow, Gerd, explained:

"We were planning to move the family to London at that time. We were counting on living in London because there was so much to do. We had given up our apartment. We were staying with my sister and brother in Copenhagen. We were wakened up by the airplanes that were hammering around, above us, towards Norway. All of us were paralyzed. We didn't know what to do. Aksel almost broke down because the planning was so beautiful. We had to find another place, we had stored our things. We had planned on April 13 to make a good-by recital to say, 'Now we are leaving for this coast-to-coast tour.'

"April ninth, we were completely crushed. When the Germans came and occupied Denmark. We were looking at these hundreds and hundreds of airplanes coming there. It was dreadful.

"We saw all these airplanes coming over us, hundreds and hundreds, black birds that were flying over. Our Navy was sunk trying to fight, but they were ordered not to fight. In Norway they fought. Danes are peace-loving and phlegmatic people. It was so unexpected.

"April eighth, the day before, we were invited to the British Ambassador's to sing because we were going to London. Their children had arrived from London from schools for Easter vacation. They were jailed, they were taken prisoners. Of course, the diplomats had to be sent back. All other British people were immediately being jailed. The Britishers were so unprepared, they sent their own children right into . . . they must have known. There were so many army movements in Germany at that time. They must have been very inefficient that they didn't know.

"All the liberal people were against the Nazis. The military was not because they admired the discipline, the marching. Our Army was cruel. They would never help anybody caught in the Resistance movement, they were actually informers. Not the Navy, it was very pro-British. The Army was infected by the Nazis. In '31 and '32, they were practically openly Nazi. Many signed up for the German Army and they were all sent to Russia." [36]

The Danish government accepted the occupation as an accomplished fact, and the Germans, in turn, agreed to respect Danish neutrality and refrain from interference in internal Danish affairs because Germany depended on Danish agricultural products. Daily life, on the surface, continued as usual.

By the end of April 1940, Austria, Czechoslovakia, Poland, Denmark and Norway were under Hitler's heel. Finland had fallen to the Soviet Army. But Hitler's Blitzkrieg was just beginning; the rest of western Europe, Belgium, Holland, and France were next. Great Britain remained the prize across the Channel.

End Notes

32 Marie and Robert LeBerre are both retired from their high school teaching jobs and live in Quimper.
33 Today Jean Powell lives in Seaford, Sussex.
34 After the war Louis Bedel returned to teaching history and geography. He lives in Dinan.
35 René de Chambrun, *Ma Croisade Pour l'Angleterre, Juin, 1940*, Paris: Perrin, 1992, p. 29
36 Aksel Schiotz died in Copenhagen in 1975; Gerd Schiotz has continued her work as a music librarian and is providing notes for the re-issue of Schiotz's recordings.

CHAPTER 5

THE BLITZKRIEG

From September 1939 until 10 May 1940, the French Army and people waited. For months, during what was called the "phoney war," no one tried to cross the Maginot Line.

The French forces had rehearsed for invasion and their success depended upon the enemy attacking at that specific location. Hitler, however, chose to go around the Line and invade Belgium and Holland. They appealed to Great Britain for help. Prime Minister, Neville Chamberlain, announced to his War Cabinet the need for a coalition government with both the Labor and Liberal parties working together. The Labor party blamed Chamberlain for Britain's lack of preparedness and refused to serve under his leadership. Chamberlain had no choice but to resign. He was succeeded on 10 May by Winston Churchill. That afternoon, Churchill made his famous speech to Parliament that he had nothing to offer but "blood, toil, tears and sweat."

Belgium's Surrender

In Belgium, King Leopold III announced he would head Belgium's army and ordered all able-bodied men between the ages of sixteen and thirty-five to report for army duty. Once of these young men was Gaston Vandermeersche, who, with his friends, left home to join the army. Instead they found themselves going from town to town searching for the remains of the retreating Belgium army. Belgium had only resisted the German Blitzkrieg for eighteen days.

Vandermeersche and his friends were still on the road when they learned that King Leopold had accepted unconditional surrender on 28 May 1940. Holland had surrendered earlier on 15 May and Queen Wilhelmina had left for Great Britain.

Vandermeersche explained the turmoil which young Belgian men experienced.

"It's rather complicated. First, when the war broke out, as a Belgian, I was given the order to go to France for the reorganization of the Belgian Army. Then we were ordered to come back, although at that time, I had the idea to go to Spain since I was already half-way there. I was thinking of becoming a pilot in the Royal Air Force, but my future father-in-law, who was my commander said, 'You can't do

that because they will take your parents and they will be captive, so you have to go back.' So I went back [to Belgium].

"Very quickly I realized I could not live in that country without doing something. I had to do something. Then I learned you had to be very careful because there were groups organized by the Germans and the pro-Nazis to pick up young people and fly them to England. That was fake. They picked them up and brought them to the salt mines in Germany. Fortunately, in time, I learned about this. Hey, we had dangerous situations here." [37]

Exodus, Retreat, Evacuation

With the rapid German advance, several events took place simultaneously at the end of May 1940: the frantic exodus to the west of Belgian and French civilians living near the Maginot Line; the epic evacuation of Allied troops from Dunkirk, where they were trapped by German forces; the retreat of the French Army toward Paris and the German capture of many French soldiers.

Mattresses, Mattresses, Mattresses

Everyone was on the road and two who were part of this exodus were a mother and daughter, Yvonne Lenoir and Marie-Madeleine Herbelin, who, at the time, lived in Nancy, near the Maginot Line. The mother recalled her concerns for her children as they fled the advancing German troops, and the daughter still thinks about her fear and bewilderment. Both women described the confusion, the clogged roads, and the frantic attempt to reach the west, only to find they had to return to Nancy after all.

Daughter: *We left, my father, my mother, brother, sister and I, to spend the school vacation of 1939 at some friends in Nancy, when war was declared. Because he had an aged father, my father's friend suggested we stay in Nancy and take care of this elderly man. This would also permit my father, who was an officer on the Maginot Line, to come home more quickly when he had a leave. Nancy was closer to the Maginot Line than Paris. There was no war movement in 1939, not until June 1940 when the Germans invaded France through Holland and Belgium by going around the Maginot Line. The French, terrified, fled toward the center and south of France, persuaded that the Germans were going to kill everyone.*

Mother: *My husband, a captain on the Maginot Line, like all the defenders of the Maginot Line, received verbal orders to quit the Line, with the orders to defend a certain village, to not let the Germans pass, but to let themselves be killed on the spot. He didn't want to abandon his men and they reached the Vosges. I decided to leave for the country.*

Everybody left. They gave verbal orders to leave the Maginot Line. They were all on the road. There were a lot of things abandoned, soldiers abandoned their trucks. There were dogs, chickens, people ran to collect eggs. . .

We took provisions, a bicycle, a mattress and we were bombarded all along the route. Barely on the way, two days, we saw quantities of people fleeing, automobiles heavily loaded with mattresses, even family portraits, moving to another place.

Daughter: There was a general panic on the part of the population, everyone wanted to flee and we walked along side of and met quantities of peasants, countrymen's carts, with their horses tied to the carts. They didn't have cars, carts with cattle tied behind, cows, calves, sheep. They thought they would never come back. Mattresses, I remember mattresses, mattresses on hand carts. Everybody was leaving on the roads.

There was an immense jumble and hodgepodge in the French Army who searched in vain their route, the Germans who arrived and wanted to set their course beyond, and the civilian population on the road which made the bottleneck. We couldn't budge. And the Italians bombarded and machine gunned the throngs of immobilized people.

Mother: We were on the road, trying to leave. Each time we arrived in a town, there were military escorts who were there and who sent us on. We went to three different towns and each time they sent us on, that blocked us. One time someone told us there was a little town in the upper zone, there were bridges that they had blown up. It wasn't worth going there because we couldn't get through.

Everyone wanted to get started. There were large military trains, there was the army, everything which hindered us.

Daughter: There was an enormous panic and it was atrocious. The Germans, in fact, they had only one desire, to advance, and they found themselves terribly vexed because they had a lot of French prisoners. And these prisoners were left along the route.

Mother: We hoped to arrive near Nevers in four or five hours, but on route, the first bombing. People were lying down in ditches and we did the same. It was near a big town called Neufchâteau and the smallest child didn't want to sleep on the ground because he was afraid of ants, and I was trying to calculate if I ought to go to sleep on Mikou [the baby daughter] or if a bomb fell on me I could protect her. My six-year old son raised his head and the little shells wounded him.

When we stopped at Neufchâteau, the hospital was bombed so we couldn't have him cared for. I found a country hospital in the woods. After a dressing for the wound, we departed again, with our wounded boy lying on the back seat. There was a house, there was a bomb which fell. I had the impression that it was earth and smoke, the house completely emptied.

Daughter: It was tragic. I remember what struck me. There were farmers who had abandoned their animals in the fields. These animals that were not lead away, howled.

One couldn't count the number of wounded we encountered. My brother was wounded, a bandage on his head, it was awful. We were seriously peppered with machine gun fire.

We were machine-gunned, I was separated from Mama, my brother wounded, covered with blood. And next to me, a dead soldier, wounded in the stomach, I remember, it was my first anatomy lesson, with the intestines. Me, I was terrified.

Mother: All the inhabitants were fleeing, even on isolated roads, because the Italians were bombing everything, and a woman, who was closing her door, gave us a glass of water for our little wounded child.

In the fields, the abandoned cows cried because their udders were full of milk. We had nothing from Friday evening until Sunday morning, not knowing how to milk the cows and jammed in a single automobile.

On route, the hub-cap blew up, the inner tube collapsed. Not knowing how to make the repairs, I was lucky to see my young mechanic coming. He changed the tire without a problem, and we started off again on the congested roads.

But a little later, when the road went up, my car went down backwards. Although I didn't know much about the mechanics, I verified that my gear box was broken. I tried, in vain, to put my car in a barn, but everyone was in a hurry and was fleeing.

I abandoned my car, taking note of the place for the insurance. We abandoned a lot of things. Two older persons, three children, the young mechanic and myself, and we walked on several routes. As soon as we arrived at the entrance of a city, the orders made the convoy turn and blocked the route in order not to hinder the military movements.

We found ourselves in another direction and finally Sunday morning, we arrived in a pretty little village with the lovely name of Combeaufontaine, the town above, where the night before had a battle. Dead soldiers on an automobile, machine-gunned, were still sitting and down below a watering trough with a beautiful fountain.

Two roads, which one to take? They told us that the bridges that spanned the Saône had been blown up. We stopped. A good woman and her husband, a little older, took pity on us because of our troubles, they invited us to stay in their house.

My mother and the children had beds under the sheep, and the mechanic and I settled down on the straw. The family fed everyone, they even killed a sheep to feed everyone.

There were quite a few soldiers, without weapons; they were put in a field surrounded by barbed wire. I learned there was a cheese cooperative. With my personal account, I bought a big piece of Gruyère to feed all the hungry mouths. They gave me all the eggs they could and a beautiful slice of Gruyère. We tried to make use of a little motor-bike abandoned on the road. They had put oil instead of gasoline and naturally, it didn't work any more.

After several days, we returned to Nancy. A little later I learned that my husband was a prisoner and that we could go see him before his departure for Germany. The mechanic with our host's automobile took us to the prison where one could easily speak and give him all that we could carry. When we got too close, we were obliged to step back.

Our hosts gave us dinner and we slept and returned to our lodging, looking for gasoline in the fields. The Germans tracked us, fearing we would find revolvers.

Daughter: *In Nancy during our absence, the house had been opened and looted. The upheaval of the invasion, fear, the news that our father was imprisoned, we settled again in the big house in Nancy. Life was reorganized in spite of the precarious food supply. We returned to school, each one back to their activities and in a way, life went on. Later we were able to return to our home in Paris.*[38]

The Epic of Dunkirk

After the capitulation of the Dutch Army on 15 May, the Belgian Army on 28 May, and the capture of many French troops, the embattled French Northern Army and the British Expeditionary Forces were encircled by the Germans. The Wehrmacht reached the English Channel at Abbeville. Hundreds of British and French soldiers were trapped, with their backs to the sea, at the Channel port of Dunkirk.

In England, the order finally went out that Operation Dynamo, the evacuation of soldiers from Dunkirk, was to go into effect. From 26 May to 2 June, a total of 339,226 British, French, Dutch and Belgian troops were evacuated in 222 naval vessels and 665 civilian motorboats, launches, tugs, yachts, fishing boats, and barges which were called into service to carry the men to the British coast. The Royal Air Force protected the operation and lost only one aircraft to Germany's three.

Mary Catherine Butland, serving in the Army Nursing Service in eastern France, was taken to Dunkirk to help evacuate the wounded on a converted hospital ship, the *Worthing*. In a taped interview for the Imperial War Museum Sound Archive, she described the chaos while the nurses tried to help the wounded soldiers.

"*Dunkirk was burning.... The town was constantly being bombed, ambulance trains and all, that made no difference. Red Cross ambulance trains made no difference to the Germans. If they wanted to bomb it, they'd bomb it. If they wanted to come down and machine-gun while you were getting your patients off the ambu-*

lances, they came down and machine-gunned. Attacks on the wounded while they were being transferred, the whole time, yes. Of course, the beach was a shambles...."

"... The troops, they were trying to get out to the little boats and failing that, trying to dig in, in the sand dunes, get a little shelter until there was a possibility of getting out to the small boats... Some of the little boats were shallow draught enough to come onto the beach, otherwise the troops walked out. In many instances, they would carry out a wounded man with them. They were just wading out and climbing in...."

"... They [the soldiers] were angry because they couldn't get on and finish the job because we were evacuating. They didn't feel relieved because they were going home, not a bit. The whole atmosphere was, 'I don't want to go back. I want to get back to the unit and I want to get on and finish the job.'" [39]

Victory at Dunkirk

In a curious way, both the Germans and the British claimed a victory at Dunkirk; one a military victory, the other a moral victory. In the text of the German Orders of the Day, Hitler sent a message to his soldiers of the West Front which proclaimed: *"Dunkerque has fallen.... Thus the greatest battle in world history has been concluded. Soldiers! my confidence in you is boundless. You did not disillusion me."*[40]

For the British, Dunkirk lives in their history as a remarkable feat of the Second World War and as a testimonial to their indomitable spirit. It was J. C. Priestley in a BBC broadcast on 5 June who referred to "Fearless Dunkirk" as "another English epic" and what was so "characteristically English... so typical of us, so absurd, and yet so grand and gallant." He was alluding to the little pleasure steamers who normally went as far as the nearest seaside resort and the role they played in the dangerous and difficult evacuation of British troops from Dunkirk.[41]

The German Vise Tightens

Just as Louis Bedel criticized the inactivity among the soldiers in the early days of the war, he persisted in chastising the lack of preparedness on the part of the French Army. He wrote in his diary:

"The tempest bursts. Germany attacks the west, May 10. The war surprises our military command. We are part of the troops sent to Belgium. Contradictory news from the first day, then the evidence breaks out. Out troops are decimated by the Stukas rush toward the North Sea, entire regiments encircled. The battle of Dunkirk rages. We feel the 'phoney war' is finished. What will happen tomorrow? Leaving the town, we see bombed out airfields, machine-gunned, fighter planes

A Time to Speak

lying tangled, unusable, big holes of concrete dug out of the runway. How could have they been surprised? They praised so much our monitoring system and the superiority of our aviation.

"April 17. We stopped in Loivre in the countryside. We got down without too much hassle, back pack, we left on a route along a country route. Suddenly the face of war was before us, we crossed a fairly important urban area in Burgundy, an impressive silence reigned over the little town, no one at the windows or at the doorstep. We understood that the entire population had to evacuate leaving everything behind. In the fields, the cows mooed lugubriously. Before leaving, the inhabitants had left handwritten signs, 'Milk the cows.'

"Where is the enemy? No information is given to us. The major general, does he know? If the Germans did not want to reach the Pas de Calais, the route to Paris is largely open. Our adversaries have taken possession of the crest on the right side. I imagine this portion of my country is already conquered. My countryman's atavism doesn't tolerate the idea of our country being trampled by strangers. I'm furious at the thought that once again, as in '14, the lack of foresight on the part of the military power leads us toward catastrophe. The poor infantrymen, looked down on, must capture the territory at what price, the sacrifice. Why haven't we extended the Maginot Line? Or at least constructed a series of casemates, permitting a line of resistance?

"Every day, without respite, a German observation plane furrows the sky at a low altitude, not bothered by the D.C.A. (Defence against aircraft) or our planes. The artillery across the way have time to prepare their next heavy bombardment of our troops.

"We are placed 200 meters in advance in another thicket, where we dig the group shelters across from individual holes where we can effectively dig in when the enemy turns up. But the crazy German observer plane buzzes over us without stopping, over this chalky land, easily singling out and photographing our trenches. . .

"We have learned of the disaster of Dunkirk. This prolonged calm bothers us. Suddenly, Sunday, June 9 it is hell. The enemy cannons belch out fire, it is not only the percussion-fuse which disperses, flashing, their machine-gun fire whistling over our heads. Like frightened rabbits, we plunge into the nearest holes.

"They have promised us reinforcements in order to take a position to form a second line of resistance. The powerful battery is supposed to crush the enemy in an attempt to attack. It is only a 'bluff' and I think our Division, drawn out, will only present a fragile curtain of troops which will quickly be routed by an attack in the grand style, like the one in Poland or the one of 10 May. We are withdrawn to the commandment post in the wood. This forces us to align ourselves, fall into line *facing the east, without protection of a trench. The adjutant passes behind the group. 'No panic, don't let yourself be spotted, don't fire, without orders.' Over us, the bombs burst without stopping, branches and leaves fly, machine-gun fire scatters whistles, whines and howls. I cling to the ground at the feet of a big fir tree, ridiculous protection. I could survey the flat country-side in the direction of Saint-Loup. Suddenly at two kilometers, rising up, a large somber beetle advances across the field, then on the neighboring road, trucks, side-cars, motorized vehicles rushed toward the south. New order to not fire. Then at my left, the burst of machine-gun fire. The balls go too high and chop off the foliage. The enemy infantry arrives by the little woods where we had been stationed yesterday.*

"*Of course, I couldn't see them. Then I heard a voice which cried, 'Don't fire, don't fire.' It was an old commander attached to the P.C. (post commander) who came out of his shelter who advanced, waving a white piece of cloth at the end of a stick. The Germans advanced toward him and told him to abandon his arms and to come toward them, arms in the air. We were face to face with those we were supposed to battle, here was the famous verdigris uniform. Somber helmets on top of their heads gave them a hard appearance to these soldiers who were not hampered by the heavy sacks and the caps sweltering from the heat. Many of them had unbuttoned their coats, rolled up their sleeves, light and short machine-gun. High leather boots with heavy soles, the handle of their grenades tucked into their boots. What a difference between what seemed to me a ridiculous uniform. We were still a band of mule-drivers with a heavy fabric cap. Orders were given and translated. 'Bring your arms, put them here. Throw down your cartridge belt, look after the wounded.'*

"*About fifty of us were taken prisoner. In the village square, the officials lined us up. In a jarring French, they gave a speech that we heard often, 'Germany had to declare war to defend itself against the Jews and the capitalists who governed. No harm will come to you. The war is going to end soon by our ringing victory and you will go back to your homes when peace is signed. You must get rid of your razors or arms that you may still have. Any attempt to flee will be punished by immediate execution.' Once more we had to get rid of these ridiculous arms.*"

The Germans continued to advance toward Paris; the German propaganda leaflets, which were dropped on French soldiers, predicted the Germans would be in Paris on 15 June. France was swept away in scarcely a month.

End Notes

37   Gaston Vandermeersche lives in Milwaukee, where he is president of his company, Gavarti Associates, Ltd.
38   Mme Lenoir lives in Chaville. Mme Herbelin, is retired teacher, still lives in Boulogne-Billancourt.
39   Excerpts, Interview, Imperial War Museum Sound Archive, Catherine Mary Butland, #6811
40   *New York Times*, 6 June 1940
41   Cited by Tom Hickman, *What did you do in the War, Auntie?*, London: 1995 p. 37

CHAPTER 6

THE FALL OF FRANCE

The civilian population in France didn't believe the German's predicted arrival in Paris by 15 June. They laughed and denied it was possible.

The Armistice and the Vichy Government

The French watched in disbelief as Hitler's army moved easily westward. Paris fell on 14 June 1940, and the German armies continued their push. For many Frenchmen, France's defeat was inconceivable and shouldn't have happened. For Marshal Pétain, surrender and signing an Armistice with Germany was the only practical solution, but for General de Gaulle, France was not defeated.

Two Leaders: Pétain

Pétain was the venerable and charismatic hero of the first World War, praised and admired for his resistance and victory at Verdun. His famous words at that battle, 'They shall not pass,' were part of the Pétain myth. Already in 1936, a little book appeared, *C'est Pétain qu'il nous faut* (We need Petain). In it, Gustave Hervé described what would happen if Marshal Pétain were elected president: a return to traditional values and social morality. Pétain's popularity was still intact in 1940, and French president, Reynaud, had named him vice premier.

As the French retreated before the German Blitzkrieg, Pétain informed Reynaud that it would be necessary to ask for an armistice. The French government left Paris and moved south, first to Tours, then to Bordeaux.

The French Cabinet asked Britain to release France from its agreement to make a separate peace. Britain, in turn, offered France an Anglo-French Union which would continue to fight even if France were overrun by the German Army. The French Cabinet refused and Reynaud resigned on 16 June.

Immediately, Marshal Pétain formed a new government and negotiations for the armistice began at once. On 17 June, Pétain, in a radio announcement, told the French army to lay down its arms, and informed the French people that armistice negotiations had begun with Germany. On 22 June, the Armistice was signed.

Pétain's Vichy Government

With the signing of the Armistice, a demarcation line cut France into two zones: in the north, the occupied zone which included about 55 percent of the territory; and in the south, the Free Zone, the "unoccupied zone." The eastern section of France, Alsace-Lorraine was annexed and was placed under a military government together with Holland and Belgium. The demarcation line could only be passed at certain controlled points and with a pass, an *Ausweis*.

By 11 July 1940, Pétain and his government had installed the French State at Vichy as the capital of the "unoccupied zone." The Chamber of Deputies and Senate conferred on Pétain the title, "chief of state," which gave him almost absolute power. His minister of state was Pierre Laval, who had served in several cabinet posts, as premier in 1931 and again in 1935. Laval had also favored the Munich Agreement in 1938 and helped persuade the government to accept the armistice so France could negotiate better terms and a peace treaty. Like Pétain, Laval was convinced that France's best course was cooperation with Germany in order to assure that France would have an important role in the future of Europe.

Pétain's program was based on a return to eternal French values and on three principles: Work, Family, Country.

Many French were more attached to the person of Pétain than to his National Revolution, and he nurtured the myth of the father in contact with the people. He cleverly used slogans, for example, "Vive Pétain, Vive la France, Résurrection." His picture was in all the shop windows, on stamps, and on posters. Even schoolchildren now sang, *"Maréchal nous voilà"* ("Marshal here we are"); they no longer sang the *"Marseillaise."* He was reverently listened to on the radio and he became a symbol of hope for peace and France's place in the "new Europe."

Many sincerely believed that the Vichy government, cooperating with Germany, would save France from the Bolshevists, and ultimately France would take its place in the new order in Europe. In fact, the Vichy government was anti-British, anti-Bolshevik and anti-Semitic. At first, the politics of Vichy were only repressive, but they became those of a "police state."

Two Leaders: De Gaulle

De Gaulle had entered the army and served in World War I. After the Armistice of 1918, he frequently wrote that Germany would return to her ambitions as soon as militarily possible. He argued for a professional French army, capable of tactical and shock action, with armored and tank divisions, but no one was listening.

In 1939, he commanded a tank unit, and for his bravery against the Germans at the River Oise, he was made a Brigadier-General. In June, Reynaud named him under secretary of state for national defense in his cabinet.

When de Gaulle learned of President Reynaud's resignation, he left for

England. He refused Pétain's request to lay down his arms. For this act, he was condemned in absentia by Pétain for refusing to obey military orders.

De Gaulle's Call of June 18

On the same day that Pétain called for the French to lay down their arms, De Gaulle arrived in London by plane from Bordeaux. The day after his arrival, he walked into the Broadcasting House, a tall imposing figure in his khaki military uniform, to make a broadcast to the French people. The script, typed on two pieces of paper, had been approved by the War Cabinet in Great Britain.

On 18 June 1940, in his famous BBC radio address from London, General de Gaulle, while acknowledging the defeat of the French Army by superior mechanical forces, refused to accept the defeat of the French. He invited all French officers and soldiers, with or without arms, engineers, and skilled workmen to join him in Britain to continue the resistance. "Whatever happens, the flame of resistance must not and shall not be extinguished," he said. He proclaimed himself the head of the Free French forces under the sign of the Lorraine Cross. Many French soldiers and future members of the French Resistance answered de Gaulle's appeal. By August, there were 7,000 members and two years later, there were 10,000 Free French soldiers.

On the other hand, among civilians, de Gaulle was relatively unknown. One of the first tasks of Resistance members was to circulate his photo.

De Gaulle succeeded in organizing the Free French forces and victoriously entered Paris, with the Allies, in 1944. He was elected provisional president of France in 1945 and became the first president of the Fifth Republic from 1959 to 1969.

Response to De Gaulle's June 18 Call

There was a new mobilization in France among civilians and military who refused to accept France's defeat and who wanted to join De Gaulle. They found routes out of France, via Brittany, with the help of fisherman and their fishing boats, or through Spain.

Albert Moline, a twenty year old soldier, mobilized in June 1940, was brought up with the idea of a free France. His father and grandfather had fought for France in 1870 and 1914 respectively. He quickly realized that he would end up in a Stalag if he obeyed the orders to stay in his barracks waiting passively for the arrival of German troops. He couldn't stand the idea of the presence of German soldiers in France and in his town. He could not accept the idea of the Armistice. His one idea was to rejoin General de Gaulle.

"*Even when we capitulated, it was a question of power, force. We weren't ready for war, it was true. If we had not given up in North Africa, if there hadn't been a pétainist government, if there hadn't been a separation between the population, we would have been like the other countries, beaten. But we wouldn't have betrayed one another, we wouldn't have betrayed the Allies.*

"I was a soldier before the debacle, I was mobilized before. I am distressed to say that my compatriots did not conduct themselves well. I was in a camp, a young soldier. Our officers brought us together, they said we are going to disarm you, don't move, stay calm, as soon as the Germans come, you will be demobilized and you can go home. I could only think I would end up in a Stalag. The others, they all said 'Yes' except for two, me and a friend. I said, 'I'm going to do something else.'

"I missed the last boat that left for England from Bordeaux. I arrived on the wharf and it was leaving. It took almost two years for me to find the channels to pass into Spain.

"It was necessary to live, to eat, to clothe oneself. I did all the odd jobs, mechanic, coal man, I drove cattle to the slaughterhouse. I did anything, with the idea in my head, to rejoin the English and the Americans.

"I spent eight months in a Spanish prison for clandestinely crossing the border in the Pyrenees. In Spain, there were no French, no English, no Americans. We said we weren't French, we said anything, any nationality, whichever was the most favored. One comrade said he was American, another English. I had declared that I was Belgian, and I had hidden my identity card in the epaulets of my uniform. The day when they started to release the French from prison, I took my identity card and showed it to the commandant and told him my story and said I was French. He looked at my identity card for fifteen minutes and said it was false. Finally, it was arranged and I was released.

"I was liberated in June 1943, and I left for Portugal. At Setubal, I embarked for Casablanca and joined the CFA (Corps Franc d'Afrique).

"The Free French Forces, 35,000, we were lost in the allied armies, ten here, five there, a division in one, a division in another.

"We [the French] had an attitude that displeased me and fifty years afterwards it still displeases me. It is difficult to swallow, difficult to explain." [42]

Everyone living and working in the occupied countries had to adjust to the uncommon circumstances and to the constant danger.

End Notes

42 Albert Moline returned to his home town, Levallois-Perret, where he was a business man until his retirement.

CHAPTER 7

DAILY LIFE

Growing Up During the War

*L*ooking back at the war years, children who grew up during World War II remembered that life was difficult: no heat; the shortages of food and clothing; life at school; and the constant fear.

The Cold

Everywhere it was cold. In the Paris suburbs, Geneviève Moline and her family lived completely in the kitchen (about 32 square feet) because they couldn't heat all of the rooms. For Midori Johnson in Tokyo, the situation was the same, *"Our house was very, very cold because gas and electricity were very, very limited. We need them to cook things, so the house was cold."*

In rural areas where there was no electricity, Robert LeBerre, a student at Collège Saint Louis near Brest, added, *"Water from the single-hole faucet was glacial; there was no question of soap (they demanded that we were clean every day), but washing was rather difficult."*

Bine Hirsch, a German refugee, learned to live an English boarding school life. *"It means sleeping with the windows open - cold, damp. All of the bathtubs had a black band five inches from the bottom of the tub and everybody in England was supposed to use no more than five inches of water. Everyone had to save power; I learned to wash in cold water every morning, to hand wash myself. We only had a bath once a week; clean underwear once a week; we changed our sheets every two weeks, the top sheet went to the bottom and it got turned. . . ."*

Even the schoolrooms were cold. Bine Hirsch sat in class with gloves on: *"A thermometer hung down from the ceiling in the classroom: when it went below 50 degrees, we were allowed some heat."* Marie LeBerre's rural school was heated with peat which served for both heating and lighting. *"We were more cold than warm,"* she said.

Shortages of Food

A common complaint was "there was almost nothing to eat," conditions deemed deficient for young people. Breakfast was a few slices of bread with a little butter. Jean Cotten ate black bread which he remembered as "inedible, like chewing rubber." Children drank either roasted barley with milk or dipped their bread in soup.

The meager breakfast was supplemented by lunch at the school canteen where they were served bread, beans and lentils; they also received cookies with vitamins added.

Boarding school students in rural Brittany received weekly visits from parents who brought bread, butter and crepes, which of course, had to be shared with the other pensioners.

Children and families living in the country benefited from food produced on the farms. Bine Hirsch's school in Rutland, England had an old English kitchen garden full of vegetables and they had goats, chickens, and ducks. *"We all took turns milking the goats in the mornings and evenings. The milk was usually fed to the sickliest children, depending on who needed it most,"* she added.

In France, the Germans requisitioned food, but the farmers learned to share food with their neighbors. According to Marie LeBerre, *"If you had a calf, you arranged to kill the calf and distribute it in the neighborhood. Later things were requisitioned by the Germans. It was necessary every week to send a certain amount. There were quotas, according to the number of cows one had for example. Depending on the number of acres, we had to produce a certain amount of butter, eggs, and so forth. And every week it was marked in the notebook. It was controlled and they could seize by force what they needed."*

In Japan most of the food produced went to the military.
"That's why we ordinary people suffered," explained Midori Johnson. *"Rice was the first thing rationed and went from 2.4 cups per day for one person to 2.1 cups. We had rice and vegetables and meat was very, very scarce. In '45 there was no meat, no sugar, no nothing. And flour, that was rationed, and we made bread at home because there was no bakery selling bread . . . other people were starving and were eating grasshoppers and locusts. And they were telling us how to cook and eat them. Most of the Japanese were hungry."*

Clothing

Ingenious mothers patched and remade clothes for their children. In the country, they had sheep, spun the wool, and knit large pullovers, wool jackets and wool shirts.

In Great Britain, clothes and shoes were not available. Bine Hirsch remembered going to a shoe exchange where outgrown school shoes were traded for bigger ones at the civic center. Her wardrobe was very simple. *"Each girl had one* school uniform, one Sunday dress, two blouses, a gym slip you didn't change, a little purse for a handkerchief, a vest underneath and your knickers."

The Japanese rationed clothes and banned wearing Japanese kimonos because they were not practical to work in. Midori Johnson explained,

"*We were told to reform. We were told to cut kimono in two, and the lower part, make it a sort of baggy pants, sleeves are very long and of course, make the sleeves short. It was a mixture of western clothing made of Japanese material.... They were khaki colors, quilted, baggy pants. Most of the Japanese clothes are very colorful. We just couldn't wear it or use it. All bright, cheerful colors were banned... we should be more stern, pink or white was OK but red was especially bad because of the Communist threat.*"

Schooling

For some children, their life centered around school and represented their social life. Marie-Madeleine Herbelin's school was located next to the Rodin Museum in Paris, where trenches were dug in the adjacent park. Each class had their placard marked with their trench number. At each alert, sometimes three times in one morning, her class went to B-41, accompanied by her teacher. Mme Herbelin said, "*Needless to say, we thought it was very amusing. We had a wonderful teacher who continued to teach us the lessons.*"

For others, because school buildings were needed for other purposes, their schooling was cut short. Marie LeBerre in Scaer, Brittany, remarked:

"*I really had a hole during the war. In '41 when I went to Scaer, the school was not yet occupied [by the Germans]. Later it was occupied and there was only the dormitory. They left us the refectory. There wasn't any courtyard at the school, it was occupied by the Germans, so we were in the street. We played there, quiet games; we were left completely to ourselves in the street. We walked from hayloft to hayloft, class to class, we had classes by half-days.*"

Midori Johnson faced a similar situation in Tokyo. "*At the end of 1943, there was no school, and our school had a big building, a concrete big building, so they converted it into sort of a factory. We worked there, anything we were asked. And the small children in grade school were moved to the country. We were making parts, filaments for vacuum tubes.*"

In contrast to these hardships, children going to school in the United States led relatively calm lives. According to Leeta Crook and Sister Jeanne d'Arc Schleicher, both teachers, school children enthusiastically participated in newspaper and scrap metal drives. "*Anytime there would be a drive for something, they would bring whatever we were trying to get,*" said Sister Jeanne d'Arc. Students bought war stamps and planted Victory Gardens. *"The students knew why they were doing it. They were very well aware of what was going on. Some of them had brothers and fathers in the service. We had maps, globes, and the war was brought out in our social studies,"* according to Leeta Crook.

Work and Community Service

In Great Britain, children helped out as agricultural workers. Bine Hirsch remembered:

"Children were let out of school at specific times to do agriculture jobs because the men were in service and the women were in the factories . . . so in the fall, we are sent out with baskets to pick rose hips and haws (from the hawthorne trees. They were turned into the government, pureed as a source of vitamin C for children. We started digging potatoes in the fields."

Geneviève Moline, at age fourteen and a half, entered the Red Cross and worked in a first aid station and helped out at the time of a bombing on the railroad station at Bezons-Bruyère.

"I was called and I went to Courbevoie and it was horrible. They asked me if I preferred picking up the dead and the wounded or working in the morgue. I preferred picking up the dead and the wounded because at the morgue there were the adults. The first person that I saw, that I picked up no longer had a head. It was hideous; it was impressive and moving.

"That was a very difficult, hard experience. The bomb entered the lower part of the station, and I saw on the street Lambreche, in Courbevoie, the boys who were the Pétain youth that we called the 'pétainists,' cleaning, sweeping until six o'clock in the evening. Then they left. There were still people screaming down below. But they left because it was six o'clock. And it was we, the first aid workers who swept and who tried to pull more people out because they continued to scream. The water pipes broke so they risked being drowned. And we worked until late at night. It was a difficult experience for me and made a overwhelming impression on me."

Parents carefully trained their children to remain silent if the Gestapo questioned them. Robert LeBerre recounted one incident in which the Germans, having been alerted that there had been a parachute drop containing arms, arrived when the family was at breakfast. The Germans fired shots, turned the furniture upside down and asked the children to tell them when and where the planes arrived. LeBerre said, *""Ah, no. We pretended to be stupid. None of us said anything. The planes? We didn't hear anything. We continued to give the impression of being stupid. They were furious but they left."* [43]

Fear

Guy Bedel lived with his mother in Pleubian, on the northern coast of Brittany, one of the strategic positions for communication with Great Britain and for smuggling people out of France to join de Gaulle in London. He recalled the arrival of German soldiers looking for men and arms.

"I remember that period, particularly, the occupation by the Germans in that region, where we greatly feared the arrival of the Germans, not knowing exactly what that would bring about. But they [the Germans] feared this coast, known by the Breton sailors and the Breton people.

"The occupying forces were very harsh toward the population. The German soldiers were prepared to terrorize the population. The stories I can tell you, one after another, left their mark on me. I have, in my child's mind, a sort of hatred toward the armed soldiers that arrived, who came night and day to look for something or other, thinking there were men hidden, that there was material hidden.

"I remember very well, that one night, I don't remember at what time, maybe at 11 o'clock at night, the Germans came beating, with the butt-end of the machine gun, on the door of the school where we lived. They were looking for crystal sets, the radios that transmitted with England. The people, including my mother, thought they were looking for ordinary radios. I have to say that the radios then, compared to today, were monumental in size, with a wooden frame. I remember my mother at the foot of my bed, hiding, if I can say 'hiding' the radio which looked like the camel's hump. And the German, coming into my room, insulted my mother, saying, 'This is not what I am looking for, I'm looking for the sets which transmit to England.' He left, very, very angry, again insulting my mother and the neighbors on the doorstep."[44]

Living with the Enemy

Another aspect of the occupation in France which was difficult to tolerate, was the obligation to house German troops which forced French families to live intimately with their occupiers. One such family was Yvonne Lenoir, the mother, her daughter, Marie-Madeleine Herbelin and two younger children. When their attempt to flee eastern France during the "exodus" was thwarted, they returned to their house in Nancy.

Daughter: *We had a very large house, an enormous house with ten or twelve rooms. I don't think that everyone was obliged to lodge the German soldiers. They saw the capacity for lodging soldiers in our house, and the fact that around there were strategic points for the Germans, they imposed on us about fifteen German soldiers (officers). And unfortunately for us which wasn't amusing, I don't* know what they were called who wore the arm band with the Nazi cross, a group more abominable than others. We lived with them for two years.

It wasn't too hard. The house was well-enough divided. There was one part of the house for them; and we had a part of the house which was for us.

My impression of them was very much mixed. They were proper, although they were assassins. They were men very well brought up. There is something that absolutely stupefied us; it was that these Germans were relatively correct in the house, and later we learned that these men who left in the morning were those who were in charge of the political prisoners in the Charles III prison and who shot them. But they were courteous to us.

We were young children and they smiled at us. They were very gentle and kind toward my little sister, two years old, blond with blue eyes who made them think of their own children. And they gave us candy. And we found this absolutely fabulous. Unfortunately, we had a chauvinistic and nationalistic grandmother who detested the Germans from the time she was born, who spent her time haughtily giving them the once over. Every time we received some bonbons, she took them and threw them symbolically in the stove so they would burn because they were German candies. That was the tragedy of my life. When they gave us candy, we tried to hide. When we had contact with these men, they were perfectly decent and acceptable and correct.

Mother: At our house, they were not dangerous. But they had arms everywhere; they had grenades in their boots.

The house, being large, with a wing a bit to the side, we had to lodge five or six Germans. As we lacked everything, we saw them arrive each one, eating a big tart for four persons.

In the stores, they were often ridiculous, especially the officers trying on women's corsets [to send to their wives], and as we had to be at their disposition. They came to weigh their packages which couldn't be over a certain weight and they sent them to Germany. They were able to get food, butter and eggs and meat, and they came to cook them on our stove. We ignored them, they were correct, a little vexed when they wanted to give candy to the children and the parents refused them. When Hitler made a speech, they came to listen on our radio.

We stayed two years then we went back to Paris to our apartment. The Germans in '40, '41, '42 were not disagreeable. It wasn't until '43, '44 that they changed."

The German Occupiers in France

In general, the German soldiers, who had been indoctrinated by Hitler and later stationed in France as part of the occupying forces, did not find the French to their liking.

Politically, Hitler regarded France as the mortal enemy of the German people. Dating from his days in Vienna, he railed at the chauvinism of the French view of themselves as the "great cultural nation," the "civilized" nation.[45]

Karl Fuchs was a German tank gunner from 1937 to 1941 and was stationed in occupied France after the Armistice. Excerpts from his letters collected in a book by his son, Horst Fuchs Richardson and Dennis Showalter, editors, *Sieg Heil!, War Letters of Tank Gunner Karl Fuchs, 1937-1941*,45 revealed his prejudices.

With some spare time, Fuchs and friends went to a bookstore and he wrote to his wife, *"You can't imagine what junk and pornography we saw! There were nothing but magazines full of erotic pictures. . . . You can truly see that in the areas of cleanliness and morality, the French people have skidded to a new low. Such an incident is simply unthinkable and impossible in our German Fatherland."* [46]

Not all German soldiers were as critical of their enemies. Adolphe Jaede managed to live with the French in relative peace. Jaede was originally from Hamburg, Germany and was mobilized in 1939 at the age of twenty. He went directly to Lorient, the well-fortified port on Brittany's coast, in 1940. After France lost the war, he stayed for the Occupation in one of the first occupation units.

"We were one of the first German units at Lorient. We formed a Food Supply Center at Lorient. I was in the navy, those ships whose job it was to provide the food supplies. I was part of that supply base, specially for the submarines at Lorient. I was in charge of food supplies for 2,500 men as well as for the civilian population billeted there. One part of our mission was to set up artillery against the English planes coming to lay mines in the narrows. Larger pieces of artillery were also mounted against a possible invasion.

"When the merchandise arrived, it had to be stocked. We worked ten hours a day. The work wasn't hard; we were young. We provided all the food for the navy; 36 to 40 pigs each day. We fed them well!

"Just after I arrived, they [the Allies] *bombed Lorient. When you have four bombs, one right after another, a ton of explosives, you have to take refuge. A bomb fell just in front of the fishing boats, a man came out, the bomb exploded. He was not hurt but we kept the family with us, a French family who were poor. We had enough space in the house that we had at our disposition; we kept them with us, we didn't evict them. His wife was young and they had three children. We had the possibility of food supplies, since we were attached to the Supply Service."*

"Me, I was against the Nazis. I was against Hitler. I was against a dictatorship.

"Now if you learn German, and you spend time with a German family to practice your German, and you want to talk about the war, they don't want to. Always, they say, 'It wasn't our fault.' That's completely idiotic. The English sabotaged the landing of the Jews because they didn't want to have too strong an Israeli population. The French, the Poles, they wouldn't give them military instruction because they didn't want Jews in the army.

"In Germany, I can swear, for the greatest part, we didn't know what the camps were. We knew they existed, but we didn't know they were so bad.

"In Hamburg, it was a mixed neighborhood, best street in Hamburg, workers, rich merchants, Jews, synagogue, the modern church.

"When I left school at fifteen, because my father needed me, I would go to that section because I had friends there. I was eighteen, three years before the war. There was the synagogue. There were windows broken.

"In Germany, there were Jews who were perfectly correct. They sold cloth and work clothes. As I knew the store well, I made a large purchase, he looked at me, and asked me, 'Aren't you afraid?' I said, 'No, since I was ten years old, we bought our clothes here. I've come here to buy clothes for my brother.' He said, 'You need to watch out.'

"There were the Hitler Scouts, I was in the Hitler Scouts, the military scouts. There were also Jewish scouts.

"They broke Jews' windows; they threw stones at the Jews. I saw a lot. They were afraid of the merchants, they were afraid of secret organizations.

"I was one of the first to go to Paris. I went for a walk, Boulevard Haussman, the Champs-Elysées. In the shops, in each shop window, it was marked 'Jew.' I didn't see any men with the yellow Jewish star, but the girls, who went for walks, wore the yellow star."

As the Allied troops arrived in 1944 to take the strategic Lorient pocket, Jaede was sent to Brittany, near Plouhinec on the right bank of the river Etel. On 10 May 1945 the German troops surrendered. Jaede was interned first in a camp near Plouhinec for eight weeks, then sent to Rouen to help in the reconstruction of the city.[47]

Denmark, Hitler's "Canary Bird"

Denmark accepted German occupation with resignation. The Danish Government decided to continue to lead as normal a life as possible with German assurances that they could remain independent in her domestic affairs. Danish bases and communications, however, became available to the Germans. Denmark was also required to break off relations with the Allied countries.

A Social-Democratic coalition government based on a coalition of the major political parties was formed. The policy of negotiation was accepted, somewhat bitterly, as a political necessity in order to avoid a greater evil, a Nazi government in Denmark.

To say that the Danes were better off than any other occupied country does not imply that there weren't difficult times during the occupation, nor that sacrifices weren't demanded. Aksel Schiotz whose singing career and tours were put on hold because of the invasion and occupation of Denmark, faced some challenges.

The family lived in a borrowed British house on $15 a month and whatever fees and grants Axsel received. His wife, Gerd Schiotz, explained how they managed.

"*Our government said, don't do anything, we have to follow the rules and have to be obedient to the Germans. Life went fairly normally and there was food enough. The play went on. Children went to school. On the surface, it was very calm. Our government was scared of Germany because they could smash us up in one night.*

"*The Germans took a line that they behaved very nicely because it was very important that they get the agriculture products from Denmark.*

"*We had some friends in the Manor House and we could stay there in the winter. That turned out to be an arctic winter, so dreadfully cold. The kids were playing in the house. We managed. Food was not hard to get. We were the food store for Germany, and they had to treat us well or we couldn't produce for all Germany. Four-fifths of what was produced went to Germany. We had points [ration points for food], and it was generous, but no coffee, no wine, no tea, no imports of any kind. When it came to having twins in '42, how about having diapers? I dug up old people's attics, 'Do you have things I can remake for diapers, for bed clothes?' So we tore them up and we mended everything. We saved a lot of things then. But when Axsel had his recitals, they knew about the twins, so they would bring him flowers, and they were wrapped into one or two diapers. On a two-week tour, 'Last night I got two diapers and the day before, I had three.' It was wonderful.*

"*In 1941, Danish people went to theater and opera. Aksel only made tours in Denmark. Occasionally he was allowed by the Germans to go to Sweden but he had to get permission. The Germans live on music and they were understanding that cultural life had to go on. The men behind, I think, they kept their hand over Axsel's head because he was spared. The Germans loved Axsel's singing. They tempted him all the time to work with them. They offered him jobs there.*

"*In '41 and '42 we still went to the summer cottage. But not later because the waters were all mined up against the Swedish coast, the west coast. So we couldn't do that.*"

Children learned to grow up quickly, accept responsibility, do one's duty and obey their parents. Adults who better understood the ramifications of Hitler's Third Reich watched and waited.

End Notes

43   Geneviève Moline has retired from her position as Adjutant for Education for the city of Levallois-Perret; Midori Johnson left Japan, married an American and divides her time between Colorado and Hawaii; Marie and Robert LeBerre and Jean Cotten live in Quimper. Until their retirement, Leeta Crook taught in the elementary school in Fort Collins, Colorado and Sister Jeanne d'Arc taught Biology at Loretto Heights College, Denver.
44   Guy Bedel lives in Quimper where he is a school administrator.
45   *Mein Kampf*, Chapter 2
46   Horst Fuchs Richardson and Dennis Showalter, editors, Sieg Heil! War Letters of Tank Gunner Karl Fuchs, 1937-1941, Hamden, Connecticut: Archon Books: 1987, pp. 68-69
47   Jaede returned to live in Groix with his French wife. He ran the Garage Adolphe at Port Trudy, Groix, until his retirement.

CHAPTER 8
GROWING UP IN HITLER'S GERMANY

Children in Germany faced similar shortages of food and clothing, but their life was also regimented by philosophical and political considerations. Hitler extended his control of political and economic life in the Third Reich to cultural life. The fine arts, literature, music, theater, radio, and films served the propaganda purposes of the new order.

Education was a critical tool of the new order. In *Mein Kampf*, Hitler outlined the purpose of education which was to give the German youth self-confidence and a belief in their superiority to others. This concept affected the school curriculum, through its emphasis on physical fitness and training; science as an instrument of national pride; history as a tool for a better political education. Germany's young were to be educated to become the educators and leaders of the future, willing to liberate Germany from its enemies, that is, capitalists, Jews, and marxists.

German youth groups originated with the *Wandervogel* movement of the late 19th century. It was a chance to rediscover nature and escape from the urban and industrial scene. Hitler saw an opportunity to make the German Youth Movement a part of the National Socialist Work Party of Germany, and in 1931 it became a unit of the SA (storm troopers). In 1932 the BDM (*Bund Deutscher Mädchen*), the girls' section, became part of the Hitler Youth. The Hitler Youth Movement was organized into groups:

•Male: *Jungvolk* (10 - 14 years of age), and Hitler Youth (14 to 18 years of age)

•Female: *Jungmädel* (10 to 14 years of age), and BDM, League of German Girls (14 to 18 years of age).

New members of the *Jungvolk* swore the oath:
"I promise / In the Hitler Youth / To do my duty / At all times / In love and faithfulness / To help the Führer / So help me God."[48]

At age 18, both male and female members entered NSDAP (the National Socialist Work Party) and had six to twelve months of labor service, including the special "land service" for general land and harvest service. For the young men, this was followed by military service, and for the women, work in field hospitals, state kindergartens and at railway stations to give food and drink to troops in transit.

During the war, times were hard for young Germans: there was fear and uncertainty, food and clothing shortages, many households headed by women, restrictions on normal teenage activities, and finally post-war problems brought on by the destruction of German cities and the failing economy.

Ultimately, for many growing up in Germany during the war years, the most difficult thing to face was the paradox: how to reconcile what they had been taught about the superiority of the Aryan race with German defeats at Stalingrad and at the Battle of the Bulge, or how to reconcile the Germany of Goethe and Schiller with the Germany of the Holocaust.

Rigomar Thurmer and Elfriede Gamow grew up under the Third Reich and first came to the United States to study.

A Lost Youth

Thurmer reflected that he is still catching up on what he missed as a child and as an adolescent.

"As I saw my children grow up and saw what they did, I look back on what I did at the same age. That's when all of a sudden I found out I had been wasted, supporting an obnoxious theory of world domination.

"I was three years old when Hitler came to power and I was living then on the Bavarian-Czechoslovakian border. In 1936, when I was six years old and Hitler had been in power for three years, we moved to a resort town, right on the Bavarian-German border near Salzburg. I was fifteen when World War II ended in 1945.

"Most of the adults accepted the notion of Hitler's dominance; everybody now says different. At the time, they gave him a mandate. In 1933 there was no question, Hitler won with a landslide. As a matter of fact, he got 102 percent of the popular vote. My father was a Nazi. He was a young forester official in a totally depressed area at the Bavarian-Austrian border. The small town he was in had two industries, one was smuggling, the other was unemployment. And in 1933, all of a sudden there was work. They were building logging roads. And my father said, 'This is it!' And he was supportive of the elected authority to the very end. No, there is no question, there were a lot were economic reasons.

"Of course at that time, I didn't realize it, but it was a very restrictive, warped childhood. Aside from not having enough to eat, I was a growing boy through all of those years, we were very isolated from the rest of the world, as children. I look at my children now; I never traveled, I had no books, I had no sporting equipment. The only thing I really had were the mountains. And those, of course, could not be rationed or taken away. Hitler never could do anything with the mountains

A Time to Speak

because it is hard to goose-step down those faces. They were really sort of my world: skiing, and climbing, and hiking, just getting away from the grown-ups, the Hitler Youth.

"It was very carefully controlled. I had to get an Aryan pass. I remember my father coming home and saying, 'It is a great day, all three of us have pure Aryan backgrounds.' And I said, 'Why the hell can't I get anything to eat around here?'

"There were ration cards; there was a black market. Over the years, a lot of my mother's linen was traded, the piano went, I cheerfully remember because it meant the end of piano lessons; and jewelry was traded. So gradually, since my father was a government official, we didn't have anything to trade. In our case, we had to have something. I was always hungry, always hungry. I grew to be 6 ft. 4 by the time I was fourteen or fifteen. Food was always on your mind. Theft for that purpose didn't really become a sin or anything. It was just something one did, stealing wherever you could, for all the things you didn't have. We never considered the loss to the other person.

"Beer and cigarettes were around. Beer was always available, very weak, but there was enough hops. I picked hops in the summers as war effort. On vacation, we had to do something for the war effort as a volunteer. Cigarettes were available. I started smoking Russian majorka, Russian tobacco was imported. Everybody grew majorka which is a Russian tobacco. And cigarettes became the ultimate currency. Everything one could desire from new tires to sex was available with cigarettes. So for many years my whole life revolved around how many cigarettes do you have to get for this guy to get a new pair of skis, a new pair of boots.

"I was able to ski. It was a constant problem, trying to get skies, they were terrible. When an Allied plane was shot down, the German field police (the sheriff's department) went out to try and capture the crew; sometimes they did; sometimes they had disappeared. After that, it was open to being salvaged. Everybody had something; that plane disappeared mighty fast. And I was interested in the foam of the seat cushions because that foam was used in padding for ski boots. So I could trade some of that foam in a round-about-way, having enough leather and thread so they would make a pair of ski boots for me, being paid in cigarettes. So this was a constant shuffle. For the skis themselves, there was a German production and I remember you could buy those, new with some wood, with coupons and through my father's profession, I was able to get the wood coupons, but some of those skis didn't last long.

"I did go to school. I did, of course, have a fairly limited education. Everything was focused toward Nazi Germany and the fact that we were the master race, the salt of the earth, which made me wonder later on why everyone was beating up on us since we were a God-sent kind of thing. I started kind of thinking.

"The idea of the master race: well, it created a certain conflict between what grownups were telling us and what the world was doing to us. It made us very suspicious. I think by the time I was fifteen, sixteen, I was a total amoral person. Neither the grown-up world, nor the church could be trusted. And I think that kind of moral kink that many of us did get is still apparent in Germany and it will take more than a few generations to change the make-up of the people. It will take a long time to get there.

"One advantage I had was I had some ancient teachers that had been recalled because all the young ones were in the war. And so I did get a glimpse of a classical education. There was a slight advantage; it was a sort of a little window. We had an English teacher who had spent thirty years in England. We read Shakespeare which was about the only English language text available. One day, he came in and he said, 'You guys, I've lost my list of books that we are not supposed to use. I can't find it,' which was a lie. 'I only have a few copies, short stories by a writer, Jack London.' This was great. The teacher was eighty-four then and he just didn't give a damn anymore. There was some punishment if you got caught. He did not get caught. They probably knew about him and said, 'It's not worth going after that old guy.'

"We had Nazi authors. We were fed Nietzsche, Kant, and Hegel. It was mainly the German classics. There was that Nordic myth in school all the time, Wotan, the Gotterdammerung. The rest of the literary world, which I suspected existed some place out there, was just not existent.

"There was music. Music was considered a stamina builder. I was always told if I listened to classical music I wouldn't be that hungry. I never quite caught that relationship. Music was available. It was Wagnerian, and Wagner of course, the court composer, incessantly.[49] I didn't even know a composer like Mendelssohn or Offenbach.

"There was very careful propaganda. The Propaganda Ministry very carefully controlled all aspects of information . The visual arts, of course, I went to the famous exhibit of degenerate art in Munich . . . we did get off from school to go there. It did backfire. It ran very briefly because all of a sudden a surprising number of people, a ground-swell, went to that exhibit because they knew it was their last chance to see some of their favorite art. So as soon as Goebbels found out about that, he closed it. One of the classic miscalculations. [50]

"The same thing, teaching about other countries, continents. They were always painted as capitalistic societies with people starving, the economies in a mess, and we were going to beat them sooner or later. After 1941 when the treaty with Russia was broken, we were taught anti-communism.

A Time to Speak

"So, movies. I'm catching up on twenty-five years of all the movies I never saw. I take four out of the library. There were movies; there were two kinds, schmaltz and edelweiss, hearts and flowers variety. You know Hitler had a philosophy about Blut und Boden, blood and earth. So there were the blood and earth movies. Then there were the propaganda movies, depicting German victories over the inferior races, countries, that sort of thing. No American movies. What would Hitler have done with Hedy Lamar or Rita Hayworth?

"Anti-Semitic propaganda was not in the schools so much, just in general, in the press and in the public statements and so on. The schools somehow felt we would be indoctrinated anyway by our parents and society as a whole, so they didn't seem to see that they needed to waste time. But of course it was all around you. You had to be very intelligent, well-educated, socially savvy, and a good liar not to know what was going on and what was planned. Hitler was very clear in 1923 in Mein Kampf what he intended to do, and he never rescinded it.

"What happened to the German Jews was often based on economic considerations. They were a tough competition. They always are. As a small tribe, they supply an incredible amount of leaders in all fields and they are good businessmen, so most of the people in my home town sort of looked the other way when the Jews were forced to sell their businesses. Hitler, in Germany, still had to watch public opinion to some degree, so unlike what happened in the Ukraine and in Poland, he used a very subtle method. He forced the Jews to sell their business; he removed their residence permit which you have to have in Europe, so the family had to move to another city where nobody knew them. Then their apartment permit was revoked and the various family members had to live in furnished rooms. There were Germans who did help Jewish people. Some of them got into trouble for that. But in general, the German society looked the other way.

"Also you are aware of the revisionist movement in Germany, claiming the Holocaust never happened. My mother, to the end of her days, did not believe the Holocaust happened. She said, 'That's all propaganda. Sure the Jews weren't treated very well and they put them to work because they needed to learn how to work harder. But the rest of it, just propaganda. I just don't believe it, I just don't. We Germans, with our Kultur, our cultural heritage, we could never do anything like that.'

"The Hitler Youth were the focal group. It was not compulsory to belong to the Hitler Youth; however, in effect, it was, except if you were mentally or physically disabled. It was really a strike against you if you weren't part of the Hitler Youth. You did get one afternoon off, no homework, Wednesday afternoon, and of course, you know, kids would do anything to get out of school. They will commit murder. So it was an inducement. Whatever travel we could do was facilitated through

Hitler Youth Rallies and Hitler Youth outings. I was part of that, yes. The Hitler Youth drew a lot from the Wandervogel movement from the '20s and '30s: hiking, see the world, that type of thing. I went to a big rally in Nuremberg, with all of the searchlights and the flags waving, 10,000 young boys raising hell in town. Anyway, it got us out of school for three days.

"I really didn't think anything about it [the Hitler Youth], because it is like being in the center of a hurricane. You have no idea of what is really going on. It was the way things were. It was just it. We tried to make the best of it. You know, you learned to goose-step, but the problem was that the Hitler Youth favored that sort of perfect Aryan type. Most of us weren't. I sure wasn't. I wasn't 'tough as leather.' I wasn't as 'fast as an afghan hound.' There was that Hitler Youth oath that listed all of those desirable things. I remember two: 'tough as leather, fast as a wind hound, an afghan.' [The third trait was 'hard like Krupp steel.'] There were a whole bunch of them. I grew up Catholic, the Bavarian version. We considered it just one other bunch of oppressors, the SS and the policemen. Of course, the Catholic Church never took a stand against Hitler the way the Lutheran Church did. Their pastors spoke out and went to concentration camps.

"At fourteen you automatically become part of the senior division. You have a different uniform and you get to bully the little guys around officially. And you get a dagger, a Hitler Youth dagger with a symbol on it. Other than that, it was just a continuation of being groomed for the nebulous future where we were going to conquer the world.

"I did have a Hitler Youth assignment in Poland which ended up in a Danish island. It had to do with swimming. I swam competitively. They were trying to find replacements for the losses of the German frogman team. I didn't know that, when I left, until I got actually to the training ground. But I did end up on April 18, 1943 in Warsaw, in the railroad station and sat there for quite a few hours. It was the date the Jewish ghetto exploded. We were told it was the Polish underground that had risen and all army leaves were cancelled. Jews didn't do that sort of thing [revolt]; they turned the other cheek. It was the first time a bunch of Jews decided not to do that, and it took two German SS regiments ten days to put down that rebellion.

"I did go through basic training with the SS in the monastery Weyarn in Bavaria, not because I was heading for the SS but because they had space available. It was a pre-military training, it was a sort of boot camp for young guys. It was mainly to break us. To give you one example, the handbook, Handbuch der Wehrmacht, paragraph one, 'A German soldier obeys an order, no more and no less.' So we'd stand out there and the Herr Oberscharführer, an SS non-com, said, 'Jump in the air.' We all jumped. And he said, 'Who said anything about coming

A Time to Speak

down?' 'You will learn to obey that order, no more, no less.' So we jumped for hours on end. Not very funny. Finally, you suck in your neck and try to keep a clean nose, keep your mouth shut and your rectum open. The universal law in all armies, and we did.

"We had to volunteer on Saturday on our day off, to work on the farm that our Herr Oberscharführer and his wife ran with all the livestock and fowl and everything. Some of the better looking guys got to clean the house of Frau Oberscharführer.

"We didn't know how to rebel against the political system. We knew how to rebel against our parents, our teachers and the cops, that's universal knowledge. But how to rebel against something that we really weren't sure about. Maybe those guys were right, so there was a instinct there not to expose yourself too much lest it backfired. So we just kept to ourselves. We talked about what boys all over the world talk about, now that I look back, 'I say why the hell didn't I try to get out?' That's easy to say. I am a grown up man, I've traveled all over the world. But at that time, I wouldn't have known how to get to Switzerland. They had the Sippeschaft which was Hitler's new legal concept of making the immediate family responsible for the misdeeds, which he used devastatingly after the 20th of July assassination attempt against him. That was the first time really, but it was a concept which was around. Your family would be held responsible with severe consequences, desertion was the big thing. Why didn't more German soldiers desert? When they already saw that it wasn't a bad thing to be in Oklahoma as a POW rather than be dead in Russia. There was that problem of severe repercussions for your family.

"Then, when toward the end of the war, I became fifteen, my birthday which is March 11, I became eligible for the Volksturm or National guard. I did my thing there and came back, which was to keep a good distance from the U. S. Third Army in front of us. We knew their patterns: they had breakfast in the morning, by 9:30 they were ready to move, so we were expected to withdraw then. The SS flying corps that cruised behind the German lines was trying to get deserters. Everything was falling apart then, in April 1945, so we disappeared and I made it home just a few hours before the first GIs crossed the river on a partially destroyed bridge, and that was the end of World War II.

"And two days later I started to work for the Occupation Force. With the principal of our high school, they needed two guys who spoke English and we saw visions of Lucky Strike cigarettes. The next think we knew we were cleaning toilets in the former German army barracks for one of the all-black outfits, one of the few black outfits that the U. S. Army had in World War II, a quartermaster outfit, which after reading Shakespeare for six years, it did improve my colloquial English. As a matter of fact, that's when I decided that some day, I don't know how, I was going to go to the place where those guys come from, when the enemy treats you better than your own people.

"I stayed on. I had no way of getting out. I did get a Master's degree in architecture at the Munich Institute of Technology. I worked for two years in construction, contributing to rebuilding the universities destroyed during the war. And the post-war years, there was nothing until the Deutsche-mark in 1948. I supported myself on the black market and after that I had no money. I had a life insurance policy which came due when I was eighteen, and it was going to finance my college and graduate school education. And it bought, probably, a dozen cartons of Lucky Strikes and I was paid off in Reichsmark. So I worked throughout school to support myself.

"Then a Fulbright and Harvard came to my rescue in 1954. So I spent the first twenty years, a third of my life, really, serving the fatherland somehow.

"To me, World War II formed aspects of my life, most of these things I wasn't aware of. At that time, I had very little idea of what was going on, that my future as a human being was really jeopardized, either being killed in the war, or being killed after the war, or not being able to get an education, or ending up digging ditches. It could very well have happened. I could have followed the millions that have disappeared in Russia after World War II. They made a lot of these Germans offers, if they were skilled laborers, saying either you become a Soviet citizen and stay here or you'll never get home, ever again. So there are hundreds of thousands of Germans now in Russia.

"It is so inconceivable to me. I went back to Germany, as long as my mother was alive, and I would look around and look at my class-mates, guys I played with. How could it happen? Did it really happen? I know it happened, I have a lot of books and information on that subject. It is just incomprehensible; it will be for many years until finally it becomes part of history." [51]

I Remember...

Elfriede Gamow grew up in eastern Germany, which later came under Communist control.

"I will start with 1939 when I was born, July 20, I was born just before the war. My first memories are of my father being gone, not there. It was a female household, my oldest sister, myself, my grandmother who was a very energetic woman (the mother of my father) and my mother who was a very soft-spoken woman. Then the baby of the family, my brother was born in 1940. A small town, middle of Germany, Sonneberg in Turingen, a pretty, sleepy, untouched place. Small industry, home industry, so it was of no strategic value at that point, also no important railroad going through. However, it had a railroad station to ship out Christmas ornaments, dolls, and toys.

"Then my memory is of hard times as far as food is concerned. Those are my first memories, not of knowing hunger, but of very tough times to get enough. And then I remember my father coming back the first time to visit, my vivid memory, in the spring of 1944, in preparation and in anticipation of my younger sister being born. I don't remember if he got special leave or not, but I remember one particular walk that we took together in the springtime, and we saw the storks coming back from Africa, coming to the villages for their nests. Then he left again and came back. And my sister was born in June.

"Then I do remember all the women, of course, were working. What they were working on, I don't know. My mother worked mainly on farms in the vicinity and this way she got some food. And I remember everyone always waiting for their husbands and fathers, and that never changed and most of them I never saw again. I have very grim memories of my mother's generation, her friends and the husbands and the ones that never came back. I do remember some men coming home on leave once in a while.

"It was very difficult on the women. The surprising thing, to me, is what women can do if they have to and how strong they really are. My mother has always been under a 100 pounds and she would go on her bicycle every day and work in the fields. She often got food to take home.

"And of course, there are little things you keep in mind. The bicycle was the simplest bicycle and it always had to be fixed because there were no spare parts, particularly no rubber tires. And the rareness of the food, three or four potatoes which would feed a family of seven to eight, nine, ten sometimes. And my mother would make a soup out of these potatoes that would almost kill me every time I had to eat it; and I called it the 'snot' soup, but that was the only way you could get some substance into this water.

"I do not remember sad times in spite of it all, it was an invigorating and happy time. We just did it! We planted food on every scrap of ground there was. Of course, there was no space for flowers which created in me this eternal lust for flowers. Strawberries were totally luxury and were totally out and no one would plant strawberries. That's why I can't stop eating strawberries now.

"Everything was recycled. That's how I learned to undo a knitted sweater and to undo embroidery. My dress for the beginning of school was out of one of my father's uniforms and it was so thick and stiff that I could have stood in the corner, fallen over, and the dress would have stood there. I remember it; rough and heavy, brown wool flannel and my mother had made a beautiful little dress out of it, all hand-sewn; it was beautiful, unbelievable, actually it was piped in plaid. The worst thing I remember is no shoes. And then, of course, when winter comes and it gets cold. You kept wearing the same old things and they never fit. They were either too small or too big because you had to pass them on. In the summertime, from April to October, we were barefoot.

"The other memories of that time are that the American Air Force flew over, with the bombing. It was towards the end of the war and the big bombing sprays were going on over other cities. We had air alerts and we had underground bunkers, beer cellars and we spent many a day and night in these underground sand stone caves. I have very, very vivid memories that were such little nooks carved out where they stored the beer barrels, and each family got one of those little caves. All I remember really, is that there must have been electric light or emergency light because I don't really remember candles. But it was pretty stuffy, crowded, babies crying and everything. We brought our own bedding.

"Then the early days of '45 we spent a lot of time underground and I remember my younger sister was very small and we always had her in a carriage. She was forever crying.

"And I remember the enormous amount of airplanes going over to bomb Dresden. At the time the word, Dresden, was mentioned and that was in very early '45. And then we always waited and wondered what else would happen. And I don't remember the exact time, then our railroad station was bombed. It was totally wiped out. They did pretty good direct hits at that point. They were very precise. The whole storage area burned. It was a tough thing. It exploded and burned. Our houses, some were badly damaged. Ours just had some holes through, some cracks in the walls. Of course all of the windows were out. There wasn't a window in the town and there was no glass. So wherever you had sheets, anything to cover the windows.

"We were there in the shelters sometimes three and four days. Actually we read, we played cards, we played games. You waited and the anxiety always was, who would peek out first and see if the house was still standing. Then you came home and you had to clean up the glass. I remember that, forever trying to clean up.

"I started schooling in '45. I don't remember too much of my early grades. We had mainly female teachers, of course, but I know then that everyone was being trained to be a teacher right after the war in our area. So we had, what you call, substitute teachers or help teachers, or poorly trained teachers. Students took school very seriously. I remember no heat in schools, absolutely no heat; we were sitting with gloves, five layers of clothes, the layered look. And hardly being able to hold your pen, we still had slate board and slate pencils.

"Then, of course, the war in Europe was over in May and I don't recall the events in Asia. Then the wait began for the soldiers to come home, which in this case, meant my father. That was interesting. He returned that same summer. He never left German soil. He was in communications. He came from southern Germany, and he came home with a horse and carriage.

"Before my father came home, I do remember what happened with the Occupation. I remember it must have been in May or June. I remember the French occupational troops coming through my home town. The railroad station was totally non-functional. There were empty spaces and the French occupational forces came through and they camped right in the middle of the road of the train station. They had their campfires, they cooked their food, they slept outside in tents, on cots. In the evening I heard them sing. They didn't get riled up about anything. They totally left the population alone. I see them there out in the open, in a sense, actually enjoying life. Then they moved on.

"And we got American troops. It was my first encounter with black soldiers whom we of course ogled at. The American forces lived in houses. They occupied immediately the best looking houses, that meant what wasn't bombed out. The families still there had to move together. In our little one-family home, we had at least twenty-five or thirty people living because they were displaced out of their own homes, and they moved in with anyone who still had a square foot, with the chickens and the cats and the pigeons. They didn't resent the American soldiers. Actually, it was a relief that it was over.

"And the American soldiers, not only did they live very well, they chewed gum. They gave you some gum. They had chocolate. But they also did not treat their surroundings very well. I remember one soldier hacking up a piano and throwing it out the window. The house is still standing. I know where it happened. That was his way of saying, 'I'm the victor.' There was no resentment toward the French or the Americans.

"Here we were in a sort of a suburb and we had a very small yard. We had this horse and carriage, of British origin, given to my father, south of the Danube by British soldiers. My father spoke English, that helped him through the lines. He was going on foot, home with a friend. So these English soldiers, 'We don't need this, here.' They made friends and they gave him a horse and a carriage. He swam the Danube, how they got the carriage across I don't know, but he swam the Danube with a horse and he said, 'It was a wonderful feeling.' The horse just swam beautifully and they came across, then they made their way north from one barn to the next. And in one barn, the horse ate something he wasn't supposed to eat. The horse was smart, he sniffed out the only grain in the barn, found it and ate it.

"This horse was a very valuable thing then because the horse was something we could trade for food. And I remember being with my parents at the time. First we tried to sell it to a moving company. They had horses then, but actually they didn't have anything to give us for it. So my father went into the farm country and found a farmer who gave us a couple of sacks of potatoes for a horse and made sure his wife wasn't going to give us the potatoes that were earmarked for the pigs.

"It was very hard on my mother to see that she didn't have enough to feed us and the farmers got rich during that time. They got everything that anyone in the city had. But she made sure we weren't going to get the pig potatoes.

"Before we traded our horse, we did go on a couple of outings. That was very wonderful. No one knew what to do but we would go. We dressed up as much as we could and we drove around from our town to some little villages and came back. So my father was home in '45 towards the fall. He was one of the very few who came home healthy and pretty well.

"Then it changed very quickly because our province was traded for half of Berlin. In the fall of '45, when the victorious forces decided, 'We'll split up Germany.' The Russians said, 'You have to give us a little more territory,' and they just drew the line. And my hometown was the southern most corner of that. It was within a couple of kilometers from my house that the border was drawn.

"After the war my father went back into the dolls and toys business; he worked for a small company. Everything was done sort of self-help and he did actually design a sort of clay substance out of which friends of ours made doll heads. We did this at home in our oven and all these things; it was how industry got going again. Then, of course, he had a good head for business, but East Germany was not made for private business. He always tried. He never gave up. And so we had a little business, and it was socialized, and so it went on and on.

"We never saw the Russians except when they were going out on maneuvers or when they moved in or out. They occupied the leftover nice places and they built big fences around and they did not mingle with our population. They weren't allowed to. It was the Soviet way. We weren't in a war zone, we were strictly occupational area after it was over. They just moved in and they stayed from then on. We weren't a strategic area.

"Right with the end of the war, there is one feeling that I got and kept with me for many years and I feel even now very vividly, and that is, the fear of another war. It was absolutely with us like something you could touch. This war was bad enough as it is and the next one is going to be total, total destruction and annihilation. This is one feeling I had as a little kid. And while picking out glass in our driveway, where we walked barefoot because we had no shoes, that was our fear as a little kid. This third world war, this feeling was immediately there. And that really didn't subside in me until I was grown-up, maybe until I was in this country. It was really building deep, an enormous fear and that, I think, if you think back, was a feeling that many Germans had, and that is something that maybe the system in the

East capitalized on, because you get people to do a lot if they say, 'This will prevent this next war.' We didn't understand, but that was really something that could have been manipulated a lot.

"That particular fear of a third world war was a young, emotional juvenile thing. I now know it is much more complicated. It was a deep, almost primal feeling. I know things have changed and we all know that things have changed. We know we will most likely have small wars. Hopefully we are smart enough to avoid the one big one that wipes us out. But there is this thing of human nature that we have to face. Hopefully we have compassion and intelligence to see what is going on.

"Besides this very vivid feeling about a third world war, I have had this big conflict of 'Germanism' in me. I felt that, after the later years and I had left Germany and returned to Germany. It has always been one of the biggest puzzles in my heart, in my whole being. How come so much good and so much bad in the German nature and the German happenings. Walking down the streets in Germany, I would suffer from this, thinking back, not just the physical war, but what came with it, Hitler, the Holocaust. It is such a conflict. The whole fight would be happening in myself. I cannot believe this. I found out it happened to many people this way. That's why people had a hard time understanding the Holocaust. You are talking about the Germany of Goethe and Hegel and Schiller. So we have to face that, that these human beings have all of these capabilities, and have all of the spectrum in them and we have to watch it and it can happen again and again. We had better watch it and make a system that will see these things and has checks and balances and prevents such outgrowth.

"The time after the war was a very cleansing and purifying time, especially in the eastern part where it didn't get economically well so quickly. Hunger disappeared; pretty soon we had the basic things. It was a time of opportunity to do something wonderful and I don't know how well West Germany did it.

"I think maybe my husband Igor says, 'Elfriede, these hard times were actually good for you because early on in life you learned how to cope, how to be rewarded by small things and you learned to be grateful in all these things.' It was a good early experience as long as you didn't suffer too much." [52]

Western Europe was under Nazi control. Mussolini in Italy was an ally; Franco dominated Spain. Only Russia to the east and the island of Great Britain were left to conquer.

End Notes

48   H. W. Koch, *The Hitler Youth*, New York: Dorest Press, 1975, p. 101, p. 112

49   Wagner was anti-Semitic and had written, "I regret the Jewish race as the born enemy of pure humanity and everything that is noble in it. . . ."

50   Goebbels had organized an exhibit of modern expressionist and impressionist paintings to show the people what Hitler was rescuing them from. Unfortunately, it proved more popular than the exhibit of official Nazi art.

51   Rigomar Thurmer came to the United States as a Fulbright Scholar, then returned to Munich to work. He immigrated to the United States and taught at the School of Architecture at the University of Colorado and pursues his private architectural practice.

52   Elfriede Gamow came to the United States in 1960 as an exchange student, where she majored in sciences and received a doctorate. Today she is the owner and manager of a fabric shop in Boulder, Colorado.

CHAPTER 9
FRENCH PRISONERS OF WAR

French prisoners of war were traumatized by their swift defeat. By the time the combat ended, 1,800,000 French soldiers fell into enemy hands. Of this number, 1,600,000 were transferred to the Third Reich. About 1,000,000 were held in captivity for five years.

Life in prison, frequent moves from one camp to another, the unbearable work details, the paltry amount of food, the fear of death were unimaginable They lived on the hope of escape and the ultimate victory of the Allies.

What kept them going was their national pride, their solidarity through the friendships made, and their sense of humor. In spite of hardships, they managed to keep alert through activities they organized for themselves.

Concentration camps opened before Hitler entered Poland in 1939. Oranienburg (Germany) and Dachau (Germany) were opened in 1933, Buchenwald (Germany) in 1937, and Mauthausen (Germany) in 1938. In general, deportation was for political and military prisoners and "undesirables," whom the Nazis wished to control. They were confined in camps where they could be watched closely, where they would provide slave labor to supplement the German work force, and in the case of Jews and gypsies, where they could be systematically exterminated.

After the occupation of Poland and the western European countries, additional camps were opened and annexes built. Among them were: in 1939, Ravensbrück (Germany) for women; and in 1940, Struthof (Alsace, France); Auschwitz (Poland) enlarged to include Birkenau in 1941, Neuengamme (Germany), Flossenburg (Germany), Treblinka (Poland), Westerbork (Holland), Theresienstadt (Czechoslovakia), Drancy (suburb of Paris), reserved for Jews; in 1941, Rawa-Ruska (Eastern Galicia, an area now divided between Poland and the Ukraine.); and in 1943, Bergen-Belson (Germany).

The Nazi Concentration Camp System

The concentration camp system was highly organized and tightly controlled. All of the camps were very much the same: a vast enclosure, a barracks or "blocks" which could hold up to 40,000 deportees or prisoners. It was surrounded by electrified barbed wire barriers. About every 50 meters, there was a lookout tower with a beacon to use at night and from which sentinels could fire at will. Inside, the barracks were divided into rooms with slatted bunks superimposed on three tiers. At the end of each barracks there was a washroom. The camps also included a prison, an infirmary, a kitchen, sometimes a gas chamber and a crematorium, and next to the camp, the house of the commandant and houses for his workers.

Hitler turned the control of the concentration camps over to the SS (the *Schützstaffel*), originally a paramilitary group which maintained security at rallies and protected Hitler. The SS became an autonomous military and police organization, under the direction of Hermann Goering. The Gestapo (the *Geheime Staatspolizei*) expanded as a branch of the SS and maintained order, administered torture, and created terror.

The administration of an individual camp included the Commandant, who lived in his military house and often had a garden and a swimming pool; the chief administrator who dealt with economic questions; the chief of the camp, responsible for the prisoners; the chief of each block; the chief inspector; the Gestapo; a doctor; and a chief of the work detail.

Among the prisoners in each block there was one person, a "trusty," who distributed the packages from home and food from the Red Cross. A general "trusty" was charged with relations with the authorities of the camp, according to the Geneva Convention concerning prisoners of war.

Camps developed a "spoken newspaper" with information they gleaned from German newspapers. They often got news of the war's progress from recent prisoner arrivals. In certain camps teachers and professors created a study center to fight against boredom, to improve conditions, and to organize lectures on various subjects.

Prisoners with special expertise, for example, with a knowledge of German, were given additional such as interpreter for the prisoners, or as a bookkeeper.

Deportees and prisoners departed in convoys from gathering centers such as Drancy or Compiègne in France, or sometimes directly from other prisons. When they arrived, the arrival was registered, the prisoners matriculated (in Auschwitz, they were tattooed on the arm), they showered, shaved and dressed in the blue and white striped garment which resembled pajamas. In some camps they were given whatever clothes were available.

Political prisoners and deportees wore a triangular colored patch sewn on the chest of the garment: red, for political prisoners, green for criminals, violet for conscientious objectors and gypsies, rose for homosexuals, and a yellow star for Jews. A black letter indicated the nationality, A (German), F (French), P (Polish), B (Belgian), S (Spanish) and R (Russian). Some prisoners were marked with N.N. (*Nacht und Nebel* or Night and Fog) which signified the inevitable death sentence.

Prisoners learned the special vocabulary, useful for understanding life in camp: *L'appel*, a huge space for roll call; the *Revier*, a barrack reserved as a hospital and primarily served by doctors who did not necessarily have medical training; *Arbeit*, work with the slogan, *Arbeit Macht Frei*, "Works Makes One Free," inscribed over the entrance to camps; the *Kommando*, the work group; the *Kapo*, the German chief of the work group.

Stories of Three Prisoners

The memoirs and interviews with three former prisoners, Louis Bedel, Pierre Moussié, and Emmanuel Poirier, all at one time, held in Rawa Ruska, a camp which Winston Churchill, in 1942, called "the camp of a drop of water and a slow death," provided a vivid and eloquent picture of prison camp life.

Convoys and Matriculation

Prisoners transferred to a prison camp by train, each car chained shut with barbed-wire on the windows, giving them a sense of being "lions in a cage." A tub in the middle of the car served as a latrine which was soon full, overflowing and splashing anyone near it. PIERRE MOUSSIE wrote his impression of the journey.

"We left in freight cars, 80 for a car meant for 40. We stood up because it was impossible to sit down or go to sleep. The trip lasted a month, with several stops to have a taste of liquid, called soup. The rest of the time, one bread for thirty people. We didn't have a knife, razor, fork or a mess-tin. They took most of our clothes.

"This was the worst souvenir of my captivity. It was there, on the day of our departure, I heard the most moving 'Marseillaise' of my life: sung out by the entire train-full, goose-bumps, tears in our eyes, becoming a single being... we were proud.

"... I lived that in a painful nightmare. Finally, broken, dulled, crushed, we arrived at Rawa-Ruska.

"There was a single water tap [for 15,000 men] in the Camp which ran only three or four hours each day. Besides the water was polluted. ...

"A smell of cadavers, decay, shit, and death reigned. ..."

EMMANUEL POIRIER shivered and was determined to escape when he heard a German commandant declare: *"Understand, you Frenchmen, that we hold the right of life or death over you. In every way, you can consider yourselves deported for life!"*

The constant attempt to undermine the prisoners' morale began as soon as they arrived. LOUIS BEDEL affirmed this when he wrote in his diary:

"On the fifth day, here was Cracow, Lemberg and in the middle of the afternoon, Rawa-Ruska. We didn't have time to look around us. It was necessary to leap on the ballast, run, in spite of stiffened muscles. Frantic yelling by the guards, with cartridges conspicuously in their guns, ready to fire at any moment. Assembly, we are counted and re-counted. We marched between guards and dogs. At a little distance, we saw the camp, it was barb-wired. Brick construction, the entry to the camp, vast entry gate, the inscription Stalag 325.

"Hungry, worn out from fatigue, I saw these events in semi-consciousness. Morale undermined, we were going to starve to death here."

"I was in Stalag XI A, my number of 78002, inscribed on an aluminum tag which I was required to wear around the neck. I became an anonymous being, a Stück, a bit of scrap, a nothing, a slave. This was 29 June 1940."

Life in Camp

Life for prisoners of war revolved around food, work, sleep, illness, attempts to escape, mail to and from home, and the little routines and activities they devised for themselves to minimize the boredom and to strengthen their morale.

Each day began with roll call, varying in length of time, in a huge courtyard, followed by work outside the camp. According to *PIERRE MOUSSIE*, "Each day we were awakened at 5 o'clock to be present in the courtyard no matter what the weather was. About 9 o'clock, roll call was over."

Work

Members of the SS watched over the work, either from their observation posts or by walking the rounds with guard dogs trained to attack prisoners. Work depended on camp needs and the camp's proximity to an industrial area in need of slave labor. The *Kapo*, carrying a cudgel, and an SS guard oversaw the work details.

POIRIER began prison life as a hairdresser and barber for the Kommando. He began his work at 4 o'clock in the morning and it lasted until nightfall. Eventually, he was able to follow his pre-war occupation. He took advantage of each work change to prepare for his eventual getaway,

"Then I stopped being a barber and was able to take up my work as a shoemaker at a shop 600 meters from camp. My boss was a nice man who treated me well and got me a map of Germany that I studied while thinking about a plan to escape."

"I was sent to a camp where, every evening, I worked in a restaurant and earned a bit of German money, useful for my future escape."

Factory work was common and prisoners worked along side regular workers. Over a hundred prisoners, including *BEDEL*, were sent to the Rudolf Sach firm, a maker of agricultural machines. He described the difficult job.

"Working with untrimmed pieces of plow discs, thousands of little needles of acid get into the ends of our fingers which are not well-protected and the skin becomes bloody, but is nothing if you compare it with the foundry where the prisoners work with a civilian. They have to carry the humid sand and put it in the molds and align it so it is ready for fusion. The bell sounds and the casting is supervised by the foreman in charge of the operation. The body is protected by a heavy apron and the face by a mask, but sometimes there is a long, dazzling jet which shoots up and hits their shoes. They keep the workers moving faster and faster. They can't stop working.

"Another time, we were sent to Wismar, a little port on the Baltic, to work in a railroad car factory, an enormous enterprise of at least 2,000 workers, with many workshops, railway branch-line, factory that makes parts of machines for aviation and sledges.

". . . We gather and bring in different recoverable materials, planks, beams, stones. The sentry finds that what I carry is too light. I answer in German. He replies, 'Dirty French, infamous race, shitty French, dirty pig.'"

Prisoners also found ways to sabotage the work they were given, adopting the principle that they had a right to cheat or fool the Germans in any way they could. *POIRIER* recalled what they did.

"We were sent to work on a state farm. Our group consisted of three escaped prisoners, one priest who was accused of being a Communist and two young Polish girls about eighteen years old. Our work was judged insufficient and we were transferred to another job: to plant fir trees that we voluntarily damaged. Later, we had to plant potatoes which we either crushed or replaced with stones."

But punishment was frequent and severe, and often made more severe by the fact that most prisoners were under-nourished and many suffered from dysentery. Any breach of camp discipline incurred a punishment such as the obligation to stand at attention for an entire day with the prospect of receiving blows from the butt end of a gun across the toes . . . if the uprightness of the position was not satisfactory.

Food

One reason that the work details were so difficult was that prisoners suffered from malnutrition. Food was a constant problem. Most prisoners would not have survived without food packages from families and the Red Cross, and their own ingenious ways of finding or stealing food. *BEDEL* wrote with heartfelt feeling about hunger and how they coped with it.

"Hunger tears at the stomach, twists the guts and is our companion during our stay, entering the brain to disorient us. The executioners count on it to weaken us, to kill our dignity, to reduce us to a disgraceful slavery.

"The menu doesn't vary much, a quarter liter or a liter of 'coffee,' what the prisoners called sapinette' warm water in which they steep some fir-tree branches gathered in the woods. At noon, a liter of soup containing two or three spoonfuls of millet. In the evening, a piece of dark bread with a spoonful of jam, sometimes a piece of potato, a bit of cheese, or a scrap of inedible meat.

"For about two weeks, Daugon [his friend] and I have only had a rusty tin can as a mess-kit. One gets at the head of the line to pass the can to the other place at the end of the line. No spoon. Near 5 o'clock in the evening, a round loaf of bread for twenty-five or thirty men. A little bit of margarine, or a little apple compote where whitened grubs swarmed.

"What bread! Compact dough, undefinable, rye, sawdust, molasses, bran between 250 or 300 grams, but it represents a very little piece. The division is a ceremony. The group gathers around the possessor of a knife. We measure the round loaf, mark the slices, we cut, we compare, we weigh. The scale, two pieces of wood, one sustains the beam, provided with two nails suspended by a string. We cut the bits to make the pieces equal in order to avoid favoritism."

A Gourmet Christmas Feast

Each Christmas the prisoners expected to be home with their families. Unfortunately, no extra rations were allowed for Christmas, so prisoners were left to provide any additions to create a festive feast as *BEDEL* described their fortune.

"It is Christmas (1943), in a camp in Buchholz. We hoped to spend the holiday with family. Fifteen days before December 25, the Soviet prisoners, in a neighboring camp, brought us the cadavers of two silver foxes. They had been sacrificed for their fur. The Russians said they wanted to eat them, but they needed to suspend them from a fir tree, in that way the odor and the taste of a wild beast would disappear. For eight days one of the Russian prisoners slept in a freezing cell, without heat, in disguise of punishment, but it didn't bother him. Each morning we found him, smiling. He overtly mocked the Germans, to whom he called out, Deutschland kaputt which got him a thrashing and several kicks. He was a strong one.

"We saved and economized our ration of margarine. In the forest we found some chestnuts and mushrooms. Sunday morning we gathered some beechnuts, some fat, for a certain price we got some ersatz soap. The sentry, bribed by some cigarettes, lent us a kettle and their kitchen. A comrade, chef at George V in Paris, browned the pieces of meat, succeeded in making a smoked sauce, so savory, that our guardian angels came to sniff it. Prima, das sehr gut' ('It smells good'). But the idea that it was fox made them nauseous. We feasted, but I tell you, today, I wouldn't dare propose such a menu."

POIRIER summed up poignantly the significance of food for the prisoners of war, *"Since that time, bread, for me, has a symbolic value. I can't tolerate that my family waste a single mouthful."*

Mail

Every week prisoners were allowed to write a card of seven lines or a letter of twenty-six lines, with a reply coupon attached. Packages to prisoners were limited to one package of one kilo a month and a package of five kilos every two months. The Red Cross also furnished one package a month to prisoners, but it contained washing products, cigarettes, and a few other useful items, but no personal items.

Prisoners often wrote for specific items which they wanted or needed. Pierre Moussié's sister, Suzanne, recalled one letter:

"In February, 1941, Pierre asked us for a pair of high shoes, strong, hobnailed, and waterproof, and a list of things he needed continued: trousers, shorts, cigarettes, candy, no bread, but Vache-qui-rit type cheese [individually packaged squares of soft cheese], *chestnuts, chocolate, almonds. Yes, he needed everything. We didn't know until later that he ignored totally that it was already difficult to get these things. We needed tickets, points, ration cards, and the stores were empty. We searched, asked friends and finally found what we needed."*

Prisoners were paid in camp money according to the difficulty of their task, and the sentinels changed it into civilian marks. With the money, prisoners could buy soap, toothpaste, a toothbrush, razor blades, books, a little bit of tobacco, porcelain pipes, suitcases, and on Sunday an ersatz beer.

Solidarity

The prisoners found ways to keep up their morale through activities: education, art, music, theater, and sports. *MOUSSIE* described one theater project:

"One day the Germans authorized us to create a theater. I was the electrician of the theater and my friend N.B. was responsible for the sets. Professionals, in civilian life, helped. The Red Cross furnished texts and we presented 3-6-9 by Michel Durand, Le Malade Imaginaire of Moliere and finally Angelica which was an homage to liberty."

BEDEL helped create classes for fellow prisoners and wrote about their success.

"Classes in French, history, geography, beginning German. I am comforted to take up again my work as a teacher, it permits me to take back some human dignity, to give some service to others. The classes are well attended, at least when, in the interior of the camp, circulation is authorized. We have managed to obtain

two rooms, and even paper, pencils, pens and ink. We had no blackboard. We use a piece of tarred paper, and a piece of plaster takes the place of chalk. The teaching is mostly oral, the students sitting on the ground, writing on their knees. Our greatest success - we succeeded in teaching a young Portuguese to read and write."

Former prisoners say that no one could have survived the prison camp experience alone. They helped and relied on one another to deal with the daily physical hardships and to bolster the low morale fostered by the Nazi camp mentality.

As a punishment, the Nazis took *BEDEL* to an isolated cabin at the factory at Dormier. He wrote a moving tribute to comrades who kept up his morale:

"In the evening a prisoner brought me a mess-tin of soup and managed to whisper that I was arrested for having false papers.

"I was transferred to II E at Schwerin, alone in a cell. The solidarity came out immediately. Unknown friends gave me a more copious meal each day, they got me German books, they wished me 'Keep your chin up.' They recommended that I deny everything. Reading kept me from falling into hopelessness, thanks to that, I escaped to other thoughts and I forgot the solitary hours. I think it is a great force for intellectuals who can continue an intense intellectual life. One week, two weeks passed. One single hour each day to go out. We turned around one another, without communicating, so carefully were we watched."

The solidarity and cooperation among prisoners was necessary if a prisoner planned to escape. Some successful escapees had a helping hand from fellow prisoners and even from sympathetic prison workers. Others received valuable help from families and anti-Nazi civilians outside the camp.

CHAPTER 10
ESCAPE

All three French prisoners, Emmanuel Poirier, Pierre Moussié, and Louis Bedel tried several times to escape. With the help of railroad workers, Emmanuel Poirier escaped and arrived in France in October 1943. After several tries, and with help from his sister, Suzanne and camp friends, Pierre Moussié successfully escaped and arrived in Paris in February 1944. Louis Bedel, in spite of his privileges in the camps because of his ability to speak German fluently, failed his many attempts to escape. He remained in camp until 1945, when he and his comrades were able to walk out of their prison as the German guards fled before the arriving Russian and American troops.

When escaped prisoners were caught, they were returned to separate barracks and isolated from the rest of the camp to prevent further escape attempts. Escapees usually were given less to eat and were frequently transported to a different and more rigid prison.

There were deterrents to escape attempts. One prisoner who tried to escape during the noon recreation was discovered, and shot down in a single blow. However, the most severe deterrent was the prisoners' knowledge that their families could be subject to reprisals.

An escape required meticulous preparations, even sabotage, and a need for precaution. It demanded ingenuity, audacious acts, and some bravado, although occasionally the lack of prudence led to failure.

Emmanuel Poirier

For Poirier, it was more than his human rights under the Geneva Convention which made him think of escape. Poirier and some fellow prisoners were brought before a German war court and tried for escape from prison and sabotage. To the question, "Do you promise not to try to escape again?" Poirier answered, *"It is a promise I cannot make because my duty as a Frenchmen is to try to escape."*

As early as 1941, Poirier and some of his fellow prisoners tried to escape from prison camp. During an escape in the winter snow, they thought of a subterfuge they hoped would confuse the Germans on their trail. He wrote:

"Fix a sole under the shoe, reversing the position of the heel, but we didn't

have a sole. My friend walked in front and I covered his footprint, walking backwards. It was hard, but we put out a false route for our pursuers.

"Reaching the middle of some fir trees, we lay down in the snow to rest and wait until the Germans leave which they did about 11 p.m. We leave around midnight. It is very dark and attached by a string from one arm to another in order not to lose each other, we walk all night in the mountains, we fall in the holes, we tumble down slopes with our food in tyrolian packs well secured on our backs. We quietly follow our way somehow or other.

"Our nights are difficult: most often we dig a hole in the snow and we stretch out there; our canvas tents in place of coverlets. But at the end of two hours, chilled to the bone, we have to leave. The snow reaches almost 8 feet, and we have to give up our plan.

"One night about midnight we come to the former Czech border near the village of Franstein where we stop for a moment in the former customs house. Then we find some protection in the woods so we can eat. At half past midnight we leave again. After a few miles of walking we have the distinct impression we are being followed. At the entrance to a village we jump a hedge and fall down on the railroad line without a single scratch. We find a railroad car which has some coal and a cook stove which we light. With melted snow, I make a delicious hot chocolate and we dry our clothes and shoes. At 5 a.m. in the morning we regretfully leave our shelter, just in time as we see a team of workers arriving near the railroad car."

They go through other villages, following routes in the forest and one night they leave and go southwest.

"Night falls on our ninth day. Mud clings to our shoes hardened by the snow. Moving like automates we find ourselves in a barnyard and we hope to find a rabbit or a chicken. But everything is locked up. . . .

"Dirty and unshaven we look for a place to hide. We decide to follow a route which will take us to a woods. We go about 50 meters when a car stops. A guard gets out, questions us and shows a Gestapo card. We say we are Italian bricklayers while we rummage around in our packs.

"Another man stops his car and asks if he can help. When he leaves, he touches me on the shoulder and says in French, 'Bonne chance les gars.' (Good luck guys).

"We come across a forest guard and a railroad worker who looks at us and asks us for our papers. We think about getting away, but the two men ask. 'Who are you? Where are you going?' 'We are Italian bricklayers, we are going camping.' 'Your papers?' 'We left them at the factory over the way.' (there was one over there!) 'What is the name of your boss?' We pretend we don't know, we have only been there two weeks. Nothing else to do but to follow them to the factory where two soldiers search us and begin to hit us.

A Time to Speak

"In the director's office we undergo an interrogation and we end up by saying we come from Stalag IV at Houeschteim. They take us to the police station at Kowotau then to Stalag IV C. The officer who searches us tells us about his escape from France during the war 1914-1918 and says, 'I hope you succeed the next time.'"

Poirier and other prisoners were moved successively to other prison camps, each time, their record of attempted escapes followed them. In 1943, Poirier was in a Juterberg, 50 kilometers from Berlin, where he was to work in a factory. With seven friends from Rawa Ruska, he began to plan his next escape. One friend worked in a slaughter-house where he gained the confidence of the foreman. He stole meat which he hid in his pants. He fed the camp with several supplementary kilos of meat, with the complicity of the prison guards who took advantage of the windfall, and the prisoners gained back their strength.

"It was at that moment that they suggested I change jobs which I accepted right away. I would be a shoemaker again.

"My patron was not a Nazi and a brave man. We exchanged views, and I could express myself freely in front of him. His wife, on the other hand was hitlerian and his son was in the SS.

"One day when the son came back from the Russian front, I refused to shake hands and refused the cigarette he offered me. I told him my opinion of the SS, reminding him of the horrors they had committed. He left, screaming that he was going to denounce me to the Gestapo. His father succeeded in calming him and the matter stayed there.

"Every time I had the chance, I stole some leather to repair my companions' shoes. I got a little money to buy some ammunition boots in view of my next escape. I succeeded in getting five pairs of boots. I had my plan.

"Just 100 meters from the barracks, a German officer stopped me. He asked me whom the boots were for. I answered they were for the friends of the commando (I was a shoemaker). He was satisfied.

"I distributed the boots to friends in exchange for chocolate.

"I resumed my work, or I should say, my sabotage.

"It was at this time that the prisoners of war had the possibility of wearing civilian clothes, could leave camp and work outside and receive remuneration.

"We decided to organize the escape of four prisoners in October 1943.

"I am at work when the alarm is given at 10 a.m. My saddler employer warned me that I was the object of serious suspicions. About 5 o'clock he received a telephone order to take me to camp. I jump out the window of the building and find myself in the gardens before heading to the center of town and the public garden. The countryside is close, but there is a cliff of 10 to 15 meters overhang. I fall upon a patrol and succeed in hiding in the darkness of a carriage entrance.

"Finally I arrive in the public garden, only to find another patrol. I plunge into a thicket before reaching the fields, then the railroad line, where I find my two friends hidden in the huts of the railroad station at Guterborg, with a third escapee, a pilferer they met on the road.

"We waited three weeks, going out at night looking for food.

"It wasn't until the 19th of October at 8 p.m., with the complicity of a civil employee of the railroad, that we embarked on the train for France, traveling with a convoy of German soldiers, headed for the U. S. S. R., who paid no attention to us.

"We get into a railroad car of merchandise. When we stop at the station in Magdebourg, I hear a German saying, 'This car is going to Breslau,' but finally it is toward FRANCE that we are headed. In the station at Kassel, our train stops since the town is bombed. Joseph, who couldn't hold it any longer, relieved himself on a piece of paper. Outside we hear the German say, 'Something smells there. . . .'

"Our railroad car is put on a repair siding where we stay 28 hours in the cold.

"Finally we start again. Going through Cologne, I can see by the slates of the car there are no longer roofs on the houses. On the other hand, the cathedral seems to be intact.

"We cross Holland and in the morning I hear the patois of Charleroi. It is 7 o'clock on the morning when I read the name of the station, Tourcoing. I wake up the others and tell them, 'Guys, we are in FRANCE!' and we kiss one another so great is our joy in spite of our fatigue.

"During the trip we opened up a part of the floor of the railroad car.

"At the time of a night stop on the same day, two German soldiers become aware of us and I hear their remarks. I wake up my sleeping companions and tell them, 'We are spotted.' One of the two, Picard, succeeds in getting out through the window of the car but falls hard on the ballast and fractures a leg. He tries, perilously and in vain, to open the car because the two Germans take him for a thief. He manages to hide in the shadows as the train departs. We manage to extricate ourselves from the car, at the next stop and we verified that we were in Longo, near Amiens.

"I think that I never loved my country as much as that particular day: it was October 25, 1943.

"After some ups and downs, we were forced to break up and I am alone and exhausted. I rest against a flat car when I see a shadow coming toward me. It is a Frenchman, whom I watch with mistrust go toward a signal station, where, he says, a German is watching. He takes me to a little barge where two guys offer me something to eat. I am very thirsty and I drink an enormous quantity of water.

A Time to Speak

"The railroad workers ask me where I want to go, and I answer, 'To Mayenne.' The train leaves in twenty minutes. They get me on the train in a car where they stay, while I listen to the shouts of the Germans who are looking for us. They offer me wine, stolen from the Germans. I haven't drunk wine for three years and I end up completely drunk.

"It is at that moment that I am surprised to see Picard get on the train. The railroad chief had picked him up, taken him to his house and put a splint on his broken leg.

"We arrive in Paris about 7 o'clock in the morning. The railroad chief took us to another railroad worker and gave us something to eat. He hands me a piece of newspaper on which is written 'Merchandise to deliver' and tells me, with that piece of paper, all of the railroad workers will come to our aid.

"I hurried to get home to get acquainted with my little girl, born after my capture and who is now three years old."

Poirier went to the demobilization center where he received 1,100 francs and was offered an administrative job. By 7 December 1943, he was re-established as a supervisor, under a false name, in a broom factory in Laval. Today he lives in Sérigné, France.

Pierre Moussie

After three failed attempts to escape prison, Pierre Moussié began to meticulously prepare his fourth try. In her memoirs, his sister Suzanne Moussié recalled two letters which the family received in February, 1943.

"15 February, Pierre wrote in a hurried manner, 'Go to Marianne, in the second office, you will find a member who should furnish you with the papers that you indicate he should give you. You will give the papers to the Notary to whom I gave instructions before the war. Ask J. L. what he thinks of this financial affair, above all, do it quickly. For the sacks of rice or semolina, double them.'

"This was scarcely disguised, Marianne, identification papers, second office, French money and the double sacks, to send all this discretely. But I didn't understand who was the Notary. The next letter, February 28, 1943, was more explicit. After writing part of it to his mother, he addressed a bit to me. "It is a question of M. Bouxaul. . . .'[Boussole is the French word for compass.] We put a compass in a false bottomed box in the packing."

Moussié became acquainted with a military nurse in the infirmary, L. Humbert, who was a butcher in civilian life. Moussié spent what free time he had in the infirmary, where be began to prepare his fourth attempt to escape. In December 1943, the doctor was replaced by a new doctor who arrived from France without an escort, with a simple paper typed on a machine. That gave Moussié an idea, and with the help of his friend, Humbert, he prepared his fourth and successful attempt to escape from prison. Moussié wrote:

"*Humbert got me a magnificent French officers's uniform, the tunic was that of a medical lieutenant, the trousers tailored by a Pole. The shoes were given me by an Englishman, with an old belt, I resoled them. And in this outfit, I was quite decent looking, suitable for a French officer.*"

Escaping as a French officer would allow Moussié a certain courtesy and perhaps a few privileges since there was always a certain respect for officers on the part of German officers.

"*My friend, Humbert, had the office of Prisoner in the Health Service and had several privileges. He knew a German woman, a secretary somewhere who typed the following document (in German):*

"'*General Headquarters of the Führer, Lieutenant Moussié is authorized to travel alone and without a guard from Leipzig to Paris. He will travel at his expense in First Class and can call on, if necessary, the German officer at the station who should facilitate his trip.*'

"*Hard to believe, but true. I added, by a process of my own invention, a seal: I designed the stamp with an indelible pencil on a cigarette paper. I applied it to the document and covered it with a wet cigarette paper. After a few seconds, I took it off cautiously and it was ready.*

"*All the material and the provisions were hidden by efforts of Humbert, and he will pass them to me through a barred window of the infirmary. Me, I will slip away at night to avoid the suspicion of the Germans. I will walk the ten kilometers to recover my provisions.*

"*In the morning at roll call, we formed by work details. I am the only one to work in the laboratory and I am always late. Several times I have run to catch up before the door is closed. So the sergeant-major is used to my tardiness. That will serve me and he will perceive my escape when I am already in France. Two wily and agile comrades replaced me at the roll call in the evening.*

"*It is a month since I returned from the Infirmary and February 1, in the evening, everything is ready. (Each time I think about this departure, I get knots in my stomach.)*

"*Toward midnight, I got up and I carefully loosen the barbed wire at the window. A cell-mate wakes up, 'You're crazy, what are you doing?' 'I'm buzzing off.'*

"*Silence. He kisses me and wishes me Good Luck.*

"*I leave and I reach the end of the barracks. There is a barbed wire and two observation posts. Where I am, they don't see me.*

A Time to Speak

"I wait on the parapet walk; the sentry passes. I count; it will take him three to four minutes to make the rounds.

"The night before I had left boards under the barracks in order to pass the first barbed wire. I get hung up, tear my trousers, I jump. I was hot. I don't budge . . . the sentry passes on the inside, at two meters. . . .

"It's finished. I break camp. I have twelve kilometers to go to reach the Infirmary. I know the route. I cut through a woods and come upon a sentry who is guarding a gun-site. I hear, 'Halt.' I walk without stopping. I hear the sound of the breech of an arm. I continue to walk. I wait for the shot; in the dark it would be unlucky to get shot. He must hesitate. I walk with a regular step. I move farther away, it's won.

"At 3 o'clock in the morning, at the planned time, I'm in front of the Infirmary. Humbert is watching; he silently passes me the material. I dress as an officer and slip the work clothes, that I won't take off until Leipzig, over the uniform.

"I must take the train at the little station at Zeitz and a uniform of a French officer will astonish and alert the authorities.

"I must still walk across the fields, I slip socks over my shoes which are polished; an officer, in the eyes of the Germans, must have polished shoes.

"Humbert thought of everything: my left pocket contains papers, my right pocket, aspirin. Inside, 60 marks because he learned that the trip costs 50 marks.

"I slip over the uniform, a military raincoat, gift of doctor Lefort before he was replaced.

"I move away in the shadow of the Infirmary, where without Humbert, nothing would have been possible. I know he has a heavy heart.

"I walk and about 6 o'clock in the morning, I am at the station in Zeitz. I wait on the platform, it is long. I am always afraid of encountering a worker from the factory.

"Finally, the train, destination Leipzig arrives; I get into a compartment where I am alone. Just before Leipzig, I take off the work clothes. I became Lieutenant Moussié.

"The train stopped. I see Leipzig, I get off and ask for the Main Lines to Paris. An employee tells me I am mistaken, I should have gotten off at the principal station. I get on the train which leaves, I arrive at the main station in Leipzig.

"I don't see the Main Line trains. I am in the middle of suburbanites on their way to work. I go back in on the side of the Main Lines and stand in line at the ticket window. I don't know the time of the train and I am a little lost. My turn comes:

"One way, first class, Paris!
"The employee answers: 'Passport.'

"I haven't a passport, I am a prisoner and I have an authorization from the General Headquarters of the Führer. I take out my paper and he reads it. 'I'm going to see the chief to find out if it is in order.'

"All of the station of Leipzig turns around me. He comes back.

'That will be 50 marks.'

"I pay and leave. In my difficulties, I can't remember whether he said 9 o'clock on platform 3, or 3 p.m. on platform 9. I don't know what to do. Suddenly I see the rapid train to Paris on the other side of the platform. It's lost.

"I got back to the waiting room and find a bench to sit on. It is 3 p. m. on platform 9.

"Everybody looks at me. I begin to feel uncomfortable."

While Moussié waits for the train to leave, he goes to the station police station and asks where he can sit until his train leaves. He is allowed to stay inside at the police station. Just before time for the train to leave, he goes back to the platform.

"There is a frightening jostling. I feel uncomfortable, everything is blurred. I get on, I move about the passage-way when I see a compartment, marked in French, 'Police.' I go in, and take a place in the corner, and wait.

"A few minutes later, a German lieutenant comes in and asks if he may sit there. He introduces himself, 'Lieutenant Schneider' and I introduce myself, 'Lieutenant Moussié.' We smile at one another. A colonel comes, we all introduce ourselves. Then several civilians come in. The train leaves, eight hours late."

Moussié slept and woke up when the train arrived in Kaiserslautern where he had lived during 1925-1930. At the new border of Pagny-sur-Moselle, everyone is ordered off the train to present their papers.

"I hesitate, but I don't budge. The door of the compartment opens and the Border Police ask for papers. I give my paper to the German Police. 'Good,' and the door closes. The door opens a second time and it is the SS. 'Papers?' I give him my paper, I am sure of myself. He gives a 'Heil Hitler,' and I answer in French, 'Good-by gentlemen.'

"The train departs again. It is France. I recognize it. I feel like yelling and screaming, 'I am free!'"

Moussié arrived at the Gare de l'Est and took the metro to the home of his cousins in Saint-Ouen, where he sought refuge. On 6 February 1944, his sister Suzanne arrived with civilian clothes. He returned to his home in Toulouse, and with the help of friends, he secured a false identity card. Moussié still lives in Toulouse.

A Time to Speak

Louis Bedel

The German invasion of Russia gave the prisoners some hope. Their opinion was that Hitler had made a mistake in opening a second front. The Soviet army was powerful and very, very large. Bedel began to think seriously about trying to escape, to think about civilian garments and the necessary German marks. He spoke German fluently which would make flight easier. He already had a pullover that he had received in the winter. He wrote to his wife, "I will try the exam." That was the code they used to indicate his escape.

The preparations demanded a lot of time. He received a jacket and pants and found a tie that the sentry let him keep, and obtained some civilian marks. Once he had everything he needed, he informed friends about the plan.

Winter was not a good season because tracks would be left in the snow and it would be easy to follow them. And where should they cross the frontier? Many prisoners had escaped at Schaffhouse.

By studying the map, they found another Swiss enclave, German territory, Stein-am-Rhein, where they could penetrate in a triangle formed on the right by a river, on the left, a railroad that joined the Stein. At the point where the railroad passed parallel to the river, they were certain to be in Switzerland. They would follow the river because the railroad was carefully watched.

The beginning of May 1942 brought good weather. In his diary, Bedel wrote:

"It is time to act. I have what is necessary to escape, even a beautiful German cap. My friends are Daugon and Thoreux. We have imagined a very plausible scenario. I will be in German civilian clothes, and I will be in charge of this prisoner who has come out of the hospital. In this way Daugon can keep his blue work clothes, his khaki shirt, transporting a sack, without attracting too much attention.

"We found two backpacks which contain a bit of clothing, the necessary toiletries and the provisions for the route, sugar and chocolate that we have saved for some time."

They were transferred to work on a farm belonging to the Sack family. One friend belonged to the night team, so that an early morning flight would give them an extra chance.

"The sentry returning with prisoners will go to sleep. The adjutant, having attended the departure of the team, will have come back to eat. At the first hours of dawn, night still reigning, a light fog hid the far end of the camp. There we had to cross the barbed wire. Under a barracks under construction, we had hidden a long ladder. After the return bell, I left our chief, I changed clothes, I had the appearance of a good German who had nothing to reproach himself with. Thoreux and two accomplices placed the ladder so it extended over the barbed wire. We scaled

up, dropped our backpacks on the grass of the neighboring terrain.

"Then we pushed against the gate which sprang open and we went out. Our friends took down the ladder. The Chleuhs [pejorative name given to the German enemy] would ask how we stole it.

"We were spared an hour before they would call me to the office. We ran toward the route, another enclosure, a bicyclist passed, just at that instance. Very loudly in German, I called, 'Is it shorter this way?' He didn't notice us. About one kilometer was the tramway stop which joined the center of the suburb. I got on with the two sacks that Daugon carried. I asked the conductor, in German, if the prisoner I was bringing to a military working party farther along could get on the train. I paid the two places and at the end of the line, we took the route which thrust into the countryside. It was so early that we didn't encounter anyone.

"First we needed to find a shelter. The Saxon countryside didn't offer any favorable, propitious grove or thicket. First village, we pretended to discuss, it was I who spoke the most because I had a good accent. At the outskirts of the village, we located a quarry which served as an interchange. Some isolated garrison which encompassed some 20 meters. We slept on the canvas of a tent. I advised Daugon to sleep at once. I went to sleep very soon. But the cold woke us up soon. Our teeth chattered. Happily the sun came up finally and made us comfortable. At noon, some crackers, a piece of chocolate, water from a pond was our dinner.

"Suddenly interrupted by the invasion of a group of kids who were playing war. We had to escape from their view and we were caught up in a game of hide-and-seek. We feared above all that they would recover our sacks and give a warning. Finally, they moved off. Toilette, brushing our clothes, we took the road. We saw several bicycles and automobiles. We plunged into the deep countryside.

"About 5 a.m., at the entry into a village, I felt completely empty, almost unconscious. I lay down on the ground. Panic! I thought I would faint. I didn't feel capable of continuing. I begged Daugon to leave me behind and take my provisions. We had already considered this possibility and had decided that the most capable should continue alone. He refused. He took out a flask of mint-flavored alcohol and a piece of sugar. I revived, got up and we left again.

"As soon as we saw a woods of fir trees, we reached it, climbed up into the branches. It was the best hiding place, where no one would penetrate. Sleep overtook us and our heads covered up in our packs, we forgot everything.

"We walked for a week, always at night, crossing the small villages. In one of them, we came across a peasant who kept watch to warn the parachutists. We went along like men who had a easy, untroubled conscience and chatted among friends. I saluted with a 'Heil Hitler.' We even cut across the town of Gera saw a local farmer who didn't pay any attention to us. I talked a lot about my garden and planting peas.

"One time we had a beautiful case of jitters. An automobile followed us, searchlight on, projecting to the left and the right to scan the sleepy countryside. The guard at the last village must have had some doubt and had pointed us out. Hearts beating, we plunged, went toward a field lower down, beside a little river. We threw ourselves flat on the ground, in a field, already high with clover. Fear seized us, we were too visible. We reached the land, next to the river. If the searchlight picked us out, we would plunge in the water, hanging on to a branch, head under water.

"Slowly the lights swept through the darkness over our heads, a minute of anguish. The vehicle drove off, what a sigh of relief. We danced for joy and it sent a shiver up our backs. Oh, liberty creates a frivolous air. The fascinating countryside under soft moonlight. If we could effect a beautiful marching song!

"The Sunday of Whitsuntide we camped in a forest, always concealing ourselves among the trees. We heard the sounds of the strollers from the village taking advantage of a spring day. Not far from us singers accompanied by an accordion. Intrigued, we emerged carefully and, in a clearing, we found a forester's lodge, people seated at a table, eating cake and drinking beer. Why not take advantage of the situation? I am decently dressed, I speak German well. I entered the hall, I ordered two portions of cake, two cans of beer and went toward the table. A dance swept up the customers and I disappeared among the trees. We clinked our cans of beer and drank to our success. In the grass, we seemed intoxicated, elated and savored living as if peace had returned.

"In the evening we left, swift-footed for a new stopping place, at dawn, an empty plain, dangerous terrain. There, very close, a little grove. We decided to stay there although the distance covered was insufficient according to our plan. Monday we decided to leave sooner in order to make up our delay. Night had not fallen and we had a large village to cross. Luck wasn't with us! What a lack of caution! Already at the edge of the village, in the open, whistling with joy, a guttural order resounded, 'Halt!' 'Kommen Sie her!' Without turning, we still whistled. Another order and a big police dog joined us. Impossible not to obey. From an ordinary house came a policeman with his arms, 'Wohin gehen Sie, Papiere, Papiere.' I began the explanations already prepared, 'We were two Flemish, voluntary workers.' 'Where go you work?' 'At the neighboring town over there.' I gave the name taken from the map. 'At whose house?' 'At Mister Fritz, to repair agricultural machines, Adolph Hitler street.' 'Keine Papiere?' 'We left them at our employer's. We took advantage of the Whitsunday holiday to join our friends in the town we just crossed.' 'Follow me, I will verify all of that.' A telephone call, Mr. Fritz does not exist. 'Open your sacks.' 'Ah, Frenchmen.' Resigned, we admitted our status. Farewell to our beautiful dream.

"Very disappointed. It would take an incredible amount of good luck to succeed. We put the matter off. That experience would serve as a lesson. The best thing would be to steal bicycles and procure civilian papers.

"Our arrival back in the Stalag caused a sensation and a bit of curiosity, just think, the fugitives, the chaps who went the distance. We told our odyssey. They gave us a good meal, hot supper, meat, fried potatoes and went to bed. We had real beds and not just straw mattresses. The sentries took away our shoes and gave them back the next morning."

Bedel succeeded in saving his good pullover but was sent to Stalag IX-C, located in Bad-Sulza, a little spa town, and eventually was sent to the punishment camp in the east, Rawa-Ruska. He was condemned for sabotage, fabrication of false papers, inciting escapes, refusal to work, theft of German goods and unauthorized use of German material in his work place. He was later transferred to Buchholz, then to a disciplinary camp at Lubthen, north of Mecklinbourg. With the arrival of the Allies, he and his friend were able to walk out of the camp in 1945.

In conversations, Poirier, Moussié and Bedel do not make prejudicial remarks about Germans or Germany. However, Louis Bedel did admit one day, *"It is not good to hold a grudge. But it is difficult for people our age not to feel resentful. Whenever I see Germans my age, I have a tendency to hesitate and step back."* [53]

End Notes

53 Poirier, Moussié and Bedel remain active in the Union Autonome des Deportés Résistants de Rawa Ruska. They nevertheless work to assure that their comrades receive their pensions and that their widows are cared for.

CHAPTER 11

BATTLE FOR BRITAIN

In the autumn of 1940, it was a bleak and desolate world. Only Hitler could take satisfaction in the success of his personal world, the new Germany. He was master of Europe from the North Cape above the Arctic Circle to Bordeaux and from the English Channel to eastern Poland. Only Great Britain and the Soviet Union remained outside his grasp.

Hitler wrongly assumed that after the fall of France, Britain would be ready to make peace. What he wanted was control of the European continent, leaving the British Empire intact. Churchill, speaking before the House of Commons, reiterated Britain's resolve to continue fighting. He concluded his speech with one of his most eloquent statements, "Let us therefore brace ourselves for our duty, so bear ourselves, so if the British Empire and its Commonwealth last for a thousand years, men will still say, this was their finest hour."[54]

Hitler now turned his attention to the battle of Britain. He ordered the Army, Navy, and Air Force to prepare plans for the invasion under the code name Operation Sea Lion.

Occupation of the Channel Islands

Britain expected an offensive against the home island. By 16 June they had decided to withdraw their troops from the Channel Islands of Jersey and Guernsey, located off the French coast because they could not be defended without weakening the defenses of Britain itself. On 28 June, the Luftwaffe carried out bombing raids on Guernsey and then on Jersey, and on 30 June German troops landed on British soil.

Although the occupation of the Channel Islands (Jersey, Guernsey, Alderney and Sark) was a relatively small part of World War II, they represented a prize for Hitler. He wanted to make them impregnable and called for fortifications of the Islands. The Germans regarded the occupation of the Channel Islands as a sort of test case for their later occupation of Great Britain. The Islanders' behavior under a military government would show them how to govern Britain after their defeat by the German armies. Channel Islanders endured deprivation similar to Continental Europeans occupied by the Third Reich. What saved them from starvation was the arrival of the international Red Cross ship, *Vega*. Their liberation came one day later than V-E Day in Europe, 9 May 1945.

The Blitz

Hitler planned a German air offensive, The Day of the Eagle, which was to begin on or after 5 August 1940. The Battle of Britain was fought in the skies over London and the over the southern Channel coast. Beginning in August and until December, Londoners were bombed almost every night. The air-raid sirens wailed and Britishers took cover in shelters.

In spite of the number of German planes, Germany was unable to break the British resolve. Churchill praised the skill of British pilots, "Never in the field of human conflict was so much owed by so many to so few." At least one Hurricane pilot never thought of himself as a hero.

"I shot down planes over Gravesend and the Thames Estuary. Of course, you didn't know there were superior numbers until you actually saw them or they saw you and you were surrounded by them. There was always a moment of anxiety being sent off into action. No, you didn't have any sense that the fate of the country depended on you. You had a vague idea that it was a serious matter. The idea of gloom, doom, and panic never entered one's head at all because one was so young. Oh, no, one didn't feel the Germans might manage to invade." [55]

Children Evacuees

With the war in the skies over London and industrial cities, the British government took precautionary measures to evacuate school children to the country where they were billeted with families who were paid by the Government for the upkeep of the children. The evacuation process was organized through the schools and the Ministry of Health. Frequently as many as 75 percent of the children in a school were evacuated.

For many children, it was an adventure to go to the country. For others there was uncertainty: "What will the family be like? Will I be chosen right away by a family? and for those who had never been outside the city, "What will the country be like?" Some children became homesick and returned home. Others, like John Bell, a six-year-old evacuee from Liverpool and among the first to be evacuated on 2 September 1939, adapted to his new life. He went to Pen-y-Groes, a market town in Wales.

"Everyone went out to see us, we were a novelty. What were these evacuees like from Liverpool? People came to select us (we were at a school). Nobody seemed to want me. I was the last. All of a sudden, then this little old lady came in. I thought she looked like she arrived on a broom. I thought actually she was a witch. When I

went out to play later in the evening, some of the older evacuees told me she was a witch and she was going to boil me in a pot.

"She couldn't speak English, she only spoke Welch. It took me a while to get used to it, and I became Welch meself, sung in a Welch chapel. She treated us like her children. It was living in a palace. . . . I was having such a good time. I stayed with the lady for five years. I loved both of them [mother and the lady]. My own mother was pleased with the results . . . everything was a bunch of roses to me. When I came back I started to lead an adult's life." [56]

The Seaford Women

The wartime crisis led to the organization of armed forces for women, the Land Army, and the recruitment of women to work on munitions, in administration, and in service industries, as well as volunteer activities. Their experiences led to the acceptance of women in the work force, altered the preconceptions that men had about womens' roles, and helped get rid of the British social and economic barriers as women worked side by side with a single purpose.

Many of the women who took jobs or entered military service were young, and by today's standards, they considered themselves naive.

A group of women, living today in and around Seaford, Sussex, agreed to answer the question, "What did you do during the blitz and the remaining war years?"

A. H.: *I think the thing that does stick out in my mind, mostly, is the way that everybody did what they thought was the best thing for them to do, the most useful thing, or the most kind thing. People helped one another tremendously. I think that was one of the reasons why we were successful in a good many ways during the war. People put themselves aside and people who had prejudices temporarily forgot them.*

There was no sense of personal gain for having done lots and lots of things for your country. And a lot of people did a lot of things that nobody knew anything about; they knitted like mad and made up all these parcels for the soldiers, these helmets, socks and scarves. There were heaps of people who just sat quietly at home and did all these things which were comforts for the forces. I really didn't do anything momentous at all. I was one of those people who did just ordinary things. They had to be done.

J. P.: *All the windows had to be blacked out. And people used to put that white tape down, so if you were bombed, the whole glass didn't come in. My father made black-out shades of cardboard and wood, so at night when the lights went out, you could put half down and open a window instead of curtains and have to 'em closed.*

A Time to Speak

A. H.: *Yes. You even had baby gas masks. They used to have gas mask practices and you had to put these wretched things on and they were in these miserable little cardboard boxes. Mine was bashed about. Everybody had them and you had them strung across you, wherever you went, all the time. And I'm not sure but I think there were some places where you couldn't go in unless you had your gas mask.* [57]

Coping with the Bombs

The Blitz was concentrated in August and September 1940. In September, the Lutfwaffe targeted the London docks, as well as the docks in Liverpool, Swansea and Bristol. Still unable to break Britain's air power, in 1941 the Luftwaffe dropped incendiary bombs on London, destroying a number of famous buildings including the Guildhall, several of the Wren churches and engulfing St. Paul's Cathedral in flames.

A. H.: *I saw the planes when they reached London and they were over the Thames. In the streets, there were all these pom-pom guns, they used to go around 'pom, pom,' firing, they used to go all over the place firing. I remember seeing the planes over Fleet Street. At the time, I thought how amazing it was that they had got through. I think it was the only time they did get that far. These were the Spitfires and they had this battle over London and it looked to me like it was over the river Thames. And the shrapnel was falling down in the yard where I was. I was supposed to be in the shelter, but we had a little shop on the corner and they sold buns . . . I had gone out to get a couple of these and I watched . . . and I saw St. Paul's burning [29 December 1941]. It really was a terrific sight. St. Paul's, it was a terrible thing. Everyone has always regarded St. Paul's as being something that has got to be preserved. And the rubble was there for a long time, until they re-built it with office buildings."*

England's most raided coastal town

Eastbourne, on the Channel coast, was notorious for being the most raided town in the southeast of England, with 1,350 general alerts and 861 local warnings. In spite of the spirit of comradeship and fortitude, the 1939 population of Eastbourne of 60,000 dwindled to 13,000 by September 1940. One woman was about thirteen years old at the time of the war.

J. P.: *We lived in Eastbourne and my father owned a news agency and tobacconist. And the Germans used to come in low, under the radar, come in below Beach Head, drop their bombs on the town and they were away before the siren went. And I'm sure that's why they did that, just for morale, because there was* nothing in Eastbourne. There was a railway station, end of the line. It didn't matter whether it was bombed or not.

I didn't hear the bomb when it came, I didn't even realize, but we were under the stairs. We had reinforced stairs in those days. Eastbourne had the ordinary siren to start with, but that wasn't effective any more because the bombs had dropped before the siren even went. They invested in something called the 'cuckoo' which was our own particular warning and as soon as that went, you knew you had to go somewhere. The 'cuckoo' went and we just managed to get under the stairs before it happened. The siren was 'boo-boo, boo-boo' like the sound of a cuckoo. That was our warning. You had to move very quickly, but it did give you those few seconds either to get down in the gutter or under the stairs.

And we had a bomb next door to us and it was very close and one poor lady died in that house. And of course, we had a lot of damage, ceilings came down, the back doors were blown in, glass windows were blown in and the soot came down the chimney, plaster and the glass was all over the place. And because we had a phone, because of the shop, the police, of course commandeered that. I remember them coming in and it still worked because that was in the front part of the house and the back part of the house was the mostly affected. And I can remember sitting on the stairs with all this dust. The shop was in the front, and my father started sweeping up and trying to clear up because he said, 'We've got to open tomorrow morning.' I was sitting on the stairs and there was this silver-backed hairbrush and comb and a silver-chained purse on our stairs and I thought, that doesn't belong to us, and it must have blown in from the next house. And of course we couldn't sleep there obviously because you could see the daylight through the roof. All the glass had to be cleared up. I can't remember how many days we were before we could go back, but we slept up the road with some friends until things started to clear up.

My father carried on, he managed to sweep all the dust up and carried on the next morning. When the bombing did start and people started to go away from Eastbourne, he did lose 500 customers in a week, and that was just one paper shop.

On a couple of occasions I was on my bike, we had to carry a dog's rubber bone with us because if you heard the planes coming or the 'cuckoo,' you had to get down in the gutter, put your hands over the back of your neck, the rubber bone in your teeth for jarring. I did that once. And another time I was in a park, Eastbourne, with my bike again and we heard this machine gunning, so as soon as you heard the 'rat-a-tat-tat' down you went in the bushes with your rubber bone between your teeth. And as children, afterwards, we heard the shrapnel dropping through the trees onto the tennis courts. So immediately when everything was over, we went to get them, but they were so hot we couldn't touch them. We were trying to take these souvenirs, that was a little bit scary because we didn't expect that. It was scorching hot, so we waited a while and then collected some of them for souvenirs.

For some reason, I don't think we felt deprived, frightened a lot of the time. It was very scary. Even now, when I hear the fire engine start, you sort of think, your tummy just turns over just slightly. You never forget it. I consider myself very lucky indeed.

The Shelters: An Underground Community

During the bombing raids, Londoners were supposed to take shelter in government air-raid shelters.

A. H.: It was a queer kind of life because, whereas now you can do what you like in the evenings, you were bound to a set pattern. At a certain time, you went down into the shelter, then you stayed there until early morning or whenever you had to go to work. People obviously went to work, just the same. You were supposed to find shelter when there was an alert. People used to go into the underground to sleep at night and they all had an allocated bunk. The bunks were three, one on top of another, they were all numbered. They saw the same people every night. It was a community. There was a lot of camaraderie in those shelters. The people went down regularly every night and sometimes neighbors used to go in each other's shelters. People took their babies and small children. They used to sing songs, have musical instruments. Some people used to read.

When I lived over the pharmacy, there was a doctor on the other side of the road. He was a Jew, and he had small children. His mother managed to escape from Germany and went to live with them. She and I used to go into the shelter with these children, and we used to sing German nursery rhymes and we used to hear the planes going 'vroom, vroom, vroom' over the top of us.

The Ambulance Drivers

Women registered at the Labour Exchange or the Auxiliary Territorial Service to do hundreds of vital jobs to release men for other duties. One ambulance driver during the Blitz recalled.

B. L.: We had a job to get done and everyone did it. I decided, Navy, Air Force, or ambulance, whichever one came first, I would take.

In the ambulance squad, we had to recognize gases in case we were involved in that sort of thing. Names, and what they smelled like; lessons which taught you to keep low to avoid everything.

We worked in London; we moved according to circumstances where we were needed, to other parts of London if there were incidents where they didn't have enough ambulances. Just two in a ambulance, a driver and one other. They had to get things together so quickly, we didn't even have proper ambulances. They chopped off the top of these cars, my particular ambulance was a Ford V-8. They chopped the top off and built a sort of side, and we could carry four stretchers. Just the driver and an assistant who had to sit in the back there.

As a driver, we had an office, of course, and someone in charge. And the call would come through, 'Go to such and such a place,' and we'd have to go wherever. We just had to know our own area and our own particular hospitals.

Sometimes we had to sit by an incident waiting for the dogs and equipment to try to get the people who were buried. We went out in the raids, in fact, I never did go underground. But it is no good working above ground if you are going to spend your time underground. It is better to stay on top.

The most difficult part was to be near London. It didn't matter if you didn't know London because we often came across a notice written out quickly, 'Diverge, because of bombs.' They took the names off the stations, and during a blackout, it was difficult to see. No headlights, you had slits, but very, very dim. So even if you knew the quickest way there, that was very unnerving because you were either going to an incident or coming away from it. And there were people who were waiting urgently.

In the beginning, there wasn't any money, it was a local authority, it was the London County Council. I went out to Simpson's and bought myself a pair of slacks at great expense. We didn't have coupons in the beginning. I forget how long it was that we were in our own civie things, but in the end, they gave us a pair of boots, sort of like army boots, that you polished very highly. I had my own slacks, and then they gave us a sort of great coat, blue, thick. So I used to sort of half stand up and turn around to see where I was going, and the coat stayed there. It was thick as a board. It was heavy.

Myself and my friend were the youngest people on the station. We were really the bottom. There wasn't any glamour attached to our situation because all of the eligible men were at the front. If you were in the Army or the Navy, they had get togethers and there was a certain social activity. We had nothing like that. What we used to do to eradicate what had happened the night before was to go up west to the cinema, and for one shilling and six pence, you could have some of the best seats and the best cinema. We used to go up there to watch a film to clear your head of the night before. And we used to quite enjoy that. We had a good laugh and then started out again. There wasn't any glamour attached to it, it was just sort of 'slog' really.

The Armed Forces

Active during World War II were the Auxiliary Territorial Service, the women's branch of the army, the Women's Auxiliary Air Force, the Women's Voluntary Service, the Field Auxiliary Nursing Yeomanry and the Women's Land Army. British Territories, for example, Canada and South Africa, organized their own military branches.

The South African Women's Air Force

A. P.: I was born and brought up in South Africa, Johannesburg, and my father had gone to war in the engineers. After leaving school, I joined the South African Broadcasting Corporation because they wanted women to release men, ostensibly to go to war. So I was behind the desk, a sound engineer. Then I got fed up with that. I thought, no, I want to be in the action. I joined the Air Force, the South African Women's Air Force and that was in September 1941.

The South African Women's Air Force did all of the radio work, we used to keep in contact with all of the flying schools, that was mainly the thing we had. When the boys went up to Abyssinia and further north, occasionally we had to contact, but usually it was just local. It was just to let them go. There was no conscription with the South Africans, it was all voluntary. They used to wear a red flash to say they were volunteers.

I was a trainee and I was sent to a camp outside Pretoria. The first night, this will show you how absolutely green I was, we were in a huge, big tent and we had to go to the wash block. We found one of the loos had been blocked off and there was a MP standing there. And we said, 'What's wrong?' 'Oh, somebody's had a baby.' And I said, 'Oh, does her husband know?' 'She warn't married.' And I thought, 'Is it possible?' And looking back, I think, 'Oh, you cabbage, cabbage.'

But we were all shipped down, 'trained' down to Bloemfontein, in the Orange Free State, which was the heartland of the Nazi sympathizers, Ossewabrandwag. There were two air stations there, one was the flying and ours was the wireless office.

We had to live in barracks. We were all supposed to do our own chores and everything, but we had one girl, she was rather wealthy girl, she was still at university, but she joined up. And when it came to laundry things, Audrey managed to get a girl, a black girl to do her laundry. We used to get twelve shillings and six pence a day which is about sixty pence, and of course we couldn't afford to get our laundry and stuff done.

And one night we were, it must have been coming into summer, and the alarm went off. 'What's happening?' the sergeant major shouts, and we all went tearing down to the mess hall. All of a sudden, two former nannies (a Scot and a Yorkshire lass) came dashing out of their billet, stark naked. Well, the sergeant major nearly had apoplexy. Of course, we nearly died laughing. Fortunately, the raid, by the pro-Nazis, misfired and we finally got back to bed at five o'clock in the morning.

One thing I remember was on Christmas Eve, we all had a service in the camp, and it was the most beautiful night I can ever remember. Clear, I think every star in the southern hemisphere must have been out, and the black service men were allowed to come as well. And I can remember the singing, the sound of white and black voices joining in joyful hymns in the middle of the veld is something I shall never forget. Oh, it was just out of this world. It was lovely.

The scariest thing that ever happened. My husband was a flying instructor in the Royal Air Force. He had done several tours up in North Africa, Italy and Sicily. He was sent down to rest and be a flying instructor. As a wireless officer, I was monitoring his flight. And all of a sudden, there was panic-station. Something went wrong with his engine and he had to come in and so I had to pass messages and things on to him. In the end, he had to pancake land, part of the engine had gone crackers, his under-carriage wouldn't come down. It was dreadful. I wasn't able to dash out and have a look. All I could hear was sirens and ambulances. And I thought, 'Oh my God.' But fortunately, he was all right.

I was in for three and a half years. I got married out there and we came back.

The South Africans had a lot to do with the winning of the battle of El Alamein. They were terrific, they really were. They were all trained in South Africa. We had the Army, the South African Navy did a lot too, and the Air Force. The South African Desert Rats, they did a lot.

You remember the funny things. It is just as well. People had to go through awful experiences. They'd go balmy if they just remembered those. It was a terrific experience. I wouldn't have done without it. It was interesting, traumatic at times.

The Canadian Women's Army

I. J.: Like so many, I was married in 1940, when I was nineteen, to a flying officer in the Air Force. We got married in September 1940 and he had been posted to Canada to train personnel in Prince Edward Island in December. So in the meantime, we lived in Black Hall in a little two-by-four that we shared with another couple. And then he went off to Canada, and I went back to my parents in Glasgow.

There was no talk at that time about wives following husbands. The Air Ministry said, 'If you can get the shipping companies to take you, that's fine,' and the shipping companies said, 'The Air Ministry will take you.' But in the end, my friend, Bunty, wife of one of my husband's officers and I went, with suitcases to Southport and stayed in digs and were there for six weeks, living in suitcases and going to Liverpool Docks every day that there was going to be a ship out in case there were vacancies on board. On this day, when we went into Liverpool, which incidentally was being bombed frequently at that time, we were told there might be vacancies and we were told we could go on board. I handed a note to a policeman on the dock, saying to my mother that I had gone. That was all we could say.

Six RAF wives were ushered to their accommodations, a tiny cabin below the propeller. It took the Baltrouver (previous a pig boat in the Baltic) eighteen days to cross the Atlantic.

"Naturally, being a small ship, we got to know people reasonably well. And we finally got into Halifax, there was one solitary figure in blue, standing on the quay. And word got around the ship that this was this girl's husband. And as we tied up at the dock, the whole ship burst into, 'Oh, Johnny, Oh, Johnny, how you can love.' Can you imagine a young officer facing this? I had a bit of talking to do when I get there. It was he. He had managed to trace us across the Atlantic.

"We had to set up home in Prince Edward Island. We lived there happily for a couple of years. Then came the time when he was going to be posted home. There were no preparations for the wives to go home. My husband and I went on his last leave to Montreal, and as we were walking along the road one day, during the last few days, we stumbled past the Canadian Women's Army recruiting office. So I thought if I can't get home any other way, I'll join up and get home. So we went in, were interviewed. 'You are just the sort of person we want, as soon as you have done your six-weeks basic training, you'll be virtually on a boat home.' He went off, and with a group of wives, I stayed in a farmhouse in Charlottetown, waiting for my call-up. I ultimately went to Halifax. I was in the barracks for a week, wondering if I had done the right thing. My papers came eventually and I swore on the dotted line to obey the King, the Queen, Canada, whatever.

"I staggered on to a train with two kit bags, wearing a trench coat in July in the hottest summer that had ever been. We were to due to go to Kitchener, Ontario for our basic training by train.

"The thing that really was the crunch was when we marched through the train to get a meal. Here are all the wives I'd been with, sitting in the civilian car, on their way to the ships to take them home. And they said, 'The commandant has been trying to get hold of you to join us.'

"'So sorry, she's already signed up.' It was such a weird coincidence that that would happen. I can visualize it now: one day, and I wouldn't have had to face that training, with a lump in my throat like this."

The rest is about the Canadian Army until I. J. managed to return home two and a half years later. Because she had taken a Cordon Bleu cooking course and done a few odd-temp cookery jobs, the Army decided she would be a cook.

"The 'cardinal' who was in charge of the kitchen of basic training, Colonel Dover, was a wonderful person. She took a great interest in me and was very sympathetic. People were wonderful, really. They decided if they kept me at Kitchener, they had more say over what would happen, rather than let me be shipped out on a draft. After one or two fatigues, they were called, where we got into a teddy bear suit which had been worn by all the other people during the week, this was your fatigues and you washed up for the whole kitchen, six hundred, or something, you washed up the porridge and the scrambled egg dishes with a pot scraper made out of key rings strung together. The water, of course, had to be near boiling, with disinfectant in it so all the other people had been in this teddy bear suit in similar conditions all week."

The Canadian Army sent her to a cookery course.

"I went to the cookery school and interestingly enough, at one time, just after basic training, I had to set up a display of the food that the British were eating in the dining halls. I also cooked for a week, and I cooked six hundred donuts and eighty chocolate pies one night on night duty."

Ultimately she trained at the National Defense Quartermaster Corps to become a catering officer; next sent to an officer's training unit to be a general duty officer to give her a chance to go overseas.

"Eventually I went to a platoon and was in Toronto for a while and V-E Day came and I thought, 'Enough of this. Where do we go?' and I sat down and penned the letter to General McNaughton himself and within six weeks, I was back in Kitchener, getting my luggage ready to bring a platoon to England. I thought that was remarkable. So there we are.

"When I arrived in England, I was stationed in a hotel in London. And my husband, who had been stationed in Ireland, was stationed in Cornwall, so we used to meet for weekends.

"It is something I really wouldn't have missed, as far as the experience of life is concerned."

Factory Jobs and Volunteer Work

Mary C., a staff member and Joyce H., a volunteer, work at the Seaford Volunteer Bureau. During the war Mary C, proved to herself that she was as efficient on the factory floor as any man, while Joyce H., like many women had a job and did volunteer work.

Mary C.: *I was in Cardiff. It was bombed. I had a scrappy kind of education. With the evacuation, we went, we came back, we were pushed out again. I left at sixteen and went to work for the Ministry of Agriculture as a clerk. I was in the butchery department where the butchers would come in with their ration books, and I would have to measure out how much was a month's worth of meat and so on.*

It was all tiny retail shops in those days. And I didn't care for it very much for the butchers were very active and very aggressive and they always wanted more. We were sympathetic because there were always queues, rationing was pathetic, so if they could get a bit of extra, a bit under the counter. So I packed that in pretty soon. I just wasn't suited for it. It was the clerical part. It wasn't that I was a vegetarian, but it was the clerical work.

Then I went to a factory that had been manufacturing pots and pans and, with the war, had changed over to preparing aircraft. I thought, I had been to grammar school and I had learned a bit of typing, and I wanted to do something other than dirtying my hands on the factory floor. Again I was allocated secretary to someone.

That's one thing that happened in the war. Women could get in next to these clever bosses and make an assessment. This man was dictating the same kind of form letters over and over again. And I said, 'I can do that... I can find that out for myself.'

So I transferred down with the men. I put a pair of dungarees on and went down on the floor. By the end, all women had joined in this, and we were identifying the parts that were missing from the aircraft, ordering them, chasing. It was what I was doing on the clerical side, but I was doing it directly and working with the men who were actually there. And they would say, 'The hole in that fuselage is missing, or that wing,' and I would immediately have all the books down there, grimy and oily, so I practically eliminated the boss's work, but it was so direct. I thoroughly enjoyed that. I was doing something that was absolutely major, to get those aircraft up in the sky.

Then the extra thing I did for extra money was working in the evenings. It was a 24-hour shift of course. I had the twilight shift, from about six until ten on the switchboards.

I was living at home at that time. We queued and we went around everywhere on our bikes to find what was going extra in the shops, and what was extra really meant a half pound of tomatoes. There was not much coming and what was coming, was coming from across the Atlantic. Many hours most women spent just getting enough food. That's what I remember, the awful dreary part. After you had finished a day's work and Saturdays you'd queue up.

Joyce H.: *I was in Cheltenham where I was born; I was fifteen then. Then when I left school I went as a secretary to a piano company in 1942. It was considered 'non-essential,' and I was moved to an aircraft factory. They were making parts for aircraft, and I worked in the cost department. I felt it wasn't really war work even though we worked very, very hard, costing the materials because these all had to go off to the Ministry of Aircraft.*

My mother, she had a big heart and her home was always open for the soldier without a bed. And I used to spend quite a few evenings each week in the local YMCA canteen and that used to get packed with all the various services around. It was nothing.. a soldier comes for a cup of tea, you get talking, they were all away from home. We would try and be as friendly as possible. The YMCA was full and the soldier didn't have a bed for the night. 'Oh, that's all right, come home with me.'

I was part of a dramatic society and we worked very hard raising money for various services' charities. We put on plays at the Opera House in Cheltenham, Pride and Prejudice, it was quite a thing, that was.

I actually met my husband while he was stationed in Cheltenham. They had dances at the town hall in Cheltenham on Saturday night. I used to go before the war, usually with my brother, and they were evening dress affairs. They continued through the war. I went this particular Saturday with my sister, and I met my husband at the dance at the town hall.

Great Britain's success during the Battle for Britain depended on all its citizens. As one of the women said, *"We had a sort of solidarity. The Germans underestimated us. They didn't know what we were made of at all."*

End Notes

54 Tom Hickman, *What did you do in the War, Auntie*, London: BBC Books, p. 32
55 Excepts, Interview, Imperial War Museum Sound Archive, Peter Derrick Macleod Down, #11449
56 Excerpts, Interview, Imperial War Museum Sound Archive, John Bell, #9778
57 Gas masks were issued in the spring of 1939.

CHAPTER 12

BRITAIN'S DARKEST HOUR

Britain alone remained fighting against Hitler's armies in the air and on the seas. They lost many RAF pilots in the Battle for Britain from Luftwaffe bombing attacks; they suffered the massive bombing of Coventry in November in which 60,000 out of 75,000 buildings were destroyed or damaged.

The North Atlantic

British forces were on the defensive in the North Atlantic where merchant ships were being sunk by German U-boats. They also suffered a major loss on 24 May when the *Bismarck*, the world's largest battleship sunk the battle-cruiser *Hood* in one tremendous blast. Only three of 1,500 men survived. Now the hunt was on to sink the *Bismarck* and three days later, British ships surrounded the Bismarck and pounded her with torpedoes. Admiral Lutjens ordered the ship scuttled. He went down with his ship and 2,300 German sailors drowned. The report was a morale builder for the British; for Hitler, it was a loss of prestige.[58]

Frank Harvey, a member of the Royal Navy, served on the *Aurora*.. Today he lives with his wife in Castlegar, British Columbia. He recalled those bleak days and the routine while chasing German warships in the North Atlantic: black nights, ferocious gales and waves, the occasional sea sickness, the cold and exhaustion, broken by only coming into dry dock for repairs.

"... *Of all the things I think was the most miserable, was the violent seas in the north Atlantic and in the Arctic.*

"... *In the winter of 1940 and '41, when nature turned on us and Britain had its worst blizzards in many, many years, freezing cold temperatures, deep snow, black out conditions when all the lights were turned out. You have to experience wartime blackouts to realize the misery they can cause. No cigarettes, no matches, no lights, nothing, total blackout conditions, and nowhere is that more exemplified that life on board ship when it comes around to the late afternoon, you get the signal over the loud speakers, 'darken ship' and at sea in wartime, the total blackout from all ships sometimes run the risks of collisions, if they didn't keep stationed in convoy. The risk was there of collisions and the total blackout at sea was even worse than on shore. Quite an experience in itself that I well remember from fifty odd years ago.*"

A Time to Speak

Harvey's ship, the *Aurora*, was the only one of four sister cruisers to survive World War II.

John L. Young, U. E., Canadian Navy served on the corvette, the HMCS *Lunenburg* and today lives in Bolton, Ontario.

For the Navy, the storms in the North Atlantic continued to cause as much concern and damage as German submarines. In Young's story, "Elements and Disasters," to be included in a reunion booklet for the crew of the HMCS *Lunenberg*, he wrote:

"*. . . Just that some storms are worse than others - and then there are the wild raging and violent storms, destructive and deadly. This is the kind that damaged our gun shield, flattened part of our bridge weather break, bruised and knocked around a few people and taught us the value of the life lines strung aft that we could hold on to prevent being swept overboard.*

"*This was the storm raging when we were detached from a convoy en route to Halifax to proceed to Sable Island about 50 miles from our position to assist in a rescue operation of a ship aground on Sable Island. It was long after dark when we arrived after a rough time. Already there were two or three RN ships at the wreck doing what they could to help. The big Allied freighter had broached on running aground, laying broadside to the sea with decks awash. The huge waves smashed against her relentlessly, slowly tearing her apart. We circled looking for survivors who may have been washed off the ship, while at the same time keeping up the search for any Subs which might be lurking nearby.*

"*What an ordeal - moving round the wreck and the other rescue ships, not knowing whether we would be blown onto the reef or not or how long we would be able to continue as we were taking a terrible beating, both by the ship and by the crew. We were like a cork in a washing machine - almost helpless to exercise much rudder or control It was into the wee hours of the morning before the rescuers had done all they could. By this time 38 men had been rescued and two others had been lost when trapped in a part of the ship that broke away and was crushed. One sailor in the rescue party died.*

"*When April 11 comes around, it's time to recall that wild and deadly night and to give thanks that we were spared a terrible fate, April 11th 1942. 'May They Rest in Peace, We Will Remember Them'*"

Malta, the Graveyard of the Royal Navy

The battle to control the Mediterranean shipping lanes was intense. The island of Malta was under constant attack by the Italians and the Germans. Malta was pounded by the enemy's Air Force. If Hitler could isolate Malta, then Allied supplies could be prevented from passing through Gibraltar and reaching Egypt.

Perhaps the only advantage of the massive bombings of Malta was to keep the enemy Air Force occupied in Malta rather than on the Eastern Front. On 13 September 1942 the much bombed island of Malta received the George Cross award for bravery. By November 1942 the siege of Malta was over. A convoy of merchant ships reached Malta from Egypt, under the protection of British aircraft, to the cheering crowds lined up to greet them.

Frank Harvey on the ship, *Aurora*, headed south to the harbor of Gibraltar, where they stocked up on ammunition, fuel, bunker oil and all available stores they would need in the future. They headed east through the straits of Gibraltar into the Mediterranean.

The blue seas of picture postcard Mediterranean hid treacherous mines. The blue skies were filled with black Stüka bombers. Harvey called the Mediterranean a vicious war.

"We used to call those Malta waters the graveyard of the Royal Navy. In those three years (1940-1943) they lost two battleships, two others were put out of action for months by the Italians, two aircraft carriers, seventeen cruisers and God knows how many destroyers. In terms of human disaster the Mediterranean was an appalling disaster.

"Malta was indeed a very strategic island in the Central Mediterranean and right from the start General Rommel of the Afrika Korps wanted it 'knocked out' of the war. The bombing did not succeed in 1941-42, and plans were made to invade Malta in the summer of 1942, Operation Hercules, with large numbers of gliders being assembled in Sicily and thousands of troops and paratroops. But Hitler and his generals were not really enthusiastic - we did not know at the time but the aerial invasion of Crete in May 1941 had caused crippling losses to the Germans, including troops and aircraft, mainly by the efforts of the New Zealanders on Crete.

"Malta was under siege in 1940 when Italy declared war until November 1942 when the first unmolested convoy of three or four ships arrived there from Alexandria with relief supplies. During those years Malta was starving, every ship arriving from Gibraltar or Alexandria was a battle of convoys, mostly under aerial siege by evening bombers from Sicily 80 miles away. The price was high and a coincidence, the numbers killed in Malta at nearly 3,000 (which could have been worse but for the 'tunnel shelters' to the number of air-raids which Malta had, nearly 3,000, the most frequently bombed target in the world.

"Those air raid tunnel shelters in Malta. Everybody had to leave the ship at night. We couldn't fire our guns as firing the guns gave our position. All we were doing was firing during the daytime. Except for fire guards and watch keepers on board the ship, the ship was evacuated at night and even we, the four-inch gun crews had to go to the air raid shelters. I hated those tunnels. They were damp, they

were dusty, they were noisy. And of course, in the tunnel, some of the signal men were connected to the Aurora by telephone because we simply had to know what was going on with the Aurora in dock, just in case she was hit by a bomb and extra hands were needed to deal with any emergencies, particularly, putting fires out.

"I can still remember the Maltese chanting all night. Of course, they were terrified out of their wits with the gunfire and the blast of the bombs that shook those air raid shelters. They were chanting all night and singing hymns, very, very strong Catholics.

"The ship did its best to keep us entertained with movies. The movies had to come from Alexandria or Gibraltar, particularly Gibraltar. It was a vain attempt to keep us entertained because they put the movies on in those air raid shelters and we would go ashore to watch a movie, particularly at that time, Dianna Durbin was a great favorite in 1941 and 1942. It was a vain attempt all right because with the noise of the bombs and the gunfire, you couldn't follow the sound track and sometimes there was so much dust, you could hardly see the figures on the screen.

"It might sound a bit dramatic, but let's face it, but there were days of hell with the screaming bombs. You felt you had been walking for days, nearly 100 days, in the valley of the shadow of death. We used to say that Malta was the island of 'hells, bells, and smells.' There were always these bells tolling, Catholic churches tolling bells, you could go ashore at 2 or 3 or 4 o'clock in the morning and hear a bell tolling in the distance, calling the people to mass.

"We were out on a Saturday night and being as the ships's crew was on shore leave and they all had to be rounded up from the pubs in Malta. Back to your ship, 'recall, recall' The ship is under sailing orders and we sailed. That happened on two occasions, rounding everybody up.... We went out to sea because Italian convoys had been seen at sea, crossing the Mediterranean, from Italy across to Tripoli and Bengazi.

"On the early hours of Sunday we made action against two Italian convoys. RAF bombers had spotted these convoys heading south and they kept it quiet and didn't broadcast it. They kept radio silence until they landed back in Malta and immediately got in touch with Captain Agnew, so we raised steam. We were closing in on what we assumed was the position of these Italian convoys. 'We'll go on for another half hour, then we'll turn back.' He no sooner got the words out of his mouth, darkened vessels, 'Green...red such and such. Where, where?' All of the binoculars were trained on these darkened vessels, brought our speed down to 20 knots. We waited until those ships were silhouetted against the moon, about 4,000 yards, the radar was in action, open fire, we can hear the 'ding, ding' of the bells of the six-inch turret and then the crash of the six-inch guns when they opened fire. And within a very few minutes, there were ten merchant ships in that convoy and *four Italian destroyers, we go within range and we opened fire with our four-inch guns. That firing when down for pretty close to an hour. By then, all ten merchant ships had been sunk or set on fire. One must have been carrying tanks, trucks and buses and ammunition because she blew up like an atomic explosion. It was such a flash as you wouldn't believe and those trucks and buses were flying through the air like little match boxes. That was the end of that ship. Of the four destroyers, two were sunk, one was set on fire and the other one skidaddled.*

"*By the second week in December 1941, it was known that the Russian winter had closed in around Moscow, and the German air force couldn't operate in those freezing, intolerable conditions. Unbeknown to us at the time, although we knew about it later, large numbers of the Luftwaffe had been withdrawn from Russia and were now based back in Sicily, only 18 miles away from Malta. And they soon let us know about it. By the 20th or 21st of December, they were coming over Malta in large numbers and more than we had ever experienced before. We were in dry dock. There were actually 100 days of air-raid warnings. My action station became quite hectic, the four-inch gun deck, along with all the others up on that gun deck, the anti-aircraft gun deck. It is not often that you have to fire four-inch guns in dry dock, but it was a case of survival for the ship.*

"*That four months until the beginning of April 1942 was another four months I'd like to erase from my memory, but it is not all that easy. Some of those air raids lasted for hours and hours. One of them was an air raid warning lasting twenty-three hours; the sirens went at 7 o'clock in the morning and the all clear didn't go until 6 o'clock the next morning which was a record.*"

American Neutrality Begins to Soften

While the British continued the fight against the Third Reich, the United States gradually turned away from the strict position of neutrality. President Roosevelt declared the United States to be "the Arsenal of Democracy." He asked Congress to pass the Lend Lease Act which was finally passed in March 1941. It allowed direct military aid to be sent to Great Britain and later to other friendly nations, including the Soviet Union and China.

In May 1941 Roosevelt spoke to the country and issued a proclamation that an unlimited emergency existed which required the strengthening of American military defenses. This prepared the way for rearmament after December 1941.

In August 1941 Roosevelt and Churchill, on board the cruiser, *Augusta*, signed a secret agreement. It left little doubt about Roosevelt's sentiments. Among its declarations was "to see established peace, after the final destruction of the Nazi tyranny." It was the corner stone for the later establishment of the United Nations.

End Notes

58 *The Rise and Fall of the Third Reich*, p. 667

CHAPTER 13

BRITAIN'S BEST KEPT SECRET

To Hitler's surprise, his Luftwaffe was no match for the RAF or Britain's solidarity and determination. Great Britain was also encouraged by Roosevelt's promise of fifty American destroyers. An even greater benefit was the work of British cryptographers at Bletchley Park, the site of the Government Code and Cypher School, conveniently located half-way between Oxford and Cambridge Universities.

Enigma, the German cipher machine, was invented in 1918. It resembles an over-grown typewriter and contains a series of rotor wheels and electrical connections. By resetting the rotor wheels' electrical connections, it could produce impenetrable codes. It was first exhibited in 1923 at the International Postal Union Congress in Germany, was adopted by the German Navy in 1926, and by 1934, Hitler decided to use its military capabilities.

Polish code and cypher experts, who distrusted the Germans, began to decipher Enigma's coding system, and in July 1939, invited British and French cryptographers to a secret meeting in Pyre Forest, Poland to update them on their findings. On 16 August 1939, just before Germany invaded Poland, Polish Intelligence handed over to the British the latest model of the Enigma machine.

Alastair Denniston, who had attended the Pyre Forest meeting, brought the machine to Bletchley Park and began the British wartime intelligence operations. The government hastily built drafty wooden huts of Canadian pine, covered either with shiplap boarding or asbestos sheets, and drab concrete bunkers constructed of thick concrete walls and topped with roofs of concrete slabs. This is where the secret code-breaking was carried on. In 1939 the staff numbered 200, including scientists, linguists, civilian women and WRENS, but by the middle of 1944, prior to the D-Day invasion, that number had grown to 7,000. The staff was housed with families in Bletchley and surrounding towns.

The first cypher, the German Army Enigma key was broken in January 1940. In May 1940 the decrypters broke the Enigma code, mostly frequently used by the German Air Force. By this time they were decoding, translating and interpreting about 1000 messages a day.

In 1941, the cryptographers achieved further successes, the code breaking of the hand cypher of the German Secret Service and then the Enigma key used by

A Time to Speak

the German Railways. At the same time, the United States received the Purple machine, the Japanese equivalent of the German Enigma.

Another success came on 8 May 1941 when the German submarine U-110 was captured in the Atlantic and the British found cypher material which expanded their ability to read German codes. In the same month, the British also broke the key to the Italian Navy's cypher machine, C38m.

In January 1942, a fifth Enigma key was broken, which carried messages Berlin sent to the Eastern Front. But in February, the German Submarine Command altered the Enigma machine in such a way that the British were unable to decrypt messages for the rest of the year.

January 1943, they broke another of the Enigma keys, which provided German Air Force messages relating to ground-air co-operation in south Russia.

Finally on May 1943, there was the Anglo-American agreement on the full exchange and distribution of Signals Intelligence. The German Enigma, the Italian C 38m and the Japanese Purple decrypts were brought into a standard form and the code name Ultra was adopted.

There was an official ban on any references to Ultra until the spring of 1974. F. W. Winterbotham first made public the role of code-breaking in World War II in his book *The Ultra Secret.*.

The technical work was done by the mathematicians from Oxford and Cambridge, called the "boffins." The laborious and dreary work was done by the WRENS (the Women's Royal Naval Service), young, skilled women who lived, ate, and worked together.

The Boffins

There are some recorded interviews, in the Imperial War Museum Sound Archives, of scientists and mathematicians who worked at Bletchley Park . One mathematician was reluctant to go into specific details about his work. He stressed instead the military importance of code breaking in Britain's war effort. It was absorbing and meticulous work for which one needed optimism, a willingness to look at a very large number of things and pick out the most profitable, and some combinatorial ability and a vague superficial knowledge of language.[59]

The WRENS
The Bombe Machine

The bombe machine was operated by WRENS. "Bombe" was the name given to the electro-mechanical machine which helped in the breaking of the coded messages brought in from the "Y" stations (the listening posts around Britain). The bombe unit was over six feet high and six feet wide, massively constructed because the machines needed to be given protection, so that the vital work would not stop, even if there were an air-raid.

Valerie Fiddelaar Knowles worked on the bombe machine and remarked, "We had to have tweezers to adjust the plugging at the back. Your nails broke." Later she wrote:

"I joined the WRENS, I was only seventeen and a half. You had to be under twenty-one to get the job because they wanted our brains."

The Silence Act Is Rescinded

After years of silence, the mystery and secrecy surrounding the work at Bletchley Park is being told. Three women, Morag MacLennen Beattie, Adrienne Farrell Jackson and Vivien Martin Young had been part of a group of fourteen who worked together at Bletchley. They returned for the Commemoration Service at Bletchley Park on 8 May 1995, the first time in fifty years they had been together and could talk about their experiences. At the time of the war they couldn't talk about their work and when the war was over, they had to sign a Silence Act that they would not talk about what they had done.

They agreed, *"In one sense, we did feel smug about the kinds of things we were doing. I wonder how important the work was when you compared it to the kinds of things other people were doing, losing their lives and we weren't in any danger, as people were in London during the Blitz, but if our work saved the life of one person, it was probably worth while."* The three women have started to recall what they did and put their recollections into booklet form, *Hut 4 Naval Section, Bletchley Park, 1941-1945.*

"We were a group of young girls with language skills who joined Hut 4 Naval Section at Bletchley Park shortly after the German U-Boat Enigma code was first cracked in 1941. We started as linguist-typists or indexers and became Technical Assistants. We were in due course given responsibility for collating and researching Ultra material and mapping references to German coastal defenses and coastal commands using Ultra and other sources. . . .

"Two things about Bletchley stand out in our memories: firstly, the total commitment to secrecy, to the extent that until recently we blacked out all recollections, never mentioning anything about it even to our closest families; and secondly, the very great sense of camaraderie that existed among us, so that when, after 50 years, we met again in 1995 as wives, mothers, grandmothers (even one great-grandmother) and career women, it was as though we had never been separated." [60]

How did we get our jobs

Mrs. Beattie: *I volunteered to join the WRENS as soon as I was old enough and filled in with dull and unmemorable jobs in the Air Ministry and Home Guard, dreaming of the exciting life to come, ships, sea gulls and salt spray.*

... At last I was called up, and had my initial training at Westfield College, Hampstead. From there about 12 of us were selected for 'important and secret work at Station X,' which sounded exciting to a teenager.

We were somewhat puzzled on arrival at Euston to be given travel warrants to Bletchley, the wrong direction surely? We went straight into Hut 11, to be confronted by our first bombes, large black machines clicking away with their tickety-tock, tickety-tock of the turning drums, a sound which became our constant background noise for the next few years. There were no windows, and a pervading smell of machine oil. Farewell sea gulls and salt spray!

Mrs. Jackson: *In the summer of 1941 I had just taken a degree in French, and started to learn Italian lying in the garden at home with a pile of books and records, waiting to be called up. Anyone with a degree was recorded on a Central Register, and I presume that was how I was summoned by Frank Birch in September to an interview at Bletchely, where they were looking for linguists following the break into the German and Italian naval codes.*

Thinking in my ignorance that the more languages I could claim the better, I learned Spanish industriously all the way on the five-hour train journey from Yorkshire to Bletchley. . . . I joined Bletchley immediately as a linguist-typist in Naval Section Hut 4, employed by the Foreign Office.

Mrs. Young: *When I went to the Labour Exchange at the age of seventeen, they said, 'We have something for you.' I don't remember arriving at Bletchley, but I recollect being shown into a room where there were other typists and being set to work typing signals. . . .*

Tickety-tock, tickety-tock

However, it was obvious to them, that as unqualified schoolgirls, they were doing the most useful job possible. They were divided into Watches which would change weekly, for example working from 8 a.m. to 4 p.m.; 4 p.m. to midnight; midnight to 8 a.m. Then they would get a four days leave. Although the work was intense, these women did enjoy some lighter moments. They were teenagers after all: dancing to Glen Miller's band in a crowded hangar, romance and marriage.

Mrs. Beattie: *In Hut 11, the bombes never stopped working, and if on a very good day the main codes had been broken, there was always a backlog of unbroken codes from previous days, or experimental trial runs with new codes.*

For every new job, we were given a menu from Hut 6, Army and Air, or Hut

8, Navy, a plan of letters and lines, which told us how to plug the great red pigtails of plaited wires into the sockets at the back of the bombes. Then to set the three rows of drums in each of the three banks at 'a' in each of the three banks per bombe and switch on, tickety-tock, tickety-tock. Every so often in a run of about 15 minutes, there would be a 'stop', a possible setting to be recorded and sent back to Huts 6 and 8.

As each run was completed, one row of 12 drums was taken off, replaced by another set, and during the next run, all the newly removed drums had to be inspected and trimmed; their circles of copper wire brushes were set at an angle, and if a single rogue wire bent and caused a short circuit, that run was invalid and had to be repeated.

... I was allocated to Coastal Defence in Naval Section. Our job was to record and plot on charts all information on enemy coastal batteries and sea mine fields gleaned from Ultra, other decodes and captured documents. Then reports were sent up to Admiralty, supplementing the automatic transmission of Ultra. We also helped the cryptographers with corrupt signals, sorting our precise map references where possible.

... Vivien Martin and I worked on the Far East, where we were understandably overshadowed by the U. S. They produced large sumptuously bound publications, while our efforts were humble typed foolscaps - photo-copying was decades away. However, when we came to plot the U. S. information, we occasionally found sea-mines laid on dry land, and coastal batteries in deep water.

...Work at Bletchley was unremitting... I can remember several of us working overnight non-stop to complete something the Admiralty needed.

... As time went by, we began to do more research, collating the information from the index. In 1943, after we had moved to a brick block by the lake, we began mapping references to coastal defenses along the Nazi occupied coastline. My job was to enter German coastal defenses and coastal commands in Norway.

... But the war was brought home to us by the personal tragedies and anxieties of colleagues who had husbands, brothers or boyfriends at risk. Among us was one girl whose husband, a senior naval officer, was killed when the battleship Hood was blown up during the chase of the Bismarck. And I remember being on duty the night the PQ17 convoy was scattered and sunk and the feeling of impotent gloom as we saw the waiting U-boats plotted on the Map Room charts and knew the tragedy could have been averted if more reliance had been placed on the information from Bletchley.

A Time to Speak

Living Conditions

The young women were housed in hotels, homes, and estates located in the neighboring villages. The neighbors knew that war work was going on at Bletchley Park, but didn't ask questions about the work, but they did feel free to ask the women personal questions.

Mrs. Beattie: *At first I lived in a hostel, then to my delight was transferred to a Woburn Sands hotel. Afterwards I was billeted at Leighton Buzzard, which I didn't enjoy because the wife was very nosey. Every time I had a letter . . . she wanted to know the contents.*

In the early days, I was billeted with a family in North Crawley, who survived on a diet of beet root and cheese, eaten at very strange hours. If you stayed back in the Park to have a bath in the Main House, you had to make your own way to your billet. So it was bliss to move into the WRENS Quarters at Crawley Grange, a beautiful house in large grounds. Sleeping in double-decker beds in a cabin of 24 WRENS, all of different watches, soon developed one's ability to compromise and cooperate.

Mrs. Knowles: *I was stationed at Woburn Abbey, the Duke of Bedford's estate. They commandeered the down stairs, and I think he lived in the back. With twelve other WRENS, we slept in bunk beds. We called it the 'Silk Canopied Room,' and it was very cold. The ablutions (they were what we called the toilet and bathroom) didn't work at all. One day we were exploring the Abbey, we were going around, looking around to see what we could find. We came across him [the Duke of Bedford] on these stairs and he said, 'Get out of here, you wretches, you are not supposed to be here at all.'*

Mrs. Jackson: *I began on a salary of three pounds ten pence a week and by the end of the war in Europe earned five pounds, with the title of Temporary Junior Administrative Officer. This was quite handsome pay, but not enough to cover train journeys home on periodic leaves. So I used to hitch-hike on lorries up the Watling Street to Barnet, then on the Yorkshire. I still remember enjoying one of the great gourmet meals of my life, in a pull-in cafe on the Great North Road - fried spam and chips! Ambrosia indeed, after the sadly undistinguished wartime fare served by the Bletchley canteen.*

The canteen was just outside the gates, so that to return inside we had to show our passes, a white card with a green line across it. One night, when I had forgotten my pass, I claimed (and after 50 years I can no longer vouch if it was true) that I managed to get back by showing the sentries a canteen sandwich, authenticated by the line of green mould than ran across it.

Once they left Bletchely, Mrs. Knowles volunteered to go to the Dutch East Indies, where she worked as a dock yard writer. When Sri Lanka came under communist rule, she returned to England, then to Wales. Mrs. Beattie took a job in a Soho cutting-room, making documentary films, then became editor. She took a short course in infant teaching and eventually spent twenty years in Marylebone Primary School. Mrs. Jackson joined Reuters new agency and for thirty years was a foreign correspondent in Geneva, Rome and New Delhi. She and her husband now live in Switzerland to be able to collaborate with the international conservation organizations based there. Mrs. Young worked as a reporter on the Sunday Chronicle in Manchester, then married in 1945 and came back to London.

Many wonder if the war could have been won without the cryptologists at Bletchley Park. An additional benefit to the Allies was the work of resistance movements in countries occupied by the Third Reich.

End Notes

59   Summary, Interview, Imperial War Museum Sound Archive, Dr. Shawn Wylie, #9453
60   Introduction from the booklet

CHAPTER 14

EARLY RESISTANCE MOVEMENTS, PART I

The Resistance in Czechoslovakia, Poland, Denmark

British intelligence also relied on information that came from the underground movements on the Continent which organized as soon as Hitler's armies occupied a country. Their first objectives were to send information to London, and to set up escape lines to enable soldiers and pilots to reach England to join the British forces.

Great Britain was the point of convergence for underground activity for several reasons. First, it was the only country still battling Hitler's armies. Furthermore, defeated countries set up governments in exile in London, Queen Wilhemina of Holland and Edvard Benes of Czechoslovakia. The Belgian ministers set up a government in exile in France, then in Great Britain, although King Leopold III refused to go and was held prisoner by the Third Reich. The Polish General, Wladyslaw Sikorski set up a Polish Government in exile in Paris. Like the Belgian government in exile, it moved to London after the fall of France. General de Gaulle also arrived in London where he established the government of the Free French. King Christian X of Denmark remained in Copenhagen.

Communication from the continent to London was possible through radio and courier lines. The Third Reich forbade radios in occupied territory. Nevertheless, radios were hidden, installed in houses or apartments, and constantly moved to avoid detection. Messages were sent to the BBC in London. Communication of plans, photos, and long reports were sent by courier across the Pyrenees into Spain, or by fishing boat from the coast of Brittany to England. Occasionally, a route across the Alps to Switzerland was used.

The activities varied depending on the country, the circumstances of the war, the practices of the war, and the occupying armies. Primarily, Resistance members looked for military information they could pass on to London. However, their work ran the gamut of silly pranks to annoy the Germans and boost citizen's morale to underground armies and overt acts of sabotage. Prior to the Normandy invasion in 1944, Resistance groups accepted parachute drops of arms, munitions and other supplies so they could destroy bridges and railroad yards and fight alongside the Allies.

Auguste Le Carpentier, historian by training and a former member of the

French resistance described the movement as "a frame of mind" or "a state within a state." He added:

"*It is difficult for anyone today to plunge into the ambiance of that time. We were only men and women, not heroes or heroines. Some were imprudent and took actions which were costly.*

"*What was difficult was the clandestine nature of the Resistance. You didn't have a name, you were on the qui vive twenty-four hours a day, you had to pay attention to your contacts. You needed to make sure of where you were, how to get out, how to kill, to kill yourself to avoid torture. You had no contact with your family, it was hard on them. You acted in a play. After six or seven years as a Resistant, it was easier to use a Bren-gun than a pen.*"

Most of the resistance members worked in small groups in a regional network. A few were involved in large intelligence networks operating in several countries in Europe. They suffered denunciation and trickery by both their compatriots and the Gestapo, and many were arrested, tortured and imprisoned.

Czechoslovakia

First to be occupied, the Czechs formed the earliest resistance groups in the summer of 1939. One of the largest was organized by officers and soldiers of the former Czech army, the Defense of the Nation. Other soldiers moved abroad to participate with the Polish Army, in which an army unit of Czechs and Slovaks was formed. After the defeat of Poland, the Resistants were interned in the Soviet Union. In France, two Czech infantry regiments were formed.

The Czech population demonstrated their disapproval of German occupation by participation in various national celebrations. The demonstration on 28 October 1939 celebrated the anniversary of the founding of Czechoslovakia. During the demonstration, a medical student, Jan Opletal, died after being shot by a German policeman. The next demonstration, during his funeral, was the pretext for the Germans closing of all Czech institutions of higher education. Students were taken to concentration camps and nine members of the student movement were shot.

Lidice

In 1941, the number of strikes and acts of sabotage as well as successful intelligence operations had increased in Czechoslovakia. Reinhard Heydrich, chief of the Security Police, was appointed to combat Germany's enemies. He declared martial law and launched a rule of terror against all illegal organizations.

Responding to Heydrich's actions, the Czech government in London planned an assassination plot against him which was carried out on 27 May 1942 by Jan Kubis and Jozef Gabcik, members of the paratrooper group, Anthropoid. Although warned of the dangers of the plot by the resistance groups at home, they carried out their orders and tossed a British made bomb at Heydrich's open Mercedes sports car as he left his villa to go to Prague. He died on 4 June.

Hitler's revenge was a frenzied attack by truckloads of German Security Police on the village of Lidice. On 6 June, the village of Lidice was shut off and instructions were given. All men were lined up for execution. The women, and those children not considered racially capable of being assimilated into the Aryan race, were rounded up and deported. The remaining children were given to German families for re-education. The buildings were looted; then dynamiters came and destroyed all of the buildings including the cemetery. What remained of houses were leveled, all trees were cut down, all trails and roads were removed, and the entire area was covered with soil. The Nazis photographed the destruction of Lidice as an instructional and cultural film.

Why Lidice? According to the brochure from the Lidice Museum, the Gestapo had information from an informer, gleaned from a love letter. During the interrogation of two families in Lidice, the whereabouts of their sons were unknown to their families except for the information that their sons had gone abroad. The Gestapo presumed they had been dropped by parachute and had assassinated Heydrich.

Hitler meant for the fate of Lidice to serve as a demonstration of his resolve and military force. Instead, the act of terror created sympathy for the town. Czech soldiers in the Soviet Union collected money among themselves to buy a tank which they named "Lidice."

Today tourists look across to the site where Lidice one existed and see a monument with its cross and a statue of a group of children, marking the spot where they were buried.

Poland's Home Army

At the outset of World War II, the regular Polish Army was defeated by Hitler's Army and the Red Army entered eastern Poland. From July 1943 until October 1944, when he became a prisoner of war, the Commander of the Polish Home Army was General Tadeusz Bor-Komorowski.

Wieslaw Furmanczyk, a retired professor and former head of the American Literature Department at the University of Warsaw, joined the Polish underground.

". . . It was in fact the 'earliest possible' movement of that kind. Poland was invaded by Germany on 1 September 1939, and the foundation of what was to be later called the Home Army (A. K.) was laid in September 1939, when Warsaw was about to capitulate. It was on 27 September 1939 in Warsaw that the leaders of

the underground movement met for the first time; Warsaw surrendered a day later, 28 September.

"As to the way the underground units were organized: the pattern was actually similar to that of the regular Polish Army. The smallest unit to which each of us belonged consisted of six or seven men; it was the so-called 'section.' Before the Uprising, I knew only the members of my section (their pseudonyms, that is, not their real names, except for my closest friend who recommended me).

"Three sections made a 'squad,' — eighteen to twenty-one men. Three squads made a platoon, up to 63 men and three platoons formed a company, 180-190 men. There were also some women (mostly young girls) who were nurses or messengers. The nurses and doctors had a separate system of training. Of course this basic pattern was no longer true in terms of numbers once the actual fighting began.

"When you read a book about the underground or the 'secret state,' it was not just the underground army, but there was a legal system; there were judges; there was a department of education. So we were used to doing things in secret. I don't know how much concern the Germans had for making trouble for the schools. I'm sure that if the Gestapo had come into an apartment where there were six or seven boys sitting around a table, their conclusions would have been obvious.

"Well, it was all secret. I could have taken you to the very place where I was recruited which was in Zoliborz. Well, a friend of mine was already in the underground, and we went to school together which was an underground school, too, because the Germans thought some kind of professional school was about enough for the Polacks, for the lower races. On a higher level, we met in private homes. You would have six or seven boys, sitting around the table and the teachers would come. So that was underground too.

"By the way, a footnote, but it is interesting how difficult it is, for an American, to even try to understand how things were happening and what was happening.

"So this friend of mine asked me if I wanted to join the underground army and I said I did. I did that pretty late. It was in April '44, months before the actual uprising and then he got in touch with his commander in chief. There was an appointment in one of the public squares in Zoliborz, the northern part of Warsaw. We went there by tram, both got off the tram and the man was waiting for us. My friend went to talk to him, and then I joined them and this fellow talked to me.

"That's the way I was somehow introduced and then we met in sections, six or eight of us, and we would meet in private homes and we had regular instruction in how to handle weapons. Some of the weapons were manufactured by Polish people after a model, a Sten. We got the Sten from England, dropped by parachute, and some of them were captured in underground actions when German soldiers were shot. I joined a unit which, relatively speaking, was very well equipped as far as weapons were concerned. Company 9, the name of our company was 'Diversion.' So we were trained in what might be considered a foolish way.

"You had to take an oath, that was actually in the apartment where we lived. One of our direct commanders, who was in charge of one of the smaller units, he came to our apartment and I and another friend of mine who was also new, we had to swear on a cross. We had to put our two fingers on the cross and we were to repeat the text of a oath, that we were going to be loyal to the Polish government. So that was it.

"One of my experiences was to carry a box of cartridges from one place in Warsaw to another on a bicycle. There were two of us and we had to leave our documents so that if we were captured we couldn't be identified and our families would not be involved. And we were given pistols and I put one under the belt, got on the bicycle and then my friend, he was in front of me. I was following him. Then the street which is now a nice street was cobblestones. Then suddenly I realized the gun was sliding down the leg of my trousers and there I was riding a bicycle. And what I saw or who I saw was not so funny because there was the village patrol approaching. How I got off the bicycle with a pistol and how I got into the doorway with it, the bicycle and the box behind me, I don't know. I somehow managed.

"Then everything went on smoothly for a time. But then my friend, who was supposed to be in front of me, slowly disappeared. And I said, 'Why isn't he waiting for me?' Then I finally caught up with him, no he caught up with me. Here is the situation: the street car line, a very busy place, and lots of kiosks and a crowd of people waiting here. When I saw the street car, I said, 'Let's not take any chances,' and I passed it on the left side which you are not supposed to do. My poor friend knocked into the middle of the crowd, he was sort of nervous and he knocked a woman and she fell. Everybody shouted. There was a policeman, a Polish policeman fortunately, who stopped him and there was poor Janus, holding to the handles with all that business behind it. The policeman asked 'What are you doing? let me see your documents.' And Janus said, 'I haven't any.' So he looked at him and then Janus said, 'You'd better let me go or there might be trouble.' And the policeman looked at him and let him go. So this was why he was behind me.

"That was one of the things that I did that was really dangerous, although I wasn't in action, trying to shoot someone.

"Another time, there was a sharp-shooter who was trying to get us. He was just in front of me and I was behind and I remember telling my friend to duck because he was fairly tall. I had hardly finished when. . . . That in a way was more terrible because the man was killed just in front of me. Then we sort of turned *around to see what had happened. Blood running out of his mouth. It was terrible but somehow I don't remember."*

Denmark

With the sudden occupation of Denmark, Aksel Schiotz, a well-known Danish tenor, was unable to leave for his coast-to-coast tour of the United States. He immediately protested against the German occupation, not in the secretive world of the underground, but through his singing. He decided to give his scheduled "farewell" concert. His story was told by his widow, Gerd.

"His good-by concert, he had a Jewish accompanist, he insisted. [Because of their proximity to Germany, the Danes were aware of Hitler's anti-Semitic sentiments.] *We went on April 9. We stick to that concert. We are not giving up, even though no people are coming, I've got to protest. People came when they found out he was carrying through, but they were in panic. No lights, people wore a white band around their arm to be seen. His recital became so impressive. Everybody was crying. Suddenly he couldn't sing, because he has a lump in his throat. People were extremely happy about that. His manager said we will repeat it, and go to the big hall. And that became five recitals in a row. He went out of his repertoire because it was so limited. We are doing all Danish songs. He became established as a singer of Danish songs because it was a national protest.*

"After six concerts, he was in demand everywhere. People made excursions for singing and he was going to lead it. People loved it because it was a confirmation of their own nationality. It was so unexpected.

"He was actually managing his own Resistance movement with his audiences, making programs with a double meaning all the way through. When he sang, there was a hidden message. I went searching through the libraries to find old hymns that had a double background. If he sang, 'Comfort ye my people,' then people would perceive it as a personal comfort to them. He sang on the radio and became very popular. We had no idea that Danish songs would mean anything as repertoire on the stage, that was not done.

"There was a famous dramatist, shot in January '45, carried out by the Danish Nazis. And we had a message in the mail box, type-written, 'Axsel Schiotz, stay away, because now it is your turn to be shot.' And that was a pressure to live under. All of his friends wanted him to go to Sweden, but he said, 'I have to do my duty, I have to fight here. I have to cheer up my audience.' He carried on throughout the war."

By 1943, there was a marked change in the attitudes of the resistance movements. They became more militant.

CHAPTER 15

EARLY RESISTANCE MOVEMENTS, PART II

Gaston alias Raymond alias Rinus

After the occupation of Belgium in 1940, Germany asked Belgian refugees to return to their native country. Gaston Vandermeerssche went back to Belgium in August 1940, where he celebrated his 19th birthday. He returned to the university to continue his studies and resumed his math tutoring.

The Nazis continued their propaganda, encouraging the Flemish people to join them in their new spirit of racial pride. Eventually they ordered all Belgian men between the ages of 18 and 50 and all unmarried women between the ages of 21 and 35 to register for some kind of war service. Political debate at universities was banned, posters appeared with threats to shoot any foreign agents along with their families. Food was harder to get, fresh meat and vegetables disappeared from the market; fuel grew scarcer.

Vandermeerssche found some useful work as a distributer of *La Libre Belgique* (Free Belgium) which reported uncensored news, most of which came from the BBC in London. Although he stuffed more and more copies into mailboxes, including those of Nazi sympathizers, he became frustrated by his inability to do anything more as he watched the number of Belgian collaborators grow. He left for unoccupied France when he learned the Gestapo had his name on a list of resistance members. He was able to find a way through the Belgian border into France in July 1941. He hoped to go to Spain, then to England, to become a pilot in the RAF. Instead he found a career in the underground, working first for Belgium. Later he organized the Dutch underground network for Queen Wilhelmine and was in charge of a network of almost 2,000 spies.

In the end Vandermeerssche was caught up in a counter-intelligence coup: the German operation known as *Das Englandspiel*. According to M. R. D. Foot, the Germans managed three break-ins in S.O.E. operations. The worst of the three cases was the Dutch one. The Germans arrested an S.O.E. officer, H. M. G. Lauwer, in Holland. After some reluctance, Lauwer agreed to send messages putting in the faulty security code to alert London he was sending messages under duress. He even inserted CAU....GHT among the jumbled letters. Unfortunately, the S.O.E. in London did not notice his transmissions were not secure. They sent back to Germany genuine and useful intelligence. Eventually, the German infiltrated and controlled the Dutch underground. Agents sent to Holland by the S.O.E. fell into German hands.[61]

Vandermeerssche was arrested 10 May 1943 in Perpignan, condemned to die, and was finally liberated by the American First Army. Today he is president of his own company, Gavarti Associates Ltd. in Milwaukee, Wisconsin.

Ramon-Raymond

"I was able to find a way through the Belgian border into France. From there on, from one patron to another one, I finally ended up in free France. In free France, I was given orders by a Belgian intelligence officer, not to go to England, but immediately to go into hiding for three weeks and learn Spanish. And I would come back after three weeks as a Spaniard because they needed a courier line, someone who could go from France to Spain, back and forth. There was no courier line so I created one, that courier line in the Pyrenees. It was the line 'Ramon-Raymond.' [September 1941] *Ramon was my counterpart in Spain and I was Raymond, that was my code name."*

Gaston (Raymond) operated the courier line from Barcelona to Toulouse to Brussels, making a trip almost every week. Ramon ran the Barcelona to Lisbon portion of the courier line.

Agents were people willing to provide shelter for couriers or downed pilots. Those with access to government offices supplied ration coupons for food and clothing and blank identity cards. The agents collected vital information, copies of shipyard work schedules, maps showing the strength and position of German anti-aircraft emplacements, tonnage and destinations of cement, brick and steel shipments, lists of uniform insignia, details of markings on tanks, trucks and vehicles moved by rail.

"I got this information to England three ways. I had a route through the Pyrenees that went through France, Spain, Portugal. I had another one through Switzerland and another one over the mountains in Sweden which was supposed to be neutral. The microfilms were all triplicates to make sure that they would get there.

"I had to get all of the microfilms to Spain, to Barcelona and the most important, I had to bring the funds for all of the different networks, all the money for this that came from England came through my hands and had to be given to the chiefs. I knew all the networks that existed. I was a very dangerous person if I were captured.

"It was against the rule that a courier would take people along. But when

you are a resistant, an agent, you do all that is absolutely necessary. And an agent can't wait until he has a ticket to go through. So I have taken people, including a Belgian minister of the government. Otherwise, very few people went with me when I went with the courier.

"I had my own system for the safe houses. Let's say I can trust you, I would not come in. I would walk along the street. I would notice that you had just left one of the window things lit. It is an intentional motion that is visible to me. I would not come in unless you had given me, 'Now you can come in - safe.' And the whole time, if it is not so, I would not come in. Maybe you have been captured or something. So I did this with different safe houses.

"But after six months, the Germans, the Gestapo, who were also in free France, they knew so much about me, that it became very risky. My boss said the normal life-time of an agent is about six months in the same area, so you have to do something else. So I was given another mission, to control all the courier lines from Holland, Luxembourg, Germany, Belgium, France, Spain and Portugal. To control the lines, that was my second mission."

Rinus and WIM

"It wasn't long before my third mission was given [September 1942] and that's where Holland comes in. The Queen Wilhemina in London, she knew she had been cut off completely from her people. There was no communication at all any more between Holland and England. She went to the head of the Belgian intelligence, who became my boss. He was asked, 'Do you have someone who could resurrect the Dutch underground?' I spoke Dutch.

"A very amazing fact occurred. First of all, I came into a country where a lot of people had been active to guard information, but didn't know where to go with it. They had groups, twenty, thirty, forty people organized, and they couldn't send the messages. They had no radio. At that time, the British were using pigeons. How anyone can catch these pigeons to get those messages, when you see the difference between using pigeons and then using sophisticated means of morse code to send messages.

"So that's how I got involved with Holland. And very quickly I was able to penetrate over the whole territory of Holland with different, independent systems. The people did not know that their boss was not a Hollander. I took a code name, 'Rinus,' and the network, I called WIM because I thought that fits, Wilhemina, WIM is short for the Queen. When I wrote instructions, it was all in Dutch. They expected to be working for a Dutch boss. You can imagine, then, during the trial, when they found out that I was a Belgian, and when they saw me and how young I was. I was a kid, twenty-two years old. 'That's the boss?' That, in a nutshell, is how I got involved in Holland.

"And the whole Dutch underground network with those 1,500 people, only about six knew me face to face. They knew me by my code name and that has helped a lot.

"There is a fact I should mention. The networks were beginning to be so upset with the fact that the couriers were so slow and that they had leakage, that the Germans had penetrated lines. 'You have to straighten this out, you have to go to London and see what those guys are doing.' We all had the impression that there were double agents in England.

"So they said, 'Ask London when you can come.' I got the OK. I started my last trip through the Pyrenees which I had done for six months. Just at that time, I got arrested in a very suspicious way. It was arranged. They didn't want me to go to London. It was part of le grand jeu (the great game [What some think was part of Britain's strategy to mislead the Germans about the location of the D-Day attack])."

Prison and Torture

The agent Gaston alias Raymond alias Rinus spent twenty-four months in prison. First, in Perpignan in a fortress, then in a tiny cell in Fresnes. From Fresnes, he was taken each day to Gestapo headquarters on Avenue Foch in Paris for questioning. The Gestapo wanted him to admit he was Raymond and give them information about the Raymond-Ramon courier line and they badly wanted any information about the rumored Allied invasion, where was it to take place and when. The prisoner's job was to feed them some information, to string them along, giving his agents time to disperse. And all the time, hoping his agents would not give him away.

"The Germans are very thorough as you know. Since I worked in Holland as head of a network and in Belgium as Ramon and in France and in Spain. Each group condemned me.

"Tortured, yes, three days and three nights without stop. They picked me up and threw me against the wall; they kicked. A piece of my chin bone is gone; most of my teeth were knocked out, my nose was broken.

"How does one resist that? I have asked myself the question, does everyone react the same way? I'm sure that some people would give in immediately. It's not their will power. I'm sure they don't want to, but they cannot resist. Some people feel pain more than others. There is a difference between women and men. Women are made to support more suffering by nature with childbirth. A man, if he had to give birth, I wonder what he would do?

"But, on the other hand when they were torturing one of my agents, a beautiful girl, half Spanish, half French, they were smacking her face, 'Do you know her? Do you know him?' She said 'No.' She was one of the very close agents.

"That was another one, while they were questioning me for three days, next door there was a Spanish courier of mine, they were pulling his nails out. Each time, the noise he made, they said, 'Well, it's your fault. If you would tell us what we would ask you, we stop right away. We'll tell him it's your fault that we are doing this,' which they did.

"Can you stop that? If you stop once, there is no way back. They will ask more because they know it works. I don't remember, even, whether it was the second day or the third day, but I was so in pain, I was going to pretend to faint. I fell down in a faint. Within two minutes, they brought in a German shepherd who jumped to my throat. You are going to resist, thinking that he is going to bite in my face. It is a horrible thought."

Staying Sane in Solitary Confinement

In between questioning and beatings, he was kept in solitary confinement. He recalled how he stayed mentally alert under those conditions:

"First, of all, the lack of food is lack of energy. If you had plenty of energy, you would do exercises. It would be a logical thing to do. That's the last thing you do. You try to stay as quiet and as still as possible. You don't move, keep your energy. The second thing is that you cannot speak, you cannot whistle, you cannot sing, you cannot make any noise. You cannot read, you cannot write - solitary. You have no news of the outside world. So what you try to do is figure out, how can I communicate? Depending on what kind of cell you are in, you can knock on the wall by Morse. Most agents know Morse, not all of them, I have a story about this. In the cells in Holland, we had a faucet of water to wash ourselves and for other things. When you turn your ear around the pipe of the water, you can hear any cell in the whole prison when someone makes the water run and he does it in the form of a Morse code. And we were communicating.

"In France (Fresnes), we didn't have a bed, we had a sort of mattress of straw and it was loaded with fleas. We didn't have forks or knives; we had two spoons. I thought, I have to do something with this, and the mattress has some kind of a seam. And I discovered that in this seam, the fleas would line up. I heard the church bell that would give me the signal of an hour. And I would count the number of fleas I could kill in an hour and see if I could beat the record. It is not easy to kill fleas. With two spoons, you just kind of roll them, then you can count them. It kept me busy. And not too much energy. Things like this, what else was there? Listen to the noise? It is easy to go crazy.

"There is another thing which is probably kind of different from others. As a kid, I was an atheist, strong, like I was strong in everything. I was already a leader because I wanted to be the president of this group, that group. I was going to *prove to the world, as a scientist, that God could not exist, based on science.*

"In prison, I did not have the help that a person who is religious did have. It is tremendous help. I don't see how you can do without it, but I did the first year. Then I said there must be something. I had been exposed to different things. My father had had a bad experience with a priest. In all those different religions, I had read a lot about Sufism which is a fantastic religion because it says, 'All of the religions should be respected and there is always something good.' And that really struck me. So I said, 'Well, let's do that, why don't I pretend to be a Jew today, tomorrow a Catholic, then a Protestant, try to shop.' It didn't work. On one occasion, I was in the upper floor of the Avenue Foch where the Gestapo was and there was a little window in the ceiling. I said, 'God if you exist, help me get out!' And I jumped, and a couple of times, I was just hanging on. Just when I begin to think maybe I can do it, the guard came in and that was it.

"When you are there, it is real. He does exist, could so many people be wrong? God is something you go through and from one day to another, you change stories, you try something, you change your thinking process, all on a slow pace. That, in itself, was kind of interesting."

The Trial

The Germans suspected that Gaston was Raymond, who created and was head of the Ramon-Raymond courier line. What Gaston did not know during his imprisonment was that London continued to send messages to Raymond, suggesting he was seen in Grenoble, later in Paris. One underground message reported he had been executed by the Gestapo. Not until a double agent recognized him and shouted 'Raymond' was the Gestapo sure they had Raymond. The Gestapo also managed to find incriminating documents about the work of WIM. Vandermeerssche and other WIM agents were taken to a concentration camp at Haaren, near Tilburg, south of The Hague in Holland.

The WIM agents were put on trial, a Luftwaffe field trial, January 1944. There, in a large office room, they saw *WIM DIENST*, a schematic reproduction of the WIM organization. The WIM agents were charged with the organization of an intelligence network that sent information to the enemy and was responsible for the death of thousands of German soldiers.

"The miracle that happened for me, I was so young, the Germans did not believe that this kid was the head of that large network. And I told them, 'Are you crazy? I couldn't have done this.'

"It was a big trial. It was the Luftwaffe. At the trial, I had a big Number One. I was tried by the Germans and no lawyers, not even German lawyers. That's the only trial in the two world wars where there was no defense. Fifty-one condemned to die. I had number 1 and I knew the chances were slim. And when I saw those big generals of the Luftwaffe, it was very impressive. They read off, 'You were responsible for thousands of women being killed, you were responsible for this.' I stood up and said, 'I am so honored that I did such a good work,' and I turned around and I yelled out in the whole room, 'Long live Holland! Long live Belgium!' But it gave the incentive to all of the others who had to defend themselves to say, 'What do we have to lose?' And it gave an impression to those Germans, which they told me afterwards, they were impressed. By the way, the guy of the Gestapo who questioned me, many times he told me, 'I have full admiration for you.' And that's typical of those guys. He was doing his duty. He was a professional.

"After we were condemned to die, for one day (they must have made a mistake), I was supposed not to see anybody because I was an "NN" prisoner, Nacht und Nebel Gefangene. [Hitler issued "The Night and Fog Decree" on December 7, 1941. Persons, dangerous to security, were seized, but were not executed immediately. They simply vanished without a trace into the night and fog, and no information was given to their families.]

"They had to put them [the prisoners] all together the next day to announce the verdict. There was another Dutch boy, who was a very fine Christian fellow with a little New Testament. He was in the same cell. My first reaction was, 'They still want to find out about me. He is probably a traitor.' So I was very closed up. But then I felt, after a little while, maybe he is all right, although he hadn't done very much. He said, 'You read that.' To make long story short, the New Testament was taken away from me also, but I had been able to read, 'If God be for us, then who can be against us.' [62]

"When we were liberated and they gave us our stuff, I still had that. Fascinating! Adding up the psychological story, the religious story, I am now a scientist who believes in God but you couldn't prove to me, in any way, that there is not something. But I am against all dogma."

A Pawn in a Deadly Game?

"Anyway, when I was arrested I began to wonder and I had twenty-four months to think about this. And many things were not clear to me.

"And when I came out of prison, I began to ask, first of all, 'Hey what's going on?' My network of more than 1,500 agents didn't exist. I had to go visit my agents and I had to put the whole thing together. Someone was a little annoyed that I came back. I was not supposed to. I am wondering. I was blaming the guys in London. They were eating and drinking. We were doing all of the work. They were sending us parachutists with labels from London in their clothes. They were smoking British cigarettes that you could smell right away. I was sending them stacks of clothing so they could do what they had to do, with new money. When the money was changing, I sent them new money. All of this was for nothing? It's too fishy.

"I found out about the testimony of one of my agents who had gone to London and saw all of those microfilms sitting in the dust on the shelves. They didn't use them. They didn't need to. As a matter of fact, the purpose was to drop agents in the hands of the Germans, have them captured. More than eighty people were dropped, only two escaped, the rest were sent to Mulhausen in an extermination camp which, by the way, was where my father also spent eighteen months. They were all murdered in a horrible way, when they had to carry those big rocks up the mountain, they couldn't do it anymore, the ones who couldn't do it were shot. The last work unit just dropped down immediately and said, 'Shoot me' because they didn't want to go through the pain.

"It took me forty-eight years to find it out. I still have a hard time believing, but it has changed my life. All of a sudden, what I did has a meaning.

"Now I understand all of this. They wanted to prove to the Germans that their intent was to land in Holland and Belgium, not in Normandy, not in Calais. So many of my agents were sacrificed, so were all those guys in Mulhausen. There were some, after much torture, said, 'What do we have to lose? I have learned that they are to land in Holland and Belgium.' So the Germans, because they got this through torture, believed this more than anything else. They said, 'They wouldn't have fought so long to hide this, so it must be true.'

"They [the Allies] *tried to confuse Hitler and there was no way to tell each one that it was happening. The more secret it was, the better it was.*

"I have been able to find out now because at the end of the war, everything that had to do with the Dutch underground and Englandspiel burned in a mysterious fire in London. And when I asked Prince Bernhard (a former German and head of the Dutch underground, who was in contact with his brother who was head of German intelligence) whether he would write a forward for my book, not knowing at that time what role he had played, 'Oh,' he said, 'I would be delighted to.' That would have been a whitewash for him. And then he said, 'You know, all those papers are burnt.' He volunteered himself to tell me, 'Don't worry, you won't find anything.' He knows about my book. And I didn't have him write a forward.

"It is the opposite with me. I was closer to bitter before than now. Now I'm not at all bitter. It was an honor that I was used for the big purpose. It is basically a miracle that I'm alive. Five times condemned to die by the Gestapo. I escaped because the American First Army liberated my prison."

Although Vandermeerssche has answered most of his troubling questions, to his own satisfaction, doubts remain. Was the information gained by his agents ever used? Or were they merely part of the military deceptions for the D-Day invasion? What was the role of British counter-intelligence? Was there a working relationship between Prince Bernhard and his brother in the German intelligence? Who ordered the information files in London to be burned? Will Britain's war archives, sealed until the year 2040, reveal the answers? (For his activities Vandermeerssche received fifteen military decorations from Belgium, France, Luxembourg, the Netherlands and England.)

End Notes

61 *M.R.D. Foot, An Outline History of the Special Operations Executive (S.O.E.)*, London: British Broad-casting Corporation, 1984, p. 129
62 Romans 8

CHAPTER 16

EARLY RESISTANCE MOVEMENTS, PART III

The French Resistance

There were two French resistance movements: the exterior movement, the Forces françaises libres (the Free French or the F.F.L.) and the interior resistance movement. French soldiers escaped to ally themselves with General de Gaulle's exterior resistance movement, the F.F.L. These Free French troops later joined Allied troops during and after the Normandy invasion. Those who did not escape to join de Gaulle formed the interior resistance movement and resisted in other ways. The common acts were cutting telephone lines, getting out propaganda through tracts, hiding downed pilots, transmitting information to London, and engaging in silly pranks. Some resistance members later joined groups of Maquis who were armed combatants who received arms parachuted from England; others joined the Forces françaises de l'intérieur.

Communication between the exterior resistance and interior resistance movements was primarily by radio, the BBC. A program, *Les Français parlent aux Français* (The French speak to the French) was listened to secretly every evening on forbidden radios hidden in someone's house or barn. As the war progressed, secret messages calling for action by resistance members were sent by radio.

A Natural Resentment Toward the Germans

The French faced occupation by the Germans for the third time in seventy years and resented German militarism. Some children had attitudes that were prejudiced by the stories of German atrocities, handed down from grandparents who remembered the war in 1914. Geneviève Moline's grandmother told her the Germans were savages and cut off the hands of children.

Jean LeBranchu explained that the Germans were always referred to by the xenophobic term, *les Boches.* "We gave the Occupants new nicknames, *les verts-de-gris (verdigris) because of the color of their uniforms, or les doryphores (potato bugs). The Germans were characterized by one-word stereotypes."*

Robert LeBerre had an image of them which remains with him. *"The first time I saw the Germans, they came out of a delicatessen and walked down the main street, eating sausages with their hands. They were greedy and fat."*

A Time to Speak

Some had a more flattering picture of the Germans. Marie LeBerre watched a column of Germans parading and said, *"I had never seen anything so handsome, marching in rows, their arms on their shoulders. They sang all along the road. They were on foot, there were cars, they were on horses, officers."*

Jean Cotten had a grudging admiration for German organizational skills, *"The Germans were, on a scientific and technical level, more advanced than the French. I saw them construct the Atlantic Wall. It was crazy, the speed at which they built the block-houses. In a few days, in a little time, the block-houses were constructed."*

The Germans were Fair Game

Everywhere in France, the Germans were targets of casual pranks designed simply to annoy the Germans. Pierre Servagnat from Epernay in eastern France, smiled as he listed what he and his group of Maquis members had done, anything you could do to annoy them was fair game:

"In the metro in Paris, there was a German sailor. I amused myself by taking the strings hanging down from the helmet and tying them up in knots. It was idiotic, but it was to annoy them.

"There were about one hundred railway men with us. They would give us the timetables of the trains that were leaving and the schedules of the trains that were to pass, if it were a munitions train or a train with Germans. We put, instead of grease in the locomotive, something the English sent us by parachute, so the train couldn't go very far.

"The 14th of July, 1943, one of the railroad workers, a gymnast, climbed up the smoke stack which had rungs on the outside. He climbed up and put a French flag on top, and while he climbed down, he sawed the rungs off. He went up at 11:00 at night and came down at 3:00 in the morning. The next morning, the Germans were furious. They had to call the fire department.

"One of the things that came in the parachutes was a powder that you could put in the Germans' laundry, their sheets, pants, shorts. So when they put them on, it made their skin itch. That was a trick from the English, they called it itching powder.

"There were all kinds of little explosives. A napkin, for example, on the table, you arrived quickly and put the explosive device underneath it, something plastic. When he picked up his napkin, 'pop,' it went off; on the sofa or the chair, with a depression, 'pop,' it went off. You could put a small explosive in a car, 'pop,' and they came out, wounded, and started to run down the street."

The Marland Group and the V for Victory

Resistance members were not professional spies. The reasons for their imprisonment were for hiding soldiers, or those escaping obligatory work service in Germany, for helping Jews, for passing information to the enemy and for possessing arms.

Some Resistants were simply unlucky in being caught, others may have been imprudent or careless. Many were denounced by neighbors or friends. Government posters were plastered in public places, with the pictures of "dangerous terrorists," along with their several aliases. And handsome rewards were offered for their capture.

Beginning in June 1940 Professor Maurice Marland was one of the first to organize the escape of English soldiers from the port city of Granville, located on the Cotentin Peninsula. He operated under several pseudonyms, "Max," "Robespierre," and "de Guibray." He was an English teacher and had many contacts in England and in Poland, where he had been an interpreter for British troops. From June 1940, with the help of several sailors, he organized the escape of several British, including Captain Stanley who was part of the intelligence service and whom Marland had known during World War I. Captain Stanley left Maurice Marland a radio transmitter and the address of an operator for the liaison. This would be the base for the first information transmitted to London.

Marland recruited his students and former students, among whom were Roger Dutertre and Auguste Le Carpentier. On 19 January 1941 their task was to get topographical information about the oil reserves found at Ville Dieu-les-Poêles to Marland who would transmit the information to England so the depot could be bombed. They got the information and gave it to Marland. They had also heard on the radio, "Make the 'V' for Victory." So coming back from delivering the information, they decided it would be fine to draw a beautiful *V* on the door of the *Feldsgendarmerie* (military police station). Dutertre said, "It was superb." The next day when the Germans saw it, they were furious.

Le Carpentier thought he wasn't seen by anyone, but there was a bistro behind them and the owner of the bistro turned him in. He was lucky since he was on a soccer team. On that particular day he had scored two points against the team from Vire. Le Carpentier said, *"So when the Gestapo came and arrested me at school, I maintained that I had been playing soccer. They inquired and it was true, and they had no proof that I was responsible for the 'V.' But my friend, he was arrested."*

Dutertre also thought he had not been seen. He told how he was arrested, *"The Germans instructed the police chief, who was obsequious toward the*

Germans, to make inquiries, because there was a guy who made a 'V,' who distributed tracts, but the people didn't know anything.

"The police chief, who pretended to be the good Frenchmen, who played the role of the good Frenchmen, made his inquiries. Then the people who hadn't said anything to the Germans told the police chief that it must be the nephew of ___. They went to see my uncle. My uncle asked, 'What do you want with my nephew?' 'Oh, it's a story about documents. It's necessary that he make some documents.' So my uncle gave them my address.

"I wasn't there when they arrived. I had gone to Granville with a thousand ideas and questions for Marland. When I came home, the Germans had gone, and I told my father, 'This is not difficult, if they arrive tomorrow and I'm not here, it is you they will arrest. OK, tomorrow I will be here.'

"And that's how I was arrested. I was held for eight months. What they held against me were the tracts and anti-German propaganda, which I absolutely denied." [63]

Helping Jews And Prisoners Escape

In 1942 Marcel Lherbette chose deliberately to settle near the line of demarcation, not far from Loches, where he worked on a farm.

"I helped war prisoners and Jews escape toward the line of demarcation at Cormery (Indre et Loire). I took them in a horse-drawn car. The property owner of the farm fed the people who passed the line of demarcation so they were able to gain some strength. I took them a little more than six miles away from the farm and then said, 'You are on your own, you are free.'

"Then I entered the Gendarmerie and was also part of the Resistance group 'Denis Buckmaster.'

"I was informed against by a gendarme in my brigade, informed against by a Frenchman. I was arrested by the Gestapo on September 20, 1943 and incarcerated at a prison in Angers, then transferred to Fresnes. At Fresnes I was in cell 373. I hollowed out part of the wall to communicate with the priest in the neighboring cell. I took the putty out of the window panes to sing the "Marseillaise" and "Flotte Petit Drapeau" (Wave Little Flag). My morale and my songs led me often to a little cell. My fiancee came to see me at Fresnes and through her, I was able to send messages to the families of Resistants in the Vosges region.

"I was judged by the high German Military Tribunal in Paris. I denied my participation in the Resistance and cited my young age. I was condemned to death, but the sentence was commuted to seven years of solitary confinement."

Lherbette was sent to the concentration camp of Flossenburg. He escaped with a friend and walked until they encountered the American Shock Troops. He received the Medal of the Resistance in August 1946. He had twenty-seven years of active service in the police force.

A Volunteer Courier

Gilles Mahé was twenty years old and condemned to die for passing information to London.

"From August 1940 we had a friend who was in the office of ship construction in Nantes. His job was to verify all the ships that were in for repairs, those that were to leave. It was an enormous source. He passed on to us the plans of the port, with the placement of the ships, their date of departure, where they were going. It was difficult at this time, but we passed this information to the English, passing it through Spain and Portugal.

"Then I left for the southern zone, in March '42, the zone that was not yet occupied. I was the courier for this young liaison agent, Polish-French. It was easier for me to circulate than for the Polish. Three months afterwards, I was arrested. I think it was imprudence on my part, however, there were denunciations. We were very much suspected because my brother had left to join De Gaulle. Perhaps we were more watched than others."

Mahé's story is a succession of internments in prison and concentration camps which left him disabled and unable to work after the war. Only through sharing with one another and maintaining their solidarity did Mahé survive.

At the Center of Eysse, close to Villeneuve-sur-Lot, the prisoners organized in small groups of twelve to share whatever arrived, food from local farmers or packages from families.

"On the train to Dachau, what was extraordinary was the esprit we had at Eysse. We organized our railroad cars, some standing, some seated. And since it was very hot and some had shirts, they waved their shirts to have a little air. We had a piece of bread, a tub, and a bucket of water. It was all, and it had to last for three days."

Transferred again, this time to Mauthausen, Mahé in a sports Kommando.

"We worked fourteen or fifteen hours a day, and we transported girders to 400 meters from there and then go back. It was done scientifically, they put the number of workers needed to carry the bar, then they had half that many, 120 kilos [55 pounds] each person. I don't know how I did that. Every day, every day."

On a beautiful day, instead of getting the small cars near the railway cars, he left voluntarily and went toward the hills of Linz.

"Suddenly there was an SS that arrived and started to chase me. Wooden cloppers weren't very practical so I dropped them. I ran barefoot along the ballast

along the railroad. There were the wagons of merchandise on the siding. I said to myself, I can pass between two wagons. One was returning, there would be coupling of the railroad cars. I passed between them and put my hand on the coupling device which was completely idiotic. I had a friend who hit me with his fist. That allowed me to avoid the head being wedged between two wagons. I broke my elbow.

"Two days exempt from work and every morning I went to the doctor. Crack! he put it back in place, bound it with a paper pad. I was like that for two days, then I went back to work. I still had my iron beams to carry, with my broken arm. It caused a lot of worry and in the middle of December, I fainted in the work yard. My comrades picked me up and took me to the dormitory, then to Mauthausen.

"I stayed in the infirmary from mid-December until the Liberation. I am amazed that I spent time in the infirmary without dying, only with the help of extraordinary comrades. I was in the infirmary, I couldn't walk. One would pass before the SS and be chosen to be gassed. One day there was a selection like that, in the last moments of the war. There were three of us, Irish, Russian and Yugoslavian, my three friends. We were warned, and since the infirmary was near the SS, I was wedged between two friends, one pushed from behind and the other in front. Just at the moment we passed before the SS, the Yugoslav talked to the SS, distracted them, and in that way, my friends got me past. I was saved by others. One could never be saved all by oneself. There were no deportees who were saved by themselves. . . ." [64]

Hiding A Soldier And Hiding Arms

Thérèse Lamotte was not a member of an organized Resistance group. She was only guilty of humanitarian aid, but was convicted of resistance activities and sent to Ravensbrück, the prison for women.

"I was arrested for something the Germans didn't want us to do. I was arrested, first of all, for hiding arms; second, for taking in and sheltering a prisoner for more than a year. When it was time to turn in the arms at the town hall, I didn't do it.

"When the Germans arrived in France, there were a group of men who escaped and camouflaged themselves. One day I was in my garden and I looked around and saw a man crouched down. He signaled me to come. Then he said, 'You saw me?' I said, 'Yes.' 'And now you must help me.' He said he had escaped from the Germans, he had hidden in the woods and had come out. He asked for something to eat, but I didn't have a lot. I had some eggs and potatoes. I have a small simple house. 'You put the eggs and potatoes where I can find them. I will take them into the woods.' That lasted three days.

"One evening, he fought with a German with a knife. My prisoner said, 'If you want, come where I am, that is all you need in order to know.' He meant there were arms. I was face to face with the 'Boche' and my prisoner was behind the door.

"He was arrested and I was also arrested and my little girl. I was arrested June 18, '42 and I didn't come back to France until July '45.

"My prisoner was shot right away. He was an officer. He made his last will: his brother was prisoner in Germany, he hoped his children would be happy, he did not accuse me, he said simply, 'A big thank-you to Mme X.'

"And if I said, I have a favorable memory of the Germans who arrested me it is because I was arrested with my little girl. One of them said, 'Oh, madame, I have little children. I don't like the war. Do you have friends for the little girl?' I said, 'Yes, I have my parents who aren't far from here.'

"They talked among themselves, I was carefully guarded. They had to take me to the railroad station to take me to prison. They looked at the little girl. My father had come to see my sister-in-law. The German put her hand in my father's and said, 'Courage, monsieur.'

"I was put in prison in Rouen for five days. I was interrogated. I was in a cell with those condemned to death. There was a cage with bars. It was panic. I kicked at the door and asked for an interpreter. They said, 'Very well, very well, you are going to take a ride on the train.'

"Then Paris to Germany. I was condemned at Breslau. I passed before a tribunal. We had with us, in the cell from Breslau, one woman whom we called Grandmère Léon. She was Jewish and I led her by the arm, barefooted. In the same cell, there was a religious sister. We told her 'Don't worry, we are in the same boat.' But she said, 'They tore my veil and broke my Christ.'

"There were Germans who guarded me in prison. I don't know whether they knew everything that was going on. In spite of everything, the night before I left to be condemned, the supervisor came to take me to a little cell. She didn't embrace me, she didn't go that far, but she shook my hand and said, 'Courage, Thérèse.' I don't know whether she knew.

"There were some of every nationality, Russian, French, only women. We swore and we promised not to cry. We decided if we cried we were done for. When we heard someone whimper in the evening then we would say, 'If you invite us to dinner Sunday, what will you give us to eat?' We passed the time like that.

"There was one woman who was forty-two years old and she went through the corridor saying, 'Never cry and don't lower your eyes in front of the Boches.' Sometimes it was hard to look them in the eye.

"We also had with us prostitutes. There was one who cried. And another said, 'Be careful we have a religious sister with us.' The sister said, 'My child, tell us your story. God is happy to listen to your stories. You must tell your story,' and she told a story every day. And the guards at the door would say, 'It's not worth telling God your story. He is far from you. He doesn't hear you.'

"What we ate at the camp: two or three potato skins in the mess tin of water; a little of that famous black bread. We never received the Red Cross packages, perhaps a week before we were liberated and we only received half of it.

"We worked. We pushed the carts filled with refuse and excrement to the woods to empty them. There were maybe thirty or forty women pushing the carts. Next to me I saw a woman and I said, 'Has it been a long time that you were here?' She made me understand that her husband was a doctor in Italy. She was Jewish. The SS hit me on the back. That's the way the SS operated. I received a blow here [pointing to her ear], I was sick. My ear was bleeding; there was pus. The doctor, when I went back, said 'What saved you was that you bled.' I have a hearing aid. It happened at Ravensbrück.

"One young woman was taken to be given some shots. When she came back from Germany, she found herself pregnant. At that time, births were at home. It was just a mass of flesh. Her husband told the doctor to take it away as he didn't want his wife to see it. The baby died a few days later. She had a normal pregnancy. Some were taken away to be executed, beheaded.

"There were German prisoners among us. They disappeared and their families were told they died of a 'heart attack.'

"I was at Ravensbrück for a year. I was liberated by the Swedes on April 23, but the Russians were arriving. Count Bernadotte arrived at the camp. I'll never forget him. He arrived at the gate of the camp and said in good French, ''Mesdames, vous êtes libres. [Ladies, you are free]. I have come to get you.'

"We passed through Denmark, we were there for five days and they gave us chocolate. In Sweden we were spoiled by the Swedish people, it was like a little camp, six each in a little chalet. It was fine. We had sheets.

"The names of those rescued were broadcast and a priest heard my name and he telephoned my parents. He sent me a telegram, 'Parents very well, brother Carolus coming back. Awaiting your return and your brother Georges' return.'

"I came back to my parents. The little girl was there at the railroad station with roses. My little girl, Thérèse, she was less than four years old and she doesn't remember the war. It wasn't all happy. When I came back, she said to my sister, 'She,' referring to me. Still there were times she said, 'I remember when you carried me on your back.' She said, 'I remember you went to Germany with Tonton Georges.'

"There were some imbeciles who said when I left I would never return. They stole my household goods. When they learned that I would return, they said,

'It was she who told the Germans that there was an escaped prisoner.' I had to defend myself. I had to fight for my rights, I made my demands. I was lucky. The mayor, a policeman and a priest were still living and could be my witnesses. It took three months before I recovered my household goods.

"After the war, I worked for the railroad and gave information about customs. One day a couple came in to inquire about registering baggage to Germany. On leaving the building, they started to turn to the left. I said, 'You turn to the right and at the very end of the street, you will find the custom officer.' My boss said, 'Oh no, Madame, you made a mistake.' I said, 'Monsieur, it is just a little vengeance.'

"I have a great grandson who is twelve years old. He said, 'Mama said you were in prison,' and he left. I thought he probably thinks I was a thief. I asked him if he knew why I was in prison and he said, Yes, it was because I hid arms. I explained it to him, the war, one side won, the other side lost.

"One day he said, 'The Germans are wicked.' Last year he told me he was leaving for eight days in Germany with the school, he had two pen pals. In front of his parents, I said, 'Sebastian, never say to your two German friends that the Germans are wicked. First of all, you don't know. And it was the war and perhaps their parents didn't know.' And I bought two silver key holders so he could give them to his two German friends. It is not good to harbor hate."

The early Resistance movements did little to halt the advance of Hitler's armies, but they demonstrated a willingness to fight against dictatorship.

A Time to Speak

End Notes

63 Le Carpentier lives in Quettreville-sur-Sienne and Dutertre lives not far away in Hudimesnil, two small villages, located near Coutances and Granville on Normandy's Cotentin Peninsula. After the war Le Carpentier was a student at the Ecole nationale supérieure des Beaux Arts in Paris. A retrospective of his work appeared at Agon-Coutainville in 1995. Roger Dutertre was a general insurance agent until his retirement. Today, he is President of the Memorial Committee for Maurice Marland and President of the Association of Deportées and Internées.

64 Because of his wartime injuries, Mahé was never able to return to work.

CHAPTER 17

OPERATION BARBAROSSA

Two military events in 1941 drastically changed the course of the war and widened its scope to include almost the whole world. Ultimately, it defined the postwar roles of the major powers, the United States, Great Britain and Russia. In June 1941, Hitler attacked Russia, and in December 1941, Japan attacked Pearl Harbor, Hawaii.

Although Hitler and Stalin were originally allies, the German invasion of Russia nullified the Nazi-Soviet Non-Aggression Pact of 1939. On 22 June 1941 at 4 a.m., Germany attacked Russia on a front that extended from the Baltic to the Black Sea, the attack known as *Barbarossa* (the familiar name of the medieval emperor, Frederick I of Hohenstaufen, who according to the legend, wished to be put to sleep until the day when he would be revived to restore Germany's past glory).

Hitler was confident of success. His armies took the half of Poland that had been given to Stalin in 1939 and then swept through the Baltic states previously annexed by the Soviet Union. Now it was the Soviet Union's turn to bear the brunt of the blitzkrieg as Hitler launched his campaign to level Moscow and Leningrad (the old imperial capital of St. Petersburg).

Russians Remember the German Invasion

Two Russian physicians, husband and wife, immigrated to the United States in 1991 because their children had previously come to America. They remembered very well the unexpected German invasion of Russia. the bombings, evacuations to the east, deaths among family members, hunger and cold. After the end of the war, the doctors returned to Moscow to begin their medical studies.

Husband: *I lived in Belorussia near Minsk, the city was called Bobruysk. When the Second World War started, I was thirteen years old, so I graduated the sixth grade. Because we lived near the west border, the first days, the 22nd of June, we had in our city, military places, military air forces, military division of tanks and other military divisions because this was not far from the border The Russian government kept the military troops in case something wrong happened.*

Before the government announced that the Second World War started, the German military force bombed our city and the military places. So, of course, we

A Time to Speak

were confused. We didn't expect that somebody could bomb our city. And you know before, maybe a week before, the Russian government and the German government, they communicate and the Germans try to explain that they took their military forces to the Russian border because they are afraid of the Great Britain bomb. And the Russian government accepted that and said to all the people, 'Ok, everything is fine. We don't expect any war with the Germans.'

At night on the 21st and the 22nd of June, some places were bombed and some of the civils' houses were destroyed. Every day we had many, many military planes who flew to our city and bombed us. And the radio announced that we should be in these special safe places under the ground. We built under the ground some special places by ourselves with wood, with soil, with other stuff to make it safe. So most of the day we would stay in these, can I say, safe places. But on the first day, on the 26th of June, the radio announced that forty-five military planes is going to bomb our city, and they asked us to leave the place, to go to the forest because it will be safer. My father, my mother, my older brother and me, we walked from the city to go to the forest and because we were told we would spend a couple of hours, maybe more in the forest, we should bring all blankets, pillows and some other to lay on the ground because we should stay for some time in the forest.

And when we passed the bord of the city, it's a river, wide enough, and it was wooden bridge above the river, so we walked the bridge and maybe were about a mile or two from this bridge. So the fire in the city started and bomb and we heard the blew up of this bomb. It was a crowd of people, it as a panic and they said all the Germans entered the city, so you can't come back. We went out of the city, it was after 4:00 in the afternoon in June. Of course the days are long. We walked, we didn't run, we walked, maybe we walked almost two miles. We had some luggage, pillows, some food, so we couldn't run. And I was thirteen years old. Maybe a couple of hours to get to the bridge, two miles. It was about 6:00 or 7:00 in the evening and we decided we should go far away from the Germans. We walked the evening, the night we walked, we were tired and my mother and my father said, 'OK, we should stay for a couple of minutes.' And we should go ahead because we tried to escape from this area.

We walked in the night and next day and the next night we were in the field, in the open place. I think we stopped for a couple of hours, we didn't sleep of course, but maybe we had a nap sitting on the ground. And the next morning we walked one evening, one night, the day and the half night next. We came to a small city, maybe about 15,000 or 20,000 people in the city. And they had a rail station and so we went to the rail station and bought some tickets, and we went to my father's sister. It was in the middle of Russia. The city called Kursk. We came to the city the first of July because we had a couple stops. We didn't have a direct train *from this city to Kursk. We had a couple stops, so we came to this city and maybe a 1,000 miles from the west border. And we lived in my aunt's house until the 8th of October.*

Of course we knew the Germans were going east, but we supposed that these Germans won't come too far this 1,000 miles from the border. So one night on the 2nd of October, our house was bombed. My middle brother was killed, my older brother was wounded, seventeen years old, and my mother was wounded and me. Only my father was unharmed in this bomb. We were in the hospital. My mother, my brother and me, we were in the hospital until 8th of October and as these military people evacuated east, we were taken to some trains and we were evacuated east of Russia to Tajikistan. This is the middle part of Russia. We lived in this area until we came back to Moscow after the war.

His wife's family came from a small town in the Ukraine. They escaped in July in a horse-drawn carriage to Kharkov, then by freight train to the Ural. She was twelve years old and in school at that time. In the cold area of the Ural, she lived with her parents, her grandparents, an aunt and a cousin, seven people, in two rooms where heating and cooking were done with wood and coal. After the war was over, her family went back to the Ukraine. She continued school, then went to medical school in Moscow in 1946, where she met her husband.

The husband continued the conversation:

"We were short in food, we were short in clothes and everything. I studied in a school because I was young. My mother was disabled because she was wounded. So my father was taken into the military and my older brother too. So I lived with my mother. I studied first of all in the school. And after that I entered a school in Moscow, medical school.

"The people who studied in this school and the people who were disabled, we had a special card. With the card we could get bread, a pound a day, sugar, one-half pound a month, maybe two pounds meat a month, some fruits, a pound a month, and some grains, about a pound. This is our limit for a month. We were every day hungry.

"Of course, it was very difficult because, first of all, I think, because the people didn't have enough food. A lot of people died because of hunger, thousands. Half of the people in the city died of hunger. The government provide some food for the soldiers but not for the civils. For a day, a quarter of pound bread, this is all. For the many, many people in different places of Russia, it was difficult to live. For women, they worked very hard from early morning until midnight, without day off, without vacations, all four years. No vacation, no day off, early morning until late night and the children too. All children worked, from ten, even nine because there weren't enough men, enough people.

A Time to Speak

"You know during the Second War maybe 15 million of men were in the Army. So because somebody should work in the plants, the agriculture, the small children worked. We worked. In some places, small children would work, very hard work, sometimes children would lift very heavy things. No men were around.

"Money was nothing. The people would only have money if they sell something. Their clothes. To exchange clothes for food. A nice fur coat they would exchange for some flour or some bread or butter. A ring they would give for two pounds of bread. I remember my aunt, she had a very nice fur coat, real fur, not synthetic and she had about thirty pounds of flour.

"The Americans helped the Russians with food. The food would go to the army, to the military, some of it to the government officials. Sometimes we would get some special ham in boxes or sausages. It was delicious. We would go to the market and of course if you have money, you can buy some things. But we didn't have enough money. We could buy, no choice for people, we are hungry. We would buy frozen, frozen potatoes, it was like a stone. And we would put it in the cold water and Mama would do some pancakes without vegetable or nothing and would bake these frozen potatoes. Sometimes we would have one piece of bread in the morning, sometimes in the evening a frozen baked potato. This is for all day.

"In the first year the school would give a small piece of bread. This is all. Some people would go to school to get a small piece of bread.

"It was not so difficult after we got our medical degrees. We practiced far east. We had an obligation if we graduated from a medical school, the government would send us to a place to work for three years. We went to the island Sakhalin near Japan. We had a hospital and a clinic. Our oldest son was born in this island. After the three years, of course, we moved to Moscow because my parents lived in a suburb in Moscow.

"We came to the United States the 22nd of May, 1991. We are citizens."

The Great Patriotic War

In the beginning, Stalin's troops were ill-prepared to withstand the onslaught, but they fought with stubborn resistance and what the Germans referred to in a *New York Times* dispatch (23 July 1941) as "an Asiatic contempt of death."

Stalin was able to rally the Russian people and his armies to fight the "great patriotic war," for the motherland and for Stalin. One sixteen year old woman who rallied to the "great patriotic war" was Maria Domas. She was a Russian spy who was parachuted behind the enemy lines in German-occupied Russia. Later, she was denounced and spent the rest of the war as a prisoner of Germany, working in a factory.

"I was a volunteer; I wanted to help my country; I was very, very active because somebody is grabbing our country, we want to do anything we can. We were considered spies, you know spying behind the lines. We were in the army, we were considered army, but we were behind the lines in the German occupied part of Russia. We had to see what Germany armies are doing, where they are moving, where they are going to hit Russian army. It was typical spying on German armies.

"It was very difficult to do. First of all, you are dropped down into occupied zone by parachute. We had to find out ways to get out of the woods from wherever we were dropped down and find way to get to live among Russians that were occupied by Germans. It was hard because we were always under suspicion. People were suspicious, where you come from, who are you, what are you doing here. We had to have some kind of history. In my case, I was looking for my mother; during the war we got separated. You tried to find a place to live. You had to feed yourself somehow because you cannot get money from Russian government. You had to live, to find some kind of work and you had to pretend that you were really here looking for mother, father, whatever. You happened to be in this area for whatever reason.

"Our parachutes were attached in the airplane because if we had to open up ourselves, we probably never would have been able to because we were not trained. I never saw a parachute in my life until I was put into it. It was attached in the airplane and when we dropped, it just opened up the parachute. There was no time for training. Many were killed, many were hurt, besides Stalin didn't really care how many people would be killed. Just send, send, send, not much preparation, not much explanation, using young people, so inexperienced in war business, it is not that easy.

"I had to work in a station where they were loading coal, coal for heating the houses. And unloading railroad cars, that was hard job for a sixteen year-old tiny, little girl. I was only sixteen because they recruited young people because Russian army thought that we would be less suspicious to Germans. We were just like real people living around. There were Russians but Germans occupied this area. It was the Smolensk area; it is a big city. Different people, different jobs were dropped down in a different area. In my case, I was around Smolensk. Smolensk was one of the first cities that fell into German hands in the beginning of the war. [65]

"We did not need to speak German, it was advantageous perhaps, but you know, we were not required and there was no time to train anybody to speak any language. We were just plain Russian people living there and so the Germans will not suspect that we are spying on them. But it wasn't always easy. We were definitely quickly suspected. And I had to go through a lot of difficult times. I have been shot at because they were interrogating me: Why I am here, What I am doing - the whole story of months and months and months of hard, hard life, walking around, being under suspicion, being interrogated.

"We were supposed to send information by radio, by Morse. We were a group. I didn't know Morse code, but we had a girl who was prepared to give information. I had to go as a spy to see where the Germans were, I had to get information to the girl who gave it by radio. It is not always easy to give information. Sometimes you put your antennas in the forest and for whatever reason, the batteries, or whatever, it doesn't always work.

"The first time, it was about three months and then I joined a group of Russian army that was working like guerrillas. And as Germans were advancing, there was no way we could stay any longer in this area. And so we had to retreat and we walked and walked for two weeks before we could cross the front line. When we crossed the front line, we came to Moscow, and in a month's time we were dropped back into a different area. It was in a big area, the Orel area; Orel is a big city. [Orel was captured on 8 October 1941.]

"I was treasoned by some people when I came out of the woods. We were dropped from airplanes by parachute in the woods, so we would have chance to cover up whatever we had and to get out. It seems it was in October and it rained and our clothes were kind of damp.

"Once you are dropped in the woods, you had to find out where you are, your orientation because you can't just get out and say 'I'm here.' You have to find out in what area you are. Once in a while you are dropped twenty miles away from originally planned. It depends on weather, on pilot, and it was always at night so the Germans wouldn't know where people were dropped.

"I had to get out and find out where we are, what is the place and of course, we had a history, saying, 'Well, I'm looking for my mother, father.' Lately they got so suspicious and they looked at my clothes, I had my change of clothes and they said, 'Well how come it is damp? You must have been in the woods. If it is damp, you must be a partisan.'

"And so they took me to, this was Russians who took me to German headquarters. They said, 'We suspect she is a spy.' And in German headquarters, you are standing before German officer, they interrogate you, take you out, shoot at you. You don't know if he is going to shoot to kill you or just to scare you. You just stand there. Then they take you back and more interrogation.

"There was one who saw me that I came back with the rest of the group who were behind the lines of the army. He was taken prisoner. He saw me with the rest when I came back to Moscow in quarters where we were quartered for a month. And he said, 'Oh, I saw her, she came to Moscow with Major so and so.' That was the end, I was thrown in the jail for a whole month of interrogation, interrogation, in jail. And at this time, they were hanging people spying on Germans, young people. Old people were not used for this kind of spying. I believe God saved my life; they did not hang me; they sent me to Germany to work in their factories. This time Germans were losing too many soldiers and they didn't have enough people in the factories that made all kinds of ammunition. So they started to bring foreigners from all over, from Russia, from Poland, from Ukraine, from Holland, from France to work in their factories. So I guess it was not to their advantage to shoot me, I would be more useful to work in their factories. To Oberndorf-am-Neckar, about fifteen miles from Swiss border. I worked and French came because it was French zone and they set us free, the French army. At the end of the war, Germany was bombarded pretty badly by different armies, American, French, Russian, and their railroads were pretty badly destroyed. And since I was in southern part of Germany, and Russian zone was far east, and to get us quickly back to Russia, it was impossible, there was no transportation. So we had to wait to go back.

"In the meantime, some brave people went to this Russian zone to go home and when they came to Russian zone, the Communist Russians were ruling and they considered us prisoners of Germans, as we were enemies, as we worked for Germans. We did not work for Germans voluntarily; we were prisoners, but Stalin did not care because Stalin knew we had seen something better than Russia. We have seen different from what we have been told all our life. So they sent us to another prison in Siberia and many were shot. I was not sent; I didn't go back to Russia; I escaped from this French zone into the American zone and then in five years, I was able, with my husband, to immigrate to Canada.

"All nationalities in prisons in Germany during World War II, they all had different experiences. French were treated badly, Dutch were treated a little bit better, but Russians were treated worse. We were their worst enemies and they really treated us badly, terribly. I have been almost killed by German commandants, the head of the camp where we were, over a little misunderstanding. He thought, if I don't understand you, what you are trying to say, so he has right to kill you.

"Russians and Poles and Ukrainians were treated much worse than any other nationalities. French were defeated; Dutch were defeated; Belgians were defeated, but Russia was still at war and drove them out.

"When I talk about it now, it is all over. But it is very hard emotionally, it is hard physically and you just wonder how you survived. When you look back on it, as a Christian, I say 'Thank you Lord. You saved my life.'" [66]

A Time to Speak

Life In Moscow

The battle for Moscow in the winter of 1941 ended with the German retreat. A grim life, marked by cold weather and hunger, continued for Muscovites who lived and worked in Russia's capital. A Russian woman, who worked in Moscow during the war as an editor, recalled the hardships of her life.

"*I was going to school, then I was going to university. After university, of course, I worked and all the time I went to ice skating during the war. After university, I was editor for popular literature and scientific literature. I worked scientific magazines. All my life I worked as editor.*

"*I can tell you that the most terrible thing was that our fathers and our brothers and our sons went to army and every day we expected to have letter about our relative who was killed. It was terrible. There were many women who worked in army in special work to be sent to the German areas and give information about army.*

"*During the war, I was hungry. We had special cards, for meat, for oil, for milk and bread. The most important, bread. And there were no people to make bread. Many people in the big cities, like Moscow, during the war, had a little area to raise potatoes.*

"*And, of course, American people helped us very much, because from America were delivered cans with pork, sausage and powdered eggs. Clothes not very good, not very new, but of course, we had, in Moscow, because you cannot live without warm overcoat and warm hat and warm shoes. I continued to wear these. And I made myself warmer in ice skating rink. We had warm pants, sweater, hat.*

"*I began to skate. In my time, when I was young, it was not for money, it was not for competition, only for fun. Moscow has very long winter and all the winter we had snow and ice. In our recreation parks, we had special big park, for walking, relaxing, for fun. And in the winter, in that park, there was special area for skating.*

"*In our apartment, there was no heating and we had ice on our floor. Each people try to alive* [stay alive]. *I lived with my mother and we together had not small apartment. We had four rooms, but we didn't use it. With my mother, we lived in the kitchen. In the kitchen we had a little iron oven and we had no wood for this and we made fire with papers, magazines, books, everything. For sometime it was warm. Very soon it became cold.*

"*Mostly during the war, I started at university. At university it was cold, so cold that ink became ice.*

"*They* [the German Army] *can see Moscow with binoculars. There were very terrible days when the enemy was close to Moscow. In that day was organized evacuation, many, many offices, many factories to the east areas of the country. I* was also evacuated and my mother and my father also evacuated to Ural and to Siberia. I was in evacuation one year and then I returned to Moscow.

"I was student. I was evacuated in Sverdlovsk, it is city in Ural. In that city was party leader, Yeltsin later. And there was a university there and I was a student in that university. And there in Sverdlovsk, the life of the evacuated people was terrible. Very cold, we had little clothes. We could not take all of our things. It was very cold and the public transportation worked badly. And I needed to go from my house to university by my leg, I walked. And I lived in one little room, within that room was four people. Our beds stayed, two beds, two beds and table, we sit in the bed by table. And that's all. And of course, we need to get our wood for own, [saw our own wood] and Army send us clothes for washing. We washed by hand, very difficult because we had no hot water. We need to warm the water.

"I had from my cards, I had one pound of bread a day, one pound of bread. I cut in three pieces, one piece I eat like my breakfast with hot water, the second I took with me to university and the third I saved at home for supper. And when I came to university and it was very cold, and I was (not only I, but all the people) was very hungry and I couldn't hear the lectures. I saw through my suitcase where was this piece of bread. And I took one little piece, then another little piece, till there was from one lecture to the other, my piece of bread was gone. And we had special dining room. When we had a plate of very liquid, but hot soup. This soup has water and a little green cabbage, but just a leaf, or sometimes it was not cabbage green leaves, sometimes it was a plant which arrives on the street, nettles. It is not bad. We cook a soup from these, we pick up, if we find.

"Yes it was difficult to study. Then, what else? There was special activity for to be 'alive.' We take our clothes and went to villages and there we changed our clothes, our last clothes, we changed for food, for salt because we had no salt, for potatoes. Another thing, the people, the adult people with whom I lived, they stayed in line in the slaughter house and they took bones, without meat, only bones. And these bones we cut, and with water, we boiled water with these bones and it was our bouillon. And so and so and so on.

"When I was back to Moscow, I also had my student card for one pound of bread. My mother she worked and she had a card for 600 grams, one pound of bread.

"Also not an easy time. Not enough food, but the war was over. Yes some of the men came home. I studied in high school, we had about twenty boys in our class. Maybe seven or eight returned after the war. My first husband lost his arm in the Army.

"Yes, it [the United States] is a different planet. Only people are the same as Moscow, kind. My daughter is here."

A Time to Speak

The war news of the Russian-German conflict reported attacks and counterattacks, successes and losses. However, by December 1941, German soldiers, ill-equipped to survive the blizzard conditions of the Russian winter, had failed to capture Moscow and were being driven back by the Russian armies who retook dozens of villages. The 7 December 1941 issue of *The New York Times* (Section E, page 5) said that for the first time since war came to Europe in September 1939, the Nazis "have tasted the bitterness of major military defeat."

End Notes

65 Smolensk, located halfway between Minsk and Moscow, was on Stalin's easterly defense line. By the end of July 1941, the German army had completed their encirclement of Smolensk and by October occupied 600,000 square miles of Russian territory.

66 Maria Domas now lives in California.

CHAPTER 18

PEARL HARBOR, DECEMBER 7

The front page of the same *The New York Times*, December 7, 1941, also mentioned the new threat in Indo-China and Roosevelt's direct appeal to Emperor Hirohito, calling on him to avoid a conflict in the Pacific. Unfortunately, the Japanese Army had already made their fateful decision.

"A date which will live in infamy"

Suddenly, the United States was thrust into the world war. On that Sunday, 366 Japanese bombers and fighters assaulted every major United States and British possession in the central and western Pacific. The Japanese declaration of war against the United States and Britain came two hours and 55 minutes after the Japanese attack.

Radio programs were interrupted to break the news of the surprise attack. Monday morning newspaper headlines screamed in bold type: "Japs Hit Entire Pacific, Far East; Claim U.S. Warships are Destroyed; War Declaration is Expected Today"[67]

Historians now confirm that 188 American aircraft were destroyed on the ground. Four battleships were blown up or sank: the *Arizona*, now on the bottom at Pearl Harbor; the *California*, the *Oklahoma* and the *West Virginia*; three other battleships were damaged. Four destroyers and four cruisers were heavily damaged. Estimates differ, but between 3,581 and 3,611 American personnel were casualties at Pearl Harbor.

Americans were shocked and surprised. Ruth Correll was in Chicago, where her husband was a doctoral student in physics. *"There I was in Chicago Lying-In [hospital]. All day December the 7th, I could tell there was something going on because the doctors and the nurses were going 'Sssshhhh' up and down the halls. Nobody told me what was going on. Becky was born at 11 p.m. on December 7th. And the next morning I was brought up to date on what had happened. My first thought was 'Where in the world is Pearl Harbor?' It was very sketchy and I thought, the Philippines. And I was ashamed to admit I didn't know where it was. People were supposed to know. I know I said something to my doctor about 'What a time to be having a baby!' and he said, 'It may be that's one of the few things that's still worth while doing.'"* [68]

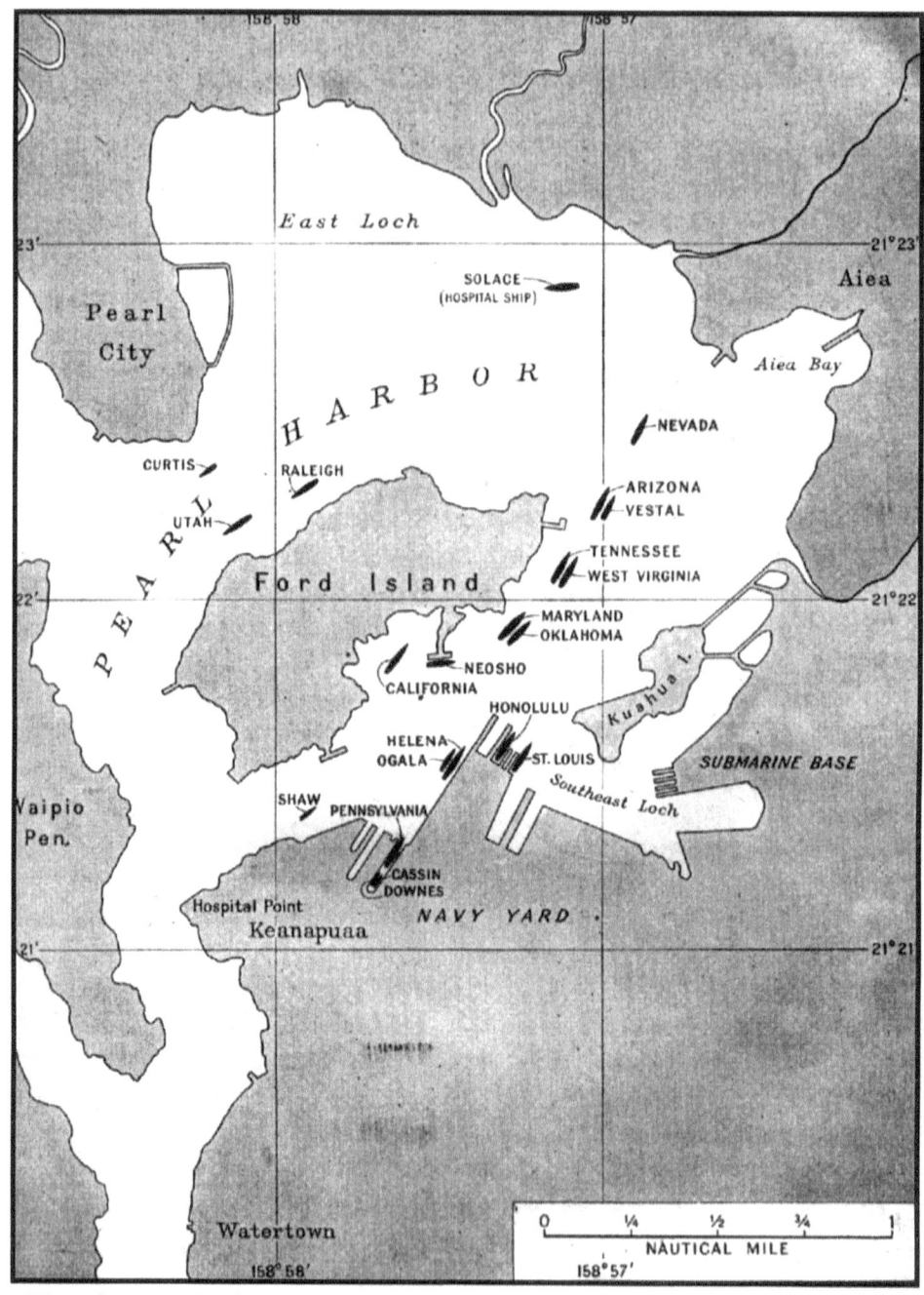

Map showing the disposition of the fleet at Pearl Harbor on 7 December 1941.

A Time to Speak

How Could it Happen?

Before the attack, the United States, trying to put pressure on Japan to curtail Japan's expansion in China and Indo-China, placed an embargo on Japanese assets in America and halted war exports to Japan.

An American note, handed to Japanese envoys on 26 November 1941, called on Tokyo to abandon aggression and to withdraw all military forces from China and Indo-China. In return, the United States offered economic concessions: most-favored nation treatment, reduction of trade barriers, removal of freezing restrictions on oil, and stabilizing the dollar-yen rate. Negotiations were still going on at the time of the attack on Pearl Harbor.

Midori Johnson, who lived in Tokyo except for six months at the very end of the war, explained the Japanese point of view - the United States was strangling Japan economically and was conspiring with Great Britain and other countries to thwart Japan's new order in East Asia.

"We, in Japan had reasons. . . . We tried to make a new world, mainly with Asian countries. . . . Japan is a very small country, and [had] *many people, even at that time. So we didn't have enough land to extend and develop our industries, to develop the new world. So we tried to extend it into Asian countries. Then those Western peoples just didn't like it. That is human nature. They tried to stop us and that was the reason we started the war."*

Why was it a surprise?

Americans know now that war had been expected both by President Roosevelt and the Japanese leaders because the negotiations were at a stand-still. The U. S. Army and Navy Intelligence unit called "Magic" had been intercepting Japanese messages which indicated the Japanese had no faith in the negotiations taking place in Washington. After Secretary of State Cordell Hull's answer to the Japanese envoys on 26 November, the War Department sent Hawaii and other outposts an important but ambiguous warning that "Negotiations with Japan appear to be terminated...Japanese action unpredictable." The Navy Department sent an even stronger message, *"This dispatch is to be considered a war warning . . . an aggressive move by the Japanese is to be expected within a few days."* On 6 December, the intercepted codes gave President Roosevelt the message that Japan's leaders rejected Hull's last proposal. War was inevitable.

"At the time of Pearl Harbor . . ."

Most Americans, civilians and enlisted personnel, remember where they were at the time of Pearl Harbor. Martha Watts lived with her family in Washington, D. C., in Alban Towers. On 7 December the family was at a football game.

"My family were great Washington Redskin fans. They had season tickets on the 50-yard line for umpteen years. They were great fans. I had never seen a professional game. December 7 1941, I was fifteen and a half and they thought, maybe it would be a treat and someone wasn't able to go so they invited me to go to the game, with seats on the 50-yard line.

"We got to the game and almost immediately, as I recall, the announcer kept calling out names like, 'Admiral so and so, report to his office, will Ambassador so and so please call the embassy, General so and so, please report.' There must have been half of the military at that game and the diplomatic corps because as I recall, the half was about 3 o'clock and we got word from the press box that Japan had attacked Pearl Harbor.

"I must say, that at fifteen and a half, I didn't know exactly what that meant. I knew we had been attacked and we would probably go to war. Some people were crying. And the game continued. I don't know whether we won or not. Sammy Baugh was their quarterback and they generally won in those days. It was an exciting experience.

"In Alban Towers, there were some of the Japanese delegation, families, wives and children. The Japanese embassy was just about two miles down Massachusetts Avenue.

"But we got home that night, we got home about 5:00 or 5:30. The lobby and the whole area where the Japanese had been was just swarming with FBI. They were lining up all of these families with little children. And I can remember saying, 'What's going on?' to my mother and she said, 'Shush, they are taking them away, they are going to put them in jail or something.' My mother wasn't sure what was going to happen. I will never forget how incredibly courteous the FBI people were to these people who had attacked us. The significance didn't hit me until some time later. But they were absolutely gentle and kind and there was none of this handcuffing. They just rounded them up and took them away in limousines. What happened later was that they sent them all back to Japan, almost immediately. I think that surprised me because almost immediately we started seeing horror movies of these evil, slant-eyed people. These were almost like aliens who had attacked us and were evil. And I had thought these people were very nice and polite. Those two experiences were an interesting December 7 experience." [69]

Pauline Parish was a college student:

"I remember so vividly December 7 when the Japanese bombed Pearl Harbor. I was in college, a senior at Ohio Wesleyan. I was a senior advisor in a freshmen dormitory and I was sitting in my room. I had been talking to some freshmen and I had turned on the radio after they had left. I think everybody came out of their rooms. It didn't make any difference who you were. Everybody came out of their rooms, just absolutely stunned. Nobody could believe that such a thing had happened. I think the fact that we were actually attacked, that an enemy killed a lot of our people, ships were sunk. We were on the brink, almost, of not being able to do anything because they had so badly hurt us with that fleet over there that we had no way to get people to where they should go. I have never seen a country come together faster than they did to begin to build those old kind of concrete ships and put together runs to different places. They took all of the big steamships which we had at that time and they got the boys overseas once they got some training. Enormous patriotism, enormous patriotism."

Bill Bower began his military training in the Air Force in 1940 and was on leave when he got the news of the Japanese attack.

"We were in Hollywood when war was declared. We'd had a leave. We started back home and were given this leave and went to Hollywood. We had a real fine time. War was declared the 7th, Sunday morning. We went back to March Field and got into our airplanes, went to Pendleton. The next day we were out looking for the Japanese fleet, did that for a month."

Living at Wheeler Field

For the regular Army stationed at Pearl Harbor before the war, life was typical of life at American Army bases, made even more pleasant by the proximity to the beach. Mr. and Mrs. Paul Postovit were stationed at Wheeler Field. Postovit joined the Army Air Corps in 1930 and served for thirty years and retired as a Chief Warrant Officer. Mrs. Postovit and recalled her easy life before Pearl Harbor and how it changed:

"We would have our monthly coffees; we all did some kind of volunteer Red Cross work. I was a Grey Lady for years. Of course, the main attraction was going to the beach. I think Priscilla was about three weeks old and we were at the beach. It was just a happy time. You just felt like you didn't have a care in the world, life was good.

"We had dances on the post. In fact, the night before Pearl Harbor, on Saturday night, we went to a dance on the base. I look back now and wonder. I guess because we were young, instead of going home, we called the babysitter to say that we were going to downtown Honolulu and eat some breakfast. And we got down there and the place was packed, every place was jam packed. There were a lot of Navy people. In talking to other people, we found out they had brought in a lot of ships because it was the last weekend they could do their Christmas shopping and mail the things back to the United States to be sure they were there on time. And so all of them were in port and on leave, so everybody was out having a good time that night."

Those good times were shattered Sunday morning, 7 December at 7:35 a.m. Hawaiian time.

"It was really just terrible. We heard all of this flying and of course, a lot of the pilots had desk assignments, and on the weekends they would fly to get their flying time in. And we thought at first that was what was going on. And we heard this explosion. And we thought one of the fellows had 'crowned out,' and so I looked out the window to see if I could find out. We were living on the base at Pearl Harbor, at Wheeler Field, not too far from the flight line and the barracks building. So I felt, from the sound of the noise, it was something on the flight line or at the barracks buildings. So I looked out the window and I saw all of these planes with the Rising Sun on them. They were flying low. The GIs were leaving the barracks building and running up toward our quarters to hide around in the bushes. And I think back, how silly I was; I didn't think about opening the front door and saying, 'Come in,' because these were cement houses, probably cement blocks, really safe as long as you stayed away from the window. I thought afterwards that I should have opened the door and said 'Come on in,' but we were so surprised.

"My husband pulled a couch across an inside corner, we had one child, she was about two and a half, and he said for us to get behind the couch where we would be safe from flying bullets but he knew that he had to get dressed and report for duty. So he went into the bedroom to get his clothes and coming out, he was carrying his shoes and kind of ducking and he said, 'I almost got my fanny shot off' and sure enough we found a bullet in the chest of drawers of that room afterwards. And we still have that.

"So Priscilla and I stayed behind the couch and he got ready to report for duty. His squadron was out on the other side of the island for gunnery practice so he had to get into the car and drive around to the other side of the island. It was really frightening, all of this flying, knowing what was going on outside, but afraid to get up and go look out of the window."

During a lull, crews headed for their squadrons and Postovit headed for the other side of the island.

"On the way over to Bellows Field with my buddy, we had to get out of the car a couple of times because the Japanese were flying over us and we didn't know if they were going to dive at us or not, so we got out of the car and went into the ditch. When they passed by, then we got back in the car. But when I got over to Bellows Field, we found out that one pilot was killed. You see the Japanese came in and strafed and they killed one of our pilots getting in there and another pilot was killed and shot down when he was taking off and the third pilot was shot down over

A Time to Speak

the ocean, but he swam back in. He got wounded in the leg. But all of our airplanes were all shot up. My job was to get them repaired as fast as possible and that's what we were doing, trying to repair all of the airplanes we had, make them flyable so they could get up in the air and protect themselves. Actually, it was just work from then on, working on the airplanes.

"The next morning I went over to Hickam Field to our depot to pick up a spare engine and a propeller so we could get two more airplanes in commission. That Pearl Harbor, it was terrible, fires all over, burning. Hickam Field was burning, it was terrible. But we got our parts and we got back to the Field. And we went back to work."

As soon as things were organized, women and children were sent back to the United States on transport ships. Mrs. Postovit and her daughter arrived in San Francisco on Christmas Day. Thanks to the Red Cross, the wives had a Christmas dinner, a place to stay and travel tickets to their destination in the United States. Mrs. Postovit returned to Ft. Leavenworth. Postovit's squadron stayed in Hawaii and in the nearby area for another year and a half.

"We bounced around from place to place. For a while we were at the Kaneohe Naval Air Station because most of their airplanes were shot up. And we were stationed with them to protect them as much as we could in case we were attacked again. But my squadron, we were very flexible, we went from place to place, to Hilo, later on to Canton Island which was 2,500 miles south and west of Hawaii for a six-months tour of duty, protecting the life line from the United States to Australia. We were in a position then, not to attack, but to protect what we had until we were able to attack." [70]

Tora! Tora! Tora!
Americans were stung by the surprise attack and its treachery. For the armed forces, it was a day marked by death and military disgrace. On the other hand, for Captain Mitsuo Fuchida, Commander of the attack, it was a proud and joyful day. Fuchida wrote his account, "From Pearl Harbor to Calvary" for *Bible Literature International* and it is cited with their permission.

"I must admit I was more excited than usual as I awoke that morning 3:00 a.m., Hawaii time, four days past my thirty-ninth birthday. Our six aircraft carriers were positioned 230 miles north of Oahu Island. As general commander of the air squadron, I made last-minute checks on the intelligence information reports in the operations room before going to warm up my single-engine, three-seater '97-type' plane used for level bombing and torpedo flying.

"The sunrise in the east was magnificent above the white clouds as I led 360 planes towards Hawaii at an altitude of 3,000 meters. I knew my objective: to surprise and cripple the American naval force in the Pacific. But I fretted about being thwarted should some of the U. S. battleships not be there. I gave no thought of the possibility of this attack breaking open a mortal confrontation with the United States. I was only concerned about making a military success.

"As we neared the Hawaiian islands that bright Sunday morning, I made a preliminary check of the harbor, nearby Hickam Field and the other installations surrounding Honolulu. Viewing the entire American Pacific Fleet peacefully at anchor in the inlet below, I smiled as I reached for the mike and ordered, 'All squadrons, plunge in to attack.' The time was 7:49 a.m.

"Like a hurricane out of nowhere, my torpedo planes, dive bombers and fighters struck suddenly with indescribable fury. As smoke began to billow and the proud battleships, one by one, started tilting, my heart was almost ablaze with joy. During the next three hours, I directly commanded the fifty level bombers as they pelted not only Pearl Harbor, but the airfields, barracks and dry docks nearby. Then I circled at a higher altitude to accurately assess the damage and report it to my superiors.

"Of the eight battleships in the harbor, five were mauled into total inactivity for the time being. The Arizona was scrapped for good; the Oklahoma, California and West Virginia were sunk. The Nevada was beached in a sinking condition; only the Pennsylvania, Maryland and Tennessee were able to be repaired. Of the eight, the California, West Virginia and Nevada were salvaged much later, but the Oklahoma, after being raised, was resunk as worthless. Other smaller ships were damaged, but the sting of 3,077 U. S. Navy personnel killed or missing and 876 wounded, plus 226 Army killed and 396 wounded, was something which could never be repaired.

"It was the most thrilling exploit of my career. Ever since I had heard of my country's winning the Russo-Japanese War in 1905, I had dreamed of becoming an admiral like Admiral Togo, our commander-in-chief in the decisive Battle of the Japan Sea.

". . . When the time came to choose the chief commander for the Pearl Harbor mission, I had logged over 10,000 hours, making me the most experience pilot in the Japanese Navy.

"During the next four years, I was determined to improve upon my Pearl Harbor feat."

The Sinking of the USS Arizona

The simultaneous attacks by Japanese air crews on military establishments were designed to destroy American planes before they could intercept the Japanese and to destroy the eight battleships anchored at Pearl Harbor on Battleship Row.

Twenty-one ships of the U. S. Pacific Fleet were damaged or destroyed (later all but three of the ships were salvaged and repaired).

The USS *Arizona* took a direct hit from an armor-piercing bomb which ignited the ship's forward ammunition magazine. The ship sank, and the explosion and fire killed 1,177 crewmen. It was the greatest loss of life on any ship and represented about half the total number of Americans killed that day.

One of the few survivors of the *Arizona* is Don Inselman, who at the time was a Seaman, First Class. He has no trouble recalling what happened fifty years ago.

"We were out at sea a week before Pearl Harbor. We were patrolling up north. That's where the Japanese were coming from.

"Occasionally we would get the word they had sighted a submarine. What do we do if we catch it? What do we do if he catches us? It was Japanese all right, but we didn't catch none. But we sighted two or three of them.

"We got back into port, we went into Pearl Harbor, we were tied up at what looks like a dock. We opened up everything we had, water-tight integrity. It was like we were going to have inspection. Anyway, Sunday morning, a whole bunch of us hanging around the quarterdeck, we had breakfast. Here comes a bunch of planes over, we had this big awning over the top, canvas awning over the top so you can't see up. So we don't see what is up there. We start running for the life lines. I'm right behind this other guy, Bob Hines. He was ahead of me, he looked out and he said they were Japanese.

"All right, they are Japanese, I don't need to see them. I'll take your word for it. We beat it back off from under that awning. Got under cover. The awning wasn't going to stop those bullets. The first thing I was supposed to do was to close the portholes. We had about three of them in our compartment there. I'm starting to close them. And I don't know who it was, a bos'n mate of some kind, I think he was ours, in our division, but he said, 'Never mind that, go to your battle stations. That won't be necessary to have them closed.'

"So I went to my battle station, I go down to the box, clear down as far as you can go, then I start to go aft. It's a long ways back through there. And you go through several compartments to get back there. I got back by the bottom of the turret and the lights went out.

"We had been trained to go up through that turret in the dark. I had been up through there several times in the dark, you can't see your hand in front of your face. I knew every one of the 'hand holds' (anything you could get your hands on). I could go up through there with my eyes closed. I knew where they all were. We were well trained in that. That was one thing I knew we had done. When the lights went out, I would have been down there with the rest of them if I hadn't known that.

"I went up there, got in the upper handling room where a bunch of us gathered up there. That's as high as you can go there, just off the deck. We sat there and you could hear the water down there below. Pretty soon, there was a smell of acid smoke. We were in the dark, we don't know. They said there were some kind of batteries down there. I didn't know if it was toxic, but I took my T-shirt and put it up over my face and it helped. It would keep you from getting poisoned by that gas.

"We sat there, we wondered about the whole thing, you know, how deep is this water? It looks like that water's coming up. How deep is it while we are sitting here? You talk about 35 feet or whatever, how far can we go down before the water gets us? So we start calculating a little bit, you know, we weren't too wrong. The water stopped coming up before it got to us. So we were sitting there, we could reach down and touch that water. It was that close to going under. It kept making bubbling noises.

"We sat there, only one guy got kind of nervous. He was afraid he was going to die. Well, so were we! but we don't say it, you know. If I had known what I know now, I would have been afraid too, a lot worse than I was.

"But anyway, we finally decided, the noise all stopped, you could hear all that shelling going on up through the hatchet that you get out on the deck, down by the overhang where you can jump out on the deck. We wandered around out there a while, looking it all over, and after while, we look up forward and the whole thing is ablaze. That's when you get scared.

"Oh, God, yeah, you'd get out on that turret and look up and see the rest of that ship, and all you could see was smoke and fire. You never imagined that much smoke and fire in your life that close. And it's on the ship you are on. I'm telling you, you just go weak. You are in some kind of shock. Somebody said, 'Did you see that fat cook?' They didn't identify him because we didn't know him, but we all knew the fat cook. 'Did you see that fat cook sittin' along side turret three?' 'No, why?' 'He had both legs blown off.' I didn't see it, but he was right there. 'I bet you looked over at him and still didn't see him.'

"You never heard such noise in your life. They hit that turret with a pretty good-sized bomb. I noticed the hole after we got out of there, the hole it caused as it glanced off the turret, it made a hole in the deck, the hole in the deck was big like this kitchen, you know.

"We wandered around and we went over to the repair ship that was tied up along side the Arizona. When we went down, they stayed afloat. So the line that was tying us to them, or them to us, it got tight, like it was ready to snap. They had to get underway, they thought. They were going to cut that line so they could get loose on the repair ship, some officer up on the repair ship. We hollered, 'We were sinking,' and he's way up, and he said, 'Don't cut that line, I don't know how you are going to get loose.'

"One officer cut that line and they popped up out of the water, and they got under way. They are gone and we are still sitting there. So we look around and we decided to put one of those life rafts (those life rafts made out of balsam). It wasn't going to be any luxury cruise, but we threw the thing over the side, on the port side. Two guys got in that thing. This is the funny part of this, if there is anything funny, and it started to sink. They didn't want to get in that thing, so they came aboard ship again. I kind of thought that was funny, even though I didn't laugh at the time. There was nothing funny about any of it.

"Anyway, this officer, he had a hat on his head that looked like he had it knocked off his head a few times, he kept throwing it back up on there, and he is chewing an old cigar. And he wanted to know why we don't get off. And he wasn't too nice about it. He was mad about something. He said we could get off. And he said, 'You can get in the Admiral's barge.' There were only two or three of us on the deck, I don't know where the other guys were. We were the only ones left on our side. So he said, 'Get in the Admiral's barge,' and we said, 'Ah, no, we don't dare do that, you can't ride the Admiral's barge.' And he said, 'Don't you worry about the Admiral, he's dead, he won't know the difference.'

"So we got in there and start over to Ford Island which is just a little ways from where we were tied up. As a matter of fact, since the war, I've been accused of jumping across there. But it was a little too far for that. It was close. So I never got wet anyway. On the Admiral's barge, there were two of us getting off the Arizona and there was somebody operating it.

"We got across. There were guys that tried to swim in that oil. That oil was four inches thick and it is burning on top. These guys are in the water, they come up and get air, then they go back down and swim a little more. They can't stay up out of the water because it will burn. And that oil is burning and that oil would burn you up. They just about had their last breath, we seen them, they were having a real rough time, they were not going to make it. I don't care how close that beach is, they aren't going to make it anyway.

"So we stopped the boat and tried to help the guys in, we helped them and got them in the boat. It is kind of gruesome when you think of it. I thought it was at the time. When you'd get your hands under their armpits and try to pull them up; that's the only hand hold you can get, everything else is slick with oil, the flesh and the skin would come right off in our hands. That's enough to cure you, you know. You don't want to do this no more.

"So we took them and went on over to Ford Island. We stayed there a little while, then we got another boat someplace and they took a bunch of us over to the receiving station. That was the last time I was aboard the Arizona.

"It was a surprise to us, to me, and I think to everybody else, to get attacked. There was no surprise that we were going to go to war. We were going to have a war with them, and the Navy out there knew it. Somehow the white hats in the Navy know. Them officers know it. They had a funny saying, when I first came aboard, when they caught you griping about this, griping about that, they'd say, 'It won't be like this under the sickle and hammer.' Now that's what they were saying, that's another enemy. That's what they were thinking. They know who your enemies are."

The survivors from the Arizona were given blue-jeans and taken to the receiving station.

"We kept hanging around the receiving station. I wouldn't report to nobody for nothing. They don't know who I belong to. Nobody knows me, and I don't belong to them.

"We found a hole over there in a lawn. Several of us got together, a bunch of Arizona survivors. We slept during the day, rested and we just took it easy.

"So an officer came by with a clipboard, he looks right down at us, laying in that hole, it's like a crater. I was the first one to speak up, 'What's your name?' 'I don't think I want to tell ya.' He said, 'I've got to have it.' 'No sir, sorry you don't have to have my name.' 'What about the rest of them?' 'They don't know their name, nobody knows nothing. They ain't going to say nothing.' He said, 'I've got to get a working party up to go an unload that ship that just came in, loaded with stores.' We sure ain't going to tell him who we are. He looked around and, 'Can you tell me where you're from?' 'Yes, sir, we're from the Arizona.' 'All of you? Forget it, I don't want you on the list. If you are from the Arizona, I don't want your name.' And he just walked away."

The remaining crew from the Arizona was put on the Chester, a heavy cruiser, to take part in one mission against Japan. They were back in the United States in March 1942, then to Boston. They joined the crew of the Massachusetts which saw service in Casablanca and the South Pacific." [71]

Nurses at Tripler Hospital

The official personnel casualties of killed and wounded were Navy, 2,718; Army, 582; Marines, 178; Civilians, 103.

The nurses serving in Hawaii were angry, frustrated and sometimes scared. They were not prepared for the chaos, they did not have the supplies or personnel to handle the casualties. Captain Dorothy Young who was stationed at Tripler Hospital in Honolulu, said that some things are hard to remember. "I can't tell you all of the horrors, so I'll have to tell you some of the funny things as well."

Dorothy Young graduated from nursing in 1938 and joined the Army Nurse Corps in February 1941. When the war ended, she became a school nurse and owner of Kickapoo Lodge in Grand Lake, Colorado.

She answered a letter from the President asking for nurse volunteers to serve for eighteen months. She signed up for duty in the Philippines but got her second choice instead, Hawaii.

After their inoculations because they were going to "some strange, exotic Pacific Island," twelve nurses left for Hawaii in October 1941, with "no inkling that there might be something going on, except on the east coast, we were more aware of Germany and Hitler's invasions, taking over much of Europe."

"So when we got to Honolulu, it was very beautiful and there was nothing like there is nowadays. It was a kind of sleepy, beautiful island, and Honolulu was busy with some Chinese junks that gave the oriental look along the harbor and the Aloha Tower which stood out. It was kind of like the smell of the tropics, fruit and beautiful flowers. It was a pleasant thing, like you were going to some exotic place.

"They picked us up and brought us to Tripler Hospital which was right across from Fort Shafter, the old Tripler Hospital, porches, lots of flowers and green grass and they were adding some more buildings there. The nurses' quarters were pretty full, so they put us in some temporary buildings, some of us out at Hickman Field as they had some housing.

"We didn't have a car so there wasn't much opportunity to take a look. But we would take the bus down to Waikiki before the war started and enjoy the beach down there. It was a really nice hospital and kind of quiet and peaceful. Some of the personnel there had a car and so we were able to take some trips around the island and it was absolutely beautiful, peaceful, quiet.

"So we were finally put into permanent buildings (they were all finished). And we were beginning to have some drills at battle stations, this would be going on into November. This seemed strange to me because it was so peaceful on that side of the world; all the war activity was in Europe where they were beginning to attack England. Who would be coming clear out here, the Germans? We'd have battle stations. We didn't have any equipment like protective clothing, or helmets, gas masks. We all had our picture taken, across the road, a big open lawn over by the church at Fort Shafter by the big gates there. And we all went over, except for about twenty-five who were on duty, to have our picture taken for the Christmas menu.

"There were 175 nurses there so you see it was a pretty good-sized hospital. It was the largest hospital on the island. The hospital out at Hickam could take care of about thirty people. The Navy base had the navy hospital there and also had a hospital ship there anchored, then at Schofield Barracks, they had a station hospital and that was maybe 40 miles from where we were.

"We'll come to that morning. The day before I'd had some dental surgery and the doctor felt I should stay overnight in the hospital. So I was a patient in the women's ward. The hospital was laid out so it looked over Hickam Field, the ocean and Pearl Harbor. It was a lovely view, so we were already awake. And all of a sudden, the building started to shake, and there was a lot of confusion. They thought maybe there had been an explosion somewhere and so somebody said, 'Why don't you come out here on the porch and take a look. Look at that, they are having maneuvers that early in the morning.' You could see planes up in the air and you could see puffs of smoke and they were dive bombing and they would drop the bombs and then the water would plume up in smoke. Actually we thought they were having very realistic maneuvers. And then they went over Hickam, and I said, 'I don't understand this, why are they doing this?' Then some of the blasts shook the building so bad the glass was breaking. So we said, 'My gosh, this is awful, what in the world is happening?' Somebody said, 'Maybe it's the Germans, why would they come clear around here?'

"So I said I'm going down to the barracks, and I was going to be off that day, but I put on my uniform to see what was happening.

"All of a sudden here come all of these trucks loaded with wounded, before I could even get out the door. They were all lined up, bakery trucks, milk wagons, anything that could bring people in. Nobody seemed to be in charge. It was just chaos.

"As I came out of the door, and out onto the lawn where I had to take a path down to the nurses' barracks, this Japanese plane flew over and he strafed, some of the patients were standing outside watching, and he strafed and got some of the cars down below in the parking lot. I could see him. He had on a leather hat, and a scarf around his neck and he smiled at me, like this, [she demonstrated with a grimace] and you could see his teeth. And here was the Rising Sun emblem on there. And I said, 'Oh, my God, it's the Japanese.' I was just out of the blue and no idea, no warning, no anything except vaguely I could remember all of these blackouts and these battle stations exercises, zig-zagging two months before coming out from the States. So I think somebody, somewhere was pretty much aware of what was going on. So what I did, I thumbed my nose at him because I didn't have anything else. So I ran down the stairs right quick, that was the only plane that went right over the hospital.

"That kept up, I thought it was about three waves, somewhere I read it was about 402 planes, different sizes and they came batch after batch. And of course, we had no idea whether this would continue or whether they planned to invade. We weren't really equipped to handle anything like this. I went down and put my uniform on and came up and they were loading the patients, some very badly hurt and some with just a little scratch.

"I was stepping over them, they were laid out on the porch, the whole front of the hospital was a big lanai. We were moving some of the patients who were ambulatory out of the wards so we could move some of them in there. The head nurse was not on duty that day, I guess she just wasn't there. So the second in command, she was a captain and she kind of took over, but it was just a mad house and we all hopefully did the right thing. What are you going to do? We had no training in something like 4,000 casualties coming in and they kept coming and coming at least for three days after that. They didn't have such a thing as 'triage,' I don't think the word even existed.

"We didn't have that many doctors to say, 'I think this fellow needs to go a little closer to the operating room.' So we did the best we could. As we went through, I'd say, 'Where are you hurt?' or if they were unconscious I'd look them over. Finally we had to have some kind of order, we were stepping over patients and some of them just badly hurt. With this many really needing some patching up, I can imagine that we had to set up an operating room in the dining room, using the dining room tables because we only had a couple of operating rooms available.

"I think we were all so angry about this, that this had happened and we were never really told that something might happen and be prepared except like these vague exercises which we thought were kind of silly. From there on, we opened up some big barracks that had nothing in them and brought in supplies and we sent word out to families and people that we needed more supplies and sheets we could tear up and make bandages out of. We had nothing left. There was no such thing as plastic and disposables in those days. We had to make our own, we had to make our own gauze 4" x 4", with a big roll of gauze and we would cut it into strips and fold it very carefully so it would be a 4" x 4". We didn't have time to do all that, we had used everything we in supplies.

"I think about the third day they started bringing in the dead because they had put them in a hanger down there or in a big storage place. They were gone and they needed a place where they could identify them. We had a recreation hall and they started bringing them in there, by the truckloads. I was out and it was kind of rainy a bit. They had this big army truck and the dead were loaded in there like cord wood and this little fellow came along and he said, 'I don't know what to do with these.' He was crying. The rain was coming down, blood was washing down the street and I stood there with my white shoes on, and the blood and water were washing across my feet and I said, 'Oh, God.' I went over to the bush, and I threw up. That was the first time...after about three days...all of a sudden...we were so busy. I rarely ever think of this because it is too hard to remember.

"You don't remember sometimes some of the patients. I remember one said, I met him in Florida at a convention, and he had no hand, but he had an artificial one. So he said, 'Were you at Tripler?' I said 'Yes.' He said, 'Do you remember me?' and I said, 'I don't know, maybe, what happened to you?' He said, 'My hand was completely severed except for some little skin there holding it on.' And I had my scissors tied around me on a piece of gauze so I wouldn't lose them. So what I did, I took out my scissors. I cut the hand off and wrapped his hand up in his shirt, don't ask me why. And I put a tourniquet on his arm. Then the doctor said 'You'd better get him in right quick.'

"We gave morphine, in those days we didn't have disposable syringes. We had to wash the glass ones and sterilize them which took time; the needles we used over and over, we had to clean them, sharpen the points and boil them in a big copper kettle. There were a lot of things that weren't available that are available now for a crisis like that. I finally got some morphine that the doctor ordered, and I had to stand in line to wait because we were running short. The water wasn't boiling fast enough. So I got back to him. I had my lipstick in my pocket. We put 'M' on his forehead and then we'd put the time so that we'd know he had his shot of morphine and wouldn't get all confused. They weren't apt to wash his face off. So that's what we had to do. When we look back, we thought we were not well-equipped for everything."

"We needed help badly, extra people just to clean up, to bathe, bring a bedpan or a urinal. If you don't know, back in those days, they had the 'houses of ill repute' all along. Word got out that we needed help so here comes all the girls from down there, absolutely volunteered. And they did very menial things, like mopping and cleaning, bringing bedpans and emptying them and God bless them. You didn't see any of the officers' wives coming over. I had a couple helping me and I said, 'You don't know how great this is coming over and helping.' It was a month or two later, a reprimand was sent to the colonel in charge that they had allowed these 'women of the street' to come in and take care of 'our boys.' It was in the Honolulu Transcript. I said, 'Somebody higher up back in Washington, maybe one of the parents wrote a letter because these "ladies of the evening" gave their son a urinal.' Maybe some of this got back to the States. But they were such wonderful help and the colonel, who was in charge of the hospital, gave them a thanks of recognition. You have to have something funny happen in all that mess.

"Things kind of calmed down. Everything was under martial law. About Wednesday, I had not been to bed yet. We hadn't really eaten because some Japanese farmers had brought in milk to the back of the hospital and the word got out that there was arsenic in the milk. They killed the Japanese drivers; they spilled the milk out in the back in the driveway. They said, 'Don't eat whatever because maybe it is poison and don't drink the water because they put typhoid germs in the water supply.' What do you eat? So we really didn't eat; we had some boiled coffee, we figured that might boil away germs, but the coffee was so bad.

"The word got out that they had invaded so we were all blacked out. We hung blankets or whatever we could up over the windows at night because we didn't want them coming in during the night. Nobody was supposed to wear navy blue because they would be shot because that was what the Japanese invaders were wearing, navy blue uniforms.

"So there were a lot of scared young people on guard. We had guards all around the hospital. We had a password if we moved outside at all from one building to another. They were kind of spread out and it was pitch black like the 'inside of a cat,' we said. If you had a flashlight to find your way, you had to put a piece of carbon paper over it. We had to find our way and then if we came to a sentry who said, 'Halt, advance and be recognized!' We had to give a password and it could be the 'Baltimore Orioles' because it had 'Rs' in it and the Japanese couldn't pronounce 'Rs.' This one guy, 'I said I think it may be the Baltimore Orioles today.' 'Well, no,' he says, 'it was changed to the 'Cardinals.' 'Please don't shoot!' I put that little flashlight up by my face and he says, 'Ma'am, I couldn't shoot you if I wanted to, I don't have any ammunition.' Isn't that silly? Some of them had guns, but no ammunition in it because they ran out of ammunition."

Finally the nurses, six at a time, were allowed to go down to the cable office to notify their parents they were safe.

"I remember, $6 to send 'Am safe' to my mother and dad back in Massachusetts. It was another week before anyone back home knew that their son or daughter was all right.

"... It was a good long time before we were allowed off the base, except to send a cable, until January when they decided the Japanese weren't going to come in. They were busy over in the Philippines.

"We finally began to feel like the nurses could go out. Curfew was 6:30 at night and everything was blackout. We were still keeping the security and we had an old plane - we called him 'washing machine Charlie' because the motor you could hear it. We had a klaxon we put up 'arruga, arruga,' and you had to stand there and crank it and we had battle stations and we went on duty and went to some shelter. They dug big holes in the ground so we could go down and carry the patients down, which we did often. We really didn't know. Nobody said, 'It's all over, you don't have to worry any more.'

"When you look back on it, it was wartime and people died and you didn't want that. You had to accept it. I hope to God it never happens again. It's a terrible thing. I never think about it, and this is kind of difficult for me to recall some things. I'm really not telling you how bad it was because then I go............" [72]

War Is Declared

The *Kansas City Star* on Monday, December 8, 1941 reported President Roosevelt's message to Congress, *"Yesterday, December 7, 1941 - a date which will live in infamy - the United States of America was suddenly and deliberately attacked by naval and air forces of the empire of Japan."*

Roosevelt also told Congress that Japanese forces had launched attacks against Malaya, Hong Kong, Guam, the Philippine Islands, Wake Island and Midway Island.

He concluded his speech, *"No matter how long it may take us to overcome this premeditated invasion, the American people in their righteous might will win through to absolute victory."* He asked Congress to declare that a state of war existed between the United States and the Japanese empire. Congress voted 470 to 1 for war.

On 11 December, Germany declared war on the United States. America was now at war on two fronts and across two oceans.

When Admiral Isoroku Yamamoto was notified of the successful strike at Pearl Harbor, he remarked, "I fear all we have done is to awaken a sleeping giant and fill him with a terrible resolve. . . ." Admiral Yamamoto was correct. The nation was united.

Pearl Harbor was a defining moment in American history, both on a personal level and on a national level. It marked America's entry into World War II and into global politics, a role from which the United States has never retreated.

End Notes

67 *The Bartlesville, Oklahoma Morning Examiner*
68 Ruth Correll later served as Mayor of Boulder, Colorado.
69 Martha Watts juggles her time between works part-time at George Watts & Sons in Milwaukee and volunteer work.
70 Postovit served in the Army Air Corps for thirty years until his retirement. Both Mr. and Mrs. Postovit are deceased.
71 Inselman lives in Commerce City, Colorado and remains active in the Pearl Harbor Survivors Organization.
72 In Grand Lake, Colorado, Dorothy Young was the school nurse and for many years she has been the owner of the Kickapoo Lodge.

CHAPTER 19

EXECUTIVE ORDER 9066

At the time of Pearl Harbor, many bewildered Americans said, "Why, the yellow bastards!"[73] That statement reflected the basic racism that underlay America's attitude.

Early California settlers, at the time of the Gold Rush, were anti-nonwhites, and that attitude included an anti-Chinese movement. Japanese immigrants to the West Coast then inherited the familiar stereotype, "the yellow peril." Pressure from working men, California politicians, patriotic groups like the Exclusion League, and the media fueled the anti-Japanese sentiment. The Japanese victories in the Russo-Japanese war (1904-1905) made Japan a world power. This only increased the fear and rumors of a Japanese attack on the West Coast.

American quotas restricting Asian immigration go back as far as the Chinese Exclusion Act of 1880 which banned entry of Chinese laborers for a period of ten years. A more severe exclusionary act, the 1908 Gentleman's Agreement, bound Japan to issue no further passports to workers for immigration directly to the United States. The 1924 Johnson-Read Immigration Act limited the annual quota to 2 percent of US residents of that nationality in 1890. However, the act *totally excluded Japanese immigrants*, in spite of a warning by the Japanese Ambassador of grave consequences if the US abandoned the Gentleman's Agreement of 1908.

The mistrust and alarm accelerated in the wake of Japan's aggression in East Asia, particularly the "Rape of Nanking" in 1937, when the Japanese marched into the defenseless city of Nanking and killed Chinese men and raped and mutilated Chinese women and girls. By the time of the bombing of Pearl Harbor, fear and hysteria on the West Coast reached a peak.

A young woman who lived in the San Francisco area in the late 1930s explained:

"The general feeling I had as a child was that the Japanese were not particularly to be trusted. And I think that feeling came from the fact that the Chinese were the preferred Orientals in the area. The real big problem between the Chinese and the Japanese, which rubbed off on to the Anglos in the area, was when Japan invaded China in 1937.

"The large tabloids that were put out by the Chinese at that time certainly

A Time to Speak

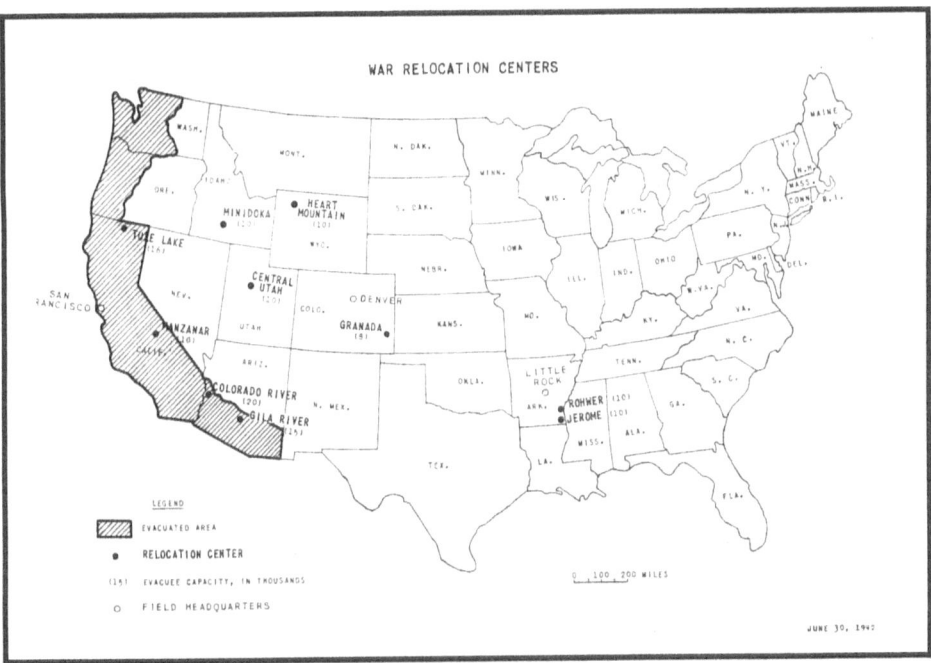

War Relocation Centers. Courtesy E. B.

got your attention. And there was a constant barrage of journalism, talking about what the Japanese were doing to the Chinese in China. I remember particularly, I wasn't more than ten years old, and there was a very large graphic picture of what the Japanese had done in Nanking during the so-called 'Rape of Nanking' when the women were raped and the bodies were from here to next Friday, and I will carry that picture forever.

"The Japanese were considered to be untrustworthy and blood thirsty and if they were American citizens, probably would be first and foremost loyal to their country of Japan and would have approved of what was going on with the Japanese expansion."

Following the bombing of Pearl Harbor, President Roosevelt bowed to the anti-Japanese hysteria from people living on the West Coast and issued Executive order 9066 on 19 February 1942. Between 24 March and 3 November, Executive Order 9066 permitted the roundup and removal of all persons of Japanese ancestry living on the West Coast and from the most westerly portions of California, Arizona, Washington and Oregon. During this time, approximately 120,000 persons of Japanese ancestry, of whom 77,000 were American citizens, were moved to temporary centers and then to ten Relocation Centers. [Issei are first generation immigrants; Nisei are second generation Japanese-Americans.]

Life in Relocation Centers

Americans are still trying to make sense of the relocation of Japanese Americans to internment camps, which was the result of this racial hysteria. Dorothy Martin, a former psychology professor still feels uncomfortable with the decision. *"So very early, I had that same feeling, how is it possible that Americans can do this kind of thing to American citizens. But we sure did! There was an awful lot of prejudice."*

Ralph Carr, governor of Colorado in 1942, was perhaps the only political figure who protested Roosevelt's Executive Order 9066 as unfair and unconstitutional. On the radio, he pleaded for more tolerance: *"There are thousands of men and women and children . . . who by reason of blood only, are regarded by some people as unfriendly. They are as loyal to American institutions as you and I. Many of them have been born here - are American citizens, with no connection with or feeling of loyalty toward the customs and philosophies of Italy, Japan, or Germany."*

Later, speaking to a meeting of the ten western governors on 7 April 1942, he said Colorado would help in the war effort and if that meant housing unwanted Japanese American citizens, then Colorado would do its part. He was the only governor present who welcomed the Japanese evacuees to his state. Today a bust of Governor Carr stands in Denver's Sakura Square as a tribute to his humanitarian attitude.[74]

The basis for the prejudice was hard for the Japanese-Americans to understand.

Granada and Tule Lake Relocation Centers

Sue Hirokawa and Kathryn Kawakami, now living in Denver, were sent to Relocation Centers. Mrs. Hirokawa, from Yuma City, arrived at the Granada Center in southwestern Colorado, and Mrs. Kawakami, from Sacramento, was sent to the Tule Lake Relocation Center in northern California.

They arrived to find half-finished barracks. What was difficult for the women was living in one room, a single room, even for those married, with children. The walls were thin enough to hear the neighbor's conversation or babies crying in the night. With wood left over from construction, some husbands picked up pieces and made partitions for their barracks room and drawers for clothes. Otherwise the families lived out of a trunk. They had no kitchens, no water, but a communal kitchen and a community bath.

Once they were settled, they made the best of what they had. The men grew vegetables and worked around the camp. The women organized cooking classes, English classes, knitting, art and flower-arranging classes.

For recreation, there was a huge cleared area with a stage for music, singing or dancing. In Tule Lake, for example, internees from the Hawaiian Islands who were in California for there education, entertained others with their electric guitars.

Mrs. Kawakami summed up the experience:

"In fact, I associate with Japanese first generation mothers and they were very humble. They do not speak out, express their feelings, what is ahead of them is the most important thing. I hear very few people complaining about camp life.

"My daughter gets angry when I talk about it, but you cannot be living with the bitterness. You have to appreciate that you are alive."

The YWCA

From the moment of the internment of Japanese-Americans, the YWCA (Young Women's Christian Association) took an interest because the YWCA had already been working with young women in Japan since the 1920s. Now they took action. Their objective within the Relocation Centers was to make life better for the women inside the camps. E. B., a former YWCA field staff worker, now retired, talked about her work which focused on activities the women wanted to have for themselves and their children.

"The Japanese talked about the things they needed, that they thought would make life more pleasant. They wanted to have meetings like they used to have outside and they wanted the Y-teen clubs where they used to go. They worried about their young people. They wanted to be sure we had something for the teens.

"We had schools and everything else in the Centers all that time. The government had to provide teachers, and those teachers didn't care one bit about the people they were teaching. They would stick them out there and they just taught. . . .

"We had our classes going for women since there wasn't anything for them. We started some embroidery and some handiwork classes. That's what they do best; they did some beautiful work.

"We got some teenagers from the Center in Granada and we mixed them up with the teenagers from Southern Colorado as a team. And they went out and worked in the fields and got paid. They came out for a certain period of time, a two-week basis. We found housing for them in town with some of the children. And that's the first crack we got to get them out to do something. And of course, those Japanese children were in the fields all the time, and they could show them how to plant a garden, how to pick your things.

"If it hadn't been for the efforts of the YWCA, it would have been dismal for those in the Relocation Centers. The government wouldn't take any responsibility for it."

Colorado River Relocation Center

Both Mrs. Hirokawa and Mrs. Kawakami spoke of the particular dilemma and conflict for young Japanese-American men of Army age. Those who were already in the Army were withdrawn and sent to camp. Others, in order to prove how loyal and how American they were, volunteered to go back to the military. But, their parents were Japanese and didn't want their children to go to war against Japan because theoretically Japan was still their country.

Tom Masamori faced just such an incongruous situation. The US Army picked him up and sent him to the Colorado River Relocation Center, Poston, Arizona. He was held behind barbed wire, yet he was asked to volunteer for the U. S. Army. He served in the highly decorated 100/442nd Japanese-American (Nisei) Infantry Regimental Combat Team.

"*This* [prejudice] *didn't just happen with the bombing of Pearl Harbor. I remember more than one occasion in California when I would be walking home from school and kids would come after me and throw rocks at me and yell, 'Get out of here, you Jap.' This is what is so wrong about people not teaching their children the difference between right and wrong.*

"*This thing was fostered by the media, radio, especially the newspapers and magazines and several organizations including the Native Sons of the Golden West, which was a California based super-patriot. The DAR and the American Legion, from the time of its inception in 1919, they passed a resolution every year at their convention, anti-Jap resolutions.*

"*It was unfairly put on us, the second generation in this country. The prejudices that were very prevalent, especially on the West Coast, would be tantamount to being a black in the South. It was that severe. Knowing that this kind of thing existed, the insistence was on (by the Issei, the first generation) that we get an education, that we prove ourselves. And this was so ingrained in my generation, that's why we had to prove ourselves in battle. We don't belong in the situation. Why are we here? Let's prove to them that we are American, that we don't deserve the treatment we got.*

"*I have to give a little background on who we are as Asians in this country, how we came here. And the big difference between the blacks who were brought over as slaves, the Asians who came to this country. First, the Chinese were under contract as laborers, there may have been some who were shanghaied. By the time the Japanese were brought over, they were under contract and most of them came from southern Japan. They came from a farm community and they were hired to work on the railroads, primarily railroads and to help with the menial jobs that were available. My father came over in 1906, toward the end of the early migra-*

tion. My mother came over about the same time, 1910 or so. She's a Nisei, born in Hawaii. They were the first migrants to what was a territory of the US. They were brought in under contract to harvest the sugar cane. And she was born on the Island of Hawaii. Technically she was a US citizen, but because of the record keeping at that time, she was an orphan when her mother died in childbirth. She was given away to another Issei family and they registered her as their own.

"Most stayed on the West Coast. Most of them went into farming as this was their background. After that they went into other things, innkeepers was one of them. To show you the success of the Japanese in the farming, in spite of the fact that they were not allowed to own land, being non-citizens, they share-cropped, and when their children became of age to buy land, they were able to purchase small plots which the white farmers would allow them to buy. But it was most marginal land. In spite of this fact, by 1941, 75 percent of the truck crops raised in California were being raised by Japanese farmers. This whole evacuation process came just at the time of planting or harvesting was going to be happening. To take them away from all this is kind of ridiculous. The cash crop might have been for the benefit of the evacuees [the Japanese Americans], and I hate to use the word evacuees because evacuation means a humanitarian action to move people from harm's way. This was a forced removal of a population.

"I was a student at San Jose State in San Jose, going to school there, my freshman year, a nineteen year old. With the bombing of Pearl Harbor, December 7, I was working my way through school as a house boy in this boarding house. I was cleaning a room and one of the fellows came rushing in, 'Hey, Tom, did you hear about the bombing of Pearl Harbor?' I said, 'What about the bombing and where is Pearl Harbor?' And he said that the Japs had bombed Pearl Harbor. I said, 'Wow!, where is that?' And he said, 'The Hawaiian Islands.' So that was my first exposure to this kind of information.

"I continued in school and then, February 19, of course, Franklin Roosevelt signed Executive Order 9066. I guess Executive Orders have an awful lot of power because they circumvented the Constitution. They circumvented the right of people to live freely in this country. And also turning over the civilian population to the military which, guaranteed by the Constitution that unless martial law is declared, then the civilian population cannot be affected by the military. Martial law was never declared and yet portions of the population were turned over to the military.

"To show you how ridiculous the whole process was, right after the bombing of Pearl Harbor, my friend who graduated with me in high school, his father owned a grocery store and had various other mercantile things. Every 4th of July, at the time in California, you could buy fireworks, so he stored fireworks in his warehouse, things he didn't sell the previous year, things for the following year. And the FBI checked his warehouse and found all these fireworks and they immediately arrested him. The rationale was that these could be used as signals to the Japanese Navy. He was immediately arrested and put in one of the Federal Detention Centers. (My classmate was killed in the Philippines.)

"First we were sent to Salinas Assembly Center in May of '42. By the end of July we were removed from there and put on the train and sent to Poston, Arizona. That was a change of about 40 degrees in temperature.

"There were nine of us in the family and we were all in one room. The largest barrack's room was about 20 ft. x 25 ft. And the only furnishings in the room were army cots. That's it, no desk, no table, nothing and one bare bulb in the room.

"There was barbed wire, and at the perimeters, we had guard towers and machine guns in the towers. We couldn't understand. These camps, you have to realize where they were situated, in the middle of nowhere. And being physically, what we look like, you couldn't wander off and not be recognized. So the question was asked, 'What's the rationale of having guard towers up there? We can understand maybe having a guard at the gate, but what's the idea of guard towers with machine guns?' And the answer, of course, was, 'Well that's for your protection in case people want to come in.'

"Coming into the camp, you could bring in only that which you could carry. Anything that you couldn't carry with you had either to be stored, and since most of the people didn't own their own homes, they had no place to store them. So they had to sell off or give away radios, knives, guns. Cameras were confiscated. That's all you could bring, clothes and necessities. That's all you had when you got into this barracks with nine cots, that which you brought with you. There was an army cot and a blanket. And on top of that there was a white bag, a mattress ticking, and in the middle of the block they had dumped straw and if you wanted to make a mattress for yourself, you went out and filled the ticking with straw.

"Meals were served at certain hours. Of course, they had communal showers and communal latrine and laundry. Everything was done in one building. Then the dining was in a separate building and that was it.

"What the camp administrators were doing was trading flour and potatoes with the military to get the rice rations. Otherwise it would be meat and potatoes, and very little meat on top of that. Of the things that were very memorable, of course, was Spam. We grew to hate Spam.

"Some were released on labor, in some areas, to help farm. The situation in most camps, there weren't those kinds of opportunities. So the only kind of work we would do would be in camp, like in Poston, there was a camouflage net factory. And the ones that were able to, or wanted to, could apply for work there. But again, the situation was that only American citizens could work in these camouflage net factories because you had to be a US citizen to work on a government project.

"And the other kind of work was, of course, necessity kind of work. We had clinics, hospitals in all the camps, and the nurses and doctors who were actually well-trained in those fields. In many cases, they had been unable to get jobs on the West Coast because of the prejudice that existed. We had schools, teachers educated to teach. We had schools, from pre-school right on through high school. Most of the camps had three or four high school graduation classes. The students were so well-educated that they had no difficulty in matriculating into colleges when they got out.

"For the women, aside from kitchen work and teaching, a lot of things to occupy their time were arts and crafts and things they would busy themselves with, making clothing for the children. The wages that were paid to us for working in camp ranged from $12 a month, the next level, $16 a month, and the top level which would include doctors and so-called professionals, was $19 a month. And this would barely keep you in things like toiletries. Food you didn't have to worry about because there was communal dining. Housing, such as it was, was furnished.

"There were PXs in each of the camps, toiletries, clothing, necessities. I don't know that there were any food items available. A lot of people sent to their friends outside to have them send food in.

"In the camps, in effect, they emasculated that Issei population, taking away the control they had on the family, the very basis of Asian culture of family and the strong customs that were generated. That, of course, stood well for us, not only in combat, but in the way we conducted ourselves when we were youngsters, not getting into trouble, not causing any problems. That goes for most Asians.

"The control of family was totally lost and that, I think, had a lot of psychological effect, especially on the Issei family. The family was literally torn apart. And kids being kids, they would go to the dining hall and eat with their friends.

"It was several months after we were in camp. Everybody over eighteen years of age was assembled and the army recruiter came and issued the loyalty oath. For the most part, the questions were fairly innocuous, but question number 27 which stated, 'Would you foreswear allegiance to any foreign government, including Japan?' You have to understand that Issei were ineligible for citizenship from the time that they were here. So if they denied allegiance to any foreign government, including the Emperor of Japan, they became, virtually a person without a country. And for the Nisei, who we are, citizens, that was not too much of a problem. So we said, 'Yes, we foreswear.' The second question was, now having foresworn to this country, 'Would you be willing to serve in the Armed Forces and go wherever sent?' Now this is being issued in a concentration camp, surrounded by barbed wire and guard towers and everything else. Yet, they are asking you if you would be willing to serve this country, in spite of the circumstances.

"We said 'Yes,' because in spite of the way the question was phrased, this is still our country and we wanted to show that we were still loyal to this country. Quite a number said 'OK' and immediately they volunteered for the service. It became very difficult for families of young men because, if the young man volunteered to go into the service, then those who believed that this is totally wrong, would ostracize that family and cause a lot of hardship for them. I saw this going on and I said, 'Well, rather than put my parents in that kind of situation, I decided to leave camp, get permission to leave camp and work.' First of all, I needed to get enough money set aside so that I could get them out of camp and secondarily, of course, once I had done that, I would be able to enlist in the armed forces.

"The camps were originally called 'concentration camps' by the government and later, with the connotation of concentration camps in Germany and what was happening in Germany, they changed it to 'Relocation Centers,' to give it a cleaner image. Eventually, there was a realization that it was a total waste of manpower to keep people incarcerated in these situations, and with the need for labor outside in the civilian market, farming was one of the great needs. A lot of people, like my brother, signed up to harvest sugar beets in Nebraska. Then, on the way back, the train stopped in Denver, they were allowed to get off the train because they were no longer under guard. Most of the young men who were in that particular crew went up to the War Relocation Authority Office that was established in various cities. Actually, its job was to implement the removal of people from camps and to find them jobs. The men went to the Office and got permission to stay in Denver, and Office helped them find jobs which were readily available because there was a shortage of labor. My brother was working at a tire retreading place up on East Colfax. Once he got a job, he got permission for his boss to bring me out. You had to have a sponsor before you could leave camp for a job.

"We couldn't bring our parents out because we had no place to house them. My dad was so devastated by the camp experience that he lost all of his incentive to do much of anything, and my mother became quite ill, especially in Salinas and from the heat of Arizona. Her health was quite weak and she couldn't work either. Since they couldn't find work and be productive, and until we could find enough resources to bring them out, we couldn't bring them out of camp."

The 100/442nd Regimental Combat Team

"Meanwhile, my draft number came up and I was inducted into the service. I enlisted for the draft in California before leaving because I was over eighteen. I was registered in Santa Cruz and then the registration was transferred to Monterey which was the nearest to the Salinas Assembly Center. But when they moved me to Poston, Arizona, I had to change my registration to Denver, so the number followed me to Denver.

"A little background on Japanese-American servicemen. There were a number of Japanese-Americans serving in the National Guard in Hawaii. After the bombing of Pearl Harbor, they were called back in and they were reclassified as undesirable enemy aliens, 4-C from 1-A. So with that, they discharged all of them. But you have to realize that the population of Hawaii at that time was primarily Japanese, over 50 percent of the population of the Islands was Japanese and Japanese-Americans.

"So if you remove them from the Armed Forces, that weakened that position there. So they decided, well we'd better bring these guys back in. There was a group of young men going to the University of Hawaii who became the varsity volunteers and they volunteered for anything that the military could use them for. And they became the manual labor force. So they were able to use them there and, finding that there was no case of sabotage or espionage, they decided they could better utilize these young men in the armed forces. That's when they decided to issue a call. It was still the Roosevelt administration that saw the wisdom of utilizing this number of young men in the armed forces. But because they didn't know what their reaction would be, whether they would defect or if they were sent to the Pacific, whether they would go to the enemy side or not, they decided to put them in a segregated unit which became the 442nd Regimental Combat Team.

"So with that formation, there went out a call. Ten thousand young men in Hawaii volunteered, but, of course, they couldn't use all of them, so they took 2,000 of those and put them to form the base of the 442nd. And that opened it up for those of us on the Mainland to also become part of that.

"The reason for the segregated unit was so they would have control over it. The 100th Battalion was the original National Guard which was sent overseas as an all Japanese-American unit. They landed in North Africa and in the southern part of Italy. Once they proved they were such good fighters, such tenacious combat people, they formed the 442nd unit. Any reference to the 442nd is always to the 100th/442nd.

"It was the most decorated unit, with one qualification, size of unit and length of service. It was organized in February 1943. Let's put it quite bluntly, we were cannon fodder and we were expendable. That's one of the reasons the unit was so highly decorated. They say there were 9,000 Purple Hearts issued, 300 percent over the complement units.

"I trained in Camp Blanding in Florida. One of the funny things, I'm sorry I threw the letter away. I had a letter from the FBI after I had finished my basic in Florida. I was visiting my folks when I came by Denver. There was a letter waiting *from the FBI, that, in effect, said 'I was not to go either to the West Coast or the East Coast.' So I said to the FBI, 'Come and catch me. I'm going to be sent overseas, but if you want to put me some place else, that's fine with me.'*

"I joined one of the replacement groups that were sent out of Camp Dix in New Jersey. We went down the Hudson River, right past the Statue of Liberty, on our way to France. We weren't told immediately where we were going, just Europe. We landed in Le Havre, France. D-Day had just finished and the 442nd had just finished liberating the town of Biffontaine-Bruyères. In spite of the devastating losses the 442nd had suffered in rescuing the Lost Battalion and the liberation of the two towns in France, they were going to be shipped back to Italy. So they said, 'We need a lot of replacements,' so that's why we were sent."

The story of the famous mission of the 442nd is told in Pierre Moulin's book, *U. S. Samurais in Bruyères, People of France and Japanese Americans: Incredible story*. The 442nd was sent to rescue "The Lost Battalion," the 141st battalion, the Alamo Regiment from Texas who were surrounded by German troops, in the Vosges mountains. The battalion had sent a coded message, "No food, no water, little ammunition, situation desperate." The 442nd rescued the 200 survivors, but also suffered 221 killed and thousands wounded in the action. The citizens of Bruyères erected a memorial to the unit which saved the town from total destruction. The plaque reads: *"To the men of the 442 Regimental Combat Team, U. S. Army, who reaffirmed an historic truth here...that loyalty to one's country is not modified by racial origin."*[75]

Tom Masamori continued:

"But I didn't get to join the 442nd until Marseille. We went from Le Havre all the way down to Marseille on a troop train, 40 and 8.

"We formed in Italy. The reason I became a medic. I thought I would be an infantry man and they issued us rifles and everything else. They went down this list, 'We need four medics, Masamori,' and right on down the list, just alphabetical. 'Wait a minute, Sarge, I haven't been trained as a medic.' And he said, 'Well, you got basic training, first aid, didn't you?' I said, 'Yeah,' and he said, 'You're a medic.'

"When we got assigned to the unit, they said, 'All we want you to do is stop whatever bleeding, pour some of this sulfa powder on the wounds, and also if the person is in pain, to use one of these vials of morphine.' But he warned us, 'Don't use the whole vial because you are not dealing with 180- or 200-lb. men. You are dealing with people who are 125 lbs. Just give them half of that vial.' That's what my medical training was and unfortunately, soon after we got on line, in fact, the first day we got on line, I had to put my training into use.

"Our job was to stop the bleeding and, with the help of a couple of other people, litter them down the hill which wasn't the easiest task in the world. It was the Po Valley campaign, just north of Florence. It is very hilly. The first task was to bring down a forward observer with the 92nd division, which was an all-black division. They had held this line for four to six months without being able to penetrate beyond the German line. We were told they were a bunch of cowards and we said, 'No, under the circumstances and having grown up with that in California,' I said, 'I don't blame them for not wanting to fight for this country.'

"When you look at rescue in Bruyères, breaking through the line in the Po Valley campaign and Monte Cassino, the taking of Monte Cassino, all these things, it really makes you wonder. They certainly thought we were expendable. All the actions we had to go through, all the battles we were involved in, gives credence to that fact, that we were an expendable unit.

"Well, you can't feel that way on the battle field. You have a job to do. And as Mark Clark said, when he was asked by a reporter, 'Why do you continue to use the 442nd battalion?' And he said, 'Well, they get the job done.'

"When you think back on the circumstances, here we are fighting for our country, parents are in a camp in the US. I don't know that it takes courage. We were not given any choice. That's my fate, that's the cards I was dealt. I had to do the best I could with what I had.

"I used to carry this chip on my shoulder, I used to say, 'Why?' But you can't live with that kind of life. I think I've adjusted fairly well.

"After the war, I came back to Denver, my brother had gotten my folks out, so they were living here. Now I talk to students. I end up my talk, at the high schools, 'The world is yours now to shape and to understand other people.'"

Redress

By 1976, pressure from the Seattle chapter of the JACL (Japanese American Citizens League) led Gerald Ford to rescind Executive Order 9066. He signed "the American Promise," the first government document to recognize that the evacuation and internment was a mistake.[76]

After a ten year struggle, H. R. 442, the Civil Liberties Act of 1988, passed both houses of Congress. The bill condemned the government's wartime action and authorized monetary payments to individuals whose constitutional rights were violated simply because of their ancestry. Entitlement legislation was signed by President Bush in 1989, and the first payments were distributed in 1990.

Remembrance

February 19 is the Day of Remembrance, when persons of Japanese ancestry commemorate the day that Japanese Americans were deprived of their rights as citizens.

Another reminder of a shameful period in World War II history will be the ground-breaking ceremony for the Japanese American Memorial in Washington, D. C. in the autumn of 1999. The monument is designed by Davis Buckley, and the centerpiece will be a statue, by Japanese American sculptor, Nina Akamu, of two cranes, reaching for the sky as they try to free themselves from barbed wire. The memorial will honor the arrival of the first Japanese immigrants, recognize the valor of Japanese American soldiers in World War II and point out the unconstitutionality of Executive Order 9066.

End Notes

73   cited in *Time Magazine, 50th Anniversary Special*, December 2, 1991, p. 33
74   *Colorado History News*, March 1995, page 1, published by the Colorado Historical Society.
75   Pierre Moulin, U.S. Samurais in Bruyères, People of France and Japanese Americans: Incredible story, 1988, p. 200. Book out of print, lent by Tom Masamori.
76   Donna K. Nagata, *Legacy of Injustice*, New York and London: Plenum Press, 1993, p. 191

CHAPTER 20

COMBATANTS AND NONCOMBATANTS

*T*he peak strength of the armed forces during World War II was 72,835,500. The men on the battlefields shared traits, regardless of nationality: a belief in the righteousness of the cause; patriotism and commitment to their cause; an appreciation and a respect of military professionalism; comradeship and loyalty to the group; a kill or get killed attitude; and a capacity for diversion.

Righteousness of the Cause

Each country believed their fight was honorable. The Allies were fighting to preserve freedom and democracy. On D-Day, General Dwight Eisenhower referred to the invasion as "the great crusade." Russians were fighting "the great patriotic war" for the motherland and Stalin; Germans were fighting for a "new world order" which would restore Germany's past glory and secure what Germans were entitled to. Italians heard Mussolini's promise of the "reappearance of the Roman Empire" and Japanese wanted to make a new world among Asian countries which would free them from Western imperialism and embody Confucian righteousness.

Patriotism and Commitment

Betty Bangs taught high school in the small town of Carmi, Illinois. She remembered the boys would graduate and go right into the service. *"At that point, for them, this was a kind of a glamorous thing to do. So they were excited about doing it. They just enjoyed the people saying 'Oh, it's wonderful, how sad,' but they ate this up. They were eighteen and patriotism was strong then."*

One former navy man said, *"In World War II, people were convinced of the righteousness of their cause."* A soldier said, *"I'm glad to have done my part."*

Enemy soldiers felt the same commitment to their country and its cause and to their job. One British soldier described the mentality of the Japanese soldier, willing to fight to the death for the sake of the Emperor. "To be taken prisoner was unworthy of a Japanese soldier; Japanese honor meant 'never to be captured.'"[77]

That philosophy was confirmed by Midori Johnson who told the story of Japanese human torpedoes sent to attack Pearl Harbor.

"The day of the Pearl Harbor attack, there were ten torpedoes driven by the men. They attacked the American battleships and they would never be able to come back. But in Japan, it was announced, very, very openly in the newspaper: nine human torpedoes dispatched and sank American ships. There were ten people who went, one was captured, so he was the first POW of that war, never talked about in Japan. Nine were raised to war heros. There was an award created, so their families were honored, but not the one. Fortunately, he survived somewhere in the United States and came back to Japan after the war."

Karl Fuchs, a German tank gunner, wrote to his father at Christmas-time, 1939: *"What is uppermost in our minds this Christmas is adherence to duty to our beloved Führer and to our Fatherland to our last dying breath."* [78]

Professionalism

American soldiers who encountered German soldiers referred to them as "some of the best troops in the world." An American infantryman said, "They were hard-bitten, real professional fighters convinced of what they were doing."

Ludger Hartmer, a former German soldier who fought in Russia, recognized the competence of soldiers. "We soldiers did not hate the Russian soldiers or other soldiers. We were all just doing our job."

Comradeship

Joe Malcolm, a Marine, explained that troops watched out for one another in a squad and took care of one another. More than fighting for the United States, they were fighting for each other and they felt a great loyalty to their unit. That loyalty is illustrated in Lt. James B. Fisher, Jr.'s account of how he was shot down, captured and imprisoned because he returned to help a pilot friend in trouble. For his sacrifice, Fisher received the Silver Star.

". . . We had just moved up from the base in North Africa. After 50 missions, you usually got to go home. I was ready to come home, but I was shot down over the Gulf of Corinth on my 50th mission [8 October 1943].

"Our job this day was to bomb the airfield that was creating havoc out of Greece. My wing man on my left, Hartmeister, got hit and lost an engine. We were coming off the target, Eleusis Airfield at Athens, into a terrible rainstorm. I could see the storm building up. I knew he didn't have a navigator and I did. Hartmeister had been my co-pilot on the way over. We were friends. . . . I thought to myself, should I make it easy for the boy or not? Finally, I said to my other wing man that I was going back to cover Hartmeister and add my guns to his guns to ward off the German fighters. Also I told him to rejoin the group and head back to base.

"I was down there flying on Hartmeister's wing and going pretty slow because he had only one engine. About the same time that Hartmeister decided to ditch and before I could get back to my group, I was shot by a German Messerschmitt fighter and I lost my right engine. . . . I flew close to the water and stayed away from the shore. . .We were doing so beautifully that I had visions of getting back to the Adriatic on the western coat of Italy, and calling MAYDAY, so someone could come out and pick us up.

"That bubble burst when the gunner in the back said we were on fire. . . . We were going into the water. . . .

"When I went down to help Harmeister, I prayed that if anybody gets hurt, let it be me. My prayer was answered. I had a busted arm, a badly broken ankle and a head wound. . . ."

French Commando Gwenn-Aël Bolloré recalled that he owed much of his success during his training to his comrades. Whatever the athletic qualities of a candidate for the Commando unit, there always came a weak moment. If the trainee didn't become one with the group, the others would leave him on the side of the road. If the contrary were true, his comrades would come to his aid. In Bolloré's case, they carried his rifle, his back-pack, even drug him along in a coma to get him to the finish line.

Bob Bradfield, with the 30th Traffic Regulation Group in the South Pacific, described one incident in which the comradery went beyond help on the battle field.

"Our sergeant-major of our over-seas unit had a little nephew dying of brain cancer. They were trying desperately to operate and they needed blood. We were out in bivouac and he came through asking for donors. I think he had six donors so fast. Good infantry units were that way. The comradery, I felt very, very comfortable with it."

Kill or Be Killed

Soldiers weren't all nice; they weren't all heroes. On both sides, Allied and enemy, atrocities were common and almost accepted. In many instances, war brought out the worst in human beings. That was part of war. The conditions were: "You shoot first and ask questions later." Men were taught, not just how to shoot, but how to kill. It was a question of survival. And many former soldiers talked about how one became hardened to death, dehumanized and desensitized. It was often a matter of statistics, "Who got it last night?"

Stories are told about German and Japanese harsh treatment of prisoners of war; about Russian troops shooting and driving tanks through terrified mobs of people; about the looting and plundering in captured European cities. American soldiers would kill a Filipino for not doing something asked of him; Marines in the South Pacific would pull out a pair of pliers and wrench out three or four gold teeth from dead Japanese soldiers, collecting them as souvenirs.

War nurtured hate and that same hate was the impulse for some horrendous but tolerated actions, as explained by one officer, Fraser Richards.

"We captured some German soldiers and my sergeant, who hated them, asked if he could take them back in the rear areas. He took them back in the woods and shot them with a machine gun. And I knew it; I could hear it. When he came back, this is your frame of mind, I asked him if everything worked out all right and he said, 'OK,' and we moved on. That was the way it was."

Other soldiers were able to get beyond their hatred of the enemy. Jacob de Shazer was a prisoner of the Japanese for forty months. After the war, he returned to Japan as a missionary. Ivan L. Hobson saw action on Okinawa. After the war he returned to Okinawa as a civilian with the United States government to see if he could learn to help people he had been taught to kill, and he found his work rewarding.

Diversions

In training or in combat, soldiers enjoyed pranks and created their own recreation.

Glider pilot, Dave Trexler, recounted what took place at Fort Sumner where they lived in tents, with a mess tent and a latrine tent down at the end. *"Somebody with access to toilet seats had tacked the seats over the holes to make a fancy latrine tent. One moonlit night, one guy suffering from the 'GIs' came roaring in, plopped down on a white seat, only to discover that someone had moved the seats to where there were no holes."* [79]

Former soldiers talked about the great poker games in Saipan, the "Salerno punch" made of pineapple juice and pure alcohol, the nightclub in Bizerte called "Madame Pissedoff's."

"It was also amazing how people could respond after adversity," said Bill Bower. *"For instance, in Naples, somebody found a restaurant, took them some food and got it started. And it had been next to the opera. The opera musicians and singers had nothing to eat and we started to feed them. As a result they played for us, beautiful music. Up at Cassino [Italy], we were just raising the top at Cassino and everybody was having an awful time, but back here you would have a little bit of normal life. The horrors, that had prevailed when the fighting was going on, left and that would kind of regenerate everybody."*

Canadian John Young's corvette, the HMCS *Lunenburg*, escorted American troop convoys from Casablanca through the straits of Gibraltar to North African ports. He wrote an account of less than staid military conduct in December 1942.

"What started it I do not know. Perhaps it was the Christmas spirit of being in harbour even if it was Gibraltar. Perhaps it was the result of drinking the saved up tots to celebrate the season. One hardy and daring matelot, in a fine state, had gone ashore and had all his hair shaved off. Five of his 'boozem' buddies wanted to share his new found notoriety and had their heads also shaved.

"They were of the faith and of course had to go to Christmas mass for the midnight service. Drunk, disoriented and devoid of hair, they proceeded noisily to church. Of course they stirred up quite a lot of humour, which continued through the service as they sat in the front row where everyone could see their shining pates in the light of the shimmering candles. The poor priest was beside himself, but helpless to do anything about this bizarre situation, he recognizing that these hairless hooligans were Canadian by birth and crazy by nature as a result of their dubious citizenship."

Soldiers could invent ways to make military life more enjoyable. Charlie Poston, chief engineer on the *Billfish* told, what happened when the submarine crew figured out how to make Coca Cola and ice cream.

"So one time, the crew got a hold of jugs of Coca Cola syrup. So how are we going to have Coke with syrup. One of my sharp engineers, he says, 'We'll get a hundred pound of Co2. They brought that down and we strapped that up, put a hose to it, then they had a nozzle on it. They'd pour the syrup and put some water with it, then they'd take this thing like a cup of coffee and turn the Co2 in there and Coca Cola.

"Another group, they wanted ice cream so they went out somewhere (I had some good scroungers) they scrounged about five gallon and a half ice cream freezers, hand-crank. That was a good idea but how were we going to get ice? You couldn't make ice in submarines. Well, they go out and hook it up to the compressors down in the pump room and what they did was to make a salt solution and put it through the refrigeration system, hooked it in there, put the coils around the drums and they would crank up ice cream. You had some really sharp people who were just having a ball."

Noncombattants

The American Selective Training and Service Act contained provisions for conscientious objectors. It allowed exemption to any person *"who by reason of religious training and belief, is conscientiously opposed to participation in war in any form."*

Deferments were allowed to those in occupations necessary to the national

A Time to Speak

interest. Local draft boards passed on the claims of objectors, and men were placed in either noncombatant army training and service or assigned to work of national importance under civilian direction. To claim conscientious objector status, men were asked questions about their religious, ethical and political beliefs as well as practical questions, for example, "What would you do if your wife, mother, sister were attacked?"

The Society of Friends

A professor, now retired, joined a Quaker group working in Vichy, France. They provided supplies to concentration camps, to groups of children, and to refugees. When American military action in North Africa began, the Germans moved into southern France (the so-called unoccupied part of France), and the Quaker group had to abandon its work. Those unable to get out of France were imprisoned in Germany.

"I had some great grandparents who were Quakers. My own parents were not. My father was an agnostic, my mother was a Baptist. But through her I became a good friend of the Dean of the University of Chicago chapel where I went as a student and met some visiting Quakers. I decided I wanted to become a member of the Society of Friends. In 1934, when I went to Washington, as a graduate student who hadn't finished his dissertation, but had done everything else for a PhD, to save the country with the New Deal, I became a part of the Friends meeting there. I didn't join formally until the Selective Service act was passed. I, then registered as a conscientious objector and a Baptist. I was working in the Executive Office of the President and when they began to administer the Selective Service Act under the Selective Service rules, I was put in the classification of doing work of national importance. That meant that I wasn't obliged to perform any military service. In fact, my draft board didn't have to consider my statement as a conscientious objector. I was classified at a higher level.

"And then I remember one Sunday I walked back from a Friends meeting to my office down at the old Executive Office Building. All of the limousines were lined up outside. I went inside as usual and asked what was all the fuss and I was told about Pearl Harbor. I knew then that we were going to war the next day and I knew that I didn't want to stay on in the Executive Office with war being its principal aim. I told my boss, the head of the Bureau of the Budget. He said, 'Well, you can try to do something else if you want, but I will oppose it. You stay right here and work on non-war activities. There is lots to be done.' But I went to my draft board and asked for permission to go and work with the Quakers in Vichy, France.

"At that time, because there was an act of Congress that prohibited C.O.s from leaving the country, I got my draft board to let me go and do what they said

was 'work of national importance.' 'Well, we think this [work in Vichy] is important too, so we'll keep this classification.'

"So I did, in June of '42. There had been a Quaker group working there [Vichy]. It was English and American, but the English had been obliged to withdraw. There were only the Americans left in Vichy, France, along with Dutch, Norwegian and other neutral people that worked with us, as well as French.

"I was based in Marseille. I was well received, as people were at that stage, because we brought in large amounts of supplies, clothes and food. And we used it, impartially, in a variety of ways. We provided supplies for the concentration camps where part of the camps were Spanish, part were Germans and Central Europeans. We helped take care of a large number of colonies of children that were stuck in France. We tried to do helpful things for refugees. We had some little villages that had been deserted in southern France in the Midi. We converted one for refugees from the Lorraine and one for Spanish refugees.

"In Montauban, we ran a canteen where we fed about 1000 people every day. We had a school for Spanish children. For a while, it was run by the former minister of Education from Madrid, who was also a refugee.

"We had workshops. In some respects, the most interesting thing we had was a workshop in which we manufactured artificial limbs. In the camps where the Spaniards were confined (there were thousands of them), they could get out of the camp if they had a work permit. We ran our own farm where we kept some of them busy. We could be the intermediaries for them to get out and work for somebody. But if they had lost a limb or leg, they couldn't get such a permit. So we had this little factory which manufactured artificial arms and legs. All of the workers in the factory themselves had artificial limbs and legs. We had the lathes and the tools, and it wasn't very hard to get supplies for that purpose.

"For other things it was hard, getting food for people in camps was hard. One of the last things we did was bring in a big shipment, freight car full of beans from Romania. How we ever got them, I don't know.

"So we were running canteens, helping people in camps, children, workshops and so on. And I was stationed first in Marseille and I was up at Montauban which was the center for a large part of our activity. There were some camps up there and we kept in touch with some of the major camps like Gurs, Rivesaltes.

"One other very important thing we did. We sent a delegation, (I wasn't a member of it), to see Laval [member of the Vichy government] who permitted us to work to get refugees out of France. His view was, 'If you can get them out, do it!' But they had to have visas to get out. So, with various other groups, we would obtain the names of people and get in touch with relatives or friends in the United States or Argentina, who would stand behind their being given a visa. We were almost every week in the position of going into a camp and saying, 'A, B, C, here are your visas, let us help you get a train and get out of here.'

"The reaction of the French was quite remarkable because it wasn't uncommon to find French who didn't know what was happening at the camp just down the road, and who really didn't know what all that bunch of kids was that you had in there in that big house. 'Why were they there?' 'Well their parents had been eliminated or shipped off to Germany.'

"Laval was one who was sensitive to what was going on. He was not going to get in trouble with the Germans, so he made no objection. Toward the end, the Americans arranged with the State Department and with French authorities to ship about 1,000 Jewish children, who were located in various places, to the United States. In fact, a ship was booked, a Swedish ship that was to come into Lisbon. We got the names and addresses of all the kids that were to go, so we had a clear record that they could all have a visa and we had the train schedules worked out to ship them first from this place, then another.

"But just as the shipments were about to start, Eisenhower landed in North Africa. And the day he landed in North Africa, the Germans started in and within two days they had come down and taken over all Vichy, France. All this was stopped and we never did get any kids out. I was told later that the State Department knew this was going to happen and this was part of a conscious program to make the Germans think the US was not going to land then.

"The French, through the Swiss who immediately took over the American interests, ordered all Americans to go to Lourdes to be interned. And almost all of our folks did. There were two of us who decided we didn't want to and wanted to stay and make sure that all of the goods and the activities were transferred to suitable non-American groups. We organized 'Secours Quaker' which had been on the books, but we got it started and set up officially. And we moved all of the supplies off the docks in Marseille.

"The French Secret Police, (the Deuxième Bureau), advised us to get it off the docks before the Germans found out what was there. We did that. We got a whole train shipment allocated to take them up to a town in the Midi, Gaillac, which I had picked out as a geographer because of the fine transportation arrangements, and we got an estate requisitioned up there by the Prefect and put all of the stuff in.

"Two weeks later, the Germans and their staff moved into town. They had an independent analysis. They never paid any attention to us. I learned that the commanding general had been fed by Quakers, as a boy, after the first World War. Nobody ever touched us. Once he sent a guard over to call on me, and when the guard marched up in front of the estate, the fellows inside said, 'Gilbert, your time has come.' I always carried a knapsack, ready to go to a concentration camp. So I put on my knapsack and went out and saw the sergeant and in pretty good German I asked him what he wanted. He said that the general's toilet wasn't working and he understood that I had the only plumber in town who would know how to fix that. Could I loan him? I said yes I would on condition that they return him. And so he did. That was my total formal relationship with the Germans during the time I was there. We went on about our business.

"There was a good relationship with the French bureaucracy in Marseille and in the Midi. They had to do their job. When you went to a concentration camp like Les Milles which was outside of Gaillac, the head of the camp was French, and there was probably a German sitting in the back room, but they were not conspicuous. They just called the terms on what was done.

"Then in late February, the Deuxième Bureau *people with whom we were working, (they kept track of what people were doing, where they were escaping and the various escape routes), said 'We know the two of you want to get out of the country because you can't stay here very much longer.' We were the only Americans left. 'But all of the Americans are being taken to Portugal next week and you can join them if you can get there.'

"They said the train was ordered for 7:30 in the morning on a certain day, and so we packed our knapsacks and said good-by to all of our friends. We had already made arrangements for a complete transition. We went to Lourdes, said we wanted to join the Americans. We were told, 'They are in the hotel over there.' But the soldiers wouldn't let us in. We said we were Americans, but they said, 'All of the Americans are inside, you can't be Americans.' We finally convinced them, through the Swiss, that we could get in. We went in and saw the acting ambassador. He asked us what we were doing there, 'Why did you come? You are the only ones who haven't come. Why did you decide to come now?' We said we had information that he was going to leave the next day and we'd like to join him. He said, 'You have very good information, don't you?' He said, 'We are leaving tomorrow, but we are going to Germany, we are not going to Portugal. Take your bags down and be ready at 7:30 in the morning.' It was just as we had been told, but the train was going in the opposite direction.

"Then we spent thirteen months in Germany. We were interned in the American diplomatic group, 'in detention.' We were in a very fancy hotel, a golden cage. We were with the newspaper people and the Red Cross and all of the diplomats. And so we spent more than a year there and finally we were exchanged.

"One of our group, the correspondent of the Baltimore Sun *had been interned once before earlier in the war. When we got to Baden-Baden, where we were guarded by the Gestapo, this fellow said, 'We don't know how long we are going to

A Time to Speak

be here. We may be here the whole war. My advice is we try to establish a university here and keep ourselves busy.' So many people thought that was pretty good advice so we established a 'Bad-Heim University' and various people gave courses and took courses. We had a group of children with us. We had about a dozen children from Vichy. I taught a course in geography, one Quaker from TVA [Tennessee Valley Authority] gave a course in accounting. We all gave courses. The mistress of the Counsel from Marseille gave a course in French philosophy. We kept ourselves busy for a year.

"I was all right until the Germans came in and then it was very difficult for the French to understand why I was there because all of the other Americans were locked up except the two of us. I didn't understand the full import of their confusion until January 1946 when I was a member of a commission of the American Council of Voluntary Agencies and went into Germany to look at the conditions of German civilians.

"Six of us went in and, on the way out on a train from Frankfort to Paris, I was in a compartment with a colonel from the French Intelligence. He looked at me for a long time and we talked and he asked if I had been in France. In my terrible French, I said, 'Yes.' He said, 'I'd like to ask you a specific question. Where did you go the weekend of October 17?' 'Well,' I said, 'I'll tell you, but you have to tell me why you are asking. I went up to visit a children's colony up in the hills, but why do you ask?'

"'Well,' he said, 'I was a member of the underground [this was the Maquis]. I worked in the garage in Gaillac, and I took care of your car. I had to report every day on what you did because we were watching you very carefully and that was the one weekend I was never able to account for. I always wondered what you did that weekend.'

"So they knew exactly what we were doing. I talked a little with him and he obviously knew what I was up to the whole time and was able to report on what my relations were with the Germans. He said they really couldn't understand why I was there. So part of his job was to track me. They kept dossiers on people. They perhaps filed it away. Or maybe I would have had a serious accident. I operated above board as far as records were concerned and I didn't keep any confidential records. I had no notebooks, anything personal that I did. That was our decision. We didn't want to be in a position to have anybody pick up our papers to use them to our disadvantage. Why was I there? Why wasn't I in Lourdes with the other Americans?

"After the war, I was still with the Friends Service Committee in Philadelphia until the Asian War was over, then I went back to academe."

Defense Plants

Roland Wolcott's first war-time job was at Consolidated Aircraft Corporation in San Diego, known for their flying boats, called PBYs during war-time. He recalled the precautions taken to camouflage the plants, the plant blacked out, machine gun emplacements on the hillside above San Diego, and the parking lot covered with wire mesh and chicken feathers, painted to look like an open field.

"I was not in any military duty. I had left my college studies. I wanted to find a job there since my father had cautioned me very strenuously not to get into any police work or any war work or anything that would be of that nature, that we needed to be peaceful people. I did not become a conscientious objector at all, but I did look for a job in non-combatant area.

"I was in the engineering department, in what they called the release group. The drawings were made up by the design engineers and various other draftsmen, then after they had been approved, they had to be inspected and compared and so forth. A lot of work had to be done before they drawings were approved. When they were approved, then they were blueprinted and released for production. So that was my work. I worked there for a couple of years."

When they were setting up a new plant in New Orleans, Wolcott was transferred, where he worked for two years.

"The New Orleans plant, taken over from American Standard who were making bathroom fixtures, then converted during the war. At that time it was Consolidated Vultee who came in there. When I moved to New Orleans, I was involved with the P4Y and the PBY in both of its versions. And that's all the work I did in aircraft.

"It was kind of interesting work. I was a materials engineer and I was trying to have the engineers use the right materials that were available. I developed a standard parts catalogue, where the purchasing department wouldn't have to search out parts the engineers wanted if there was some already available. That was an important part of trying to keep the economy and their materials and supplies in a little better control.

"They always watched for sabotage anywhere, whether it would be inside or whether it would be an intruder. They had to watch within the plant, too, because there were people taking advantage, carrying things out, for instance. I remember one story. The guards would check you as you went out. One guy, according to the story, he wore his raincoat and he had ropes around his neck and he walked bow-legged and he was carrying an anvil between his legs. They caught him. But there were all kinds of things going on in there. The shop workers, they would do a lot of their own little things instead of making parts, fooling around, and they'd make toys.

A Time to Speak

"When I moved to Denver, it was Gates Rubber Co. and it was still war work ('44). My work there was involving drive belts (v-belts). They made lots of belts for war vehicles. I stayed at Gates until the end of the war." [80]

Lumbering

In the 1940s, Fraser, Colorado was a lumber town. Morris Long was born in a logging camp and started working in a logging camp at the age of thirteen. He worked for Koppers Company, first in Del Norte, Colorado in 1929, then transferred to Fraser. After working for the Ford agency in Granby, he returned to Koppers in 1944, to their logging and lumbering operation in Fraser, Colorado, where Koppers manufactured railroad ties and telephone poles.

In 1944, 200 German Prisoners of War from the main POW center in Greeley, Colorado, arrived in Fraser to work at the Kopper's logging and lumbering operation.

Since most men were either in the military service or in munitions work, Koppers was glad to get laborers, reliable German POWs who worked in the lumber camp as loggers, skidders, horse-shoers and carpenters. The Army was delighted to turn the work operation over to Morris Long.

The Army published a German-American dictionary of wood terms for wood workers which included phrases such as *Rufe Achtung wenn Baum fällt* (Always yell "timber"); *Schneiden Sie die dürren Äste* (Cut limbs off flush); *Die Klinge ist stumph* (The blade is dull) and common words, *Mannschafts Führer* (Crew leader); *Klotz* (Saw log); words for tools, *Axt* (Axe) and safety rules with pictures.

The government assured that the prisoners were clothed and fed. In fact, some civilians from the area remember that the prisoners had meat when they themselves couldn't buy meat.

"They, mostly sergeants and corporals, were captured at Anzio and were anxious to stay together. They lived in Army barracks. They had no physical freedom, but were in a prison compound with woven wire across the top. The gates closed at 10 p.m. and the Army had ten men to guard and be responsible for them.

"Actually, they were quite free, they worked as cutters, but a guard was also taken with a group. They had a place to play soccer and they organized a band. They were paid 75 cents per day which they could spend at the PX: smokes, beer, candy, gloves, soap and shaving cream. The Army was credited with the work they did.

"I was assisted by an interpreter, Rudi Prause. He was a college boy and knew English. We worked like father and son.

"I taught them the dimensions, how to load the lumber, the instructions for use of tools and equipment. By the second year, the prisoners ran the whole operation. Those who worked in the woods had to produce enough to meet the quotas of those who were cooks or tended the horses. We had the best operation of any camps in Wyoming or Colorado because the prisoners ran it.

"We did not use the men to drive logging trucks or to use the power saw, as the Geneva Convention rules prohibited the use of prisoner labor near hazardous machinery or near vehicles they could use for escape.

"When they loaded a carload of lumber, I told them they could quit for the day. They did have a secret cabin where they sometimes went and played cards. They were excellent carpenters."

Long said he discussed the jobs to be done each day. He put them on a point system, 400 points each team to cut strips. If they didn't perform, they would go back to Greeley. [Greeley was a major POW center for about 30,000 men]. The prisoners worked things out for themselves because they didn't want to lose their piano player for the orchestra they formed, so one team who finished quickly would help out somebody who didn't get enough points.

The carpenters were especially skilled and tended to build too carefully and well for the temporary camp buildings. Long remembered that when the mess hall burned down, he wanted it built a certain way, *"But the prisoners added ten feet because they thought the cooks needed more room. They really put one over on me."*

The prisoners were allowed to cook their own food, which often included German cakes. And Long frequently supplied them with fresh elk and deer (in season).

"At the time of the Allies' liberation of the concentration camps in Germany, the Army reduced their rations, cut out the choice meat and gave them more starchy food, beans, potatoes and poor cuts of meat. They blamed the Army, and for the first time, they felt abused. They weighed themselves, to prove they were going to lose weight, but they found they had gained because of the starchy food.

"They were friendly, I was never afraid to go in the barracks, and when I went by, everyone always waved. Everyday there was something - fun, sad, interesting - to report at dinner time."

Long found other ways to bend the rules for POWs. He arranged for them to see a movie in Fraser. They would goose step from the camp and sing German songs on their way to the movie theater.

Most of the prisoners were Catholic. *"I had Mother Gertrude from the Boulder Abbey who found a German-speaking priest who came up for services."* (After the war, Long and his wife sent CARE packages to the former POWs.)

Even with the available men in vital wartime jobs, the United States still lacked enough people in the work force to supply the demand for war materials.

End Notes

77 Interview, Imperial War Museum Sound Archive, John Hewlett Nunneley, #10203
78   quoted in *Sieg Heil!* , p. 45
79 Trexler stayed in the service and retired in 1974. He flew fighters in the first air-to-air combat in the Korean War in the Seoul area. In Vietnam, he flew F-4s, air to ground, carrying bombs. He is especially proud of the Gilder Museum in Terrel, Texas, east of Dallas.
80 Later Wolcott set up a food service distribution system in the mountains while his wife handled the bookkeeping. Now he is writing a family history.

CHAPTER 21

INDUSTRIAL MOBILIZATION: WOMEN IN THE WORK FORCE

The big change in wartime industry was that women were needed in the work force to replace the men who were drafted. In the United States however, attitudes toward working women were still traditional. In 1936, 82 percent of the population felt that wives should not work if their husbands had jobs.[81] Those who worked did so out of economic necessity as teachers and nurses.

Not all businesses and industries were eager to hire women or minorities. President Roosevelt, after returning from a tour of war plants, was impressed by the number of women doing skilled manual labor. He predicted that as more and more men entered the armed forces, the proportion of women working in war plants would increase. In a radio address, he tried to dispel the bias against hiring women and blacks, *"In some communities employers dislike to hire women. In others they are reluctant to hire Negroes. We can no longer afford to indulge such prejudice."*[82]

For most of the women, it was their first work experience, their first chance to earn their own money. They gained independence as they realized they could "do it." Many were away from families for the first time, sharing apartments with other women. They went from being naive, protected, and dutiful daughters and wives to being competent and self-reliant women. They valued their wartime experiences.

DEFENSE INDUSTRY
Rocky Mountain Arsenal

Sally Griffin, graduated from college in 1942, married a young man in the Air Corps in 1943 and came with her mother to "sit out" the war in Boulder, Colorado, her father's home-town. Like many women whose husbands, fathers and brothers were overseas, she described her city as a female world.

"Boulder was an interesting place during the war. There were very few men left in town. It was a woman's world here, let me tell you. There wasn't a family in town, whom I knew, who didn't have somebody who was involved in service in one way or another and most of them were overseas.

"Gene Wilson was one of the few men in town and we all just loved him. Poor Gene would be called to come when things arose such as malfunctioning furnaces and electrical problems. Wayne Nuzum held the town together. He was the

fireman for most of the coal furnaces in town. He would come by in the winter to shovel the coal and shake something you used to shake on the old coal furnaces and to see that everything was all right. And he had mammoth job because there were no men left in town to do these sort of things.

"*I got a job at the Rocky Mountain Arsenal, a chemical warfare base, run by the Chemical Warfare Service. I chose it because it was a wartime job. I wanted to help. Wartime jobs were fun. There was a spirit behind it that kept you going. I did not work on the manufacturing line at the plant where the gases were made. I had a secretarial job in the administration building because I could type.*

"*It was an interesting time, fraught with a lot of heartache, tremendous losses that people endured, that are hard to remember.*" [83]

DEFENSE INDUSTRY
Consolidated Vultee

Women often worked side by side with men. Although she worked at the same plant as Roland Wolcott and later married him, Jewell Wolcott said, "*I had this big drafting table, and I sat on a high stool. We were all lined up, and he had to pass by to get a drink. So you get to know each other.*"

Her work at Consolidated Vultee was in a different section and she described the work from a woman's perspective.

"*I graduated from high school in 1937 and then I worked a few odd jobs as secretary and office work and that sort of thing. The women got a taste of what it was like to earn their own money, have their own paycheck, and I'll tell you, it went to our heads. When I got my first job, which was right out of high school working in a woolen factory, doing stenographic work, I bought things from any salesman who came to the door because I had no experience in earning my own money. I was really gullible. I remember those days.*

"*Then war was declared, and the men had to go off to war and there was no one to build the bombers and the equipment that they needed, so the government asked the women if they would come in and do some of this work. So we all remember "Rosie the Riveter," that type of person who did the actual construction.*

"*Well, I went to a class for maybe about three months, six months, I'm not sure how long it was, and studied engineering drawing, drafting. So I drew the parts, and assemblies and blueprints were made from that, and the blueprints were sent down to the shop where "Rosie" took over. So after my education, I went to Consolidated Vultee. I made drawings for PBY planes that could land on water.*

"*And of course, we as women, came into the plant with a bunch of men who were still there and not required to go into the military because somebody still had to build these things. They were there and of course, we took a lot of guff from* them. I can't remember some of the things they did, but they played real tricks on us. But we survived. They would probably have done it to any newcomer, a little more so to the women because they thought we were more gullible.

"The girls got together a team to play soft ball on our lunch hour. And so the men got on it, and of course, they took over because they could throw the ball faster and harder and hit harder than we could. So they just broke up the game. It's like school grounds.

"There was a comradery among men that did not exist between women. However, we were very close. We understood each other's problems very nicely. However, there was this bridge, this gap between the workers, like the riveters and the welders who were women and the women who were upper echelon. We did not associate with them. Whether it was that we did not talk the same language, I don't know, but I distinctly remember. I cannot tell you the name of a person who worked actually building the planes and yet it was right in the same place. We were upstairs, they were downstairs. Of course, they were in a two-story area and we were in another area.

"We were the newcomers and the pay had nothing to do with sex or gender. A man had been there before and he would have made more. We were just beginning so we would have been the lowest paid. "Rosie the Riveter," who had been there longer than I, probably made more money that I did. She might have made more anyway. She was an important person, building the plane.

"I found the work fascinating. I really enjoyed it. I think I was proud of the work I did and I was proud that I was contributing to the defense of our country.

"So I worked there, actually a total of nine months because that's where I met Roland and when he was asked to come to work at Gates Rubber in Denver, then I came along with him. And we have lived here ever since. I enjoyed it. I felt it was my duty. I did it willingly and I have never done that type of work since.

"During World War II, everyone was proud to contribute to the war effort. There was no bickering, there was no group of people who said this was wrong, we should not do this. Everybody just towed the mark willingly. We didn't gripe. It was just what was expected of us and we did it. We were proud of it, a far different cry from the Vietnam War.

"We were married in 1944, and then I became a housewife as we did in that day. I did not go back to work until in the '70s when my children were nearly well grown. So you see how long I was at home." [84]

DEFENSE INDUSTRY
Boeing Aircraft

Turza Briscoe Pflug graduated from the Colorado Springs High School in 1943 and took a job with Boeing Aircraft.

"*A friend and I had both been in drawing class at high school and Mr. Albrecht said we were qualified and would be good candidates to go to Seattle to work for Boeing if we so desired after graduation in June 1943. We applied and got a place to train to go to Seattle.*

"*I left after my 18th birthday, after 13 November, 1943. And of course, my folks gave the conductor so much money to watch over their poor little girl from the hinterlands who was going away. And I had an upper berth which was a real experience.*

"*I arrived in Seattle the next morning real early and I'll never forget the feeling as the train approached Seattle. I passed by Boeing Aircraft Company, big hangars, and I was so surprised because they had little towns built on top of them, to show up from the air as cities because they were trying not to show where the aircraft companies were in case of bomb attacks. These little towns, the houses were probably no larger than a shower stall and they had net over the top of them. It was just like a little toy town. I was surprised to see miniature towns atop airplane hangars.*

"*The street lights were dimmed by paint, cutting out half the light, paint on the top. It was dark, but they were afraid of someone coming in and bombing. Of course, since then we've heard where they* [the Japanese] *did come in. They found places where fires were started.*

"*I started to work immediately. Shortly after that they moved us to the Volker Building in down town Seattle to work on drawing, on drafting. Now our drawings, were very, very long, but they were rolled up. But they were on vellum which is a very fine linen covered with a covering. Of course they checked to make sure that no one was carrying out squares of linen, because if they would soak it out, they would have a very fine piece of linen for a handkerchief.*

"*We'd roll these along our drawing tables and these drawing tables must have been 10 feet by 4 feet, and the drawings themselves extended much, much beyond that. One person at a table; I worked by myself.*

"*Shortly after we got there, we had an opportunity to apply for a scholarship at the University of Washington and my friend and I both got a scholarship. It was not the same thing as regular college, they were people who were working for Boeing. It was two different types of calculus, strength of metals. That was sort of fun for about a semester. We went half day to the university and half day to work.*

We worked nine or nine and a half hours a day, I'm not sure which it was, but on the sixth day, we got off after only eight hours.

"After the university work was finished, we moved to the main plant. I started working for flight test analysis. I worked on a monometer board which showed the pressures on different parts of the plane after a flight test.

"My cousin had gone out to Seattle earlier. Every week, we'd take one night a week and we'd meet in the University district and we'd have dinner together. But it was terribly wearing and terribly tiring, not much play time. Saturday seemed like a vacation because we only worked eight hours.

"Time was so precious, we were trying to do as many planes as we could. Of course, the B-17 was the one we were working on at that point. Our work was preliminary to putting together the planes, done by 'Rosie the Riveter.'

"I walked along the catwalk and watched them working ['Rosie the Riveters']. Mostly women, but also midgets because they could get into the wings and do the riveting whereas people of normal size can't.

"When I came home for vacation, my dad was so afraid that I would go back and not finish college. So I sent my badge, all the things they needed on my special employment, by special mail and retired or resigned and stayed here [Colorado Springs]. I started at Colorado College in November 1944.

"I think I would do the same thing again. It was a good experience. It gave me the freedom I felt I needed. You know kids that age needed to get away. I came from a family that built in me their values. I knew what they expected of me, I lived them.

"Our experiences were not adventurous, but we thought we were doing something worthwhile." [85]

DEFENSE INDUSTRY
Pratt-Whitney

Dolores Divine's wartime job was only the first of many jobs she has held.

"I had many jobs and I felt each one was a life experience. I worked at Pratt-Whitney in Kansas City. We made the WASP engine that was in all the big bombers. That was the only thing we made and that was quite a place. There were 77 acres under one roof. To me, at that time, it seemed like an awful big building. It took me a half an hour to walk to my department after I got off the bus.

"My family lived on a farm at that time, in Lenexa, 71 miles south of Kansas City. My husband was in the Army and I had gone back home; and I needed to be busy and I needed to work.

"I worked the second shift, from 3:30 p.m. to midnight. When I first went there I was on a turret lathe and what we made on the turret lathe were the tools that were used in making these engines. They made their own tools. And of course, they had a precision inspection and that's where I went the next time. And I was there in school and trained as a teacher in this particular kind of inspection. But when I finished, they did not have an opening and I went to the magnetic inspection. They called it magne-flux. And the parts were magnetized, and then dipped in a solution of iron and oil. And if you took that, you could see the cracks or particles that shouldn't be there because there would be two deep holes set up there for the magnetism and that should show you that there were things there. It was a neat way to find flaws in metal: to magnetize it and then inspect it.

"My particular parts that I did, knuckle pins and push-rods. The knuckle pins were probably about 18 inches long and about the size of my thumb and they were hollow. But the inspection I did was the final inspection and the piston pins were silver plated.

"For the inspection, those motors were all put together and run for 72 hours, then they were taken down, part by part, and all of them were re-inspected. And I did the final inspection on those two pieces.

"I took my inspection very seriously and a lot of people did not. Six o'clock, pay day and they were through. And I felt that if I missed a flaw in one of these parts, a plane crashed and people were killed, I might just as well have taken a gun and shot them. I really felt a concern about doing the job well. And that was a part of our bringing up. I still remember my inspection number. It was B-25. I didn't want my inspection number to show up on some faulty part.

"I considered it a good experience in my life. That was really my first real job. I had lived at home until I was married, then when my husband went in to the Army, I went back home again, so I had never really been on my own. And that was my first experience of being alone. It was a good experience. We all have to have that first job.

"I shared an apartment with a lady who had a little boy about two years old whose husband had gone into the army, so she was quite happy to have someone with her. She did not work outside the home. There weren't nearly as many places for children as there are now.

"When I think back to the wages I made, I don't see how I hardly afforded that ticket to go home to Lenexa every weekend. I made $2.05 an hour, that was my time and a half. And I thought I was filthy rich. I was earning my living, I had to have rent and groceries and utilities and things like that. And I did save money. I collected $100 bills, I liked those very much. I bought a fur coat that I'd never had before and had always wanted one and a few things that I really did want. And I bought gifts for my family and things for my home when my husband would be home.

"There were slackers then and I think part of it was, that it was big money. We had older women that worked, women who had never worked before in their lives outside their home. But who could resist all that money?" [86]

DEFENSE INDUSTRY
Redwood City Factory

Leeta Crook, a primary school teacher, enrolled in a shop training course to prepare people to take wartime jobs and worked during the summers.

"In this war, so many women went into work. With so many of our men gone, women took over so many of the jobs that men had done. A lot of women went in who had never worked before because the men were gone and there were openings. Women began to realize how much they could do, if you gave them the opportunity.

"I went out to California and stayed with relatives in Menlo Park and I drove back and forth from Menlo Park to Redwood City to a factory, making parts for airplanes. I had a machinist's grade. I got the machinist's pay but I worked wherever they needed help.

"I worked there two summers, and there's where I felt rich, getting money from school and a machinist's pay was one of the best and I got good pay for the work I did. I had more money then and less things to spend it on than I had ever had before. I bought myself a suit.

"I started out working cutting leather washers and I'd cut them with a diamond cutter. That is what I did at first. We did the leather cutting all day long. If anything went wrong, you just sat there until somebody could come along and fix it for you. You wasted an awful of time. That amazed me. We had been taught and trained in fixing our own machines if something went wrong. I could have fixed my machine more than once, but I didn't dare touch it as it was a union factory.

"Then I worked in one spot and we sat around and we had to sort these parts, little ones, and so forth. It was fun for me because I knew I was going back. I didn't mind it, but I thought how awful I would feel if I had to spend all my life doing that type of work. Then they put me on the conveyor belt. I couldn't take it, I darned near went down the conveyor belt with everything that was on it.

"The nurse was going to take her vacation and she was going to be gone two weeks and I had had training in first aid. And I got to work in the nurse's office for two weeks and it was fun. We could just take care of little things. Anything that was at all serious, we had to recommend.

"I went to work at 4 o'clock in the afternoon and got off at midnight. We had time off to eat. The department I was in (leather department, we took our lunch in a sack and someone every night would bring the dessert. They always had a big

A Time to Speak

picnic in the summer for all the war people. And did they ever drink beer. I learned an awful lot.

"When I left, they gave me as a gift, the book, A Bell for Adano. And there was a little German lady that worked. I noticed she was alone a lot, but I didn't think too much about it. I used to visit with her. And when I left, she gave me a loaf of bread because she said, 'You were so good to me,' she said, 'All the rest of them looked down on me because I was German.'

"It was an experience that I'm glad I had because I met people I would have never been around or known or seen, all different ways of living. And I said, I really got an education. I learned more dirty jokes that you could imagine. I couldn't remember a darned one of them. But you know it was worth it. I was always glad I had that experience." [87]

Wartime Office Work

Manufacturing companies which converted to war-related work needed young women to fill the extra clerical jobs. Three women from the midwest remembered their contribution to the war effort.

Steno-Clerical Worker

Bernice Janssen, at age nineteen, was invited to come to Indianapolis to stay with an aunt who advised her to look for an office job. Her aunt believed that although girls were making enormous salaries in factories, afterwards those factory jobs would be given back to the men.

Her aunt advised her on just the "right clothing" for job interviews and the importance of having all of her references and samples of her work - stencils, dittos. "I had a purple jersey dress, not bad at all for work, at least it was dark."

Mrs. Janssen found her letters which her mother had saved. At the U. S. Employment Office, among several offers, she chose to work for Curtiss-Wright, an airplane manufacturer. Excerpts from her letters [with no changes in punctuation or spelling] give a glimpse of her wartime office work and social life.

Nov. 12, 1942 ". . . But I really do think I have a grand opportunity in this organization. . . . By the way my salary is 22.50 a week for five days 8 hrs. a day. Saturday is compulsory with time and a half making my weekly salary 28.60 and my monthly 123.90. Not bad, eh. And our working conditions are perfectly marvelous. Everything is brand new — and lots of everything. They get priorities galore you know. And the cafeteria — well, it is almost worth working there just for that. I pay about 40 cents a meal and get a perfectly scrumptious one.

"I like the work just loads and there is just oodles of room for advancement. They have plants all over the country.. And I asked him about after the war work and the man said that he believed the factory would run at full speed then too. I'd not be working myself up to dismissal after the war. . . I'm a 'steno- clerical' worker.

"My wages will come in one a week — and then I'm going to save 10% in war bonds, give Aunt Lois $20 on the loan, spend about 35 or 40 for food. You can't get anything down town without paying 65 cents a meal, about 10 for rent I guess, about 20 for clothes and 4 or 5 for carfare with a little for shows and church."

Nov. 26, 1942. "Well, today is Thanksgiving. I'd scarcely know it tho, it's just like another working day.— I did get me a real nice dinner today tho — had the swellest chicken mixture in a pastry cup with mashed potatoes and gravy, cranberries, real good muffins, and a large piece of coconut cream pie. . . . I'm going to be in the Waltz Girl's and Parade Girl's Numbers in this big stage production of Curtiss Wright. All proceeds are going to the U. S. O, while the producer is being paid $1200 by the company. He was brought in from N.Y."

Christmas Day, 1942. "The man who drives me to work in the morning invited the other girl and me to dinner today so we really had our food over at the cafeteria and didn't shell out a cent. He also bought a large box of candy and one of cigars to keep on his desk for today.

"We got out at four today. Marvelous, isn't it and even got a ten dollar bonus. But then we have to work New Year's day. . . . Well today is Christmas and we're listening to Basil Rathbone playing Scrooge."

January 13, 1943. "We went roller skating again Monday night. . . . Am enrolling at I. U. Extension tomorrow night for Spanish. . . ."

January 23, 1943. "The course cost 12.50 and my textbook was 1.45 I'll get 2 1/2 college credits tho. . . . But I shan't take anymore this semester as I would like to take a dancing lesson or two sometime and then do as so many of the girls have been urging me to —to join the U. S. O. and go out to the various dances. I guess the girls are pretty busy if they attend all as they have one somewhere almost every night. They're held in different places and by different organizations but wherever the soldiers are invited, I guess the U. S. O. girls are too. They have a sponsor for each girl who calls them up by turns and special invitations are then given out. It sounds like fun."

February 10, 1943. "Wish I'd bought another pair of shoes for spring before the shoe rationing went into effect. Under ordinary circumstances, tho, I guess most everyone will be able to manage with the three allowed a year . . . I bought a new black Chesterfield coat. . . . I'd hunted for some (dresses) Monday night - the only time I get for shopping and my gosh, there just isn't anything worth bringing home. Everyone has more or less gone hording mad as there's a terrible selection to choose from for us poor defense workers who can't get down for the first picking. Even if we had the selection of goods available, well, my gosh the

A Time to Speak

quality seems to me is perfectly awful for the price we have to pay. Aunt L. brought a 15 dollar dress, tried it on and was disgusted.

"... Got a couple of good books — "The Lady Means Business" and "The Woman You Want to Be" — both seem to be of a nature that will really help me get ahead in business. If I can only find time to read them now."

February 17, 1943 "... Curtiss is organizing another skating club— meets and skates costing us only 30 cents."

July 1, 1943 "Just a line to tell you I broke the news yesterday and really started quite a commotion here at work. . . . I won't have any trouble getting my release and availability papers, I don't think, as my reason is a change of residence. Sooo, July 10th, I shall pull up stakes here."

After reading the letters, Mrs. Janssen commented:

"My two aunts were writing my mother telling how I was getting along. It was a very protected life, but it was a very happy time. I know I loved my work. It gave women a taste of the work world and it brought that freedom." [88]

Young, Foolish, and Patriotic

Mary Mulhollon and Bernice Mittig, from a farming family, grew up Wisconsin. Young and energetic, they were ready to do their part, working in plants that converted to wartime activity. They looked back on their experiences and impressions of the war days: no dates, no nylons, but patriotism and commitment to the war effort were hallmarks of midwestern attitudes.

Mary Mulhollen: *I had known my husband-to-be since I was fifteen. The war was in December, and he went into the Army Air Force in January. Looking back, I think it was an injury to me that I was deprived of what I thought were the normal activities of dating. All the boys were gone. Being so young, seventeen at that time. I thought it was a great sacrifice, you could only get silk stockings. And really it was nothing. It was so minor.*

And I went to work at Cutler Hammer and it was a war-time job. And we were all finger-printed, investigated by the FBI. We were really very patriotic, and anything we could do we did. So Cutler-Hammer, my husband's folks had worked there. So I thought I could help in some way. They made controls for the submarines and war-time things like that.

I joined the Red Cross, and every week we went and rolled bandages for the wounded. We mailed lots and lots of packages to the service men. I had a girl friend who would bring home boys from the U. S. O. for dinners and we would entertain them. I was just a young girl and my main thing was writing letters. We didn't have the boys around. It was mostly girl activities.

We were engaged during the war and we were married in '45 before the war was over. He wanted me to come to California in the worst way to get married. I was such a mother's baby. I was old enough. But my mother and father just didn't like the idea of me leaving home and going to California and getting married out there. They wanted us to wait until the war was over. Anyway, he got a very short leave and he came home and wanted to get married. But he had to ask my father's permission to get married. They thought the war was already over in Europe and they figured it would be OK. I wouldn't have dreamed of defying them, saying I was old enough.

Bernice Mittig: I was that much older than Mary. I was in school. And I had two brothers who were in the service. My brother was working at the Allen Bradley Company and I was working in a little dime store in West Bend. And gas rationing was on and my brother said, 'Why don't you come to work with me? You drive one way, I drive the other way'. I said, 'OK, but I don't know how I'll work out on that because I like to meet and talk with people.' To work in a factory wasn't my thing.

I had one younger brother at home who was going to be deferred because you were allowed one son to stay home on the farm. So he stayed home on the farm and I went out to work.

I went to Milwaukee to work in the Bradley Company and I wasn't just too happy to work in a factory, but I worked at machines that I didn't really care for. And finally one of the managers and supervisors came up to me and asked me, 'Would you like to work in the office?' I said, 'I really don't have much training, but I would be willing to go to school for that.' So I went to school and took shorthand and typing.

Then I finally got a job in the office, but it was a war plant. We were on security. You had to be checked in and when you went out again, there was someone watching that you weren't just somebody off the street.

I really enjoyed working in a plant where we had government inspectors coming to check our work. We had a very good social program, we had our own band; you could join the band, you could join the basketball club. There were little USO groups that would entertain the boys. We had these activities at Allen Bradley. We had these women drill teams. If I had lived in Milwaukee, I would have liked to participate. As it was, it was twenty-four miles to work every day.

That was the best part of my life, that job. They made cards for Singer Sewing machines, they made switches and big control panels for ships. When my brothers came back, they both came to work there. I was so serious about my job. I worked there seven years.

Life on the farm was not that easy. The gas rationing was definitely difficult for us. My father had quite a few tractors and it went according to how much *acreage you had on the farm, how much gas you were allowed. We had 100 acres.*

You would come to Milwaukee to the stockyard, your grain went to elevators. Of course, my father raised a lot of potatoes and red beets. The government used a lot of red beets for servicemen, peas, beans, potatoes and grain. Especially the canning factories were after the farmers for red beets, peas and beans, navy beans.

The farmers would take their produce right to the factory, a lot of them would take it with horses, horse-driven you would haul it to the factory. They had German prisoners of war, they had housing for them and they made them work in the factories. They were actually well-off compared to our prisoners of war. These fellows had nice living quarters, they had nice jobs. Being a German area, they sort of accepted them. Everyone spoke German out here. The Lutheran churches all spoke German.

My husband and his family were into dairying. I had been dating my husband at that time and he was a farmer. He was deferred due to the fact that he was the only son at home, so he could farm with his parents. They didn't have enough land to raise more than their cattle would eat. You had to get your cows into production. The government needed everything. I remember my father saying, 'Don't be so heavy on the milk, we have to ship our milk.' [89]

CIVILIAN NURSES

The Surgeon General's office and the hospitals appealed for nurses to work during and after the war.

Cadet Nurse Corps

Some young women were attracted to nursing for its heroism, like Sister Damian Mary Simmons.

"I went into nurses training and became what they called a cadet nurse. We had the cadet nurse corps and we had uniforms. It was wonderful and they treated us as if we were in the service. We got into the movies free, we could ride on the street cars free and all kinds of privileges that other people didn't have. And I remember the reason I went into nurses' training rather than taking a music scholarship at Drake was because I saw a movie with nurses. Veronica Lake was in it and Paulette Goddard. It was called Victory something. Anyway I just remember her in one of the battles, where the Japanese were attacking this one camp and she put a hand grenade under each arm and walked into the Japanese and blew them to bits. And I thought, any nurse that can do that - I wanted to be like her." [90]

City Hospital

Katherine Welch started nursing school in September 1943 because she wanted her contribution to the war to be a healing one and not a military one. Her account is revealing for what it tells about the state of medicine in the 1940s, which was limited because of the medical needs of the Armed Forces.

"By the time I arrived at Yale, the Yale Unit had left. It left soon after Pearl Harbor. It was the second medical unit to be called up. It ripped the Yale-New Haven Hospital of physicians, nurses, lab technicians. Unlike Harvard, which used several hospitals, it was very devastating to Yale's one hospital. We didn't start working in the wards for perhaps six or eight months, but when we did get on the wards, it was a rat race, so little help, so much to be done and very poor equipment.

"About a year and a half into nursing school, the US government started Cadet Nurse Corps. By that time, we had paid most of our tuition and I didn't want to be committed into going into the military. Our class graduated in January of '45 and I was head nurse from '45 to '46.

"New Haven had a large military industry, especially the Winchester arms, so all the non-skilled labor that might have been working in the kitchens, working in the wards, being orderlies, were receiving comparatively high salaries and had deserted the hospital. We did have some very nice volunteer people from the community who were nurses' aids and men who pushed stretchers, an elderly man who pushed stretchers and one thing and another. But it was a wartime hospital at its worst, from a civilian point of view, because it was so under staffed.

"And the equipment was terrible. Today's nurses can't imagine what we had to deal with. Every single needle had to be filed because they had burrs on them. Then they had to be put into the sterilizer; every syringe had to be washed and then sterilized. The way the nurses do it today is so simple. Of course it is not as ecological. Even the bedpans and wash basins were scummy because there was no easy way to sterilize them. They did get sterilized. The nurses had to do everything, sterilizing, preparation, and we gave the first penicillin. There were four hospitals in the country that were given penicillin in 1943 which was used only for osteomyelitis. We had a whole huge ward of men who were mainly skin and bones and we were supposed to take three inch long needles and put them into their muscles every two hours around the clock, day after day after day after day. It was pretty gruesome. These people had been in the hospital already months and months. And this is their one hope of getting out of the hospital. And that's the way penicillin was given.

"One of the things that was most frustrating were the safety pins. They were all rusty. And in those days we had to put all the newborns and sick babies in diapers, heavy cloth diapers. It was all you could do to get the safety pin through the fabric and get it pinned up, also not jab the baby or yourself.

"Of course, there was rationing. And I think the hospitals bought very little equipment during the war. What was made went to the troops. The need was much greater. In the civilian hospitals they were desperate for trained people. The minute I got through nursing school, I was a head nurse. That would never happen during normal times. I was the head nurse on the men's orthopedic and neurology ward. It was the only ward in the hospital that had a paid orderly. We had an elderly orderly who somehow or other managed to turn over the body cast. Medical students did a lot of work on the 'old men' as we called them in those days.

"All food was rationed, oleo, sugar, meat. And I think we did what we did in the civilian hospitals and never thought of complaining. We all had friends who were going through terrible times.

"In New Haven, I was inside a building all of the time. No air conditioning, hot as hades. One of the jobs the nurses did in the O.R. was to mop the brow of the surgeon so perspiration wouldn't drop into the wound. It was unbelievably hot and buildings weren't built to be well insulated from the heat.

"The patients were all civilians and since there weren't very many young around, they tended to be fairly old. So there tended to be a number of prostate operations and the old men would hobble around carrying their bottles. It was something, that's all I can say. We worked terribly long hours. We were supposed to be working eight-hour shifts, but you never got through. You were racing the whole time, supposed to be giving a bath here, something there, and you had to do your charts. You never got away, two hours afterwards maybe and you were dead tired. It was just very high pressure.

"The undergraduate part of Yale had been taken over by the Army or the Navy, so the undergraduates and the medical students were walking in uniform and in platoons. The medical students were all in barracks and they were pretty well marshalled in what they could do. They got some time off. There was very little social life between the medical students and the nursing students.

"Bill Welch came at one point and you might have a date from getting off at 1:00 in the morning until 4:00 in the morning, every night for a week and then he would be gone.

"In the war years, medicine was still primitive. The first use of sulfa drugs was in 1937, and it was experimental. There were no new supplies for hospitals during the war as they all went to armed forces. Wartime budgets for state hospitals were at a minimum existence level.

"TB was a dreaded disease. Hospitals had isolation wards for polio where *the patients' limbs were wrapped in hot towel compresses, and the limbs steamed; patient in iron lung; there were lots of very sick children, for example, from whooping cough. There were children hovering between life and death.*

"Student nurses had to spend time in the psychiatric ward of Connecticut State Hospital in Norwich. The patients were treated like cattle; their diet was soup and bread (with no butter). And the nurses' job was to walk them. Now, in the last ten years, we have made advances.

"During the war there were a lot of jobs that needed to be done and there were no men to do them. And women got the chance. And I think women in the services, even though they were separated from the men, I think they began to get confidence that they could get good jobs." [91]

Women's entry into the work force not only contributed to the Allied victory, but helped the women achieve self-confidence in their own abilities to do whatever they chose to do in the post-war period.

End Notes

81 Sherna B. Gluck, *Rosie the Riveter Revisited, Women, the War and Social Change*, Boston: Twayne Publishers, 1987, page 8
82 *The New York Times*, 13 October 1942, p. 5
83 Sally Griffen retired from her job with Boulder Travel but continues to work part-time when she has a chance.
84 Jewell and Roland Wolcott moved to Boulder and studied at the University Colorado.
85 After her children were in school Turza Pflug taught mathematics and later fifth grade.
86 A widow since she was thirty-six years old, Dolores Divine worked many different jobs until she moved into a retirement center.
87 Leeta Crook, 91 in 1996, has retired from teaching, but stays active with church groups and her bridge club.
88 Mrs. Janssen lives in Mequon, Wisconsin where she is a Christian Science practitioner.
89 Mrs. Mulhollen and her husband celebrated their 50th wedding anniversary in 1995, with three sons, seven grandchildren and four great-grandchildren. After fifty-two years on the farm, Mrs. Mittag has now settled in a retirement center.
90 Sister Damian taught Health and Wellness at Loretto Heights College in Denver. She died in April 1995.
91 Mrs. Welch's volunteer work has been health-related, the Community Hospital, Planned Parenthood, and she is president of the Hemlock Society of Colorado.

CHAPTER 22

WOMEN IN THE ARMED FORCES

There was a critical need for women in the military services. In 1943, at the height of war activity, the need seemed more pressing and women were offered a chance to serve their country.

More than 265,000 American women joined the Armed Forces, including the Women's Army Corps (WAC), Navy Women's Reserve (WAVES), Coast Guard Women's Reserve (SPARS), Women Airforce Service Pilots (WASPS), Army Nurse Corps, Navy Nurse Corps and Marine Corps Women's Reserve.

They took over jobs that enabled men to be released for combat and worked as everything from clerks to airplane mechanics. They learned to march, to have rifle practice and to find romance.

Their motives were primarily patriotic; most of the women in the service never intended to make the military their career. From a personal point of view, it opened up opportunities to women and gave them a chance to do something that had never been done.

SPARS

The Coast Guard recruited 10,000 women during World War II, most of whom were assigned to office and clerical jobs to free office-bound men for active duty.

One of the thirteen original SPARS was Elizabeth Lipstreu.

"The Coast Guard in wartime went under the Navy Department. They were under the Revenue Service in peace time, the Treasury Department. They decided then to start the SPARS as the Women's Reserve of the Coast Guard, as the WAVES were the Reserves of the Navy. And this was 23 November, 1942 that it was approved by Congress. They had a group of WAVES, who had trained at Northampton who transferred to SPARS, which gave them a nucleus to start with.

"Then they brought thirteen of us in who were civilians, no military training whatsoever. People who had been recommended got a letter or a telegram. As it turned out, the person who was the first commanding officer of the SPARS, Dorothy Stratton, had been Dean of Women at Purdue University where I had been. But this was the telegram that I got, with the commission, the approximate pay, uniforms, travel, if you qualified.

"Dorothy Stratton was the one, I think, who came up with the name of SPARS which is 'Semper Paratus, Always Prepared' and that is the SPARS.

"We were from all over the country, an interesting group of people [the original 13]: one of them had been an actress, another had been a dean of women, a head of resident halls, both at Purdue, one from St. Louis who had a real responsible job. I had been out of college two years by that time and had done Girl Scout field work. These thirteen people were going to command and be sent out to who knows what.

"So I went down to Detroit and this time I had to go to the Coast Guard office because they had the papers for swearing me in. I went into this office and the man in charge had been in the Coast Guard for a long, long time, although he hadn't been an officer for very long. It threw this recruiting office into a tizzy, a huge room with all of these men typing up papers for enlisting men in the Coast Guard. So when he finally called the Cleveland district office and got instructions to swear me in and send me off to the Coast Guard Academy, he drew himself up and said, 'Attention,' and all these men stood up until I was sworn in.

"The first officers began training at the Coast Guard Academy on 10 June, 1943 for three weeks, giving it to us as fast as they could, trying to make military people out of us in three weeks for a bunch of civilians who had been out there working. That says something about the kind of days we had and what we did - learning to march which was pretty funny. There were an awful lot of people in the group who had two left feet at that time. Rifle practice, Coast Guard history, it was interesting.

"The Coast Guard Academy was an interesting place to be. Oh, sure, they were prepared for us, 'Semper Paratus.' It didn't take them long. But you know to go to chapel services there on Sunday, you would march in. It really was quite an experience just to be part of it.

"SPARS did all kinds of clerical work. They did Loran Stations (Long Range Aid to Navigation), a highly secret radio signal system which passed information between coastal stations and U. S. military ships and planes. We took on the recruiting in our offices, things that could be done in offices.

"What happened was that they sent most of us back to the general areas we had come from because we knew the area, particularly if we were going out on recruiting as was the case with me. Knowing the area was helpful. I was sent back to the Detroit area, recruiting and I was there until January 1945.

"We had a lot of publicity. I had to go and speak a lot, Rotary, Kiwanis, women's groups, schools, and we traveled, we might be in Grand Rapids, then somewhere else. I would tell them, 'It was wartime and it was a matter of releasing men, it was a matter of taking over shore jobs.'

"One funny thing that happened. We were up in the Alpina [Michigan] area or some place like that. We were supposed to be at a ship launching. In order to get there, we were going kind of cross country to save time and we stopped at a crossroads and he [Coast Guard member] took his foot off the clutch and the clutch didn't work. We were out in the middle of nowhere and so he got out and got under the car to see what was the matter. There was a place where two pieces of machinery come together and the cotter pin that holds it had apparently worn out. Our station wagons were not the newest. And so he got out from under the car and started looking around to see if he could find it, in case it had just dropped out. And of course, it was not there. So I got out to see if there was a nail that we could put through. And all of a sudden, he said, 'You wouldn't have a bobby-pin, would you?' And I said, 'Yeah, here.' And I happened to have one in my hair and I passed it to him and he put it through where the cotter pin was supposed to have been, bent the ends, got in, tried the clutch, it worked and we got there on time. So he says in this little article that he wrote, 'And so we can flush a bit and the SPARS deserve to use our motto, "Always prepared."' So there was a lot of kidding about this bobby-pin.

"The Motor News in Detroit commissioned John Coppen, who was an artist in Detroit, to paint a picture for their Motor News, using a service person. John Coppen talked to our public relations officer, and they came up with the idea of doing a pin-up of some kind. And so they wound up asking if I would go and sit for this and let him paint this. So this is what he did and it was used for the Motor News. Then the Coast Guard picked it up and used it. When Tex and I were married, the chief petty officer, went to see John Coppen and sent me the original painting.

"In January 1945, they had decided that WAVES and SPARS could go out of the continental limits of the United States, meaning that we could go either to Alaska or Hawaii.

"I was sent to Hawaii and I was out there a year. We went 'blacked out,' to Hawaii. They didn't know where submarines were and it was a troop ship. And as we had more SPARS and WAVES out there, we lived out toward Pearl Harbor right across all the roads from Hickam Field and we had a quonset village out there. For the first few weeks I was there, they transferred me out to that quonset village, and I was the liaison between the Coast Guard and the Navy. I was the only SPAR officer on that base.

"I met Tex out there, my future husband, and he was Coast Guard. He was commanding officer of the training station out there at Guadaloupe. I still have the uniform, the hat, and the heavy coat. I went in as an Ensign and finally made Lieutenant. I could hardly have any regrets about my service of three and a half years. I met an awful nice husband and we were married after the war." [92]

WAVES

Similarly, the Navy accepted about 100,000 women into its ranks. Most of the WAVES were also assigned to traditional office jobs to relieve men for service on ships. The WAVES were not allowed to serve overseas, except in Hawaii.

A former WAVE officer and retired Dean of Women at the University of Colorado, Pauline Parish, trained young officers and decommissioned them as training centers shut down.

"I went in 1942. I had graduated from college that year and the war was on. A number of people in my class, the boys, had already gone, and we were getting information about the first ones being killed and things like that. I had two brothers, both of them over the age, but somehow it was a way that women could contribute, in a kind of different way. And I suppose I was interested, as a woman, of doing something a little bit different. Also I'm patriotic and it just felt right.

"I was in the second class of WAVE officers that trained at Mt. Holyoke. We had dormitory rooms and they had been cleaned out of everything. I'll never forget it: a wooden table, four wooden chairs and four double-decker bunks and that was it. It was a little sparse and I can remember thinking, 'What have I done?' I went through training up there at Mt. Holyoke. We had regular classes as far as things about the Navy was concerned, even airplane identification and, of course, ship identification. You had to learn the navy lingo and you had to learn a lot of things about the navy as such. And then we had to learn how to march and to drill and do all those kinds of things.

"Then I was transferred over to Northhampton to become a part of the training program, training young women to be WAVE officers. So I spent several years in Northhampton, Massachusetts living in a big old hotel that the Navy had taken over. Smith College was where the classes were taught, but my job was, in effect, to take care of the troops. I had a company of women assigned to me. They weren't all young, that's for sure. I would say, up into the 50s. Some of those had special commissions because of special abilities. The head of the whole show was Mildred McAfee. A man was a captain, he was in charge of the whole program, but they had a woman who was his counterpart, of course. Naturally, he had the final decisions.

"What we did was train these young women: how to march, how to drill and in naval procedures. And we're the ones who took them all over the place. If they needed somebody to parade around some place, we were called on and we'd take the company of young women. I can remember marching down the street in Holyoke, along with the sailors, the soldiers, the WACS and the marines for some kind of celebration.

"That's what I did for several years. Then after that, I was transferred to

Brooklyn, New York, and I suppose because of what I had done in Northhampton, I had to open up WAVE barracks. It turns out it was a low-cost housing project. They had moved all of the people out of it and they were going to put a lot of the enlisted WAVES in there. So I had to get it all opened up, furnished and all that stuff. Actually we had to set up a mess, feed them and house them, provide recreation. They went out to these various jobs, working in places like the Armed Guard center and the Brooklyn Navy Hospital and the Navy Yard in Brooklyn. My job was to see that they were well taken care of when they were not on the job. I was the officer in charge of that; I was there about two years.

"We had a recreation area. There were about 1,500 to 2,000 of them (WAVES) in this area. That's a lot of women. They had their own boyfriends and they could come and go as they chose. We would plan different kinds of outings for them. We could get tickets to theaters, to the theater in New York, primarily those were balcony seats they were giving away. It didn't make any difference, people got to see plays. We had some kind of organized activity, like softball, things of that sort. Maybe it was a big Halloween party, a big Thanksgiving dinner and they could sometimes bring their boyfriends.

"They transferred me back to Manhattan to a hotel called Manhattan Towers which had been taken over. There I had to close it. They called it 'decommission.' That had been the main area of the WAVES. That was the headquarters, New York City, for the lady who was the lieutenant commander in charge of all of the WAVES. So we had to take all of the furniture and equipment out of, probably a fifteen, sixteen, seventeen story hotel. Then we had to get the furniture out to warehouses where the Navy stored things, and I had to do the same thing over at what they called the Fort Green Barracks, which was the one I was in charge of. What we did, we had a whole group of young women and we took everything apart and I used to ride trucks, loaded with furniture. I had to sign papers saying that I was responsible for all this. And who would know whatever happened to it, once it got off the truck and stuck in a warehouse? So I must have signed my name millions of times, saying I was responsible for all this.

"The WAVE officers were not sent overseas. Apparently, we were being protected. There were many of us who thought we could go just about anywhere anybody else went, but that was not allowed.

"The WAVE's job was to replace men. They did all kinds of things. They did a lot of work in the area of communications. They were in the supply corps. They were in all the different aspects of the Navy. Some of them taught people how to fly. They had what they called 'link trainers' and these WAVES were trained to handle the link trainers into which they put the prospective pilots. And they worked with them, originally, before they got out into the airplane, on what it was all about and

A Time to Speak

helped train them. They did almost anything a man would do ashore, but they obviously didn't do what a man would do out on ships at sea, fighting the war.

"I didn't get that feeling that the women were frustrated because all of this was still so new to all of us. We were doing something that had never really been formally done before. So I don't think there was a lot of feeling along that kind of line. And also people were being sent places and meeting different kinds of people that they would probably never had those sorts of experiences as a younger person. And it has meant a tremendous amount to me all my life, the experience I had in the WAVES, the kind of responsibility I was given in the WAVES and just told to 'Do it' without a lot of people standing over me telling me exactly what to do.

"We all felt, even though I wasn't out there on the firing line, I felt that I was doing something very worthwhile and we were all fighting, and in effect, we felt we were fighting for the world. We felt we were fighting for democracy and we were making our contribution. There was no question about that. I don't think I ran across anyone, man or woman, who didn't feel like they were making a contribution in that way. They were fighting for their country and for the other people in this world to have a democratic form of life.

"It opened up a lot of opportunities for women and as you know, they stayed on in the service afterwards. Any woman could apply to stay on and they chose a small number of them. That was not the thing that I wanted to do the rest of my life.

"I went in December '42 and got out in November four years later. And I had to find a job. I thought I wanted to stay in New York City, only I discovered that looking for a job in New York City, unless you really had what they called 'work experience,' was hard. They did not count military service as work experience. The only thing I could find was 'Well maybe we can find some kind of secretarial work.' I said, 'I'm not a secretary, I don't even know how to type.'

"So I ended up finally by going down to Washington, D. C. to visit some friends and heard about some openings. They were setting up a whole new office in the Bureau of Naval Personnel and what it was, it was encoding the classifications, qualifications and work experience and what people had done in the war as naval officers and they were looking for people like me who had been in the Navy. So I got a job in civil service in the Bureau of Naval Personnel, first as an analyst, analyzing and encoding the language backgrounds, the degree backgrounds, the job backgrounds, the naval experience backgrounds, all put in code and put on IBM machines because there was no such thing as computers.

"As a result of that I had a fun experience which has probably has held me in marvelous stead all my life. I was moved into and had to develop what they called a mobilization system, should we have another war. And they wanted to use this classification system as a call-up method, to call people up based on the experience and qualifications they needed. So another WAVE officer and I were given the task of developing this system which was all going to be put on machines. A part of my job was to go out and set it up in all the naval districts all over the country. So I did that and we sent out to each naval district, the people who were living in their district, the cards and equipment that was need to do a call-up. My job was to go out and see that it got set up and then supervise it.... As a matter of fact, they did use the system when the Korean war came along to call back some officers who had certain kinds of backgrounds."

WACS

The WAC began as the Women's Army Auxiliary Corps in May 1942. In 1943, the Women's Army Auxiliary Corps was legally given full army status and the word "auxiliary" was dropped, and it became the Women's Army Corps. With her degree in dietetics, Thelma Foster decided to join the WACS soon after it was organized.

"Then came World War II and that old feeling to make a worthwhile contribution for the war effort. Right after the bill was signed in May '42, I went in November so I was one of the early ones. We were called auxiliaries instead of privates. I was on active duty until May 1946, helping discharge people.

"If people find out I was in the service, they will tell me, 'Oh, my husband wouldn't let me go in the service,' or 'My boy friend wouldn't let me go in the service.' I listen to this whole thing, well, my mother and dad wouldn't have let me go into the service either, but I went and enlisted and then told them. I was twenty-two years old. Mother and Dad, they were heartbroken because my brother had already left and it was leaving them home alone. But I had to live my own life.

"I was teaching in my second year out of college at the time. I was being paid $1440 a year and I was taking a private's job at $21 a month. My mother thought I was absolutely crazy to give up $1440 a year for $21 a month. But I said, 'They are going to pay my transportation, what do I need money for?' It was that kind of an attitude.

"In the WACS, there weren't an awful lot of options as I recall. You could go in the motor pool, bakers' and cooks' school, or you could do office-type jobs. Oh, they looked at what you had been doing.

"My assignments had to do with food. The Bakers and Cooks School which was hilarious. It wasn't much fun for me, remember I'm only five feet tall and the size of those pots. I could have camped in some of those pots they were so huge, and I couldn't reach the bottom of them to clean or anything like that. Anyway, I had a dietetics degree and they didn't know what to do with me because I was an enlisted person. That's why they were pushing me to go to OCS because the instructors and

A Time to Speak

all the hot shots in the feeding situation were officers.

"I was promoted to corporal, and made an instructor in Bakers and Cooks school in Daytona Beach, Florida. The other instructors were officers. At this time, I had very little interest in moving up in rank. Dating the handsome navy pilots nearby and having them dip their wings as they flew over our quarters was great fun. And riding a bike on the beach was a lot better way to spend that winter than OCS in Des Moines, Iowa.

"In Daytona Beach, what they had done, since it was a resort, they took over a store which had been vacated and that's where we had class and the feeding was done in churches. Church basements were great places to eat. The Clarendon Hotel, which was right on the ocean was an elegant hotel, but it was housing WACs only, and we had a big mess-hall there.

"That was one of the problems in the early days. The original training units were at Fort Des Moines, which was very cold, and those first women who went there in the first winter, they didn't have the right clothes for them and they were issuing them men's overcoats. Because of difficulties in getting fabric to manufacture uniforms fast enough, they decided that a warm climate was the thing to do for their next training center. They chose Daytona Beach where they wouldn't have to supply all of those woolen fabrics.

"One of my problems was, because I was five feet tall, they had no uniforms to fit me. They had told us to go to camp, basic training, with minimal supplies. The only thing I was issued was a pair of shoes, army shoes. And I was wearing army shoes with a couple of little cotton dresses I brought along, and I was going to Florida, so I didn't need anything warm. And I thought I was getting a uniform. I went through basic training, six weeks, with no uniform. I had army shoes and my civilian clothes. I made quite a splash. I was really awful.

"I became an instructor and I taught in the store front in Daytona Beach and that's how I got a uniform, as a matter of fact. Somebody came by to observe my class, some colonel or general or somebody to see whether or not I was doing what I was supposed to do. He saw me in civilian clothes, teaching a whole class of people who were in uniform. And so what they did, he ordered that they cut down a large uniform and put it together to fit me. It was the worst looking uniform you ever saw in your life. The pockets weren't in the right places and it was horrible. Eventually they found that not everybody that was going into the service was 5 ft. 6 in. and hefty. And they did make uniforms in more reasonable sizes. But we really had difficulty getting uniforms because there were so many other uses being put to fabrics that were available. Everybody wanted to wear some sort of uniform and this made a terrible shortage of fabrics.

"Florida was to be short-lived. The company commander had put out several calls for those interested in becoming officers. I never responded. Finally, I was called into her office and lectured on my patriotic duty.

"I gave in and was on my way to the cold, cold Fort Des Moines, Iowa for officer candidate school, graduating in May 1943 as a second lieutenant. My assignments were based on three things: first, my training in dietetics and quantity feeding; second, my ability to play swing on the piano and organ; and third, my brother was missing in action and later was a prisoner of war in Germany.

"When we first started, they had no separate ration sizes or portions for women and we were being shipped these humongous quantities of food for men and trying to figure out what to do with them. I was a mess officer then. I had three dining rooms. I was assigned a weapons carrier. For me, it was a truck. We would load up everything we couldn't use and I would go around to the men's mess halls and try to trade and try to swap because the guys didn't really care that much for the fruit and the vegetables. They liked the beans and the potatoes and the stuff that really stuck to the ribs whereas the women were not getting enough of that kind of thing [fruit] and it was a long time before they adjusted the rations to fit the size of the people they were feeding. I got to be very well acquainted on the base.

"One evening at Fort Campbell, Kentucky officer's club, soon after I arrived, I was playing the piano and had quite a good sing-a-long going. I was invited to join the post commander at his table where he was entertaining the commanding general who had an idea. He was looking for someone to put together a GI art show at the Columbus, Ohio art museum and to also put together an orchestra, using GIs from posts in Kentucky, West Virginia, Ohio and Indiana. The next day orders were cut and off I went, did a fine show, with the help of a few very talented GIs, the orchestra was wonderful. All of this expense and the result was good PR and maybe we sold a few more bonds.

"I was sent first to Special Services School because of music and that's how I got involved in that art show and putting together the orchestra. Then eventually I was made a post exchange officer because the post exchange had taken over the operation of all of the cafeterias in the service clubs at the posts and they needed somebody to oversee all those kitchens and cafeterias. In addition to that, I purchased all of the women's merchandise for the post exchanges.

"I was sent to this school to learn post exchange procedures. It was at that point I had one of the most humorous experiences of my career. There was a group of men who were accountants, business men, retailers, the type that would be involved in post exchanges. They had been given commissions directly from civilian life. They barely knew their left foot from their right. Here I am the only woman in this whole group and basically the only one who knew how to march. And they took a vote on who was going to lead their platoon when we had parades because we had to parade to class, we had to parade to this and to that. And you know who. I was it. We would have to practice a little bit on the side. This is your left, this is your right, 'Hup, two, hup, hup, hup two.' Those guys laughed so hard at what they were doing that they had great difficulty in staying sincere and serious. And finally came graduation day in the stadium, all the proud wives and everybody were there, and I gave that platoon a talking to. 'I want you to be as serious and military as you can be.' It was really funny. When we came on the field, it was the only platoon led by an itty, bitty lady. They applauded, they whooped, they hollered, they laughed. And I had to go up to the commanding general to get the graduation certificates for everybody in my group. It brought down the house, this little gal going up to get the certificates because there weren't that many women at that facility at that time.

"The British had experience in establishing women's services and they warned the US to expect a slander campaign. OK, everything went swimmingly for almost a year and then it started on the East Coast. It was traced to Fort Devons, Massachusetts. What they were saying was that whole boat loads of WACS were being shipped back from Europe pregnant, and the WACS were a bunch of whores basically. And the men who had sisters who were in, or who had mothers, were trying to get us to come out of the service. When we went from WAAC to WAC, we had that opportunity and it was a about that time when it all started, 'Get out of that organization' [1943]. Originally the FBI thought it might be an Axis plot because it had a great effect on recruiting all women in all services. And it was found to be, as it spread, moving from one military base to another, spread by an interesting list of people. It was timed to get hot when the fighting got hot in North Africa, and men were being shipped out fast for combat and people realized it was no longer a phoney war. The people passing this along were ladies playing bridge in the officer's clubs and in the country clubs at home, whose husbands had gone on active duty and who were being replaced by WACS and service women. And the women hated us. We stood for something which they didn't - we stood for total involvement in the whole thing and I really, at the time and since, many times had to be very patient about listening to women telling me why they didn't go in the service.

"We [the service women] never wanted to be equal. We didn't want combat pay. We were in for the duration. Our purpose was to win the war. We never thought the Corps would endure in peace time.

"Women did not go in, intending to make it a career. I view the current women as so serious and I can't help but ask, why? Why do they want to be in combat? Is it just to earn combat pay, or is it to prove they can do the same job a man can do? I don't know." [93]

WASPS

Less well-known are the members of WASP (Women Airforce Service Pilot). Their story is the history of women who flew military aircraft in a special program designed to release male pilots to fly overseas.[93b]

England, in 1940, had already established the Air Transport Auxiliary made up of female pilots who assisted in ferrying military aircraft. Jackie Cochran, winner of the 1938 Bendix Transcontinental Race, thought a similar American program was needed. With the influence of Eleanor Roosevelt, she finally convinced General Henry H. "Hap" Arnold, Chief of the Army Air Corps, to allow her to take twenty-five American women to England to fly for the British Ferry Command and the Air Transport Auxiliary.

Meanwhile, Nancy Love organized a group of experienced female pilots at New Castle Air Base in Wilmington, Delaware.

In the summer of 1943, Love's group and Cochran's group merged into one organization, called the Women Airforce Service Pilot or WASP.

The women who became Airforce Service Pilots did so because they believed that everyone needed to pitch in on the home front. Everyone was doing something for the country and their contribution could be to support the air effort at home. While they were never militarized, they had rigorous screening and training standards. After twenty-four weeks of training and tests in physics, math, navigation, aircraft engines, and Morse code, they received their silver wings. Of the 1,830 who were accepted, only 1,074 graduated and received their wings. They were credited with over 60 million miles during their brief service.

They ferried light weight military aircraft and later more powerful airplanes. They were trained to ferry planes from one point to another. They also flew planes to repair depots or to scrap yards. They towed targets behind their planes for ground troops to practice their anti-aircraft gunnery skills. Their insignia, "Fifi," the good gremlin, was designed by Walt Disney.

By December 1944, they had flown 60 million miles, qualifying in 78 kinds of planes. They checked out in ten or twelve different military planes, including the P-51 fighter, the B-17 and the B-29 Superfortress.

In spite of the record of WASP, it was not assimilated into the Air Force, but disbanded. In fact, they found that trust and respect was hard to come by. Even though thirty-eight of their comrades died in service, they received no death benefits. In some cases, the women themselves took up a collection so that the body could be flown to the woman's home.

In 1978, it was announced that the Air Force would train women to fly military aircraft for the first time. Indignant, those who had served in the WASP set about to correct the record. With the help of Senator Barry Goldwater, Colonel Bruce Arnold (son of General Arnold), and Congresswomen Lindy Boggs and Margaret Heckler, legislation was passed in 1979 to grant military recognition and veteran status to women who had served in the WASP.

Army Nurse Corps

There was an appeal for nurses to take care of American troops in military base hospitals, and they also served near the front lines. Roberta Trexler was a physical therapist who worked with the wounded after they returned to the States. She went into a one-year training program for civilians paid for by Civil Service. When she finished her training, she was sent to McCloskey General in Temple, Texas.

"I didn't have the feeling I was in the military. We were in uniform and that was about it. At the hospital there was no shopping in the PX, no dances. We worked so much and so hard and such long hours.

"It wasn't that it wasn't a great thing to do, it was. It was good to have it. It gave me a wonderful career. It was something you felt like you were really participating in. But we didn't have the fun a lot of people had, nor did we have the danger that some people did who went over-seas.

"They could hardly spare us for basic training. And they had a hard time when we spent three weeks at Camp Swift in basic training. I came right back in my same patient schedule that I'd had before even though I'd changed uniforms and now was in the service rather than a civilian.

"One thing I think that to me was kind of interesting about basic training was my realization that women really don't have any part in some of the aspects of the military. You need muscles.

"The thing that happened was that we were supposed to go on an overnight bivouac and so we were each carrying a half of a tent and our bedroll, not our food. We didn't have to carry any ammunition, guns, or food. They were being transported up to the top of this hill. It was supposed to be about a six hour hike to the top of this hill. There was a steady drizzle of rain. We had rain things we could put over us, but when we put them over us, we got so hot under them that we couldn't stand it so we couldn't wear them.

"At least an hour before we got to the top of this hill, it was really like a mountain, an ungraded road that went up and the mountain itself was all pine trees with lots of pine needles on it so you wouldn't be in the mud when you got up there. But we had absolutely the muddiest road you ever saw. It got muddier and muddier. Every time you put your foot down, it just got sucked down and you could hardly pull it up to put the next foot down. So girls were dropping out all over the place. They were absolutely not going to fight the mud. We had a captain who was in charge of this. She got out of her jeep, got in front and she said, 'Come on girls, you have to come,' so she stayed right in front of us. There were 300 of us and the majority got up there, but I remember sitting down every once in a while and my heart was just pounding because it was so exhausting, yet we weren't carrying much of anything.

"We got there and they already had their kitchen set up which they evidently had brought up the day before and they had hot food for us, something you wouldn't have in ordinary combat. But we had to put up our own tents. My tent mate and I got our tent up, and we got our pegs and everything. I think we had a more sheltered place, but an awful wind came up during the night. You could hear the screaming. All these tents began to go down. It was a real hard wind and rain storm and I thought, women don't belong in situations like this because they didn't have the muscle power to do the things they needed to do. It was a revelation. That was basic training!

"We got to the clinic at about 7:00 in the morning; we broke for a little breakfast, then we started our patients at 9:00. We worked until 5:00, then we did clinic work and things like that until 6:00, book work, what have you, and had supper. And we had Sunday off. The physical therapists, in Temple, for example, there were thirty physical therapists there. I don't know how many patients, but thousands, and we carried a patient load that was way beyond what we could do. Our schedule, everyday when we picked up our schedule, in addition to our regular schedules, they slipped a few more in.

"They divided the patients in the army hospitals by the type of hospital that it was. McCloskey, where I stayed the longest, was an amputee center, a spinal cord injury center, and peripheral nerve damage from gunshot wounds. When they came in from overseas, from the ships or planes, they looked to see which hospital would be more apt to be able to take them. During the height of getting so many wounded from overseas, we had spinal cord injury people which meant they were either paralyzed in all four extremities, or just the lower extremity.

"And they had them on hospital ships coming over, and they had so many people in bunks that they couldn't change their dressings, couldn't turn them enough. Then when they got them into the East Coast, they put them on troop trains, a lengthy ride to Texas, and when they came into Temple, they were just half dead. They would get off. They would have bed sores that were so extensive they were unreal. We treated bed sores as well, we used ultra violet for bed sores. Then the usual types of things that are still being carried on.

"This physical therapy was a relatively new field up until the Second World War. They described physical therapy when I went into it: treatment of physical disabilities with natural means, such as water, heat, massage. To give a good example, suppose you had someone who had a gunshot wound to the arm and it clipped some of the nerves and perhaps had limitation in the joints in the related swelling. The treatment, as soon as the doctor said he was ready, the doctor would send in the physical therapist. First, he would go into a whirlpool bath with his arm, then range of motion. He'd start stretching whatever joint was limited and you keep pushing and pushing up to their endurance to get the flexibility; then they went into a gym where there were pulleys and all the other things that you see now. And not quite as sophisticated as you see in some of the places.

"If the legs were paralyzed, they went into braces after a period of time. You worked on strengthening their muscles in their back and in their abdomen, shoulders and everything so they could lift themselves when they went into braces. Then it was your job to teach them how to walk with braces. If it was an amputee, the physical therapist had the walking aspect.

"I never had any feeling that there was any self-pity, with few exceptions, no matter where they were lined up in the wards, there was always someone worse than they were. And it was very edifying to work with these men. No matter how sick, I never heard anyone, very rarely heard anyone complain.

"The only thing that disturbed me along that line, and was sad to watch, was a man who had a head injury. It's one thing if the head injury means you have no control over one side of your body, but when it affects your personality. Yet, they have enough awareness to know that they are affected. That's when I saw the depression in this one man who had been a teacher and now was a little boy again. It was sad to watch, and it was sad to watch his young, little pretty wife who couldn't deal with it when she came around him. And the sadness that his parents felt of their son's personality change. For the most part, you admired them so much.

"We lived in nurses' quarters. In our particular building were all the physical therapists, occupational therapists and dieticians. Those three categories and nurses wore the same uniform. We had a different insignia. The non-nurses, we always felt we were step-children. The head nurse ran the whole system and the nice quarters went to the nurses and what was left over went to us. But it was still fine. Believe it or not, we had maid service.

"On Sundays, the whole base was really lively except for our wing, and it was just real quiet, we were so tired.

"It was a privilege, it truly was. I still correspond with some of the physical therapists I was in the service with. I had some very special friendships. It was a very special time.

"I've always said, if you survived the war pretty much intact, for your own personal experiences, it was an upper. But lots of sad things happened." [94]

To support the war effort, women willingly accepted the changes and challenges of entry into the work force and into the military.

End Notes

92	Elizabeth Lipstreu still lives in Boulder, staying active in church and university affairs.
93	After her discharge, Mrs. Foster married, had a career as a home economics teacher, a dietician for a school district, and a second career as a life and health insurance broker.
93b	Information cited, with Ken Magrid's permission, from TV program and booklet, "Women of Courage."
94	After she was out of service, Mrs. Trexler worked in polio epidemic centers in Texas and Arkansas, in a general hospital in Chicago and in California.

CHAPTER 23

THE WAR ON THE HOME FRONT

Millions of other women went to war on the home front. Grandmothers, mothers and wives learned to make do with whatever was available. Common items were scare: gasoline, rubber, electricity, heat, food, shoes, clothing, soap, food, especially sugar, coffee, meat, butter and fats, even wine.

Wartime priorities forced families to forgo purchases of refrigerators, washing machines, alarm clocks, bed springs, hair pins, metal office furniture, lawn mowers, residential oil burners.

In spite of increased industrial production in the United States to provide arms and munitions to the Allied Forces, Americans were asked to pitch in and save materials needed for the war effort through drives for scrap metal, tinfoil, rubber, aluminum and tin cans, newspapers and waste paper, silk and nylon stockings. Women were encouraged to save cooking fat to be recycled into glycerine for explosives.

FOOD FOR VICTORY

"Eating for Victory" was a vital part of the war effort. The food saved enabled the men and women in the armed forces to eat well. In the occupied countries, the limited amount of food available was due to several things: the lack of food production, the destruction of the transportation system that could have brought food to cities, and the ability of the German Occupation troops to buy what foodstuffs were available.

The major efforts to provide food for the Allied Armies and still maintain adequate staples for civilians were home gardening and food rationing.

Home Gardens

People were asked to plant gardens. "Grow your own and can your own" was the motto in the United States. Americans worked in their "Victory Gardens," and by 1943 these home gardens provided more than one-third of the vegetables grown in the United States.

The British were encouraged to "Dig for Victory," the slogan to promote wartime gardens in any spare ground. Bine Hirsch described the city parks which had been dug up so people could plant vegetables, *"My brother and I and my father, we spent all of our weekends digging and culling. One is nothing but potatoes and cabbages to get us through the winter and the other one is the onions, peas, beans and everything else. I remember my mother 'bottling' food, making jam which we never did before the war."*

In Paris, tomatoes grew in the Tuileries Gardens, potatoes and cabbage were cultivated on the grounds of Les Invalides. The French raised vegetables and rabbits on their balconies. They bicycled to the country to get eggs and vegetables; they sent any extra food in the monthly packages to the men in prison. But Geneviève Moline pointed out that their principal preoccupation was not what happened outside of France, but the fact that they didn't eat. Housewives got up early and hid by the doors to be the first at the butcher shop to get meat.

RATIONING

The British, the French, and the Americans all had a system of ration stamps and points for food, established by their governments, with allocations which often varied according to the food supplies available. The black market did flourish. Grocers often put aside rationed commodities for their preferred customers. There were also false tickets made in print shops and sold to those with enough money. Mme Moline remembered that her family had the same baker. But one day, her mother was warned, "Listen, your tickets are too badly printed, we can't accept them."

HELPS FOR THE HOUSEWIFE

Armed with ration books and ingenuity, encouraged by clever slogans and bombarded with help and guidance on how to prepare meals under the rationing restrictions and use substitutions for commodities no longer available, women still managed to feed their families.

The Ministry of Food in Great Britain employed cooks to give advice in centers, for example, school kitchens, the foyer at Harrod's. There were food facts in magazines and a five-minute daily radio program, "The Kitchen Front," with clever jingles to remind the public,

> *"Those who have the will to win*
> *Cook potatoes in their skin*
> *Knowing that the sight of peelings*
> *Deeply hurts Lord Wooton's feelings."* [95]

A young Brit in a reserved occupation (public utility), who lived in a rented room with "cooking facilities," received this wartime letter (late February or early March, in 1941) from his mother giving him ideas for using his rations skillfully.

"My dear son,

"Thanks so much for the chock [probably chocolate]. I shall enjoy them. I have a tin of syrup by me so will send it on to you.

"Your list for dinners covers a good bit of ground, but here are one or two hints.

"Corn beef minced and made into a savory pie with a little OX for gravy. Mince corn beef. Boil potatoes and mash with milk and margarine and seasoning. Moisten beef with a little OX gravy. Put meat in pie dish and spread on potatoes and bake until browned.

"Just a vegetable dinner, with gravy, also made from OX if none other is available. I had one the other day. Potatoes, carrots, turnips, brussels sprouts. You can put onion if you like it and any other kind of vegetable. Mix all together when cooked and add hot gravy. With a pudding after it is very nice. I had macaroni after — no egg is needed for that, just milk, sugar and a bit of margarine. Vegetables with fried rashers or eggs.

"Have you had sausage in batter made with egg powder instead of egg? Also a savory pie could be made with sausage. Another way with sausage is to wrap it in a rasher (after taking the skin off) and bake.

"Baked beans on toast is good for a first course. Also a tin of soup with toast. Dad and I had a tin of tomato soup on Sunday, a small tin. I emptied it into a sauce pan and add an equal quantity of milk and brought it the boil, but not let it boil. With dry bread or toast it makes a good meal.

"Another way with vegetables is to pan cook them. Put them in a pie dish and cover with a pastry crust and bake. I cannot get any steak and kidney puddings just now, but am on the watch.

"... Tinned salmon could be mashed and made into little pies with a pastry crust if you liked and served with potatoes. Of course you know what to have for 2nd course, all kinds of puddings, jam ———, treacle, apple, marmalade, bread pudding. I made a roly pudding with mince meat for Reg while I was there and he enjoyed it.

"Well, I hope I have given you some new ideas but so many things require eggs or egg whites that it is no use sending those as eggs are a bother to get and it is expensive using them for cooking. We were lucky enough to get some eggs this weekend, the first I have bought since before Xmas.

"... No more now, love, Mother"

French women's magazines like *Marie-Claire* provided many suggestions for substitutions, as well as economies of hard to find products.

To replace wine, one could make a drink of pea pods infused in water; for tea, do as the Chinese, use the leaves of red currants, raspberries and wild strawberries. A substitute for unavailable vegetables were nettles (found in fields and along the roads) which could be prepared like spinach. By 1944, the magazine told French women how to wash clothes without soap which was becoming more and more scarce. They could simply pound into a pulp either soapwort root, ivy, or the seeds of the Indian chestnut and mix with water.

By comparison, American women had an easier time feeding their families. It was more of an inconvenience than a privation. However, newspapers and women's magazines and advertisements were filled with suggestions and recipes to help families cope with shortages, and cook books printed wartime supplements.

> "To market, to market
> To buy a pot roast
> Home again, home again
> To peas and milk toast." [96]

One of their recipes was Sautéd Lamb Kidneys, which the contributor noted, *"This is an economical meal and kidneys take no points."*

Wartime cookbooks suggested women use stretch meat dishes with peanuts, soybeans, peas, beans, and lentils. There were suggestions for coffee stretchers, adding roasted chicory, cereals and legumes like chick-peas before the coffee is brewed. Nothing should be wasted.

Cakes and cookies were a problem for many cooks because of sugar rationing. The "Corn Syrup Cake," substituting corn syrup for sugar, was typical of most sugar-less cakes. Mrs. Gablehouse, who found this recipe, commented she didn't know how her mother could have baked this cake for one and an half hours, as the recipe stated, because they lived on a ranch and had no electricity.

The Joy of Cooking (probably the 1941 or 1942 edition since the cover was no longer on the cook book) referred to the wartime challenge as "the time new order for the cook" and suggested women make the changes an interesting and thrilling adventure. After all, the shortages and ration cards would become legendary.

JUST MAKE DO

Margaret Duncan summed up the attitude of women during the war years. Her husband was in construction work, first in Ogden, Utah, at the time of Pearl Harbor, building the largest hanger in the world; later building barracks at Lowry Air Force Base in Denver, Colorado, and in Leadville, Colorado building barracks for the ski troops who trained near there.

The couple had two small daughters, ages two and four Mrs. Duncan recalled her double challenge: to cope with wartime shortages and to live in a relatively primitive and isolated setting near the Moffat Tunnel which is west of Denver and under the Continental Divide. Her husband was heavily involved in war work.

"I guess you just learn to contend with it. We had an old coal stove in the kitchen and then the oil stove. At that age, you accept things easier. It was the thing to do and the way it was. Oh, yes, I could bake with an old coal stove, with a kitchen oven but I was kind of used to it. Heat your bath water in a boiler on the stove or for washing or whatever. It just took a long time to do all those normal things.

"The first cabin we had we didn't even have a washing machine. Finally my father thought that was unheard of, so he got an old washing machine that I used on the outside with an old motor. And you would hang things out and they would freeze dry in about three days.

"It kept you busy. We had the water, what you might say, piped in, one pipe. My husband had fixed it up so it came in from a spring from one pipe. We caught water inside so you didn't have to go outside to get water which helped.

"The food rationing was quite a problem, especially with the men working out in the forest. They were pretty hungry on one roast a week so my husband would go fishing nearly every night, and we'd have fish, many a time. Nothing else.

"You just did things with whatever was available to do with. It was an experience, and you felt if that was the only way we could help out the war effort, we were helping out and did a real good job!"[96b]

These sacrifices made it possible to provide food to feed the Allied armies and to feed them well. The menu prepared by Don Look, the cook on the USS *LST 511* for Christmas dinner 1944 is a good example.

"Fruit Cocktail
Chicken and Rice Soup
Roast Young Turkey - Raisin Dressing
Baked Virginia Ham - Hawaiian Sauce
Mashed Potatoes   Candied Carrots
Giblet Gravy   Buttered Sprouts
Combination Salad   Sweet Pickles
Stuffed Celery   Cranberry Sauce
Parkerhouse Rolls   Butter
Mince Pie   Vanilla Ice Cream
Coffee
Oranges   Apples
Candy   Cigarettes   Cigars"

At home, women coped. On the battlefields, the Allies suffered military defeats. Successes would came later.

End Notes

95   Lord Wooton was Minister of Food;*Ration Book Recipes*, p. 4.
96   Author unknown, p. 12, *Ration By-Pass, War-Time Recipes Collected by the Members of the Garden Club of Halifax Country*
96b   Today, Mrs. Duncan volunteers, helping hwe neighbors with sewing and tailoring.

CHAPTER 24

SOUTHEAST ASIA

The news from Southeast Asia continued to be bleak. Only a few hours after the bombing of Pearl Harbor, Japanese forces landed on the Malayan Peninsula and bombed Singapore and Hong Kong. Japanese bombers struck Manila and Luzon in the Philippines, and their troops landed on the northern island of Bataan.

The Fall of Singapore

The British had surrendered Hong Kong on 25 December 1941. But the fall of Singapore, the "Gibraltar of the East," 15 February, 1941 was not only a serious blow to Britain's ability to control east-west shipping lanes, but it was a "severe blow to British morale."[97]

Defended from the sea by guns on the hill top fortresses, Fort Silosa, Fort Serapong, Fort Connaught and Berhala Point Battery on the island of Blakang Mati, and from the north by the jungle, the British thought Singapore Island was indestructible. A quotation from *The Malaya Tribune* of 3 December, 1941 is an example of Britain's over-confidence, ". . . the Japanese are caught in a trap of their making . . . neither by land nor sea nor in the air do they have even a glimmer of chance of victory. . . ."

On 1 December 1941, however, the defense of Fort Silosa consisted of only two 6-inch BL guns, a 12-pounder QF (quick firing) gun and Lewis light machine guns as anti-aircraft defense. Like the German Blitzkrieg around the Maginot Line, the Japanese boats came around the British forces and invaded from Malaya. The cannons at Fort Silosa were pointed the wrong way and were designed to fire shells to pierce ships' armor and not to deal with land forces. By 13 February, the Japanese destroyed Singapore's coastal defense. Singapore surrendered, and 32,000 Indian, 16,000 British and 14,000 Australian soldiers were taken prisoner.[98]

Francis John Docketty, a member of the British Territorial Army, 306th Battery of the Royal Engineers, was in Singapore and taken prisoner. In a taped interview at the Imperial War Museum Sound Archive, he described the dismay over their defeat, his capture and imprisonment.

"If one order had been given in advance, which was what we wanted, we could have pushed them off Singapore. We know that. I think every prisoner of war

you have spoken to would be of the same opinion to tell you that what we wanted was the word 'to go forward,' just leadership.

". . . And they said, "You've got to pack it in, the war's over." And Major G. took us to the top of the hill and we went up there and he said, 'Well fellows, the war's over. . . .

". . . Everybody was cursing, 'Why can't we go ahead. We've got the men here,' but that's only a soldier's point of view. We could be wrong, but there's lots of things behind the scenes we don't understand."

Docketty and other prisoners were marched to Bukit Timah, to Changi Prison in Singapore, later to Surabaya, to northern New Guinea and to Kokopo where they were put in tents with little food. He described some of his punishments and his solitary confinement.

". . . They used me for bayonet practice, you see. They stand you up against a tree and they get broomsticks and they come dashing at you with these broomsticks. You are supposed to parry them off when they come at you, otherwise you are going to get bruised ribs, only my hands, nothing else. They had broomsticks or like a broomstick, and when they charged you, if you swing your arms out sideways like that, you can divert the blow; when the next one comes, you can divert the blow. If you miss and they get you, you are in pain because you had to go for some time. It depends on their whim. . . .

" . . . [They] decided to isolate me, I think it must have been an experiment. They put me into a pig pen and they threw sweet potatoes on me, the same as the pigs fed on. Of course, you couldn't eat them . . . but I think it was their sense of humor, mostly, but they soon put me to work. I was only in the pig sty about three or four days. Then I built my hut, I had to build my grass hut, you see."

In response to the interviewer's question about his attitude toward the Japanese, Docketty revealed an extraordinary tolerance of a different culture.

". . . You see there were two different sides to the Japanese. As I told you before, one Jap gave me his cape when it was pouring with rain and another one when I was dying, Hagaki, he placed an egg on my chest and put my hand over it and then gave me a bashing so the other chaps wouldn't see his kind act. Because he did a kind act, he didn't want it to be seen. . . . They were of a contrasting nature. No doubt there was good in them, but you see we live in different upbringings. We are taught different ideals, so a Japanese and an Englishman are two entirely separate races, with different ideals. What is good for us would be bad for the Japanese and what's good for the Japanese would be bad for the English. So therefore, there is a lot of understanding to be done. We look on things as atrocities, but the English and the Australian atrocities were just as bad. In New Guinea, they called the Japanese prisoners of war and asked if there were any volunteers to go on bombing

A Time to Speak

practice and the Japanese that volunteered were tied hand and foot and put into those bombers at Lei. That was in August in 1945 and to my disgust, they was taken up 3,000 feet and let go. They were the bombs. I mean these atrocities are things that happen with the Australians as well as with the British, you see. . . I didn't see it happen, but I heard the story of what they had done because they bragged to me what they had done." 99

Force 136

After the fall of Singapore, the British organized an underground resistance group, Force 136, code name, Operation Gustavus, to operate in Malaya. Its job was to gather intelligence for Allied headquarters in India and to train guerrillas to fight against the Japanese. After their training in India, the resistants established an Allied base camp behind Japanese lines in the deep forest on Pangkor island, off the eastern coast of Malaya and kept in touch with British headquarters in India by radio and by messages sent by submarine. In turn, they received military supplies and financial aid.

By January 1944 Jian Yik Jan, the food transport firm established as a cover for the intelligence work, had branches and affiliate offices all over Malaya. Resistance members information from local people in social gatherings, or while playing mahjongg.

Operation Gustavus was eventually crushed by a Japanese counter-espionage unit. Meanwhile, Allied submarines succeeded in breaking through the Japanese blockade, re-established communications with British headquarters in India and by February 1945, began to parachute para-military personnel and supplies to more than thirty posts all over Malaya.

The Capture Of The Philippine Islands

American troops, unable to withstand the Japanese onslaught, were being pushed back into the Bataan Peninsula. General Douglas MacArthur withdrew to Australia [11 March 1942], vowing, "I came through, I shall return." It was three years later that he was able to keep his promise.

The survivors' stories record the despair over their defeat, the horrible atrocities endured at the hands of their captors, their survival and finally their strength and willingness to forgive their enemies.

Sister Mary Louise Kroeger of the Mary Knoll Sisters went to China in 1935 and became ill with TB. She went to the Philippines in 1938 and was stationed in Bagal, a mountain province, where the sisters had two schools, one a preschool for the children of the Gouant tribe which were a head hunting people, another school located in the city proper for the Filipino people. She remembered vividly the arrival of the Japanese.

"I shall never forget it. It was about 8 o'clock in the morning, it was a special feast day for us, the Immaculate Conception, December 8 and it was a holiday. I remember we had visitors and we were sitting at the breakfast table when the phone rang. I think it came from the Spanish Fathers. Then no sooner had we been told about it, the planes were overhead and we went outside to cheer. We were convinced they would be American planes. What other planes would there be?

"They had organized the civilian people prior to the war; they allocated their captains, as they called them, and what they would do in case of war, but it was still not real. What happened when the first bomb was dropped, we saw nobody, all the planning, all the drills, everything kaput. The men naturally ran to their families. They were being bombed, they grabbed and they went. The terror of the bombing, I remember in the afternoon, we were just stunned. We just stomped around, truly alone up there, nothing, isolated from neighbors of any kind. We were far from the city. I remember going out there and looking at my watch and it was 2 o'clock. I walked and walked. I looked at my watch again to see what time it was and it was two minutes past 2 o'clock. I had passed a lifetime then, we were just dazed by it all.

"I wish I knew how I passed the time between the 8th and the 20th of December. I have often thought afterwards, even in the concentration camp, really what did we do. Mostly I think we were talking about the boys, the boys this, the boys that - when were they coming? how were they coming? Yes, the relief, they were on their way, as far as we were concerned. As far as MacArthur was concerned, he thought so too. . . .

"The Dominican Fathers up on the hill, just above us, they could see the Lingayen Gulf and they could watch it [the Japanese landing] and they would call and tell us exactly what was happening. I think if the 'Star Spangled Banner' ever had any meaning for us, every morning, we would say 'Old Glory is still waving.' Then one morning, it was down at the American camp at Lingayen. I've often wondered since if that was the first time the American flag went down in surrender. I think that was the first place that it fell.

"They just came right in up the mountain. Anytime I hear the 'Star Spangled Banner' now, I can't hear it without crying. Those words meant so much because you just lived them. You heard what Francis Scott Key was hearing. The bombings were constantly over Baguio, but on the other, hand when they stopped, there wasn't a sound any place, not a sound. Until all of a sudden we heard this screaming coming up the mountain path. They just came with thousands and thousands of them with bayonets and guns, all kinds of things and they were horrible looking men. We never knew where they really came from. It must have been upper Mongolia.

They were massive men, massive, massive, fierce looking and very cruel. The Japanese who came in later were not. Don't misunderstand me, they weren't delicate by any means. But these almost inhuman people, they almost frightened us, just frightened you to death.

"The Japanese came through the convent precincts. They went through with their bayonets, slashing things, cutting them up, banging doors, throwing things around. Of course, you can't blame them. There wasn't an officer there who treated you with respect, not in the beginning. No, they were as hard as nails. I remember our bishop. He was a Belgian and they went to his house at night, they were mean to him. They kicked him, they beat him. He was a very tall, frail man. Then the next night he heard banging again around midnight and he went down and opened the door and here was one of the men kneeling on the floor. He said, 'Bishop, I am a Catholic. I know how I should treat a bishop, but last night in front of the others, there was nothing for me to do but hit you as they did. I've come back to ask pardon. If they find out I came here, they will send me to the front line, but I couldn't live with my conscience without coming back to say I'm sorry.' But that was unusual, very unusual.

"The first time they came, they grilled us and grilled us, kept up this constant batter of questions. They wouldn't believe us. They always thought we were connected with the military guerila groups. Some of the priests were tortured. One of the priests was deaf and he had a hearing aid. He was tortured because they thought it was a spying system connected to Washington. He was an American. When they took his hearing aid from him, he was like a moron. . . .

"I remember once, one of the Americans had given us a huge radio. In those days, they had great big radios. It was so heavy that two of us could hardly lift it. We were listening. You weren't supposed to have a radio, that was instant decapitation. We were listening this night and we were getting all the news which was then, of course, very optimistic and we were so thrilled to hear it all. All of a sudden, we heard them tearing up the mountain side. What would we do with this radio? we couldn't move it. One of the sisters, and she was a tubercular patient also, picked up that radio and carried it on one hand and went up that ladder which was perpendicular to the whole in the attic, I think it was called. She went straight up there. We had some bug powder so we dusted it with bug powder so it looked dirty because it was still warm if they had touched it."

Sister Mary Louise was imprisoned, along with Dutch, Russian, and American allies and twenty-five different religious sects, first in Camp Hay, then at Camp Holmes (1943), and finally in the Los Banos prison camp, south of Manila.[100]

Surrender on Luzon

The Japanese landed on Luzon 24 December 1941. Fighting in northern Luzon against overwhelming numbers of Japanese troops, and unable to receive reinforcements, General MacArthur ordered a retreat to the Bataan Peninsula.

The Battling Bastards of Bataan

With control of Manila, Japanese troops reached the northern part of the mountainous Bataan Peninsula, just southwest of Manila in January 1942. American troops held out for three months against their superior numbers, awaiting reinforcements which never came. In the wake of renewed fierce attacks and weakened by short supplies of food and medicine, the Bataan defenders, under Lieutenant General Jonathan Wainright, continued to hold their stand until 9 April 1942 when they finally surrendered.

One of the survivors of the three-day march, known as the Bataan Death March is John Sedillo.

"All these memories, they are not all good. There aren't too many of us left.

"I joined the National Guard way back. In fact, I was so young, my sister had to sign so I could get in.

"I did have a choice. I volunteered. At that time, there was nothing. If you didn't belong to the National, Guard, girls wouldn't even look at you. It was during the Depression, there were no jobs. That $21 a month, that was the whole thing. My people were poor, although they lived on cattle ranches and farms. But in town, there was nothing. We didn't have it hard, we had food. We had a cattle ranch and farm so the Depression didn't hit us that hard. There were no jobs at all, that is one of the reasons I joined the National Guard because it was something to do and it seemed like everybody looked up to you because you were in uniform.

"Of course, at that time, it was cavalry, horses. So then the second year, it was just a couple of weeks a year; the second year they mobilized us. I had never seen such big trucks in my life, 1938 or 1939, somewhere in there. After we saw those big guns, I fell in love with them. I always wanted to be a gunner. Then we had anti-aircraft three-inch guns and this is what we wound up with. Then we went down to Ft. Bliss, Texas as a sort of a training camp. There we broke all kinds of records in tracking and shooting down planes. So then I guess they thought we were ready and then they put us on a troop train from Ft. Bliss, Texas to San Francisco. There they put us on boats and off to the Philippines we go.

"I think we were supposed to go to Europe because we had the clothing, the old ODs [olive drabs]. We wound up in the Philippines with ODs. It was so hot, humid. It didn't take them long to issue khakis.

"So we were there for about three months, then Pearl Harbor happened. I was a pretty good soldier by then and our captain had granted about five of us soldiers leave to go up to little Baguio, that's a nice, little resort up in the mountains in the Philippines. And here I had bought myself a $12 sharkskin suit. Anyway, that leave was cancelled because shortly after they bombed Pearl Harbor, they invaded the Philippines. We were stationed at Clark Field.

"What I remember most was that we had P-40 fighter planes and the B-17 bombers and we had them all over Clark Field. And what I remember is that we had a lot of bamboo planes, made to look like the others. And the Japanese didn't touch them, they knew exactly where the dummies were and where the real ones were. And what was really sad was that they hit us with the pilots in the planes. Just very few P-40s got off the ground. And there were so many Zeros up there, Japanese Zeros, and they just gobbled up all our Air Force.

"Immediately after that, we lost our Air Force there and at Nichols Field, also at Cavite which was a naval base. Then we started the withdrawal back to Bataan, we called it a 'strategic retreat.' We were supposed to go back there and find gun emplacements, but there was nothing but jungle back there. So MacArthur really screwed up there. He didn't have anything back there for us. Right at the end of the peninsula there were rivers, very hard for our heavy equipment, but we did manage to get our guns in place. What was even worse was, we had 1918 ammunition. We spent all night scraping the fuses, we had 18-second fuses only. The Japanese knew it, so they would fly up here at about 19,000 feet. We'd fire, well, my gun would fire 27 rounds and we were lucky to get reports. Oh, the ammo was bad. We didn't stand a chance. About a month, I remember that a ship came in to pick up MacArthur, the records, the gold, what have you, and they did bring us some 21-second fuses.

"So here comes the Japs, arriving in formation right over and they didn't know that we had 21-second fuses. We hit them, and we knocked out a lot of them that day. Those crazy guys, those Japanese, I'm sure they had parachutes, but they would not bail out. They would go down with their planes.

"We were awfully green. We gave a hell of a battle for three months. We held them off until the United States could at least get back on its feet. But it took them so long to get me out of there, three years, eight months and five days! That's a long time!

"We were scared, once the first bombs fell, you just didn't know. They hit us the following day [after Pearl Harbor] approximately the same time, at 8 o'clock in the morning at Clark Field. They really bombed the heck out of us. And they hit Nichols Field and they hit Caviti which was a naval outfit. They didn't touch Corregidor for some reason. I think they wanted it intact. Without Corregidor, they couldn't get into the Bay. I don't think they wanted to destroy it. They had to take it.

They held out for a month after we surrendered. A lot of our soldiers swam across because it is only two miles from the tip of Bataan peninsular to Corregidor. Some of them would take a log, a barge, anything to get across there. I don't think there were any deserters, there were some, a few that escaped from concentration camps. But it was worse on the outside. Then too, the Japanese would reward a Filipino a bag of rice for information of any American soldier, so that made it pretty dangerous. And then you stood out like a sore thumb among the Filipinos.

"We ate everything. Even on Bataan before we were captured, the monkey population was sure down. We were eating them. It's better when you dry it like jerky. Just dry it out in the sun and it is a lot better dried than it is cooked. You take the skin off and hold it up and it looks like a little baby. We ate just about anything, we ate the whole cavalry. I think the mules tasted a little better than the horses. Horse meat is very sweet and the mules are a little tougher. And those water buffaloes, their skins are about that thick [measures several inches with his hands], we ate those too, we ate everything that was on the island. We had to. We didn't have any food back there.

"We were cut off from the world, we were cut off. The Japanese here and Corregidor was over here and they had big guns, although they weren't functional. The Marine on the rock there would push these out so the Japanese could see that we had big guns. So there were battle ships that would stay at a distance. They really didn't get in close enough to bombard Corregidor because they were afraid of these guns. Every once in a while, they would lob a shell and scare them off a little bit.

"I think most of us blame MacArthur. Most of the people thought he was a wonderful man, maybe he was, but he let us down. Instead of having all of those polo fields and officer's clubs, fancy deals over there, he should - they knew this was coming. The Japanese had ammunition, guns up in Subic Bay. How many years they had been doing this? And why they didn't know it? How the heck they could allow the Japanese to manoeuvre over there in those waters, do their training, have their guns buried on the seashores and back of the lines? I just don't understand what MacArthur was doing in the Philippines outside of playing polo. He had beautiful horses and beautiful clubs for the officers. And the Philippine Army that we had, the guys were fairly good soldiers, very loyal, but they weren't trained either.

"We were prepared to fight to the last man. None of us wanted to surrender. I think it took President Roosevelt to surrender us. He gave the order to MacArthur and then, of course, to General Wainwright who was the commander in chief of the peninsula. He was the one who surrendered us. When he turned his 45 gun over to the Japanese to surrender, they nailed him down because he would give them nothing but his serial number and rank. They were going to chop his head off. Then this

Japanese officer figured that he was such a brave man, they came out and fed him because he was hungry too, you know, put him in a car and took him back out. All of our ranking officers captured on Bataan and the Philippines were sent to Manchuria, an officer's camp.

"The only thing you are allowed to give as soldiers is your serial number and your rank. That's all they have to know. 'Sergeant so and so, number so and so,' and that's it. That's all they are entitled to. Then they can get pretty mean. The Japanese actually thought we had a tunnel from Bataan to Corregidor and they wanted to know where that tunnel was. And they beat up a lot of soldiers trying to find out. There was no such thing, but the Japanese were convinced there was a way to get to Corregidor.

"When a soldier surrenders, he automatically loses his colors, rank, so forth. But in this particular case, it was not an individual surrender. It was Congress, President Roosevelt, it was a Congressional surrender. So I did not lose my colors. I can still fly our regiment colors, the United States flag which I still do. Oh, they gave me a bunch of medals. They could have given me a sack of beans, it would have been better. All those medals, they are pretty, I've got them in a drawer there."

The Death March

"That Death March, it was horrible, it really doesn't do me much good to talk about it. At Chris' funeral, he was one of my soldiers, I was a staff sergeant in the Army and he was one of my men. It kind of hurt me. We had lost touch, I hadn't talked to the man for fifty some years, his wife, there she was crying, the whole family, so I broke up too. But I think it helped me. I think I'm out of it all right.

"Bataan, after the surrender, it was unconditional, but the Japanese never honored it. At Mariveles, we started there. I would think about sixty miles all the way up to San Fernando Pampanga. We walked all of this, and the only reason I survived was because of sugar cane. Just as soon as we were mobilized at the little airfield we had, and all the soldiers gathered, the Japanese right behind us were moving their heavier artillery to start shelling Corregidor. Corregidor didn't stay quiet; they started answering back, they started their big guns and shooting right among us. That created a big panic as there were civilians and Filipino soldiers, and we all started running away. And that's what started the so-called Death March. The Japanese just let us go and go. Along the way, not too long, there was, one of these shells had hit a water buffalo and a cart. The buffalo, of course, was dead and the cart was turned over. And in this cart, the Japanese (they are kind of dumb), they thought it was firewood, but it was sugar cane. The sugar cane in the Philippines is about three inches in diameter and maybe four to six feet. I had been wounded in the leg, it was wrapped, it looked worse than it really was. It was just two flesh wounds, the bullets went right through. The Japanese seen me pick up this thing, using it as a cane, so I guess he thought, 'Well that's all right.' And I had three salt tablets. About one day I'd take a tablet and I'd chew on the sugar cane. That was nothing but energy, you know. So I got to San Fernando. There was no food, San Fernando was the first rice they gave us. We had no mess kits, so you put your hand out like that [he cups his two hands] and you get your rice in your hand and you gobble it down as fast as you could. That was the first meal we had, that was about the second day.

"It was sixty-five miles to San Fernando, in the heat, the dust, no food and artisian wells all over the place and you could count anywhere from fifty to sixty bodies around those wells. Because when you would break the ranks to go and get a drink of water, you had a bayonet in your back or your head would be chopped off. And they were just laying all over the place. You just didn't dare get off the road. The road, the dust was about that thick [measures with his hands, six inches]. We had regular army shoes and my khakis were in good shape. This dust was created by so many trucks going back and forth, the Japanese moving their equipment to the southern part of Bataan, the peninsula, heavy tanks, heavy equipment coming along those roads. They just pulverized it. It was ankle deep. There were times, whenever another Japanese group was coming with equipment, we would have to double step, trot. They were there with the sticks.

"A lot of guys, I seen healthier guys just put them on their back and push them all the way through. You had to have help. Once you fell, that's it. The Japanese would stab them and kick them off to the side of the road.

"The Philippine people were wonderful. Most of the people would risk their lives to throw a banana at you, or throw a rice paddy. When the Japanese looked the other way, they would throw food at you. A lot of them were punished, a lot of them were killed for doing it. When we left the battlefields in Bataan, from there towards San Fernando, even up to Camp O'Donnell, the Filipinos were lined up, to try to see if they could recognize some of their own. We were losing more Filipinos than Americans. They sure died off there at Camp O'Donnell. They put them in a blanket on a pole and take them over and bury them in the swamp. You could see those lines a mile long, day in and day out.

"I didn't like the country, I didn't like the people over there, the Filipinos or Japanese, and I told myself, 'I am not going to die here! I'm going back home to die!' And there is one story, and this is a 'believe it or not.' I had a sister who was quite religious, and in her bedroom she had a little makeshift altar in the corner. And every day she would go in there and have a glass of water in my behalf. To this day, I don't remember being thirsty, I don't remember going thirsty when so many were dehydrated. Believe it or not! How that happened, I don't know.

"We didn't get any water at all, but the sugar cane is so juicy, and it's sweet and energy, filled with sugar. There were several people using them as canes. But I think I was the only one who knew what they were really.

"There they put us on these little old narrow gauge flat cars, you couldn't even stand up in there and everybody was sick, everybody had the 'runs.' It was just one big mess. I don't remember how long it took us to from there to Camp O'Donnell. Camp O'Donnell, that was really bad because we were losing anywhere from 60 GIs a day, malaria and so forth. And we couldn't bury these guys. We were right there. I was on the burying detail there. You would dig about two feet and you'd hit water. So the only thing we could do was just stack these bodies and then put dirt over them. Then of course, the flies would penetrate that dirt. Boy, it was just one big mess.

"After I'd been at Camp O'Donnell about a month and a half, I volunteered. I had to get out of there, that was the only salvation or I would have died there on working details. By that time Corregidor had already surrendered also. On the battlefield we had trucks, tanks, all over the peninsula of Bataan. And the detail I got on, what we were doing there was picking scrap iron, anything that was metal, cutting them with torches and putting them on barges. Then they would ship them back to Japan. And lucky enough, we were working pretty hard with them [the Japanese] and they weren't too bad there. They were feeding us pretty good because we were working and doing a good job.

"We wouldn't have made it if we hadn't stuck together, especially if you get sick. There were so many ailments in these concentration camps. When you would get sick, you would try to help. One incident, this was at Cabanatuan, a little better condition, at least it was up on a hill, a concentration camp. One incident there that happened that I remember. We had outdoor latrines and this pig-weed. The Japanese used to think we were using it for bedding. That wasn't the case, we were eating it. It's very good, in salads. We would boil it, drink the water and also eat the vine. It's very soft, very tender, very good. And this fellow had dysentery so bad, his rectum was upside down. I said, 'There's only one thing to do.' I made him eat this vine and you know, that stopped it.

"At Cabanatuan, the Japanese, they made us farm, casaba. It's a root, it doesn't mature for about seven years. They mash it up and make a flour out of it. We were growing that and okra. And every time a Japanese would blink his eye, I would get me a little okra and eat it raw. To this day, I like okra.

"I was a guard. We had an electric fence and Japanese sentries around the compound. And we had to have guards over here because some of these prisoners would go berserk and they would head for that electric fence. As soon as they hit it, *they're dead. And it was our duty to intercept them, to tackle them or whatever it would take to keep them away.*

"When you have been laying on the concrete until your skin sticks to it, you are going to get up and run and kill yourself. That was a common thing every day, especially at Camp O'Donnell. Conditions at Cabanatuan were a little better, and the camps in Japan, oh, and the Bilibid Prison there in Manila. At least we had our own doctors there. We had a lot of amputees there and fellows that had been pretty badly beat up. We did have our own doctors there and some source of medicine. The Japanese would allow the Philippine hospitals to issue a minimum. We were getting some. I spent some time there at Bilibid. It was an old Spanish prison and they still had the dungeons and that sort of thing."

Fukuoka Number 4

"Then, after about two years of this, the Americans were beginning to get a little closer, so what the Japanese would do there was to ship all POWs from the Philippines to the mainland, to Japan. And they had all these boats, unmarked. By that time, we had the Flying Tigers in China and they were sinking anything that moved out of the sea. Twenty-four ships, that I was on, that left Manila Bay, four of them got to Kyushu. The rest were sunk at sea with prisoners in them. It was just slaughter. Our ship was hit by one of the bombers, but it hit in the front port, killed a bunch of them there, but it didn't damage the ship enough. It finally hit bottom at Kyushu, one of the southern islands of Japan. And there we went to a concentration camp 'Fukuoka Number 4,' that was the name of our camp. In that area, there were about three or four concentration camps. Conditions there were not good at all. By that time, even the Japanese were short of rations. You had three rations: the soldiers rations, which was fairly good, the working people rations, and the sick - they got nothing.

"The concentration camps in Japan, outside of the shortage of food and the hard work, the Japanese didn't slap us around like they did in the Philippines. On the march, they were extremely cruel; they were mostly kids, young Japanese. The older soldiers, the Mongolian Japanese, they were more of a general type, a career soldier, but these young kids they had just brought in, those were the mean ones. They were taught to be mean.

"Then on the working details there, like a dummy again, I volunteered. They needed some electrical engineers. I knew nothing about electricity, but I volunteered anyway. So they put us on this little flat train and we would go down about twelve miles to the factory. Well, all these engineers, they had scoop shovels out there and we shoveled pig iron. Pig iron is real heavy and it took us forever to convince those dummies to put a steel plate in the bottom where we could scoop it.

A Time to Speak

We were just getting deeper and deeper into the dirt. In the winter time, it was good working there because we could get heat from the electrical furnaces. They were making bomb casings, melt the steel and put them in and make a casing for a bomb. They were so desperate that they would take these darn things on the side of the ocean there and spray them with water to cool them down where they could go and put the explosives in and take them out. That's how desperate they were. When the salt water would hit these things, it would create little beads and that's the only salt I had for we had no salt for the rice. I have a lot of respect for it [rice] for it kept me alive for three and a half years.

"It was almost close to the end of the war when they dropped the first A-bomb at Hiroshima. Here's Kyushu and here's Nagasaki where they dropped the second one. And I wasn't too far from it. I remember, I can't say it was the A-bomb mushroom that I saw because every day the Navy was already in Japan's bays, and every night the subs would fire into these ships and most of them were carrying oil and that creates a mushroom almost like the A-bomb.

"The A-bombs - that saved my life. Right there at 'Fukuoka Number 4' there was a little hill in the back. What these Japanese had done, they had dug the side of that hill and anytime there was a heavy air-raid, they would move us in there. Later, we found out that this hill was, in other words, if the Americans had ever landed there, all of the prisoners who were in this camp would have been covered up in that hill. That was their plan. On the islands there, they discovered mass graves where they put the prisoners in these holes and poured gas on them and burned them and covered them up. They found a lot of those. There are a lot of gruesome stories.

"From there I walked close to Nagasaki and I never seen such horrible looking people in my life. They were speaking English, but they had on these radiation suits. We knew nothing about radiation. They finally picked me up in a hurry and put me on a little boat and shipped me over to this aircraft carrier. They were flying American and British flags. It was a big aircraft carrier that was actually a laboratory. When they got me in there, they washed me down with all kinds of colored water. They wouldn't feed me and I was hungry. Finally they would give me only the yolk of the egg, about three yolks of egg every once in a while, and tea. They kept me there about four days, delousing and what have you, shots.

"From there they flew me to Okinawa and from there they put me on this great big airplane. By then the B-29s were going strong, back to the Philippines, a hospital there, they had all these pretty little girls, striped shirts. Of course, it was a tent hospital and my gosh, you should see how they treated us, every time you'd turn around it was either a shot, vitamin pills, beer, candy, all day long, they wanted us to eat and eat and eat. What I remember most of all was the last shot that I got.

Here's a pretty little nurse and she says, 'Sergeant, this is your last shot!' You know, I was sore. And she says, 'I'm even going to make it a double shot.' 'Oh, no!' You know what it was? A double shot of bourbon! Then she says, 'You're free to go!' Stupid me, there were planes flying back to the States, Hawaii, then San Francisco. But there was a ship leaving that afternoon, and I wanted so bad to get off that stupid island, the Philippines, that I chose the boat rather than the following day on the plane. So here twenty-seven days on ship. Of course we got on board ship, two petty officers that had quarters on the ship, an icebox full of beer. Those guys were so nice. They picked me out and another sergeant and let us have their little cubby hole there, I don't know where they slept. And they'd come and fill up that ice box with goodies all the way through. So that was very nice.

"We got to San Francisco and, of course, we had bands and all kinds of welcome home. Then we went over to Angel's Island to another hospital for some more shots, delousing they call it. From there they put us on a train to Santa Fe, New Mexico, Brauns' General Hospital for more treatment. And I always vowed, I'm going to marry the first green-eyed babe I meet. It happened to be Delia, she was just a skinny little girl. I followed her around and finally she said 'Yes,' and we got married.

"Shortly after we got married, we went down to Ft. Bliss and I got my discharge. I wanted out of the army! After that, it has just been work, work, work.

"Quite an experience. I wouldn't want to go through it again. It made a better person out of me, really. I've seen them stand them up and bayonet them four or five times before a guy would die. I've seen them chop the heads off. It is a horrible sight. Every once in a while, I say to myself, 'How in the hell could I stand it?' Stand there and not being ABLE to do anything?' Like my captain, when his head was chopped up there. I could see his head and he was trying to say something and the dust and his blood just became mud. Nothing I could do. It's a hell of a feeling, I'll tell you. You can't do anything. A lot of them did, a lot of them broke down and took after the Japanese and they were dead immediately. You didn't stand a chance.

"For a long time I had dreams, especially about that head and other things. It's in my mind. And I remember just about all the good things and the funny things that happened, just like it happened yesterday.

"You know we were in there for a purpose. We were supposed to hold off the Japanese until the United States could get back on its feet. And three months, it took four months with Corregidor effort, we did help. And we were highly decorated for that. We have a lot of pretty medals. And I think the United States really appreciated our efforts there. All of the people I work with, who were in Europe, the Battle of the Bulge, they just treat me like a king.

A Time to Speak

"I think I have a better feeling for other people. For a long time, I kept quiet. It took me a long time to say, 'Goddammit, you were there, talk about it! Help people!' I'm with the DAV [Disabled American Veterans]. *I don't like to go to the veterans' hospital, but we go over there every once in a while. We hold bingo for the patients, we go over there, pat them on the back, try to make them feel a little better. Some of those guys are in worse shape than I'm in. They just can't get over it, especially some of these soldiers in Vietnam. They just can't get over what they went through and they are still holding it instead of getting it out."*

After the war, Sedilla returned to school on the GI bill. He worked with various companies in the nuclear field and retired from Stearns Catalytic.

In February 1946, General Masaharu Homma was executed by a firing squad. He was found guilty of being responsible for the Bataan Death March.

Americans were disheartened by the surrender on Bataan and General MacArthur's evacuation to Australia. Americans badly needed a victory.

End Notes

97	Martin Gilbert, *The Second World War*, p. 300
98	*The Second World War*, pp. 268, 293, 300
99	Excerpts, Interview, Imperial War Museum Sound Archive, Francis John Docketty, #4822
100	Excerpts, interview, Imperial War Museum Sound Archive, Sister Mary Louise Kroeger, #5022

A Time to Speak

CHAPTER 25
ALLIED SUCCESS IN THE PACIFIC

Three military offensives were planned to counteract Japan's victories: the Doolittle Raid on Japan, the battle of Midway, and the first ground offensive on Guadalcanal.

Doolittle's Raid

The idea of bombing Japan in retaliation for Pearl Harbor was on the minds of military men. The U. S. Navy conceived of a bombing raid, launched from an aircraft carrier, on the Tokyo-Yokohama area. The purpose of the raid was twofold: to raise morale at home and to demonstrate to the Japanese that they could be attacked on their own soil.

The plan was a daring attack, led by Lieutenant Colonel Jimmie Doolittle, an aviation pioneer who was known both as a daredevil pilot and as a scientist. He had a doctoral degree in aeronautical engineering from MIT. He developed techniques and instruments for flying blind and was responsible for helping develop high-octane aviation fuel.

The sixteen planes involved in the raid would bomb their targets and fly to airfields in unoccupied China, where friendly Chinese would help them return to safety. One of the members of the volunteer crew was Lieutenant William Bower.

"I volunteered for this mission. So I picked my airplane up and went to Eglin Field in Florida and met the others. There were a number of us who had been together in Minneapolis. We all got together in Florida, and I filled out my crew. I got a fellow named Thad Blanton, Waldo Bither, an old soldier I'd known at Lowry, he was the bombardier, Bill Pound, somebody new, who was the navigator, and Duquette, I just picked up casual, he was the gunner. We went down to Florida and began some intensive training.

"And in a day, General Doolittle came in and said he had this special mission and laid it on the line. He said, 'Keep your mouths shut, do what I ask you to do, I'll show you how to do it,' and all that came out to be true. We worked hard and we got our airplanes into shape. I was the engineering officer which means I had maintenance responsibility for these machines. I don't know why, I guess because I knew how to fix a Ford.

"Anyway, we did our little job and learned how to fly that airplane [B-25].

We did all those things we had to do, like learn how to take it off in short distance, how to fly 2,000 miles, make sure it was in good shape and take all the stuff out of it that we didn't want, didn't need. That tipped us off that we were going to do something. We took the radios out except one, put some tanks in it, bullet proof tanks, added some tanks. We had about 1,000 gallons of gasoline, added fuel to it, more than we were supposed to have. And we were sworn to secrecy. We did that. We didn't contact our families, we just disappeared. I must have called Lorraine once or twice. I didn't tell her where I was. And we went out to San Francisco and we had a last night on the town. We loaded our airplane on this carrier, we were going to go on a carrier, we knew that. We went into town and had a big deal, on the Top of the Mart. Lorraine's cousin was the only woman there. She lived there. I asked her to come and have dinner with us. She didn't know what the heck it was all about either, put her in a taxi and sent her home. The rest of us went down and got on that liberty ship, got back to the Hornet, pulled anchor and steamed out across to Japan, eighteen days worth, picked up most of the navy, the viable navy in the Pacific, the Enterprise, couple of cruisers, a number of destroyers and went on and were found to be twelve hours ahead of time.

"We had been briefed by a naval attaché who knew Japan. He'd been over there. All we had was oral descriptions by Lieutenant Jurika. That's all we had. We had pictures, but we had no maps of Japan. We picked our targets from what he said and he described what we would see. We took off between 8:20 and 9:20 in the morning after we had been discovered and went about our business one at a time, all by ourselves. We didn't have any formation, just a stream of airplanes went in, which was pretty good because they didn't know what the devil was coming.

"I saw just what Lt. Jurika said we were going to see. I made land fall above Tokyo, upstream, and then turned southwest and went down right on the shore line and went across an airfield, went across the bay. There were barrage balloons there. There was an American sub in the center of the bay; we never heard a word from him again, never heard a word from those people. But we were to see these barrage balloons; they were there. We climbed up above them and this target I picked out, jokingly, I called the Ford Motor Company. It was some sort of subsidiary of Ford, but it was an arms manufacturing company at Yokosuka. We hit it and went down across the peninsula and out to sea, down the coast until the weather got bad. I didn't see Mt. Fujiyama. I remember thinking about that later on, gosh, 'Where was that mountain?'

"And we headed for China. The weather turned bad, fortunately, so we climbed up into the weather and flew on instruments. We hit a pretty good wind and it made up that distance we were shy and we got to the place we were supposed to go and ran out of fuel. Most of us were thirty or forty miles from the intended place to land. One person, who must have been a miser, went on in another 100 miles. All of these planes landed in China except the one [one plane landed in Russia]. Three of them crash landed and were able to see the shore line. Most of us just stayed up in it until we ran out of fuel and then jumped out.

"The Chinese had to get us out of China. They were to put in this beacon at this airfield at Chu-hsien and the airplane was shot down or didn't get in there. They had evidently warned the Chinese guerrillas, friendly Chinese, Chiang Kai-shek's Chinese (even though he didn't agree with this whole thing). Evidently he had told the people they were coming in. And we were in rather a remote part of China, these people didn't know what an airplane was, or a man in a funny looking uniform was. They didn't recognize my pictures of a flag that I drew like this (picture of American and Japanese flags) on toilet paper. They didn't know an American flag. I drew a railroad and I drew a train. I remember this person didn't know what a train was. Finally somebody did. I was on a mountain, a pinnacle, in south China there are volcanic extrusions and I was up on top of one of those. It took me all day to get down.

"Then somebody led me into a village, just a system of valleys. We finally got into this little village and I stayed there part of the night. Then they brought some of my crew members in. The Chinese guerrillas brought them in. We got together. My gunner was injured. Then we started out and they took us to the place where we were intended to be. Within a couple or three days, we were all there. We were in a cave and there was a Christian mission. And we would go there and they fed us at this Christian mission. Then they would take us back to this cave because the Japanese were bombing this town all day long and all night. I don't think we expected it, but we didn't know they [the Japs] were coming for us. We didn't know what we had done in Tokyo for that matter.

"Then we started out and we went by rickshaw and we went by car for a while. Then we got a train, went on the train until they kept shooting that up, jumped off the train and got into the rice paddies and got back and got into the train and they'd shoot it up again. We got on a bus, I'm not quite sure of the details yet, but we finally came to a place where we met the Flying Tigers coming out of Burma.

"Later on we found out that they [the Japanese] killed 250,000 Chinese people who tried to get us out. They'd go through and wipe the village out. We'd stop there and they would give us a party, a dinner, we'd meet the Chinese officials, the next day the Japs would come and wipe it out.

"We went on to Chungking and met General Doolittle, who had preceded us, and had a pretty good time there for a couple of days, drank milk from madame's cow which was in her compound. Went into Chungking and walked around and found out that wasn't a place for white people. Well, we got into a C-47 and went into India and the darned Japs attacked as we landed in a place called Dinga and then we went on into Calcutta and came on home on a Pan American. That was the story." (Bower stayed in the military service for thirty years until 1968.)

Of the seventy-five flyers who landed in China, one died on bailout; two more drowned trying to swim ashore. Eight were captured by Japanese tropps, given a mock trial, and sentenced to death. Of those eight, three were executed by a Japanese firing squard and one died of malnutrition. The other four, their sentences commuted to life imprisonment without hope of parole, survived forty months of torture, beatings, and starvation. They were released after Japan agreed to an unconditional surrender in August 1945. [101]

Captured by the Japanese

One of the fliers captured by the Japanese was Jacob de Shazer. He was a prisoner of war for forty months, thirty-four of them in solitary confinement.

"We were captured in China and flown back to Tokyo. We stayed in Tokyo prison for sixty days. After we traveled by train and ship back to China and were kept in Shanghai for about seventy days. We finally moved to Nanking where we stayed until we were moved to Beijing, and that is where we were until the end of the war. It was about August 15, 1945 when the war ended and I think they began to release us and take us to a hotel. We must have been in the hotel for three or four days and then flown back to Washington, D. C. on American airplane. Eight men were captured and three were executed. One died from malnutrition. Only four survived."

De Shazer also wrote *I Was a Prisoner of Japan*, published in 1950 by The Bible Meditation League. It contains a more detailed account of his experiences and is cited with their permission.

"When I flew as a member of a bombing squadron on a raid over enemy territory on April 18th, 1942, my heart was filled with bitter hatred for the people of that nation. When our plane ran out of petrol and the members of the crew of my plane had to parachute down into enemy-held territory and were captured by the enemy, the bitterness of my heart against my captors seemed more than I could bear.

"Taken to prison with the survivors of another of our planes, we were imprisoned and beaten, half-starved, terribly tortured and denied by solitary confinement even the comfort of association with one another. Three of my buddies were executed by a firing squad about six months after our capture, and fourteen months later, another of them died of slow starvation. My hatred for the enemy nearly drove me crazy.

"It was soon after the latter's death that I began to ponder the cause of such hatred between members of the human race. I wondered what it was that made one people hate another people and what made me hate them.

"My thoughts turned toward what I heard about Christianity changing hatred between human beings into real brotherly love and I was gripped with a strange longing to examine the Christian's Bible to see if I could find the secret.

"I begged my captors to get a Bible for me. At last, in the month of May, 1944, a guard brought me the Book, but told me I could have it only for three weeks."

For a year, De Shazer began to read chapter after chapter, the Old and New Testaments and found the strength to bear the physical beatings and lack of food.

"Then one day as I was sitting in my solitary confinement cell I became very sick. My heart was paining me, even as my fellow prisoner had told me his was paining him just before he died of starvation.

"I slid down onto my knees and began to pray. The guards rushed in and began to punish me, but I kept right on praying. Finally, they let me alone. God in that hour revealed unto me how to endure suffering.

"At last freedom came. On August 20th, 1945, parachutists dropped onto the prison grounds and released us from our cells. We were flown back to our own country and placed in hospitals where we slowly regained our physical strength."

Jacob De Shazer completed his training at Seattle Pacific College and returned to Japan as a missionary. But the story doesn't end there.

At the end of the war, General Douglas MacArthur's staff chaplain contacted Bible Literature International (known then as The Bible Meditation League) and asked for a pamphlet which would help heal the wounds between Japan and the United States. The pamphlet in question included Jacob De Shazer's story and they were distributed at railroad stations. One person took a pamphlet, stuffed it in his pocket, and decided to read it later. By a curious coincidence, that person was Mitsuo Fuchida, who was the commander of the attack on Pearl Harbor. He read De Shazer's account of how Christianity changed his life. He purchased a Bible and eagerly read it. Mitsuo Fuchida converted to Christianity in 1950.

The Doolittle raid inflicted very little physical damage on Japan, but the psychological damage was important to Admiral Isoroku Yamamoto, commander in chief of Japan's combined fleet. The military had failed to protect Japan's homeland from attack. His rationale was that the Japanese would need to expand their protective defense to the south to include Midway. The American military feared a retaliatory move on the part of the Japanese. They were correct. The next target was Midway Island.

The Battle of Midway

The Japanese planned to invade Midway and to initiate a diversionary attack on the Aleutian Islands. Fortunately, the interception of secret Japanese radio messages gave the Americans much needed information about the Japanese intentions.

In spite of the fact that the American forces were outnumbered by Yamamoto's 200 ships, they destroyed four aircraft carriers, one destroyer, 332 aircraft and killed 3,500 men. American losses were only one aircraft carrier, one destroyer, 150 aircraft and 307 men. It was a decisive victory in the Pacific for the United States.

Almost a year later, in April 1943, another Japanese message was decoded, giving the time and itinerary of a visit by Yamamoto to the Japanese on Bougainville Island. The American Chiefs of Staff decided to shoot down Yamamota's plane. Operation Peacock was successful. When Japan mourned his death, the American role was not announced in order to protect its secret code-breaking ability.

Guadalcanal

The first real ground offensive in the Pacific took place on an obscure island, Guadalcanal, in the southern Solomon Islands, located below the Equator. Marines landed on Guadalcanal on 7 August 1942, but the complete defeat of the Japanese forces wasn't achieved until 8 February 1943.

The Marines dealt with stubborn resistance from Japanese troops who hid in the thick undergrowth and in caves. They endured months of jungle fighting, hand-to-hand combat in their foxholes, air attacks at night, dropping bombs and flares, and bombardments by Japanese cruisers and destroyers. What made the Marines' progress even more difficult was the climate: hot, humid with torrential rains. Not only did they suffer from battle casualties, but from diseases, such as malaria and tropical fungus irritations.

The fiercest battles were fought at Edson's Ridge, known as "Bloody Ridge," where Marines and soldiers fought side by side to defend Henderson Field, named for a Marine aviator killed in the battle of Midway.

The victory at Guadalcanal marked a crucial turning point in the Pacific War. But the cost was high: more than 1,200 Marines were killed and 3,000 wounded; the Army units had approximately 450 killed and 1,900 wounded; and the Navy had more than 3,600 killed in naval battles. Thirty ships were sunk and 76 were damaged. The military personnel losses were costly, and the most serious casualties needed to be evacuated to Hawaii and back to the United States.

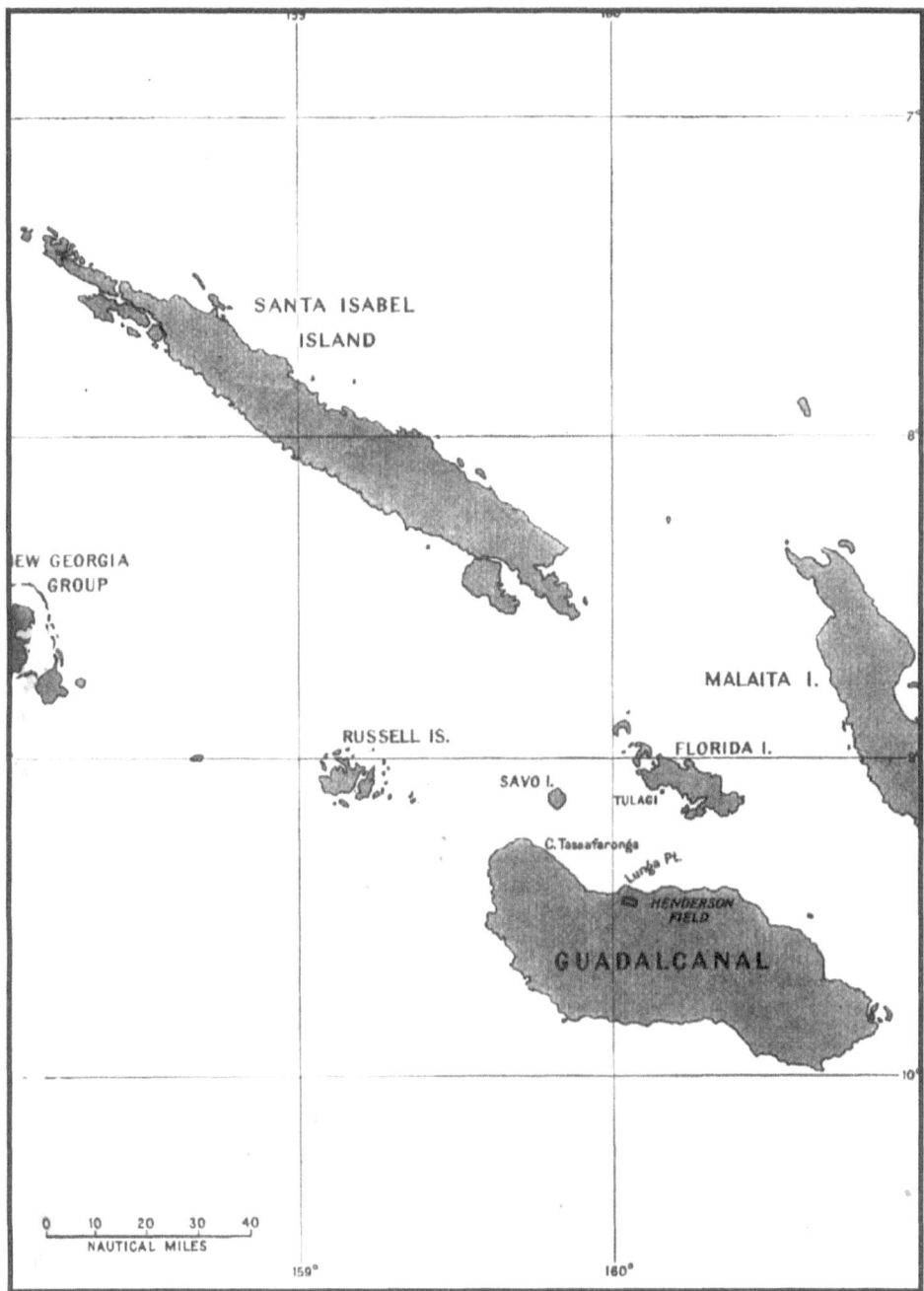

Chart of Guadalcanal Island and surrounding Islands, showing the location of Henderson Field

Evacuation of Casualties

Dorothy Young, the Army nurse at Tripler Hospital at the time of Pearl Harbor, volunteered to help evacuate casualties from Guadalcanal. The nurses at Tripler Hospital were experienced and knew what to do.

"We nurses had first hand knowledge of what we had and what we would need. When the time came, Guadalcanal was your first positive invasion into their world [the Japanese world]. They had spread themselves all up and down, into Indonesia, and they were trying to get into Australia and New Guinea. They had really spread themselves out. They needed more land, more supplies, more food because they were running out of space.

"The United States did have a hospital at Guadalcanal after it was secured. But what happened, they didn't send women in. They weren't expecting 10,000 casualties. So in the tropics like that, nothing heals. They were up against the same kind of thing we had, no supplies. At Hickam, they fixed up the inside of a B-17 and they put in bunks with regular pipe, bunks, layers and layers in the bomb-bay. They came over to the hospital and said, 'We'll just have to evacuate because we have so many casualties.' It was the 31st bomb squadron that were piloting the planes and we were on one of the planes. We went from Hickam. They were expecting us to make as many trips as it was going to take, to bring in casualties. Since we were baptized by fire [at Pearl Harbor], I volunteered.

"We went out of Hickam. This was a big deal. We went into Guadalcanal and brought casualties out. I just went down twice. It was pretty grueling. Because there was a lot of aerial activity around, they had the bomb bay doors open and we were maybe 5,000 or 6,000 feet up. We would lay on our bellies and take turns and watch the ocean to see if there were any downed pilots or wreckage. There were two nurses on that first trip and a doctor. We managed beautifully and it worked.

"They started bringing all the casualties that needed to be sent back to the United States, and to save lives if we could, maybe hold them over there in Hawaii until we could ship them back to the States because transportation was a problem.

"They had to be taken care of. We stopped once on Johnston Island which is south of Hawaii. We already had a secure base there and kind of broke the trip up. It was still a pretty hard trip. That was the only time we went in and evacuated. They sent Navy hospital ships. We just evacuated those more seriously injured It was a mess to try and say, 'You go, you don't.'"

Rehabilitation

The Marines who came home wounded were determined to get back to normal as quickly as possible. Some of those evacuated were in the Army Hospital in Fort Lewis, Washington. Bob Levine, who had joined the Army immediately after graduating as an electronic engineer, was in the same hospital, but not terribly sick.

"While I was there [Fort Lewis], I realized that the people who were really sick in the hospital were guys who were coming back from Guadalcanal, Tarawa, and all of those terrible places in the South Pacific where they had been shot up and some of them came back essentially as vegetables."

Levine was looking for something to do and organized classes in electronics.

"I wandered around and talked to some of the other people and I said, 'Anybody interested in learning about electronics?' I got a couple of hands and we found an empty classroom, part of the hospital was set up as if it were a school. And so I went in and we started from the beginning. We had two or three guys, the next day I had four or five guys. By the end of the week, I had about twenty guys.

"So I taught sort of beginning electronics and then in order to make the thing real as a lot of these guys wanted to be electronic technicians as soon as they got out of the Army, I discovered a Signal Corps close by with a huge warehouse with electronic parts to fix radios.

"It didn't take me long to set up a lab and before long I was conducting these classes in the lab where we would have a little demonstration and experiment. I started building little electronic devices. Soon somebody came in and said, 'Do you fix radios?' and I said, 'Yeah, sure,' and in the back of my mind I thought it would be a great thing for them to learn on the job. People came in and brought their radios and they would say, 'How much will that be?'

"Before long we had a long stream of broken radios. I had all these wounded guys learning how to do it so they could have some direct hands on experience. It was one of those serendipitous situations. I did that until they discharged me from the hospital.

"Some of them were too sick to come to classes. So I would actually go into the wards and sometimes do some teaching right there.

"Morale was surprisingly high. I remember seeing one guy with literally a hole right through his knee and you could see through it. He was staying there until they could patch it up. I said, 'What are you going to do?' 'As quick as I can get out of here, I'm going to go, I've got a girl friend, I'm going to get married and who knows, I may be an electronic technician or something.' They were anxious to get out of the Army and go back to civilian life and do the things they had been dreaming about for the last three to five years. I don't remember meeting anybody who was depressed, but maybe it was the way that I sought out people who were interested in doing something." [102]

The Occupation in Guadalcanal

Although organized resistance on the island of Guadalcanal ceased in February 1943, bombings and air raids continued to be common and the United States used Guadalcanal as a base of operations. Gil Pannebaker enlisted in the Navy Seabees in the supply area and was stationed on Guadalcanal.

"Originally, the unit was formed as a naval construction battalion. That's why we had the letter 'C' and 'B.' Of course when we got to boot camp, there was a lot of joke about the 'C and B' being 'confused bastards,' so we had all that to contend with.

"But later on, Seabees was formed and we had more identity. Our reputation had to grow from the very beginning. There had been civil engineering departments in the Navy, but this Seabees thing was a new adventure."

The 4th Special Construction Battalion landed on Guadalcanal on 11 May, 1943. During their tour of duty there, they earned the reputation of moving more cargo than any other unit in the area. Pannebaker recalled his first night on Guadalcanal and the big June air raid.

"The first night we arrived on Guadalcanal, of course, we had no tents to sleep under. The view above was something easy to see and they had this Japanese plane in searchlights, following it along. We hadn't seen this routine before because one of those P-38 night fighter planes was up there, unbeknownst to us. All of a sudden, the two big searchlights went out and we thought, 'My gosh, they've lost him.' But instead we saw this string of tracer bullets come from this fighter plane, hit the Jap plane, set him on fire, and all of us cheered. It was the best sight we'd seen because we hadn't seen any damage done to Japanese. That was the first night.

"We went through five and a half months of bombing after that. Some of it was nuisance bombing by a single Japanese plane and other times, I think it was June 14 of '43, 120 Japanese planes came down from Rabaul, their base, and our fellows shot down 96 of those 120 planes. That was a daytime thing that we could see very well. We could see the destroyers and other ships out in the bay there.

"Our main task was to unload ships because, as the Marines had landed on Guadalcanal and left their gear on the beach and moved inland to fight, here was all this gear, materials and even ammunition that they couldn't possibly take inland with them. Then the commanders of ships were complaining too that it was taking too long to get stuff off those ships. They wanted to get out of there, they didn't want to get bombed. Our primary object, besides having a lot of men skilled in various construction trades, we had a lot of men who were assigned to the companies as stevedores to get those ships out of there. We got a lot of commendation *for that because that was a shortcoming that all of the forces had over there in the Pacific, to get the stuff off the ships and send them back.*

"The most memorable thing about time spent on Guadalcanal was probably that 120 planes coming in that noon. That was a grand sight and to see so many of them shot down. After all, we were there for one purpose. It made you happy to see that we could win." [103]

The Doolittle Raid, the victory at Midway and the campaign at Guadalcanal were strategic and moral victories for the United States and its Allies. The Japanese were kept from establishing lines to Australia.

Although the tide began to turn for American troops in the Pacific, British troops did not celebrate a military success until their victory at El Alamein in October 1942.

End Notes

101 *Air Force Magazine*, November 1993, published by the Air Force Association, "An American Hero,", C. V. Glines, pp. 24-25
102 Levine lives in Princeton where he gives wine appreciation courses.
103 After the war, Pannebaker was in the printing business in Pueblo and later in Boulder, Colorado.

CHAPTER 26
ALLIED SUCCESS IN EUROPE; THE GERMAN REACTION

As Midway and Guadalcanal were turning points both in military success and morale on the home front for the United States, the dramatic victory at El Alamein was a success for the British. General Montgomery's Eighth Army defeated Field Marshal Rommel's German-Italian Army on 1 November 1942. Later, the Allies opened a second front in Europe, Operation Torch, on 8 November 1942. Finally, after a long series of battles, the Germans, under General von Paulus, surrendered to the Russian Army on 31 January 1943.

El Alamein

In North Africa, German and Italian troops were on their way to Alexandria when General Montgomery launched an attack at El Alamein [Egypt]. This time the British had the advantage: the decoders at Bletchley had received information about German positions and German weaknesses in fuel oil; and Montgomery had tanks, aircraft and guns.

Australians, New Zealanders, South Africans and British fought side by side. In spite of Britain's superior military strength, victory at El Alamein depended on the preparedness, skill and courage of the armies. One Scottish officer, Colonel J. D. MacGregor, who participated in the battle of El Alamein, told his story in a taped interview for the Imperial War Museum Sound Archive.

"Everyone spent some time in the front lines with the Australians, carrying out duties to get the feel of things. A fortnight before the battles, we went into intensive training, to do the set piece attack over and over again on ground well to the south of Alamein with tanks, guns, firing, ammunition, etc. We did the advance we were going to do on Alamein in absolute detail, every timed move, the formation on the start line, the advance, control pitch, flanks being in touch with the center. Everybody was completely familiar with how the movement would take place. We practiced our skills, with our weapons, with our first aid, discussions - what would happen if this went wrong or that went wrong? how did we reinforce? how did we counterattack? - every possible contingency was discussed. Nobody except senior commanders knew about dates - we knew it was getting closer because of the intensity of activity around us and in the air above us.

"... Every company had made a sand model of the ground over which we were going to attack. Every single man was shown where he would be... Cooks, supplies were already in their base headquarters and every night they practiced what you do in battle, come up in hours of darkness with hot meal, replenishment of ammunition with mail pouch and disappear into the night. They came every 24 hours.

"... We moved at night, arrived in final assembly area at one quarter past midnight, Friday, 23 October 1942. The area was pre-dug by our own people, slit trenches laid out in the exact formation we would cross that ground, a slit trench for two men, camouflage nets over the top of it When we arrived at that area, we had a hot meal brought up to us. Before first light we were inside our slit trenches, hidden from view, thousands of soldiers hidden from the view of the Germans, lying in the whole of that Friday, no movement was allowed above ground except emergencies.

"...At dusk we came out of our slit-trenches, had another hot meal and very soon we were on the move through the front line. They had been out earlier and marked with cable pegs where the battalion would form up. From those cables, we could, in the dark, find out center lines. Came through about 8 o'clock through the front line into no man's land and got into position we would advance in, company by company, platoon by platoon, man by man and we settled down in the dark to wait. At 2140, the whole of the eastern sky erupted in flashes of light and everybody knew that's the 650 guns that Monty talked about. And soon the whistle of shells overhead, tremendous crashing roar as they landed in front of us in the enemy lines. Then the planes were silent and we stood up every man and started to advance.

"At 2200 hours the two big search lights that had been in the sky behind us swung down and over us and crossed beams which to us was the cross of St. Andrew, but it was indicating the line of advance of the whole of the 8th Army. This time it was a creeping barrage and suddenly the German fire came back and we were under heavy shell fire from then onwards.

"... It happened, not only once but many times, I was constantly amazed and tremendously proud of the behavior of the men, not the biggest or the strongest, but quite often ordinary little chaps, who just got up, shook the dust off and carried on. In the midst of all the noise, you had the pipers. Every company had a piper who played the company tune.

"We reached our objectives, the objectives were either known German positions or higher ground (ridge) positions and that been noted in pre-battle intelligence.

"The breakthrough at Alamein was November 1, 1942. There was tremendous elation. It was a stunning victory, the first major land victory of the Empire forces; that was the first phase, and when you saw day after day droves of prisoners coming back, there was the evidence, the battlefields showed the rest, burned-out german tanks, supply units, vehicles - one had this feeling of elation.

"On the first Sunday in November, we went to El Doba airfield for a rest. In the sand dunes, there had been rain, flowers blooming. . . The Signal Regiment had been able to tune into the BBC in England, and with as much amplification as was possible in these wartime sets, and we gathered around and we heard the most remarkable sound. It was the church bells which Churchill and the King, between them, had arranged that they would be rung to celebrate Alamein. Otherwise, ringing of church bells was the national signal for invasion of our country. To hear them rung and realize we had played some part in that was quite incredible." [104]

Stalingrad

The German Army was prepared to take Stalingrad at any price and fulfill Hitler's boast that Stalingrad would soon be German. But the Russian defenders were equally determined to achieve victory and save the city which was dear to Russians. The soldiers fought bloody battles in streets and in buildings, the Russian soldiers without regard to danger.

The Russian and German armies were locked in a deadly combat within the city, fighting bloody battles in streets and in buildings. Russian troops fought without regard to danger. They were also helped by military aid from the British and the Americans, by the horrendous conditions of extreme cold, and the fact that German soldiers were exhausted.

By Christmas time, German soldiers were eating cats and dogs, and even horse meat was scarce. The soldiers' morale was very low.

On 8 January 1943, the Russian General Rokossovsky sent General von Paulus an ultimatum to surrender his troops which were trapped in Stalingrad. When von Paulus refused, Red Army troops encircled the German troops and continued to push onward on all sides. They overcame enemy resistance and captured German military equipment and men.

German newspaper editorials talked about serious setbacks against the Bolshevist armies who had become dangerous and stubborn opponents of the Wehrmacht. [105]

German pessimism was confirmed with the surrender of von Paulus on 31 January. Russia's victory at Stalingrad and the victory at Leningrad the week before marked a turning point in the war in Europe, but at an enormous price. Among the 284,000 German soldiers caught in the Stalingrad trap, 160,000 were killed in action; 34,000 were evacuated by air; and 90,000 were marched eastward to Siberia.[106]

Two Stories from Russia

Ludger Hartmer served in the German Army and served in Russia in January 1945. He was at Stalingrad and later he was a prisoner of war in Russia. In a letter he wrote his two war stories:

The Orchard Story

"I came to the Russian front late in autumn 1941 immediately after my promotion to the rank of a lieutenant in the artillery of the 18th Panzer Division. After relatively 'peaceful' weeks - static warfare - at the front north of Briansk we had to move to the front south-east of Orel where I was in the front line as artillery observe. There, it was in February - at the time when the battle of Stalingrad came to its end - our lines were attacked by masses of Russian soldiers. They came in huge numbers as I had never seen before and they attacked our weakly manned lines several days and nights without a pause. It was bitterly and most of the time there was heavy snowfall and even snow storms. I did my job as I had learned at the artillery school and finally managed to stop the attacks. After that, at the first light of day there was a wall of dead Russian soldiers in the snow in front of our lines. Fighting was over, there was no shot, only dead silence.

"Then I left my cover to have a look especially at an orchard where the attackers had tried to get shelter. There, when I opened the door of a garden hut, I found among the some dead Russian soldiers, three little children about three years old. They were trembling with cold and fear, wearing only torn shirts. They were starved and their bellies were swollen. I took the poor children to one of the undestroyed huts nearby where I asked two women to look after them. Then I gave them some blankets, food and chocolate, admonishing the women to help the children to survive. Leaving the hut, I told them firmly that I would come regularly and see what they had done. Unfortunately this, however, was impossible for me because we had to move to a southern part of the bent front lines between Orel and Kursk."

The Tank Story.

"On January 12th, 1945, the long-awaited Russian offensive on the Vistula (Weichsel) began. We knew from aerial photographs that in the Russian 'bridgehead of Baranow' where the course of the Vistula river makes a big bend to the west, there was an immense concentration of artillery (there were more than 240 heavy guns on one kilometre in that bridgehead. We knew equally well that there

were more than 3000 tanks ready to attack the German lines. The number of infantrymen was ten times higher than ours. At about three o'clock in the morning on January 12th the Soviet guns began with their 'preparatory fire' to lure out the German barrage. Some hours later all the Soviet heavy guns began with their devastating fire which lasted nearly for two hours.

"Shortly after the heavy gunfire had begun I was sent to the commanding staff of the 17th Panzer Division (I had to change from the 18th to the 17th Panzer Division after I had been wounded in the 'biggest tank battle of military history,' in the battle of Kursk on July 31st, 1943). Among other officers from different units we were waiting for special orders in the hut of a little Polish village about 40 kilometres south of Kielce. It was still dark with snow covering the fields and houses standing in a long row along the village street. All of a sudden I had a strange feeling that something was wrong. We were more than 30 kilometres behind the front line! I looked out into the darkness and suddenly realized that at least one hundred Russian tanks, all in white camouflage paint were rolling towards our village. I gave the alarm signal, left my car behind and ran into the snow covered fields together with my chauffeur. We heard the tanks rattling along the village street, heard the guns being fired and all the noise of fighting. The scene was absolutely chaotic. We two, up in the fields, had the feeling of being secure, but not for a long time. Suddenly a single T34 tank followed us who were running and falling down again and again. When we were lying on the ground we expected to be shot by the machine gun or to be rolled over by the tank. I do not know how long they played cat and mouse with us. Was it a quarter of an hour or more? To us, it seemed to be hours. Finally the tank stopped again, about three metres behind us. The commanding officer appeared in the hatch, moving both his arms and shouting something which we could not understand and then ... the tank turned round and want away towards the burning village. Why didn't they kill these two 'fascist soldiers' which should have been their duty especially according to Marshal Zhukov's appeal to his soldiers before January 12th, culminating in the words, 'We'll cruelly take revenge on them for everything...Woe be to the country of the murderers! Stalin is with us - the victory is with us!'

"After this 'adventure' we went cross-country until we met German army units on their way to the Oder river.

"There were some more breathtaking adventures for me later till the end of the war and even after the capitulation, but now I think I should bring my letter to a close."

Operation Torch

Roosevelt and Churchill decided (July 1942) that the hoped-for second front would be in North Africa and not on the Continent. The first combined Allied initiative in the war, Operation Torch was in the Mediterranean on 8 November 1942 when troops and tanks landed in Casablanca, Oran, and Algiers in North Africa. It brought together troops and generals from various countries and combined military staffs, all needing to cooperate and understand their differing military strategies, as well as the dissimilar characteristics of combatants from various countries, in order to succeed in gaining control of the North African coast.

Complete victory in North Africa did not come until May 1943 when the Allies controlled the North African coast. De Gaulle claimed North Africa as a base of operation for the Free French.

Collaboration and the Vichy Government

After their defeat at El Alamein and their losses against the Soviet Army, the Third Reich became less and less tolerant of Jews. Now Jews were forced to wear the yellow star on their clothing. The French police of the Vichy government cooperated with the Gestapo and rounded up Paris Jews for deportation. Members of the Resistance were considered "Communists" or "terrorists," and were often denounced by neighbors, or picked up by the Gestapo and deported because of their anti-Vichy and anti-Nazi activities.

Collaboration with the enemy included what were called "passive collaborationists," those who adopted a wait-and-see attitude, assuming the Allies would rescue them, or that Germany would fall from within. Others wondered what General de Gaulle could do from London and thought perhaps it was more prudent to listen to the voice of reason which was Pétain and Vichy, even though submission to Germany was displeasing. When they saw Rommel's defeat by Montgomery and the invasion in North Africa, some changed their minds.

Collaborationists denounced their neighbors for several reasons: out of jealousy; to receive the monetary reward [at the time, it was 100 F]; or because they fervently believed in the Nazi cause.

Je suis partout

The collaborationists had a semi-official newspaper, *Je suis partout* (I am everywhere), whose editor was Robert Brasillach, a writer and journalist, and politically a fascist. The newspaper reappeared in Paris in February 1941 after eight months' interruption of its publication. Brasillach and his fellow writers wrote articles of virulent anti-Semitism. These writers claimed that it was the Jews who wanted war, who were at war against Germany, and therefore at war against the French. "They are our enemies and shouldn't have any more rights than a prisoner of war." (23 May 1942)

They also were anti-British and were convinced they would be present at the crumbling of British power. (21 February 1942)

In their writings, they called the United States weak, a country whose raw materials and resources were not enough to guarantee the potential for war. What characterized Americans was their "amateurism," their complete lack of experience. (2 October 1942)

Certain that everyone was awaiting the spring invasion, so hoped for by the Germans, the editorials deplored "the systematic destruction of Normandy by the Anglo-Americans" (16 June 1944). There was a somewhat pitiful entry (23 June 1944), "England will pay."

At the end of the war, Robert Brasillach was tried, found guilty and condemned to death and shot 7 February 1945.

Vel' d'Hiv

By July 1942, in all territories occupied by the Third Reich, the Gestapo and the SS organized the great round-ups of the Jews, often aided by the local authorities. The Vichy government ordered the arrest of all Jews in Paris, the roundup known as 'Vel' d'Hiv.' The Jews were sent first to the Drancy prison and later deported to work camps and concentration camps in Poland. Roger Dutertre deplored the fact that the roundup was conducted by the French police.

"And the roundup at Vel d'Hiv, it was the French police who did it, not the Germans. It is tragic to admit that. There were some police who told the people, 'Hide, save your yourselves.' It was the French who brought other French to Vel d'Hiv. *They treated them like cattle. They rounded them up like cattle like one would round up cattle at the fairgrounds. The conditions of* Vel' d'Hiv,'*in which they lived were appalling conditions. It was frightful to grasp that it was the French, a certain category of French. Why? They wanted to be properly seen, for malice, sometimes for the bounty, other times to take vengeance on their neighbors."*

The Vichy Syndrome

The French obsession with Vichy, sometimes referred to as the "Vichy syndrome," has become as controversial for the French as the debate over the atomic bombs dropped at Hiroshima and Nagasaki has become for Americans.

For years, French presidents, beginning with de Gaulle, refused to recognize the Vichy government as a legitimate government of France and therefore not responsible for its actions of government collaboration with Nazi Germany, or for its politics of anti-Semitism. Some French, like Geneviève Moline, still feel guilty about the attitude at the time.

"For me, this time was difficult, an ugly moment, something that profoundly

wounded my own self-esteem. We the French were not good. We were contemptible. A good half of the population accepted the government of Vichy."

In July 1995, President Jacques Chirac, on the anniversary of Vel d'Hiv, recognized the Vichy government as the legal French state at that time and therefore responsible for the deportation of Jews.

The actions on the part of the Vichy government and the Third Reich had the opposite effect of what Hitler hoped: it escalated the actions of Resistance movements.

End Notes

104 Excerpts, Interview, Imperial War Museum Sound Archive, Col. J. D. MacGregor, #12572
105 *The New York Times*, 25 January 1943, pp. 1-2.
106 *The Second World War*, p. 398

CHAPTER 27

1943: THE MANY FACES OF RESISTANCE MOVEMENTS

In 1943 the acts of resistance and defiance against the Nazi regime became more militant. Several factors contributed to the shift to combativeness. The Nazi government became more repressive: persecution of the Jews intensified; heavy German losses created a shortage of machines, ammunition and workers for the German military complex. Rumors of another Allied invasion in Europe encouraged resistants to react more aggressively.

STO

The Vichy government in France collaborated with the Third Reich to furnish the manpower which Germany needed. At first there was the "Relève," a call for volunteers from France to go work in Germany. In exchange for three volunteers, the Reich would liberate one prisoner. Since this invitation met with complete failure, obligatory work service laws were passed, *Service de Travail Obligatoire*, known as STO. The law passed on 4 September 1942 and again on 16 February 1943. These laws required Frenchmen, ages 18 to 50 years old to register for work in Germany.

Yves Briand was twenty-one when he was called.

"I can tell you that I did not respond to the STO. I found out that with a medical certificate, you were classed in such and such a category. I found a doctor who gave me a false certificate out of kindness. Later he was arrested and deported."

Briand escaped only temporarily. He was arrested in his classroom by the Gestapo on 23 November 1943 and sent to a series of prisons. Later he was transferred to a concentration camp at Mauthausen and a work camp in Melk in April 1944, where he worked in a subterranean factory for a year until 6 May 1945 when an American jeep arrived to liberate the prisoners.[107]

Raymond Paris from Sainte-Mère-Eglise was nineteen when he and escaped from being rounded up.

"The STO, it was promulgated by Pétain and by Vichy. I left on bicycle to come back to Sainte-Mère. Before arriving at St. Pellerin and St. Hilaire Petitville, I came across these Germans. They were everywhere in the road. I turned, went

down the hill, always in the middle of groups of two. I saw a truck with a chevaux-de-frise. To leave for obligatory service, there is a roundup; you embark in the truck, then a cattle car to be taken to Germany. I panicked. What to do? There was a passageway to go to the house. There was an old women and I asked her what was happening. She said, 'Since morning, the Germans have been here and they are rounding up all the men.'

"*I saw a young girl about my age going up the hill on foot, with a bicycle. I had to think fast. When I saw the girl, I went down the passageway. I arrived and took her by the waist, and I said, 'We are engaged.' Lucky for me, I ran into a girl like that. She said, 'There are a lot of guys in the truck. She played the game and thanks to that, I got out. We kissed on the mouth. We were very much in love and locked in a passionate embrace all along the route. The Boches made fun of us, 'Monsieur fuck, fuck, up yours, Mademoiselle,' And I replied, 'Ja, Ja.' I didn't want to annoy them. We passed by all of the Germans and a little farther along, we got our bicycles. She lived in the last house on the left. I managed to escape.*

"*Years later, I went to the same spot. No one could tell me her name or where the family had gone. We all presumed it was a immigrant family, like so many others that had arrived in Normandy.*" [108]

Alsatian Workers

Once Hitler incorporated the region of Alsace-Lorraine into Germany, Alsatians were recruited for obligatory work. This was a sticky situation for those who were Alsatian, were they French or German? [Alsace-Lorraine, separated from Germany only by the Rhine River, became part of Germany at the end of the Franco-Prussian War in 1870. At the end of World War I, the region was restored to France as part of the Versailles Treaty.]

The threat of forced labor convinced many Alsatians, when possible, to engage in Resistance activities. Sabotage was made easier because most Alsatians spoke German fluently. Georges Kieffer served in the French Army until the Armistice in 1940, then returned to his home in Strasbourg. On 30 July 1940, he was called for obligatory work.

"*It wasn't just that Alsace-Lorraine was occupied, but annexed. We were considered as German subjects since our country was annexed by Germany, therefore we had become German. It was very difficult. We were liberated as prisoners of war at the beginning, but they realized they could have us work for them in Germany. It was a calculated program, as everything they did.*

"*Eight days after my liberation as a prisoner of war, it was necessary to register for obligatory work. Then eight days after, depart to work in Germany. I* worked as a manual laborer for the auto routes they constructed at that time in Germany.

"We worked for a German firm. This firm considered us as 'free workers.' We were not imprisoned. We were paid. It was located about fifty miles from Strasbourg where my parents lived. Every weekend we went home. That lasted almost a year."

Their next construction job was in Krasnia, forty miles from Moscow where they maintained the route and reconstructed bombed-out bridges for the TODT organization. [The TODT enterprise was named for a German engineer, Fritz Todt who conceived of it as a way to combat unemployment. Before the war it constructed the Siegfried Line.]

"Then the firm we worked for had a construction job in France. So it was necessary to transfer us to France. So we were to be repatriated, but we didn't know where. But for us, it was France. There was a team of eight, nine or twelve Alsatians, all from the region of Strasbourg. We arrived at Dinard/St. Malo.

"We were hired to construct the Atlantic Wall all along what was called the 'Emerald Coast.' There was construction, we were stationed at Dinard and we worked on the construction at Pleurtuit.

"Each morning there was a car that came to transport us to the construction site. I ran a diesel engine machine, transporting material. And it was there that I had contact with the Resistance, it began then. The organization TODT, we had a uniform, but we were always in civilian clothes, never in uniform except when I needed to. It served me all the same. When in civilian clothes, I couldn't get entrance into certain areas. For information, one needed to be in uniform. You understand the tactic. Since I was Alsatian and I spoke German as well as French, it was an enormous advantage. I could take the documents in a corner and get all the information. I spoke German and I would say to the workers, you should do this, do that - easy to do, but dangerous for me.

"I arrived in February '43 and I was arrested 29 November '43. I worked almost eight months, it was an English group, the group 'Buckmaster' which was in this area. I furnished the chief information as one does in a Resistance group, making sure never to give everything at once in case it was intercepted en route - the plans in one part, the installations in another. So I worked like that. And one day they asked me to go to the Pas de Calais in the north to begin a work to fabricate concrete. I didn't know until later it was to construct the runway for the V-2 rocket. I stayed there four or five weeks, and there I could naturally furnish information about the installation which never functioned because it was bombed.

"All of the twenty-eight members of the Resistance group were denounced. I had a situation of being in two camps. The Germans didn't know whether to consider me French or German. I was arrested with the others and we found ourselves at St. Malo. We left for Rennes. Naturally, they began the interrogations.

"It turned bad for me: I was convoked before the tribunal, before the German officials. They judged me as a deserter. In addition to my work for TODT, I had also received a mobilization order for the German army and I had to leave. In fact, I was supposed to leave for Strasbourg the day I was arrested. It was that day (D-Day), I was condemned to death. What saved me was that my condemnation was made at Rennes and they couldn't execute me without the confirmation from Paris. It was sent and it never came back. It saved me from execution but it didn't save me from deportation.

"I was still considered a German deserter and I couldn't be mixed in with members of the Resistance. They made a distinction, military and deserters had separate prisons. . . I didn't think they knew I was condemned to death; I didn't think the papers had followed me. . .

"Then one day, the cell door opened and I saw two Gestapo. Finally the papers had followed me. They had my dossier, and I knew I had been condemned to death.

"I was then put in a cell, all alone, handcuffs on both hands and feet. What was the hardest was the complete isolation, for one's morale. Nothing to do, no book to read, no one to chat with, not even the possibility to sleep on your bed which was folded and attached to the wall. You slept on the floor, on the concrete. There was nothing in the cell, absolutely nothing. You turn around like a savage beast in a cage. I stayed in that cell for two or three months. Then one day the fortress was bombarded."

After that bombing in January 1945, Kieffer was evacuated and taken to Dachau, then to Neubourg. He managed to escape into a nearby forest, then to a farm not far from Munich, where a French prisoner, working on the farm, was willing to hide him. He was repatriated fifteen days later by American troops. [109]

Tracts

August Le Carpentier and some members of his Resistance cell in Normandy distributed tracts to different constituencies.

"What we did before was information, tracts, composing and printing tracts, putting forth the problem for all the population. We had tracts differentiated according to social categories, tracts for women, for agriculture workers to tell them not to do certain things, and tracts for workers."

One tract, prepared for all of the patriotic youth groups, including Catholics, Protestants, Young Communists, Sports, and the Union of Patriotic Students, urged them to *Resist the STO!*

To counteract Petain's Mother's Day Festival in which he gave out medals for large families, one tract told mothers to ask for supplementary bread on Mother's Day, May 31. "No lying speeches, no decorations, no pacifying gifts". *We want BREAD!"*

The most detailed tracts were designed to prepare the French for the eventual Allied invasion and liberation. Tracts were targeted at the French gendarmes, to the working class, and to the general population.

Gendarmes were reminded not to be deceived by Pétain and aid the German invaders. A call to workers, employees and civil servants asked for a national insurrection at the time the Allies were going to land.

Distribution of tracts might seem like an easy task and free from risk, but Le Carpentier said,

"In the Resistance, there were some bizarre things. In '43 I had left the tracts in Ville-Dieu, in the house where I was living, on a buffet in plain sight. I was warned in St. Georges Montcocq (just above Saint Lô) of the arrest of some friends. I was there with my liaison agent. As soon as I learned about my friends' arrest, I said, 'This is serious, I must go back to Ville-Dieu,' and I went back by the route that I knew.

"They had searched everywhere, the armoire, the linens. At my parents, it was the same thing, they had rummaged through the linens. I learned that if you want to hide something, you leave it like that, in plain sight of everyone. We didn't keep many of the tracts because we had a network that distributed them in mailboxes.

"And I left Ville-Dieu, I left over a cliff, like the Rangers at Point du Hoc. I spent a month in the Calvados region and I came back at the end of June, in the middle of the afternoon, to Ville-Dieu where I picked up contacts again.

"Do you know how I came back? Dressed as a woman. In the Resistance, all my friends called me 'Jacques.' From then on, they called me 'Jacqueline.' I was superb; I had a beautiful, broad-brimmed sun hat, a beautiful dress. It was the shoes that bothered me, a little narrow, especially for the feet of a soccer player. I dyed my hair. Friends gave me a bottle of dye and told me to use all of it. I put it all on my head. I had dark black hair. I came back in a horse-drawn cart with a farmer.

"This farmer took those risks involved in transporting me. What I had in my bag was my gun. If a German wanted papers, I would have been obliged to shoot him. And the farmer, what would have happened? Condemned. He had a lot of courage.

"It is difficult for anyone today to plunge into the ambiance of that time. We were only men and women, not heroes or heroines. Some were imprudent and took actions which were costly.

A Time to Speak

"What was difficult was the clandestine nature of the Resistance. You didn't have a name, you were on the qui vive twenty-four hours a day, you had to pay attention to your contacts. You needed to make sure of where you were, how to get out, how to kill, to kill yourself to avoid torture. You had no contact with your family, it was hard on them. You acted in a play. After six or seven years as a Resistant, it was easier to use a Bren gun than a pen."

Letter From Paris

Written in English in March 1947, this letter was a thank-you to a family for a CARE package they had sent. E. P. summed up, in these excerpts, how she felt about the occupation.

". . . I will go over my 'experiences' again. I understand now, as I did not before, why returned soldiers or, in fact, people who have lived through 'fire', are reluctant to relate details...There is something so much bigger in the 'living of these things than can ever be put into words, written or spoke, that it comes easier to just think about them than to speak of them. There are also the things one could wish to forget, were forgetting possible. Although perhaps, it is also a duty to remember...."

"There were no atrocities in our neighborhood during the German occupation, except during the middle of August 1944, when the beginning of the end came for the Germans around here. It is very difficult to give you the impression of what it was like to live under German rule, after the first shock of knowing that they were nearing Paris, and then that they were there. There was a feeling of 'choking' about it - of being in a huge prison within which certain liberties were tolerated, but where there was a hidden meaning to everything that was done and said around us, and where we were without direct contact with the rest of the world. A prison where certain questions were allowed but where the answers were known to be lies - a prison so huge as to give an impression of liberty - and yet where nothing could be said or done according to <u>truth</u> that did not bring its immediate punishment in total loss of freedom, or death or things worse...Yes, choking, stifling slowly, describe the feeling better than anything else I can think of. And it lasted four years.

"While my brother was, unknown to us, first among the "fire-fighters" in the battle of London and then in the RAF, I joined the French Resistance, which meant signing a voluntary declaration of loyalty to the French Fighting Forum, which declaration was registered in London; a number was given to me, a word or fictitious name was chosen as a counter-check over there; I chose another name by which I was henceforth to be known by my fellow agents here, with whom I was to work, - and from then it was a question of having no known past, living a very real present, and never speaking about the future except in terms of optimism. Of course, it was not possible to ignore everything concerning ones fellow workers, because some were old friends, and then there were daily contacts and addresses...and it was to avoid the possibility of telling the truth, under torture in case of capture, that the liaison agents were given phials of prussic acid, to be used at their own discretion, if they thought the time had come to do so.

"The chief of our 'Reseau' or network was a professor of philosophy at the Sorbonne. (He was to be shot in Arras, in January 1944; his 'second' died in a camp in Germany). I used to handle the mail for England, transmitting the information that would come in from all and any quarters - numbers, figures, dates, maps, stories, data of all kind concerning the enemy and written on any kind of paper, - sometimes the inside of a paper-bag, the back of an envelope, a subway ticket or again maybe perfectly set-up records, according to the conditions under which the information was obtained and transmitted.

"At the beginning, I carried the documents to and from Paris in a bag or attaché case which I would put under the seat in the train or the subway so as to deny ownership of same if the car would be unexpectedly searched by the Gestapo - but precious and unique documents had been abandoned that way and I took to carrying them wrapped around my body, under the clothes, leaving my hands free - and empty. But the risk was then that people carrying papers that way could not deny knowledge of their presence if they were taken to the police station to be searched for such a possibility, as it happened when the Gestapo would make a "scoop" in any designated neighborhood.

"Luckily, that never happened to me, but what did was that, in May 1943, I walked blindly with three other agents into a "barrage" or "cordon" of plain-clothes policemen and Gestapo in the entrance to a subway station. One, a young girl, was caught and released on the spot as she carried nothing; another a young French lieutenant, who had 40 wounds from this war and only one arm left, was caught and kept as he was carrying the mail prepared for London that I had given him some minutes before.

"I was carrying a large bag full of data and documents "in the rough" that he had given me a few minutes before, in exchange of the finished mail. Both loads of papers, those he had and those I had, were exceptionally interesting and important that time. This man was eventually sent to the German camps from which he was lucky enough to return two years later, after we had tried, and failed, to 'buy him back' from his captors.

"The other man and myself managed to get through, thanks to Providence granting me a cool-headed inspiration. As soon as I realized what was happening around us, I said loudly, in an attempt to give the "cue" to our friends, that <u>this</u> was not the way <u>out</u> of the subway; we were making a mistake, it was the way <u>in</u>, and then laying my hand on my friend's arm, we turned on our heels and

A Time to Speak

walked...slowly...up the steps we had just come down and back into the street, hoping the other two were able to follow. But they had been caught, as I said above. I was never in my life more tempted to run (which would have cost the show) than just at that time, when all depended on acting with a calculated lack of apparent speed, and yet never were my legs nearer to refusing all service. Then the man I managed to escape with was arrested later, released, then arrested again and sent to the camps in Germany, from where he returned in 1945, broken in health, if not in spirit. I must have been providentially protected for I was, in the end, one of the few remaining of our group who had not been caught and sent to Germany - or worse."

The Later Resistance in Denmark

Victories at Stalingrad and El Alamein helped change the Danish attitude from compliance with the Occupation to more overt defiance. The turning point was August 1943. There was a wave of sabotage; there were spontaneous strikes in factories. The Germans reacted with a strong police force in the streets, a curfew and a threat to take hostages. On 28 August the Danish government was given an ultimatum which demanded the death penalty for sabotage, the declaration of martial law, and a ban on strikes and meetings. The Government rejected the ultimatum and the Germany military took over the executive power. Gerd Schiotz described the activity:

"August '43, That was the turning point of the war for Denmark. Now we are in open warfare. Everything became different, the sabotage went everywhere.

"May 23, There was a people's strike, a folk strike. Everything was in chaos, no police, no government, no authorities, the Resistance movement, Germans shooting all the time. People had been throwing their furniture out, building barricades. Aksel came in and people said, 'Oh, Aksel, come sing,' and he sang in the streets. He went up to the barricades and sang. Germans loved oratorio. I know there was one who had his hand over Aksel. He got warnings, but they saved him. They were taken by the singing.

"We had our apartment in Copenhagen that we are not using because we had the kids in the suburbs further out. It was safer there, with the shooting in the streets. And we couldn't keep the twins in the shelters because they wanted to get up and see. The schools were going on, on and off, it was only in '44 that the schools were closed. They were commuting to their schools from the suburbs.

"So we gave our apartment to the Resistance movement. Of course, it was a risk to give our apartment, but that was the least we could do. The Resistance movement rejected Aksel's help completely because he was much too well-known. 'We cannot use you at all because every kid will know you.' He was tall, he didn't conduct himself very modestly, he kept strutting, you know. They laughed when he came to offer his services. 'Go on doing what you are doing.' He refused to go to Sweden in danger, he wanted to stay. We got warnings from the Resistance movement, 'Mr. Schiotz, you have to go underground because you are threatened, they are talking about shooting you.' So he got a pistol from the authorities, just in case. He was open to be shot on the stage or wherever. I didn't sleep very well when he was in other places.

"We had meetings in our dining room. People could go undercover and meet in our home, and they [the Germans] wouldn't be suspicious as long as we had a normal family life. They told us, 'Please keep your normal family life.' At one point, we had a birthday party with kids playing. And finally the kids ended up in our bedroom, disguised themselves in all our clothes, and had a wonderful time. But there were photos in bookcases, another bookcase with secret transport information to the VIP refugees in Sweden to be warned of something.

"It was very dangerous for us to tell anything about what was going on because the kids, because they would tell somebody, 'You know some people came here.' So we had to be careful. Michael was silent, but Brigette would tell anyone in the streetcar what was going on, 'I'll tell you what...'

"We had telephone calls, 'Some boxes of apples are being sent, would you please pick them up.' We had a young girl working and we warned her that these boxes were not to be touched by the kids. We thought it was ammunition, but it was two officers. Later the boxes were used for playing on the lawn.

"We never knew the names, in case of being captured and being tortured. Of course, we didn't know at the time that we had (in the apartment) the file of all the resistance members.

A Saboteur Hero

"The strong winter in '43 and '44, you could practically walk across to Sweden, but there were open waters in between. It was so dreadfully cold, that was when our saboteur hero swam. His name is Hans Keiser-Nielsen, and I have known him since high school.

"On the dock in a corner of the harbor, a destroyer sitting, having pulled up from the bottom by the Germans to be restored, to be put into use again. It occupied this dock for a full year. He was part of the Resistance movement. He had taken this job to put two bombs around his neck, tied down, and the cords to make the explosion. In 20 below temperature, he came, the destroyer was actually finished, there was a German team, an armed guard on the bridge, and some were hammering and giving it the finishing touches before it was to sail again.

"He came there and it was so quiet, no wind, no waves, only the movement *of his swimming would be heard. As long as the party was working it was all right because there was this hammering. But suddenly it stopped and here he was. He had to go along another boat, next to it on the dock, and dive under to the other side, come up with his heavy bombs close to where the guys were walking. He figured out any tiny little splash, they would hear that. Now he was doomed. He finished it very slowly. He got the explosives mounted and ready for explosion and he had to dive under the destroyer again to get across the harbor. When he reached the other side, he couldn't move his legs, they were absolutely dead from cold. What was he going to do? He had to swim a third time over and try to reach a schooner. He didn't know if it was Danish or German, but he had to knock on the side to be pulled up because he couldn't lift his legs, they were lame from the cold.*

"*It turned out that a man came from the schooner and helped him come aboard and to reach the harbor and the town. He was lucky enough that it was a Danish schooner. Finally, he came as an ordinary person walking, wet all over, but he managed to flee. The destroyer was blown up so that there was no hope that it could ever be remodeled. He escaped. He had to find hiding. He is a doctor and he received a Medal of Freedom in 1947 for meritorious achievement which aided the United States during the war.*"

Rescue of the Danish Jews

The most dramatic act of resistance came in October 1943, the rescue of the Danish Jews from annihilation. In September 1943 the Germans decided to deport the Danish Jews. Hitler's action was leaked to leading members of the Social Democrats by D. G. Duckwitz, a German diplomat, who in turn, warned the Jewish community. The German action was planned for the first and second of October. The Danes went into action. Danish Jews went underground and, within a few days 7,000 Jews were illegally sailed to safety in Sweden. Only 481 ended up in the concentration camp, Theresienstadt. Mrs. Schiotz said:

"*The King had an agreement with Hitler. The King had made it clear that he would have the promise from Hitler that he would not touch the German Jews. So when it came to August 23, and everything broke out, they were going to be sent to concentration camps, the old Jews would not move. They would stay in Copenhagen on this holiday [Rosh Hashanah] where they were not supposed to move. They would not believe that Hitler would break his promise. Some orthodox didn't want to go on a Holy Day and just sat there. They had to be forced so they could save their lives. They were brought to Sweden under protest.*

"*It was a shock to the Danish Jews that they weren't safe here. They were entirely assimilated in the Danish population and we had never felt that there was a difference between Jews and other people. They were no different from any other Dane.*

"We did whatever we could, the Jews waited for transport in our apartment. They could come up there until they could be helped, by fishermen mostly, weather depending, to go to Sweden. It was amazing what they did. These fisherman were so brave, some of them were sunk, shot down and lost, and some of the Jewish people were lost, some of them even swam over.

"Later, Aksel had some of these Swedish tours, and he was stormed by the Jewish people, having arrived safely with the fisherman under the boxes of herring.

"The Jews who had escaped wanted to send messages back with him. And he said, 'I can't have any written messages.' He had music and piano scores and between the notes in the lines, he wrote a text in the music. All these messages were sent in his music. When he came to the Danish customs, he was searched, undressed, pants, shoes, soles and there was not a message. His bag with the music case was sitting there next to the German customs officers and they didn't look through that."

One of the Rescued Jews

One of the Jews rescued in October 1943 was Ruth Woldike, a long-time friend of Gerd Schiotz.

"I'm Jewish, and in October '43, the Germans started the prosecution of the Jews. You see, only my mother was Jewish. My father was not Jewish. During the first part of October, practically all the Jews in Denmark left their homeland and escaped somewhere, most of us to Sweden, some to other countries like England, if they were lucky enough.

"How did I know boats were available and how did I escape? That was on account of a German official who actually thought that Germany was going to lose this war anyway, and there was no reason really to make things worse than they were. So he decided he would like to give a hint to some Danish foreign ministry official, so he did. And this official in the foreign ministry passed on the information to the head of the Jewish Community in Copenhagen. And from there it was read to all the Jews in Denmark.

"Many Danish committees, or small groups of people, arranged escape lines to Sweden, mostly by approaching fisherman along the coast, asking them if they would sail with Jews. Many of them did. Of course, many of them also required quite a lot of money. That's understandable because, if they were caught, they would have been shot and their boats taken.

"Along the coast, from Copenhagen to Helsingor, boats were going out with refugees. It was not only Jews. The Resistance movement had really begun to be efficient, and among the resistance movement people, many of them were very young, many of them had been living underground for some time and they had to escape to Sweden.

"In the boat that we came with, there were some young Resistance people, but most of them were Jews. I remember, among them was the director of the Danish Music College, his old, old aunt and his son and some other people I still know and still see.

"I remember my mother was terribly nervous. I think it was for her sake that my father went with us. He was active in the Boys' Choir, busy with conducting and very active in the whole musical life. He had no need to do it, but I think he felt we would be better off with him along. Actually, he was employed by the Swedish radio in Stockholm.

"My father had a very good friend, a little younger than he, but not very much. He was unmarried. Shortly before we escaped to Sweden, he called my father and suggested he might marry me so that I could get a better name, a pro forma marriage so I could stay in Denmark and finish my schooling. But my father felt that it would be too hard on my mother to get away, so he refused and said, 'No thank you.' And the funny thing is that when we came back after one year and a half, I actually married that man. Then it was not pro forma and I was married to him for forty years.

"Not very much could be taken with us, a handbag. We left the flat of course. You had to empty your flat otherwise the Germans would occupy it, so my father's sister and her husband emptied our flat very quickly. They put something in their basement. I know I had three goldfish and they disappeared.

"On the fishing boat crossing, it was scary, terrible. It was a very small boat, we came from Tarbaek, just north of Copenhagen. We landed on the little island, Ven. So it wasn't very far, but of course, it was scary. My mother was shivering and terribly afraid.

"We came to Ven and they took the women to a hotel and the men to a cinema where they stayed one night. The next day, they transported us to the mainland.

"We were taken to some house. We were scared and it was dark and everything had to go very fast so I've never been able to find the house. But I know that we sat in their living room quite a while and then finally we were told it was safe to walk through the garden and down to the fishing boat. The group that arranged for us to come over was a group consisting of university people, a man who was president of the student union at that time and a professor of classical languages. They organized it.

"It was Swedish soldiers who were called out to pick up all those people who arrived; they came by the hundreds every night. They took us to some interrogation on the mainland; they tried to find out if we had any diseases; quite a lot of people had stayed underground for some time and some were dirty. He asked my name and he had been to one of my father's concerts a year and a half ago, so he said, I gather you have no diseases.

"So then we were posted on to a camp in a lovely village, in the middle of Sweden, and we stayed there almost a week. That is where I celebrated my 18th birthday. Everybody wanted to go either to Stockholm or Goteburg - any of the big towns. They made an arrangement that if you went to Stockholm or Goteburg you had to have a Swedish person who would guarantee your support. My mother had some friends in Stockholm. We telephoned them and they said, of course we will guarantee your stay here. Then we were allowed to go on to Stockholm at the end of October. We had taken all the money we could possibly lay our hands on which proved very good. We went to a small hotel and my parents stayed there for almost a year."

The Underground in Norway

In Norway, the Germans encroached more and more on people's lives. They demanded that radios be turned in; that blankets, heavy clothing and boots be given to German troops. They established a curfew. According to Oddvar Solstad, a former high school student in Oslo who lives in Marblehead, Massachusetts today:

"The teachers were quite courageous in holding forth their opinions on the Occupation. I recall one English teacher that I had was arrested and taken to the Gestapo headquarters in Oslo. After about a week or two we suddenly found out that the teacher had jumped out of the top floor window of Gestapo headquarters and killed himself. It was obvious to us he had information the Gestapo wanted. That really left a tremendous impression on us.

"By 1943, by the middle of the war we heard of sabotage action taking place. There was obviously an underground movement going on. I, as a young fellow, young and crazy I guess you might say at that time, thought I would like to participate in some of these underground activities. So I happened to mention it to my Dad. 'Give me some time and I'll see what I can find out.' He came back to me and he said, 'You're supposed to go to the east corner of this graveyard, which wasn't too far from us and you will meet a man there who might help you out. And he gave me a question to ask the gentleman who should answer back with a certain phrase my Dad told me. That I did and that was my first contact with the underground.

"He asked if I would be willing to organize a platoon. I was very anxious and very happy to say yes to that. Over the next week or so I contacted old Boy Scout friends of mine. There were twelve of us in a platoon. After we had organized this, I contacted my contact again, he informed me on how we were to get training."

Norway's underground was organized into two parts, the Military Organization (Mil Org), organized into regular troops, guerrilla troops and the intelligence branch and the Civilian Organization (Civ Org). Solstad's father was a member of the Civ Org which tried to find food and clothing for families whose husbands had been killed or put in concentration camps. Solstad joined the Mil Org.

They met in attics, basements, warehouses and received basic training on handling and caring for weapons. Later in a park outside Oslo, the platoon received instruction on using weapons, shooting at targets, hand grenades. Their instructors were Norwegians who had fled to England and returned by parachute.

Since Solstad's platoon consisted of young men with no families ties, they were asked to accept training in explosives and sabotage techniques as guerrilla troops. Solstad said, "Of course, we were gung ho for that."

"We were involved in reconnaissance. We were given orders to recommend certain areas which were planned for sabotage action. We had to find out where the guards were, how often they changed the guards, a map of the area.

"About a month before the end of the war, my platoon was assigned to a different group, to the intelligence branch. My platoon's job during the last month of the war was to guard the intelligence headquarters outside Oslo.

"About a week before the end of the war, I was assigned two other platoons for guard duty for the intelligence headquarters. On May fifth, the Germans capitulated in North Germany, the Netherlands and Denmark. There was a lot of uncertainty in Norway about what was going to happen. At that time there were 350,000 German soldiers in Norway. There was serious discussion among the German headquarters in Norway as to whether they could keep on fighting in Norway. We heard afterwards reports that they wanted to bring in other Germans to help hold their stand in Norway.

"From May fifth to May eighth, there was much uncertainty, Nobody knew what was going to happen. There were a lot of negotiations were taking place between the Allies and the Germans and between the underground and the Germans.

"Over the four years a lot of Norwegians had fled Norway to go to Sweden and they were organized into Norwegian police troops, something like 14,000 police troops in Sweden, ready to come into Norway. So there was a lot of activity

"On May 8, my troop was still guarding the intelligence headquarters outside Oslo. Intelligence was able to take over, in central Oslo, the Norwegian Nazi archives, where they kept the list of those who participated with the Germans, traitors as far as we were concerned, before the Norwegian Nazis were able to destroy it.

"Our whole group moved into that building in Oslo and that became our headquarters for the next two months. At that time, my group was also assigned to go out, according to the orders of the intelligence people and pick up all the Nazis. We did this with great pleasure! We spent the next two months picking up all the Nazis in the Oslo area.

"At one point and this was shortly after the capitulation and we were asked to go out to a farm, a large farm. It turned out that in this particular farmhouse the Norwegian Chief of Police in Oslo, a fellow by the name of Lie and two other Nazi collaborators, Minister of Justice and the Chief of the State Police in Norway. They had holed up in this farmhouse to negotiate some kind of settlement. We found out afterwards that in the basement they had a tremendous amount of explosives to blow this place. My group was trying to guard and support the people who were trying to negotiate with these Nazis over a period of a couple of days. It turned out that two of them committed suicide and the third one finally gave up. An unnerving situation!

"We were young; we were eager to participate and fortunately we were able to participate. The whole underground in the Oslo area consisted of about 7,000 men in the Mil Org group."

OTHER ANTI-NAZI UPRISINGS

In 1943 there were three other revolts against Hitler and his Third Reich.

The Warsaw Ghetto Uprising

In 1941, the Warsaw Ghetto, one of the largest ghettos, contained some 450,000 inhabitants who lived in a small area of 758 acres...an area smaller than the size of two average American farms.

The Polish Jews had developed an underground culture whose primary task was to save the inhabitants from starving. It soon became a fighting culture with the idea of armed resistance. The armed organization was made up of twenty-two fighting groups, whose commander was twenty-four year old Mordechaj Anielewicz.

On 19 April 1943, the uprising broke out in the Warsaw Ghetto. In the first few days, the Nazis, taken by surprise, suffered losses, but General Juergen Stroop, the Major General of the Police, systematically destroyed the underground bunkers where the underground forces had taken refuge. On 8 May, the Nazis surrounded the command bunker at 18 Mila Street and filled it with poison gas. Choking from the poisonous fumes, Anielewicz, together with the whole command of the organization, committed suicide. On 16 May, Stroop gave the order to blow up the Warsaw synagogue.

The Ghetto uprising was a struggle against uneven odds, but it demonstrated to the world that the Jews would fight against the Nazi regime. The surviving members took up arms again during the Warsaw uprising in August 1944.

The Military Coup

In February 1943, some disillusioned military officers, General Friedrich Olbricht, General von Tresckow and Fabian von Schlabrendorff, one of von Tresckow's junior staff members, made plans to stage a coup to rid Germany of Hitler. Using a British-made bomb, the scheme was to make an attack on Hitler's life by luring him to army group headquarters in Smolensk; this then, would be the signal for the coup in Berlin. In Berlin they waited for news, but no bomb had gone off.

Undaunted, the conspirators tried again on March 21 at the Heroes' Memorial Day ceremony at the Zeughaus in Berlin. This time, Colonel Freiherr von Gersdorff agreed to carry the bomb in his overcoat, and when he could get near enough to Hitler, he would detonate it. Again, the conspirators were thwarted as Hitler only spent eight minutes at the exhibit hall before he left. There would be a further attempt on Hitler's life in July 1944, also doomed to fail.

The White Rose

The student revolt against Nazism was led by Hans Scholl, a medical student and his sister, Sophie who was studying biology, Christoph Probst, Willi Graf and Alexander Schmorell, all medical students, and Kurt Huber, a philosophy professor at the University of Munich.

Originally an enthusiastic member of Hitler's Youth Movement, Hans gradually became disenchanted with the Hitler doctrine. What changed his attitude were the Jewish question, sanctions against singing songs of other countries, and the suppression of the poems of his favorite poet, Stefan Zweig, and the mysterious disappearance of a young professor who did not belong to the National Socialist Party.

The students distributed their tracts, known as the "White Rose Tracts," in which they called on people to resist by whatever means they could: sabotage in the manufacture of armaments; sabotage in the cultural and economic domain; sabotage in all aspects of propaganda, including the applied arts and the press.

In February 1943, as Hans and Sophie Scholl arrived at the University to distribute tracts in the hallways, they were glimpsed by the building concierge who alerted the Gestapo.

All five students and their philosophy professor were put in prison, brutally questioned, found guilty of treason and were condemned to death. As Hans Scholl put his head on the block, his strong voice was heard all through the prison, "Long live liberty!"

Hitler's warning was clear: opposition and resistance movements were not tolerated.

End Notes

107   After the war Briand returned to his job as a teacher and school administrator.
108   Paris still lives in Sainte-Mère-Eglise and gives students copies of his memoirs so they will not forget what he calls "the great pages of history."
109   After the war Kieffer went to Dinard to work in a bank. He also found his former comrades from the Resistance group.

CHAPTER 28

CITIZENS CAUGHT BETWEEN BATTLING TROOPS

Budapest

First, Hungary was a German ally in 1939 and in 1941 fought alongside German troops against the Russian Army. Hungary remained a part of Germany's zone of influence. The country was officially and peacefully occupied in March 1944 and at the same time, the Red Army arrived on Hungary's eastern border.

On 4 December 1944, the Russians were able to cross the Danube at Vac, only fifteen miles from Hungary's pre-war border with Czechoslovakia. Fighting between the German and the Soviet troops continued in and around Budapest. When the Germans refused to surrender, Hungary declared war on Germany on 31 December 1944. By April 1945, the Soviet Union was the master of Hungary, eastern Czechoslovakia, and had reached Vienna and signed a treaty of friendship with Tito in Yugoslavia. The Russian-controlled eastern portion of Europe became part of the post-war Soviet bloc.

Civilians in Budapest were trapped between fighting German and Soviet troops and forced to hide and hunt for food. One woman, a retired professor of literature, grew up in Budapest. She lived and hid there during the war until she was able to leave for Sweden in 1946. In thinking about the war and Hungary, she said,

"I don't belong any more. I prefer to think about it in my childhood when I had a good time. I had a very good life before the war. I managed to absorb the war thing and distance it. It is more like a story than an experience.

"I was aware of the war when I was sixteen because we had a lot of refugee children to feed from all kinds of places, from Poland, from Germany and so on. As a sixteen year old I volunteered in a camp run by nuns for young children, who were brought from other countries because they were very hungry. They spent their summers there.

"Things really became bad around '42 when the Germans came in and the bad things started. The Germans occupied Hungary, which was fairly late, it was late '42. I was a teenager, eighteen years old. And it was a very methodical take over. They immediately had all the lists of all the people they started deporting and killing. I was living with my mother and step-father. She divorced my father when I was five years old. My father's family was three-quarters Jewish. And so the prob-

lem was that my grandmother lived in Czechoslovakia, which previously belonged to Hungary; they had factories and farms there. Eventually the Germans were told of my grandmother and my uncle and his family, his wife and two children also in their early teens. And they had to dig their own grave and they were shot into it. And so my father was very upset and joined the underground before the Germans came in. They knew that things would happen, so he organized people in the underground.

"For a few months I wasn't bothered, but one day when I was in school, I was in the gymnasium. The Germans came to our house and wanted to deport me or take me because they wanted to get my father. And so when I came home, there were my mother and step-father, the cook and a friend standing on four corners watching for me to come home, saying, 'You can't come home because the Germans have come. You'd better not come home.' So I had to go into hiding for a long time, for nearly a year.

"And it meant moving every month. Usually people helped, it was a sort of underground situation. For one month I was a nanny, not a real nanny; I worked in a factory for a while, where the Communists were organized; and I spent a month in an attic while the bombs were falling. We had practically every day bombing from the Germans. The people who took me in were either friends or people in the underground, Communist, simple workers. And there was another type of underground; the Catholic Church was very strong and very brave in Hungary and so nuns, Jesuits and Benedictines had hiding places. I spent time in an attic in a six-story house, where everyone was down in the basement, and I watched the bombs. And then I spent a month in a basement sort of watching the rats running around, and I was getting food once a day through a door. And that was a very bad experience because I was beside the Danube and a couple of times a week they took a group of Jews to the Danube and shot them. So I had many experiences like that until the Germans and the Russians started fighting. The Russians came from the east after a year. I spent a year like that.

"When the Germans came in, for example, one sequence, in hiding, I was with the underground. What they did was, many Jews were deported from Hungary and at least my job was to hang out with a companion, close to a school because Germans raided part of the town. The underground knew what it was, or heard about the raiding. When they raided it and took away the parents, we were waiting to get the children in school. And I remember many trips going to various schools and picking up school children and they took them to two different places - one was the basement of an insane asylum (there was a huge park with many, many buildings and the doctors there were part of the underground). And that was a fairly safe place because the Germans didn't come in there. I remember spending nights with little kids in the basement while the patients, usually when the bombs fell, they made a tremendous noise, very eerie, like dogs howling. It was '42-43, when I was hiding and I did that kind of job.

"Then we had about two months which I think were the worst months I can imagine because, by that time, it didn't matter what you were. Two-thirds of Budapest was shot out, burned out. And food was a tremendous problem. We ate beans mainly, at least for a year before, and then beans two years later. And also utilities were gone from the bombing. Water was a problem. We were really down to basics. Budapest was a big city so it was difficult to transport any food into the city so you relied on people in the country.

"My mother and step-father were bombed out, so they moved. The second house was bombed out and then they got an apartment briefly before the fight between the Germans and the Russians. And we couldn't stay in that apartment, especially with me. And so we went to an apartment house. For many years we had a butler and a cook and the butler was very drunk but he loved the cook. So my step-father got them a position as a janitor in a house and so we went into the house where they were the janitors.

"On the eastern side of Budapest, there one expected the Russians quickly to come through. The thinking was that the less fighting we have between the Russians and the Germans, the sooner we get through, the better it is.

"Those were two months which were absolutely hairy because we had intensive fighting, door to door, back and forth and so on. And all kinds of horrible things. The upper part of the six-story building was more or less bombed out. There were fairly simple people living in that house, and everybody crowded into the basement and no sanitary conditions. There was no water so they tapped where they kept the bathroom water in this heating stove and the toilet, any drop of water that you could get hold of. And eventually there was no water, but there was a house about two blocks away, and every day somebody was assigned to crawl over there (because they were shooting all of the time) with this container to bring a little bit of water. And then you were given a half a cup of water. You were thirsty.

"Eventually a bomb hit the house, and the house caught fire and the people were trapped in the basement. And for a day we listened to those horrible cries. And after that nobody dared to cook, no fire to cook anything. So what they did, there was a stray army horse, an old nag, and they shot it and everybody got raw horse meat. And eventually, everybody got sick. After we heard people screaming for a day as they slowly fried in the basement, nobody was very interested in that kind of demise.

"Eventually the house was hit and some died and some got terrible sores and then you watched them die in that house. There was one person especially, a young man who was a teacher in the country and was drafted as a soldier. His leg was shot and gangrene set in and everything like that. He asked me to be with him when he shot himself. This kind of thing. We were starving and full of lice because we hadn't washed ourselves and I must say that is one of the most difficult thing when bugs are crawling on you and you can't do anything about it. That is something so revolting. You stink and you are full of lice.

"People lived in open houses. A woman was giving birth to a baby and there was no front to the house. She was in a room, in a little corner, and then by the winter, they managed to get some other room.

"And then the Russians came (1943). They were very interested in raping anyone and anything. And so the upper part of the house was bombed out and what the older women did for the young girls, six young girls. They managed to get a wooden ladder. When dusk came, we went up the wooden ladder where the stairs were bombed out and pulled up the ladder and slept there in a very windy and cold February. This was still better than being gang-raped in the basement or the lower part of the house. By the time the Russians took over, I was pretty sick. I got paratyphoid and I was already half-starved, dehydrated, and sick like a dog. The only man who escaped the paratyphoid was a man who sold liquor and he drank up his own liquor and that kept him healthy.

"My step-father and mother were not in very good shape. He was very much a gentleman, and he was told he must go with the army and fight. We obviously didn't want that so that anytime any kind of military came, we made him hide in a shaft and in the lower part; there was no window and he had to sort of stand there.

"But after this experience, we had to go to my step-father's uncle who lived even more east, in a more garden section of the town which was already occupied by the Russians. I had to crawl, I don't know how many miles. I couldn't walk, so I walked and crawled just to get there and then I collapsed. And I was fabulously ill, nearly died. You get diarrhea and you are completely dehydrated, no medicine. I was told I spent six weeks lying on the floor, on a blanket, and then I recovered slowly. I was very weak.

"It was time, by that time, to go to another city. I remember there was an event. It was spring and the sun was shining, and in Budapest there was a big hill where the royal castle was, 16th and 17th century old houses, very beautiful. Hungary was occupied by the Turkish people for 150 years. What they did to hold Hungary, to hold the city, was to excavate the whole hill, and there were labyrinths where you could hide and have ammunitions without having them bombed out. The 15,000 Germans were holed up there. And Budapest was all occupied by the Russians, and the Germans tried to break out and all of them were killed. And you had

Germans lying all over the place. They were lying in the streets up to three weeks. There were human bodies all over, rotting and smelling. And I had to sort of stumble many, many miles with my mother and step-father through this scene.

"And that is where things snapped for me and I lost my memory. It was already during this illness and that was nothing uncommon at that time. It was a temporary memory loss due to trauma, and when you went on the street and somebody looked very familiar to you, you said, 'I think I know you but I can't remember you.' And they said, 'Well, I'm your cousin, or I am your friend from school.' That was perfectly normal; that happened to many, many people. And it took about half a year before I put things together and got into some kind of shape.

"After the fighting, the Russians were a bad lot. They were Mongolians, mainly, I think the cannon fodder type of people and many women. They were peasants, huge, Russian ladies, most of them terribly uneducated. The Mongolians, for example, drank water out of the toilet and killed people for a watch. You couldn't go out in the evening. The moment it got dark you stayed home because they got drunk and roamed the street. If they didn't get the watch, they shot you. You woke up on the morning. In front of your apartment house, there was a tree, and there was a person hanging there and his pants were taken off or something. So it was chaos for quite a while; it was chaos in terms of food or any transportation.

"Eventually, the trains started going and I remember that I and my two boy cousins had to go out once a week for things which were left over, like pillow cases, sheets, silver forks or whatever, anything you could carry, and take the train into the country and barter to get food. I remember once coming home and holding out a live chicken from the train for hours because it was so crowded that the chicken would have croaked. And the big victory when you arrived home with a live chicken or a piece of bacon, or flour or whatever you could get. And we had a rather nice apartment close to the Danube, close to the Parliament, but there was no heating, obviously. No one was prepared yet for gas. No coal was coming in. So we had a little iron stove. That was for heating and cooking for a while, but we had a butler because we had a butler before the war. He was a very nice man, very lonely and he liked the family so he drifted back and discovered us. So we had a butler cooking our beans. So there were many incongruous kinds of things.

"After three or four months of the Russians, they started drafting people for public work. Anyone who was young worked three days a week, free, doing anything. I was taken out to trains to clean up train tracks. There was no school yet, nothing, all the young people were drafted and we had free labor cleaning army things, anything from scrubbing floors to carrying heavy things, cleaning streets. Free labor for several months.

"You couldn't let a man go alone on the street because the Russians just packed up everything they could see and took it to Russia. So if they needed labor, whoever was on the street was put into a train and taken to Russia. They got their slave labor because they needed clean-up crews and building crews. So I remember when my step-father wanted to go out on the street, it was mother who went in front and I went in the back and the moment there was a Russian in sight, we ducked into a door.

"They were hordes of incredibly primitive, especially the first wave. And even then, the German terror was a meticulous organization, knowing in every place where everybody is, prepared before they came in, down to the last 3" x 5" card with the last name. So they were terrifying in their organization and their conscious cruelty. To me, in Dante's Hell, that is the bottom, premeditated evil, you planned it and premeditated it. That is the icy part of Dante's Hell, the rock bottom, the closest to Lucifer who is frozen in the Lake of Ice.

"The Russians were spontaneously evil. They shoot you, bang, bang, bang, or they get drunk and beat people on the train, especially in the beginning, or 'Give me your bread or I'll shoot.' When you hesitated, then they shot you. Or I want your pants and took off your pants and hung them on a tree. What they did with our apartment, there was no fuel. They came in the winter, so they took all of the paintings and furniture and piled them in front and lit a bonfire. They were bonfire makers. The Germans packed our paintings.

"The same underground works, the priests, the Benedictine priests that I had contact with, they tried to save national treasures and there were some caves. I remember going one night to a museum and hauling pictures away, and they were hauled to this cave and walled in and preserved. The Germans took a lot of national treasures, robbed the museums. The Russians mainly burned them up because there was not enough fuel. Eventually the Russian Secret Police took over, but that took them a year until the mess was organized and then they started. It was more a spontaneous kind of thing: we need a hundred men, get into the train and we take you to Russia and people disappeared. Where did you see them last? My cousin, the one who died, was taken to Russia. And we never learned what happened to him. When he came out, he never talked about it. And he was not himself.

"To go to the Opera, it was a thing to show that you are civilized. There was dust and rubble and bombs, and no food, but everybody dressed up, washed themselves, and went to the Opera. That was a demonstration that we were human beings, civilized human beings. Somehow some Russians got knowledge of this event and they robbed a lingerie store and arrived in night gowns because everybody had on evening dress. That was a wonderful joke, the first joke. The Hungarians love to tell jokes and make fun of things. That was a big joke in Budapest, how the Russian women arrived in lingerie at the Opera.

"In the beginning, when the Germans came in and started running out the Jews, they were not allowed to perform in the opera or anywhere else. This kind of restriction was one of the first things. They found a little theater and gave a light opera, Don Pasquale. It was one of the things one did, solidarity, to show up for those performances and they were sold out every day. People showed up to show their solidarity, a protest against the Germans. So there were many, many events like that. But to assert your humanity and dignity, that you haven't become a worm. That was the crushing part, the psychological part, reduced to nothing. And all of the indignities of the wars: starvation, rape, sitting for a year and waiting, bombings three times, listening in the basement to the bombs falling down. We were bombed once by the Russians, once by the English and once by the Americans. And in some ways, it was welcome. In theory, it was a good thing. But in practice, you still had to go to the basement three times.

"After six to eight months, things became, I couldn't say liveable, but somehow one managed to survive. [Russia was in charge in Hungary in April 1945]. I already went to the Academy of Fine Arts before the war, so I continued with that. I was a painter. Until I left in 1946, that is what I did.

"I won some prizes in the Academy of Fine Arts, so I was offered a fellowship to another country and I chose Sweden because I think it was emotional. Sweden was very important to me. It was an untouched country. I like Thomas Mann very much. I don't know if you know his Tonio Kroger, but I always considered myself the dark-haired, the one who loves the blond, I always wanted to have long blonde hair and I always wanted to belong to somewhere, a story-tale princess which was somewhere in Scandinavia. So Sweden seemed to me the dream country in many ways. . . And I arrived in Sweden on the 14th of December. I remember it because the 13th of December is Lucia Day and they put stars in the windows. They have lanterns made out of paper and put a light bulb in it and every window had a star. And snow fell and it was very pristine, with snow and the whole city was untouched by war and I went in there and every window had stars in it, white snow and food and it was like coming into a fairy tale kingdom, which is what I needed after this rough kind of life. I met my husband in Sweden and married him.

"This wasn't a picnic. It slowly got to you. I don't even remember. It takes you twenty years. I didn't speak about it for twenty years and then some how you begin to heal. That's why you get such late World War II writings because people didn't heal and couldn't talk about it."

A German Woman in France

Friede Metzger was caught between the Germans, the Russians, and the Americans. Her family had been living in Russia for many years, she didn't know how far back. She explained that "Kaiser Katerina" invited many Germans to Russia.

Catherine the Great was born a princess in the German principality of Anhalt-Zerbst and reigned from 1762-1796. Part of the government measures relating to land, under Catherine the Great, included sponsoring colonies of foreigners, particularly of Germans along the Volga and in southern Russia.[110]

"We are Germans, not Russians. We were big farmers in Russia. We had lots of land and cows and horses, and we had a good life. We had German schools in Russia, but we had two hours a week so that we could write Russian and read Russian because we need that because everything was Russian. Then my father sent me to college, all of us went to college. I was a kindergarten teacher and my husband was a carpenter.

"The Russians took everything. We didn't have land any more, we only had a garden. The state took it and in the fall, they gave us so much we could live on. The Russians are good people. . . But then when the Communists came, in church, they took the tower off, the bells and everything. Oh God, that was something. Our older people, they screamed and cried, 'God help.' But then they said, 'Who believes in God? There is no God.' You don't know what that means. And they wanted me to cut my hair, but in our time, we did not cut hair. We braided the hair. They put me in the paper all the time because I didn't cut my hair.

"When the war started, I don't even want to think about this; this war was just awful. And then they [the Russians] *took my father and took my brothers and sent them to Siberia. My brother, the one who saved his life, he told stories about what they made them do in Siberia. They took my father, my oldest brother and they shot them together. They put them on the wall and one guy counted, 'One, two, three,' and they shot them and they threw them way out in Siberia in the forests there. They sent us a picture, I want to show you, like animals, it was awful. I look at the picture* [a picture of nothing but skeleton heads] *and I wonder which one is my father.*

"I was hiding my husband in a barn, we dug a deep hole, we put him in and he was in there the whole day, and at night because they took all the men first.

"I was running and looking for my mother-in-law and they came, four policemen, Russian, with the guns at me and said, 'Get on the wagon.' So I had to go on the wagon on my way to Siberia. My poor husband was still hiding. The train went real slow; the other train, he saw it coming, so he had to stop and when he went real slow, I 'pshht,' jumped off that train and threw myself in a ditch; there was water in there and it was cold. Here comes the police, looking for Germans. They drove right on by that ditch. Then I walked out of a corn field and looked just

over the highway. I wanted to go and look for my husband. I thought my mother-in-law and my husband, they are gone.

"I got away, I knew I had to go home and look for my husband. But then I came [home] and he was gone, and I thought, 'Dear God, they found him.'

"His sister was hiding him in there (in the border which was dirty) and had boards over him. So she told me, she said, 'Go there so he knows that you are safe.' And I went there and I lifted up a little board and I called his name, his name was Hermann. And he didn't even recognize me. He thought now they found him again. And the other guy said, 'No, that is Friede.'

"We were close to town and that was what was so dangerous. The bombs were just like rain, German bombs, they wanted to get Russia. They bombed the railroads and everything.

"And that night they came in and captured the city. Oh, God, the Germans from here [she points] and the Russians from here [points in the other direction]. Nothing but fire. We all thought this is the end. We are all going to die. It started to come down at night, and here the Germans came in with the motorcycles. They didn't come with the cannons, first with the motorcycles, four of them to see if the Russians are gone. And they were gone. And then they came in and we were in their hands. And they said, 'Don't go home in your city, everything is burned down in fire.' So we lost everything, only the clothes we had on. And nothing to eat, God when I think and I don't even want to think.

"But then when my husband was saved with the Germans, he said, 'Don't cry Friede, we are together and we have saved our little son,' because I had him all the time with me.

"Well, we went home and started again, you know with the Germans, but they helped us. They gave us bread to eat and everything again to plant. We had lots of sunflowers to make oil. So they helped us and we started again.

"After the war, we lived in barracks; and then the Americans built apartments in Nuremberg and they give us the apartments.

"And then it came out, who wants to go to America? The Lutheran Church announced that America wants people who wants to go to America. Of course, I didn't want to go. My husband said, 'Friede, let's go to America. Go get the papers. We fill them out, if we can go, fine.'

"Then I had again a tragedy there, my little son, he was three years old and he had nothing to eat. He had no toys, but there was a blacksmith, who give him nails to put in the ground and he played with the nails with a little hammer. He ran across the street. Here comes an American soldier and ripped him to pieces, my little boy. And I thought my life was over. I couldn't stand it. You couldn't cry in a guest house with all of the people. But you have to let it go; you have to cry. Me and my husband, we went to the cemetery where he was buried. We were sitting there and we cried and just screamed, let it go. Then a man came and said, 'I think you are the parents of that little boy who got killed.' We said, 'Ja,' and he said, 'Those bastards, one day we are going to kill their little kids in their cradle.' Here we want to go to America and now they say that.

"So then I got the papers and you had to go to the police for papers that you did nothing wrong. We had a good record. So I went to the Germans and so there were lots of people and soldiers too. When I had to go to the desk and tell them what I want, they had to give us a paper that we are good to go to America. And a soldier came and grabbed me, a German soldier. He said, 'You want to go over to those bandits. Those criminals had no reason to come and take over here.'

"But we didn't listen. We came over here in 1946. It was not good in the war. I hope not another war." [111]

Innocent people were victims of the military aggression. For many rehabilitation to normal life came long after the Allies won the war. Ultimately, the resiliency of the human spirit was the victor.

End Notes

110 Nicholas V. Riasanovsk, *A History of Russia*, New York, Oxford: 1993, p. 254, p. 263.
111 After her husband died, the Lutheran Church helped her find a job and she bought a house in Denver.

CHAPTER 29
AFRICAN AMERICANS IN WORLD WAR II

Tuskegee Airmen

While escorting bombers over Italy, Charles B. Hall downed an enemy plane. For this action, he received the Distinguished Flying Cross, the first African-American fighter pilot to down an enemy aircraft, July 21, 1943 [112]

However, to prepare for their participation in the North African and Italian campaigns, African-American airmen's attempt to be part of the Army Air Corps had a long history of struggle because of segregation and racial prejudice.

Laws were in place to accommodate African-Americans in the armed forces. President Roosevelt's Executive Order 8802 established the Fair Employment Practices Commission to end discrimination in the defense program and the Armed Forces, but implementation of the Order met resistance.

Public Law 18, approved 3 April 1939, provided for the expansion of the Air Corps, with one section of the law authorizing the establishment of training programs in black colleges to employ Blacks in various areas of Air Corps support services.

In October 1940, a release was issued by the War Department stating that "Negro Organizations will be established in each major branch of the service." In January 1941, the War Department announced the formation of the 99th Pursuit Squadron, a black flying unit, to be trained at Tuskegee, Alabama, the home of the Tuskegee Institute.

James H. Harvey III tried to enlist in the Army Air Corps but was drafted into the Army and served in the Corps of Engineers. He applied to Tuskegee in 1943. In an interview he told about his struggle, typical of other African Americans, to be part of the Tuskegee Airmen.

"They weren't taking Blacks in the Army Air Corps at that time. Well, they were taking Blacks, but they were putting up resistance in taking them in. The Tuskegee Army Air Corps project started in January '41 and the first class graduated in March '42. So when I tried to get in, it was January of '43, but they said they weren't taking enlistments at that time.

"A couple of months later, I got a draft notice which said 'Greetings, you've been inducted into the Army and you have to report to your draft board.' I did and I went off into the Army in March of 1943.

"Everything was segregated. I came into my first taste of that when I arrived in Washington, D. C. from Pennsylvania on my way to Fort Mead, Maryland. I got to Washington, D. C. That's when we got off the train, they put us in the back, car all to ourselves. That was my first taste of it. I didn't like it, but there was nothing I could do about it. That's the way it was and I had to go along with the program.

"Where I went to school, it was a little small town, I was the only black in the school. I was captain of the basketball team, anchor man on the tumbling team, class president, valedictorian. I didn't have any problems, none. They didn't look at me as being black, they just looked at me as being another person.

"So I went to Fort Mead, Maryland and I arrived there in the late afternoon, got my uniform, all the stuff you get when you go into the service. They gave me a physical, gave me shots, and the next day they started to take psychological tests. I took the tests and based on my score, they put me in the Army Air Corps. So they sent me off to the Jefferson Barracks, Missouri for basic training. And after Jefferson Barracks, Missouri training, they sent me to Fort Belvoir, Virginia, for the Air Corps Engineers, driving bulldozers and graders, this big earth moving equipment. Our mission was to go into the jungle and doze out an airstrip for airplanes to land on, to build an airfield. And we used to go out every day, a little town called Akketink, Virginia, churn up the dust. That's where we practiced. I'd get dusty and sweaty and I'd say, 'No, this isn't for me.'

"Anyway I got to Fort Belvoir, Virginia. So I applied for cadet training again. And this time I was accepted. I had to go to Bowling Field which was across the river. There were ten people, I was the only Black, I was the only Negro, so I took the tests, the physical again, the psychological test again, and two of us passed, myself and a white. So from there I went back to Fort Belvoir and they sent me to Biloxi, Mississippi, another month of basic training. And it was segregated down there. And from there I went back to Tuskegee and started into the program at Tuskegee.

"Mrs. Roosevelt was at Tuskegee. She went to the flying school. She went up with one of the pilots. Before she went up, the Secret Service called Franklin D. Roosevelt, 'You know what Eleanor is about to do?' He said, 'What Eleanor wants to do, Eleanor will do.' She went up and flew around with Chief Anderson, came down, landed, her picture was taken. That picture was in all the white and black newspapers throughout the country. That's what got the program going. They told us we were nothing, just a step above the baboon, second class, we were nothing.

"Now this program at Tuskegee was designed to fail. A lot of people don't know this, but the program was designed to fail. First of all, they put the program in the south. They knew the program was going to be segregated and what better place to put it than in a segregated surroundings.

"The majority of the cadets were from the north, a few of them were from the south. The people from the north weren't used to the segregation that they had in the south where it was sport to go out and pick up a Black (or Negro, at that time), castrate him or hang him.

"Our instructors were white. Our basic and advanced instructors were white. Our primary instructors were Negro. We got our primary training at Tuskegee at Moton Field. The Field belonged to the Tuskegee Institute. We lived at the Institute for our primary, we took our ground school at the Institute half-day, and flew half-day.

"When you finished primary, then they shipped us to the main base, Tuskegee Army Air Field, where we took basic and advanced. Our instructors were white. They were white southerners and they did not care for Negroes at all. Our base commander, he was white too. He was from Kentucky, but he was behind the program 100 percent. He was the only one. It affected his career. Any time a white is in charge of Negroes or Blacks, it affects their career.

"I've got something I'd like to read to you. Many of the officers in the Army, the majority of them from the south, believed in the stereotypes perpetuated by the Army War College studies of the Negro, produced in the previous decade in the War College reports of 1936. The War College studies were primarily unscientific surveys and interviews of white officers who commanded Negro troops in World War I.

"According to the studies, 'Negro soldiers were child-like, careless, shiftless, irresponsible, secretive, superstitious, immoral and untruthful. They were more likely to be guilty of moral turpitude. The Negro soldier was also branded as a comic, emotional unstable, musically inclined with good rhythm and if they are reasonably well fed, they are loyal and uncomplaining.'

"Every commander had a copy of this. That was some of the things we had to put up with. Service jobs, that's all we had in the military. When I took my exam for the military, the guy said, 'How would you like to go into the Navy?' I said, 'What would I do?', and he said, 'Be a steward.' And I said, 'What's that?' 'Oh, you can cook, shine shoes.'

"The ground crew for the Tuskegee Airmen, they were trained at Chanute Field. When they finished their training, they finished before Tuskegee Air Field was completed, so they sent them to Montgomery, Alabama. There was a flying school there to wait until Tuskegee was finished. While they were there, aircraft was sitting on the ground, needing maintenance, but they didn't have enough people to maintain them. Here are these men, right out of school, trained as instructors, they knew the aircraft. They were black, so therefore, they could not work on these aircraft for white pilots. In the meantime, they gave them service jobs: washed trucks, cleaned up the base, washed windows, worked in the mess hall. It was bad, but you couldn't let it get to you. That's what they wanted. They wanted to get to you.

"Not only that, but when they built the Army Air Field, the War Department let the contract to a Negro outfit. They designed the field, and they also let the contract to a Negro construction firm. Normally the whites would be doing it. They let it to Blacks. And they gave them eight months to do it - to build the airfield, the ramps, the taxi-ways, the buildings, the headquarters, the whole ball of wax, in eight months. They knew they wouldn't finish it, they wouldn't complete it, but they did, they did, they did.

"The instructors were white, they hated Negroes, but they had to train us. The washout rate for whites at that particular time was running around 63 percent and they didn't dare have the washout rate at Tuskegee lower than the white schools. So they had an unwritten quota system that the washout rate would be higher than for the whites. So we lost a lot of good people. Colonel Parish used to go to Montgomery, Alabama which was about 100 miles away, they had a flying school there. He'd tell the commander over there, 'We wash out better pilots in Tuskegee than you graduate over here.'

"We knew it. There was a guy in the class before me, he washed out graduation day. We wore the pinks and greens in those days, the officers did. He had a spot on his pink trouser, they washed him out. They did everything to wash us out. The instructors would get in your face, call you all kinds of names, to provoke you to do something so they could wash you out. Everything was designed to wash us out.

"That's something else. I've talked to other pilots. We were flying P-40s at the time. We'd fly at night, we had missions where we would fly with no lights, formation flying. The only reference you had was the exhaust coming from the stacks, the cylinders in the aircraft. It is hard to fly with just one point of reference. No one else had to do that. Talking to other pilots who came through flying school, I know what it was: they were hoping we would kill ourselves.

"Plus the requirements in flying school were much higher for us than they were for the whites. We had to be precise. You know what a figure-eight looks like, well a lazy-eight between 1,500 and 2,000 feet. At the top of the lazy-eight, you had to be 2,000 feet, not 1,990 or 2,010, 2,000; and the bottom had to be 1,500. You couldn't be ten feet off, you had to be precise. You came in to land, you had to land on the numbers on the end of the runway, in a three-point attitude, 360-degree tight turns, 140 miles an hour, at 2,000 feet. White flying schools didn't have anything like that. They just had to get the airplane on the ground. But, by us having to do this, we were the best and that's why we were able to do what we did.

"We had each other, just us. We relied on each other, we helped each other. But I never thought I would wash out, personally because I always strive for perfection. So by them saying this is what they wanted, nothing I wouldn't have wanted for myself.

"You could go in to town [in Alabama] but I didn't. Some of the guys did, just go see what it was like. You'd have to go to the black community. I never left the base. I stayed on the base the whole time I was in the south. Biloxi, Mississippi, I even stayed on base in St. Louis, Missouri. Tuskegee, I stayed on base.

"We couldn't go anyplace, sit on the back of the bus, separate water fountains. When I came through Augusta, Georgia, going to Godman Field, Kentucky [the first all-negro base of the US Army], got off the train in Augusta. We had about an hour layover there at the station, I went to the rest room. Four signs: 'White Men,' 'Colored Men,' 'Colored Women,' 'White Ladies.' Oh boy, you look back at it and ...but you can't let it bother you. Colonel Davis, our commander, he went to West Point. He graduated in 1936. There were no Blacks in West Point. No one talked to him for four years. He didn't have a roommate, he ate by himself, he swam in the pool by himself. No one talked to him, the instructors talked at him. He wanted to go to West Point and he wanted to graduate a second lieutenant. Two hundred sixty in his class and I think he was number 30."

99th Pursuit Squadron

"They also said, 'We will make this a pursuit squadron.' It is the most difficult flying there is, aerobatics, navigation and gunnery. Their thinking was, if we graduated from Tuskegee, if we graduated, they'd put us in a pursuit squadron. We know this flying will be too difficult for them, they cannot handle it. Well, we proved them wrong, we proved them wrong all along the way. And we went on to Italy, North Africa.

"My group got to North Africa. Our only mission was strafing and dive bombing. We did that, we were the best. We became known as the experts in dive bombing and strafing in North Africa and we were attached to a white outfit. We got over there and they didn't care for us. They would put up a briefing time, say six o'clock, Colonel Davis, our commander, would tell us, 'OK, briefing is at 6:00 a m' Get there at 6:00 a. m., they are already briefing. 'So, well you are late, why are you late?' We said, 'Briefing is at 6:00 a. m.' 'No, check the board.' They had changed it to 5:30 a. m. Just little things like that.

"Also the commanders over there, one commander started a negative or derogatory report about the 99th, saying that they could not find targets, they could not locate secondary targets, they would turn in the face of danger, all kinds of derogatory things which were untrue. As it went up the chain of command, each commander would put his two cents in, comparing the 99th flying P-40s against other P-40 squadrons over there in the whole European theater.

"Now they gage a fighter squadron by the number of kills they get, how many airplanes do they shoot down. The 99th didn't shoot down any airplanes. Why? They never saw any. Colonel Davis had come back to the States to talk to the McCloy Committee to talk about the utilization of Negro troops. And he went to the War Department and he rebutted this report and he explained the incidents in each battle they were talking about. And based on what he said and what the figures said, all of these commanders were wrong.

"General 'Hap' Arnold, he hated Blacks with a passion. He did not want any Blacks in his white Air Corps. In the meantime the 332nd fighter group was forming. As we graduated pilots from Tuskegee, they sent them up to Selfridge Field (Michigan) until they got enough. Then they formed the 332nd fighter group. So General 'Hap' Arnold says, 'We'll take the 99th out of combat, we'll send the 332nd to a noncombat outfit.' There were also plans for a 477th bomber squadron, four squadrons of Black pilots. And we will not have the 477th bomber squadron. But, after Davis went to Washington and rebutted this report, the War Department said 'No!' These commanders were wrong. So he had to back off.

"The figures were there, figures don't lie. Davis went back to North Africa and that's when the 332nd went back with him. And they all moved to Ramitelli in Italy and started flying out of Ramitelli. And their mission had been changed from dive bombing to bomber escort. Over 200 missions, they never lost a bomber to enemy fighters, never, not one. Bomb units started requesting us as escorts.

"In North Africa and Italy, we stuck together. The others didn't want to have anything to do with us. We had guys who would go into town overseas. They were treated very fine. We had one guy in Northern Italy. He was invited to dinner to an Italian family's home. So they had the hard chairs. They went in and he noticed they sat him on a chair with a cushion on it. They got ready to go to the dining room, picked up his cushion and put it on the chair he sat on there. So he asked them why. They said, 'We heard you had tails. We didn't want you to hurt your tail.' Yes, very bad. That's just one of many things.

"Overseas, the 332nd group was supposed to fly an escort mission. They were supposed to relieve the fighter group escorting the bombers, take them to an area south of Berlin, where they were supposed to be relieved by another P-51 outfit and they were to take the bombers on into Berlin. It was a long mission, an 1,800 mile mission, they'd gotten tanks for the mission. So they took off, rendezvoused with the bombers and fighters, relieved those fighters, and they were supposed to be relieved by another P-51 outfit. That P-51 outfit was not there, so they took the bombers on into Berlin. The Germans put up twenty-two jets that day. They shot down three of the jets, damaged two and did not lose a bomber to the jets. Here's what I think happened. The P-51 group, that was supposed to relieve the 332nd fighter group, was not briefed. Why weren't they briefed? Here's their thinking - the 332nd will get there, they are not relieved, they will be low on fuel, they'll go home. Big headlines in the States, 332nd fighter group runs in face of enemy, something to get the 332nd fighter group out of Europe. Didn't work that way, went on into Berlin. I think our Intelligence knew they were putting up jets that day, big headlines, we go in, see these jets, we turn tail. They run in race of enemy jets.

"The Luftwaffe called us the 'Black Airmen.' They feared and respected us. We shot down twenty-five of their aircraft in two days, that's a whole squadron. They knew we were good. The Luftwaffe was good, but we were better. We were the best flyers in the world! But no one will give us credit for it. A lot of people don't want us around.

"At Tuskegee, we didn't let that stuff bother us. You couldn't. Same food, same kind of uniform, but we were known as the Black Air Corps. There were two Army Air Corps. When they changed over to Air Force in 1947, we were still the Black Air Force and then the regular Air Force. Yes, we are proud. But no one knows."

Prejudice After the War

"I stayed in the Air Force and retired. A lot of us stayed in after they broke the group up. We were a good group and we had a good leader, Colonel Davis. No regrets whatsoever, it was a good experience. We had co-pilots who were white. We socialized with them, partied with them, squadron parties and they never thought of us as being black or white, while on the base.

"In May 1949 the Air Force had its first weapons meet in Las Vegas, Nevada and we were invited to participate. It was a four-man team, three primaries and one alternate. I was one of the primary participants in this weapons' meet. We flew into Las Vegas, we were flying P-47s. We were the only outfit in the Air Force that were flying them, they were obsolete. We landed at Las Vegas, the other pilots laughed at us, number one, we were flying this big P-47, number two, we were Black. They were flying the P-51s, the P-82s, nice sleek aircraft. To make a long story short, we won the meet. The Air Force Times puts out an almanac every year, and one of the articles in this almanac was the winners of the Air Force weapon's meet. In 1949 through 1995, 1996 will be out shortly, but for 1949, listed 'Unknown.' In 1993, my commander, Colonel William A. Campbell was commander of the 332nd fighter group at the time, started working on this, trying to get that changed. And as of April, 1995, it says 332nd Fighter Group, 46 years late. If he could find out who won, they could have found out who won. All of the records were in the Air Force base, but they did not want us to be recognized as winners, but they also destroyed Tuskegee Army Air Field. They didn't want it as a reminder.

"Now that I'm retired, I go around and talk to kids, Brighton, Colorado, in the Youth Services Center, kids are incarcerated and, if I can just get through to a few of those. What we are talking about is overcoming adversity.

"A teacher was talking to her students about World War II and this little black girl, raised her hand and stood up and said her father was a fighter pilot in the war. The teacher told her to sit down, 'There were no Negro pilots in World War II.' The next day she took her Dad to school, show and tell. The teachers play a part in this too, they are always downing blacks, telling them they can't do this.

"What can we do? We have to learn to get along together, don't pre-judge and don't listen to these stories that have been told for years and years and years about people, stories that are untrue."

Commendations of Black Airmen

James Harvey III provided the following information about the military record of Black airmen and their commendations:

Lee Archer, Wendell Pruett, aces, sunk a destroyer with bullets only
Record of 332nd fighter group:
> Aerial aircraft, destroyed in the air, 111, damaged 25
> Aircraft on the ground, destroyed 150, damaged 123
> Barges and boats, destroyed 16, damaged 24
> Boxcars and other rolling stock, destroyed 58, damaged 561,
> buildings and factories, damaged 23
> Gun emplacements, destroyed 3,
> Destroyers, destroyed 1
> Horse-drawn vehicles, destroyed 15, damaged 100
> Motor transports, destroyed 6, damaged 81
> Power transformers, destroyed 3, damaged 2
> Locomotives, destroyed 57, damaged 69
> Radar installations, destroyed 1, damaged 8
> Tanks on flat cars, damaged 7
> Oil and locomotive dumps, destroyed 2
> Total missions - with 12th Air Force, 1,267; total sorties, 6,381
> Total missions with 15th Air Force, 311; total sorties, 9,152

A Time to Speak

Grand total of missions, 1,578; grand total of sorties, 15,533
Total number of pilots overseas - 450
Number of pilots graduated at Tuskegee - 992
Prisoners of war - 32
Total killed in action - 66
Legion of Merit - 1
Silver Star - 1
Soldier Medal - 2
Purple Heart - 8
Distinguished Flying Cross - 150
Bronze Star - 14
Air Medal and clusters - 744

The Golden Thirteen

In 1944, another group of African-Americans became part of an experiment to integrate the U. S. Navy. This came about under pressure from the National Association for the Advancement of Colored People and with urging from both Eleanor Roosevelt and Adlai Stevenson, assistant to the Secretary of the Navy, Frank Knox. Knox agreed to a program to create twelve commissioned Naval officers. Sixteen black men, chosen from enlisted ranks, received sealed orders to report to the Great Lakes Training Station, Illinois.

The *Great Lakes Bulletin* [113] reported the black trainees arrived at Camp Robert Smalls [named for a former slave who had been a hero for the Navy during the Civil War]. These trainees were separate from the rest of the black sailors being trained, and the camp was located away from the main side of the Great Lakes Station. It had a barracks, a recreation hall and a drill hall. The black trainees were to undergo intensive indoctrination in six major fields: Fundamentals of Naval Service, Seamanship, Ships Ordnance and Gunnery, Navigation, Physical Training and Military Drill.

Their headquarters were in Building 1902 which housed the school's classroom and study room. In fact, they were isolated from the other sailors on base; they attended classes from eight until noon, had chow, then classes from one to five. They lived and studied together and drilled one another after lights out. They went in together and they were going to graduate together.

At the end of the training, twelve were commissioned as ensigns and one as a warrant officer in March 1944. The group later became known as "The Golden Thirteen."

Among the sixteen who arrived in January 1944 was Jesse Arbor from Chicago. Arbor, like many of the other sixteen, was college-educated and a good athlete. He had worked as a doorman and receiving clerk at the Chicago Beach Hotel and as a Pullman car porter. Then he began his job making clothes at Kuppenheimers and finally opened his own shop.

Hard to catch at his home in Chicago for a telephone interview, Arbor was free to talk about his experiences.

"*I had four brothers already in the Army and I can remember when my mother's brothers came home from World War I. I was about seven or eight years old and I wanted to join. I tried to join the Army and the Navy when I finished high school in 1932. I went to one place; I tried to join the Navy. They said, 'No, they weren't going to take nobody in the Navy. They said the Army might take you.'*

"*When the fighting broke out, I had to go somewhere and I didn't want to go in the Army. We were the very first when the camp opened up in June 1942 and they started accepting us about the latter part of June or first part of July. I entered September 11, 1942. We were all volunteers.*

"*Then we had sixteen weeks recruit training, then we all had to go to service school. I went to Quartermaster service school came out as a Third Class Quartermaster.*

"*I was sent down to Boston. They couldn't send me nowhere at sea, so I got aboard a minesweeper, coastal minesweeper. Then when they found I knew my stuff, they sent me out to the school of navigation at Harvard University. I was there six months and made Second Class Quartermaster. I was too big for that little ship.*

"*Back in December '43 they were talking about making an all-Black Navy, manned by all black sailors. So they called my name, 'Jesse Arbor, Quartermaster, Second Class.' So I got down to get aboard ship. One of my best buddies came up to me and said 'They've scratched you off the list, I'm going.' So they told me to step aside.*" [The destroyer-escort, the USS *Mason* was the test ship, with a black crew of 160 out of 191 crew members. The Commander was Norman H. Meyer and among the thirteen wartime officers, only one was Black, Lieutenant J. G. James Hair, who was coincidentally among "The Golden Thirteen." White sailors referred to the *Mason* as "the nigger ship." However, during a frightening North Atlantic gale in the fall of 1944, the *Mason* successfully led twenty ships from the Convoy NY-119 to safety in Falmouth Harbor, England, then returned to help the rest of the convoy's scattered ships. Commodore Alfred Lind recommended a "letter of commendation" be placed in the files of every man on board. Nothing happened until February 16, 1995. At a ceremony, the surviving crew members were finally honored for "meritorious service."] [114]

Scratched from the list of those scheduled to make up the crew of the *Mason*, Arbor got a leave to go home.

"*All of those who lived fifty miles from Boston could get Christmas leave.*

A Time to Speak

Chicago was further than fifty miles. I went right downstairs that night and caught the Michigan Central, stood up, there was no place to sit down; so I stood up until I got to Niagara Falls. People started getting off, so I went in and sat down. The conductor came around and wanted to know where was my ticket. I said, 'What ticket?' (In those days, if you got on a train or a streetcar, and you were in uniform, they couldn't put you off.) So they gave me a seat. I got off here in Chicago and stayed here for thirty-one days. Didn't have no money, and I was ashamed to ask my sister or my mama for any. I wrecked my car one night.

"When I got back to Boston, all my clothes were dirty, went to the washing machine, threw everything into the washing machine. The machine would run thirty-five minutes; then you had to dry them. When I got up there, they were playing poker and I was busted. 'Why don't you get in the poker game?' 'I'll have to wait 'til payday anyway.' Everybody knew me and felt sorry for me and loaned me some money to get in the poker game.

"As soon as I sat down and started playing, somebody ran up and said, 'Quartermaster Arbor Second Class, report to officer of the deck,' and I said, 'Hell, I just left there.' I had a good hand and I wanted to play this out, and before the officer could get up the ladder, a voice came out, 'Quartermaster Arbor Second Class, report to officer of the deck.' Well, he was standing right up over me. So I said in that case, 'Yes, sir.' A full commander, what did he want? He said, 'Captain Anderson is waiting for you at the bottom of the ladder.' I got down there and he said, 'Arbor.' 'Yes, sir.' I didn't have anything but a borrowed pair of blue pants, a borrowed blue jumper until mine gets dried. 'Go upstairs and get your bag. You've got thirty-five minutes to get down to Back Bay Station. You're going back to Chicago.' I said, 'Sir.' And he says, 'Shut up and follow the orders,' and he handed me a sealed brown envelope, marked for 'Eyes Only.' [Your eyes only] I went back upstairs, so I got a borrowed uniform and a pea coat.

"They had arranged for all sixteen of us to meet at Great Lakes at 4:30 p.m. that evening, that Sunday evening, so we'd all arrive at the same time. And we all came from different bases.

"To this day I don't know who recommended me. There were thirty-some that were recommended. Now there were sixteen of us who went up there.

"And at that time, we didn't know who we were in competition with. There was a white enlisted group officers training right across the highway at Camp Green Bay. Most of them across the highway had been there six months before we got there; those white boys, all from colleges, would get a commission anyway and they would outrank us. Some of those infants over there had diapers on, but they knew how to drill. We didn't know how to drill; nobody taught us. We don't know anything about that, except three boys in my outfit. One had had ROTC training and he was twenty-one and he had one year in college. The other one was thirty-three years old, a Merchant Seaman who hadn't finished high school.

"We were at Camp Robert Smalls. We had the same classes, the same instructors, the same everything. When we graduated, they took our papers and the papers from over there. Came back, our marks were so high they said, 'Hell there's got to be something wrong. Have them take it over again.' So we took it over and it came out four points better than before.

"All sixteen of us passed, everyone of us. We all graduated; they called off our names and they gave us our commissions. I don't think they said, 'Congratulations' to me. My name being the only one with A, I got the first and I never shall forget...the man was Daniel W. Armstrong. He thought he knew everything about black people, how capable they were. He was the battalion commander. [Armstrong's father had founded the Hampton Institute for the education of Blacks.] He called me in and said, 'Arbor, who recommended you?' I said, 'Commander, I don't know.' He said, 'I just don't know how you got in the group.' Well, three of those he had recommended himself, and one of them didn't make it.

"Some of those officers who came out over there, some were twenty-one, twenty-two. All those who were twenty-one to twenty-three were ensigns. Those who were twenty-three to twenty-five came out as lieutenant junior grade. You went by age groups. I was from twenty-eight to thirty and was supposed to be a full lieutenant, but they made me an ensign, all of us ensigns.

"The first orders I had: they gave me a piece of paper, 'Don't go to the Officers' Club,' the white Officers' Club. And none of us ever went into the Officers' Club until we came back from overseas.

"Lear and myself, we were the first ones to go overseas. Funny thing about it, they gave Lear his orders to ride the train out there to Frisco and they wanted me to fly out there. I'd never been on a airplane before, so I went to the officer of personnel. I said, 'Since we are going to the same destination, why is he going to ride the train and I the plane?' So I said, 'Get Lear some flying papers or me a train ticket.' We're both going to end up in Pearl Harbor. It might be two weeks before he'd get out there.

"There were twenty-six white Army officers on there and they looked up and Lear was real white. Then they saw me coming out there and I had on a Navy uniform. They all were leaning out the portholes, looking to see what plane I was going to get on. And I walked over and got on that old boxcar. When I stepped up that ladder to get on, there was a sigh of relief. They wanted me to get on their plane. Me being Black, I had 'black cat bone' and was lucky. They all took a one dollar bill and made everybody sign. And I've still got it, that one dollar bill.

"When I got to Pearl Harbor, they had all these junior grade officers just waiting to go to sea, all of them just fresh out of school. They had announcements that I wasn't supposed to see, to the effect that there were two of us coming and what would happen if they disrespected us.

"We'd been there about three weeks. They had a Officer's Club at this hotel, and I didn't have any way to get out there. Talking to this officer about going to the Officer's Club. 'I don't know where it is and I have no way of getting out there.' 'Well, I've got this jeep, want to ride along with me? Aw come on.' When we got there, one officer, he was a full lieutenant, we all went to the same Officer's Club. So at the door, the guy made eye contact, Lear was from Rome, Georgia, so he was just as green as we were. So we all stepped inside the Officer's Club together. There were two Jews and me. They didn't know what Lear was. Those officers wanted to know why I was born and where, and what for. They asked the damndest questions.

"I had a little old lieutenant commander, every night, 'Arbor, come on up and join us in poker.' Sometimes I'd go to the barracks, sometimes to Officer's Club, the whisky was free. You had to get out of there before the curfew. Drink that free whisky and play poker. I had four or five decks of cards. I played about two or three times a week. Every time I'd get a good hand, that old captain, I'd let him win.

"Everyone of us had a degree. It was a good experience; they picked the right people. Yes, it was worthwhile."

Arbor stressed over and over in his interview the academic achievements of "The Golden Thirteen." They had the choice to stay in the Navy. Only one made the Navy his career and retired as a lieutenant commander; one was recalled and served the Navy in Korea. The rest chose to return to civilian life and entered careers in teaching, coaching, business, social work, administration and law.

The members of the "Golden Thirteen" may have perceived they were pushed harder and their training made more difficult than their white counterparts. However, Paul D. Richmond was the white officer who set up the training curriculum. According to his interview with Paul Stillwell, in *The Golden Thirteen, Recollections of the First Black Naval Officers* [115], Richmond set the curriculum course based on his own training at Annapolis. It was designed to be a course in professional naval subjects, abbreviated to correspond to the short time allotted for training. His assignment was to make them officers. He admitted in his interview that he made it as difficult as he could so they would get the best training possible in a short time. If he scared them into thinking they might not pass, it was only to motivate them. He said, 'They were bright, serious men, and I was impressed by their degree of motivation. "The Golden Thirteen" were pioneers in desegregating the Navy. According to the figures cited by Paul Stillwell, today African-Americans represent 15.9 percent of the total U. S. Navy Force.

92nd Infantry Division: The Buffalo Division

In addition to the Tuskegee Airmen and the "Golden Thirteen" of the Navy, a third black group was formed, an Army division. The 92nd Infantry Division (the Buffalo Division) was activated at Fort McClellan, Alabama; their commander was Major General Edward M. Almond, a Virginian and a graduate from Virginia Military Institute. The entire Division assembled for the first time at Fort Huachuca, Arizona in May 1943. The 370th Combat Team, the advance detachment of the 92nd Infantry Division, landed in Naples, Italy on 30 July 30 1944.

They were not the first "Buffalo Soldiers." The first were the Ninth and Tenth United States Cavalry Regiments, fighting against the Indians on the western prairies in 1867. As protection against the cold weather, the soldiers made huge robes out of buffalo skins. To the Indians who saw these black soldiers for the first time, they resembled buffaloes. And they were formidable in battle, so the Indians called them "buffalo soldiers."

The Buffalo Division, which took part in the crucial spring offensive in Italy from 5 April to 2 May 1945, was composed of the 473rd Infantry, the Japanese-American 442nd Infantry and the black 370th Infantry. The situation in Italy in 1944-1945 was difficult. The American Fifth Army was south of the Arno River; the Germans had fortified defense lines in the Apennines; the Germans were fighting tenaciously. The task of Company C, 370th Infantry, commanded by Captain John F. Runyon, was to attack the entrenched German Army in mountainous terrain and destroy their position, helping to open up the way to the Po River.

One of the officers of Company C was Second Lieutenant Vernon Baker. Under heavy attack, bombarded by mortar and machine-gun fire, Baker was able to destroy one enemy position, killing three Germans; then to attack an enemy observation post, killing two more Germans; and with the aid of one of his men, to charge two more machine gun nests. Runyon, the commander, radioed for reinforcements which never came, and he decided to withdraw. Runyon and Baker organized their withdrawal in two groups. Baker volunteered to cover the first withdrawal and to remain to help get the more severely wounded to safety.

"When Baker came off that hill holding tight to his courage, having served his country and his comrades well, his body betrayed him. He vomited. Maybe there were tears. He doesn't remember." [116]

Hondon B. Hargrove described the spring offensive in Italy and Baker's role, for which he was awarded the Distinguished Service Cross. Hargrove comments, "Many felt he should have received the Congressional Medal of Honor."[117]

A Time to Speak

The Congressional Medal of Honor

Among the 433 Medals of Honor in World War II, none were awarded to Blacks.

In 1993, the Army awarded Shaw University, the 130 year old historically black college in Raleigh, North Carolina, a contract to find out why no Blacks had received the Congressional Medal of Honor. There was a team of three white men and two blacks, all military historians. They interviewed white and black veterans, enlisted men and officers.

Among their findings was evidence of prejudice against African-Americans, similar to what James H. Harvey III encountered. It was a climate which guaranteed that Blacks would not advance far enough in the military organization or have adequate combat experience to earn the Medal. There was the pervasive bias, mentioned by Harvey, that black soldiers were lazy and cowardly. Furthermore, they were commanded by white officers.

In Vernon Baker's case, with declassified documents, the Shaw team found evidence that Captain John Runyon, at least in part, disagreed with the general consensus that Blacks were inherently incapable of becoming infantrymen. Runyon was Baker's superior officer and fought beside him on 5 April 1944. Elliott Converse, one of the authors of the Army study noted, "The senior white officers had falsified Runyon's account to support their view that inherent racial characteristics prevented black soldiers from becoming effective."

Runyon's original report praised Baker. He had recommended him for the Distinguished Service Cross. Some of that praise was edited from the report. Contrary to other officers, Runyon felt that black forces were not properly trained and that they suffered from a constantly changing white leadership. He suggested training deficiencies, and the men not knowing their leaders or each other, could partly account for disappointing results.

In light of the climate of racism which existed during World War II, the Shaw investigative team recommended that the Army review the deeds of several black servicemen for higher honors. Seven men were selected, including Vernon Black, the only surviving member of the group of seven.

On Monday, 13 January 1997 President Bill Clinton awarded the first Congressional Medals of Honor to these seven black soldiers.

Baker's comment to Maureen Harrington, made before he actually received the Medal, *"If I get the Medal it will belong to all black soldiers. It will be a kind of restitution."*[118]

It wasn't until after World War II that segregation in the Armed Services was eliminated. President Harry S. Truman issued Executive Order 9981 on 26

July 1948 which put an end to segregation in the military.

By 1954 the Armed Forces were completely desegregated. In the Persian Gulf War, 20 percent of the soldiers were African- Americans, compared to 8.7 percent in World War II and 9.8 percent in Vietnam.

End Notes

112	*Fact Sheet, 50th Anniversary of World War II*, Commemoration Committee, Washington, D. C.)
113	Vol. XIX No. 12
114	*Boulder Daily Camera*, February 26, 1995
115	Paul Stillwell, *The Golden Thirteen, Recollections of the First Black Naval Officers*, Naval Institute Press, Annapolis, Maryland, 1993, pp. 41-42; p. 288
116	Maureen Harrington, "His Finest Hour", *The Denver Post Empire Magazine of the West*, June 16, 1996, p. 13
117	Hondon B. Hargrove, *Buffalo Soldiers in Italy, Black Americans in World War II*, McFarland & Company, Inc., Publishers, Jefferson, North Carolina, 1985, p. 153
118	Maureen Harrington, "His Finest Hour." p. 19.

CHAPTER 30

BURMA AND THE SOUTH PACIFIC

The Japanese had a firm grim on Burma in April 1942. In July 1942, in order to bypass the sea lines of communication, the Japanese had begun a railway link between Burma and Thailand, using British, Australian and Dutch prisoners of war to construct the railroad. In 1943, British and Gurkha troops set off for the jungles of Burma on a mission of sabotage against the railway.

The Burma Campaign

Since 1886, Burma had been a province of British India. It gained independence after the war was over in 1948. The Burma campaign to oust the Japanese lasted from 1942 until May 1945. The British Colonial Army engaged in battle against the Japanese, aided by the Gurkha troops, who together with the British made up the 77th Indian Brigade, known as the Chindits. The Askaris from Southern Rhodesia also served the Colonial Army in Burma.

Two taped interviews from the Imperial War Museum Sound Archive in London give some insights into the British Colonial Army, particularly the relationship between the officers and the Gurhka troops and the Askaris.

What comes through in these accounts is the British troops' lack of tactical training for jungle fighting, the "gut-strangling fear," and the extreme hunger and exhaustion in the jungles of Burma. Their survival often depended on help from the native Gurkha troops and the loyalty and friendship of the black African troops.

The Gurkhas

Colonel. D. F. Neill transferred from the 60th Rifles to the Indian Army, the 77th Indian Brigade, made up of British and Gurhka troops, known as the Chindits. Colonel Neill participated in the first Chindit expedition (February 1943), going from India into Japanese-held northern Burma. His job was to take his small group of Gurkhas into the hostile territory of the 33rd Japanese Division.

Moving out of a village and heading north on 14 April, out of the blue, there was a Japanese ambush. Neill and his troops crashed through to the jungle. He was left with only twenty of his men. Now their aim was to get back to India with as many men as possible. In his taped interview for the Imperial War Museum Sound Archive, Neill recalled the terror of being hunted and how the Gurkhas knowledge of the jungle saved them from starvation as they headed to the Chwindin River and friendly territory.

"We had to pit our combined skills of evasion and survival tactics against those military skills of fresh well-fed professional killers of the Nip's full strength 33rd Division. We were the quarry, they were the hunters.

"The men's knowledge of what could be eaten in the jungle turned out to be our salvation - a favorite was the tips of fern (nuro), tasty if boiled together with one's rice.

"We met the buffalo, three or four. One shot and a buffalo was killed and dragged out of the chaung (river). It was butchered as quickly as possible. They cut one-fourth inch wide longish stakes to use for cooking and smoking while we ate the chunks in the fire itself. The men knew exactly what to do. We ate, and ate, and ate, and ate until we could eat no more. Apart from the hide, blood and bones on the ground, and dried strips in our packs, the buffalo had disappeared. Strips of meat, shared on the march. We even ate it when it was too late and covered with flies - it tasted a bit bitter."

Racing against time, the monsoons, and a fear of Japanese troops, they reached a friendly village and crossed the Chwindin River (June 1943)

"We got news that the Japanese patrol had been only one-half hour behind us. We had been sorely defeated but we still had our pride. . . I knew we had been routed and had to retreat through hundreds of miles of hostile wilderness, but we had achieved our aim. We had escaped, we had outwitted the Japanese of the 33rd division. We could now fight them on another day in another place." [119]

The Askaris

The Burma Campaign did not end easily or quickly. John Hewlett Nunnely arrived in Burma in 1944. He was commissioned in 1941 and was posted immediately to the 9th Battalion of the Somerset Light Infantry. Later he was posted to the Tanganyika Battalion, King's African Rifles, which included British officers and about 1100 Askaris from several tribes, Wagogo, Wangamesi, Yao, and a smaller tribe, the Wahehe. The black African troops, the Askaris were mercenary soldiers. However, contrary to what many thought about these African troops, Nunnely commented on the extraordinary loyalty and friendship of the Askaris who served with him.

"I counted myself very fortunate to have been posted to a Tanganyika Battalion. I felt an affinity with these different tribesmen; I enjoyed their company; I had a great respect for them. They were after all, in the main, plainsmen. They were not jungle men and yet, in the end, in Burma, they acquitted themselves with enormous courage and the application of their innate skills, such as tracking in the jungle. I was very happy with the King's African Rifles in that particular battalion. I think the affection and trust they obviously demonstrated if one liked being with them, their readiness to put up with all kinds of discomfort. After all they were, in a sense, mercenaries. They had perhaps answered a call, uttered by their tribal chief, to serve 'Kingie George,' a remote figure. The aspirations of power by the British government meant very little to them, but they were prepared for two shillings a day to be Askaris to 'Kingie George.' That seemed to me to place a great responsibility on everyone who was a European not to let those people down, and to develop their best qualities and generally set them an example that one would not be ashamed of.

"There are those who believe that the African was a mercenary and therefore he would have been prepared for, in exchange for pay and rations and accommodations and uniform, to have fought for anybody. But I don't believe that. I believe there was a patriotism which had developed since the late 19th century as Kenya, Tanganyika, and Uganda began to see European settlers. I want to believe because I can hardly credit that Africans would otherwise be prepared to put their lives at risk simply for two shillings a day, and the pay is not exactly munificent, and only merit of the rations were that they were balanced and regular. It was just accepted that we were going to fight the 'Japans,' as they called them." [120]

31st Japanese Division

Facing the British Colonial Armies in Burma were well-trained Japanese troops, taught to kill themselves rather than be captured by the British.

Hirakubo, educated in Japanese expansionist policies as well as European culture, techniques and literature, was obliged to go into the Japanese army after two and a half years at Kobi University (1942). In a taped interview from the Imperial War Museum Sound Archive, he talked about the war and his experiences in Burma in 1944.

"At the time of the outbreak, actually I was astonished and I thought it was a bad decision. I expected it, but it was not a wise decision. Many people thought it was mad. Nobody expected Japan would win. I didn't know anyone who thought Japan would win. Japanese wins were pleasant news."

In 1944, he joined the 31st Division, a new Division which was made up of regiments from China and Thailand. Hirakubo was the supply officer, which in the case of the Japanese Army, meant responsibility for procuring, supplying and even cooking food; for equipment, except ammunition; and responsibility for clothing and payment.

"The Army didn't arrange any transport for us. We were obliged to find trucks. We went by ship from Japan to Singapore. Young officers like us were asked to watch, even at nighttime, for any torpedoes. Five [ships] arrived safely in Singapore, one was sunk off Saigon. From Singapore to the southern part of Burma, we were escorted by Japanese planes."

Hirakubo's first impression was "Burma was sandy, muddy, easy life, easy climate, no civilization or culture, Buddhism people, lots of monks." He took up his duties as a supply officer for the 31st Division Headquarters on 26 February 1944 and found serving in Burma just as difficult and harrowing as did his British enemy. It required ingenuity to survive air strikes, lack of food and jungle illnesses.

"The campaign was decided by headquarters in Japan, we must carry it out. Four out of seven were ordered to work in front lines. He [the commander] said no grain of rice will be delivered from behind to the battalion, so he said, 'It is entirely your ability how your battalion will last long fighting.' I was astonished and my very militaristic idea has been broken down at once, and equally I pledged myself to serve and get the food for the 3rd battalion as long as I can. That's how my war started.

"We took over British warehouses before being burnt. Fifty kilo carried on shoulders to prepare for campaign. Our rations? Rice, nisal, paste beans, canned fish, biscuits.

"We did the cooking for 1,000 people. We started bringing water from the valley to the cooking place in the evening and we started cooking rice for 1,000 people. Two each [rice cakes] for each person, pressed by hand, added by some pig's meat, bottle of water. Before dawn we put it in bamboo basket on shoulder and we all went to the front line and we put there and take yesterday's bottle of water back before the sky becomes light because otherwise British aircraft started to go around in the sky when dawn comes.

"We were attacked ten times in Kohima [India]. Very much casualties. In the daytime, generally speaking, all Japanese soldiers were hidden in the valley or in the cave. Ordinary officers didn't move, but I did move to ask for cigarettes for my battalion and also we set up pig collection point in remote village about ten miles from Kohima. I also go to divisional warehouse. Always I was obliged to walk in the daytime. So ten times enemy aircraft coming. My orderly was shot and I wasn't.

"Ambulance truck to bring back wounded to camp, and I convinced the commander that way of going to Kohima to carry our pig to the front so we could add some meat in the campaign.

"After 2 June, we started to retreat from Kohima, that is the only tragedy. Everybody is sick, beriberi, malaria and dysentery. No food, just to die so those people are scattered in the way. We had no time, no way to bury them. We left, we passed among the dead corpses. We walked all the way from Kohima to Chindwin.

We decided to walk at least fifteen miles a day because we believed otherwise we'll be catched by the British. We were taught to kill ourselves by hand grenade anytime, and everyday in the jungle there was such a noise of grenade.

"I went to the river and crossed the Chindwin river searching for food. High fever of more than 40 degrees and I got a lot of stuff but I had no way to get it back across the river. I lie down, and after seven days, my orderly came to my place. It was a sort of miracle. I continued to lie down for thirty days. I couldn't move. And after that I walked to the east, to the railway side with him. And finally we chased my battalion in the railway.

"We walked to cross mountains and we found Burmese house or cottage and asked to sleep inside. They just took us inside and washed my feet and gave food and let us sleep on the floor and sometimes gave us some medicine, some leaves crushed. It is good for the malaria. When we left I wanted to pay (Japanese Army money). In almost all cases, they refused to accept money."

By November, the British controlled Kohima and launched a drive across the Chwindin river. Hirakubo was captured in October and his Division handed all weapons to the British side.

"Supplies from the British to the camp was rice, dried potato and corned beef. So we must collect vegetables and other things and the sweet and fruit we must collect by ourselves, from Mudon Dematuway to Maudong in the plantation area. We were allowed to go to the Thailand border to cut and collect bamboo and we made a house, but the supplies were the same, added by some fruit.

"Compared to time of fighting, it was very easy life. We were ordered to go to the British camp to make any work: painting, cleaning, digging ditches, repairing of the road, railroad. We went to that work once a week. I was teacher of English, somebody was astronomic lecturer and also sports and games and also theater. It was exciting. Each company, as a unit, had a performance and competed in performance.

"In Moudon, the gum of the mouth was bleeding; that was lack of vitamin C and we asked British supply officer to supply more fruit. The next day we were supplied with a durian, very strong fruit, very expensive and then it stopped at once. Enough to eat? Actually not quite enough in quantity. The soldiers exchanged shirt and those things with the Burmese people." [121]

THE BILLFISH

The struggle to control New Guinea was long and arduous and not completed until 1944, the campaign in Burma not until 1945. Meanwhile, American submarines, operating out of Pearl Harbor, the Marianas, and Australia were the sentinels on watch.

A Time to Speak

Charlie Poston enlisted in the Navy, because in the 1930s he couldn't afford to continue at the university after the first year. He was sent to the East Coast to go to submarine school and never left submarines. When the war broke out, they were looking for men with submarine training.

"We went out on the *Billfish*. Well, in some places it was exciting, other places it was pretty dull.

"We operated out of Perth, Australia. We had the Australian pilot take us up north to Port St. Charles, then we went out on our own. And we had a big operation there and we had another group operating out of Pearl Harbor. I was chief engineer. We started the wolf pack, we'd have three boats in a wolf pack. If we'd had communications then like we have now, but we were trying to use walkie-talkies and silent radios. We were stationed in different quarters, so if we'd see a convoy coming, and it looked like we were going to miss him, you'd alert somebody else, the three of us would gang up on him. That worked and it was a very interesting operation.

"We did take beatings. It seemed like every depth charge in the world hit our boats. It was not pleasant. One of the worst ones was right off of Borneo, 'Smoky Charley' we'd named him, and he was pretty good. Everyone was trying to sink him, but it was so shallow that the torpedoes would run under him. Then he would come and bring these depth charges. They would just oscillate and get you down. This one time they got us down, and they had a destroyer on us and we submerged. We ran silent and we ended up about 200 feet, and we couldn't get him off of us. He just kept going over and dumping ash cans and bombing us. Of course we were running silent and there is no ventilation on the boat. You couldn't smoke. The air was getting thick. The condensation on the boat would start dripping down, and we would just strip down to nothing but our drawers. We were down for over eighteen hours and our batteries were almost dead. Finally, it got dark and we finally lost him. That was the worst depth charge. We took them pretty nearly every run I had, two or three depth charges. They'd drive us down.

"The most scary one I had was out of the Marianas. A gun-boat got after us and he was gaining on us. We were on the surface and finally we dove because he was shooting at us. He kept missing us on both sides. Finally the skipper says, 'Take her down.' I had quarterdeck at the time. We went down...we were doing about 20 knots. We shut the engines down, pulled the plug, closed the hatch. As soon as we hit underneath, we slowed right down. And then we'd have to make an approach off to the side to get away from him. But that's the closest time we ever got shot at.

"But this one trip, they kept us down so long, we had a lot of water coming in, lines leaking and breaking loose, the crews fixing them.

"Japanese submarines, they got them. They didn't have too many but before, the end of the war, they had quite a few. If you can imagine, we ran into it once out there, we were playing cat and mouse with a submarine submerged. If you don't think that is a tricky thing. We played with them for about eight or ten hours. I don't know who gave up first. We didn't give up; we were still trying to track him and nail him but we never did. He got on us and we lost him. He had lost us but we turned around and picked him up. You never know where you are at with that. Strictly sonar, we had sound people there with their equipment. They are quiet and you've got your sound domes. And you are playing with them all of the time. And they are doing the same thing. That get's pretty hairy when you are playing submerged, 100 to 150 feet where you can't see anything. And of course, we didn't have the equipment on there that we have now."

Chicken or Lobster

"While we were on our last refit at Fremantle, they had just brought the Orion and a couple more tenders out there. They had refitted us and we had a full load of chow that had just come out from the States. They had issued us, we being the submariners, we had the best food in the world. They brought out this canned lobster, canned turkey, canned chicken, all this stuff in the cans that we could store aboard.

"Well, we had all of this canned stuff down in the bilges; the water got in and flooded. Guess what happened to the markers on the cans? They disappeared. Which was chicken, which was lobster, which was turkey?

"They pulled us in to Speary. It was in the Marianas. They had taken over one of the islands as a temporary submarine base to refit there and get more torpedoes and more chow. We'd be there for two weeks. Well, we pulled in there and over at the island. The Seabees were on one island, the Marines were on another island, and we were on an island of our own. We went down and found out all these cans were missing the markers and I said, 'Well,' I said, 'Skipper, I bet there are some Marines over there who would just love to gamble. They probably hadn't had a full meal for three years.' So I went over to the Marines and I said, 'You got a flat boat over here? Here's the problem. I've got a boat load of lobster, chicken, turkey, anything else you need, but I don't know which can is which.' 'We'll take it, we'll take it.' Over they came and we loaded them up; took all this stuff on and gave it to them. That was the happiest bunch of guys! Man, they had a ball over there.

"As far as the Billfish's damage is concerned, it wasn't very much. I think we only got seven or eight ships the whole time we were out there.

"We took the submarine back to San Francisco, the Billfish had seven runs. They sent me back to the East Coast to another submarine, the Achievo at the

A Time to Speak

Electric Boat Company. I put the Achievo in commission. This was in '45 and we were headed for the Pacific. We went out there and went out to Pearl and had our training session at Pearl. They had us slated for going into the Japanese harbor and in through the mine fields and go in and sink the battleships that were anchored there. So they had set up a mine field out of Pearl for training and they brought the old Achievo in. We practiced for about three weeks.

"We were ready to go, so we headed south. We got on Midway and the war was over. We never got to go through the mine fields. We had to turn around and come back to Pearl. It was an interesting time during World War II. It was for me."[122]

Harry Tate's Navy

From the beginning of the war the British Royal Navy Patrol supported military activity where it was needed. The Patrol operated in the South Atlantic and across the Indian Ocean to Ceylon (now Sri Lanka) and Burma.

Jimmy Brown's history, *Harry Tate's Navy*, tells the story of the Royal Navy Patrol. Harry Tate's Navy is more properly known as the Royal Naval Patrol Service. Its nickname was given, in derision, by regular British navy men because of its motley fleet and its crew of fishermen.

It began, in fact, in 1907, when it was suggested that the Admiralty purchase fishing trawlers for use as experimental minesweepers. Trawlers were used during World War I as minesweepers. At the end of the war, when the trawlers had finished the dangerous task of clearing enemy mines, as well as Allied mines, the men returned to their peacetime fishing business. The Trawler Section of the Royal Naval Reserve was reconstituted as the Royal Navy Reserve Patrol Service.

When war broke out in Europe, the Admiralty saw the need to requisition trawlers. The Admiralty Surveyor of Lands found an assembling point for the Patrol Service. They chose Sparrow's Nest, a country estate, once the home of the Marchioness of Salisbury, and located in Lowestoft, a thriving fishing town (in East Suffolk on the North Sea). Fisherman heard of the emergency and lost no time in arriving at Sparrow's Nest. They were fishermen of all ages who had undergone three weeks' annual training.

After Pearl Harbor, the Germans sank US ships on the east coast and President Roosevelt appealed to Churchill for help. Trawlers were dispatched in 1942 where they were in active service for about six months. The ships were then withdrawn to South Africa to combat U-boat activity in the South Atlantic. At the time of D-Day, fifty-eight trawlers, manned by shipmates from Sparrow's Nest took part in the landings.

Demobilized in 1946, one by one they left Lowestoft. The sentries vanished, the wartime buildings were removed, and all of the naval trappings were removed. In 1953, a Memorial, a tall fluted column, topped by a bronze ship, was erected above Sparrow's Nest, with a clear view across the North Sea.

Brian Brown, a member of the Royal Navy Patrol, wrote about his experiences, "a great adventure."

"*Starting from the beginning of my first relationship with wearing a naval uniform would be in 1942, when, as a sixteen year old, I joined the newly formed Sea Cadet Corps in Chesham. As you might imagine, as it was in wartime, the Sea Cadets was a thriving organization, with five or six officers and instructors and approximately thirty cadets.*

"*It was possible under a scheme called the 'Bounty Scheme' for sea cadets to join the communication branch of the Royal Navy at the age of seventeen and half, this I opted to do in the hopes that perhaps one day I would meet up with a brother, two years senior, who was already serving in the navy, having joined as a boy of fifteen in the early days of the war.*

"*After finishing training in one of Butlins Holiday camps in Scotland (these camps were taken over during the war by the Admiralty), I qualified as a wireless telegraphist suitable for drafting to small ships.*

"*After spending a short spell at the communications ratings camp near Devonport, one particular morning parade, all ex-sea cadets were told to 'Fall out', which we did and those remaining were informed they would be transferred to the Army.*

"*Having escaped the possibility of becoming a soldier was my introduction to the Royal Naval Patrol Service, based at Lowestoft, Suffolk.*

"*Our HQ was situated in some pleasure gardens, a theater was the administration block.*

"*All the young ratings were billeted out to homes in the town, as in my case, housed in an old brewery building. But not for long, because very soon after arriving, my next move was aboard a troop ship bound for Durban, South Africa, where I was to join my first ship, a converted yacht H.M.Y. Virginia, a small escort and anti-submarine vessel of approximately 800 tons (about the size of a corvette).*

"*So I became one of Harry Tate's Navy which was the nickname given to all Patrol Service personnel. On the Virginia, there were two more telegraphists, my friend who joined with me and a more senior rating who was already on board. The crew consisted of about thirty men including four offices, the C.O. was a Lt. Commander R.N.R., a pre-war officer in the Merchant Navy who was a fine seaman.*

"*At the time of joining, the Virginia, she was undergoing a re-fit which if course gave the crew plenty of opportunities to visit Durban and sample the de-*

lights of a city not restricted like those at home. Eventually, the 'good life' came to an end, so after sea-going trials we departed Durban docks and headed north to Mombasa for a short visit. From Mombasa, we escorted a troopship to Aden. Both trips were uneventful. To the passengers on the troop ship, our little ship with its main armament of twelve-pounder guns and Oerlikon machine gun amidship would seem scant protection against some enemy craft, at least that was the impression we formed whenever we came close enough to see the looks on their faces as they leaned on the ships' rails.

"From Aden, we sailed across the Indian ocean to Colombo in Sri-Lanka [formerly Ceylon], whilst at anchor in a line of minesweepers, one day one of my mates and myself, decided to swim down the line, where to my surprise, on one of the ships was a seaman from my home town of Amersham, who I last saw when we were at school a few years previously. It was during our stay in Colombo that news of President Roosevelt's death was announced.

"From Colombo, our next port of call was Calcutta where we received orders to proceed to Burma, where our forces were engaged in various landings along the coast. I remember our ship towed a motor fishing vessel between two of the areas, our ship having had to take up survey duties, along with another converted yacht called 'White Bear.'

"You may remember my telling you that whilst at anchor in the River Tharrawaddy at Rangoon, during my watch in the radio room, we received news about victory in Europe, at the end of the message it said 'Splice the mainbrace', which meant a tot of rum for each of the crew. As I was only eighteen I wasn't entitled. One of the officers, though, brought me a tot to the radio room, this I duly drank and when my watch was finished, feeling a little light headed, I went down to the mess deck where my mates had saved a part of their tots, collected in a glass. As I sat down, they said, 'Here you are sparks, sippers.' Needless to say I was more than light headed when I reached my bunk.

"One evening the quartermaster had us scrambling up the ladder double quick time with the news we were about to be rammed. We arrived on deck to see a hugh tank landing craft (which had broken loose from its moorings in the swift current) bearing down on us. Two of our small boats which were swung out on davits disappeared with the impact. We never knew where that L.S.T. finished up, because we sailed back to Trincomalee in Sri Lanka soon afterwards.

"Soon after the Virginia was due back in the U.K. I was to leave her in Bombay to spend a few months ashore before my return to Lowestoft, where I received my leave pass for fourteen days, so off home I went.

"My next ship was among a group of mine-sweepers based at Dover which meant a busy time cleansing the English Channel of mines so that shipping could pass freely once again. These ships, by the way, were built in America, made of wood and very light, about 250 tons. They were called B.Y.M.S. followed by a number. This particular operation was to last a few months towards the end of 1946, when, because of winding down the service and with the closing down of our HQ at Lowestoft, ships were de-commissioned and sold to various countries or were just broken up.

"At Sheerness in the Thames estuary, there were scores of B.Y.M.S. sweepers lined up awaiting their fate. Twice I became part of a crew to sail a ship around the coast to Milford Haven in Wales to leave them in the hands of breakers.

"However, in December 1946, my number came up for de-mob; having refused the offer to enlist in the Royal Navy as a regular, I returned to civilian life, a few months over the age of twenty. But I did enjoy the satisfaction of being eligible to receive a tot of rum for four months."

Speculation continued about where and when the Allies would invade Europe. In anticipation of an invasion, the French Maquis intensified their activities.

End Notes

119 Summary and Excerpts, Interview, Imperial War Museum Sound Archive, Colonel D. F. Neill, Reels 5, 6, 7, #13299
120 Excerpts, Interview, Imperial War Museum Sound Archive, John Hewlett Nunnely, #10203
121 Excerpts, Interview, Imperial War Museum Sound Archive, Hirakubo, #11516
122 Poston stayed in the service. After twenty years at sea, he got shore duty in St. Petersburg, Florida as commanding officer of the Naval Reserve Training Center. Then he was sent to Korea to Chinhae as commanding officer for the American shipyard and ended his career in Indiana in charge of all the classified material for all of the factories who were making navy materials in Indiana.

CHAPTER 31

THE MAQUIS IN FRANCE

Late in 1943 and early in 1944, for two main reasons, resistance activity involved overt action and sabotage by the maquis. Allied bombing raids of German military and industrial targets affected the capabilities of wartime production in the Third Reich. However, as the bombing activity expanded, so did the risk for downed crews. To avoid their capture by the Germans, they often depended on a maquis to rescue and hide them, then evacuate them by plane to England.

Prior to the D-Day invasion in Normandy and during the Allied attempt to move westward, the maquis devised ways to delay the German Army on the ground, aided by parachute drops of arms from England. They derailed trains, cut telephone lines, blew up lines at hydro-electric plants, and engaged in active combat against German troops. Codes indicated to members, listening on the BBC radio, the various activities to be carried out: "Plan vert" (Green plan) for railroads; "Plan violet" (Purple plan) for telephone lines; and "Plan bleu" (Blue plan) for electrical installations. The maquissards were armed, generally located in a woods, and acted as guerrilla troops. Later, they joined the Forces françaises de l'intérieur (FFI) and fought alongside the Allies. In some instances, as the Allies liberated cities and the troops moved east, the maquis were left in control. Roger Dutertre, a Resistance member, joined a battalion [FFI] which was assigned at Redon and given control in several cities, La Roche, Royan, Redon, Lorient, and St. Lazaire.

MAQUIS IN THE REGION OF EPERNAY
Everett Childs and Pierre Servagnat

The region of Epernay, southwest of the Marne River, had five sections of the maquis. Pierre Servagnat was both the Chief of the maquis and a captain in the Forces françaises de l'intérieur (FFI). Everett Childs was the navigator for the squadron leader of the 544th Bomb Squadron, 384th Bomb Group and participated in the second Schweinfurt raid.

American bombers, based in Britain, had carried out two heavy raids on 17 August 1943, one on the German ball bearing factory at Schweinfurt and the other on the Messerchmitt works at Regensburg. Both factories were badly damaged, and the raids accomplished their purpose of setting back German military production. German industrial production recovered however, and a second raid was planned for 14 October 1943.

Two hundred twenty-eight American bombers, flying the B-17G, the newest bomber available, went on a daylight raid at Schweinfurt. They flew in tight formation without bomber escorts. Childs said,

"This raid has been publicized as the greatest air battle ever fought. The Germans were determined that they would turn back the bombing raid and the Americans were determined that the Germans couldn't do this. And they both changed tactics after this because the Germans decided they should do frontal attacks instead of attacks in the rear, and the Americans decided they couldn't take these long range bomber raids without fighter escorts."

Childs' plane was shot down over Bar-le-Duc in eastern France. His number four engine was on fire; the plane flipped into a spin; his arms were pinned up because of the centrifugal force and the plane exploded. He found the parachute rip-cord around his knees but he was able to bail out. Bleeding from cuts, Childs walked until he found a ditch where he could try to get some sleep. In the morning he hailed a man who took him to his employer, a farmer, and Childs was put in touch with members of the maquis, headed by Servagnat.

From October until 20 August 1944 when he managed to get inside American lines, Childs and other downed pilots stayed with a variety of underground groups as they awaited evacuation by plane to Spain or England.

From Bar-le-Duc, Childs was to go to Reims, by train, where the airmen were to catch a plane to fly them back to England.

"My trip from Bar-le-Duc to Reims [November 1943] was kind of interesting. There were three of us and this Frenchman, Robert L'Heurre, an English teacher in the schools, was going to take us on a train. He said there will be a lot of soldiers on the train, but don't worry about it. You can say 'bonjour' and 'merci' and they'll think nothing of it because there are a lot of workers over there who don't speak French at all and they are trying to be friendly to the French because they are occupying the country. The fellow, George Hill, escaping with me, spoke pretty good French.

"So we get on this train. He said if there was a troop compartment he would try and get in there. He said, 'I'll do all the talking, you won't have to worry about anything. If they talk to you, just say you don't understand.' We sit down in these seats in the compartment and pretty soon, he snuck away and came back. 'Come on with me,' and we went into this troop train. So here we are, three of us in with fifteen German soldiers, we had on civilian clothes. So he talked a blue streak to these soldiers and of course, the soldiers were all using their French on him. It

was a great thing for them and so they didn't pay any attention to the three of us who couldn't speak any French at all, three Americans.

"So we made a mistake. It was raining and we couldn't see the signs. We missed the sign for the stop we were supposed to make. We bought tickets for Reims and we were supposed to stop before, about two miles before, in a little village. And there was somebody in a car that was supposed to pick us up and take us to where we were going to stay. This was like ten o'clock at night. We missed that stop. Well, he stepped out and he let us hide some place. But then he had no contact with the people who were supposed to pick him up. They were looking for him. So he had to use a telephone. He went to Gestapo headquarters to use the telephone. He said, 'You wait outside here, I've got to go in there.' So it makes you a little nervous. We asked him afterwards, 'Why did you go in there to use the telephone?' 'Well,' he said, 'it's the only phone I know of that wouldn't be bugged.'

In Reims, Childs moved from place to place, first to the home of a champagne maker, then to a Marcel Tavernier's butcher shop, then to the home of a baker in Fismes, and finally to a small nearby village in preparation for the plane trip to England. About fifteen airmen were in this small village, scattered among different homes. It was there that Childs and two others experienced a narrow escape (31 December 1943).

"Here we were in this town and a Frenchman said, 'Oh they are going to bring a plane in next week.' We were there about a week. 'Oh, it's still coming and it's going to be next week,' then he said, 'It's going to be three days now.' There was some message that had to be sent and received and so we moved to another house.

"So we moved to this other house and we were just there the very next morning. The night before we were acquainted with the little girl who was crippled. We were in bed and they brought up coffee for us, ersatz coffee, they didn't have coffee. And they thought we should have breakfast in bed. And here we are having coffee and this little crippled girl comes running to the house, 'The Gestapo are coming!'

"Immediately we forget all about the coffee and started putting on our clothes. We had an escape plan. If anything happened, we were going out the back way. It was a kind of house attached to a barn. We would go over and slide down this pipe and be in the barnyard.

"There we are ready to go out there, and there is a troop of soldiers in the yard. So we had an alternate escape plan which was to hide up on top of the room. We dashed around that corner and as we dashed around the corner, the Gestapo agent is running up the stairs. And we were almost certain he saw us. He didn't. We climbed up on top of the room, with our feet sticking out, however there were shoes, there were hams hanging there, there were rakes, shovels hanging from nails, including our feet, shoes with feet in them. And somebody did come around and look around down that little hole and didn't see us. And they searched that house all day.

"So when it got dark, we made it out across the fields. It turned out there was about a half inch of snow, new snow on the ground. So if we had gotten out the back way before the soldiers got there, we would have probably been tracked down. The old couple were arrested and they died in a concentration camp about a month later.

"The French thought they were going to get planes in to land at night and take us back to England. This never happened for various reasons, one of which was that the Germans knew enough about it so that they had spies in the unit and were arresting the French as soon as they assembled people to fly them back."

The three airmen walked in the general direction of the southeast, intending to reach Switzerland.

"Near the end of the sixth day we decided to stop at a particular house on the edge of the village. The two sergeants hid to watch me while I approached the house. A woman answered the door and directed me to ask her husband, who was around the barn. I walked over to the barn and around the barn. I was confronted by a French policeman, her husband, in full uniform. I must have stopped in mid-air, I didn't know whether to bluff it, or run, or what. He tried to assure me things were OK. His name was Charles Forney, and we were in the underground again. He was later to lose his life because someone turned him in to the Gestapo. We learned the local chief of police, this policeman's boss, was a chief of the underground in this area."

In 1944 Childs together with another navigator, Bill Rendall, moved in with a baker, Lucien Mouillet, in the village of Coligny, where they were grateful to have the warm rooms over the baking ovens. Then Childs and Rendall were housed in Pocancy, hidden in Mme Mauclin's upstairs storeroom for about six weeks. Neither her daughter nor the people who worked for her knew she had airmen hiding upstairs. The airmen learned to be quiet during the day, but took walks in the woods in the evenings.

In April they were moved again to the Chateau de la Charmoy and later moved to a cabin on the estate, where they lived with Serge Tartas, the game warden and his family. Here, in the Forest of Charmoy, the wait for a plane to take them to England was less tedious because they enjoyed the freedom to hunt wild boar, deer, and cheviot, and to fish in the lakes. During their stay in the woods, they met Pierre Servagnat who came to check their name, rank and serial number as they still hoped to fly back to England.

"By May, myself and another friend, George Hill, decided this was enough of this waiting around. Let's go for the Spanish border. We had so much encouragement. Anytime we would ask anyone for help, why they'd give it to us.

"We started out and we'd have a Frenchman buy us a ticket to a big town, and we'd ride and get off before we got to that town. And we did two or three of these and nobody checked our tickets so we thought, 'Well, they are not checking tickets. Let's just ride on right through and not stop to buy another one.'

"However, when we ran into this ticket problem, we had been talking with a Frenchman. We decided we could trust him and we told him who we were. Along comes this conductor, collecting tickets and we didn't have any. So the Frenchman says, 'Well, why don't you go into the rest room there and I'll try to talk with him and we'll buy a ticket for the Canadian.' But it ended up, we both had to buy tickets. The Frenchman paid for them, by the way. However, I think he was part of the underground.

"We were captured right near Pau, about ten miles from the Spanish border. We had some kind of underground arrangement. We were supposed to knock on a door and use a certain name. Somebody opened the door, the knock was supposed to be a code. I forget whether it was four knocks, then hesitate, then another knock. And we knocked on the door, no answer, we waited about five minutes, knocked again and still no answer. So we decided to go back to Toulouse. That's where we had stayed in a hotel the night before. On the way back, they searched our ID's. The Canadian had one that was identified as false. Of course, they were all false. Usually when you flew, you had pictures taken of you in civilian clothes which you carried with you. However, in my case, I lost mine because the plane blew up when I was in it and so I lost my pockets off my clothes. So a Frenchman took my picture and made some false papers in the underground.

"This Frenchman talked us out of this ticket thing so smoothly, we thought he could talk us out of this. He didn't."

Like most prisoners of the Germans, they were transferred from one prison to another and finally to the large prison, Fresnes, fifty miles south of Paris. Childs was in cell 414 on the fifth floor. Through the Morse code grapevine, Childs learned that his friend Bill Rendall, from their days in Pocancy, was also imprisoned in Fresnes.

On 10 July 1944, the airmen were assembled on the first floor and told, through an interpreter, that they were going to Germany.

"On the way back to Germany, they handcuffed us and some of us had bleeding wrists. I think I had bleeding wrists. We were waiting in the station and there was this German Air Force captain along with a couple of other Germans. He went over to the Gestapo who had us as prisoners. Pretty soon, he came around

A Time to Speak

with his keys and loosened these handcuffs. And mine was loose enough so that I could slip it. I was handcuffed to the guy next to me. So we made plans. I was thinking our train ought to be strafed or something. It was after the invasion and there was a lot of air activity. We could just scamper if they strafe us. So it turned out they had a party going on. This operator wanted to get in on the party so he takes off and assigns an SS trooper sitting in the hallway. So the fact that he was going home on leave, there was lots of liquid. He went to sleep. I headed for the window and dropped out, rolled and that was it. The train had just gone through Bar-le-Duc, so I was near where I had been shot down."

After the D-Day invasion, the resistance movement changed its tactics. Many became members of the Forces françaises de l'intérieur (the French Interior Forces) and were armed to fight against the German troops. Anyone who escaped from the Germans found it more and more difficult to move safely without encountering a French ambush.

"Then trying to walk across the country was a little bit hazardous because here are these little French groups that had their arms that had been dropped to them. They were put in charge of a big group, a captain in charge of 50 or a 100, and they would set up ambushes and anyone caught walking along the road, riding a bicycle or in a car, why they'd get ambushed and shot up. . . We would be with one group for a while. The Germans coming in with their squadrons and attacks and breaking it up. And so we would leave and get in with another group. And this last group, the Frenchman said he thought he could get us through the lines. Actually, he had been through the lines the day before and talked to an American colonel. There were seven of us. But anyway we had an elaborate plan in case we would get attacked. We drove down back roads.

"All at once we came to this village and there was this big crowd there, we got closer to the crowd. There is an American soldier standing on a table. There was a crowd and we were behind the lines. I got back to the American lines three days before Paris fell."

It had been ten and a half months since Childs' plane had been shot down.[123]

The Chief of the Maquis

Pierre Servagnat oversaw the rescue of downed pilots, received arms parachuted into the region by the English, and established plans for the defense and attack in the five sectors of the maquis. He explained how a maquis was organized.

"I entered the Resistance for a very simple reason. I detested the Germans because they killed my father in 1915 and when I was demobilized from the army to find my country and my town and my house occupied by the Germans. They left us one room on the ground floor, and they occupied all the rest of the house. And to hear them singing in the streets of the town, the curfew, to have to go back home at eight o'clock in the evening until seven o'clock in the morning. Certain cafes were closed, the theater also. Everything for these German men. We didn't like it very much. For example, if the Germans inhabited a house, they put barriers on the sidewalk and the pedestrians who came down the street were obliged to go in the street. You couldn't pass in front of a house inhabited by the Germans. One didn't like that kind of vexation. That's the reason, that little by little, the vast majority of people entered the Resistance.

"When they sent the young to work in Germany, those who were eighteen to thirty-five years old, there were some who went because they couldn't do otherwise because they were well-paid. On the other hand, there were others that we gathered up, put on farms and then in the maquis. So the maquis grew in larger numbers at this time. Our region was not very favorable for the maquis. We never had groups larger than fifty-five or sixty people maximum. We had them in all of the region, we had twenty-five or thirty groups.

"It was the Resistance that made the maquis. The maquis concealed American aviators who were shot down in the area. It was too dangerous to keep them at home, so we put them in the maquis.

"You didn't concern yourself with politics. It was not a question of politics. And it was the greatest surprise after the Liberation to learn that when these men came forward at the time of elections, before, they were just French. Our region was a large territory of the Resistance, 2,000 resistants, all the way to the river, Aube, Dormand, Chateau-Thierry, Chalons.

"We organized the networks in the area, five sectors and each of the five sectors were divided into smaller groups. The sectors were delimited and each sector had a chief, and chiefs of each of the smaller groups. It worked well, they got along with one another, head of a group, head of a sector. It was organized in a military fashion.

"Everything was organized secretly. We even had a medical service, also well-organized who took care of people, for example, the pilot who had been hit in the shoulder. That was also done clandestinely.

"Your friend, Everett Childs, he arrived near Fère-Champenoise and immediately he was put in touch with men in the Resistance. We put him in a little maquis. He was there and another American came. The men were very kind to him. They were very happy to have an American with them. They were the aviators who had fought. They were delighted to save a combattant.

"There were groups hidden in the woods. When a crew needed asylum, they were camouflaged in a grove. They were wounded. I remember one, an American, he was put in an automobile and brought to my house in Epernay. I had a friend who was a doctor, a surgeon who operated on him in my house. When he recovered, he left by the usual route. We kept two other Americans at the house and took care of them. When they were capable to moving, after about two weeks, they were able to leave. The Germans didn't know about it right away. They found out later, when there were arrests and when the resistants were tortured and they talked. Then they came to my house and my wife was deported to Ravensbrück because of that." Mme Servagnat's imprisonment was avenged later by her husband.

"I had occasion to take one of those who arrested my wife, one afternoon, in Epernay, June or July, he was in the Gestapo. He was in his car. With two friends, we passed by and saw the keys to his car. We left at the same time, I had my revolver and we took him to the woods. I asked him why he arrested Mme Servagnat and her three children. He answered, 'Because he [Servagnat] was head of the communists of the region.' I said, 'He was never a great communist, but I am M. Servagnat.' He went all white. Likewise, we gave him a civilian internment. We dug his grave.

"We had identification papers we could give the pilots. We did this for all of them. It was necessary to hide them. When it was an American or an Englishman, we tried to give them a name easily pronounced. You are called 'Mr. Good.' So if they ask you what your name is, you say, 'Good.' We had tricks like that. On the identification card, it was written 'Goud.' There was another one, 'Black,' 'Blaque.' We found names that would correspond.

"Communication between the groups was done by bicycle. The liaison agents would leave by bicycle, to carry the orders and the instructions for each group. With London, on the other hand, we had the liaison by radio, well hidden and well protected. The radios were never left more than two days in the same safe house, then the location was changed. There were specific hours for each pianiste [the radio operator]. The radios arrived by parachute. They were put in several different places, the bell tower of the church, at my house.

"The parachute landing fields were given names. For example, 'Cloitre' was the one located in Pocancy, the radio signal was L./.-.., and the code words were the sentence, 'La gelée grille les bourgeons' (The frost nips the buds).

"You had to be careful. There were always some ill-intentioned people who could get a little money from the Germans, who were interested monetarily and would betray someone.

"It was difficult to be sure of someone, but after all, it was by personal relationships. You had good friends. You had your pals. A friend had a friend in his neighborhood.

"It was dangerous. It was also a question of luck. It was done through groups, for example, sports groups, again by affinity. Tennis teams, football teams, they had their friendships and that helped enormously. It permitted us to know one another very well.

"In town, you had to have the tickets: tickets for everything, bread, meat, butter, tobacco. In the maquis, you had the farmers in the area, usually 100 percent for us. They furnished us, in large part, butter, milk. On the other side, in the woods, hunting was forbidden by the Germans; we practiced it. We had a lot of game, turkey, deer, roe deer. It was rare not to have two or three, we had plenty, plenty, plenty! We had pals who cooked, cooked over a wood fire, we had delicious meals. In the afternoon, when the Americans took a walk in the woods, we asked them to pick fraise des bois. We made crepes with strawberries. We fished in the streams, the crayfish. Since it was a small maquis, about forty people, the food provisions were massive.

"Occasionally, they lacked butter in town and we had a good farmer who gave us butter and we distributed it in town. To sleep, we had a kind of trench, covered with wood, straw to make a good bed. We managed to find some feather quilts and we slept like the Pope. We were young. We slept in the forest, tranquil. The Germans didn't dare be so adventuresome. They didn't dare come into the forest. During the war, when it was the Germans in the woods, we didn't go look for them. When you are well hidden in the woods, you are afraid to go in and look for someone. They wouldn't come out. The German follows, the Frenchman is a go-getter.

"All of the cachets, in the prefectures, we had them on reserve. We had false papers for bicycles, you had to declare bicycles to the Germans. You had to have a work certificate and a ration card.

"Sometimes the maquis burglarized the tobacco shops, always with the agreement of the tobacco shop owner. We simulated an attack, took all of the tobacco, he reported it to the authorities and the administration replaced it and so we had tobacco for those in the maquis. Nine times out of ten, it was done with the full agreement of the owner.

"We got the arms from the English. It was from the Bureau d'Opération Aérienne (BOA) of which I was the head of the region. We were given thirty-eight localities for the parachute drops in our region. We had a certain number of operations, arms, explosives, sometimes men, radios. They arrived about two or three o'clock in the morning. It was impressive, as a operation, very enticing. The first parachute drop that we had was in June 1943, a good year before the landing. In July we had a lot, September, October, almost every month in '43 which was good, but perhaps too many. It was revealed to the enemy since we engaged in a lot of sabotage. We had the material. We amused ourselves in using it.

"For an operation of sabotage, there was an extraordinary excitement in the maquis. Those who were designated for a particular job were ecstatic; the others were furious. 'I want to go, I want to go.' 'We only need three or four for this operation.' They waited until they came back, 'How did it go?'

"We cut the lines that supplied the electric current; we cut the rails of the train; we cut the telephone wires that were underground between Berlin and Paris. They were the distractions that were irresistible. Each time something like that happened, the Gestapo was there.

"One thing that the English sent, with each parachute drop, they sent a package for the receiving team. In this package, there were English cigarettes, tobacco, coffee, chocolate. We shared it equally. But there were some of the younger ones who had the English cigarettes in the bistro in the evening, or a packet of tobacco. They would arrive in the cafe in the evening to impress their friends. They didn't think about the consequences. It came to the ears of several collaborators and they were denounced. They were arrested. That night, they arrested nineteen of my friends and, among those nineteen, seventeen were shot the same day. Good friends of mine. In February '44. The Germans were without pity, without pity! I telegraphed to London not to send the packages because they were a permanent danger.

"We attacked the isolated vehicles. When there was one in the evening, we knew that French cars couldn't pass because of the curfew, so it was the German cars. When you had two or three, not too many, we would eliminate them. The Germans were interred rapidly, a little civilian internment in the woods and recover the car. It was thrilling. We were so much against these occupants that we didn't have any pity for them. They didn't have pity for our friends.

"There was an extraordinary ambiance, a patriotism. We stayed in touch through letters and Christmas cards, it was an epistolary relationship. At the Permanence, [local museum and meeting room], we get together every Saturday, among friends, and talk over the old stories. We have stayed very close friends. It was a part of my life that I won't forget. For the Germans and Germany, one doesn't forget. Eventually, one can pardon them, but not forget." [124]

The Maquis in Boquen

Jean Lebranchu created the maquis in Boquen on the northern coast of Brittany. Part of his group included Mme Lebranchu, then Aline Gauvin, the liaison agent, Dr. Louis Dalibot and Charles Coulombel. Lebranchu was the only one of the maquis to be arrested. Mme Lebranchu, for her efforts in helping Allied soldiers escape from the enemy, received a formal certificate of gratitude on behalf of the President of the United States, signed by General Dwight D. Eisenhower.

They acted as a clandestine army and were involved without thinking of the danger. Lebranchu said, *"We were very mobile and we gave the illusion of being everywhere. And when they came to look for us, they couldn't find us. We were nowhere and everywhere."*

Coulombel remarked, *"We were told to divide ourselves in little groups, six or seven who had to find a little corner to hide in, either in the woods or on farms. After D-Day, the Americans were coming and the Germans retreated, we took the little side roads to hinder the German troops; we formed little groups of maquis."*

They took risks but received help from neighbors, for example, who gave the Germans the wrong directions to a house. The sisters in a convent hid Coulombel; a teacher colleague, who lived in a room above the city hall, did not call for help when Lebranchu secretly entered to take guns and ration cards. According to Dr. Dalibot, *"Some of the gendarmes saved our lives. They would come and warn our parents that we should leave quickly because the Germans gossiped in a cafe."*

Communication between the groups took place through the liaison agents, often the women like Mme Lebranchu. She commented, *"I knew all of them. We were friends. It all happened naturally. When there was something important to pass along, we did it. I knew what I was transporting to an isolated houses. I went on my bicycle and carried the documents on my luggage rack, even during the day."*

Originally the purpose of the maquis was to provide information to the Allies and to rescue pilots. In December 1943, the acts of sabotage began. Dalibot stressed the importance of the parachute drops.

"There were radio sections that were able to organize the parachute drops. In the beginning we only had revolvers, no arms, no explosives. It wasn't until we had the parachute drops that we had the means to undertake an important defense...

"I still remember, we were alerted by the radio, the following message, 'Six hirondelles viendront vous voir ce soir' which meant 'Six airplanes would come tonight.' And in fact, they arrived, they released their cargo, only five... All night we gathered the arms, munitions. There were even arms we didn't know, the bazooka. There were parachutists who dropped specifically to show us how to maneuver the arms that we weren't familiar with."

Well-equipped, Lebranchu was able to organize the acts of sabotage.

"It was quite often the electric line, connected to the factory at Tréfumel. We had the complicity of electricians who worked at the factory, and we were given information about what line the Germans were going to make ready at such and such a date. I kept a plan of the line, and then I was given a sign to intervene on such or such a section. In general, we chose the section at an angle because the work was not as hard. The concrete had a certain height, and when we lay down

flat, we could calmly prepare the explosives. The fuse line was broken, or sometimes of poor quality, so it was necessary to light it several times which reduced the security. It was dangerous.

"There were fourteen expeditions to sabotage the railroads, one Paris/ Brest. We had the keys of the SNCF in order to create a bottleneck. We arranged the rails crosswise to derail the trains. We had the cooperation of railroad workers because we needed to know the exact time the trains would pass. We decided to disrupt the line between Caulnes and St. Jouan de l'Isle and to immobilize it as much as possible. It was after the June 6 landing. It was a parachutist, among the parachutists who were entrusted with the mission of sabotage just before the D-Day landing, that gave us the plastic [explosives].

"So that day, with Georges Le Gac, we placed the explosives according to the instructions of the parachutist, our plastic charges on a certain number of rails. We chose the automatic release for the explosion at the moment that the train passed. The train was blown up, a single wagon."

On 6 July 1944, Jean Lebranchu was arrested, taken to a school at Uzel, interrogated and tortured by the S. D. (*Sicherheitsdienst*, the security service) and the Milice (the Vichy armed police force). He managed to escape and was transported in a farm wagon to the maquis at Mûr-de-Bretagne where he was able to recuperate.

At the time of the landing in Normandy, members of the maquis who joined the FFI often found themselves face to face with the Germans. Dalibot watched one encounter, *"At the cemetery, the German car and the FFI car met, crossed one another, the German with a machine gun on the hood of the car, and the FFI with an arm on the hood of his car, and they fired at one another."*

Dalibot concluded, *"The few things we did had a positive effect. It was the little things that facilitated the advance of the Allied troops."* [125]

Genevieve From Cherbourg

Aïde Mahé was from Dinan but her code name was "Geneviève" and she was to be from Cherbourg. She is reputed to be the only woman resistance member, from the region on the northern coast of Brittany, to organize and receive a parachute drop by herself. She heard de Gaulle's appeal to resist Germany's occupation and joined in early resistance activities. In 1941 she became a liaison agent and carried messages between Saint Cast and Saint-Jacut, and between Dinard and Saint-Malo. Later when the Gestapo was looking for her, she joined a maquis.

Mme Mahé referred to the maquis as a "mask" because they had to invent a new identity, never go by more than a first name, and always be ready to pack up and leave, since they never stayed in the same maquis more than a month or two. It involved constant espionage, lies, cunning, camouflage and risk.

"I admit, I flirted a bit when I saw a German patrol. I went with them and crossed the bridge. And one day I saw an old Breton who said, 'Watch out, young lady, you will have your head shaved.' They [the French] shaved the heads of the young girls who were too friendly with the Germans. I never had a revolver.

"After '43, Maurice Barré, the Resistance leader, said, 'It's not going well, the Gestapo is looking for you. You have to stop.' I left to study nursing at Saint-Brieuc. He gave me a five-franc note which he cut in half. 'When someone gives you the other half, you can have confidence in that person.'

"I left to start my nursing studies at Saint-Brieuc. I had work right away. There was the STO, and we helped them escape. We helped them escape from the area where they were being picked up. I wasn't afraid of those who really wanted to escape, but I was afraid of those who weren't sure they wanted to escape because they might denounce me.

"Then one day someone came up and said, 'Hello,' and he had the other half of the five-franc note in his hand. There were a lot of STO who left and who formed the maquis. They took refuge in farms, in the woods. And I made contact with the group, Movement de libération nationale (MLN). I should say, that in the early days, the Resistance was a voluntary decision by someone; then there were small groups; and afterwards, there was a Movement. And after that there was the FFI, Forces françaises de l'intérieur.

"The MLN was a group in charge of information and supplying food. I stole the vitamin-fortified crackers from the Red Cross. Since I was a nursing student, I had access to the vitamin-fortified crackers. We had ration tickets for food, in order to find food for the hungry boys who were hiding in the country-side. It was there I met Petit Pierre, whom I encountered again in the maquis.

"Then I was obliged to leave my nursing studies because the Directress of the Hospital received a visit from the Gestapo. She warned me and I joined the maquis. She did something that certainly did me a favor. She buried, in my name, an old woman from the hospice, with the result that three years after my marriage, the mayor of Saint-Jacut called me and said, 'You can't vote because you are deceased.' They looked in the register and found that it was the Directress of the hospital who had done it. I already had two children. Finally, there was a tribunal and with all of the information, they declared that I was living.

"On one mission, I was sent to join a agent at the crossroads of L'Hermitage and Boquéo to pick up a radio transmitter. The password was 'Il faut beau aujourd'hui' [It is a nice day] and the response was 'Le temps est superbe' [The weather is superb].

"Everything went well. On the way back, I was amazed by a field of yellow marguerites. I picked an armful and put them in my bicycle basket on top of the radio transmitter which was wrapped up in a carton. A little farther along, I was stopped by a German patrol who wanted to know what I was carrying. One of the Germans got ready to verify what I had in my bicycle basket, and I remembered a maxim from my grammar book, 'Tell people the truth, they won't believe it.' So I said, laughing, 'Don't ruin my flowers. Underneath there is a modern radio transmitter which is going to transmit messages to London.' The German looked at me, dumbfounded. My luck was that he understood French very well, and the noise of a motor was heard, and he signaled me to move on. I got back on my bike, but a few kilometers farther, I stopped, my legs shaking, crying my eyes out.

"Another time I was stopped by the Gestapo who were on the road. I can tell you there was a miracle. In the Resistance, I was called Geneviève and was supposed to be from Cherbourg. The Gestapo asked, 'You live in Cherbourg?' 'Yes.' 'What are you doing here?' I said that my house was demolished and I was looking for a shelter. You know I had the message on me. I was sure he saw me swallow the message. This German, he had dark eyes, a young soldier. Then he said, 'Your name is Geneviève?' I said, 'Yes.' 'Are you Catholic?' I said, 'Yes.' Then he said, 'I wish you a happy feast day.' He said, 'What day?' I said, 'January third.' I'll tell you why. I was a Girl Scout. I was a Senior Scout. Sainte Geneviève's day is January third and together, we drew for the king [from the Twelfth Night cake]. When I said that, that was the miracle. I returned to my friends.

"I was afraid afterwards. I wasn't afraid at the time, but afterwards. I said, 'I am mad to continue like that.'"

Mme Mahé had to arrange a parachute drop of arms because several members of her maquis were arrested, arms destined for maquis members were seized, and the hiding places of arms were becoming suspect. Other comrades were engaged in a small battle with German soldiers. A new parachute drop was planned to provide additional arms.

"I had a message to get out that there was to be a parachute drop. [9-10 July 1944] It was a Sunday at noon. The personal message was 'Buvons une bolée six fois!' [Let's drink six bowlfuls] and the letter was 'A.' The name of the landing field was 'Cadoudal.'

"My comrades were fighting about four kilometers from there. I could hear them fighting, and I thought maybe they won't get free. I absolutely have to get out of here.

"The members of the maquis were engaged in combat with German soldiers and were captured. The farm, where I had changed clothes in order not to be recognized if I met the Gestapo a second time, was surrounded. Making my way back to the headquarters of the maquis, I encountered my friend Petit Pierre, also a member of the maquis since he escaped from the STO. He immediately offered me his services for the parachute drop. Then Thérèse, another friend, asked to be included. We were three; I was the oldest, twenty-three years old, twenty-year-old Thérèse and eighteen-year-old Petit Pierre. We were three who made One.

"The parachute drop. 'I know how to arrange the parachute drop. I have sent the messages. The three of us can handle a parachute drop.' It was decided like that and I told them, 'Here it is: you need to find an electric lamp and then we will arrange ourselves in a triangle and we'll have a letter in Morse code for the planes who come. If they see us, they will illuminate a white light.' It is what we did. We found an electric lamp at a farm house, and then we found a field. It was about five or six kilometers of land agreed on by London.

"I thought, 'What if they don't see us?' Then I thought they would have to return. 'We'll see.' We heard the airplanes and we saw them leave. We made the Morse code, 'A' (the letter agreed upon). Again, fortunately, I had been a Scout and knew the Morse code. The last plane illuminated his white light, and we saw the parachute drop - seventeen containers of armaments. I had to wake up the farmer. We hid them and camouflaged them. I told Pierre to take a revolver. Fortunately we didn't receive machine guns. 'Pierre, you guard the arms. I will return and tell them that we made the parachute drop.' It was necessary to find someone to come and get the armaments because I was afraid the farmers would be sought out by the Germans and arrested.

"Thérèse was sent to the head of the Resistance group which was at Chateau Breffeuillac. There was a maquis there, with some Frenchmen who had escaped, pilots, those who were to help with information, resistants and they could give us help.

"Unfortunately, those comrades engaged in combat with the Germans were arrested and taken to Uzel where they were tortured and shot on July 14. Every July 9, I think about them.

"It wasn't extraordinary. I had lots of friends who did that. Some were arrested, deported, shot.

"There were no heroes. We were friends: 'You do this, you do that, it's going to work.' I cried sometimes on the road because my hands were cold or I was demoralized. When you knew that a friend was arrested ...you thought about their wife, their mother...."

For her heroism, she received the Médaille de la Résistance. Until her retirement, she worked as a school nurse. The men and women of her maquis wanted to be the ones to liberate Saint-Brieuc. They were armed and ready to attack, if necessary, the retreating German troops in order to protect another parachute drop of Allied troops, including French troops arriving in their homeland. They were disappointed when American jeeps entered Saint-Brieuc on 6 August 1944 and liberated the city.

End Notes

123 Childs stayed in the Army one extra year, then left for college to study chemistry. He worked first in Ames, Iowa where he had studied, and later at Rocky Flats.
124 Pierre Servagnat was an officer of the Legion of Honor and the National Order of Merit and received the Croix de Guerre and the Medal of the Resistance. He stayed active in community affairs until his sudden death on 6 December 1995.
125 Jean Lebranchu returned to his teaching, Dalibot opened his medical office in Plumaudan, and Coulombel was a carpenter and poultry farmer.

CHAPTER 32
D-DAY, PART I, PREPARATION

Years after the event, people are perhaps influenced by the cinematic version of D-Day of legendary proportions. Was it, in fact, the epic event that marked the turning point of the war? Many tend to forget that two days earlier on 4 June 1944, while soldiers were waiting to land in Normandy, Rome fell. And for Americans awaiting the end of the war, the conflict in the Pacific was still to be won.

Early in 1943, Winston Churchill and President Roosevelt decided that Germany should be defeated before Japan and that an invasion of the European continent was essential to defeat Hitler's armies. A fifty-mile stretch on the Normandy coast was chosen.

The Germans realized, strategically, that either Normandy or the Pas de Calais (located on the northeast coast of France) were logical places. As early as 1941, they began to fortify the Normandy coast, with the construction of the Atlantic Wall (bunkers, radar stations and gun sites). The Todt Organization, headed by the German engineer, Dr. Todt, was charged with its construction.

In February 1944, Field Marshal Rommel criticized the defenses of the Normandy coast, especially those along the coastline from Colleville-sur-mer to Vierville-sur-mer. Franz Gockel, a German soldier who served in this area remembered the fortifications and Rommel's impression of them. In his memoir, "Normandy," Gockel wrote:

"Since Rommel's inspection, we constructed tank barriers on the beach at low tide from logs topped with taller mines [called Rommel's asparagus]. *Other beach obstacles were the so-called 'Czech hedgehogs', made from crossed iron beams, and 'Belgian Doors' from thick steel stakes. Running parallel to the water line before us was a low wall made of water-worn stones enclosing the beach, and along the wall was laid a mine field for the purpose of protecting us from surprise attack during darkness. Recently a tank trench had been dug between WN62 and WN61. There was also a short stretch of tank trench in the direction of St. Laurent. In front of and behind the tank trenches were mine fields, and our position was protected with a tangled ring of barbed wire 'K' rolls."*

The Germans also flooded the swamps and estuaries in the countryside to impede the infantry once they advanced beyond the beaches. Once inland, the Allies would face dangers from the snipers, hidden in the six-foot high hedgerows, and from what, the soldiers would call, the "Betty Boop" mines that exploded at the waist.

In spite of these precautions, German military strength was weak. According to one observer, Vincent Beach, a retired professor of history, who served on *LST 378* landing at Gold Beach on D-Day:

"In pre-invasion bombing strikes, the Americans and British had effectively disrupted communication in Northern France which made it difficult for the enemy to bring in reinforcements. German armored divisions lacked sufficient infantry support and the Allies had complete control of the air and the sea. But over and beyond the situation in France were the general and overall trends that indicated German defeat everywhere was inevitable. The Russians had torn the guts out of the German army by June, 1944 (2 million German soldiers killed). Germany was terribly overextended by a two-front war. Allied bombing of industrial and civilian targets was devastating and gradually left Germany during the last months of the war short of tanks, guns, ammunition, fuel, and submarines."

The Big Snafu

Allied forces trained for the invasion for over a year and a half. There had also been unsuccessful practice raids. In 1942, Canadian and British troops took part in a raid on the harbor town of Dieppe, sixty-five miles across the Channel from Britain. The casualty rate was high, and war vehicles and equipment had to be abandoned on the beach. The Allies had learned a tragic lesson about cross-channel invasions. Unfortunately, this was not the only tragedy before D-Day. Don Look, serving on *LST 511*, was part of the preliminary practice for the invasion in Normandy.

"I guess the real action part of the trip would have been the Slapton Sands, the invasion before Normandy, 'the big snafu.' This was a horrible night. This was April 28, and it was so close to the invasion. We were in the middle of it this night when they sunk the ships. They sunk two ships. I was on the third LST. We were loaded down with troops. That was a wild night.

"We just thought it was a practice or something. We had no idea what was going on. No, this was just a rehearsal. We would just load up the soldiers, tanks, trucks, everything and have a dry run and practice at Slapton Sands. But this particular night, and I think it was just by accident that the German torpedo boats...it was a big snafu, the radio waves were not tuned in right. They lost almost one thousand men in two ships. But Eisenhower, not a peep out of anyone so close to D-Day.

"We still didn't know anything about it until ten years ago. It was so secret. There were eight or nine officers that had the secrets for D-Day and because of

that, Montgomery wanted to call D-Day off.

"Most of the soldiers were buried in a common grave. They finally found all of the officers [American], the bodies of all the officers with the exception of one and they decided they'd take a chance and let him go even if he had the secrets of D-Day. That's a fascinating story. That cooled down and we got ready for D-Day."

In 1987, the United States government acknowledged publicly one of the most disastrous incidents of World War II, the rehearsal for the D-Day invasion. The simulated attack, Exercise Tiger, took place on the southern coast of Devon, England, and according to official figures, 749 American soldiers and 197 Navy men died when German torpedo boats slipped through the poorly guarded convoy and sank two landing craft. Today, near the village of Torcross, at the southern edge of the beach, there is a commemorative plaque bearing the names of those who died in Exercise Tiger.

When and Where Will They Land?

Many times during the Occupation people asked themselves, 'When will the Allies come?' People listened to the BBC in secret and waited, among them two French women, Marie-Madeline Herbelin and her mother Mme Lenoir.

"It was mysterious. We received messages. We listened and listened. I believe, at the time of the invasion, the message was precise. There was a precise code, 'Les sanglots longs/Des violons/De l'automne' [The long sobs of the violins of autumn], heard on June 1. We didn't know what it meant until later. The messages arrived in great numbers. They insisted, in particular, I remember the speaker saying, 'I will say that again, I will say that again. I repeat....' We felt, without knowing, that the messages had a significance. There were people, like the resistants, who knew what the message meant."

Each Resistance group listened to the BBC for their particular message, signaling their special mission. But the German radio had also picked up cryptic broadcast messages destined for the Resistance, including the June first code, "Les sanglots longs des violons de l'automne". From a captured Frenchman, they knew this was the alert for the invasion. On 5 June, they heard the second line of the poem, "Blessent mon coeur / D'une langueur / Monotone" (Wounding my heart with a monotonous languor). This meant the invasion was coming within forty-eight hours.[126]

But where would the Allies strike? The most obvious point for the invasion would have been the Pas de Calais, the point in northern France closest to Britain. But the Allies effectively used deceptive tactics to confuse the Germans. A phantom First Army Group, under General George S. Patton, seemed to be stationed in Kent, opposite the Pas de Calais. Dummy tanks and landing craft made the Germans believe that this was the main Allied force. Constant radio communiques sent false information to Germany. And on the day of invasion, the Allied planes scattered tons of mylar confetti which, on German radar, appeared to be aircraft.

A double of Bernard Montgomery, the British invasion commander, turned up in the Mediterranean to make the Germans think something might be happening there.

The invasion, as planned, consisted of several parts: heavy bombardment of the German fortifications; parachute troops jumping behind enemy lines; glider troops to take Sainte-Mère-Eglise and to capture key points such as the Merville battery, the bridges over the Caen Canal and the River Orme; and the Rangers, whose mission was to scale the 100-foot high Point du Hoc and take out six enormous guns. Finally, approximately 135,000 men and 20,000 vehicles were to come in by sea to land on five beaches: the Americans to land on Utah and Omaha beaches; the British and Canadians to land on Gold, June and Sword beaches. It was the largest amphibious operation in history.

"OK, we'll go"

The invasion was postponed for twenty-four hours because of the weather, low clouds and strong winds which would have made the landings hazardous. On 4 June, discussion of further postponement would mean waiting two weeks until the tidal conditions were favorable and the Allies would risk losing the element of surprise. Eisenhower consulted the Chief Meteorological Officer, Group Captain Stagg. Stagg announced he could forecast twenty-four hours of settled weather from late on 5 June with fairly good conditions for the rest of the week.

Eisenhower consulted his commanders, but as the Allied commander, he made the decision to go.

The soldiers who had trained for Operation Overlord were emotional, pumped up after anticipating the day of the landing. Some were seasoned veterans of the campaigns in Africa. Many, however, were young, eighteen and nineteen years old, inexperienced, seasick, apprehensive, even petrified. In battle for the first time, under machine gun fire, mortar fire, they would suddenly encounter horrendous sights. Those who had never seen a dead body before soon saw comrades blown to bits and bodies stacked up on the beaches. In spite of this, they acknowledged they were well-prepared and well-equipped. Each one had a mission to accomplish. Not only would they discover the shock of battle, but the shock of two cultures: American chewing gum encountered "le calva" (calvados).

Those who were involved did not find the sea conditions perfect. The waters were choppy, some recalled five-foot waves, making the infantrymen seasick. The skies were cloud-covered.

A Time to Speak

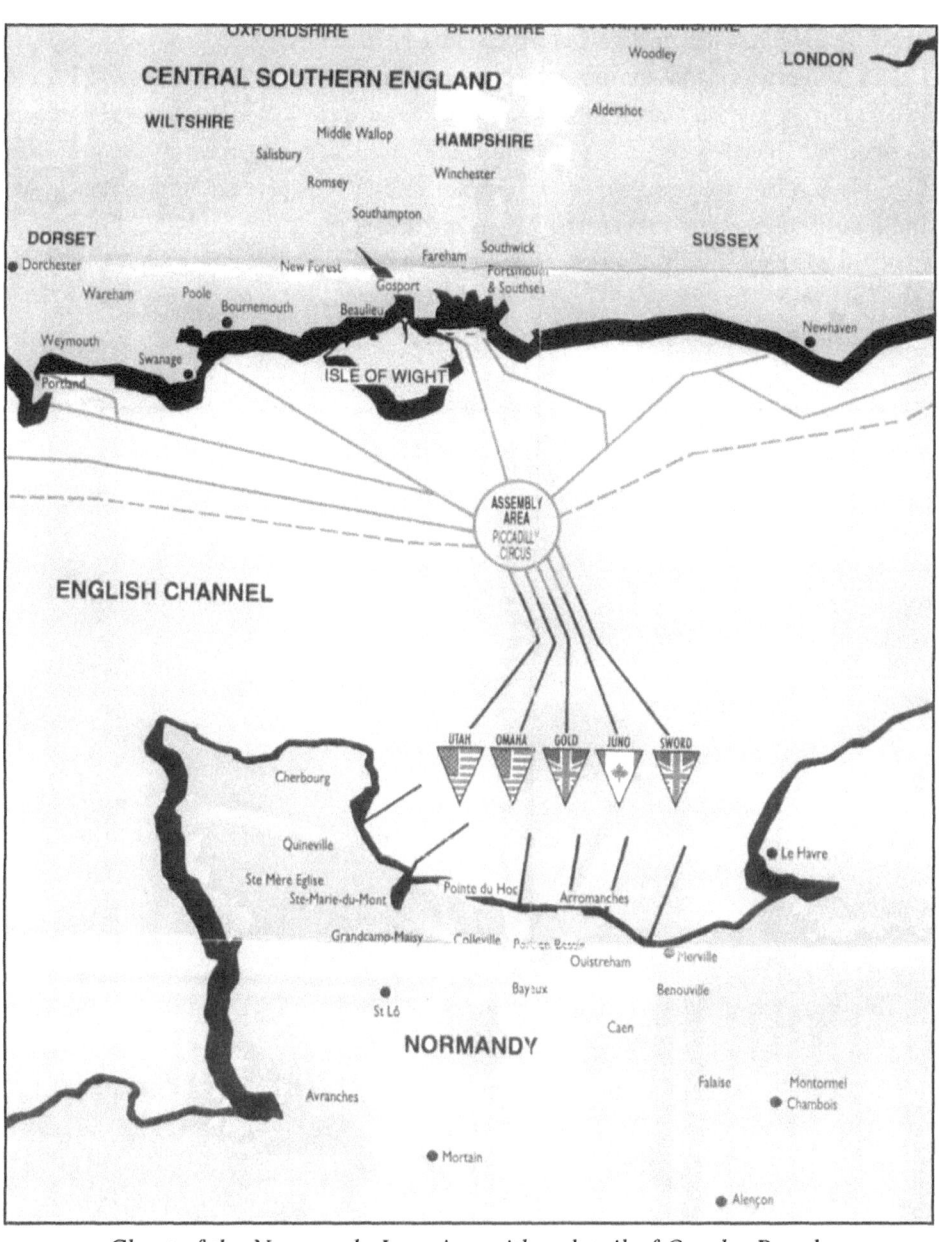

Chart of the Normandy Invasion with a detail of Omaha Beach.

None the less, during the night of 5 June and on 6 June, Allied troops landed in Normandy. It was the long-awaited invasion and "liberation" from the German occupiers. In reality, it was only the beginning of the end of the war in Europe. It would be eleven more months before Hitler's armies were defeated.

What was it like for those who were involved on D-Day, for American and British pilots, a Canadian infantryman, a Belgian priest, a French commando, a paratrooper, the cook on an LST, British and American glider pilots, and the FFI (Free French Interior Forces), and a German soldier stationed at Omaha Beach. No single individual could take in the whole picture of the gigantic D-Day landing. It involved roughly 10,000 aircraft, over 5,000 ships and landing craft, 2,200 gliders, 156,000 ground troops and 10,000 tons of bombs. Yet all participants saw it from their particular perspectives and their special missions.

End Notes

126   The verses are from the poem, *Chanson d'Automne* by Paul Verlaine.

CHAPTER 33

D-DAY, PART II, SAINTE-MERE-EGLISE

According to the military plans for the invasion, the parachutists and the gliders were to be the first to go into Normandy. Their mission was to parachute and land before and after dawn of D-Day, and to take and hold Sainte-Mère-Eglise and the towns around it. Each man carried of copy of Eisenhower's order: "You are about to embark upon the Great Crusade, toward which we have striven these many months...The tide has turned! The free men of the world are marching together to Victory!"

One Who Watched the Parachutists Arrive

Parachutists jumped into the black unknown and were watched with excitement by the French inhabitants of the town, and with concern by the German soldiers stationed there. Gliders silently arrived next, landing in the town square and astonishing people by unloading jeeps and men.

Raymond Paris was living in Sainte-Mère-Eglise at the time of the invasion.

"I was part of a Resistance group, two electricians in charge. The evening of June 5, I was at my parents, we didn't have any Germans lodged at the house anymore. There were two companies of D.C.A. (Defense Against Airplanes) based at Fauville, a village of Sainte-Mère. I was the only one listening, because there was only one set of headphones, and I heard the message, Les dés sont sur le tapis, (The dice are on the table) *the message for our Resistance group O.C.M.* [Organisation civile et militaire]. *Excuse me...it was such an emotion to hear that because it was the end of the nightmare. For me, the invasion was the end. That's it! That's it! We tried to imagine what it would be like. For years we had said, 'When the English invade.' We didn't think about the Americans. There was such a long coastline from Bayeux to Hendaye, they could land almost anywhere. We didn't think it would be close to us, false thinking since the Vikings landed at Sainte-Mère du Mont, at Utah Beach. The invasions of the Hundred Years War always were in our territory.*

"There was the curfew and we went to bed. My bedroom was on the second floor, but I was in such an excited state that there was no question of sleeping. I lay down, completely dressed, on my bed and I opened the window. It was calm. Mid-

night sounded. The church was across from our house. I saw a friend who said, 'Come quickly, there's a fire at Julia's.' It was the roof that was burning. I called my father who was a fireman. We ran to find the fire pumps. We woke up another fireman who sounded the alarm bell. We had all of the material ready to fight the fire.

"Then arriving from the west was an important formation of planes. They were flying very low and we didn't hear them come. Right away we lay along the walls because we feared the bombs. It was the first reaction. It was the first time we had seen on the wings and on the cockpit, black and white stripes, to make them easier to identify.

"We started the fire pump. The Germans stayed in the street. And we established our fire brigade. It was my two Resistance chiefs who were there too.

"Another wave of planes, just as large and just as low. Everyone looked up. The Germans fired. It was not night yet. In June, night comes quite late and it was a full moon.

"Two minutes after the second wave, a third wave of planes arrived. And this time we saw that the doors of the planes were open, just above our heads we saw these men jump and their parachutes open. Then I realized it really was the invasion. And I literally cried out, 'It's the landing force!,' risking being killed by the Germans, but Germans had other things to do. They were firing at the men who landed.

"They had sacks of material of different colors, blue, violet, red, yellow and orange. All the men, sacks fell around us, and there was panic on the square. Contrary to what you see in the film, "The Longest Day," it didn't happen like that. The filming lasted two months at Sainte-Mère. They asked us how it happened and they found it wasn't spectacular enough. In the film, it was a complete butchery, you see Germans and Americans firing at one another, with men falling everywhere.

"First, you have to say that each parachutist had a considerable charge, at least 45 kilos and they had attached to the harness, a strap with a sack that hung to their feet, a sack that had munitions. As soon as they landed on the ground, they fell backwards, there was a little wind and the parachute stayed puffed out so they could get out of the parachute first. They had a knife in the inside lining of their vest and they cut the sack from their parachute. And when they were free of the parachute, they were standing up and they disappeared.

"In the parking area, surrounded by a big wall, the parachutists who landed near us ran across the street, jumped over the wall and escaped. Those who landed closer to the church, where there were bushes, also escaped.

"I was near a lime-tree and I heard a noise and saw a parachutist caught in the branches of the tree. Two Germans on each side of me shot him. Another one in the acacia tree, same thing. I did see about twenty Americans who were dead.

"The noise from the airplanes was dreadful and terrifying, and the alarm bell continued to sound. The alarm bell is very mournful, lugubrious. It is two tones and very rapid. 'Dong, dong, dong; ding, ding, ding.' There was the alarm bell, the fire, the Germans who were giving orders, and the women screaming with fear.

"I was in the street. There was a parachutist who fell right at the town pump between my two Resistance chiefs who helped him get out of his parachute harness. I found myself about ten meters away, in the street, next to a German who raised his machine gun to fire in their direction. With some authority, I lowered his machine gun and cried, 'No, civilians.' Luckily for everyone, the German didn't insist.

"Everyone got out of there, abandoned the house on fire, the fire equipment. You have to have lived it to realize the panic it produced.

"In the street, we found a parachutist dead, right there in the street. We thought he was a black. We lifted him and put him at the side of the street and covered him with his parachute. My mother, a bit frightened, told us it was a TODT who had killed him. TODT was the organization that constructed the Atlantic Wall. Their uniforms were very clear; we called them caca d'oie [gosling green], reserving the name verdigris [grayish green] for German infantrymen. [Both terms were derogatory].We didn't hear another shot. The parachutists had disappeared.

"The Germans ran from place to place. They had an officer in charge, then they left for Fauville. They saw so many parachutists come down that they panicked and thought they would be shot down like rabbits. They rejoined their company with the intention of coming the next day. So that Sainte-Mère was liberated June 5, in the evening because the German detachment left Sainte-Mère.

"It was calm but everybody was too excited to go to bed. There was a common courtyard. In the interior, three families were together.

"During the night we saw arrive from the west, no noise of motor, only the whistling of the wings, with a beacon on each wing. It was a glider that transported three tons. He landed a few feet away from my garden. The glider broke the wing against a transformer. Inside there was a truck and anti-tank gun. At 4 a.m., the baker went to get bread and returned completely upset. It's full of soldiers and they aren't Germans. We went up and looked out the window and the square and the street were full of soldiers. Sainte-Mère was the first objective of the 82nd Division. During the night, all of the men arrived at Sainte-Mère. There was a mass of soldiers. Looking at a distance, we had the impression that there were a lot of blacks. The smell of white tobacco (I smoked dried potato leaves, whatever) was in the air. They made signs of friendship, and we rushed out to the street, and the enormous surprise. They were Americans, they were whites, but painted with black.

"My father went to look for bottles of Calvados. They offered the Calvados to the parachutists who didn't want to drink. They were distrustful because they thought all French were collaborators. There were people who entered into commerce with the Germans, but there weren't collaborators. They just wanted to make some money, but they weren't pro-German.

"The Americans didn't want to drink the 'calva.' They wanted my Father and my neighbor to drink it first. A bit of 'calva' in the morning? They quickly learned to appreciate it. Finally, they stood in line to get their ration of 'calva.' We didn't hear a single shot during the night, we thought it was the fête. The Americans were also joyous. They clinked glasses.

"An automobile in the square with soldiers in it. It was our first jeep. It wasn't the automobile in itself that was astonishing, but that the automobile was there! It came in the glider.

"I went across the street to see if I could find the body of the parachutist we had carried the night before to the side street. His parachute was there, three German trucks that had been forgotten, but there was no body. There was a soldier, holding his right arm, sitting on the running board of one of the trucks. He called out to me in French, in the patois of the region, 'What was I looking for?' I told him that we had carried one of his buddies who had been killed to the side street. He burst out laughing. It was he. He received a bullet in his shoulder and he pretended to be dead so the German would not finish him off by firing at his head. I was astonished to find a soldier who spoke such good French. He explained he was from Louisiana. There were a lot of people from Picard, Normand, Breton who left for Canada and later left Canada for Louisiana. He employed the same words, old French, that we have preserved in the patois.

"In all of the houses, we had a French flag. Everyone was very patriotic at that time. And everyone had a French flag flying in their window. It was a fête. We embraced, we sang the Marseillaise. For us, the war was over. The fête continued until June 6. We understood that it was just the beginning of the war for us. I understood the word attack, counterattack. It wasn't long before the first shells exploded on Sainte-Mère. They began to attack us with the D.C.A.

"We evacuated our trench. I was more than twenty and a half years old, my brother was sixteen, and my sister was fourteen. I am not exaggerating, fifty shells per minute. It was not only the bombings that began the sixth of June. They were shooting from the west and from the north. And there was the German counterattack. There were tanks that arrived here. There were the troops that landed from the sea.

"It was very painful because in a small community like ours, you know *everyone. There were horrible things. There was a family, mother, father, son, daughter and a nephew. They went into the storeroom for shelter, not only those five persons but their neighbors. A shell fell. It was unbearable; it was dreadful. It was necessary to go find gas masks. For all of these dead, there were no coffins. So we carried them to the cemetery in parachutes.*

"*And we looked for all of the Germans who were killed. The Americans gathered up their dead. It took about a week to gather up all of the dead Germans. There were relatively few at Sainte-Mère compared with those found in the countryside. By the hedgerow, I have a photo, there were about 250 dead.*

"*When you went to look for someone in the fields, you always went with two or three others, walking in front of the horse. We were always afraid of...there were torpedoes, grenades, there were shells, there was a bit of everything.*

"*There were four nurses to treat the wounded. There weren't any medications. They went to the town hall, forced open a cupboard where a Red Cross woman kept medications. There were terrible wounds; there was a little boy, eleven years old (his family was burned in the fire). How he got out, I don't know; he was burned from head to toe, he was like a leper.*

"*We paid dearly for our liberation.*" [127]

A Parachutist Lands

Gerald Willen was a private of the S-2 (Intelligence) Section of HQ and HQ Company of the 505 Parachute Regiment of the 82nd Airborne and landed in Sainte-Mère-Eglise on D-Day.

Willen gave an interview before he died 12 June 1994, to the Boulder, Colorado *Daily Camera*, "Insight and Opinion" section, "D-Day" by Gerald Willen for the D-Day Special, 5 June 1994. Excerpts from that interview are cited with permission from his wife, Mrs. Willen-Henrichsen and the *Daily Camera.*

"*The 'day' finally came. I was assigned to a 'stick' (a stick consisted of 12 men and every C-47 carried two sticks, one stick on the metal bucket seats on each side of the plane) in Company C, First Battalion. At about 2200, I was driven to a C-47 parked with dozens of others on the runways. I can't say I was welcomed by the men I was to jump with, since they didn't know me, or I them, but everyone was pretty quiet, anyway.*

"*Assigned a place in one of the two sticks, I began to put on my gear. It all weighed about 70 pounds and included my disassembled M-1 rifle; gas mask, K-rations* [K Rations were designed for troops in combat, derived from American Indian's concentrated venison or pemmican. It included meat, biscuits, coffee, chewing gum, candy, and cigarettes]; *two canteens; a morphine syringe strapped to one boot (for the medics to use on you if you were wounded, or to give to the medics for* use on others if you were not wounded); a bayonet strapped onto the other boot; a roll of communication wire I was carrying for the communication squads strapped across my belly; four hand grenades attached to some straps that held all this together; ammunition for my M-1; a shelter half (something you could spread beneath your blanket to keep yourself water-proofed, or which, combined with someone else's shelter half, would make an entire pup tent); a spade; and a chest parachute, strapped over the roll of communication wire straps, for use if my main parachute did not open.

"And I carried among other things, a blanket; a poncho, toothpaste, some toilet paper; a package of regulation-issue condoms; a razor and its accessories; soap; and a letter from a buddy to his wife to be mailed in the event he was lost in action.

"So we loaded up, took off and found ourselves in the air, the only sound that of the C-47's twin motors. Some men lit up. There was no talk. Occasionally, we could see anti-aircraft shells rising slowly from the ground. At one point, the sky was full of them. Then complete darkness again.

"The cockpit door opened; a sergeant went to the back of the plane to talk to the jumpmaster. Soon the jumpmaster stood up, stuck his head out the open door from which we would jump, drew back in and barked at us to stand up and hook up. At the time, the air was full of anti-aircraft shells, the plane was bucking, and I had the sensation that it was descending. . .

"Suddenly from the jumpmaster, the command 'Go!' My stick began to move; I found myself standing at the door's edge looking down. Just for a moment before the man in back of me pushed or the jumpmaster kicked me out, I remember thinking that we were far below the 400 feet we were to jump from; in a flash, I estimated about 200 feet and hoped as I went out that my 'chute' would have time to open.

"It did, but I had only about two or three seconds to prepare for a landing. Actually, I lurched to the ground, turned a somersault, landing on my head, protected by my helmet.

"Stunned, unable to move, I lay there. In time (I don't know how long), I felt someone standing over me. Opening my eyes, I saw and felt a bayonet poking at me. In the darkness beyond was a human form holding the bayonet. German or American? Not waiting to find out, I shouted frantically that I was an American, repeating it several times. The man above me bent over. I saw the American flag on his left shoulder. Another American paratrooper! So I said loudly, still unable to move, I'm a trooper, don't shoot, don't shoot!'

"He wasn't going to shoot since the paratroopers had been given orders not to shoot during the first few hours of the landing, but to use bayonets and hands, if necessary. The trooper asked for the password.

"Naturally, I couldn't remember it. Pushing slightly on his bayonet, he growled, 'Thunder, Lightning. Remember that trooper.' Then, he was gone.

"Dazed I lay on the ground for a while, watching the anti-aircraft shells go up, listening to the C-47's flying overhead.

"Finally, I was able to stir. With all my equipment, especially with the heavy and awkward roll of communications wire strapped onto me, I was unable to sit up. I was, however, able to lift myself onto my side. But in that position I could not reach my parachute buckles in order to unbuckle. I was able, though, to reach my bayonet strapped only my boot. With it, defying the strict order not to do so, I cut myself out of my 'chute,' stood up, shook myself, assembled my M-1 and loaded it, rearranged my four hand grenades, slung my gas masks over my shoulder, and took a swig of water.

"I then set off, solitary and anonymous, right out of The Red Badge of Courage in the charcoal darkness, to find other American troopers, who like me, probably had not much of a notion of where they had been dropped."

Willen finally found some of his fellow paratroopers and they headed for a collecting point. On 22 June, he and two other men ran into an ambush and were captured. Although he escaped, he was recaptured and was taken to a prison camp in eastern Germany. He was released by the Red Army on 31 January 1945.

Before her return to Germany, Christa Willen-Henrichsen talked about her husband's participation as a paratrooper:

"He enlisted and volunteered as a paratrooper, knowing it was dangerous. He was a rebel, a liberal thinker. It was the adventure of his life. His motto was from Henry James, 'You have to live.'

"Because, as a child, he went to school in Switzerland and knew French, he was assigned to give French lessons to groups of troops while they waited for the invasion to start. Soldiers wanted to know the words for wine, women, conversation for getting a women into bed, and the phrase for 'how much?'"

According to Mrs. Willen-Henrichsen, her husband occasionally talked about the war, mentioning the fear the paratroopers felt when they landed in Normandy and weren't sure where they were; and how the soldiers fed on the food they could find and calvados, since most of the farmers had left Normandy.

"It was while they were 'on the run,' that he rescued a British fellow. An Allied soldier wanted to kill the Brit because he had no idea who he was. My husband looked at his watch which was an RAF watch, and because of that, that British soldier was not shot. He had a great depth of feeling for his buddies. When we went back to Europe, he saw all of the names of his buddies on the crosses. In fact, the night he died, he talked about his guilt because he was sure he had killed someone in the war.

A Time to Speak

"I'm German, although I left in 1938 to live in Switzerland. While Gerald always said the ordinary German soldier was a decent person, he felt uncomfortable in Germany, he felt awkward entering the German house of my brother and sister-in-law.

"He was a gutsy person. I must tell you what he did when he was a POW. The food was terrible. He made up some menus and they took the menus to the Commandant of the camp. Gerald told him he was going to denounce him to the Geneva Convention unless the food improved.

"He was liberated by the Russians. A tanker arrived at the camp gate, the turret opened, and out of the tanker came a woman. And what does she lift up? A child! Isn't that symbolic?

"He was proud of having been in the war and kept his uniform and his medals." [128]

A German Soldier In Sainte-Mere-Eglise

German soldiers were already stationed in Sainte-Mère-Eglise when the Allies landed in enemy territory. The following letter was written forty-five years after D-Day by a young German soldier who returned to Sainte-Mère-Eglise on a visit. His letter, written in English, was mailed from Germany in 1989. It is found in one of the display cases at the Musée des troupes aéroportées (the Airborne Museum), Sainte-Mère-Eglise. His letter echoes a sentiment common to soldiers of all nationalities, a longing for friendship and peace.

"My short History of Invasion. I was a soldier of the German Army from October 1939 till of the war end 1945. My military unit was the 91st Infantry Division - Regiment No. 1058 Strabscompany - Rad Fahrzug (soldier with bicycle). Four weeks of May 1944 we stayed near Ste. Mère. I was corporal and leader of six soldiers. We were since on 2nd of June on the church tower, this tower were our day and bedroom. A young soldier, 17 year old Rudolf May of my group were standing at the beginning of the invasion on the tower, the other man and I stayed on the church-place and the 1st U. S. Paratroopers came down. Alfons Jakl, soldier of my group was killed on the place, he lay in Orglandes in the cemetery of soldiers. At four o'clock in the morning of 6th June, John Steel, paratrooper of the U. S. Army was hanging in the town, my comrade, corporal H. Schmitz, leader of the other group (he now lives in Augsburg, Germany), we had see him and we thought he is death. After we started with our bicycle to our military unit, 2 kilometres of Sainte-Mère. Our military unit started of 7th June to Carentan and of 8th June in the afternoon, we capitulated in Carquebut by the U. S. Army. We were prisoner and went by ship to USA till February 1946 after we were in England till october 1947. This time of prisoner was better than war. I visited Sainte-Mère at 6th June, 1984 and I meet Rudolf May again 40 years. I didn't know where he lives, now he is death. After 45 years I come back to Sainte-Mère and to you my friend Philippe. Friendship is better than a hostility. Excuse my bad English. I didn't learn it. Rudi Escher."

Gliders

Also on display at the Airborne Museum in Sainte-Mère-Eglise is a Horsa glider like the ones which landed in the town square on 5 June. It was a fragile-looking craft with a small space which carried men and equipment, even jeeps, and startled the French who saw them for the first time.

On D-Day, American and British glider pilots, all handpicked volunteers, were in the vanguard of the invasion. They set off in pre-dawn darkness in Horsa gliders, which were made of plywood and weighed eight tons apiece. They transported men, machines, fuel and ammunition. Borne aloft by a towline, they would cut loose over the target, descend, and hopefully set their craft down in a field. Once down safely, they assembled and launched attacks on the enemy, if necessary.

Carmel Lopez, originally from Alamosa, Colorado, flew a glider into Sainte-Mère-Eglise. He kept a diary, "Motorless Morons." His son, Christopher Lopez, a *Denver Post* staff writer, loaned a copy, and the extracts are cited with his permission.

In England for training in formation flying, ferrying gliders to other fields and flying paratroop missions, Lopez and other Horsa pilots were kept busy.

"All this, of course, was to lead to one thing and that was to set off the invasion. We all knew that it was to come but when, we did not know. It wasn't long before we were going round making bets on when it would take place and where we would go in. Guesses ranged from one month to one year.

"The day grew nearer and we all knew it because of the activity that was taking place at our base [Greenham Commons in southern England]. Paratroopers began to arrive and later airborne troops. Our area was fenced in by barb wire and mail was stopped from going out. Then came the day that we had our first notice of the invasion. As our CO told us we had been picked to lead the invasion. Maybe it was because we had the best group or for other reasons, but the fact was that we were picked to lead it. Our CO gave us that vague but vast picture of the invasion and assured everyone that according to intelligence there was nothing to worry about. Immediately after the briefing we were put under armed guard and not allowed out of our area or allowed to talk to anyone except those who were concerned with our activities. Not one of the enlisted men was told what was going on, although I am sure they could sense what was taking place. The idea of the whole thing was secrecy and surprise.

A Time to Speak

"Later on we were briefed thoroughly as to what was to happen. I did not attend the briefings of the tow plane pilots as we were briefed by the airborne. We were briefed on the enemy situation and given a thorough picture of what was to happen. We were to join the airborne once we had landed and naturally we were more concerned about ground situations than we were about flying there. The problem was presented something like this: Our group would take off at 2200 on D-Day, fly to the DZ, drop zone, where they were to drop the paratroopers then return and fly gliders with airborne troops who would reinforce the paratroopers. Our mission was to reinforce the paratroopers and to form a left flank guard for the men coming in from the beach by seaborne. The paratroopers were to have secured our landing zone which was to be in the vicinity just south of Ste. Mère-Eglise on the Cherbourg Peninsula. From here the airborne together with the infantry, motorized, and other divisions, were to proceed to the port of Cherbourg which was to serve as our main source of supply. We were to be evacuated as soon as possible with the idea of coming back for more reinforcements. All possible information was given to us and we felt very confident as to the outcome of the mission.

"At 1600 we all went to mess and at 1800, we were all at stations ready to take off. I had a good sized load in my glider consisting of a jeep, a trailer, and ten men, myself and the co-pilot Flight officer Donovan. At 1852 the first tow ship with its glider labored down the runway and soon they were both airborne and on their way. We sweated out our turn. . .At exactly 1907 our glider started to roll down the runway. I could feel the load was rather heavy but at 90mph, it lifted off the runway and we were on our way to France.

". . .The air was very smooth and I enjoyed looking round and watching our air protection above us. I could see P-47s in twos and threes weaving back and forth across our long column of two ships and gliders. I don't recall that I gave it a thought but I guess it was an assurance to us because we did not carry any fire power. . .I don't know whether it was due to nervousness or not but it seemed to me that I was very calm all the time.

"It wasn't long before we spotted the coast of the Cherbourg Peninsula and I expected any minute to start turning but it seemed to me like we flew indefinitely before we finally did turn on our final approach. . . . The air was full of gliders and I was trying to keep my eye on the other gliders trying to find a field and turning to Donovan for reassurance and in my heart I as praying to God and also His court in Heaven. . .I finally made a decision as to a landing field. By that time I had my glider slowed down to about 75 mph and it was mushing on down. Donovan put down full flaps and we were on our straight approach when in my mind I could see that we were going to hit the tree up ahead. In a fraction of a second a good field appeared to our left and we turned into it. We set down very nicely but our brakes did not hold due I suppose to the heavy load and we rolled until we hit a ditch which stopped us very abruptly. . .In spite of the fact that we hit a ditch and tore the nose wheel and damaged the undercarriage, we all came out without a scratch or without damage to any of the equipment other than the glider.

"Upon landing I immediately jerked off my flak suit and seeing that no one was hurt I stepped outside the glider and was greeted by an artillery officer. We had landed almost in the midst of a battery of our own 105MM Howitzers. I could hear machine gun fire as well as mortar fire when I stepped out but it wasn't until this officer told me that the front lines weren't over 300 yards away did I realize how close we were to enemy fire. . .

"As soon as we unloaded our glider we proceeded upon instructions to an assembly point. Our original point was blocked so we had to assemble somewhere else. . .We were taken to a first aid point where already there were wounded men being taken care of by those great men with a Red Cross on their sleeve. . .All this time the gun fire continued, and I realized that this time they were really playing for keeps." (Carmel Lopez died in 1990 at age 68).

End Notes

127 Both Paris and his father had bit roles in the film, "The Longest Day."
128 After the war Willen earned a PhD in English and taught at Hunter College.

CHAPTER 34

D-DAY, PART III, THE LONGEST DAY

One of the amazing aspects of the D-Day invasion on the Normandy beaches was the coordination of activity and the almost simultaneous actions of Allied air, sea, and ground troops on 5 and 6 June. After the paratroopers and the gliders established and captured certain key points along the Normandy coast, the Second Ranger Battalion made a daring assault at the fortified position at the Pointe du Hoc, scaling the sheer 120 foot cliff to take out a German gun emplacement which had a long enough range to wreak havoc on the Omaha and Utah beachheads.

Meanwhile, the Allied air divisions prepared the way for the landing by dropping nearly 1,760 tons of bombs on the Germans. A vast armada of ships transported men and machines to five landing beaches: American troops to Omaha and Utah; British troops to Gold and Sword; Canadian troops to Juno. The objectives fixed for the evening of D-Day were the capture of Caen, Bayeux, Isigny, and Carentan. Although these objectives were not all achieved, the general operation was a success.

IN THE SKIES

Three airborne divisions took off from British airfields. Approximately 12,000 aircraft assaulted the beaches to make them safer for the landing troops. Each plane had its special mission.

Fighter Pilot on a British Spitfire

Christian Chapman served with the Free French Air Force from 1941 to 1945 as a fighter pilot on Spitfires.

Chapman left Princeton in February 1941, took a banana boat, and arrived in Liverpool in June 1941. Not sure what he would get involved in, he stumbled into some young Frenchmen who asked him to consider joining the Air Force. He said yes. At that time, the Royal Air Force had incorporated all nationalities from countries occupied by the Nazis and organized them into individual squadrons. Following early training which took place in Canada because the British weather was not good for training, trainees returned to England.

"We went back something like September '42 and then there was still some

training, we went to a gunnery school and to a night flying school. You had to know how to fly in English weather, day and night. Then eventually to the advanced training, the training place I went to was in Scotland. And the instructors were Poles from the 333rd Squadron which was one of the great squadrons of the Battle of Britain in 1940. They were all crazy, wonderful pilots; they drank hard and lived hard, flew hard, but they launched me on the Spitfire which was a wonderful plane. Anyone who has flown one of these planes like the Spitfire remains very attached emotionally.

"And when you have flown a great many hours and you get into combat, you really become as one with the machine, like a 'centaur in the air.' Taking off and landing is terribly exciting. When you get in combat, it is so crazy, you don't have time to think.

"For months prior to the invasion, we had run missions over northwest France and Brittany. These missions carried specific code names: 'Rodeo' for fighter sweeps seeking out the Luftwaffe or harassing ground movements; 'Ramrod' for bomber escorts; and 'Noball' for dive-bombing attacks against the V-1 [the first flying bomb] sites.

"In the weeks before the landing, we were moved to Cornwall, to Chichester, which is due south of London, and we were put into tents. There was a very heavy concentration of Allied troops, army and air force in that area. And so we waited through April, May, until June. Everyone knew we were there for the landing. But at least at our levels, secrecy was very well maintained. And we did not know that the landings had been postponed by twenty-four hours because of the lousy weather. And it was very bad weather, very heavy rains, very heavy winds. Even on D-Day, June 4, it was just not good. It cleared in the evening. And on June 3, the evening before, Group Captain Malan, who was the commanding officer of the group, (there were four squadrons) called us to the intelligence tent, a big tent, and said, 'Chaps, this is it!' Very emotional, very pumped. We were all pumped up. You can imagine spending three or four years waiting for this moment. For the French, it was going home and finally getting a crack at those...

"You have seen the films of D-Day. You have heard the sounds. In the air, we had only the sights, and there is a disconnect with the reality on the ground. In a plane, one has the impression of being a distant observer, disassociated from the rest of the world. It takes a wrench of imagination to grasp what is happening there. But what sights they were! What unbelievable scenes! Hundreds of ships with their protective and somehow festive balloons. Hundreds of aircraft. Swarms of men and material on the beaches.

"And on D-Day itself, I personally flew three missions, one at dawn, one at midday and one in the evening. And our mission was to fly to protect the forces on the left flank of the front, of the line over the Canadian and English army, Sword and Gold. I essentially flew back and forth 2,000 feet over those beaches, never saw a German plane. The Luftwaffe, throughout the summer and fall, just did not show up because they had been very heavily damaged in the months before. The Allied Air Forces had conducted a very heavy campaign of attrition.

"That evening we escorted the British 6th Airborne that was flown over in gliders, towed by four-engine Lancaster bombers.

"It was a spectacular spectacle: these hundreds of ships, these hundreds of planes. Remember, we were in a box seat at 2,000 feet, watching all of this. The countryside was so beautiful, so green, the sky was so blue that the whole thing was unreal.

"Battleships on the southeastern end were pounding Caen, and we could see the yellow flashes of their guns and of the fire they had ignited. When the gliders we were escorting arrived on target near Caen, a cluster of antiaircraft opened up. The Lancasters and gliders were sitting ducks. Many were destroyed, and we watched helplessly as they exploded into great yellow and orange balls, each carrying thirty young men to their deaths. Transport aircraft that accompanied the division were dropping equipment and supplies by parachute, red and orange and yellow parachutes. The whole scene was an extravaganza of color.

"Normandy is worth visiting to this day, to drive along the coast, visit the beaches, visit the little museums, to visit the cemeteries, then you appreciate the violence of that day." [129]

Squadron Bombardier on a B-24

Howard Teague was a squadron bombardier aboard B-24s in the European Theater of Operations. His D-Day mission, one of twenty-nine bombing missions completed, was to bomb the beaches ahead of the troops. Teague received the Air Medal on four different occasions and the Distinguished Flying Cross on three different occasions.

"I have several memories of D-Day, when we went across the Channel. First of all, there was high cloud cover. We had a terrible time forming on D-Day. We formed over southern England and when we went across, I still have a picture of that mass of boats going across. It was just, you can't picture it, just hundreds and hundreds, as far as your eye could see.

"Then there was cloud cover. Right in the middle of the Channel there was a break in the clouds, an interesting break because it was north/south and probably a mile or two wide and you could see down to the water. It was early in the morning, just after daybreak, and the battleships and cruisers happened to be in that break in the clouds, and they were bombarding the shore that we were going to drop our bombs on. The salvos would go from those ships. The flash of the guns would light up the dark walls of the clouds, and that would silhouette the ships, so that, as the gun flashes would make the ships vivid. It was a picture that, once you see it, you never forget it. Those are things that are coming back." [130]

Pilot on a B-26

Bill Herron was a pilot with the Army Air Corps and retired after thirty years of military experience. His mission D-Day was to fly a Martin B-26 along the English Channel to the Normandy beaches.

"The buildup toward D-Day was anticipation more than anything. The papers were full of it; the news broadcasts were full of it. So it was no secret. The only secret was where, and of course, we didn't know that. We didn't know when, and the Germans were outguessed on this thing the whole way, fortunately. However, the invasion itself was still a tremendous, tremendous operation.

"They woke us up about two o'clock in the morning on June sixth. We nodded to one another and said, 'This is it'; went to our briefing at about three o'clock. Our takeoff was about 4:00 a.m. or 4:30 a.m. But it was extremely bad weather, 800 foot ceiling. We formed in six-ship flights under the overcast and then climbed through 9,000 feet of weather, night-instrument formation. It is probably the most difficult mission I ever flew, just because of that. It was terrible; we were turning constantly, almost on a racetrack pattern, on a radio beacon from the ground. The leader of the group I was in was an exceptionally sharp individual. I was flying number two, flying his right wing and, ironically, the squadron commander had flown more combat flights than the group commander wanted his squadron commanders to do. So he didn't fly that night except as my copilot. He sneaked aboard the last minute. My copilot always blamed him for his not going on that mission.

"The flight, climbing up through that weather, was extremely difficult. And out of our squadron, we lost four airplanes, just flew into the ground. Again, we were not experienced instrument pilots. We never practiced it. We practiced it some and we had to fly an examination every year to get our estimate cards. That was a mandatory thing. But we weren't real exceptional instrument pilots because we were still pretty young.

"Almost every airplane that could fly was on its way down there, had its mission. So we went on. Our mission was gun emplacements, German gun emplacements on the Continent, probably fairly deep into the Cherbourg peninsula. We then flew across the Cherbourg peninsula, went out over the Atlantic and back by a circuitous route to our base in England.

"By this time the weather was nice, the clouds had dissipated. Shortly after landing, they formed another mission and I happened to be on that one too, so I got two chances to fly on D-Day. The targets were close to one another, just a few miles apart.

"The most impressive thing about the mission itself was actually the tremendous amount of things going on in the harbor or on the shoreline. It was just huge, that is all you can say for it. One of the most impressive things I saw, I just happened to see it, was a battleship. I think it was the Texas. I would have to confirm that, but anyway, it was out there and it was lobbing broadsides in on the shore. It had targets too, just like the rest of us. And every time it would fire, the whole side of that boat would light up. It was just a tremendous sight. I can't help but believe that boat almost took in water from the recoil of all those guns."

The Work Horses

About 700 warships, 2,700 support ships, and 2,500 landing craft headed for the five beaches. Many considered the LSTs (Landing ship, tank) the work horses of the Navy, carrying men and machines back and forth between England and the Normandy Beaches.

LST 511

Don Look enlisted in the Navy right out of high school (1943) and served as a cook on *LST 511*, a hospital equipped ship. "When I enlisted I was going to be sent to Pensacola, to the Naval Air Station photography school. And the fellow said, 'Just in case you don't get it, what is your second choice?' And I said, 'Why don't you make me a cook?' And the next morning they needed three cooks. It just popped into my head. I didn't think there would be any question that I would get the photography end of it. I just did it as a joke. I said, 'I've got it, I might as well make the best of it.'

"It was fun. I went to Samson, New York, six weeks, Cooks and Bakers school, big galley, 5,000 men out of a mess hall and they give you a stripe and you go to Saunders, Maryland, amphibious base, a little training there, then the big day comes and you are hoping for a ship. The worst thing is to be setting on land. The big day comes, the captain, with his papers, and picks out his crew. And you go on to Great Lakes, had to wait there two or three weeks, a month (it was cold that winter) until the ship got ready. We left from Boston to Halifax, Halifax to Port Talbot in Wales, then over to the southern coast of England. We spent most of the time, Falmouth, Southampton, Bournemouth.

"LST 511 was 360 feet long, but the tank deck when you opened those doors, inside was the size of a football field. We could carry thirty-six Sherman tanks, 1,000 prisoners, everything you could think of. . .

"We had thirteen air raids we went through, twenty-four different ports, five countries, 508 days overseas. We carried 10,000 personnel, 34,000 miles and 111,000 individual meals.

"A small ship is unique. It was a family. And you don't worry about the other fellow, you don't worry about the engine room because you know its done right. They don't worry about the cook. We were all seventeen and eighteen years old. Fellows running the engines, signalman, he was eighteen, fellow steering the ship, he's only eighteen. Our captain was just a lieutenant, junior grade. He had been in the Navy as a chief, fifteen years. He was an old-timer. I had a lot of respect for him. He was a great fellow.

"Ship broke down. This fellow, eighteen years old, with his little tool box, down in the engine room, because they had more than that going on, but they got the thing fixed. It got going, that's his job.

"There were seventeen in the crew, that's running the engines, cooking, helping clean up the store, doing the paint work, steering the ship, it's like a little city.

"And our compartment where we slept, we had 10 ft. by 20 ft. long, and eight of us slept there. A couple of black fellows, supply division, a couple of blacks stewards' mates, they couldn't hold rates at the time, but they were neat fellows. It teaches you to get along with your neighbor there in a hurry.

"When you take a thing like that and make it home for a couple of years, it is quite an event in your life. Two Christmases, two birthdays. There were still thirteen of the original crew left (you know they get transferred on and off, back and forth), Seneca to Norfolk, the long way around, 34,000 miles. We had a big dinner that night. It was kind of sad, took the flag down for the last time.

"I wasn't sorry when it was over, but it was good experience. It did me a lot of good — how to take orders, keep your things clean, a little respect, a lot of things. I'd do it again if I had to. Everybody was in the same boat. Your neighbor was in it; the guy across the street was in it. It was just such a neat bunch of people. But I think you put all that stuff behind you and get on with today.

"About a week before D-Day, we loaded up. They sealed the ship and then we knew something was going to happen, two or three hundred soldiers, just sitting there. We knew something was going on because the old man came back with his roll of 'blueprints' we called it. He knew what was happening, he was the only one.

"Then we started out, a storm came up, and we turned back. Then they finally said, 'Go.' We were taking soldiers over and we were hospital equipped, not a hospital ship, but hospital equipped. We took soldiers over, two navy doctors and twenty hospital corpsmen, an army surgical team. We evacuated about 1,000 wounded. We went back and forth quick on D-Day.

"The soldiers were petrified of the ship. They could hardly wait to get off the thing, scared to death of the water. D-Day, it was hard, they were seasick. It was a rough day that day. We fed them and half of them couldn't eat.

"I was the cook. They got three hot meals. On D-Day, the captain said, 'Feed 'em good.' We served them steak, mashed potatoes, peas, and my buddy cranked ice cream.

"D-Day itself was quite a sight. You couldn't see the sky for the bombers, wave after wave after wave of bombers. You couldn't begin to count them, just unbelievable, and ships as far as you could see, 5,000 or 6,000 ships. The battleships behind us would fire those guns and my LST would pop right out of the water. The eeriest part would be at night when the German planes would drop flares and it would light the place up. You are just sitting there, you can't move or anything. Then they would open up these antiaircraft guns, but by then the German air force wasn't as bad, but it just had a eery feeling. We survived it and got on with it. Everybody had a job to do and we got it done.

"We made just one trip D-Day. We didn't get there until about eleven o'clock on D-Day. We stayed there for two days, unloaded, loaded, and waited until we got the casualties on, the wounded fellows.

"Then after D-Day, everyone got fed, a lot of the soldiers we had to hand feed, the wounded fellows during D-Day. When they were wounded on the beach, they didn't do anything for them. They couldn't, they'd put plaster on, you know like you have for burns, similar to that. A lot of them we had to hand feed. We even had German officers, prisoners, but they got fed though. I fed a German officer.

"Our wounded fellows got our regular menu, whatever we had. But if you had a big bunch, like the German prisoners, beef stew was a good one. And I would get them to do the cooking. Captain said to me one day, 'We're going to load 1,000 prisoners,' and I was the boss cook and it was about noontime, and he said, 'I want supper at 4:30 p.m. and I'm going to start loading in about an hour and everyone gets a hot meal.' Then he said, 'Now goddamnit, use your head.' All I did was say, 'Yes, sir,' and turned around and walked out.

"I got my buddies and they said, 'What did he mean by that?' So I figured that out of 1,000 prisoners, they've got to have some cooks. So I went right down in the middle of all the prisoners on the big tank deck. My German and some English, I got about seven or eight German cooks and they made beef stew. That was a good meal, too. Then he called me in about a week later, and said, 'That's using your head,' and I got another stripe out of it.

"After D-Day, we went right up on the beach which a lot of people don't realize. Up on the beach, we'd play baseball there. We'd walk around the beach and play baseball at low tide.

"These LSTs were work horses. At high tide, there was this big anchor and a winch, and we'd pull out and go back to England. We'd get those wounded soldiers back, then we'd load up with something else. It could be anything, tanks, guns, ammunition, fuel, troops and go over again.

"I can remember after D-Day, we would leave religiously. They would make up a little convoy, three or four LSTs, a liberty ship and the escort ship. They'd open the submarine nets and we'd go out at 4:30 p.m.; they'd close the nets; they would get the convoy together and wait for the escort ship to show up. That's all we worried about, make sure that thing was there, AK-88. When we saw that, we would go to sleep. After dark you didn't have to worry going across the Channel. It was at the wide part and our ship only did eight knots an hour." [131]

THE LANDINGS ON THE BEACHES

The American landings were timed to go in first at Utah Beach where the 4th Division encountered little resistance and at Omaha Beach where the 1st and 29th American Divisions encountered heavy casualties. To the east, the British 50th Division landed at Gold Beach, the Canadian 3rd Division at Juno Beach, and British 3rd Division followed at Sword Beach.

Among those who landed and who won't forget their impressions were a Belgian chaplain, an American lieutenant, a Canadian soldier, a British glider pilot, and a French soldier, part of a commando battalion. From the enemy side was a German soldier, who with his comrades, waited and watched in their fortified positions.

Utah Beach
(Saint-Martin de Varreville, Sainte-Marie-du-Mont)

Victor Dossogne, S. J., a Belgian who had escaped in the wake of Hitler's advances, came to the U. S. in 1940. In 1943 he signed on for active duty and began his training at an American chaplain school. In May 1944, he was on his way to Europe, where he joined the 90th Infantry Division in England.

Once in England, General Devine took Fr. Dossogne inside to show him an enormous map of the French coast and pointed to the base in Normandy and said, "This is where we are going to land." It was Utah Beach. It was a beach Fr. Dossogne knew as he had visited there with friends in 1913. In his memoirs, he recalled:

"After a few days orientation and visiting with the troops, we were finally preparing to board the ship. It was Sunday, June 4th, 1944. Each person was lightly loaded. I carried only two musette bags, one with my personal belongings, the other with a Mass kit. Each of us were given a C-ration and a piece of chocolate. It was supposed to feed us for a day, and was usually used by the paratroopers. With my chocolate, I was ready to move.

"...It was not until after dark that we started moving during the night, turning east toward the island of Wight, and so started the preliminaries of the biggest invasion of the war, D-Day. Hundreds of ships slowly moved toward France.

"As soon as we left port, I held a service. Everyone on board attended the Mass, except for the commanding officer...I talked and prayed and all the soldiers were in high spirits as I attempted to give them confidence in the future, saying, 'You are in the hands of the Lord.'

"...At about 5.00 in the morning the ship stopped and I went on deck to see what was happening. Just ahead I could see land. Now it was just a matter of waiting our turn.

"All day long we waited and watched wave upon wave of men landing. We saw and heard the German artillery, but never saw any German planes...Finally, at about midnight of the 5th, it was our turn to land. I got into my jeep and it was loaded onto a barge. My driver came promptly, and we slowly approached the shore. It was not an amphibious jeep and about 200 yards from shore, the jeep suddenly stalled and got stuck in the mud. We were in shallow water, but for two hours my driver and I just sat there helpless, literally up to our necks in water, soaked to the bones.

"Could I have swum to shore? I think under the heavy load that I carried, I'd surely have sunk! Eventually an amphibious jeep came and picked us up, and we finally reached the beach, wet but so far, safe.

"...On Friday night we reached Ste.-Mère-Eglise... Friday, at 2:00 in the morning when we reached Normandy's main square, there was the church and the rectory and the city hall. There were extremely tall trees growing along the side of the square, and as I glanced up, a horrible sight held my eyes. Hanging in the trees were the bodies of four paratroopers, and there were more paratroopers hanging from the spires of buildings. It was ghastly. We brought the bodies down. There were no survivors. They had landed on the 4th, and we got there on the 9th, so they had been dead several days.

"...I realized that evening [after an evening with General Devine] what it took to be a great leader. It took a sense of humor, and an ability to take the good things as well as the horrible things in stride. Unmistakably, the war was deplorable, and I must say that I saw the most horrendous sights I have ever seen, in all my life, shortly after we had landed.

"On Utah Beach there were not so many men lost, but at Omaha beach it was a different story... The bodies were buried here and there along the beach, but there was not enough room.

"The army had to open a huge, vast cemetery, and on June 20th, by the regular service time, the graves had all been dug.

"The Protestant chaplain and I had service at 3:00 o'clock every day. While we were praying, the trucks started arriving. There were carloads of bodies buried as we prayed."[132]

Omaha Beach
(Vierville, Saint-Laurent, Colleville-sur-Mer)

Of all the beach landings, Omaha was the worst. It was known as "Bloody Omaha." Estimates vary on the number of casualties: accounts put the number at between 3,000 and 4,000 were killed or wounded; but the casualties were fewer than the 10,000 predicted by officials.

Troops landed in four-foot surf, under machine gun fire. From the landing crafts they leaped out into deep frigid water. Veterans describe how they saw men dying all around them, being hit and blown to bits by artillery fire, machine guns or land mines. Many of them died before they could reach the shore.

Mal Walker was a cellist, but on D-Day, he was a first lieutenant and a member of the 29th Division, 115th Regiment. He left England, landed with the second wave, and finally reach Saint-Lô forty-three days later (an objective they were supposed to reach in nine days).

"The 29th Division, 115th Regiment. They were in southern England in Cornwall, and I joined them in Bodmin which is in Cornwall. Before May twenty-eighth, we were moved into what were called 'sausages,' a restricted area. That was about May first. Then 28 May, we started loading on boats, small landing craft, then out to the LCIs, then we moved into Plymouth harbor. Incidentally, D-Day was supposed to be May first or second. But in the early planning, they decided to have Utah Beach in addition, so they needed more landing craft so they had to delay a month. So they waited, then the weather delayed it a day. If they had waited, the worst storm in the Channel occurred 19 June which completely destroyed the American 'mulberry.' ["Mulberry" was the code name for the artificial harbors.]

"All of the officers were briefed several days ahead with maps and the men were briefed on the ship. We had already sailed on 5 June. 'Picadilly Circus' was the line of departure [southeast of the Isle of Wight]. It was ten miles out and all of the ships were to assemble in that area."

The Password, "Mickey Mouse"

"I still have the plans for D-Day, the orders. We had maps and aerial photos, orders for the day. The men under me had sand maps of the area. I'll never forget, though, the password for D-Day was 'Mickey Mouse.' Actually we didn't have to use it, but we might have had to use it if we were challenged.

"Where we landed wasn't where we were supposed to land. We were about a mile east of where we were supposed to land. Things were different.

"About two o'clock in the morning, the signal was given 'Move out.' The sea was still rough. Those LCIs [Landing Craft, Infantry] held 230 men, but the landing barges would only hold 30.

"I'll never forget the meal we had at two o'clock in the morning on June sixth. It was beans, hot dogs, donuts and coffee. It was on the ship before going in.

"A lot of the men were seasick. Those pills didn't do anything. There were five columns, one for each beach and we were on Task Force 'O' which was Omaha. We loaded into the landing barges. Those are flat-bottomed, and everyone was sick and they were baling out on the side, and the water was coming in over the tops.

"They told us it would be a weak group, but it was the 716th; they were a different breed. Everybody said, 'You can just walk in because the Air Corps is going to flatten it, bomb craters on the beach.' Of course, none of that happened. Eisenhower vetoed the use of bombs that would make a crater because that would make it too difficult for vehicles to come in. The vehicles couldn't come in without driving on dead bodies. So it was a good thing all of the tanks didn't make it.

"People who say they weren't afraid are crazy. Fields were burning where some of the artillery shells had dropped. And by the way, the Air Force didn't help. They bombed three miles inland. They were supposed to bomb, but it was overcast and they couldn't see, they didn't help a bit.

"At Omaha, there were 8 concrete bunkers, 35 pillboxes, 4 batteries of artillery, 18 anti-tank guns, 35 rocket launchers and 85 machine gun emplacements and that's just at Omaha.

"I was in the 115th Regiment. When we landed on the second wave, there were bodies all over. The tide was low tide, but by noon the tide comes clear back 150 feet, and the bodies were just washed up, acres of just bodies and parts of bodies. The water was red. You can't describe it really. Unless you were there, people can't understand. All of the artillery pieces were sunk at the bottom of the sea, so they didn't make it ashore for our unit. Twenty-seven of thirty-four tanks were sunk. 8,000 yards out they were lost, they were amphibious, they had canvas sides and they sunk. Only three of them made it to the beach. When we got to the beach, all small arms, that was all, rifles, mortars, small mortars, all 81-mortars. Machine guns, but a lot of them didn't work.

"The 116th landed right at the Vierville Draw. We landed just below the cemetery; there is a path still there. The Vierville Draw took all morning. We were a little bit luckier because, actually, we landed in the lst Division's area which was called 'Easy Green' and 'Easy Red.' It was about noon before we got up. You had to watch for mines, snipers, machine guns and artillery, mortar, so it wasn't a walk-in.

A Time to Speak

"One of the reporters asked me, 'Well, why didn't you just turn back?' And I said, 'Where are you going to go, in the water?' You have to keep going. And as General Cota [Brigadier General Norman Cota, assistant commander of the 29th Division] said, 'Let's get off this beach. A lot of men are dead and the ones that are left are going to die. So get up on top.' He came in at 7:30. He came down and said, 'What are you waiting for? I've just been up there, and there is nothing up there.' He started to organize things. The engineers were to clear the obstacles on the beach. And there was no way; they would get butchered. As the tide came up, they hit those obstacles with mines on top. Many of the crafts were blown up or sunk by the motion of the sea. Everyone was glad to get off. They were sick.

"That night we were supposed to take St. Laurent-sur-Mer and Colleville was supposed to be taken by the 1st Division. It wasn't cleared until the next day. At night we were at the edge. It was all new. The 29th Division hadn't been in combat. I saw one of my men, he was a real nice fellow, he was picking flowers in the field.

"You had a job to do and you had to do it. Death got to the place where it was commonplace. On the beach, there were 3,000 dead, and a lot of them in the water, they never did find their bodies. And some of them, when the tide came in, it washed them back out.

"German troops took advantage of natural obstacles to impede the progress of Allied troops. There was the inundated area near Colombières and Canchy. At Isigny-sur-Mer, for years and years, it was always flooded when the tide came up. They put a dam and sluice gate, but the Germans opened that so this was all flooded. It was only about three feet of water, but there were cuts below where streamlets would come through which made it another three feet. You couldn't walk across that. Some tried and they'd drop into one of these stream beds and it would be over their head. Finally the engineers developed 'weasels.' We used 'weasels' to cross. A weasel, they used weasels to come in on D-Day, is a boat-tank combination with treads. Then they took us across to Colombières. It was the ninth before we got to Colombières. There was no deadline, but it was suggested we get to Saint-Lô in nine days.

"We kind of zigzagged to get to Saint-Lô It took us forty-three days to go to Saint-Lô. The British were supposed to take Caen on D-Day. It took them longer than it took us to get to Saint-Lô.

"In an area of eight square miles around Saint-Lô, there were 3,900 hedgerows; in fact, they were all over Normandy. [Old mounds of earth, topped with brush and brambles, that stretch the length and breadth of a field, existing from the time of Julius Caesar]

"You can't communicate because these hedgerows are over your heads sometimes and trees on top of that. Some unit might push four hedgerows ahead and find there are Germans on both sides because they had no way of contact with the others. It was just taking one at a time. The Germans would dig down behind the hedgerows. Then they would sometimes use periscopes so they wouldn't have to stick their heads up.

"And the Germans would have the next hedgerow behind them already prepared. So they would cut out and must move back into the next one. Tanks couldn't maneuver. In the hedgerows, for the tanks, it was deadly. But the 2nd Armored devised a scheme, with some prongs up on top, on the front of the tank. They'd go to a hedgerow and they would punch a hole and put dynamite in it. Then they got some metal extensions, prongs, and they would go up to a hedgerow and they would move the whole hedgerow.

"One German who surrendered said, 'I saw that tank coming and I was ready with ..and when I bellied up to hit it, the whole hedgerow moved and that was enough for me.'

"*Bradley* [Lt. Gen. Omar Bradley, commander of the American First Army at Utah and Omaha] *was contemplating calling it off and sending the additional troops on farther east because of the devastation at Omaha. And General Cota got word to him that we were on top and things were progressing. But there was so much debris, boats, tanks, everything destroyed, it was difficult to get in. Even the 2nd Division that came in the next day, they had to fight off snipers that were still on the beach.*

"I would never want to do it again, but it was an interesting time." [133]

On Widerstandsnest 62
Colleville-sur-Mer

The German troops, 50 infantry divisions and 10 armored divisions were waiting for the Allied forces. Among the young German soldiers was Franz Gockel.

In 1994, Gockel wrote his recollections of the invasion of Normandy on Omaha Beach, "Normandie," and had them translated into both English and French.

Gockel joined the German army in 1943 and was trained as an infantryman in Holland for seven weeks. Then he was transferred to Normandy, where the German soldiers were instructed that their appearance in public always had to be correct, and as a result, their relations with the local people were good.

There were commonalities among German and Allied troops: youthfulness, worries about families at home, calm anticipation of the events to unfold, and the tension before the invasion. There were conspicuous differences. The German troops were not as well-prepared as Allied soldiers; they received no help from German defenses, in aircover, manpower, or additional ammunition. Their heavy weapons were preset on defensive fire zones, limiting their flexibility. They were misled by the deception forces; they expected the Allies to come at high tide, not at low tide, and certainly not in bad weather. They were caught in the miscalculations on the part of Hitler's commanders. They had placed their confidence in Rommel and his reinforced defenses at Colleville-sur-mer, only to see the defenses demolished by superior Allied power. Rommel went home for his wife's birthday, realizing too late that this was the main invasion. Field Marshal Gerd von Rundstedt, on the other hand, was not convinced Normandy was the main landing and delayed committing reserve troops. Hitler, a late sleeper, was not informed until noon on D-Day. Newspaper accounts quoted him as saying "In Britain, we couldn't get at them. Now we have them where we can destroy them."

Gockel wrote a graphic description of the landing at Omaha Beach. Selected excerpts from the English version of Gockel's account describe his reactions:

5 June 1944.

"During midday from 12:00 until 14:00 I stood behind a twin-barreled machine gun on aircraft watch...I was still very young. I had celebrated my 18th birthday here on this position, and almost half of my comrades were also only 18 or 19 years old.

"Sometime in May an Artillery Observation Point had been established with a Lieutenant, a Feldwebel, an NCO, and two crewmen. They supported an artillery battery located about 5 kilometers behind the coastline in a field position.

"The 105 mm guns were situated along a coastal strip in front of WN 62 and WN 61, [Widerstandsnest or fortified point] *and were zeroed in on pre-planned target areas. They were to serve as support for the WN crews when needed.*

"I sat behind the mount of the machine-gun and gazed out over the sea. . . Nothing moved on the calm surface of the water, only the slow swells made their way slowly to the beach.

"The fishing boats from Grandcamp and Port Bassin remained in the harbor. Several months ago they had routinely made their excursions along the coast, but now the sea was empty.

"There were many hours when no one thought about the war. Experiencing the sunsets upon the horizon would permit thoughts to wander from the war, but then would come news from home, news that would serve as a brutal reminder that not only on the front, but also at home a horrible conflict fiercely raged.

"With mixed feelings, letters from home would be read daily. Many comrades were from the large cities in the Ruhr area, and a number of them had already lost homes, possessions, and family members in the hail of bombs.

"Several days previously a friend from my city had received news that his sister and grandmother had been killed during a bombing raid. . .A few weeks ago

those members who suffered losses at home would receive special leave, but because of the deteriorating situation this leave was no longer authorized.

"With the short report: 'Nothing new on the position', I was relieved at my post.

"...During the evening hours on the 5th of June, like so often before, debate raged in the bunker over the possibility of invasion. The opinions were varied, and with heated argument one group was convinced that the English or Americans would never attempt to land here. The other group could be persuaded from the opinion that within no more than four weeks the Tommys and Amis would be attempting to land on this beach.

"After being relieved from my post, I and other comrades resumed the task of digging a trench line that was to connect a recently completed gun casemate with the bunker...On the evening of the 5th of June, a comrade remarked: 'Guys, we've got to get this trench finished. If there will be any possibility at all to survive an attack, it will only be with the help of this trench.'

"With the twilight came always the relieving of the sentries on the positions. The password for the evening was given. The company commander was briefed on the situation and on progress made on the defenses. In the bunker the most recent letters from home were read. Letters were written. In a corner an unconcerned game of cards was played. On a bunk played an old gramophone, screeching with the sounds of 'When you once give your heart...' and 'When the white flowers bloom again.' We had heard the few old records countless times daily.

"A comrade sat on his bunk and packed together some things to send home with the outgoing mail the following day. We had no electric lights for some weeks, and the fluttering candles and smoking oil lamps gave a soft light. Soon everyone was lying in the bunks, which were stacked three high. In accordance with orders we slept in full uniform, only pulling our boots off and carefully placing them next to the bunks.

"...During May and through the beginning of June the aircraft activity increased over us, passing our positions and dropping their deadly load on key railway junctions and road crossings to the rear.

"...The attacks on the railway stations and roads led to increasing transport problems and to a lack of required weapons and ammunition.

"Only once or twice during the week would two German fighter aircraft be seen flying along the coastline. We named them Max and Moritz.

"...The alert condition had been raised since the end of May. It was reported that in southern England strong troop units had been embarked.

"On the sea and in the air the sounds and light signals increased. The "landsers" [infantrymen] *with experience at the front were saying, 'Something is in the air.'*

"Additional machine gun positions, including a dummy gun position with a long barrel, were added to the defenses. Mortar shells were stored in a shallow concealed dug-out. The watch personnel had been increased, spread out to cover the entire position, each man within calling distance from another.

"Night foot patrols with trained dogs were sent out to cover the open areas between the support positions of the mine field along the beach.

"A patrol from our company was returning from Vierville-sur-Mer as it approached the first position near St. Laurent-sur-Mer. The dog suddenly became excited and began straining violently against his leash, not in the direction of the position, however, but toward the sea on the opposite side of the patrol route. . . suddenly a shot rang out from close range. The patrol dove for cover, and it was immediately known that enemy forces had infiltrated the beach. A flare was fired by the patrol leader, shots rang out in rapid fire. The other positions came to life. The sentries opened fire with weapons fixed within pre-set fire zones, and the fire soon ceased as quickly as it had begun. . . Several dead English soldiers lay on the beach. . .

"In the evening hours of 5 June I stood at my sentry post. Like so often before, the duty seemed to last an eternity. Finally, I was relieved, and I trotted to the bunker to try to get a few hours rest before I had to be awakened again. At the bunker stood a comrade who had also just been relieved at his post and was reporting to the sergeant of the watch over the radio. I said to him, 'I hope that we don't have more of those damned exercise alerts tonight' as we so often had in the past, and I disappeared into the bunker deep under the ground. Quickly the overcoat and boots were pulled off and I dove into my bunk."

6 June 1944, 0100

"The alarm call into the bunker woke us from a deep sleep. A comrade stood in the entrance and continued to shout the alarm, to dispel any doubt, and urged us to hurry. We had so often been shaken to our feet by this call in the past weeks that we no longer took the alarms seriously, and some of the men rolled over in their bunks and attempted to sleep. An NCO appeared in the entrance way behind our comrade and brought us to our fee with the words: 'Guys, this time it's for real. They're coming!' We sprang to action. With carbines in grasp we ran to our positions. All weariness evaporated. Machine guns, heavy guns, and mortars were prepared. We stood next to our weapons ready for action. The night remained quiet. Soon the first message came from the company. In Ste.-Mère-Eglise enemy paratroopers had landed. Large numbers of ships had departed southern English harbors and were headed toward Normandy.

"Our coastal sector remained quiet, nothing moved. Was it again a false alarm? The minutes slowly ticked by. Was this time for real? We stood at our weapons and shivered in the thin summer uniforms. The cook prepared hot red wine. Our senses were again alerted when an NCO appeared and checked our readiness, saying, 'When they come, don't shoot too soon.' Then I was again alone at my machine gun.

"The silence weighted heavily upon us. The tension continued. Soon the sound of bomber squadrons could be detected in the air and faded again in the distance. Like always before, they would fly over our sector. It remained quiet for only a short time and with the morning dawn came more bombers. Dark shadows could be detected on the horizon, and we first believed them to be German patrol craft. Soon the shadows grew and became so numerous that all hope was dispelled, the vessels were not German. The detectable wake from large and small ships increased in number. More bombers approached the coastline. A few kilometers from us in Port-en-Bassin, the first bombs fell.

"Again bombers approached our sector. Before me stood my heavy machine gun on its lafette, the sights trained on the sea. Once again I inspected the ammunition belt. I attempted to concentrate on my weapon to take my mind away from the impending events. In a recess of my gun position stood ignition switches for two flame-throwers which were aimed at the beach and the tank trench. Also within reach was a pile of hand grenades.

"The bombers were suddenly over us, and it was not too late to follow through with the plan to spring into the prepared dugout for cover. I dove under the machine gun as bombs screamed and hissed into the sand and earth. Two heavy bombs fell upon our position and we held our breath as more explosions fell into the hinterland. Debris and clouds of smoke enveloped us. The earth shook. Eyes and nose were filled with dust. Sand ground between teeth. There was no hope for help. No German aircraft appeared. This sector had no anti-aircraft guns, and unimpeded the bombers could drop their deadly load upon us.

"An endless fleet lay before our sector. Heavy warships cruised along as if passing for review. A spectacular but terrifying experience for those of us who survived the naval gunfire.

6 June 0600

"The heavy naval guns fired salvo after salvo into our positions. In the beginning the ships lay at 20 kilometers distance, but range slowly decreased. With unbelieving eyes we could recognize individual landing craft. The hail of shells falling upon our position grew heavier, fountains of sand and debris rose in the air with the impacts. The mined obstacles in the water were partially destroyed. The morning dawn over the approaching landing fleet exhibited for us approaching doom. Bombs and heavy caliber shells continued to slam into the earth, tossing tangles of barbed wire, obstacles and clouds of dirt into the air. The fight for survival began.

"...The overwhelming superiority in material made possible only a slight token of resistance. Our heavy weapons were pre-set on defensive fire zones, thus we could only wait, and continue to wait. It appeared as though the enemy would land in the approximate beach center. We had planned on the enemy attempting a landing only at high tide, in order to drive the boats over the open beach. But now was low tide, the water-line lay about 300 meters distant.

"The shells and bombs had destroyed many of our positions, but we had not suffered heavy casualties.

"... With the bombardment the landing fleet had approached the beach and was close enough for us to recognize details. Along with warships of every description were troop transports, landing craft and assault craft preparing to set the invading army upon the beach. Suddenly the rain of shells ceased, and a strange quiet enveloped us. But only for a short time. Again explosions of gunfire from the ships could be heard, and again shells slammed into the beach. Some of the log obstacles were splintered, some burning. Slowly the wall of explosions approached, meter by meter. Worse than before, a deafening torrent of smoke and dust rolled toward us, cracking, screaming, whistling and sizzling, destroying everything in its path. The wall of destruction took its time, as if knowing that for us there was no escape. We crouched small and helpless behind our weapons. I prayed for survival, and my fear passed.

"The first shells of this barrage landed among us, but miraculously no one was wounded. Over us and within our positions the explosions pounded and rattled. Hissing and screaming, the shrapnel and splinters flew through the air. They slammed against concrete or thudded into the ground. Suddenly it was again silent.

"Now with great speed, dive bombers approached our positions at low altitude, board weapons rattling, bullets whistling and popping around us. There were six of us in the position, and still no one was wounded. A comrade stumbled out of the smoke and dust into my position and screamed: 'Franz watch out! They're coming!'

"The sea had come alive. Assault boats and landing craft rapidly approached the beach. The first closely packed landing troops sprang from the boats, some in knee-deep water, others up to their chests. There was a race over the open beach toward the low stone wall running parallel to the water-line which offered the only protection. The defenders sprang into action. It had been futile to attempt to defend against air and naval bombardment, and until now we could only attempt to save our own lives. Now we heard the first machine gun bursts. Within seconds the first waves of assault troops collapsed after making only a few meters headway.

". . .I had opened fire with my heavy machine gun with short bursts aimed at the landing boats, when the sand-covered ammunition belt caused it to jam. I tore the belt from the feed tray, shook it clean, and slapped it back into the tray. At that instant the machine gun was torn from my hands, and still today it is difficult for me to imagine that I escaped this blast without the slightest injury.

". . .On came the second wave of assault craft. Again a race across the beach. Again the defense positions opened fire. The resistance from the defenders grew weaker. More and more comrades were killed or wounded. The tide came slowly forward, the water-line creeping up the beach.

". . .The battle raged back and forth for some hours, the beach became strewn with dead, wounded and shelter-seeking soldiers of the landing fleet. The tide crept forward, the water coming ever closer. Anything that could move on the beach sought shelter, with many falling victim to the defenders. We began to notice our own losses. The lightly wounded were bandaged and sent to the rear. The seriously wounded were carried to a sheltered area. Dead comrades were left lying where they fell, there was no time to look after them.

"Some of the assault troops reached the low stone wall, seeking protection from our gunfire. The safety offered here was temporary. Our mortar crews had waited for this moment, and began to lay deadly fire upon pre-set coordinates along the wall. Mortar rounds with impact fuses exploded on target. The shell splinters, wall fragments, and stones inflicted casualties upon the troops. Hour after hour boats and tank landing craft assaulted the beach, attempting to gain as much ground as possible upon the flat sand. With great confusion and haste soldiers, weapons, and equipment were pushed onto the beach. Soldiers attempted to organize. Despite constant fire upon our positions from naval guns of all calibers and heavy machine gun fire, the waves of attackers broke against our defenses. The tide continued to rise, the unprotected stretch of beach became more narrow, and the surf brought a gruesome cargo to shore. In the swells wounded soldiers fought for their lives, the dead troops floated and tossed in the water, the waves dumping them on to shore.

". . .With rifles we continued to attempt to stop the onslaught. . .we continued to replenish our rifle ammunition from the belts of my machine gun.

". . .About mid-day, between 1200-1300 some comrades and I made our way to the upper command position. . .A half ration of bread and a mess-tin of milk offered a welcome respite. . .

"From the upper command position I once again had an overview of the entire beach from Colleville to Vierville. On the sea were even more large ships than observed earlier and between these ships and the beach was heavy traffic in boats of all descriptions. Also seen were burning and torn apart landing craft in the surf and on the beach. Dead and wounded lay everywhere, especially in front of WN 62. A tank was burning near the Steinbrecher, and numerous tanks were knocked out between WN 61 and 62. Weapons and equipment were seen in the tide. A large number of ships flew barrage balloons for protection against the aircraft, but they also made a good target for our artillery batteries behind the coastline.

"The landing troops had first captured those positions to the west and east of us which had suffered heaviest damage and casualties through air attacks and naval gunfire. From these captured positions they penetrated further inland, making it necessary for us to defend ourselves from attack from the hinterland. There came no supplies or reinforcements... The enemy continued to bring more troops. Our resistance became weaker. About mid-day two landing craft struck mines attached to the 'Rommel asparagus' anchored in the sea. Heavy explosions ripped through the boats, leaving only wrecks behind.

"The pressure from the assault troops on our flanks grew stronger. The first enemy soldiers penetrated our position, surprising us while we were concentrating on the landing craft on the beach."

Wounded, Gockel joined other wounded comrades. Crawling and running, he made his way toward Colleville-sur-Mer. At the outskirts of Colleville, he learned that Colleville had been taken by the Allies. With fifteen comrades and a captured American, they climbed aboard a transport truck and drove to St. Honorin.

"Ruins of bombed houses covered the streets. Dead cattle lay in the pastures and along the road. The supply units had also suffered their share of casualties, giving mute testimony to the deadly effects of the landing preparations."

When they found it impossible to proceed any further, they continued on foot; then requisitioned a horse and wagon from a French farmer in order to reach Bayeux and the field hospital.

"In Bayeux the field hospital had already been evacuated. With a truck we passed destroyed and burning vehicles on the way to an assembly point in Baleroy. This route ended at the entrance to the heavily damaged and still burning city of Vire. Almost the entire city had been destroyed by air attacks, and progress with the vehicle was once again impossible. We established quarters in a farmhouse at the edge of town, the inhabitants having fled the premises at the beginning of the bombardment. Food remained on the table, and we helped ourselves to bread, milk, butter and eggs. A cask of calvados was discovered, from which a few bottles were filled and taken with us.

"The following morning I attempted to find another route for our vehicle when suddenly on a side street I was confronted by a number of Frenchmen. I instantly feared that they would attempt to vent their wrath for the destruction on me, but their anger was directed otherwise. They encircle me and one of them in broken German asked about my wound and about the situation on the coast. Another pulled a dagger from under his shirt and muttered in French: Pour l'Américain (For the American). So great was the rage and disappointment for the destruction brought upon them. After receiving directions I was permitted to continue. I returned to the farmhouse in order to assemble those remaining wounded who could still walk, and we made our way on side streets toward the other side of town in hopes of finding further transport. Dead and wounded French civilians lay scattered on the streets and in the ruins."

With the help of French civilians, the group found another route.

"Completely exhausted we reached the next village. Despite the tragedy brought upon the population of Vire from the American Air attacks for which we were also responsible, the inhabitants who had lost belongings and homes, whose family members and friends lay under the rubble as victims of the American air attacks, offered us their few remaining portions of bread and apple wine.

"Not without incident we proceeded to Paris under cover of darkness. We reached the city several days later, only after our accompanying medical officer was shot by the resistance in a wooded area in which we had sought shelter from enemy aircraft. In the Achillea Melituria in Paris, transportation to Germany was assembled.

"On the 6th of June only three men had escaped unwounded from WN62. On 7 June these men were taken prisoner by the Americans. After being loaded onto landing craft on the beach of Colleville, they were transported to the USA by way of England.

"After suffering heavy losses our company was withdrawn from the front line and transferred to Perpignan on the Spanish border to be re-equipped and rebuilt. From there the company began a withdrawal. While taking many casualties, through the Rhone valley and the Vosges, ending the journey in Alsace.

"None of my comrades who had survived the invasion on the coast continued to believe in a victory.

"This overwhelming superiority in men and material could not be fought against.

". . .Many of our comrades lost their lives. Others still today carry the scars of this battle. Both sides fought fiercely in Normandy, each fighting for what they believed was a righteous cause. The many crosses in the war cemeteries in La Cambe on Omaha Beach and near Bayeux bear testimony to this bitter battle. For the French nation June 6, 1944 brought freedom." [134]

A Time to Speak

Juno Beach
(Courseulles, Bernirères)

Joseph G. Rouleau served in the Canadian Army. In a letter sent from his home in Englewood, Colorado, he enclosed his account of D-Day, "An Odyssey from Sherbrooke, Quebec, Canada, to the Normandy Beaches on June 6th, 1944 and beyond."

"*Landing on Juno Beach, we waded neck deep, holding our rifles above our heads.*

"*On D-Day we liberated the first town, Courseulles. I remember the most heroic action that day while house to house fighting still raging; a private running to the flag-pole lowering the enemy flag and hoisting the beautiful Canadian flag. On that first day we advanced about a mile inland, all day long while fighting was still going on the landing beaches. We picked up supplies and gasoline and transported same inland. It was the longest day. We did not rest for the next 24-36 hours. On D+two, on such a pick up, I saw Captain Eaton being hit by an enemy 88 artillery shell. I saw comrades of my unit blown to pieces with their explosive cargos, our cargo in large heavy duty trucks was for front line troops. Lion-sur-Mer was the next town liberated, flag procedure same, lowering the swastika, hoisting the Canadian flag. On D+3 or 4, we liberated Bény-sur-Mer. At D+7 or eight we liberated Fontaine-Henry. We moved inland as fast as humanly possible. We did have just one fear, the German Panzer divisions. If they break the Allied flanks, they may push us to the sea, a repeat of Dunkirk. The combined air forces of the Allies destroyed every bridge, junctions behind enemy lines. The strafing and bombing did continue day and night without any let up, rail lines and over passes and underpasses and river traffic destroyed too. . .*

"*More than two weeks elapsed before we had a hot meal or a change of clothing; the underwear, socks, uniforms we wore on D-Day landing were still covering our bodies. The communication system is being rebuilt by the Allies, in addition to our regular transporting supplies to the front line troops, we also stood guard duty. My unit was camped in an orchard. It has been raining for days without any let up, no tents or buildings so we slept under a truck. On such an occasion I was called for guard duty, while crawling out from under the truck, someone lowered the tail gate. It hit me on the head, made my helmet fly away. I needed medical attention and stitches, as a souvenir of that night I still have the scar on my head. The dispensary was in a large truck: M. S. and orderly on duty.*

"*I was involved in the capture of the Carpiquet Airfield. When we entered Caen, that beautiful city was a heap of rubble, only building was still standing: a cathedral.*

"On D+28 we liberated the Reichs Wald Forest. It was a wild game resort, a recreation area and a convalescent area. We captured many, many POWs. I recall trading a pack of cigarettes for a watch. All enemy flags lowered and the combined Allied flags hoisted - what a beautiful sight never to be forgotten in my memory.

"The combined Allied forces met at Falaise: the American and French off to liberate Paris; the British and Canadians to liberate Belgium and Holland and into the heartland of Germany.

"On V-E Day, May 7th, I was in Bremen."

Sword
(Ouistreham, Hermanville-sur-mer)

In the British sector, Horsa gliders crash-landed on the approaches to two strategic bridges: on the canal at Caen and over the river, Orne, marking the left flank of the Allied invasion force. Their mission was to unload men and equipment. British glider pilot, Jack Elford, participated in this operation.

Elford first volunteered for the RAF at the end of 1940 when Britain was running out of pilots because of losses during the Blitz. In 1941, the British decided to form an Airborne Division to train glider pilots for special operations. RAF pilots were asked to volunteer to become glider pilots.

"I said 'Yes.' Gliders were limited to what was called 'circuits and bumps,' take-offs and landings. That's all you were really bothered with. The rest of the time you were towed. I really enjoyed it immensely. I thought it was great. It was hard physical training. There was commando training, and you had to train as a weapons expert at the same time.

"I suppose about one-third of the total strength of the glider pilot regiment was involved in D-Day, or in various operations in D-Day. There were, in fact, three. The first operation was six gliders, two on each bridge over the Orne canal and Caen river. And it was remarkably successful, they all got there. You know, every landing was a crash landing because you landed obviously in a field. The fields were very small. You usually bashed through a couple of hedgerows on the way down.

"The second one which I was on was sort of a backup to land reinforcements which got down about three in the morning. And the main operation was on D-Day itself; the evening of D-Day, a considerable armada landed. Our orders were (we all carried letters, all of the ones on the night operations) from General Montgomery, saying, in effect, that every facility must be given the bearer to get back to the UK as soon as possible, which I thought was great. I was all for it. It wasn't the sort of place to stick around in. So we all had orders to make our way back to the beachhead as best we could. And we did this mostly in pairs, those who weren't hurt.

"I carried a jeep, an antitank gun and crew of eight, which was one of the configurations. The other one was a Horsa glider. The Horsa glider was not the biggest glider; it was excellent for the job it was supposed to do. And we landed. It wasn't much of a night really, there were clouds around. The targets weren't very well marked, there were a few flares. Most people got down, well anyway two-thirds got down without too much mishap, a little antiaircraft fire, not a great deal. It was mostly the fact that you were flying blind at night and you wondered what was underneath because although you had seen all sorts of pictures, photographs, and you knew the name of the commanding officer of the enemy unit which was in that area, what he was likely to do, how many men...the intelligence of the operation was amazing. There was some mortar fire on the landing zone which was near Ranville, I suppose about a mile from the canal. And there were some casualties, my friend was killed, or he died of wounds that night and I had a second pilot, whose name was Perkins (I can never remember his first name) and I really don't know what happened to him. I lost touch with him because we got split up after D-Day and formed different squadrons.

"You don't remember these things in sequence. You get these odd pictures: the mind remembers something you saw which might have impressed you at the time. Little things come back to me now. I just remembered something that I didn't mention. We all carried, and I think this was only true of the British, we all carried morphine because there were no medical facilities, there were no doctors dropped. We also carried all sorts of little gadgets, there were buttons. The British had a camouflage smock, much like the German paratroopers. You could use this for almost anything, umpteen packets of cigarettes. In one of the buttons was sown a compass. What else did we have? We had maps and we had French francs and nobody ever had a chance to spend anyway. In fact, I think we gave it away as we were leaving. They were very concerned when they saw us making toward the beach. They thought we were evacuating, so they were concerned. They suffered a lot. The bombardments were quite horrendous on the French in Normandy, on the farms.

"We went back together to the beachhead, we went to a little town, Ouistreham, where, by that time, the bombardments had started from the sea. And the Germans had evacuated. It wasn't a defensible spot, and we sat down on the pavement there outside a cafe. And the proprietor came out with a bottle of wine. I couldn't believe this, drinking wine when the first troops arrived and they said, 'What are you doing here?'

"We were told to meet at a rendezvous point and they would arrange to get us back somehow to England. And I got down to the beach, one of the main invasion beaches, Lion-sur-mer. The beach commander said, 'You can get aboard that.' The beach commander was a naval officer, and he said, 'OK, you can hop aboard that thing. It's got hulled a bit, but the pumps are working.' So we waded out to this landing craft.

"The beach was a mess, actually. They had bodies stacked up, a bit like cord wood, and as you went through this water, you saw a hand with a glove on it or something, and nothing else. So we waded out to this thing and climbed aboard. Whoever had been on this landing craft had left all of their rations behind so we had these cans of soup (I've never seen them since). And this they did for D-Day. Cans of soup with a filament around and you put a cigarette or a match to the filament and within about ten seconds, you had a can of hot soup. So we had all these cans of soup. It took about eighteen or nineteen hours to get back to England on this old landing craft which didn't make more than about three or four knots an hour, if that. And that was it." [135]

The Men of Commando Kieffer

A second mission on Sword Beach was given to a British-French Commando Unit, led by Philippe Kieffer. It arrived at 5 o'clock in the morning on 6 June in two landing crafts. Its task was to open Sword Beach and to take the seaside resort of Ouistreham, where the Casino had been converted into a blockhouse.

Among the Commandos were 177 Frenchmen, including the youngest member, 18-year old Gwenn Aël Bolloré. These French Commandos had the honor of being the first Frenchmen to set foot on French soil on D-Day.

Bolloré used the false name of Gwennaël Bollinger so that his family in Brittany would not be worried about him. At the age of seventeen, he escaped clandestinely and left for England in March, 1943 in a patched sailboat.

"There are a lot of motives for an escape to England. If you wish, there was the fact that in our country, there were soldiers in uniform who had us under constraints, who kept us from going out in the evening after a certain hour, who rationed you. We didn't have any butter, we didn't have anything to eat. All that is a motive. This is not the only one. There are other motives. There is the motive among the young who have a little drive and don't want to be apart from the events. Then there are the less glorious motives. I had a lot of friends who went to England to go to school. And finally, we think about a decision, we don't make it, it is imposed by all of the circumstances. Patriotism is a thing which comes out of its hole when it is needed."

On his arrival in London Bolloré discovered he was too young for the Army. He was convinced that the invasion would come soon and he could join the Navy.

He signed his enlistment in the Forces navales françaises libres (Free French Naval Force) for the duration of the war plus three months and joined the Bir-Hakeim barracks, located near Portsmouth. Ultimately, he trained as an apprentice nurse, but was frustrated by being far from the military action.

Toward the end of 1943, a group of soldiers came to the Bir-Hakeim barracks to train for the Commandos. Originally created in 1940, the Commandos consisted entirely of British soldiers sent on secret missions to prepare for the 1944 landing. Commander Kieffer had the idea to form a French force, integrated into the elite British Commando group. They would render valuable service because of their language expertise.

Bolloré was accepted and began his extensive training which was meant to eliminate the weakest.

"Nighttime maneuvers. It was necessary to cover, with a compass, the eighteen miles set up ahead of time. Then the next morning, after two or three hours sleep, be present on the parade grounds, closely shaved, brass polished, arms polished; and having left behind a clean room.

"Then the 'seven miles.' The group had to run that distance in less than an hour, with a pack on your back, weighing about sixty pounds, and carrying a rifle. It only took one time of missing the arrival to be eliminated."

After three months of this training, Bolloré and his friends were awarded the "green beret." The French formed two troops of seventy men each and were attached to Commando 4 under Colonel R. W. P. Dawson. "We were ready," Bolloré said.

"We reached early May 1944 and it became more and more evident that our easy life with our English hosts could scarcely be prolonged.

"For the June sixth invasion, there weren't any French. We were a French unit, the commando battalion which had been integrated into the English Commando Number 4, under the orders of Lord Lovat.

"The invasion began well before June sixth. We were confined to a camp and then they explained things halfway. We knew where because we had buddies who were local. The invasion began the evening of June fifth. There was still bad weather, there was storm two or three days before. They delayed the landing a little. I think most of the French soldiers were seasick.

"When we arrived, we stopped because it was night and there was no shore light or sound like there is today when you enter a port. We were obliged to wait until day to reach our objective. What is extraordinary is that a similar landing would not be possible today. Any little fisherman who fished five or six miles away from the shore would have seen the fleet of five or six thousand ships. And the Germans didn't see anything.

"On the 40th anniversary, I had occasion to discuss with a German colonel, the first one to see the fleet at daybreak, and he was flabbergasted because it wasn't a single boat - you could have walked from one boat to another. I think he exaggerated. It was very impressive. Exaggeration or not, it is true that the Germans expected the invasion to take place at the Pas de Calais. Hadn't the Allies planted their deceptive forces in Kent just opposite the Pas de Calais?

"The boat stopped, and when it was daylight, we could see the coast of France, and, for a short time, we were moved; then there was silence.

"There was a storm, waves against the shore. There was no artillery, and when the Germans saw us, they fired on us. The warships that we had with us fired back. Then we disembarked, and from that moment on, we didn't think of anything, except we thought about our jobs. We had learned to do our jobs, just like any worker.

"I'm not talking about the ridiculous films which show men who knelt to kiss the soil [of France]. No, I think the only moment was when we remained motionless in the hush and silence before the landing. I can't tell you how long it lasted, it didn't last hours. But afterwards, we did our job. We tried to do it.

"I should explain. Before I was a commando, I was a medical orderly in the Navy. When we lacked an orderly, they asked me to replace him. I agreed. June sixth, my medical chief was killed, the quarter's chief was wounded and evacuated, and I found myself alone at the head of the medical service of the Commando. Impossible to evacuate toward the English because their doctor was also killed. This was the context of the most dramatic experience.

"It was in front of the Casino at Ouistreham, about noon. I was alerted to go into a house that was cut in two; destroyed by a bomb. At the rear, there was a comrade who had probably received a mortar shell in this right shoulder and he had a hole from his collarbone to his hips, and you could see his heart beat and his lungs breathe. He wasn't dead, he had his eyes open, and he tried to talk. That was something that can never leave you. There are lots of other examples, but I think this one is the most characteristic.

"You know, there is always the question, from what point of view you look at the problem. For example, in France, they are persuaded that the landing was the turning point of the war. It is true in a sense, but I think in all of the conflict, what interested the Americans was the Pacific, and the landing in France, and the war in Europe was secondary, and we [the French] don't recognize that.

"It was already the second war; there was the war of 1914-1918. From my point of view, there is only one world war, which began in 1914-1918 and ended in 1945. During the fifteen years that war ended, and it was very short, it was the same protagonists and the same war." [136]

In spite of the enormous casualties and losses, Operation Overlord was a success. But the battle for Normandy and the rest of Europe was just beginning, and the war on other fronts accelerated.

End Notes

129	Chapman is a former American diplomat and is an Associate in the international consulting firm, Global Business Access.
130	Teague volunteers his time to Habitat for Humanity in Lafayette, Colorado.
131	After the war, Look returned to Masschusetts and after a few years, he moved his shop to Colorado.
132	*Victor*, pp 101-103; pp. 105-106. Dossogne, Victor, S.J., *Victor*, privately published by friends and colleagues. Fr. Dossogne died March 16, 1995.
133	Walker was in the music profession at Butler University. When arthritis forced him to give up playing the cello, he turned to writing music.
134	Gockel was in the hospital in Neheim, a small town in the Sauerland. After being released, he went into American captivity north of St. Die on the Meurthe on 20 November 1944 and returned after the war to Hamm-Rhynern to the family roofing business, Gockel Dachdeckermeister.
135	Elford stayed in England for four years then immigrated to the United States and found a career in aviation. He retired in 1982 as sales manager for British Airways.
136	After the war, Bolloré returned to Brittany and worked for thirty-five years in the family paper business. He also created the Musée Océangraphique de l'Odet.

CHAPTER 35

WAR IN THE AIR: DESTRUCTION ON THE GROUND

More than in any previous war, bombing raids played a crucial role in the Allies' success in World War II. Bombing by British and American planes continued over northern France to weaken the German military as the Allied armies moved west. Targets also included German cities in an effort to destroy German factories and to demoralize the enemy civilian population. Later, Tokyo also became a target for American bombers in the war in the Pacific. The Germans launched their pilotless aircraft, the V-1 flying bomb.

Whether the Germans or the Allies did the bombing, whether citizens were injured or not, recollections of watching bombs fall and experiencing a bomb raid left powerful memories. For city workers, the alerts were an inconvenience. They had to go down into the subways and often spent an entire day below ground. Most people talked about the spectacle of bombardments: the showers of fire, the smells, the fear, and the impression "of night turned into day." So strong are their memories of the bombings, as one man said, "When I took our children to the fireworks [on Bastille Day], I always saw Lorient and Brest. It is haunting."

Brest and Lorient

Two of the major bombing targets were the large ports of Lorient and Brest. With the fall of France, Lorient had become the principal German submarine base and Brest was a heavily fortified port for German U-boats and also provided a haven for naval repairs. The Germans' strategy had been to make Brest and Lorient impregnable bases to protect the Atlantic coast.

Jean Cotten, a student in Plougastel, was close enough to see the bombs fall on Brest.

"*We spent entire nights when the bombs were falling. In July and August 1944, just before the fall of the city of Brest, the bombings intensified and there were thousands and thousands of planes that bombarded the city of Brest. You saw Brest on fire, night and day, several days, maybe several weeks.*

"*At the time the planes passed over to bomb Brest, it lightened the sky, there was a lot of noise from the cannons shooting at the planes. Another time there was a beautiful spectacle, a dogfight between planes. The English fighter planes* who came directly from England to machine-gun the German munitions depots; they came quickly and then went back. I remember harvest in 1944, one day I saw the fighter planes after they bombarded one of the railroad stations and razed it to the ground. They were so close to the ground that I fell flat in the field, scared. I thought they would fall on me.

"When Plougastel was liberated, my aunt returned to her house and she found it had been burned. I still remember her crying and saying, 'Oh my mementos, not the house, but the keepsakes.'"

Lorient was another target of bombings by the Allies. Mme Marguerite Dravalen, a former teacher, lived near Lorient, not far form the zone of the German submarine base.

"There were bombings from the beginning by the English to keep the Germans from taking Lorient. Every morning when we woke up there were houses burnt. The English dropped a lot of incendiary bombs. We spent the night in the basement as soon as we heard the alerts, we went down. I didn't sleep. That went on for a year.

"It took a quarter of an hour to take a simple route to cross the road because of the debris. It was very hard. People don't like the English. I don't like the English. They left things a blazing mass for days and days. They demolished the entire city.

"There wasn't anyone left in Lorient; there was nothing left standing; the streets were nothing but fields. It was razed. The Germans destroyed everything before they left. My worse souvenir of the war was my parents' burned-out house.

"We accepted life as it was then. I could not relive the war. One can't forget the war, it is not possible to forget." [137]

Saint-Lo

To get to the port of Cherbourg as quickly as possible and to move inland south and east, the bombing of strategic cities in Normandy was considered necessary. By the morning of 7 June, the city of Saint-Lô was practically wiped off the map. With bombs falling, houses and buildings were destroyed, and the entire city became a gigantic blazing mass. Inhabitants of Saint-Lô refer to these days as the "Apocalypse."

Jean-Pierre Crouzeau lived in Saint-Lô. His father, René, a postal inspector, was a member of the P. T. T. Resistance group involved in receiving arms which were to be used to divert the German troops away from the Allied troops on D-Day.

"At the end of the morning [6 June], *the planes were more numerous, the* first bombardments were not at Saint-Lô but in the direction of Coutances, at the electrical transformer which cut off the electricity. In the afternoon, the planes came back and bombed the railroad station again.

"At 7 p.m. we hurried to our perch to listen to the first BBC announcement, 'This morning the landing began on the Normandy coast.' Then we heard a noise and we saw a huge formation of bombers. My sister said, 'Oh, look here, they are dropping bombs.' No, they weren't bombs, they were tracts, but having said that, we were in the dark. [These tracts contained a "Message Urgent," to the inhabitants of a village from the Supreme Commandment of the Allied Expeditionary Forces. They warned of air attacks on vital transportation and communication centers and urged families to leave the danger zones and seek shelter in the country, but not to encumber the roads.]

"Bombs fell in front of the house, another one in the courtyard, demolishing the wall. I was under the table because there were no windows left. I said I would be better protected there. The French windows were gone. My sister began to scream. I put my hand on my head and felt blood running down.

"Janine, a neighbor about my age, arrived and gave me a handkerchief to swab my head. We couldn't stay in the house. Where could we go? I lost my shoes. There was a pharmacist nearby and he was also in a catastrophic state. He said he couldn't do anything; we should go find a doctor. Where? at the hospital? It was hit, there was no one at the hospital. Find another doctor?

"No place to go, we finally settled in a doctor's office. Suddenly a noise, a frightening drone, it was terrible, it descended, descended, the windows were blown out. We couldn't breathe because of the stinking odor. The dust prevented us from breathing. We couldn't stay there. We would die inside. The house was going to crumble. We felt the one next door fall. It was burning, burning, burning everywhere.

"Then about 12:30 at night, there was a pause. The first wave had passed. We waited for the second. We couldn't stay there. The doctor said, 'Do as I'm going to do, take the route to Bayeux. Get away!'

"We left toward Bayeux, my mother taking each of us by the arm. People had to escape. We went three or four meters and arrived in a worker's garden. Another wave of bombers arrived and dropped bombs. There were flames everywhere and we stayed under an apple tree. I remember we took a bottle of Calvados with us to raise our spirits.

"At daybreak, we couldn't stay there so we started off again for Bayeux. We spent two hours and the bombardments continued. We went to a friend's farm where we were welcomed. We weren't the only ones. There were about fifty people who arrived from various places. I remember I saw my gym teacher arrive.

"We stayed there several days, maybe ten or fifteen days. It was at this same time that my father came to find us. And my mother said, 'Good, now that the sabotage is finished, I hope that you will stay with us.' He answered, 'No, I can't stay, I won't abandon my comrades.' He left, and I never saw him again. [René Crouzeau and ten resistants were picked up by the Germans on 14 June, interrogated, then shot in a field in Beaucoudray.] Every year on 15 June, Jean-Pierre Crouzeau holds a memorial service at Beaucoudray in honor of these resistance members.

"With our house burned, it was useless to go back to Saint-Lô. A neighbor friend went to our house and told us that it was burned out. He brought back a rabbit that was in its hut. We kept it for a long time, a long time....."

Crouzeau, when asked if the American bombs dropped on Saint-Lô made him anti-American, responded, "What a strange question!" Then after thinking about it, he answered, "No, because the same thing was happening to German cities and it was all part of war." But he remembered seeing posters put up by the Germans reminding the French that it was their "friends" who were responsible for the damage to their cities.

Saint-Lô was not the only city in Normandy destroyed; even cities with no military significance were 75 percent destroyed: Lisieux, Valognes, Coutances, Falaise, Villers-Bocage, Isigny and Martain.

Dresden

The objective of the fire bombing of Dresden was to delay German troop reinforcements, coming from Norway, Italy and Holland, to join the Eastern front around Breslau. Led by Air Chief Field Marshal Arthur Harris, 245 British bombers struck the railway marshalling yards of the city of Dresden on 13 February. Three and a half hours later, 529 more bombers hit the city. On 14 February, 450 American bombers took part in the raid and on 15 February, a second wave of 200 American bombers attacked the still burning city, creating more havoc. The city was leveled, and the fires that followed destroyed many of Dresden's historical and cultural landmarks, the 18th century Church of Our Lady, the 16th century Dresden Palace, and the Semper Opera. The death toll was tremendous; 135,000 deaths was the largest number of civilian casualties in a conventional bombing raid during World War II. A comparison of deaths in major raids: Hiroshima, 140,000; Dresden, 135,000; Nagasaki, 70,000; the London Blitz, 40,000. Many Germans see the firebombing of Dresden as a war crime.

A German woman who lived and worked in Dresden talked briefly about the devastating bombing of Dresden and her eventual escape.

"I was from Dresden and Dresden was the 'Florence of the Elbe.' Because it was such an international city, we felt there would be no need for air raid shelters, so we had no shelters. We lived during the war with no light; it was living in

the dark all of the time. In order to walk around, you held on to houses, and felt your way along. There were only slits of light in windows.

"I was called to work. I worked thirty-six hours in a chemical factory. In the evening I taught dance. People who had been working all day still came in the evening to take a course and they danced in the dark. I was not a Nazi, not a member of the Nazi party, but in order to teach dance, I had to be a member of the Dance Club. But after the war, when questions were asked about whether I had been a member of various Nazi organizations, I could answer 'no.' So I was cleared for work.

"During the war, in Dresden, there was no food, no freedom. Even when you had a week's vacation, they told you where to go. It was existing and not living.

"I was in my house when the bombs fell, and the city lit up, and you could see one part of the city. At that time, people heated with coal, so like the others, I took refuge in the coal cellar. When we walked out, all three of us, and went to the beautiful parks. There was one little moment of humor because we all looked at one another and we all had black faces from the soot. That was February 14.

"Dresden was bombed on February 14, Valentine's Day, 1945, only a few months before the war ended. There were no men, there were no factories, there were only women and children. Dresden was not a vital target. People consider it a war crime. I died there. I can still smell the smell of burned bodies. We carried champagne bottles in our pockets and wore masks against the stench. We had to put people in mass graves and shovel them in. What I and other people did was to dig with our hands to find friends.

"Many people took refuge in the catacombs in the churches. The monks had put in kegs of wine. People who hid in the catacombs, where there was some air space, lived on wine. Some of them stayed in the catacombs for four or five weeks, and when they came out, they were really just crazy. My mother was in the countryside, so she was safer.

"Later in April, on April 8, there was another bombing. We had deep flyers and we could see them and we hid in the gutter. We had rescued a feather pillow, so as we hid in the gutter, we put the pillow over our heads. The guardian angel was taking care of me.

"The people who fled the earlier bombing and were living on the river, women and children who were washing their clothes and bathing in the river, the planes just strafed all those people on the river.

"I was still searching for my best friend. When I was looking for my friend, I found a hand holding on to a briefcase. Everyone had a briefcase, at the bedside, in which you kept a bottle of water, your rations, some sort of sugar product that gave you energy and all of your documents.

"I never went back to Dresden but stayed in the suburbs until the Russians came. I still say, 'The Russians are coming, the Russians are coming,' and I used to say this to my children when there was some dire circumstance.

"The time between February and May was a time of great mental anguish. My sister and my friends would go looking for people who were missing. You would find basins full of bodies; there would be whole families in a basket. Then you would bring them to a mass burial.

"To get out, we used our bicycles. We left on May 8, 1945 and we left because the Russians were coming. Everyone was being raped, the Russians were the victors; they were often drunk and they regarded certain things as victor's spoils. I left, with a knapsack on my back, on my bicycle. The Russians were coming in one direction, the Americans in the other, near the Elbe River. We went west, then south to Bavaria. We slept in the woods. Soldiers would come along and they would throw bottles of cognac in the woods. So for a few days, we lived on cognac. Once we got some eggs from a farm and we cooked the eggs over a candle, so the eggs and cognac were our food until we could get to the American zone.

"When we got to no-man's-land, my sister, who had been head of a factory, had some connections. The only way we were going to be able to get into the American zone would be to bribe American soldiers. Because my sister had connections in the firm, and former clients, she was able to get some whiskey and she bribed the American soldiers with whisky and we were able to get out of no-man's-land.

"We went to Munich. My sister, relatively quickly, got a job in a steel factory and started collecting steel scraps. All I had to offer was teaching and school English. In Munich, it was very hard to find a job because I was a Protestant and Bavaria is Catholic. I was able to find a job in the police department which had both American and German counterparts, MPs. I acted as an interpreter. It was a horrible job. What would happen is that the MPs would pick up very bosomy girls, take them into the woods, bring them back and say they would have to be put in jail because they were under suspicion of venereal disease. I would talk to the girls, get their telephone numbers, promise to call their mothers. I would say, 'Don't worry, I can't get you any food because I don't have any food, but I will help you get out of here.'

"I had one meal a day which came from the Americans, and it was corned beef hash, green peas, and bread.

"I stayed with a friend. The friend would only let me stay a few days because I was a Protestant and the friend was Catholic. I met a Polish girl working in the police department, who decided she didn't want to work in the police department and she was going to find a job in the Military Government of Munich. The Polish friend got me a job, and we were in the Denazification Department which was to look through files and find out any dangerous or harmful people. That was not very satisfactory because many people who were really not Nazis, for example, professors, found themselves trapped because they had been forced to say, in order to teach, that they belonged to the Nazi party. They had to sign papers, making them members of the Nazi party.

"Eventually I was transferred to the Religion and Education Department and they helped me find an apartment. They had no prejudice against women or against Germans. I was an alien, I was a former enemy. I was put in charge of the clerks, although I didn't have to do any typing. I met an American girl, who became very friendly, who had a lovely southern name and was in charge of the American contingent. I knew I could not go back to Dresden, although I was very homesick.

"I met an American, a former army officer, who had volunteered to go to work in the Military Government. But there was no fraternization among Americans and Germans. When I left the building, I was searched. The law was changed in 1946 so we could speak to one another and could fraternize. One morning, I found an orange on my desk. I hadn't seen an orange for years, and I still love oranges. The officer, who got provisions from the American PX, had put the orange on my desk."

Doodle-Bugs in Great Britain

The Luftwaffe had not succeeded in bringing Great Britain to its knees during the Blitz. In 1944, during the final phase of bombing in Britain, the Germans introduced the pilotless aircraft, the V-1, the flying bomb, nicknamed in England, the "doodle-bug." It was named for the midget racing cars, called the "Doodle-Bug," introduced into England from America. The V-1 jet engine sounded like the noise of these cars. The roar of these bombs continued until they reached their target when it would stop. Then the bomb would dive silently to the ground.

Having survived the earlier bombings, the British took these bombings in stride, although not knowing where they would land increased the apprehension. Jean Powell, who was living on the coast at Eastbourne, remembered her family took precautions: *"When the 'doodle-bugs' and the rockets started, we then had a Morrison* [a metal table often used as an indoor shelter] *in the living room and we slept in this. It was big enough. I slept in first, then my mother, and my father was just on the outside so he could roll in, if there was an air raid or 'doodle-bug.' We did sleep in that for quite some time because the 'doodle bugs' were another thing. You heard those, but as soon as the noise stopped, help! You knew it was overhead somewhere, but you didn't know where it would come down.*

"I remember also seeing our aircraft turning them back, on the wing, overhead. We got quite blasé after while and used to go out and watch them. With the

'doodle-bug,' you could see the flame, then our aircraft were coming this way, and they used to tip this and send it back again, turn it round, so it came down in the sea instead of on land. They were very clever at doing that. I saw them do it several times over Eastbourne because that's where they were. I suppose they came from Beacon Hill, the aircraft station there."

Tokyo

Late in the war in the Pacific, Americans bombed Tokyo. Midori Johnson explained:

"Bombs in Tokyo started summertime of '44. The biggest bombing was March 10, 1945. The Americans began a new offensive against Japan. A firestorm bombing, more devastating than the bombing of Dresden, destroyed much of Tokyo. The official death toll, according to the Japanese was 130,000, almost the same number as were killed in Hiroshima.

"Fortunately, at that time, my house was not bombed. But it was a big thing. That was the time we saw the B-29 come. They had captured Saigon and they could come almost every day, but March 10, that was carpet bombing. It was night. I barely saw the B-29 dropping the incendiary bomb. The fire happened very close to our house, and my school was bombed, but not my house. Then my father was determined to evacuate, so I was not there when my house was actually bombed. That was a memorable night.

"There is a river running through Tokyo like there is in Paris. People thought it must be safe if they would flee to the river, which they did, but fire swept all over. The peoples' houses were small wooden houses, with paper inside. The walls and roofs were broken."

George Watts, who as a Marine, went to Tokyo as part of the Occupation Forces, confirmed the devastation he saw.

"All of Tokyo, when I flew over it, was orange, orange. And that's because all the buildings had burned down, big and little ones and tiles were orange. And the tiles went right to the ground. It was much worse than the atomic bomb, more vast, square miles after square miles just burned to the ground. And they burned them up in great fire storms, I don't know, thousands of civilians must have died."

Bomber and Fighter Pilots

American bomber pilots were aware of the risks that they might bomb civilians or their own troops. They also were fearful of being shot down and landing in enemy territory to be captured or killed. Nevertheless, they were also aware they had a job to do before returning safely to their base, with their equipment intact. They had to recognize the reality of war and the need to follow orders.

Howard Teague flew with the 392nd Bombardment Group pointed out:

A Time to Speak

"I led the bombing, when Patton broke through at Saint-Lô and did the bombing, and stayed up most of the night to make sure I knew the target. I had to get an absolute perfect picture of those to be sure I didn't sight on the wrong thing because our troops were close by. For months afterwards, I could still draw you some of the roads around Saint-Lô.

"They started you, usually about midnight or a little after midnight, on certain missions and they showed you all kinds of pictures of the area from different view points so that you fixed it in your mind what you were looking for — railroads, trees, forest, towns — and it was very important that you picked the target up from that mental image.

"Well, the Allies did bomb Saint-Lô. As you know, the Germans were out there, and they were well entrenched and had all the defensive positions in many hedgerows. It was extremely slow going for the American troops. If the city got bombed, it was a natural consequence of what was happening."

Bill Herren belonged to the 394th Bomb Group, the only group that was given the Croix de Guerre by the French during all of the missions over there.

"What was I thinking about when I was flying over a target? Thinking about getting home, mostly. After you fly combat for a while, you get a little bit used to it. You are never used to the fact that you are being shot at and are in danger, but fear is an emotion like all emotions. You can control it. And you did in one way or another.

"Of course, in the military you do what you have to do. Actually, prior to our move into France, when we were bombing in Germany, our targets were always military. We had marshalling yards, we had bridges, we were called bridge busters and we never, I can't ever recall bombing (with the possible exception, we bombed near Paris, the Renault factory which was being used to build military stuff). But other than that, I don't recall ever having bombed cities.

"In bombing Cologne, I think again we had a military target and, I think, if I'm not mistaken, that the bombing was very careful there, and that beautiful, beautiful old cathedral was never touched. And so, in spite of what they think of military people, we do have a certain amount of compassion."

Not only did they have compassion, but Bill Bower, who had been on the Doolittle Raid on Tokyo, actually questioned his superior officers on the necessity of bombing a town.

"So I called and I said, 'What on earth are you trying to do? That's just a tiny, little town with a church in the center of town (Marsala, Italy), marsala wine.' We'd seen it, we'd flown over the town and there wasn't anything there at all. I said, 'I think that is ridiculous, what are you trying to do?' Carpet bombing, we were to carpet this town. So about an hour later, I got a call back from General Doolittle and he said, 'Bill, I plan these things, you carry them out.' Click.

"So I didn't know what it was all about until a long time later. It was a reaction to Coventry. They did it to us and we had to strike back. We were trying to get the Italians to give up in Sicily before we had a big battle with them on the eastern end of Sicily. We were having a big race between Patton and Montgomery.

"So I went ahead and did it. Then a friend asked, 'Did you have any feelings after these missions about killing people, women and children?' I said, 'No recollection of it, no recollection whatsoever.' I completely blanked that out of my mind. I never thought about killing anybody. We were immune to that as aviators. We went over and dropped our bombs, came back home, and we had no idea what happened except that we hit the bridge, or hit this, or that, and it didn't make any difference what it did to anybody. I don't ever remember having any reaction to it, other than the fact that I told General Doolittle and the fellows that it was silly, it [Marsala] was no military target.

"Coventry was military in the sense that it was to break the will of the people. That is part of the military action, to break the will of the people, and we did it from then on. War is war. But the whole human reaction to war, once you are committed to it, is totality, and I think that was the day that I decided that war was to do what we had to do, keep marching on. But before that I don't recall that I had any reaction because the war we fought before we went to Italy was not people."

Robert Cherry was a pilot on a P-47, in the 56th Fighter Group, as a fighter escort on bombing raids over Germany, his most exciting mission was the 8 March 1944 bombing raid on Berlin.

"We tangled with a horrendous number of FW-190s and the initial assault there was just one squadron of us, even though we had the two groups up. We lost a bunch. It was four pilots; that's a pretty big loss. That was also the day I got my first confirmed victory.

"We did get confirmed 29 victories that day, which was a new record for one outfit in one day. That was a pretty memorable mission. They lost about 62 bombers or something."

"Survival. Well, you do your job. I know I've read the books that say you think about flag and country and all this, and your family. Maybe some people thought that way, but I didn't. I thought strictly of survival. You've got to win, period! The loser does not go home. Yeah, they could bail out — we had people who bailed out, and we never heard from them again." Cherry spends his winters in Denver, his summers in Pitkin, Colorado, where he and his wife run a pottery and gift shop.

Bombing attacks created the immediate trauma of losing possessions or loved ones and also the long-lasting memories which stayed in the subconsciousness. Even now those who watched or survived bombings have flashbacks to the war years.

End Notes

137   Lorient was liberated a year after Brest in May 1945. By then the city had to be completely rebuilt. Brest was not liberated by the Allies until September 1944. The port had been destroyed and the city reduced to rubble.

CHAPTER 36

INTELLIGENCE ACTIVITY

INTELLIGENCE ACTIVITY IN EUROPE

By May 1943, there was an Anglo-American agreement on the full exchange and distribution of Signals Intelligence. This included the German secret message system, Enigma; the Italian Navy code, C38m; and the Japanese Purple decrypts. They were brought into a standard form and the code name "Ultra" was adopted.

Individual and group reconnaissance provided still another means of acquiring vital information about enemy emplacements, and a means of sending deceptive information to the enemy.

Tactical Deceptive Troops

Colonel Clifford G. Simenson was a member of the 23rd Headquarters Special Troops, a group developed specifically for tactical deception. The unit operated over a large area, serving in France, Belgium, Holland, Luxembourg, and Germany. Simenson was Operations Officer for the Tactical Deceptive Troops.
Colonel Simenson explained that successful deception was based on three principles. First, you needed to determine what you wanted the enemy to believe and make that story plausible. Then you needed to implement the story by using the enemy's information gathering channels so that the enemy made up its own mind that the deception story was genuine. Lastly, you needed to consider the risk factors: What is the value if it is successful? What is the disadvantage if the deception is discovered?

Simenson, and six others flew to England in April 1944 and were joined by others in May and June, then they gradually moved into Normandy. "We did not have our full complement of Deception Forces until August (1944), it was put in piecemeal. At the end of the war, when we disbanded, we thought it would be forever classified, but they did declassify," he said.

As Allied troops moved inland from Normandy toward the east, the Deceptive Forces used rubber dummies, sonic machines, artillery flashes with rubber artillery guns to give the impression that a military gap was filled in with active forces.

"*Not all deceptive actions were successful. The first operation we had was* to move the 2nd Armored Division into line between our First Army and the British Second Army in Normandy. We were prepared with our deception forces to hold them in their bivouac area for six to eight hours while they moved up into line. It would give them that much grace period. We didn't do any good as far as deception went.

"Our second operation, we made four columns and went out and merely threw confusion into the whole thing. And one column came back with prisoners. It wasn't deception as much as it was adding to the confusion of the breakout in Normandy.

"In one operation we used the 6th Armored Division, which was available but which was unmarked and in hiding, so we put the 6th Armored Division initially in a big gap between the 3rd and 1st Armies. And until the 6th Army could physically arrive, the deception worked very well. There we used rubber dummies, rubber tanks which four men could pick up and turn around, trucks, sound machines, artillery pieces, spoof radios, command post signs, bumper markings, shoulder patches, any way we could to get a little information through to the Germans that the 6th Armored Division was physically in that presence. It did, it was a successful operation. When the real 6th Armored Division arrived, we were relieved. I don't think the Germans ever knew we [the deceptive force] existed.

"Before we went to Luxembourg, we had one rather interesting operation, a river crossing at Yucons, on the Meuse, where actual engineering equipment was poised for a river crossing. On the river crossing, we merely threatened the river crossing and built up the area. We bore artillery fire and did lose a lot of air where they punctured our rubber dummies. But the Germans moved in to defeat the phony river crossing and the 90th Division moved across the Meuse ten miles up the river and took the whole German division in the rear without losing a man. So that operation was successful.

"Unless you are like a cat, you are not going to survive. Time after time you hit the dirt. You never walk down the middle of the road." [138]

Chemical Warfare Reconnaissance

Reconnaissance work included secret experimentation in chemical warfare on the part of the Allies and covert searches for poisonous gas being used by Germans. Lieutenant Fraser Richards, a meteorologist, went in the Army as an enlisted man. In California he was offered the opportunity to go to chemical warfare school at the Edgewood Arsenal, Officer's Candidate School.

"And that was my entrance into chemical warfare. That was '42 or so. We went through that business, got transferred down to Texas, and were transferred over to France in the fall of '44. It was right after the summer of D-Day.

"While I was in chemical warfare, I worked covertly. We were working out about the different gasses and how we could deposit gasses at 40,000 feet over England and have them float into Germany. It was very confidential at the time. I ended up in Marseille with this chemical combat outfit. Basically, we kept track of all the poisonous gas throughout Europe, France, Germany. My job as a Second Lieutenant: we were combat outfitted, we were basically reconnaissance officers. I spent probably five or six months in a jeep, starting in October, November '44.

"We had to stay in Marseille and that was the time when they were still parachuting troops in there. One of the first exciting things I did, I had to go from Marseille on a French freight train with two Frenchmen, and I was camouflaged, dressed as a Frenchman (my French was not good, but I had a good accent). They did the talking, I didn't have to say much, but strapped to me was all of the information about poisonous gas locations. I took the train outside of Paris. From there, they transferred me, in this little car, through Belgium. And I took a ferry on up to Rotterdam and joined the Canadian Air Force with this information. This was just prior to the Bulge, and I didn't realize at the time that was what it was. The RAF wanted to know where they stood as far as gas was concerned in reference to the Allied front lines which was the Bulge. [December 1944 in the Ardennes.]

"It was interesting because the person that drove me from Paris up through Belgium was this young blonde prostitute, so I was totally camouflaged. Nobody stopped us at all. We got to Rotterdam and nothing would do, this was midnight, but to have a big party. So they (the RAF) poured me on the ferry the next day and I worked my way back slowly from Paris back to Marseille and never a word was said. No one knew where I was. To me that was fascinating.

"The Germans were reputed to be using poison gas. But on our side, we had enough mustard gas to drown every German in Europe.

"We were very versatile. We were all in jeeps, combat ready, worked in with the infantry, with the armored forces. We worked our way from Marseille all the way up through France, up to Worms, Germany which I'll never forget. And there we waited, 22 April. We had to wait for the Russians to cross the Rhine at which point, we moved on into Germany, then down into southern Germany.

"About that time we crossed the Rhine river and into Germany and down to Stuttgart. It was a mess. Everything was shattered, and again our job was, we hooked up with Patton's armored division, to be with them, to run the reconnaissance at any time, which means going out, looking, and seeing what we could smell. We'd get sniped at, shot at, and so all of a sudden we end up in Munich. We didn't find anything, but they [the Germans] were well aware that we were there which was part of it. I think that was important. We heard rumors they were using gas, but it was never verified. I think the fact that we had all of this equipment there and the capability was very much of a deterrent. And they hated us." [139]

The Helmsman Mission

Reconnaissance for the Allies was also carried out by members of the French Resistance. In July Allied troops were paralyzed during the battle of the hedgerows in Normandy and badly needed information about the rear guard German troops in order to plan for Operation Cobra [25 July 1944]. Without this ground information, the breakout from the Cherbourg peninsula would be hampered.

John Bereford Hayes, pseudonyme, "Eric," an officer in Churchill's Special Operations Executive (SOE) was given the task of recruiting volunteer French Resistance members to infiltrate German lines and to obtain precise information about troops and materials for General Omar N. Bradley.

Thirty-two volunteers left, each team choosing its own route through enemy lines. Twenty-six succeeded in crossing the German lines and reached the rendezvous point with the 8th Division of the American Army at St. Sauveur le Viconte, west of Sainte-Mère-Eglise. With a map spread in front of them, they provided precise information about the weakness of the poorly equipped German rear-guard, their lack of trucks and the nonexistence of fortifications, except along the coast.

The information supplied to American troops by the line-crossers was invaluable in planning the line of defense for Operation Cobra. So successful was the mission that subsequent missions of this type were known by the name "Helmsman." [140]

INTELLIGENCE OPERATIONS IN THE SOUTH PACIFIC

Communication between troops fighting on the islands in the South Pacific relied on radio communication and the use of the Morse code and specially designed codes for transmission of information.

Philippine Islands

In preparation for reconquering the Philippine Islands, American forces in the South Pacific began to bomb Japan's defenses on Leyte. On 20 October 1944, they landed on two separate beachheads on Leyte, near the town of Tacloban. The island of Luzon was invaded a week later; General MacArthur had returned to the Philippines.

Before he landed in the Philippines, MacArthur began a campaign to maintain communications with the guerrillas left in the Philippines and to intensify a propaganda campaign, known as "I shall return."

Stanley Hendrickson went into the Army in 1943 at Fort Carson, Colorado as an enlisted man, then was assigned to a group for six months of weather training in Grand Rapids, Michigan, learning how to do pie-balls and to work with a satellite. He wanted to be more active and noticed a bulletin board posting, "For hazardous duty in a tropical climate." Hendrickson signed up for it. He was sent to Kearns Field in Utah for a rigid training program to learn demolition, combat, and field situations, then was sent overseas to Port Moresby (New Guinea). Finally, he was attached to MacArthur's headquarters.

"MacArthur's headquarters really was on a major theme of 'I shall return.' He was very much aware of the communications between people who were still there and part of MacArthur's entourage. He wanted to keep communications going some way, somehow. His 'I shall return' theme was supposed to be prefaced by people like me going into the islands and reestablishing contact with the Filipino people; and, more specifically, with certain people.

"MacArthur had his 'druthers' about how to do this; he had created this group which I was in. Before we went in we became part of the Allied Intelligence Bureau. They assigned us, it was a worldwide unit, but what my official capacity was, I was on detached service from the Air Force to MacArthur's headquarters and, at that point, I joined the Allied Intelligence Bureau.

"Radio work. It was important. It was the only communication between the islands and MacArthur's headquarters for us. And to get radios to the right people. We took in several radios and got them out to the different guerrilla groups we hoped. I know we lost one; two guys were drowned when they took it across the river. That was extremely important to that whole scenario, communication within the islands. It was our life blood, it was our only contact, very extensive. It was a network of communication that was pretty sophisticated for its day. Most people don't know what the Morse code is. It was an essential ingredient in that whole war.

"Our radio station was U 2, 'didida, didida, didida, da, da,' Morse code. And I can remember it was so easily detectable. There are a million stations that all come on the radio. Every bit of dial, you'd get a new station and static. The radio transmission in the South Pacific was very antiquated. It wasn't updated. To keep our radio, it was the battery we had to charge.

"I had my own code book; it's a onetime code book, where there is no system to it, it is a random code book. I can't even remember how it works, it was a little tissue paper notebook. You use one message. You write your message underneath the letters and then they would radio in the letters that the message corresponded with and then they would type that off. And that would be our message, then they would throw that tissue paper away. There was no way it could be broken; there was no rhyme or reason to it; there was no system; it was just a onetime deal. That's what we sent our messages with. We could voice message, we had a difficult time with Jap search patrols. They had a very antiquated method of vectoring, of finding where you are. It was difficult for them because their equipment wasn't so sophisticated to vector on radio signals, but voice, they could vector easily. So we couldn't use any voice at all, any place; we did it a couple of times just before we'd leave a camp, before we'd move. We only did it a couple of times because it was so dangerous; they could find out where you were."

Hendrickson left Darwin and went, by submarine, to the Philippine Islands. His special mission was to meet a small guerrilla group. He recalled they carried twenty-two tons of supplies: guns, ammunition, bombs, dynamite, 2 or 3 million dollars in money, half in American currency and half in Filipino currency, which was to be distributed to certain elements in the Philippines, people who had stayed behind and were friendly to the United States. After fourteen days in cramped space, he and ten Filipinos arrived on the island of Luzon.

"We got to the island of Luzon, the town of Baler. My primary mission was to go into this area, join a guerrilla force, and report weather every four hours back to MacArthur's headquarters and any coast watcher. We had extensive training in coast watching, the configuration of ships, American ships and Japanese ships, and aircraft of all kinds. We had quite thorough training in that so we could report any troop movements.

"There was a commander. He went in with us. The first night, when we got onto the surface, he got into a small boat alone. They had signaled from shore. We were a long way offshore, a couple of miles offshore. He went in alone. He had been in the Philippine Islands and he had escaped. He had gone from within MacArthur's group and had gone to Australia. He spoke Tagalog, a tremendous person. He got in that damn boat and paddled alone into shore. The next night he came out and met us and how he ever got us in that dark, I'll never know. They flashed lights.

"I was in the conning tower and I had a walkie-talkie and he had one. We couldn't see, the only way you could see was to flash a light. And of course, nobody wanted to do that, but you really had to. So he flashed a light and I started talking to him on the walkie-talkie. He was 'farm-house' and I was 'barn-yard' and I said, 'Hello barn-house, this is farm-yard.' I got them mixed up and I was nervous as heck. I'd never been in a conning tower before and I tried to get this guy out there who was all alone. Finally, he came back and said, 'The coast is clear, there are no Japs within four or five miles.'

"We unloaded, we pulled our rubber rafts up on top of the submarine, midnight, pitch black and you couldn't see anything, it was overcast. We got the boats in the water. This large submarine, 300 feet is very stable in the water, it didn't move with the swells. The swells were about eight or ten feet high and getting ten rubber boats into the water off that submarine was no fun task. It took us several hours, about 3 a.m. in the morning, we finally got everything loaded. After the captain yelled out, 'Get your ass in gear and hurry up' because he was worried. So they were throwing stuff in the water because we couldn't get it in the boats fast enough. Of course, everything was designed to float, cans were all weighed out. We finally got all of the stuff and started toward the shore.

"And we landed at the beach and pulled in all the boats and just worked like dogs for twenty-four hours to get everything in and the boats out of sight. We hid this in the jungle. It is on the east side of Luzon, all jungle and mountain territory. It was not difficult at all hiding in the jungle. I met a guerrilla leader there who was an American who had escaped from the 'Death March' and he had hid out in these hills all this time and had got together a group of ex-Filipino soldiers and created this nucleus guerrilla band. And the headquarters knew that he was there by reason of a radio contact they had established with the other side of the island. By courier, they had gotten word in that Anderson had created one at Dibut Bay and that's where I went in to meet his group.

"So that was all there was to it. I worked there for a couple of months. I developed a kind of network. When I got there, I had purposefully taken four sets of complete weather instruments. What I did when I first got there, there were two Filipinos who were part of the Philippine elite army, I can't even think who they were, they were young kids, smarter than a whip, talked beautiful English. I trained them in weather operation. I couldn't move freely, so I trained these two guys and they picked it up in a hurry and they went and reported weather from the mountains overlooking Manila for about six months before they came back.

"Bob Ball came to camp one day, just a tremendous guy and told his story. I was so impressed with what he had done and we became very close friends. He was ordered to go over to the island of Polillo. He radioed in and asked if I could go with him. I was there at Dingalan, I was sending stuff out of Dingalan Bay and he was ordered to go over to Polillo to check out some Japanese installations. Radioed back that Hendrickson could go along.

"Then after Polillo, we were ordered back up to Dibut Bay to the town of Baler and we were to establish some place in the mountains of Baler so we could establish a camp right next to the town. There was a garrison here of about 500 Jap soldiers.

"And the Americans landed up here at Lingayen Gulf in January or February of '45, and all during that time, I was over there between Dingalan and Polillo. One of the interesting aspects we ran into; we found several flyers who were shot down and this process was interesting in itself. We had picked up probably six or seven who found their way into our camp. Some of them were sane and rational and some were insane and irrational because they had been in the jungle. One of our missions was to pick these guys up and put them back on a submarine. So during the course of all this time, six months or so between the time I got there and the time

I left, we had met probably six or seven submarines at night taking guys out at night and putting them on submarines. There were two instances when we had taken civilians, American civilians who had found their way into our camp and put them on submarines.

"I can remember my birthday on the seventeenth of January and we didn't have any food. Finding food in the jungle was almost impossible. You had to barter. Rancid rice was really the menu. On my birthday, we didn't have anything. I hadn't eaten for a couple of days. And we were hiking up to Baler Bay. One of the guys said, 'We've got to have something to eat.' He climbed a palm tree and cut out the heart of the palm which is called 'ubud' which was raw, very tender and very tasty, very good, tastes like coconut. There is the soft pith of the palm flower. That's what I had for my birthday dinner. They also make that palm into a very strong drink; it's really strong. I can't remember what it was called, but boy it was strong, almost one-hundred-proof.

"There were many occasions we would run into Japanese on the trails. They always had scouting parties out; hide out in the jungle and they would walk by, twenty feet away from you, they are really mind-boggling situations. Bob and I were swimming naked on this black sand beach, which was stupid, but we had been hiking all day, and we wanted to take a dip in the water. It turned out as we got out of the water, a Jap Zero came down about fifty feet off the water. And here we were, out there, on this black sand beach and we were right on the edge of the water. It came right over the hill; it swooped down on us and curled back up and made another pass; and while he was doing that, we just 'ran like sixty' for the jungle. It was kind of comical because we were both stark naked. And there were Filipino people around laughing at us. They didn't shoot or anything. We just had a lot of encounters like that. You were just on your edge all the time.

"One of the interesting things was the relationship with the Filipino people. 'Tense' is probably the best word to describe it. 'Mistrust' was another one. You didn't know who you were talking to. I slept in a hammock every night with my gun on because I never knew when I was going to need it. And many times I've awakened with my gun in my hand because I heard something. There were loyal Filipinos and there were disloyal Filipinos and you, of course, you never knew, without being able to speak the language. I couldn't communicate except through somebody else who spoke both languages. And the Filipinos always had a way to protect themselves.

"The Americans were well-received and so glad to get back and 'We're going to do this.' But there was just a general undertone of mistrust that seeped into this whole relationship which was difficult. I had met several other guerrilla leaders who had come in to get supplies; when we had met submarines, we had taken off supplies and the guerrilla leaders, through the grapevine, would come over, thirty or forty bearers, and they would haul off the stuff. And I got to meet several of them - inhuman people. The control element is so - the network didn't work; it wasn't cohesive at all, these were guerrilla bands and the Americans led these. They would fight each other.

"This was a very discouraging thing for me. This is one thing I never did comprehend or understand and came away with a great deal of resentment about the Filipino people and about some Americans because they weren't all nice guys. They were not all heroes; they murdered at the drop of a hat. If a Filipino would not do something, they would kill him. Those kinds of stories were just so prevalent and you never hear about those kinds of things. War brings out the worst most of the time.

"There was, this whole tone of mistrust and resentment. I can think of an incident where I was in my nepa hut [hut on stilts made from the large pinnate leaves of the nepa palm tree] and I was about to send out some radio message, and here come three or four Filipinos and an old lady and brought me this big bunch of bananas that was really something. I remember those big old green stalks and I thought, 'Oh, boy that's going to last me for a week.' They were all very nice and everything. The next day they all showed up again, walked over and took my bananas and walked out. They had gotten the wrong guy; they given them to the wrong guy. But for some strange reason, I remember something like that. That epitomized the whole attitude and atmosphere.

"I took in all this money; I had it in tin cans, my whole thing was to give it to Anderson who was head. He was a major and I was an enlisted man. I resented this because he ate and I didn't. He took all the food and I didn't get any. This was the kind of mentality that these guys who were head of these units had. They were very protective and they were very rigid about the people around them, the way they treated them, the soldiers around them. They really toed the line. And if they didn't, they'd disappear, bingo.

"That was one of the difficult things. Every day you woke up wondering if the Japs had got your radio message, and some Filipino would run in saying, 'Search party,' and we'd all run from camp into the bushes and wait until the 'All clear' sounded. The Filipinos were really pretty good about that. They were protective of us on the one hand, and on the other hand, they had their bad ones.

"Living in that, having that background, let alone having to fight the Japs. The Japanese war was subordinated to survival in those mountains, food, healthwise and with the other Filipino groups, you just never knew. And I just saw things happen that shouldn't have happened, that's all.

"It's questionable whether the guerrilla groups were important to prepare

A Time to Speak

the way for MacArthur's return. He may have made a mistake there. He relied too much on their allegiance; there was a lot of collaboration with the Japs. On the overall, I doubt very much that strategically, war-wise, it helped. The strategy of encouraging the Filipino people by sending in 'I shall return' gum, candy and stuff with labels; try to give the stuff out to the Filipino people and they wouldn't take it. They didn't want to be caught with 'I shall return' stuff. I know a lot of it sat there and rotted, or they would eat it and bury the papers."

On a mission to check out a Japanese garrison, Hendrickson and his friend, Bob, found they were out of gasoline. They saw a Japanese supply truck going by and went after it. The Japanese soldiers scattered, but a bullet went through Hendrickson's neck as he ran across the road to the supply truck. The bullet pierced the right laryngeal nerve and destroyed his voice box and his right arm was paralyzed. He was evacuated over the hills by Filipino soldiers, then flown to a field hospital in Lingayen Gulf, then to Leyte. He was sent home to a nerve hospital in Walla, Washington, where the doctors advised lots of therapy. He was discharged in September 1945, married in October 1945 and finished his studies at the University of Colorado.

The Navajo Code Talkers

Unable to send voice messages for fear they would be picked up by Japanese patrols, the Marine Corps needed another way to send coded messages. The Marine Corps established the Navajo Code Talker Program in 1942. It came from a recommendation by Philip Johnston, who had been raised on a Navajo Reservation, to Major General Clayton B. Vogel. The rationale was that because Navajo is an unwritten language and its vowel tones rise and fall, changing the meaning with pitch, and contains complex glottal sounds, it is almost impossible for a non-Navajo to master it. It is only intelligible to another Navajo.

The first group of recruits underwent basic boot camp training at the Marine Corps Recruit Depot, San Diego, then were assigned to the Field Signal Battalion, Training Center, Camp Pendleton. John Benally, one of the original twenty-nine recruits in Platoon 382, stated that the twenty-nine men developed the actual code. "We all contributed to the code."

The Navajos devised a system which substituted clan names for military troops and gave names of birds and fish for airplanes and ships; for example, "jaysho" (buzzard) for bomber. They also used a multiple alphabet when it was necessary to spell out proper names. For example, there were three words for each letter of the alphabet, they would use one word for the first E in a work, then another Navajo word for the second E, and another for the third E. It was really a code within a code.[141]

James Nahkai, Jr., llth Marines of the First Marine Division, an artillery regiment in Headquarters and Service Battalion of the regiment, explained that it took two or three months to go through Code Talkers' school, a lot of classroom work to get the words and the alphabet transposed. It was all memorization, with nothing written on a piece of paper. This was followed by field work with the radio, the TEX, a small hand generated radio. Overseas they used a smaller walkie-talkie size radio, the SER300, which they had on their back, with batteries. [142]

The importance and value of the Code Talkers was best expressed by Dan Akee, in the Fourth Marine Division. In Saipan with shells coming through, Akee described how they used the code.

"And one time we, somehow we got into a mistake with our platoon there and we went too far beyond the enemy line there. And we were getting shelled from our own artillery, and from the other side we're, we're being machine gunned by the enemy. Right there they told me to send this message, you know, and quick. And I did. And I think it was worth the lives to choose this, Code Talker, instead of being a paratrooper [his original choice]. *Because there are so many people are saved because of this, very secret message would have easily been intercepted by the Japanese. Now, afterward, I think about this, how important it was the Navajo used communication at same time. It saved so many people, you know, because otherwise they were intercepted by the Japanese. Look how, just how many people would have been dead, you know. This was because the Japanese don't understand, they were all confused and we, they can't locate us, and our own men can be located what's going on, you know. Afterward everybody really realized that how important the Navajo was, you know. So we was very, we were protected very good by them."* [143]

The Navajo Code Talkers served and transmitted messages for the campaigns on Guadalcanal, Bougainville, Tarawa, Peleliu, Saipan, Iwo Jima, and Okinawa.

From July to October 1944, intense military battles took place in the islands of the South Pacific in the struggle to reach Japan and on the Continent in the campaign to move east toward Berlin.

End Notes

138 Colonel Simenson was back in Germany as an attaché and returned to the United States in 1947.
139 Richards returned to St. Paul and went into the family clothing business. He moved to Jackson Hole in 1956 and owned a Ford dealership, then moved to Denver.
140 The official record of this mission by Resistance members is found in the Archives nationales, Paris, Code 72 AJ 2009.
141 Information from interviews with John Benally, Jimmy King, Sr., Window Rock, Arizona, July 9-10, 1971 (MS. 504, Navajo Code Talkers, Manuscripts Division, J. Willard Marriott Library, University of Utah, Salt Lake City, Utah
142 Excerpt from interview, July 15, 1971, MS 417, Doris Duke Number 1162, Manuscripts Division, J. Willard Marriott Library, University of Utah, Salt Lake City, Utah
143 Information from interview, July 15, 1971, MS 417, Doris Duke Number 1159, Manuscripts Division, J. Willard Marriott Library, University of Utah, Salt Lake City, Utah

CHAPTER 37

ON THE WAY TO JAPAN

The excitement of the D-Day landing didn't overshadow the goals of the American troops to reconquer lost territory in the South Pacific and reach Japan. But at each island, Americans faced determined Japanese troops who refused to surrender. The military learned from the experience of taking Tarawa in November 1943 that the Japanese defense consisted of networks of dugouts with machine-gun nests, hazardous coral reefs, and tenacious Japanese troops. At the end of three days fighting, there were 1,000 Americans killed and 90 out of the 125 amtracs (amphibious tractors) were lost. On the enemy side, only one Japanese officer and sixteen men and 129 Korean laborers were still alive.[144] The Americans ultimately succeeded in capturing Saipan, Tinian, and Peleliu, but at a terrible price in men and weapons.

Saipan

Joe Malcolm, a retired Marine colonel, enlisted in the Marine Corps as a private. He joined a unit at Camp Pendleton and trained about six hours in amtracs and went overseas.

A few days after the D-Day landings in Normandy, Marines went into Saipan Island. During the three week battle, 20,000 Japanese were killed and 3,426 Americans were killed.[145] Later, 7,000 Japanese committed suicide, a further testament to their fanaticism in battle.

Malcolm's unit encountered Japanese troops and their expertise and doggedness in jungle fighting.

"Our first thing was the island of Saipan which is interesting. So our battalion loaded up and we went to Saipan, June 15th, 1944. Anyhow, they had the reefs and up over the reefs our vehicles went. The Japs had navy guns they got at Singapore and they were putting holes through everybody. And they had the anti-tank gun which could pop in one side and out the other, and the mortar shells. But we got through, landed our troops. But we usually ended up losing so many vehicles, the Marine Corps never wastes anything. And we'd end up with infantry duty, scouring out this and that and the other.

"But Saipan was a very interesting operation. It was the first time we came face to face with Japs. They were well dug in and they were well trained and highly motivated. I can remember at the far end of the island, the Japs had a lot of Korean

laborers there, we didn't know that at that time, everybody had slant eyes. And they were jumping off a cliff, women and children jumping off cliffs. We had loud speakers, 'Don't do this, don't do that,' but some of them were smart and didn't jump.

"In the jungles, I remember the first time I went in, I could see this beautiful island. Oh, we all wanted to get ashore. We got ashore and stepped in there, God, the heat, the humidity, the bugs. The Japs were very good at that [fighting in the jungle] *and they were very dedicated. I remember when we were making a thing around Saipan, clearing out the resistance, I came up and here's a Jap soldier sitting at the base of the tree, I said, 'Let's take him!' We circled around him, I kicked some dirt, he opened those little squinty eyes at me, looked this way, that way, and started to shoot, just like that. Of course, we nailed him right there. Never a bit of hesitation, he was going to get one of us.*

"In Saipan, we could always tell when they were going to pop a grenade on us. Our grenades, you pulled a pin and it had a spoon and as you threw it, the spoon would flip up and you would have so many seconds. Well, the Japs, theirs was a percussion thing on the end of grenade and you had to hit it against something and they used to hit it against their helmet. Then you knew a grenade was coming.

"Absolutely no qualms about shooting Japs, I'll tell you that. It was well done. Talking about Japs, they mounted an amphibious attack against us on the island of Saipan. On the other end of the island, they had landing craft; here they come around the island; here the Marines were waiting for them. They dropped their raft, wham, it was the other way around. We nailed those damned boats..and I remember before we left the island and here are those old boats full of skeletons and dead Japs.

"The kamikaze pilots, they didn't mind getting killed, but they killed a lot of our people on ships, those guys. I can remember a Jap plane come over Saipan one time. It was on fire and that front gunner with the machine gun, he was spraying it just like that. He was trying to get somebody before they piled right on. They were very dangerous people. You couldn't take any chances. But you know they didn't want to be captured by Marines. I can remember working through caves and you'd here that thing pop and they would put a grenade up against their chest. They didn't want to be captured. I guess they thought we would treat them the way they treated us. Anybody who got taken prisoner, his wounds got dressed. We didn't like him, you know.

"We did a lot of sweeping. Of course, the Marine Corps said the island [Saipan] is secure. They left us, and the 2nd Division. So we built camps and all that. I remember the flies were so bad. Here are dead Japs, and we are trying to eat our rations and there were flies. So they sprayed it later on with DDT and we thought that was wonderful. They treated us well all of the time. Things got settled down a little bit and we had tents and we made a place to run a movie, we thought that was wonderful.

"Our morale in the troops was pretty good. We never had any trouble. I remember our Marines were absolutely fearless, they would go anywhere, do anything."

Field Hospital on Saipan

As soon as the island of Saipan was secure, a field hospital was set up. Dorothy Young, an Army nurse at Tripler Hospital at the time of Pearl Harbor, helped evacuate casualties from Guadalcanal and also worked setting up a field hospital on Saipan.

"*The United States was not really ready for something like this, so not only hospital supplies, medication, everything, we ran out of beds, linens, blankets, everything, sterile supplies. We didn't have running water, so when we had to set up field hospitals, we used oil drums and one of these little bulbs that you baste your turkey with and put a rubber hose in it, so we could pump water. We couldn't boil at night in enemy territory.* "*Now we are moving on up into the Marianas* [Islands which include Tinian and Saipan]. *We brought a hospital of seventy-six into Saipan. We lived in tents. We had a big canvas fence around us and a ten-holer down at the end. We had water in tanks up above, and we could pull a chain and the water would come out, soap up, then we'd rinse, because we couldn't use too much. So we had a lister bag which held water so we could have a drink. It was a big lister bag, hanging on a tree. We also had a field phone, which was a new innovation. It was wired in case the nurses needed to call. We had a guard at the gate.*

"*All of the wards and units were all in tents with mosquito nets. We had tents and mosquito netting because the mosquitos were really bad, and the flies. So we had DDT or FLIT. We had it in a can and sprayed. We did that around our cot and into our mosquito netting in order to keep all of the mosquitos out. Then you would quick sneak in there and nine times out of ten, there would be one damned mosquito that would get in there. You were swatting because if you had gotten out, fifty more would have come in. There, it was the danger of malaria. That was a problem; the flies were really bad.*

"*We'd take a spit bath in our helmet, olive drab, GI issue. We could collect rain water because it would rain frequently, and we could take a bath and never expose an inch of skin because we didn't know whether someone was laying on their belly underneath the canvas tent.*

"*And you never went to bed without your underwear because you felt you were in enemy territory. And if they did have an air raid, you had to go out of your cot into a dirt foxhole which you had dug to fit you.*

"And we had C-rations by then and K-rations. They were really busy back in the States getting all kinds of things. They even sent us penicillin out there. And they said, 'This is a new miracle drug that has just been discovered.' It was in a powder form in a little vial. And you put a little vial of sterile water with that and shake it up and give them a dose or two. Then you refrigerate what is left.' I think it held five doses in that little bottle. Thank you very much, where were we going to get a refrigerator? We laughed, and we said, 'If we don't use up all five doses, then we'll have to throw it away because we don't have any refrigerators.' We didn't even have electricity in Saipan.' 'What, you have no electricity? What do you do?' We did beautifully. We had batteries.

"Eleanor Roosevelt came, on behalf of the Red Cross, to visit. She had on a uniform, she was very efficient and they showed her around the nurses' accommodations and the facilities. I'm sure she meant well, but when she looked around at our facilities, and I thought they were first-class, she said she felt that we were living like pigs. She said, 'I am going to see that no more of our women, Army and Navy nurses, are going to be put under such grueling circumstances.' We thought we were doing a good job and had all of the amenities. How many people had a lister bag? and water with iodine in it to drink?"

Tinian

Moving closer to the Philippines, Americans landed on Tinian in July 1944. The Japanese fought to the bitter end, losing 6,050 defenders of that island, but only 290 Americans were killed.[146] Once again, Joe Malcolm was part of the invading Marine forces.

"Then we took the island of Tinian. That was a cakewalk to the Marines. Tinian town was here, they would set the battleships around and they started bombarding the town. And the Japs thought they were going to land here. So there was a very narrow beach over on the other side and they landed the 4th Division right there, just a few Japs.

"They got smart and bypassed a few islands. After Tarawa, they thought we don't have to take every damned island. So we stayed there on Saipan and got new vehicles and got fixed up, trained out replacements for the ones that got killed and we were in pretty good shape."

Peleliu

In September, American troops landed on Morotai Island and on the Palau Islands, both strategic locations near the Philippines.

The battle to capture Peleliu, one of the Palau Islands, had the highest casualty rates among amphibious attacks: 9,171 Americans and 13,600 Japanese killed.[147]

Given those statistics, it was not surprising that Ivan S. Hobson, a machine gunner in the First Marine Division on Peleliu referred often to how Marines became hardened to death and came to accept the statistics relating to "Who died last night?" It was often the "luck of the draw" to escape death in battle. Marines had their own way to keep their minds off killing while they faced enemies that were willing to fight to their death.

"I was a PFC, then later a corporal in the First Marine Division. We needed to take the island of Peleliu before others were to go into the Philippines. It was not a success. Out of three hundred fellows in my company, only two of us returned. The rest were either killed or sent back to the States with wounds. All of my friends, for the most part, were killed. I refused, in the future, to make friends.

"When I was wounded on Peleliu, we had just gone up to a little knoll, nicknamed 'Bloody Nose Ridge,' and we were digging in that night because three other attempts had been made to hold the ridge and they were beat back each time by the Japanese. We dug in our position for the machine gun next to a little narrow dirt road, about the width for a cart.

"And then, at the last minute, as it got dark, we were told to move back about twenty or thirty feet, back closer to the perimeter of our company as we were encircled in enemy territory. We were kind of disgusted as we had already dug our fox holes and camouflaged our machine gun. It was a great blessing to us because it happened that the Japanese watched us digging in our first gun emplacement and after dark we moved back. The enemy started shelling the first gun emplacement, thinking we were still there. That's the only thing that saved us that time.

"Right across this little dirt path or cart road, the Japanese were on the other side of the road. We were about fifteen to twenty feet apart. I had a turn, with another Marine, to man the machine gun. We took two-hour turns manning the gun. Six of us would rotate two at a time. Sometimes you had 100 percent alert, so nobody went to sleep. But on this occasion, there were three groups of two each. Right about time we were to be relieved, we heard a noise further up at the bend in the road, but there was no silhouette to show what was on the road until a head sort of popped up over the tree line. The silhouette of a person was very close to us. The silhouette in the trees told us there was a figure there. I wouldn't have normally fired the machine gun under those conditions because it would give one's emplacement away to the enemy.

"Machine gun bullets are of three different types: one is armor-piercing, one is for regular personnel, the third, a tracer. The light coming out of the machine gun would also let the enemy know our location. I pulled the trigger and hit my target. I had a very unfortunate experience. As the person was dying, just in front of the machine gun, he spoke in his native language. He spoke in English. I was very concerned that I had killed one of the US troops that had come up several days before. But it was dark and I couldn't see.

"Well, I was relieved of duty and moved back just behind our gun pit. When you are four feet behind the line, you think you are in safe territory.

"The Japanese started throwing rocks instead of grenades because we would quite often take their grenades and throw them back. The Japanese had a longer-timed fuse on their grenades. And the Japanese, also you knew when they were throwing a grenade; they had to hit the grenade on a rock or on their helmet or something solid before they threw it. That would start the timer, whereas United States grenades had a pin which one pulled and would then throw it. And typically when we threw a grenade, we would pull the pin, let the handle flip off and the grenade would start to time to explode. We held the grenade in our hand for a few seconds, then would throw it so the Japanese didn't have time to throw it back before it would explode. Sometimes, if you held it too long, that was the end.

"Anyway, a Japanese grenade hit me. I was laying flat on my stomach and my arm was sort of covering my head. It hit me on the left side, it blew up and did damage to my side and winged my left elbow. There was no light to see by, I just felt with my right hand the places from where the blood was flowing. The corpsman, the medical fellow, just poured sulfa on my side and arm and started a heavy wrapping of gauze around my body. The next morning I was going to be taken to a hospital ship, but one had to wait until daylight to leave the front lines. I was the only one wounded in my company that night. I refused to leave for the hospital ship until they took me back up to the road so I could see that it was a Japanese person I had killed. I had to have satisfaction that I hadn't killed one of our own.

"About an hour after I got on the hospital ship, another fellow from my company came aboard. I was quite disheartened. I might get a little religious here, as I thought, my Father in Heaven had deserted me. I saw others dying around me and wounded and being taken out. I thought I would be protected as I didn't think I'd been that bad a kid. So when I was wounded I thought, 'Who is here to protect me?'

"Another fellow from my company informed me that shortly after I'd left the line, a single shell came into the line and killed everyone of the fellows who were in my machine gun crew. Had I not been taken out, being the only one wounded that night, I would have been right there with the rest of them. I had a number of similar experiences like that.

"I was sent to New Caledonia where I was rehabilitated. We had previously trained on an island called Pavuvu, which is in the Solomon Islands, very close to Guadalcanal where the first Marine Division had fought. I was not on Guadalcanal for that battle. I did go to Guadalcanal for some training exercises. I was sent back to the little island of Pavuvu and, of course, we received a lot of new recruits from the United States to replace those who were dead or missing from the previous battle.

"There's one thing, of course, when that squad was killed, and throughout combat, many times it became very materialistic. You become hardened. I never took revenge on an enemy. I protected myself. I did what I was supposed to do. Often, in the morning, if there had been a battle during the previous night, the word would be passed up and down the line, 'Who got it that night?' And you'd say, 'Well so-and-so and so-and-so.' It was a matter of statistics. You became so hardened to it.

"Prior to each combat when we were at Pavuvu training, the leaders made our lives as miserable as possible while getting us ready for the next projected action. If it began to rain, then they got us out and we started hiking. If the sun was shining, we had to do something indoors (in tents). They made life so miserable, intentionally, so as to make one feel, 'Let's get to combat, it's better than this.' That's hard to believe, but you wanted to get out of this mess when they had you training.

"I was in the first wave that went into Peleliu and our amphibious tank was supposed to carry in the American flag. Well, there was a coral reef that was some 500 yards out from the shore and our tank got hung up on that reef. There were about thirty-five of us in the little enclosure in the tank and we all had to pile on top of each other so the back treads of the tank could get off that reef. The two navy fellows, who were driving the tank, backed it off. All of a sudden, they went full speed ahead to get over the reef and they hung us up totally. We had to evacuate. Enemy shells were starting to target in on us. Due to the delay, we were not the first to land, nobody knows who got the first American flag to shore. Our tank was left out on the reef.

"The water was maybe four feet deep and, as we waded ashore, it was almost like a movie. But in a movie, you see almost a constant battling and bombing, that's not totally realistic. Sometimes one would have intense enemy shelling. We had two enemy machine guns and mortars trying to drop in on us. You'd see spits from these machine guns coming in the water. As the bullets were hitting the water and as the machine gun bullets came close to you, you'd go under water, hoping the water would deflect the bullet. Some of the fellows came up too soon and they were killed.

"Of the thirty or thirty-five of us, half got ashore. We started singing the Marine Corps Hymn, and we also sang the song, but we varied the words of it, 'Oh what a beautiful morning, everything's coming our way.'[from *Oklahoma*] You think, here men are being killed all around you and you're maybe going to be hit,

A Time to Speak

how can you sing? I don't know who started or how it started. It sounds very childish, but I guess we were psychologically trying to keep things off our minds.

"When I got ashore, my pants were full of water because they were tucked in the leg guards. I knew I had to get up on that beach so I wouldn't be hit by something. I was falling to the ground about five yards from the water's edge. A Marine, who had come in just before me, yanked my arm, while I was still in midair, and pulled me over to him. He saw where I was going to land and there was a land mine there. I have always been very grateful for his assistance.

"Then we had to try to make our way back up to our company because the rest of the company was up on the front. Because of our delayed arrival, we were with troops who were part of the third or fourth wave. As we moved forward, we noticed the palm trees on the island were all pretty well stripped from the heavy bombardments from the battle ships and planes. That's what they had done to prepare for our landing. But there were still some Japanese that had tied themselves to palm trees to be snipers. Most of them were dead and they were still dangling out of the trees. There were some that were still alive and active. It was necessary to take cover behind a log or tree when they fired at us. There were a few that were assigned to have shotguns for such occasions. The shotguns would splatter pleats. We couldn't have found the enemy otherwise. But in that area, there were as many dead as passing by, both Marines and Japanese.

"Actually, when I left the tank to wade ashore, I only kept with me my carbine rifle because the machine gun and ammunition was too heavy in the water. So we had to leave almost everything in the boat or leave it in the water. I kept my rifle and the one clip that was in it which had seven rounds. My pack which had my two-day supply of food, some dry clothes, et cetera was left behind. My belt, I had to also take it off, which had two one-quart canteens for our water supply, a little first aid kit, all that was left. I went ashore just with a rifle and seven rounds of ammunition. I used one round, as soon as I got ashore, to fire my carbine in the air so as to dry out the barrel. That left me with six rounds, so as we were moving forward, I searched out some Marines that were dead and I took their belt, their water, and their backpack. That's how I tried to re-equip myself.

"They [the Japanese] spent sometimes a whole night, maybe crawling a distance of twenty feet toward our line. Americans didn't have that kind of patience. Sometimes, the lines were so thin between foxholes, sometimes there was ten feet between holes and literally, sometimes, they crawled in between our foxholes without one knowing it. One is always intense. One night on Peleliu, the ocean was too noisy for us. We were surrounded by the Japanese on three sides, with the Pacific ocean on the fourth side. Just by chance, the Japanese had cut off the antenna of our company radio with a bullet. It snapped and left us with no radio and then they cut our telephone line which we had just laid. That night I heard a crackle. It was dark, couldn't see anything. I threw a hand grenade out in front of me and I happened to catch one of the enemy. The next morning, we found that all the corpse had with him was a knife, and he was about six feet directly in front of our foxhole.

"At that time, our company was trying to get supplies to us. A lieutenant who was stationed in the rear, our supply officer, said they were going to send in reinforcements with supplies. We needed the ammunition, our gun supplies. This happened just before our radio communication went out. We could care less about food or anything else at that point. We also needed a flamethrower, as the one that had been with our company had been destroyed. Six Marines advanced carrying cases on their shoulders, and we all felt relieved as we thought this was ammo. They had sent seven men, carrying six cases of grapefruit juice and one flamethrower that didn't work. If anybody had ever found that rear lieutenant, I don't know if he would have been around very long, as our lives were in danger at that time as we were fighting for our own lives.

"The rear signal depot was going to send an amphibious tank with supplies to us from the ocean side and just above our area. A 'volunteer,' (he was considered the joker of our company) was sent out of the perimeter to strike matches every once in a while if he thought he could hear what sounded noise from the direction of the ocean noise, and if it sounded like a tank, so as to let the tank know where to come in. Nobody heard a tank. Two of us were told to leave the circle and go back up the trail into enemy territory to locate our buddy and bring him back. We located him and the three of us started walking back into our company line, and the one fellow that went with me went in the front and the fellow who had been striking the matches and I were covering the rear. We were walking down the trail, and suddenly there was an explosion. We didn't know whether the fellow in the middle touched a land mine or whether a mortar shell had hit between his legs. As I was in the rear, I ran forward as we weren't very far apart. I wasn't affected by the shell. I think it was a land mine. I held the young kid in my arms. He was younger than most of the guys. In fact, we thought he lied about his age to get into the service. He was always a joker. It was a touching thing for me, to hold him momentarily in my arms while he died. I always remember, he said, 'Well, I guess the last joke's on me.' Those were his last words.

"On the island of Peleliu there were supposed to be 25,000 US Marines and their support groups and it was figured there were about 13,000 Japanese, most of them being buried in the raised hill tunnels. When we would capture the gun emplacements, we found that they were using anti-aircraft guns to fight us. The shells would explode over our heads. At some guns, we found Japanese had chained their own men to the guns. They had nowhere to go. They were to fight to their deaths."[148]

A Time to Speak

The Philippines

To regain control of the Philippines was important to American forces as a step closer to the home island of Japan and the planned invasion. In September and October 1944 there were air raids on the Philippines to prepare to retake the islands. Then, in October 1944 American soldiers landed on two beachheads on the east coast of Leyte Island, near the town of Tacloban. It took sixty-seven days to conquer Leyte. In January 1945, American troops landed on Luzon; in February they landed on Corregidor. MacArthur finally returned to Manila on 27 February 1945. He was not able to announce the complete liberation of the Philippines until 5 July 1945.

Japanese soldiers inside Manila refused to surrender and a savage battle continued until the American forces finally controlled a city in ruins on 23 February.

Bob Bradfield went into the Army in 1943 and eventually joined the 30th Traffic Regulation Group and went into the Philippines in 1945. The unit was made up of one officer and four enlisted men who combined together into a very small battalion, trained to operate independently.

When Bradfield arrived in Manila, he saw the result of the Japanese attempt to hold on to Manila: destruction and chaos.

"We came in south of Manila, over the beaches, of course. We were much later than the original invasion that came in, in two places, Lingayen Gulf which is on the northwest coast from Luzon and then from the south at Tacloban Ridge which is near Bataan province. The 11th Airborne came in there and both sides converged on Manila as fast as they could get to it.

"Coming in, landing in landing boats. Fortunately, again, we had had a chance to do that at Eniwetok and Eulithe. They called it a 'swimming party,' we had to go down the nets. I still remember coming on deck, at anchor, we were probably not too far from Caviti, and the colonel saying, 'Are you ready to go?' 'Yes, Sir.' 'Down the net you go,' and the coxswain was holding the boat and it was going back and forth, so was the boat, and so was I. I was black and blue from the knees on up to get down to that landing craft.

"By the time we got there, there was no place in Manila. All of the docks were a mess. In fact, as I look back on it, we were exposed to it in such increments that we weren't quite aware, but Manila was a reeking mess, a wreck. They hadn't even picked up all of the bodies off the streets. They decomposed very rapidly in the jungle. There were bodies every place.

"They found out we were there and they were having such a terrible mess with the movement of their quartermaster trucks and supply depot (that's partly what we were created for). We set up check points all through Luzon, picked up

these guys in their trucks and headed them where they were needed and not where they thought they were going to go. We had our own radio command cars. We patrolled the entire southern half of Luzon.

"It was difficult to move toward Manila, difficult to the degree that there were no bridges left, so the bridge across the Pasig River was a 'Bailey bridge,' rapidly constructed from interchangeable latticed steel panels, coupled with steel pins. You are looking down and you are looking through the open webs.

"But everything over one story tall was just smashed flat, that entire metro area. Looking at the legislative building, there was a Japanese corpse floating in the water, there was a Japanese skeleton, drooped over the parapet of the Red Cross Club which was there when they took over, and it was still there when I left Manila.

"I think this came as a rude shock to some of our group. Manila had an open APO, 'Oh boy, we are going to a metropolitan area.' It may have been at one time, but it certainly wasn't. It was about as primitive as you can get.

"We were regulating the traffic in Manila, diverting trucks. The Manila area, southern Luzon was a massive staging area for the upcoming invasion. There were supply dumps the size of Boulder, Colorado before World War II [three square miles]. There were actually Japanese units based in the center of those supply dumps. The Military Police would guard the roads in, but who knew what was back in there. You didn't go in for supplies even in the daylight unless you were armed. They were just out in the middle of the nearest field, piled in, just as fast as you could pile the stuff in. It is unbelievable how much material was there.

"Right in Manila, English was OK, that was the second language. But there are forty dialects on the island of Luzon alone. And while we had an interpreter, he spoke Tagalog which was spoken in Manila. If you got him twenty miles out of the city, he was as lost as we were. We did what all Americans do when you run into somebody who doesn't speak your language, you talk louder and louder and louder and you don't understand why he doesn't answer.

"There were so many American troops in the islands that it wasn't much of a problem. We didn't often find ourselves someplace where it depended on our ability to get along in Tagalog.

"Dust, you just can't believe. We were there at the tail end of the dry season and the dust was probably six inches deep over everything. Every time you moved a vehicle, just clouds of dust. We were living out in San Fernando Del Monte, which was the old pre-war movie-making district, and we were camped in a buffalo wallow outside some of the big, lovely homes there.

"Then on either side of the highways were rice paddies and that was mud. We had one of the funniest episodes there. Coming along a back road, there was one of our company jeeps sitting in the middle of a rice paddy. It had to be somewhere because all you could see was the colonel sitting in it. 'Whatever, Sir, are you doing out in that rice paddy?' 'I'm sitting in a goddamn jeep.' It just settled right down on him. We had to go over to the motor pool, then winch him out of the paddy and they had to take the jeep to pieces to get it cleaned off. He slipped off this very slippery road and slid right in.

"Then before we left, right after the war was over, you were running into the rainy season. Then it would be like somebody dumped a bucket. You were just soaking. And we were on volcanic soil; it was so soft.

"And that led to another funny thing that happened. The Colonel, manning our outfit, wanted to climb Mount Mayon which was a blown-out volcano which is right down on the seacoast. It took us three times before we could make it up. We had to drive a little ways to get to it. We came back after one expedition and couldn't find our jeep. We had taken it up as far as the volcano as we could get. There were ruts on either side and the rain had come up during the day and washed all the dirt out from underneath the wheels and just left the jeep sitting on its axles. Of all things, we had a jeep that didn't have a shovel on it. So we dug it out with our mess kit spoons. That was typical of the soil, it was fertile, you could stick your rake in there and it would grow leaves.

"And the Japanese were just all through and around us. We killed Japanese infiltrators in our camp. One managed to sneak in during the night and surrendered to the officer of the day sitting in his tent. Some of them were trying to exact the last revenge for Asia and others were trying to surrender. The trouble was you didn't know which was which.

"They were familiar with the ground. We were pretty green, but after while we realized that you don't used fixed guards around the camp. We found we couldn't use regular guard posts. We had roving guards, we had no idea where they were. And we were running twenty-four hours a day, so if you came in at two in the morning, you yelled your head off and made all kinds of noise because you didn't know where that guard was and how jumpy he was going to be. It was a very spooky experience.

"We saw a lot of interesting things toward the end of the war. There were 70,000 or 80,000 Japanese still on Luzon. They were all over the northern half of the island. This was the first time there was any number of Japanese soldiers captured. And that was astonishing to see that. The German prisoners I saw in 1943, the prisoners from the African Corps, there would be a twenty-man work party and a half dozen MPs with machine guns. In the Philippines we saw two or three hundred Japanese soldiers and maybe one MP with a 45. They weren't going anyplace.

"If they surrendered, they considered they were dead and they were reborn into the American Army and they couldn't understand why they even needed a guard. It was to keep the Filipinos off of them.

"Very few surrendered willingly and only at the last. That's one of the things you found all over the urban area of Luzon, dead Japanese who had blown themselves up, and booby-trapped bodies, you had to be very careful of. I watched a kid fresh from the States pick up a booby trap from a dead Japanese and said, 'Gee, what's this?' He was lucky it didn't go off. The rest of us were flat on the ground.

"The Filipino population hated them deeply, to the point of killing them with their bare hands. It had been a very brutal occupation. Down toward Lake Taal, more of an excursion than anything else, we came to this back country town. The villagers flagged us down. They had this absolutely terrified Japanese kid, a soldier, and he tried to surrender, but there weren't any American troops around. The town officials were absolutely certain that the villagers were going to get their hands on him and kill him. And they were trying to get him away from them. We didn't have anyplace in the jeep for him. There were five of us in that jeep. So we tied the kid on the hood with tent ropes and brought him like a deer to the next military police post, about twenty miles down the line. It saved his life. He was so frightened he would have done anything we said.

"And I was on duty in Manila harbor one night when they did catch a Japanese soldier and they tore him to pieces, limb from limb right in front of us. We couldn't do a thing to stop them.

"I was in the Philippines when the war was ended. We were actually slated for the invasion of Kyushu. We only had 133 men and 33 officers. Half of them were sent to Japan and the other half went to Korea. And I spent the next six months in Korea." Bradfield, retired from Bradfield Lumber Company, is editor of his Rotary Club's weekly newsletter.

The pace of Allied successes accelerated. In Europe, the Allied Armies broke out of Normandy and marched toward Paris and eastern Europe. In the South Pacific, although the Philippines were under American control, the conquests of Iwo Jima and Okinawa were still ahead for American Marines.

End Notes

144   Martin Gilbert, *The Second World War*, p. 476
145   *The Second World War*, p. 541
146   *The Second World War*, p. 559
147   *The Second World War*, p. 592.
148   After the war Hobson went to George Washington University on the GI Bill. He worked in Washington, D. C. in the Office of Price Stablilization and in the Department of Agriculture. He is active in the work of the Mormon Church.

CHAPTER 38

LIBERATION OF PARIS

*T*he liberation of Paris was a complicated military effort. On 17 and 18 August 1944, the Communists put up posters calling on all Parisians, and those living in the suburbs, to participate in a general insurrection to open up the route to Paris and to welcome the Allied forces. The Resistance Forces were now established as the French Forces of the Interior (FFI) with Colonel Henri Rol-Tanguy, regional head of the FFI, d'Ile de France and member of the French Communist Party, as the head. He was determined that Paris would be liberated by its people. They set up barricades, seized the Hôtel de Ville (City Hall) and other buildings. Although these groups were poorly armed and badly trained, they fired on German soldiers and armored vehicles and convoys.

Meanwhile, for more than a week, Allied troops advanced toward Paris. The French Second Armored Division, under the command of General Jacques Philippe Leclerc, followed the route from the south and southwest, some troops passing through Rambouillet and Versailles, others through Longjumeau, Antony and the Porte d'Orléans to converge in Paris. American troops moved to occupy the eastern district of Paris, going through Chartres, Palaiseau to Athis-Mons. On 25 August, General Leclerc entered Paris, and in the afternoon, German General von Choltitz surrendered. What followed was a day of confusion, with snipers firing and small groups of German soldiers unwilling to give up and continuing to resist.

On 26 August General de Gaulle walked down the Champs-Elysées to Notre Dame Cathedral and the celebration of the *Te Deum*. Much to the dismay of General de Gaulle, Communist leader, Rol-Tanguy, claimed partial credit for the liberation of Paris.

Letter from Paris

After E. P.'s involvement with the Resistance (from Chapter 27), she witnessed the arrival of American troops in the eastern district of Paris, Athis-Mons. In her letter, she wrote:

".....As days went by, "Liberation" was in the air; the Germans became restless, and arrested people right and left, sending whole trainloads to Germany. Air-raids on points of vital interest for the Germans became more frequent, and hardly a day or night passed without the RAF of the US Air Force "unloading"

A Time to Speak

bombs in the vicinity. One night, the most important junctions in France, the railway yard of Juvisy was smashed up by the RAF. This yard is on the territory of Athis-Val, down in the valley, while we live in Athis-Mons, up on the hill. In a straight line, it is about 800 yards from here. That neighborhood was thickly populated for a suburb. It was a night of horror. 300 people are in the cemetery now; whole families were wiped out, - some bodies were found only a few months ago and there are still unexploded bombs in the valley. Yet not one word was said against the Allies. It was wonderful. Even those who lost four and five members of their family in that one night found the strength of soul to says "<u>it had to be done</u>..." They knew, as we all knew, that those victims had been called upon to give their lives for the liberation of their country, just as soldier, sailors and airmen are called upon to make the same sacrifice. But it was a nightmare, and the horror continued for days afterwards, when the "time" bombs went off. We had several within 50 yards from our house, and some of the ceilings, walls and windows were blown out or cracked but that was all.

"...And then on August 24th, Thursday, at about 6 p.m. our last Germans, about 30 of them armed to the teeth, finger on trigger and grenade in hand, came up our hill...We watched them out of one of our dining-room windows, on the first floor, flattened up against the wall, my husband and I, for all windows were supposed to be closed and no one was to go near them...And then, out of the other window in the same room, at right-angles from the first, we saw our first Americans coming....They were on foot, some twenty or more, gun in hand and walking stealthily close to the gardens bordering the road. The Americans and Germans could not see each other, until they were almost due to meet at the apex of the angle, just beneath our windows, and we thought: 'Now, this is where it happens.' But it didn't. The first Germans coming to the tip of the angle below our window, caught sight of the first Americans who were still some 50 yards away and, with a yell, the Germans turned and tore down the hill, their firearms and equipment rattling with their speed, turning and hiding in the several little lanes that branch out right and left. The Americans had seen them turn and they hurried forward, cautiously, however, for as they were placed, they could not see if the Germans had gone <u>down</u> the hill or if they had only gone far enough to be out of sight around the first bend in the road... So when the Americans were within hearing distance I called to them in English from the window, telling them how and why they were to go slowly and where to look. I shall never forget the surprise registered in the one eye and the one eyebrow on my side of the American nearest the window! He heard and understood and yet could not be sure that it was not a trap...and he kept the 'off side' eye and eyebrow bent in search down the hill....

"That was the beginning of the end. An armored car (American this time) stationed outside our house. I photographed it next morning. I will send you a picture next time. And that night I acted as interpreter for the liaison agents who were coming and going with information between the Americans on our side of the river and those who were 'clearing up' the little towns on the other bank. In the morning I was sent for to get down the hill to the American H.Q. to help transpose on their maps the information that had come across in the night; this was done in a house at the riverside around which the Americans mounted guard, with guns trained on a German 'nest' of machines across the water. Some of the boys had been going since days without rest, we had had no sleep, either for long and anxious hours, and we were, all of us, drunk with joy and fatigue and the August sun. And we were FREE! FREE! FREE!....

"I don't think there is much more to tell. Things gradually shook themselves down and that wonderful, unique, never-to-be-forgotten week of our liberation (when people were happy and helpful and grateful with the best that was in them) went down into the past, giving place to the disappointing, discouraging spirit that seems to be universal these days...I suppose it is too much to ask of a world that has been through such terrible times to be generous and kind and good, but there are days, many of them - and all my friends agree, - when we look back with regret on the days of the underground with its unity of purpose, its spirit of aid and sacrifice, when ideals and actions were pure and clean....."

The First to Liberate His Home Town

Albert Moline, who refused to give up when Germany occupied France and joined de Gaulle's Free French, entered Paris from the south. He ultimately had the satisfaction of liberating his home town, Levallois-Perret, a suburb northwest of Paris.

"We had to take Paris from all sides. We arrived at the Porte d'Orleans, others by Sèvres. I was in the 2nd Division blindée, 14th American Corps. General LeClerc was directly under General Patton.

"The division blindée was divided into tactical groups: autonomous groups that could, each one, go in a certain direction because they had everything they needed in arms, tanks, machine guns, artillery. It was an army unto itself. Each tactical group was commanded by a colonel, all under LeClerc.

"After Longjumeau there was a battle, then we battled at Antony, at the prison of Fresnes. I slept in at the crossroads of Croix de Berny, and we entered Paris the 24th in the morning. The morning we entered Paris, LeClerc launched the five or six tactical groups who surrounded and entered Paris by all the routes available. Some arrived by Versailles, some, like us, by the Porte d'Orléans. All of the tactical groups converged on the center of Paris with average success, average battles and an uncertain number of deaths.

"Paris itself was not liberated at all, it wasn't finished. After the Rue Monge, we arrived at Rivoli. [Rue Monge, 5th arrondissement, near the Jardin des Plantes across the Seine to Rue Rivoli]. *The Resistance for eight days had constructed the barricades to hinder the Germans, but it also hindered the Allied troops. They* [the Resistance members] *didn't have arms, they had a lot of courage, but they didn't know what to do.*

"*By evening, Paris was liberated and the day after we left on reconnaissance.*

"*I was the first to liberate Levallois. I don't know if I can tell all of it. I was not on special duty. The company was stopped at the Jardin des Plantes. We worked for a while to get to Levallois. To come to Levallois, it was necessary to find a jeep, some arms, someone to drive the jeep (me) and someone else to come with us. It was necessary to be well armed to defend ourselves.* [There were pockets of German soldiers heavily armed and unwilling to surrender.] *We borrowed a jeep, with a machine gun in front, we had our individual arms, lots of grenades, an Indochinese who had been in the campaign with us. Then there was another comrade, Jean-Jacques. He wanted to come if I would bring him to his house. We decided to leave; we started off; very quickly we arrived at Jean-Jacques' and I continued with my Indochinese friend. We didn't encounter any opposition until Levallois. In Levallois, upon arriving, we were fired on by soldiers in the church steeple. We weren't in the habit of firing back. We fired, and I learned later that we eliminated them. In the evening we were going down the street, Anatole France; I turned at Aristide Briand, then rue Carnot and in front of my house.*

"*I wasn't very calm because I said to myself, 'If there were any Germans at the corner of the street, there was a mob around us.' I thought, 'What could I do, I couldn't fire if there were a lot of civilians around us.' It went well. I ate at a place on Henri Barbousse. Then they called us by radio, saying that the captain was looking everywhere for his jeep. We said goodby and took the same route back. We weren't fired on, there was no one. We picked up Jean-Jacques who was waiting at the door. I said the captain had bawled us out. We went back as fast as we had come. We got back and he came out and said, 'My jeep!'*"

A Wild Celebration

For Parisians, like Geneviève Moline, it was a joyous occasion.

"*In the evening, we heard the bells of Notre Dame which hadn't rung for four years. When we heard the bells, we covered pieces of boxes, since there wasn't any paper, with red, blue and white. We designed a French flag to hang on the balcony of the building, as well as English, American and Russian flags. We made* bracelets, red, white, blue, to create garlands for the house.

"For me the Liberation was the wonderful, unprecedented fête. Everyone embraced in the streets. Everyone was delirious with joy. You can't imagine. Everyone sang, everyone was in the street. We were happy, we yelled 'Vive de Gaulle, Vive les Américains,' it was wild, wild, wild!

"I was at the parade; I was on the shoulders of my father to see it. I saw de Gaulle, Leclerc, all the great who saved us and who paraded down the Champs-Elysées.

"We were machine gunned by the former militia members who shot from the roofs. I remember we were behind the Pavilion of Elysée. We tried to hide ourselves. My mother found a taboret and put it over me to protect my head. We weren't afraid.

"We went home on foot to Levallois. And we heard them say there was a detachment which came to Levallois. It was my future husband, but I didn't know him then."

The Warsaw Uprising

With the Allied armies moving east and the Red Army moving west, these victories encouraged other outbreaks of violence against the Nazi Regime.

The short-lived Warsaw Uprising was launched on 1 August 1944 and by 2 October, it was over. By the end of the uprising, 85 percent of the city was demolished, trees cut down, underground water mains and sewage pipes blown up, telegraph poles and tramway tracks torn up. Between 200,000 and 250,000 people were killed, including 15,000 insurgents.[149]

Wieslaw Furmanczyk, a former member of the Polish underground, survived the Warsaw Uprising and wrote:

"Just before the Uprising, because we were in one of the crash units, we were mobilized a week or so before the Uprising. First, we stayed in the house of a man, whom I later discovered was the vice-mayor of Warsaw. His son was in our unit. Except for my close friends, I didn't know the names of the other ones. A company would have hundreds.

"We were part of a platoon and there were three platoons in a company. In a platoon, there were three smaller units and each was about sixteen people. We were waiting for the Uprising and we were not supposed to leave. We had to stay until the beginning of the Uprising.

"The Warsaw Uprising was the only time I was actually in combat. I was eighteen. Most of boys were, our commanders some of them were pre-war officers. Our commander was a captain and there was one lieutenant. Otherwise there were some, (I don't think you have that equivalent in America), people who had a secondary education, then get to a military school and they are somehow noncommissioned officers. They had some training after they left the secondary school, so some of them might have been twenty-one or twenty-two.

"But there were quite a lot of boys who were fourteen, fifteen. They served as messengers, carrying messages from one place to another. In fact, when we were taken prisoners of war, they were with us. We were in Germany, working as prisoners, there were two or three boys who were with us who were fourteen or at the most fifteen.

"I fought in Zoliborz all the time. I saw plenty of military action. During the Uprising we got some food, but not regularly.

"The day before we surrendered, we were stationed in a building which, like most of the buildings, had been heavily shelled by German artillery fire. As a result of this, most of the casualties were among the civilians. As I was moving through this building, I entered a staircase and when I looked up I saw a woman's leg, still in a stocking, somehow suspended, just hanging there, part of a human being or what had been a human being. The sight of this 'poor leg' has somehow survived in my memory more strongly than the sight of so many of my friends who died in battle literally next to me. If I were a poet, I would probably write a brief poem about the leg.

"My parents were across the Vistula. My parents didn't know whether I was alive, I didn't know whether my parents were alive. When the Russians came, there was one of the soldiers who was rather sympathetic. He talked to my parents, 'Well, what about Warsaw?' 'Well, our son is there.' And this Soviet soldier said 'Oh, yes, we know, the guys are fighting.' We've come to help them, we'll rescue them in no time.' Then after a few days, all of a sudden they [the Russians] disappeared.

"There was a meeting; they called it a meeting. Instructions were given obviously. He came back and said to my parents, 'Well, now, you'd better not talk about your son'. We've just discovered they are Fascists.' And that's when Stalin decided he would let Warsaw suffer.

"They [the Russians] just went through the movements with helping us. When they came to the Vistula, they were in Prague, then they went through the motions of trying to help us. They were supposed to give information, to get artillery support, they weren't even trying.

"They dropped quite a lot of weapons, but all of this was much too late. There wasn't much we could do. Our troops in Zoliborz surrendered on 30 September 1944.

"As prisoners of war, we were first transported to a camp in Pruszkow near Warsaw and then to Stalag XI-A, Altengrabow in Germany. After a few days our group was transported to Arbeitskommado 301/3 Groningen, where we worked in a sugar factory twelve hours a day, day and night shifts. So, changing from day to night shift we had to work twelve plus six hours. We lived in wooden barracks in miserable conditions, hungry most of the time. A loaf of bread for eight men daily, watery soup, etc. After a month or so we got some food parcels from the Red Cross which contained some cigarettes. Since I did not smoke at that time, I was able to swap them for bread with one of the German workers. On one occasion, I was beaten up by a German worker because 'I didn't move fast enough.'

"When the sugar refinery stopped working, a group of us were transferred to a kind of big farm where we did all kinds of work. We lived in what used to be a stable. No heating, damp walls, our clothes never quite dry. The place was called Hamersleben.

"On April 11, 1945 we heard the guns of the approaching American Army. We were evacuated to the east, on foot, but after a few kilometers, while we were marching through a small town, Oschersleben, we were liberated by the American Army which was moving towards Magdeburg. The Americans took no more German prisoners at that time, so our guards were set free.

"Towards the end of May 1945 we were transported to Hameln, situated on the Weser River, where we stayed in a kind of semi-military camp. Getting sick and tired of 'camp life,' I decided to go back to Poland, though I knew that the political situation there wasn't too good. So, with a few friends, we arrived in Poland on September 15, 1945." (After the war Furmanczyk began his studies in the English Department of the University of Warsaw. He has received numerous honors, including Ford Foundation and Fulbright scholarships.)

The uprising failed for military and political reasons. The insurgents believed the Germans were beaten on the eastern front. They also received erroneous reports that Soviet tanks were entering Prague and would be entering Warsaw soon. This would have allowed the insurgents the opportunity to capture Warsaw before the Red Army entered the city. The pro-London resistance leaders hoped that a successful insurrection would encourage Roosevelt and Churchill to reaffirm their support for the Polish Government in London and minimize the Polish Communist Party and its relationship to Moscow.[150]

Operation Valkyrie

Another form of resistance against the power of the German Third Reich was Operation Valkyrie, the second attempt to assassinate Hitler. Although the earlier attempt had failed, there were still German Army officers who wanted to try again.

The key man was Count von Stauffenberg, promoted to full colonel and chief of staff to the commander of the Home Army, a post which gave him easy access to Hitler. He and his fellow conspirators hoped to kill Hitler, Göring and Himmler with a single bomb at Berchtesgaden on 2 July, but the attempt was called off.

On 20 July 1944, von Stauffenberg reported to Hitler at the "Wolf's Lair" at Rastenburg. Hidden among the papers in his briefcase was a time bomb. Carefully pushing the briefcase close to the work table where Hitler was studying a military map, von Stauffenberg whispered he had to leave to make a telephone call. The bomb went off at 12:42 p.m, but fate had intervened. Colonel Heinz Brandt had earlier shoved the briefcase to the far side of the table; it inadvertently saved Hitler's life, but cost Brandt his own. Fellow conspirators in Berlin were slow to carry out their part of the Army revolt and failed to secure Berlin for the anti-Nazi government. Their coup was crushed, and Hitler took his revenge. Those who hadn't committed suicide were tortured, tried, and condemned to a horrible death by strangling. The victims, like cattle, were suspended by piano wire from meat hooks; their relatives and friends were sent to concentration camps. William L. Shirer, in *The Rise and Fall of the Third Reich*, concluded that the revolt of 20 July 1944 failed because some of the ablest Army men were inept and most of the German people, in spite of their misery and the prospect of defeat, were not ready for a revolution.

Operation Valkyrie and the Warsaw Uprising took place a few months after the invasion of Normandy, but they were both aborted attempts at unseating Hitler and his Third Reich. While Allied victories continued, not every campaign was easy. Still ahead for the armies were the campaigns in Italy and in the Ardennes.

End Notes

149 George Bruce, *The Warsaw Uprising, 1 August - 2 October 1944*, London: Hart-Davis, 1972, p. 206.
150 Jan M. Ciechanowski, *The Warsaw Rising of 1944* ; Cambridge: 1974, pp. 312-315.

CHAPTER 39

PIVOTAL BATTLES: MARKET GARDEN, BATTLE OF THE BULGE, RIVA-BELVEDERE

The Allies celebrated in 1944: Rome fell on 4 June, almost forgotten in the enthusiasm for the D-Day landing on the Normandy beaches on 6 June; Paris was liberated on 25 August.

The Allied armies still faced important battles: Market Garden in Arnhem, Holland, the crucial Battle of the Bulge in the Ardennes, and the Italian campaign which had begun in 1943.

Market Garden

The move eastward to cross the Rhine and then enter Berlin proved to be more difficult and more costly than anticipated as German armies stiffened their resistance.

On 17 September 1944 an attempt to land British and American troops behind German lines in Holland and capture the bridge at Arnhem proved to be a disaster. After eight days of fighting, the Germans recaptured the bridge. Casualties were high: out of 35,000 men, 1,400 of the airborne troops were killed; more than 6,000 were taken prisoner. It wasn't until 15 April 1945 that Canadian troops succeeded in capturing Arnhem. [151]

One American glider pilot, George F. Brennan, 442GP, 305th Troop Carrier Squadron, was shot down on the mission into Holland, but was saved by luck, resourcefulness, and the courageous Dutch nuns who hid him in the maternity ward of their hospital.

"We had two glider missions. As I remember, the first echelon which went were the guys who didn't make southern France or Normandy. We thought, 'You poor bastards, you are going to get lambasted.' As history showed, D-Day in Holland, the seventeenth was a quiet day. The Germans were caught with their knickers at half mast. There were several missions into Holland. The seventeenth, our guys got in with very little flack and small arms fire. We thought the rest of these

outfits were going to go in by sea echelon and this at the end of the glider operation. That wasn't to be. We were told they needed the artillery and needed them badly. On the nineteenth, the weather was horrible, visibility less than a mile, the ceiling, I estimated, was between 500 and 1000 feet. I thought they wouldn't launch a mission in that kind of weather.

"We did launch. We took off, we went over the channel, and we had to keep on dropping. I estimated we were 30 feet over the Channel. We passed over gliders that had to cut loose because they got in instrument weather and, of course, we weren't equipped for instrument flying. The gliders would be flying wing tip to wing tip or the glider's wing tip with the e tip of the horizontal stabilizer. Guys had to ditch. It sounds impossible, but it did happen. And accidents were possible, if the rope got over or behind the wing and started to tighten, it could pull your wing off. So guys had to ditch. We saw at least ten gliders ditched with people on the wings. They waved at us, and I know they were hoping we'd do something to get them, but what the hell we could do, except wave back at them? We were so low, the tow ship splashed water back on us. We had to pull up to go over Dunkirk, and the weather was still horrible.

"I looked round and there was no more formation. I was leading the right hand element of this column of twos. My friend in number one in the left column was gone, I couldn't find him. I was carrying one jeep with two men in the jeep and an airborne sergeant in the copilot seat. Couldn't see any gliders around us. We had telephone wire going up to rope to the C-47. It was WWI signal corps telephone wire, brittle as hell, and it broke almost immediately. I managed to get some good stuff, and being the glider engineering officer, I took care of number one, and was able to talk to the pilot. He was a damned good C-47 jockey. He had a lot of guts. I never had to worry about getting cut off. He said, 'I can't find anybody, Hang on! The damned fool navigator doesn't know where we are either.' We found out later, the little SOB was kneeling between the pilot and copilot on four flack suits. He was scared spitless, and didn't want to know where we were.

"We started taking small arms fire right away, and small calibre flack, I estimated was 20 mm. One hit me smack in the left foot, took half of the foot with it, and blew the rudder pedal away, and detonated over my left shoulder and peppered me with all kinds of fragments. I took a hit in the left hand, and hits in the chest, butt, thigh, and stomach. I had seven holes in me before I got on the ground. I kept praying. The two young field artillery soldiers riding in the jeep yelled that the gas cans and gas tank of the jeep were punctured and were leaking gasoline. The damn stuff soaked the floor and got up under my foot in the nose section. And I was thinking, 'Oh my God, please, please, no tracers.' We took a tracer and it went 'whoosh' and blew out the windows and blew out the fire too, thank God. But my eyes and my face and hands were burned, and the sergeant's left leg was on fire. He was a comedian. He kept taking his helmet from his head to his crotch. The flack would start busting around and I told him a crotch without a head is no good. He put it back on and immediately took a hit that went through the thigh and scrotum. Poor guy, he thought life was over.

"The floor of the glider was burning. The fabric was burned off on either side of the fuselage. Things were getting pretty hairy. I took a hit in the jaw which knocked me damned near unconscious. With no copilot, and with only one hand and one leg serviceable, I decided I couldn't stay on tow. I said, 'Hit the release.' The poor bastard was frozen with terror, I guess, he couldn't do it. So I put my arm through the wheel and released the tow and told him, 'Hit that nose release.' We were headed for trees and I didn't want a jeep nudging me in the back of the head, I wanted that nose to go up. He couldn't do that either. I managed to do it. I saw a little field and made a skidding right turn because I could only turn right because I couldn't use my left hand and had no left rudder pedal. The nose went up and the wings just went plop when I put it down. We stopped and got out and really started taking small arms fire, so we ran like hell to a ditch. I hopped, skipped and jumped. The sergeant got out, dropped his pants, gave himself a minute examination, with small arms fire popping all around. I said, 'Thompson, come on, what the hell?' He said, 'I want to see if this hurrying was worthwhile.' He had taken a hit in the scrotum.

"We went into this ditch. The two guys in the jeep were not wounded, they bandaged us up as best they could. They were trading small arms fire with an advancing Kraut patrol. I directed them to get the hell out of there. I saw no point in getting them captured and told them where I thought Zand was. They got down to the end of this field and started taking small arms fire, turned around and let fly some shots, and then kept going. Evidently this confused the Germans; they must have thought that the two who had taken off were all that came in the glider. They came around the glider which was still smoking and burning; all the fabric had burned off the glider. They proceeded to loot the glider. They came around and laid their weapons down. I told Thompson, 'Don't fire, hold your fire.' We waited until they got their weapons down, there were only two guys standing on either end of this squad or patrol. I said it was twelve to fourteen. Thompson said it was fifteen to twenty. When we opened up on them, we dropped everyone. There were some more around the other side though.

"Thompson had used up his ammunition. It was quiet and I told him to go out and get the ammunition in the jeep. He crawled out and immediately some more fire started coming. He came back and so help me God, he brought his goddamned mandolin. I said, 'Are you out of your mind? We needed the ammunition.' Well, he didn't want to leave his mandolin. He then crawled out, under a hell of a lot of fire, and got that stuff. I said, 'I'll cover you. Get the hell out there and get some M-1 ammunition and if there are any grenades left, bring them too.' Thank God he wasn't hit. We proceeded to trade shots. I think there were probably six or eight more of these Krauts, but they kept pretty well concealed. Two of them started coming from the left and I opened up with the Tommy gun and they decided it wasn't too good so they went back. By then, I had used all the Tommy gun ammunition. I had a 45 with a clip in the magazine and a clip in the pouch. They started coming again. We used all the Tommy gun ammunition, had the 45, two grenades. I used the 45, and the two grenades, all that was left.

"To make a long story short, I used all my ammunition and Thompson used all the ammunition he brought. When everything was gone, I said, 'We'd better get the hell out of here.' We went down in this ditch. My face was burned and it was very painful. My jaw was painful too, the inside of my mouth was torn up. My right eye was watering like hell and I couldn't see out of it, and my left hand was useless. We were sad sacks. We hopped, skipped and jumped down in the ditch and the water came up to our waist. Immediately I said that something was wrong. It smelled like hell. It wasn't an irrigation ditch but a sewage ditch. We got down about 100 yards and crawled into a barn and just about passed out. We were in shock. I was freezing and had lost lots and lots of blood. I was bleeding pretty badly from a chest wound. My hand and foot, were pumping blood out of me. I didn't think we had long to live.

"A Dutch woman brought hot milk. I tried drinking it, but I couldn't get it down and threw up. Of all the damned barns in Holland, we went into a Nazi sympathizer. She sent her thirteen year old son to tell this nearby German outfit we were there.

"The first Germans that came were a captain of paratroops and a sergeant, he spoke excellent English. He put a bandage on my chest, and then took my watch, zippo [lighter], carton of cigarettes I had in a musette bag, and a bottle of Scotch. He did pour a healthy dollop of schnapps, out of a silver flask that he carried, down my throat. My cigarettes that were in my upper left hand pocket were soggy, He took that pack out, threw it away, opened a pack out of the carton, pulled out one and put it in my mouth. He told Sergeant Thompson I didn't have long to live, so to stay with me until I died, then turn himself in. 'Yes, Sir, yes Sir,' (he told me later, 'Like hell you damn Kraut.'). This guy was a gentlemen. He told me he was on battalion staff of this German parachute regiment, and they were looking for positions to move into to oppose airborne landings. He was coming from Germany. We were supposed to be in Zon, south and west, thirty-six miles, south and west from where we came down. That gives you some idea of how far off course this navigator had us.

A Time to Speak

"To make a long story short, Thompson and I passed out or fell asleep, and I was awakened by some damned severe kicking, all the ribs on my right side, my jaw was fractured again, my cheek bone fractured, and my skull on the right side was fractured. We were awakened by this SS outfit, part of the patrol we had encountered. Evidently, they had found what was left of the patrol and somebody had told them where we had gone and they came after us. They proceeded to kick the hell out of Sergeant Thompson too. He had his ribs kicked and clavicle fractured. The kick in the jaw loosened some bone fragments. I had a mouthful of bone fragments, blood and saliva. This Kraut got his face down and said, 'Where were you supposed to land?' I said, 'Berlin,' and I spit everything I had in my mouth right in his face. I got the kicking again and passed out.

"Thompson woke me, it was black out. There was small arms fire going off all around us and other explosives. Thompson said they had two guards on us. He lifted me up. I could see one guard sitting in the doorway, slumped over, fast asleep. The other guard was sleeping stretched out. He [Thompson] said, 'I have two knives in my jump boots.' Thompson was a paratrooper, broke an ankle in the jump in Normandy, and was put in the glider field artillery. It made him very unhappy, but he was a very resourceful guy. He says, 'If we are here in the morning, they are going to knock us off. We'd better get the hell out of here. You take that one, I'll take this one.' I agreed with him. He got the guy, and I got the one that was sleeping.

"We crawled out of the barn and somebody said to me, 'Komm!, Komm!' and picked me up and started running across the road with me. It was so damned black I couldn't see who it was. I didn't know whether it was German or what. He put me in a two-wheel horse drawn cart. I said, 'The sergeant.' He said, 'Ja, ja,' and he went back and got Thompson, put Thompson next to me, put a blanket on top of us, covered us with hot, moist cow manure (I can still smell it to this day). He was driving down this blacked out road and was stopped twice by German patrols. The first time, he told the German patrol (he told us later) that this manure was for the vegetable garden of the hospital in Schijndel. And the boys, probably from farms, said, 'Ja, ja,' and let us go. The second time some SOB was pushing a bayonet through that manure. Although I was in a bad way, I didn't want a bayonet pushed through my vital organs. I got very nervous.

"Anyway we got there. I was taken to this hospital, I was in surgery for four hours. They patched me up, I received the last rites of the Catholic Church (they didn't expect me to live). I was placed in this maternity ward; my face was all bandaged, my hand was bandaged. I had a broken ankle and broken fibula. My knee was dislocated. The 20mm. that hit me threw my left leg over my shoulder, my foot and leg were in traction. I was there for eleven weeks in the maternity ward. The Kraut patrols would come through looking for Thompson and me, stop and say *something. I would grunt and groan, and the little Mother Superior, who was 5 feet 2, would come running in there, stomp her feet and say, Raus, Raus, and the damn Krauts would get out of there - they were afraid of her.*

"*I was there eleven weeks. They got a little nervous. I was in 'labor' too long. They decided to put me in a room with a TB sign on the door, and the Krauts never came near me. The British 51st Highland division came in and liberated the town and we were free.*"

Jim Swanson, whose tow ship was blown up, was hidden in the basement with Tipton Webb, a glider pilot from another group. The crew of a C-47 was also hidden there. This hospital had been a way station on the underground railroad that got RAF and US bomber crews out of Holland. They kept photo albums of these evaders. The Mother Superior, Sister Veronica, was awarded the U. S. Medal of Freedom, the highest medal ever given to civilians by the U. S. Unfortunately, President Roosevelt died before he could present it to her. The government flew her to the U. S. and President Truman pinned it on her at a White House ceremony with other Dutch, Belgian, French and Luxembourg awardees.

Battle of the Bulge

Another critical battle toward the end of the war in Europe was the Battle of the Bulge in the Ardennes on the eastern front in Germany where the Allied Armies raced to join the Red Armies on the Elbe River.

Hitler made a decision to retake the military initiative with one of the greatest German counteroffensives of the war. From 16 December 1944 until the beginning of January 1945, he amassed 250,000 troops who advanced from the Siegfried Line into the Ardennes, the forests of Belgium and Luxembourg, an area known as the "bulge." The German objectives were to push the lightly-spread Allied troops back and possibly reach Liège, Antwerp, the English Channel and Paris. To achieve their goals, they attacked with the new 75-ton King Tiger tank, jet-propelled planes, and flying bombs. A number of English-speaking spies were dropped behind the Allied lines, some of them in American uniforms, with instructions to kill Allied commanders.

Facing the German troops were 75,000 to 80,000 Allied troops. Their objective was to stem the German push to the west and to cut through the Siegfried Line, cross the Rhine and get to Berlin.

In December, the 117th Infantry Regiment of the 30th Infantry Division (which made its reputation in World War I as the "break-through" or the "Old Hickory" division) moved from an area near Mariadorf, Germany to Belgium, to halt and contain the powerful enemy army advancing toward the Meuse River and toward the sector Stavelot-Malmédy. Then they headed toward La Glaze and St.

Vith in Belgium and into Magdeburg, Germany.

"Dutch" Westerberg, member of the "Old Hickory" division, was drafted at age thirty-five, already married with a three and a half year old boy, and in business for nine years with Metropolitan Life Insurance. He was the last draftee to go out of Boulder County, Colorado. He received a Bronze Star and the Purple Heart decorations for "heroic achievement" in Belgium.

"I said, 'It can't get to a point where it is so tough that they are going to draft me.' When I was drafted, I went in, took that physical, passed it, and I was in the service. They were going to defer me, but I didn't want the deferment. If I'm needed, if they draft me, I'll go.

"You know it's hard, fifty some years, it's hard to get the sequence just right. But you'll never capture combat the way it is on the line. You've got to live it!

"But it started on the sixteenth of December and ended on the nineteenth of January. That was the length of the Battle of the Bulge. The 117th Regimental Infantry hit the Bulge the night of the sixteenth of December. It broke out that night. We were in Malmédy. We got to Malmédy from way up in Germany. We were guarding a town and a dam. The Jerries were going to blow that dam and wipe out a whole town, and we had some soldiers billeting down below that. That's what they were after. We were up there to keep them from blowing that.

"And the Bulge broke out and they put us on trucks and they trucked us into the Battle of the Bulge at Malmédy and we were strafed almost all night. The trucks didn't have any lights, just feeling their way, couldn't make very good time, but we made it to Malmédy. By the time we got there, it was snow all over the ground and my gosh, we didn't have any camouflage, nothing. We got in some billets there and got some sheets and we tore those sheets up and we had sheets for camouflage. And we were dug in that night at Malmédy. I was on an outpost and my squad of men out there, not for combat purposes, but to find out where the enemy was. They were on all four sides of us. Boy, they were alive and you could hear them. Were they close! And I said, 'Boy, this is not good.' We didn't make a move until dawn and then we went back. We sneaked back before dawn because we didn't want to be seen, and came back and reported to Captain Abbey that the Germans were on all four sides and they were headed this way. So the 120th regiment moved up in our foxholes and we took off in the attack and, by golly if we hadn't of, I think I wouldn't have made it home because at that time, the first time the Air Force got into that part of the country and was dropping these bombs. The smoke was so diffused and so wrong that it wiped out about half of our guys, with those bombs from our own planes.

"We were in the point, we kept going, we kept hitting them. We started at Malmédy, we had Bastogne, we had Stavelot, we had Spa, we had Liège, we had all these towns that were in the 30th Infantry assignment sector to check what was going on. Of course, we found out that the Battle of the Bulge started at St. Vith and it moved down and they were after all the supplies the American army had in Liège, Belgium.

"We had enough stuff in Liège, Belgium to run that German army for another year and they were after it and they needed it. By golly, within sixteen or eighteen miles we stopped. We set up a line of defense there and we kept them from going further, and it was touch and go, there for a while because they were determined they were going to get that cache in Liège, Belgium. Well, they didn't.

"Then they had to get another plan, so then they started spreading out on us, and some of them were down in the southern sector going into Bastogne so we had to pull out of Malmédy and help Patton. Patton was coming up from the south into Bastogne, and this was all taking time and they had him surrounded, the Germans did in Bastogne, and we were on the north flank, attached to Patton's army and trying to keep them from going in from the north; they were coming in from the east and the Malmédy massacre took place right there.

"They put these guys they captured, about four squads, and they run them up and opened up with machine guns and leveled and killed them all right there. It was snowing. They covered the bodies up and nobody knew it until it started to thaw out and they found them. And of course, they tagged them all, and got them taken back." [The Malmédy massacre took place on 17 December 1944 when seventy-two American soldiers captured by a German SS unit were led into an open field, lined up, and machine-gunned. After that the Americans had "Avenge Malmédy" as its cry].[152]

To Capture La Glaze

"Well, the Battle of the Bulge really was one of the most important battles of the war. And it was a magnificent operation once they got underway. But we had a lot of experiences. We hit the Battle of the Bulge; our mission was to capture the highest point in the Battle of the Bulge which was La Glaze, Belgium; fifty mile observation every direction. The Germans had been backed up; they had 32 Tiger tanks, 368 armored vehicles, half-tracks and all that in La Glaze, Belgium.

"I only refused one direct order while I was serving in the Army and it happened right there because we had fought for three solid days, trying to take the town of La Glaze, Belgium. It wasn't very big, but it was high, and we hit them from three different sides; and we hadn't gotten in yet.

"That night the captain says, 'Sergeant, I want you to take a platoon of men (which is about forty guys) and I want you to rid that mine field.' We had to go through that mine field in order to take the town. I had gone through a mine field before at night and I lost about seven guys with their legs blown off. I said, 'I left that up to the good Lord above and I can't worry about myself. I've got a job to do and I've got to do something about it.' We went through that mine field. When the captain gave me that order, I said, 'Captain, you know, do you really know what you are asking me to do?' 'Well, Sergeant, we've got to have it done.' I said, 'Well I'll make you a deal. I'll take my men and I'll lead my men, but I'll be right behind you. If you'll lead that mission, I'll go.' I said, 'It is a suicide mission, you know that.' And I never heard another word. And we didn't go and I saved those guys.

"We had night patrols, we had combat patrols, we had information patrols, and I was taking these kids, and I'd go if it was reasonably practical, not kill a bunch of my men. But they turned over so fast, it worried me because I would try to get them oriented before we ever left on a mission and tell them the pitfalls that could happen and, boy, they paid attention, because I said, 'Boys, it is a matter a life or death and if you follow my orders, I think we can get through and make this.' I was like a dad to these kids. But as long as 'Old Pop,' (when we got in combat, they called me 'Pop') would take a combat patrol out, they were there. They wouldn't move without me.

"The next day we hit those guys with a surprise attack, coming out of the woods, and we just planted that thing with M-1 rifle fire. And we went on in there, we got the tanks in there and boy, we captured all that. They didn't even have a chance to get out of there. They were caught, and from there it was the beginning of the end, because they were trying to get out of there. This was on Christmas Day, December twenty-five. The next day it cleared up and that's the first time the sun shone and the first time the planes could fly. And boy, they came in there with those P-38s, those fighter planes and they strafed whatever was trying to get out and burned that stuff right at the side of the road and just crippled the Germans. They were trying to get back there and get on the Rhine River for their last stand."

Into St. Vith

"We could look into St. Vith, we were about 1000 yards and we had fought and it was getting toward night and the Jerries had put up a line of defense and were going to make a last stand. My outfit was in pretty good shape at that time until they opened up with these doggone 88s and put a bunch of tree bursts in on us, and it practically wiped my outfit out. I had one guy, shrapnel hit him and it just laid his stomach wide open and there he was with his guts hanging out and everything else. We got him back and I really don't know whether he lived.

"I had a little company runner by the name of Joe V. He was twenty-one years old and he had four kids. That was my foxhole buddy, and I was like a dad to him. I said, 'Joe, they really have riddled us,' and I said, 'You know, we've got to fake something and the only way I know that I think we can do it. I want you to run back to the weapons, just back of us always. You go back there and tell those guys to send up a water-cooled 50 caliber machine gun.' (We had 30 calibers but you can burn those things up. There's no way you can keep firing those all night.) So he went back and got a water-cooled machine gun. 'Tell 'em you've got a guy out there that can fire that thing and you just get it up here.' And they got it up there in my foxhole.

"In the meantime, I had shrapnel in this right arm and I put a tourniquet around the thing and it was almost pitch dark by that time and if I didn't do something, we were going to be taken prisoner or they were going to get wise and do more damage —they didn't know this. But when I got that water-cooled machine gun in place, about every fifteen minutes, all night, I'd spray a blanket of lead all over that valley and across the other side and let those guys know that we're in good shape over here. By gosh, we didn't have but five men. They could have walked through that. But they didn't know that and that's the only thing that bluffed them, to hold them off until the next day. And the next day, then we got help. We got air power, we got tanks, plenty of help, and we went right on into St. Vith and I went back to the hospital. The doctor laid me out on this table and pulled all the shrapnel out of that arm, except one slug which is still there, still in the elbow. He bandaged it up and sent me back to my outfit, went into St. Vith that same day and the Battle of the Bulge was over."

In the battle of Auchen, Westerberg's Division went through the Siegfried Line. Now they were ready for the big push to cross the Roer River and the Rhine River, 169 miles from Berlin on the Rhine. The Russians were 75 miles coming the other way. The two armies were trying to coordinate; the Russians arrived in Berlin by the time Westerberg's Division got to Magdeburg.

Magdeburg, Hitler's Headquarters

"We got into Magdeburg and this was the headquarters, Hitler's headquarters for the Siegfried Line. He had it all staked out. He had ribbons running to every gun position, from Magdeburg, Germany into the Siegfried Line. He could fire any one of those guns, in pillboxes down there from Magdeburg. And it was five floors underground.

"Magdeburg was wiped out, I mean everything, but this bomb shelter, this communication center was intact. It was a round dome and it was probably 12 to 15 feet thick. They bombed it and it just bounced off everything, didn't even faze it. That's where they had this communication center. Right across, about a block from us, was an apartment house and an old professor that taught school there (he had to teach Hitler's way, all Hitler's books), and his mistress still was there. And he took to me, for some reason or other, and I was nice to them. In fact, I would take some of my rations from my platoon and we fed them and fattened them up for the time we were there. His office, he had a couch, one of those old-fashioned ones, and I had my squads there, when we had a change of guards.

"We guarded that bunker with our lives. We were down where they made all the decisions and where they fired all those guns and it was a fascinating place, really. I pulled that map, which was on the communications room wall, that Hitler looked at. I took it off the wall very carefully, folded it very carefully, and put it under my shirt in back; it just fit my back. I got it up to the place and I told the professor, 'Could you find me a box that I could ship this in?' Well, he did. I've got that map at home.

"We didn't stay very long. We went down to Oelsnitz. They were having some trouble down there, sniper fire and all that, and they weren't settled yet and my outfit took off down there, that was south of Magdeburg. And we got that quieted down in about three or four weeks.

"So it was a wonderful experience. You couldn't put enough money on the line to ever get me to go back again, but what an experience it was to get through something like that and get back home and be sane and have your faculties. A lot of them didn't. I still support a lot of hospitalized veterans. I think of them because, boy, I know the situation they are in and most of them are there for life. They are stuck in there in the hospital and can't get out and some of them with legs off. We lost a lot of men and that was real tough. We turned over so fast. You know you go into battle and you are bound to lose them. You get close to those guys if they stay four or five days. The life of a guy in combat is not very great. I mean, the mortality rate is pretty grim, but there were a lot of good men. It was an experience that I'll never forget. I should have written a book.

"I don't know. I grew up a Lutheran when I was a kid. My parents were Lutheran. I grew up in Iowa and I seemed to develop a very strong faith in God. I've never been an overly religious individual, but I've believed in God. And I believe in prayer. I've devoted a certain part of every day in talking it over with Him. Boy, that saved me in combat, I'm telling you, because it relieved me of my responsibility. I just turned it over to God, I just said, 'I've got a job to do and I just hope You are going to go with me because I need all of the help I can get.' I said, 'I'm not going to worry about it. I'm just going to turn it over to You and I've this job to do and I'm going to do the very best I can to accomplish it.' And through mine fields and all that stuff, I can't take any credit for that. It wasn't me, I was guided with the higher power to get through it. I just believe that He had a mission for me more, fighting the war and winning it. I can see it, when I look back at all the things He guided me to do and to get me through and always be there. I think I can see where He spared my life." [153]

Italy: Riva Ridge and Mt. Belvedere

Although the Italian government capitulated to the Allies on 8 September 1943 and even declared war on Germany on 13 October, German troops remained on Italian soil to fight desperately to keep the Allied troops from moving north.

For the United States, the first military campaign on European soil began south of Naples, at Salerno, on 9 September 1943, and after murderous fighting, the beachhead was secured on 16 September. The Salerno invasion proved to be a real challenge. The Anzio campaign, in the mountainous terrain of Monte Cassino (January 1944), led to the liberation of Rome in June, but it was costly in terms of combat casualties. Allied combat casualties were estimated at 30,000 and the German combat casualties were 28,000 to 30,000. Furthermore, the Allies needed control of the north-south highways through the Apennine mountains, giving them access to the Po Valley.

Another pivotal battle loomed, 18-20 February 1945. The mountain troops needed to scale the 2,300 foot Riva Ridge and assault Mt. Belvedere.

The 10th Mountain Division was sent into the Apennines because this east-west mountain chain was a powerful base and vantage point for the German Army. From the high peaks, the Germans could control troop movements between northern and southern Italy. Three times the Allied troops had tried to scale Mt. Belvedere, the highest of the peaks, and three times they had failed.

Their orders read, "The 10th Mountain Division will attack on D-Day to seize, occupy, organize and defend the Mt. Belvedere-Mt. della Torraccia ridge, prepare for action to the northeast."

Although the ski troops were formed in 1942, Max Peters didn't join until 1944. In fact, Peters, who already had a Master's Degree in Chemical Engineering, had trouble enlisting in the ski troops. His Dean thought he was "an absolute idiot and not a patriot" because the armed services needed chemical engineers rather than infantrymen.

The 10th Mountain Division was first assigned to Fort Lewis, Washington, then up to Kiska, Alaska. From there, the ski troops went to Camp Hale in Colorado to do their basic training in the mountains to prepare them for the assaults to come in Italy.

"There was a big argument about how they could best make use of the ski troops. We thought they were going to send us to Burma because we were mountain climbers. We got on this train. The big shots knew where we were going, but the rest of us ordinary guys (at this time, I was a buck private). We watched carefully to see which way the train went, hoping it wouldn't go west. It went east to a port in New Jersey. Right at Christmas time, we loaded on a boat, all 10,000 of us, the whole division loaded on this boat. We left about the second of January, 1945. The war only had a few months to go. It ended for us in May."

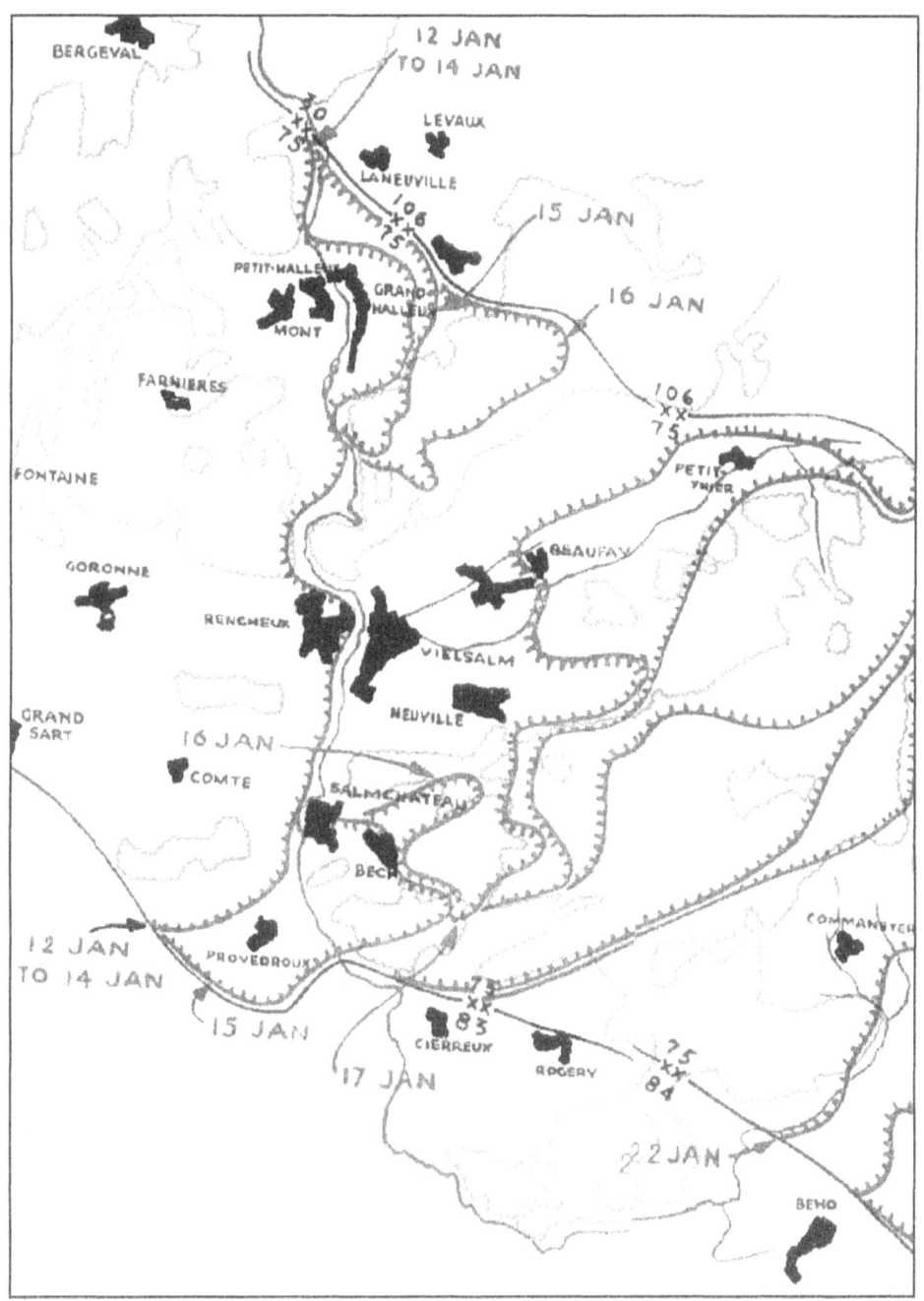

Division routes- Battle of Ardennes

The German Welcome to Italy

"Occasionally we would notice the ships were zigzagging and that meant probably there was a submarine around. In any case, we went through Gibraltar and the Mediterranean. We landed at Naples. We landed there and marched up into part of the town and German airplanes came over, and we saw them dropping these things. All of us rushed around trying to catch them; they were little leaflets. The little leaflets said, 'We welcome you Mountain Troopers to Italy. You will not live long, but it is nice that you are here.' That was the way they welcomed us. I think we spent one night in Naples.

"The next day we got on LCIs and went up along the coast there, from Naples all the way to Leghorn [port of Livorno] which is just ten miles from Pisa, where the Leaning Tower is, at the base of the Apennines. We got a chance to go into town and see the Leaning Tower and we got used to the general atmosphere. We were there about two weeks.

"Then they took us up into the foothills of the Apennines and this was probably about the end of January. And we started going patrols, ski patrols, we'd go on skis. Occasionally we would see a German ski patrol group and we would shoot at them, and they would shoot at us. Then we would both go in opposite directions and nobody was ever killed in that part until about twentieth of January."

Mt. Belvedere

"They had this place called Mt. Belvedere and that was the key to getting into the Po Valley. They tried it three times with United States troops, and the Germans held a ridge that overlooked Mt. Belvedere which was named Riva Ridge. They were on top of Riva Ridge. Three times the United States had tried to go up Mt. Belvedere and they had been beaten back because they shelled them from Riva Ridge. So they said, 'What we've got to do is take Riva Ridge and then we'll have a chance to go up Belvedere, which was tremendously well defended.' So they said, 'We'll go up Riva Ridge.' But the people said, 'You can't climb it. It's got a cliff and the Germans are right there at the top of the cliff.' Our guys scouted and found out that the Germans weren't protecting that cliff because they knew it couldn't be climbed. So here was this cliff with the Germans ready to shell us if we try to go up Belvedere. We laid all kinds of plans, practicing. They took my outfit, A Company, 85th, and we were taken out at night and put into this place and we were told, 'Don't you move at all for the next day!' We lay there all day, hidden away where nobody could see us. Next night, if it went right, we were going to be able to go up Belvedere. In the meantime, these other guys, at the start of the night, were all set to begin climbing this unclimable cliff. They had all the climbing gear and all the rest. They started out climbing by about ten o'clock at night. They got up to the top of

Riva Ridge, went over it. And the Germans couldn't believe they had done it. They killed a few Germans up there, but they captured all of them. They captured all of the emplacements, so now there is no protection on Mt. Belvedere because our other 10th Mountain Group had gone up this cliff and gotten the place.

"So then they said to us, 'Go,' and we started walking up Belvedere, very steep and they are shooting down and it's hard to run up it. You can walk up it; it's not a mountain climb. In any case, we went up there, we lost a whole lot of guys in my company, either killed or wounded, and by the time we were done, of the 10,000 people that went over there, 997 had been killed and probably three or four thousand wounded, not in that one battle, but the whole way through.

"Later on, when I ran into a nurse someplace, she said there were all these Mountain Troopers being brought it. She said you could always tell it was a Mountain Trooper because they were always shot in the shoulders, in the face, and in the head and front, whereas, other people were usually shot from behind. They were moving away. Our guys were always shot going up.

"In any case, we managed to get up this thing; a lot of guys got hit by the mines. There were trenches dug at the top and the mines were in the trenches, but we cleaned them out and went on down on top of the ridge and we finally got down to the place where we actually got Mt. Belvedere."

Letter from Northern Italy, March 15, 1945

Although the mountain troops were on Mt. Belvedere by 7 March, German artillery and mortar fire continued to be directed at them. Some were lucky enough to get time away from the shelling for rest and relaxation. Among them, Max Peters, who wrote this to his family.

"Dear Mother and Dad:

"As I am writing this letter I am probably the most contented man in Italy. Yesterday I was hungry, dirty, cold, and tense while today I am completely relaxed, warm, clean, and full of good food served with the best of service.

"Day before yesterday I was there with shells never letting me relax and every night I was up all the black hours creeping around in no-man's land. It looked like there was no relief in sight and I was not very happy about the whole thing. Then - Bango! Somebody walks up to tell me I've just been given a four-day pass to an amusement town in a rear area.

"Promptly I packed, and after hiking, I caught a truck back to my rear area. It was really a marvelous feeling to sit slumped in the back of that truck going further and further back with the muscles of my body slowly relaxing as all the tension drained out of them.

"A long ride, a warm night's sleep, a hot bath, clean dry clothes, a haircut, a shave, good food and I'm living again.

"This town has excellent eating, sleeping, and amusement facilities for the G.I.s Last night I walked in for supper expecting only regular C2 food and I got the surprise of my life. I ate (free of charge) in a huge hotel with mirrored walls, an arching, decorated ceiling, and an orchestra playing softly in one corner. As I went in I was taken to a table completely set with plates, napkins, table cloth, silverware, glasses, and all the rest of the trimmings. A waiter brought me my first course of soup, then a huge plate piled high with chicken, mashed potatoes, peas, and beets, chocolate milk to drink along with hot rolls and jam finished out the main course. Then I was served two huge chocolate eclairs with their sides fairly bulging with delicious whipped cream. After that the waiter asked me if I wanted anything more and I could only ask to be helped to the door.

"After my meal I couldn't decide whether to go to the opera La Boheme or to a stage show and movie. Finally I went to the stage show and movie where I settled back comfortably in a soft theater seat to watch pretty girls dance, comedians crack jokes, a highly entertaining stage show and finally, an excellent movie.

"Then I went to the Red Cross for some more free coffee and sweet rolls and on to bed. I have a room with two other fellows in a large modern hotel with a private bath. It's a large airy room with mirrors and pictures covering the walls and a huge soft bed which is so comfortable I was almost afraid to lie down on it.

"After a dreamless slumber, I got up to continue on today in this paradise. The same eating treatment was given me again today with my eyes still popping in amazement.

"This afternoon I have been loafing around in a deep easy chair in the reading room listening to good music, reading, and going over to the snack bar every 20 or 30 minutes for some coffee and sweet rolls, cookies or cake. Later on this afternoon I'm going to a movie. I've got about five choices of the movie I'll see and they are all good shows. Then this evening after a dinner of good food, good music and good service I am taking in the opera The Barber of Seville. Tomorrow I'm planning on seeing the opera Madame Butterfly. Lots of food, lots of rest, lots of entertainment. I don't know when I have ever appreciated anything so much as this or enjoyed anything so much. I guess a few hardships make one enjoy the good things in life much more.

"You never heard of the town where I am, and I won't tell you its name because the censor might not allow it. I'll be here two or three more days anyhow, and then I don't know what will happen. No matter what happens, though, nothing can take these days from me, and I'll always hold their memories.

"I should be getting my second class mail within the next few days and I'll bet I'll really have a stack of newspapers. I hope there are some packages too.

A Time to Speak

"Send me some packages of food packed in readable newspapers if you find time.

Sgt. Max S. Peters, 33767761
Co. A., 85th Mountain Infantry
(10th Division)
APO 345
c/o Postmaster
New York, N. Y."

Into The Po Valley

A few days rest and Peters was ready for the next stage of the Italian campaign.

"Then we started for the Po Valley. That was the breakthrough for us. With Belvedere, there was no way the Germans could stop us. They would stop and fight occasionally. We got to this place, Castel D'Aiano, the only spot where we had any resistance. I stayed in that church. We knew the Germans had this one hill, out about two miles from us. And this was the day after Roosevelt died, about April fifteenth. That day the decision was made that we were going to take that next hill, which would open the route to the Po Valley. We shelled that hill and I watched the shells go in there. The hills disappeared. You couldn't see anything. I knew there couldn't be anybody left alive on that hill. Our airplanes were doing it. They obliterated that hill. Yet when we got there, the Germans were all over the place. They killed a whole bunch of our guys. In any case, early in the morning, we started out to take this hill and I got down on this road, which is right above that place with the holes in the wall, about 200 yards from that. I went around a corner, a shell landed right beside me. It came up and hit me on the arm here and tore a huge hole in my pack. I stopped and looked at it, it was bleeding. Very shortly, we got a little break and a medic came along and I said, 'Put something on that.' And he said, 'I'll bring you back.' 'Oh, no, just put some Band-Aids on it.' He put about ten Band-Aids on it and I kept on going and that's when I got the Purple Heart. The Medic turned me in, put me on his list as a guy who was wounded, but kept on going and they gave me a Purple Heart.

"Then we went on farther down and we got up this one hill. There was a tremendous amount of fighting and we dug in and spent the night there. The next day, they sent my squad out on a patrol, and we went sort of back and around and we came to this one house. We went across a mine field, dodging these wires and when we got to the top of this, there was a house. We shot into the house a couple of times and I was the only one who knew any German at all and I yelled, 'Kommen Sie heraus mit den Handen in der Luft und ich werde nicht schiessen!' which is supposed to mean, 'Come out with your hands up and we won't shoot you.' And they did, about seven of them. They surrendered to us. And we went up and checked them out. Every time you do this, everybody steals their watches. I decided I was never going to do that. But this one little lieutenant, I said, 'Gimme your watch!' and he handed it to me and I looked at it and handed it right back to him. And he put it into his pocket and I think he decided I was a pretty nice guy."

Peters and his men continued under sniper fire and checked each house and each hayloft while bullets were hitting on the steps, wounding the lieutenant and another sergeant. Peters went in, pulled them out, and got the patrol to take them down to the medics.

"We were going pretty good and all of a sudden somebody came back and said, 'I saw something white go into that little shack over there at the left. I think we've got problems again.' So I said, 'Well, I guess I'm in charge.' So I went up in front. Here was this stone shanty and they said, for sure, they had seen something go in there. So I crawled up to the side and threw a grenade in the window. The minute it went off, I jumped around and jumped in the door and I got all ready to shoot and two sheep came out of the door.

"Now we've got a clean run and we go back up on our hill. We got shelled completely that night, it was an awful night. We managed to get through it, although we did lose an awful lot more people. Then we started running like mad and every place we went the Germans were trying to surrender. We went to one place; we were being shelled; a friend of mine was killed by a shell that went off about fifty yards past that.

"We came to this place and I was told the Germans were up that ravine and they were shooting anybody that goes across it. So I said to my squad, 'Run!'. . . And just about this time, we were sitting, and out came two Germans, one of them smoking a cigarette, trying to surrender and I got up and knocked the cigarette out of his mouth and he just sort of stood there. They were carrying their rifles but all they wanted to do was surrender. As soon as they'd surrender, we'd send them back.

"From then on, they just surrendered right and left. You'd go some place and there would be twenty or thirty of them waiting and begging to surrender. Some of our guys would go through and take all of their watches. I saw one guy with his whole arm full of watches. And because of what had happened with this nice lieutenant, I would never take anything. Some of the guys had their pockets full of pens and things like that. They just stole all this stuff. But the Germans didn't care. All they wanted to do was surrender and get out of there.

"Then we kept on going and pretty soon we had it all cleared and got on some trucks and went to the Po Valley. My company was the first to get a man into the Po Valley. I watched as this one guy ran ahead, Eddie Storms. Eddie was the *first guy to get into the Po Valley. Then a lot of people followed us. We got up to the Po River and we didn't have a way to get across. So we got some pontoons, boat-like things and went across and got on the other side and just kept on going and going and going until we finally got up to Lake Garda. Then they posted us there. We were leapfrogging each other."* [154]

The Battle of the Bulge and the assaults on Riva Ridge and Mount Belvedere were decisive battles for the Allies in the winter and spring of 1945, and the Allied troops moved steadily toward victory in Europe.

End Notes

151 *The Second World War*, p. 593; p. 666
152 *The Second World War*, p. 620
153 Westerberg returned to his job with Metropolitan Life Insurance which his wife had taken over during the war. He died September 15, 1999.
154 Peters retired as Dean of the College of Engineering, University of Colorado, Boulder.

CHAPTER 40

THE HOLOCAUST, PART I
THE VICTIMS

In spite of the hope generated by the Allied military successes, it was a war-weary world in 1945. An event in January deepened the war-time horrors when Soviet troops entered the Auschwitz-Birkenau concentration camp on 26 January. As more and more camps were liberated in April and May, the world became aware of the extent of the German plan of the systematic extermination of the Jews.

People were overcome with disbelief by what is now called "the Holocaust." (The word "holocaust," understood as a reference to the planned annihilation of the Jewish people by Hitler's Nazi party, occurred as early as 1942. However, the phrase, "The Holocaust" did not become established until the late 1950's. The Nazis referred to the extermination of the Jews as *Endlösung* (the final solution); Jewish people, in the postwar period, referred to it by the Yiddish word *Hurban* and by the Hebrew word *Shoah,* or catastrophe.

Anti-Semitism had its origins in the belief among some Christians that the Jews were collectively responsible for killing Jesus and therefore rejected God through deicide. Martin Luther in his 1543 essay, "The Jews and their Heirs," wrote that a Christian has "no enemy more cruel, more venomous and violent than a true Jew." This concept of Judaism versus Christianity persisted through centuries.

In Medieval times Jewish settlers were confined to ghettos, or separate city quarters, the largest in Prague and Warsaw. The purpose of ghettoizing Jews was to restrict contacts between Jews and Christians and to confine them to certain economic activities. In Russia from the 1790s, the Pale of Settlement confined Russian Jews to the western provinces of the empire. The main centers of industry were outside the Pale which left the Jewish settlers within the Pale in poverty.

These ghettos should be distinguished from the Nazi-instituted ghettos which were camps where Jews were held under duress and their lives regulated by the Nazi regime. In Warsaw and Krakow they referred to ghettos as the Jüdishcher Wohnbezirk (Jewish residential quarters).

In the 19th century, anti-Semitism was a powerful political and social force. One well-known example was the Dreyfus Affair in France, where anti-Semitism permeated the French Army. In 1894, when secret French documents were discovered in the German embassy, Captain Alfred Dreyfus, an Alsatian Jew, was convicted of treason, sentenced to life imprisonment and sent to Devil's Island. The

Dreyfus Affair divided France: the royalists, militarists, nationalists, and Roman Catholicswere anti-Dreyfus; the republicans, socialists and anti-clerics were pro-Dreyfus. In 1898 it was discovered that much of the evidence had been forged. The results were: the separation of church and state in 1905; the exoneration of Dreyfus in 1906; and the rise in power of the French left-wing.

The United States Immigration Act of 1924 had quotas against Jewish immigrants. During the depression years, Americans feared the refugees would take jobs away from American citizens. As late as 1939, a Roper poll revealed that 53 percent of the Americans asked believed that Jews were different from everyone else and that these differences should lead to restrictions in business and social life.[155] It is not surprising that there were quotas to college and university entrance, discrimination in employment and in social clubs.

One of the earliest opportunities to accept Jewish immigrants in the United States was in May 1939. The ship St. Louis sailed from Hamburg, Germany with 936 passengers, 930 of them Jewish refugees escaping from Nazi Germany. They were bound for Cuba, a temporary sanctuary, as they had fulfilled U.S. immigration requirements which would permit them to enter the United States from three months to three years after their arrival in Cuba. Cuban officials retroactively invalidated the landing permits before the ship sailed, then refused them entry. The Jewsih passengers were confident of a waiver from the U.S. government, to save their lives. The State Department cited American immigration policy and refused to admit the ship. President Roosevelt did not respond to their request for temporary haven and the ship was forced to return to Europe and docked in Antwerp on 17 June 1939. They were finally welcomed by Belgium, Holland, England, and France. Only those who entered Great Britain found safety; the other refugees faced Nazi regime when war broke out. [156]

The Allies did know about the massacres of the Jews and newspapers reported the information. On 28 October 1941, *The New York Times* (page 10) acknowledged "Nazis seek to rid Europe of all Jews," and the complete elimination of Jews from European life was an established German policy. *The Seattle Daily Times* (1 June 1942) had a banner headline on page one, "JEWS SLAIN TOTAL 200,000" and the lead paragraph referred to it as "the most terrible racial persecution in modern history." [157]

Great Britain, the United States, the Soviet Union and eight other nations issued a declaration on 17 December 1942 which condemned Germany's "bestial policy of cold-blooded extermination" of Jews and vowed that those who perpetuated the crimes would not escape retribution. [158]

On 1 March 1943 a huge rally was held in Madison Square Garden, New York City to demand the immediate action by the United Nations to save as many as possible of the millions of Jews threatened with extermination and to halt the further liquidation of European Jews by the Nazis. The demand was made by religious, civic, political and labor leaders to an audience of 21,000 inside the auditorium and to thousands in the streets listening to the speeches through amplifiers. Support for the demonstration came from overseas with messages from the Archbishop of Canterbury and Chief Rabbi J. H. Hertz in Great Britain. A resolution was addressed to President Roosevelt and through him to the governments of the United Nations. [159] But no attempt was made to rescue Jews.

No one knows how many people were victims of the Holocaust. Martin Gilbert estimates that the number of Jews killed in Europe between September 1939 and May 1945 was six million.[160] These are conservative estimates as thousands of infants and children were murdered before their births could be recorded. Many others were deported without a numerical register of their existence. Research continues to establish Jewish losses.

Statistics don't tell the real story. That is best left to some of the victims and survivors and how they remember their experiences.

Mr. and Mrs. Zesa Starr

Mr. and Mrs. Starr, originally from Poland, spent five and a half years in concentration camps. They met and married after the war. As they began to talk about their experiences, Mrs. Starr remarked, *"There are no happy moments in this story."*

Mr. Starr: *Poland was anti-Semitic before Hitler. They would not let the Poles come in and buy from Jewish stores. It was like a boycott. Still, we make a living. We were tailors, we were working. We were not rich people, not poor people. We lived in a little town, a few hundred Jewish families. We lived very peacefully together because we make a living.*

In 1938, November the ninth, the Kristallnacht. That time I remember on Friday night we were together, eating supper, and I said to my mother and to my children, 'I don't like what is going on. What they are doing to the Jews over there? Throwing them out of their homes, knocking the windows out, taking over the stores, burning the synagogues, books? We are neighbors. We don't know what will happen to us.'

So that time we lived, it was scary; we didn't have any place to go, we had to stay over there. One mistake was the French and England. If you give me Poland, there will be peace, this is what started the war. So this is what happened about September first, 1939.

I was drafted into the Polish army and the war. The Poles were not able to fight against the Germans. So we start fighting and by the fifteenth, 1939, the Germans catch me. I was together with two Polish soldiers. The Jewish lieutenant said to me, 'You know what the Germans are doing to the Jews in Germany, they will do worse things to us.' I started crying. It didn't help. He killed himself.

After two hours, six German soldiers arrived on motorcycles, and the first question was, 'Are you a Jew?' I said, 'I am a Jew.' They knocked me down on the ground and they started kicking me, each and every one, kicking and hitting, I was beaten all over. Later they said to everybody, 'Take off your clothes, we want to see if we have more Jews here.'

Two hours walking, we came together about 5,000 soldiers sent to Germany, Stalag 21B. Right away all the Jews go on the right side. We were about 1,200 soldiers. And they said, 'From now on, you are not a prisoner of war, you are a Jew. You can wear the uniform, but you are not entitled to be a prisoner of war.' And the punishment started right away. They put us in a labor camp. We do the work. At night they wake us up to make us exercise.

The worst thing we saw over there some boys sixteen or seventeen. They could kill anytime.

I was sent to a labor camp in Poland until 1943. Everybody, in 1943, arrive in Auschwitz. We didn't know the reason for being moved. I was in about fifteen camps, the biggest were Auschwitz, Buchenwald and Dachau. I was liberated by the American Army from Dachau. [29 April 1945] What I understand, they didn't want us to have too much friendship...

Mrs. Starr: ...or knowledge of what's going on. So you were sent to another camp, and you were new over there. They tried to break our morale and spirit. They tried to break us. We went to a ghetto in 1939. He [Hitler] tried to send people out to concentration camps. My home town, Lodz, was a center. They brought people in from all the small towns. From there they sent us to Auschwitz, Treblinka and to other camps.

In the ghetto, we used to work for the Germans, work for uniforms, to make from straw shoes, our hands were bleeding. It was at the time they prepared themselves to go to the Russian border, and straw keeps dry. As long as they needed us, they kept us. If you were capable to work, you are OK, you could go home and next day return to work.

I worked in a place where they brought all the clothing from Auschwitz and we ripped it apart; we took all the valuables, we put sleeves and sleeves; and linings and linings; and back to back, collars, it has to be numbered, according to the size. And all the valuables we sent to Germany, diamonds and gold. Not just little boxes, huge barrels, a lot. They robbed all the people from all over, for all these countries.

Mr. Starr: I was in these camps five and a half years, actually, five years and eight months, from September 15 to April 29, 1945.

Mrs. Starr: And I was in the same years. We met after the war. I was liberated to the British.

Mr. Starr: I spent three months in the hospital. I couldn't walk. I weighed 80 pounds. Everybody asks the question, 'How did you manage to survive?'

Sometimes, miracles happen, so maybe it was a miracle. Of course, the doctor told me when I came to the hospital, 'If you have lain over there another two days, you would not have survived.' My body was about 95 percent dead.

No food, no water, no nothing. Six days and six nights, no food and no water. We were laying out to be thrown into the crematorium. So it was lucky the American Army arrived.

Mrs. Starr: There was no system for deciding who was to be sent to the crematorium. Most of them were the disabled, not capable.

Mr. Starr: The last six weeks, I couldn't work anymore. My strength was going down, down, down, down.

Mrs. Starr: Our morale was very low. I just didn't care to live. I fought another war after the war, when I started searching for relatives. And I just couldn't find anybody so I didn't care to live. I was in a strange country and I had a setback, a very bad setback. Bergen-Belsen, the camp I was liberated from... about five days before I was liberated, I had typhus and I was in the hospital.

Mr. Starr: I worked in a coal mine for a year and half. We didn't have overcoats. In the winter time, it was very cold and rainy, so I find a paper bag in the coal mine, so I put it under my shirts to keep me warm. We came back into the camp and the SS looked us over and found I had a paper and called me into his office, knocked me down on the floor and started kicking me, took off the belt and was beating me with the buckle. Later, he picked me up and he said to me, 'You know why I was hitting you?' I said, 'Yes, because I had a paper.' 'No, because you are a Jew.' And he said to me, 'Why are you not committing suicide? You will never come out alive from here.' Because in the morning when you went to work, you could see sometimes, one, two, three Jews running into the barbed wire and committing suicide. 'You will never come out alive, you will be punished every day.'

I didn't answer him. I had my answer inside. You can kill me, but I will not commit suicide.

Sometimes in the morning, when I have a chance to wake up, and I start crying and praying, 'God, look what punishment we Jews are going through. Why? Help us. Give me strength to come out alive from here.' Maybe God listened to my prayer. It was a miracle to survive.

We worked twelve hours in the coal mine. We'd come home and lie down like dead people. We had no lunch over there, twelve hours straight. How could someone have the strength to work twelve hours? I don't have the answer myself. Lucky.

Mrs. Starr: *They say the human body is strong like iron.*

Mr. Starr: *In five and a half years, you could see things unbelievable. Once we were walking home from work, a Jewish man about twenty years old. When he came back into camp, he was with his father, and they called his father out and said, 'You have to hang your son.' And he said, 'I will not hang my son,' and they hanged them both.*

Mrs. Starr: *They were cruel people.*

Mr. Starr: *The most educated country was Germany.*

Mrs. Starr: *That's why it is difficult to understand.*

Mr. Starr: *They taught them and taught them.*

Mrs. Starr: *They brainwashed them; he [Hitler] didn't teach them, he brainwashed them.*

Mr. Starr: *It was unbelievable what kind of things they were doing with us.*

Mrs. Starr: *The people you had over there, they didn't see zero, they didn't see anything. You get immune to it, seeing the horrors day after day. I don't know how to describe to you. They really didn't care. Without a reason, they hit you. They did so many catastrophic atrocities, it is just hard to describe.*

Mr. Starr: *You can see what kind of monster was Hitler. When he took over Germany, what he did with the handicapped people, even Germans.*

Mrs. Starr: *He wanted a perfect race.*

Mr. Starr: *Just kill, kill, kill. He has in his cabinet, Goebbels, Göring, Streicher, Ribbentrop, Eichmann, they were monsters. If I had known in the beginning, when the lieutenant killed himself, I would have to spend five and a half years, I would have done the same thing. I thought a year, maybe next year, someday has to come help. When the SS kills my friends, what can you think about? Who will be next?*

Mrs. Starr: *Unborn children, women had babies. What they did to those babies? Just take an infant and tear to pieces, like a rag, or take their teensy weensy bodies and smash them against the wall.*

Mr. Starr: *Who faced Dr. Mengele?* [Dr. Josef Mengele who experimented on twins in his laboratory in Auschwitz.] *I faced him every day. I work over there* under his command. He was happy he could send about 4,000 Jews to the gas chamber. He had a smile on his face. He made experiments on twins.

Mrs. Starr: In one camp, on a Sunday, there came a bunch of SS ladies and a gynecologist and they tried to monkey around with us, 4,500 women. I knew when they took us to work, they were not doctors, they were talking, laughing, playing the guitar and they were telling jokes on our bodies, just to break us. They were so cruel. No mercy. I tell you, over in Auschwitz there was an SS lady whose name was Irma G. She was with Mengele. She was so cruel. She had a whip, a horse whip; she had a grin and she would split your head with that whip. They didn't have to have a reason to punish you. That was their joy.

Mr. Starr: When I was in the labor camp in 1940, they took out ten Jews in January in freezing cold and hanged them up by their arms, took off their clothes, naked, and they took water and they sprayed on them, in about five to ten minutes, they were frozen to death. You have to stand and watch it and they do it with a smile on their face. Why were you doing this? For fun. You stood like this each and every one. You couldn't cry even.

We all were friends. We were friends because we were in the same boat.

We remember one thing. Comes September, the high holidays, the day we didn't know. We were like animals. Wake up in the morning, get some coffee, go to work, come home at night, get a little piece of bread, a little bit of soup. If you find a potato, you were lucky.

In one coal mine was Italians and French people. We couldn't talk to them. It looked like they had better treatment than we had.

Mrs. Starr: In one camp, I went to rest room, one of the SS ladies had left a paper. I picked up the paper (we were guarded even then). I tried to read, but no way. We did hum when we came home. Our biggest thing is reminiscing, day in and day out.

Mr. Starr: In the coal mine, four or five Jews, and one Pole was over us. We were afraid even to ask him a question. We couldn't trust him. Se we couldn't find out nothing that was going on. The Americans start coming and bombarding in the daytime so we were watching how the bombs were coming down. We said, 'Maybe, maybe, help is coming.' The SS was screaming, 'Lay down, lay down.' We didn't care if the bombs killed us. We were watching how the bombs were coming down.

Mrs. Starr: When the Red Cross came, they showed them the nice places, for propaganda, they didn't go beyond to see the catastrophic things.

Mr. Starr: It was about January 17, 1945 when the Russians came in, the Russians started invading Poland. We were 6,000 Jews in the coal mine camp and we were walking out from there and we were walking 400 miles until we come to Buchenwald. The whole way you hear the machine guns. We walked, this was the 'Dead March.' [Death marches were forced marches, under heavy guard, of long columns of prisoners.] *When we came into Buchenwald, we looked around and there were only 500 left. 5,500 were killed, laid down and frozen to death. The machine guns were going and going and going. We couldn't walk. One held the other one, 400 miles in thirty days. We walked during the day, and lay down at night.*

I don't know how I survived.

Mrs. Starr: *After the Liberation, we couldn't digest the food. People were dying, they were heavy foods.*

Mr. Starr: *When Eisenhower liberated the first camp, he said to the soldiers, you know why you were fighting, for this you were fighting. You were fighting to liberate the camps. He was crying with what he saw at Buchenwald.*

I went to the camp Bergen-Belsen. There was a Jewish committee with a list of all Jewish survivors. I find my brother there. We were young, twenty-nine and a half; I met my wife over there. We married in January 1946.

Mrs. Starr: *When we got married, we had nobody. I was so sick, morally. I had no desire to go back to Poland.   In my heart, I'm still young.*

Mr. Starr: *I am thankful to the United States. It liberated me. It let me in the United States. We visit schools to teach children about the Holocaust. We make a short presentation and then we ask them to ask lots of questions. In the schools, some asked, 'Are you telling everything that is true that happened in the concentration camp?' My answer, 'Yes, I spent time there.'*

Walter Plywaski

Plywaski was a secular Jew born in Lodz, Poland in 1929. His father was a pharmacist, Maksymilian Jozel who was politically active and led demonstrations against the occupying forces. His mother, Regina helped save his father's business. He had a half-brother, actually a cousin, adopted in 1941 after his parents died of TB. The Plywaski family was forced to move from Lodz to a ghetto then to a series of concentration camps.

"To start with, I sort of object to the word 'ghetto.' It is an urban concentration camp. Even under West German law, it is considered that.

"I was ten years old. We were not rounded up. What happened was that two of my father's pre-war card-playing buddies, who were so called ethnic Germans, Volksdeutsche, walked into the pharmacy wearing swastika lapel buttons, pulled pistols and said, 'Max, we're friends, we'll give you half an hour to get out.'

"So, they relented and gave us an hour. We grabbed whatever we could and put it on handcarts and one hansom cab, horse drawn. That transported all this shit to the area designated as the Litzmannstadt ghetto, where we were crammed into a room with a kitchen with some other thirty people in it already. A third of these people were relatives. That was probably at the turn of the year, in the winter

(1939-40), either December or January, I don't know, perhaps even February. It is difficult to say.

"The ghetto itself, a large camp, was closed by March; barbed wire, dynamited buildings for better firing areas and so on. That's how we went there.

"What she [his mother] did to protect our house, one of the few houses in the Lodz camp that had, for some time, city gas. Most of the place was very primitive; 95 percent or more had no running water, even the apartment houses did not have connection to sewers. That was one of the main reasons why in Lodz we were much more strongly isolated than in other places: because they had sewers they could use for communication, but we didn't.

"Anyhow, so what she did, she swapped and borrowed a whole bunch of gas hot plates and put up notices that people can come in to cook. And the fee was one-fifth of what they were cooking. It was very important, especially at the very beginning.

"We didn't stay there, maybe half a year. Very, very fast, the overcrowding was diminished, disease, starvation, shootings, people leaving or escaping for a while. Some did [escape].

"Then the ghetto administration came into being; it was run by Jews, the name whom the Germans designated to be the 'king of the Jews,' so to speak, was a guy by the name of Chaim Rumkowski. He was an insurance salesman before the war and, at one time, and another part-time, he was working for my aunt, who was running the Jewish orphanages in Lodz. For that reason, for instance, her son-in-law, by the name of Jakobson became the chief prosecutor in charge of the ghetto. Of course, positions like that, not only obtained better living quarters, but much and better food, actually luxurious food.

"For that reason, my father was able to get an assignment to a ghetto pharmacy and, at one point, after all this gas business ran out, my mother got an assignment as being in heaven, peeling potatoes for the communal kitchen. You could eat and steal the peels and bring them home and cook them. We made either soup out of it or potato pancakes or by adding saccharin and German ersatz coffee grounds, a so-called cake. You had to use everything and anything.

"So that was our start. At first, there were sort of schools for us. After a while, the Germans stopped it. By then, my cousin was adopted and my father hired an old man by the name of Ginsberg who, before the war, looked like Falstaff. But by then, his skin was hanging like drapery fifteen sizes too large on a mannequin. My dad paid him with two slices of bread for tutoring us two hours a day, three times a week.

"Because of the protection we had, because of the extra food, our aunt was able to smuggle us into the orphanage that was receiving heavy doses of food because Rumkowski was the angel of the orphanage. It was a showcase. The only way you survive a meatgrinder of this sort is by luck, mostly.

"By end of May '44, the ghetto is down to about 50,000, from about 320,000, because of transports and everything else. [Figures in the *Encyclopedia of the Holocaust* mention 204,800 in the Lodz ghetto in 1942 and by May 1944 only 77,000.] Because of my father's activities, we knew what was happening to those who went 'east to work.' He didn't change stripes; he was active in listening to BBC broadcasts, a little group and they would type up the news on little pieces of cigarette paper, very thin paper. Of course, listening to the BBC was punishable by death. If you are smart enough about it, and maintain security tightly, you could get away with it, at least for some time. There were some suspicions at one time. Both he and I were arrested because I was distributing those little pieces of paper. They were rolled up like a little match and you would shake somebody's hand and then leave it in their hand.

"There was an outfit, calling itself Kripo, which is German, short for Kriminal Polizei, and they were a branch of the Gestapo. [Kripo, the criminal police department of Göring's Prussian ministry of the interior. In 1934 the Kripo and the Gestapo became part of the Security Police Main office. Within the borders of the Reich, they wore plain clothes but in the German-occupied countries, they wore SS uniforms. From time to time they were called on by the Gestapo to assist it in operations against Jews and political opponents.] *They had quarters at the cathedral which was inside the ghetto. They were actually living in the parish house and that's where they were interrogating. They simply made a big sweep of people. They didn't really know. They fed us two big spoons of castor oil before interrogation and you shit in your pants every time you were hit in the face or anywhere else. In the case of me and my dad, they would beat him and ask me; then vice versa. Just as we were being taken there, he whispered to me, 'If you sing, and if we live, I'll kill you.' And he would have. And I would have deserved it.*

"If it had gotten much worse, I don't know if I could have held out. It was extremely bad. It depends on your motivation; it depends on everything. I was fully aware that if I break down, I'd probably kill my father effectively. Worse yet, I would subject him to much worse torture before he is killed. That was on the top of my head, below that was his threat to kill me. It was what saved me from breaking down. I was only twelve years old.

Hiding In An Attic

"We were hiding in an attic near my aunt's house on the outskirts of Lodz ghetto. It was an abandoned house. By then, the ghetto was constricted to a much smaller area, less than 50,000 people. [probably about May 1944] *Daily Jew hunts.*

"In the summer, being in the attic is very difficult. You are lying flat between big beams in the attic. When they shine lights, nothing shows. And it goes on like that eight to twelve hours a day. It's like an oven: you can't fart, you can't do anything. You cannot even shit in the house because they would smell it. We left all feces on the staircase, broken bottles. We never cooked inside, so it looked totally abandoned. And also there was still some protection because we were near my aunt's house. At least, the Jewish police who were helping them would sidetrack them if they could. They [the Jewish police] *enjoyed it; they reveled in it; they were being treated special.* Many of them adopted high polished high German boots, they lorded it over others. They exacted sexual favors for extra food they had.

"Eventually by August '44, we were running out of strength. The protection was removed from my aunt's house which was also the house of Jakobson who was the big cheese of the justice system. They told us that they are going to go the next day to the small railroad station where people were getting loaded. I knew what was awaiting because of my father's activities. We said, 'We can't hold out any longer either.' So we all marched two miles to the railroad station. About one hundred to a freight car. The journey lasted about four days. We were stacking people like cord wood in one corner.

Auschwitz-Birkenau

"On arrival, we were rushed out of the cattle cars, women left, men, right. Knowing what was coming, I wanted to run to my mother and say good-by, and of course I didn't. I could have. They would have led me to the crematorium. I still sort of feel guilty about that, regardless of rationality. And my father and my brother and I, we were then selected to go into the quarantine camp rather than directly to be killed.

"Auschwitz was two camps, Auschwitz and Birkenau. The mass production was Birkenau, the more refined shit was Auschwitz. The holding camp for men was just that, a cattle yard for a slaughter house. There was at least one selection daily. For one reason or another, we survived. We always managed to fade away or to appear very healthy. We were healthier than most because we had a little more food before that. We knew that my mother was murdered the next morning when we saw a woman we knew against the wire in the women's camp, where my father signalled to her. He pointed at me, my brother, himself and then to an empty space.

"At least we [my brother, my father and I] survived Auschwitz. My brother and I almost got ourselves into a difficulty by being too clever. We heard a rumor that there was a barracks where twins were getting extra food. We were hungry, so we lied that we were fraternal twins. Sure enough, it was the holding barracks for Mengele. There was a Polish gentile, Kapo (block supervisor), male nurse. For one reason or another, he took me aside and told me, 'You don't want to be here. If I can help, I'll get you out.' And he did. He had a lot of power. He created, at one point, an assembly at one end of the barracks. Lots of commotion was created, and meanwhile he slipped a door open for us to get out. We rejoined my father in quarantine barracks.

"Then I would guess, in about six weeks after arrival, it was stated that there was to be a selection for a transport for Germany. Again, you don't know, because you might get selected for something you don't expect. But that's part and parcel of playing the 'German roulette.' But it turned out that it was a real transport. We managed to get through it even though the place had this law, this regulation, that children under sixteen must be murdered, must not leave the place alive.

"My brother got through because I threw a rock at a group of people who were already selected and created a commotion. He disappeared into the group that was already selected while I ended up discussing with the guy that was doing the selection, who, I think, was the assistant crematorium chief of Auschwitz.

"By 1943 my father started teaching us how to die. That was in large measure a good reason why we survived. Because if you know how to do that like a human being, you no longer become panicked. And if you are not panicked, you can still exercise judgement. And you don't run with the crowd like a cow going down the shoot to the butcher to be hit over the head. And so I was actually able to maintain my composure.

"Sixteen, you are already a liar. At sixteen our boys are already fighting the Bolshevik monster on the eastern front. What I said to him [the assistant crematorium chief], 'I've been fed your shit now for almost four years, and if your boys were given the same shit I've been given, how fit do you think they would be?' 'Oh, you're right, Go.' But mainly because he recognized me as a player in the 'dance of death.' And if you wish to perceive that kind of thing, there's an old black and white Czech movie, Closely Watched Trains. You'll notice the reason they spare the little boy is that they perceive he attempted suicide. He is part of the cult of death.

"My father went through because he was a rather powerful man still. Before the war, his parlor trick would be to take a half inch manila rope around his biceps, tied tight, and pop it. He was not like that in Auschwitz. He was already descending."

Under Dachau Supervision

"And we were taken again in freight cars, again maybe a week to a place in Germany near Landsberg. The first camp wasn't all that bad, but it was under Dachau supervision. That's when a Dachau number was assigned to us. 112-406 was mine. My father's was 405 and my brother's was 407. We lived in barracks that were really rectangular holes in the ground, with a roof on top of it. And there was a deeper hole in the center, and there were two shelves made of earth where you slept. But it wasn't all that bad because we were being used, at the beginning, to clean potato peels which allowed us to steal some potatoes and eat some potatoes raw.

"Another part of the prisoners were working on a fighter airplane strip, concrete work. Some sabotage was done. Under the concrete they put a bunch of cement sacks and newspapers, so the first fighter or two that landed, crashed.

"We were sent then to a place called Riederloh, near Kaufbeuren, all of this in Bavaria. Riederloh was a punishment camp, where we stayed two months, then left for Dachau main camp, half of us walking. The casualties were being beaten to death, hunger, worked to death, losing running the gauntlet (different from being beaten to death). It was winter, near the Alps, very cold. My fingers froze off, working in the woods, digging holes. The SS had this very nice sense of humor, so they referred to our parade grounds, where we would be counted, as the 'red square,' it was, frozen blood. Every counting, every morning, every evening, a minimum of three or four would be pulled out or dragged and stamped to death with boots into human pancakes.

"My father was beaten to death in Reiderloh, by the camp commandant, primarily because my father decided he was going to illustrate his lessons in how to die. He also recognized that he was becoming, what was called in the camps, 'muselman,' or someone whose entire body begins to collapse. And if you go into that stage any further, you lose all volition. Because of the brutality that was extended to him, and because of that, he had a rather stentorian voice and excellent German. He chewed that guy's ass up and down and through the middle. It was so surprising that the man stood stock still for quite some time while my father went on. Then he grabbed a shovel and started beating him over the head. And I rushed up. I was a runner in that camp, meaning between the trustees and the SS. He, at least, knew my face. So he stopped, but my father died a couple of days later, only once regaining consciousness. Just before that took place, he left me with a kind of a mission. 'As for you, make sure, if your brother dies, you're dead!' That was very helpful because it was a black and white mission, no shadows, no grace."

Dachau Main Camp

"We arrived in Dachau main camp, where by brother was sent to the quarantine barracks and I was sent to the so-called 'hospital' because I had a disease called 'phlegmon' which is a kin to 'quashiorkor,' animal protein malnutrition disease. It causes holes in your body, even tiny scratches. Oh, yes, they had medicine; they assigned me to be a malaria guinea pig. First, I was to recover a little before the experiments. Again there were two Polish prisoners who showed up at my bedside, and covering their numbers, started bringing me sausage, eggs, butter. And my holes started healing within days. Then they put a corpse into my bed and smuggled me out into quarantine barracks. Why? I don't know. Possibly because my real name is Wadiswa Plywaski, very Polish. Probably that had an influence, most likely. They also warned me that I have to get out of the quarantine barracks, with my brother, on the next transport because typhus was starting. So the Germans were going to clean it out in their usual way.

"We managed, with many difficulties, to get on that transport. I had to risk refusing to go to an SS man unless he put my brother on the list as well. Again, it was a question of this 'Fuck you buddy.' I told him, 'I know what you are going to do in the barracks.' That alone would have qualified me to be shot. Instead of that it won the day. Defiance, especially unexpected from a little shit. We were sent to camp in Augsburg, the whole camp was inside a huge aircraft hangar. Three layers of bunks. That camp was run by criminal Kapos, wearing the green triangle. I made buddies with them, defiance, so they started helping out a little bit. Then we went on to another small camp called Burgau, right in the town of Burgau. In both camps we worked in Messerschmidt factories, slave labor, shit work.

"Out of Burgau, by this time, it is the end of the war coming. We were marched to an even smaller camp near Turkheim where there was really no work. By then I knew that the 'death march' was getting ready. But I didn't know if they were going to march us out into the woods and shoot us, or march us somewhere else and shoot us. We set up an escape. By then, discipline was quite lax. There were only a few work details in the woods. The way we did it. I picked up a great big beam, something like a 4 x 4 ft., 20 ft. long and put it on my shoulder and marched out the gate, and the guard at the gate said, 'Where are you going?' and I said, 'I was ordered to take this to this work site.' So I went; then I went to a little hill about a kilometer and a half overlooking the camp, covered densely with a tree nursery, because in an hour, my brother was supposed to do the same with another beam. I could see him walk, and he was turned back. So I dropped the beam, went to the nearby village and begged a whole bunch of food from women in kitchens, had a run-in with an SS officer recuperating from wounds. I went back into the woods, hid my sack of food, picked up my beam and walked right back in with the beam, a different guard by this time.

"So then we had to arrange to steal some leather boots because, on a march, if you don't have leather boots, you are dead. We had wooden soles, canvas top. So they marched us back to Dachau, about five days, those who couldn't march, obvious solution.

"The main camp of Dachau was full so they turned us aside. The main Dachau camp was really three camps, Dachau 1, Dachau 2, Dachau 3. Dachau 2 was the closest to Munich, only about ten kilometers, by a little town by the name of Karlsfeld. Dachau 3 was Alach.

"As we marched in, there was a long line of freight cars, just outside the camp, with cars stacked full of rotting bodies. We are not going to get out of here unless we do something. Most of the nights we spent outside the barracks, watching the outside, some shooting. This was close to mid-April '45. This one morning, when it was still gray, cannon rounds, maybe bombs fell, and one of them ripped up the wire in front of us. And of course, the big fucking heroes were hiding their ass in underground bunkers. So we split. There was a potato field about a kilometer and a half, maybe two. And on the other end of it, I could see, there was a German ack-ack battery. I saw them already before the bombs fell, run up a red flag, explode their guns and take off in trucks. So it was empty. Then some crazy machine guns started shooting at us, then some other forces started shooting at the machine guns. Potato fields are good when machine guns shoot at you, especially if the rows are at right angles to the line of fire.

"The best meal of my life was in the ack-ack battery because there was a big pot, on the stove, of hot corned beef stew from German field rations. I'll never taste anything like that in my life."

Escape And Rescue

"There was a bunch of uniforms, weapons, and DDT powder. We were covered with lice and fleas. We got into nice, woolen German uniforms, took a bath in DDT, saturated our camp jackets, German helmets, Lugars, potato mashers, Schmeiser machine pistols. We took off in the direction of firing. We were captured by an American infantry reconnaissance. We pretended we couldn't understand German. They could have put us in a German prisoner of war camp. They took us back to the battalion field headquarters. There was a Polish sergeant from Chicago. He said, 'Hey guys, these are Polish Jews. Give them anything they want.' They took the weapons, unfortunately, and gave us the smallest GI fatigue uniforms, rolled up pants, American breakfast: Cream of Wheat with butter, sugar and condensed milk. From that point on, we became Army mascots.

"There was still was some fighting going on and I acted as an interpreter for reconnaissance units, speaking Polish to the guy who would speak English to the rest of them. And at one point, I had a small victory over myself, not becoming an assassin. I was told by the guy, 'You stay here and kill the fucking woman and her children,' because they were hiding five SS. I told them I didn't see anybody.

"We drifted around with various units. We decided we were going to march to Hamburg on the Autobahn to stow away to the United States. We lived by picking up cigarette butts and putting them into cigarette packs and swapping it with the dumb farmers, as real American pipe tobacco, for food and for sleeping in a barn. One day we were marching past a small lake at the side of the Autobahn. We were sweaty and dirty. 'Let's go take a swim.' We went there and there were a bunch of GIs fishing with hand grenades. We started talking, we spoke a little English. They said, 'You have a long way to go. You are tired, why don't you stay with our outfit, artillery.' It turned out to be the 278th Field Artillery Battalion, Battery C, under *the command of a Captain John Van Arsdale. The next morning, at the reveille formation, he made a little speech: 'These guys lost everything. You can't give them that back, but they also lost a lot of education. So anything you know, teach them.' These guys were just waiting to be shipped back to the States. He tried to get us back to the States, he couldn't."*

Pylaski's brother got to the United States in the spring of 1946, Pylaski himself arrived as a stowaway in June 1946. His entry was legalized by an Act of the US Congress, signed by President Truman, in recognition of his services to the US Army in Europe. Plywaski served in the Air Force, used the GI Bill to study Electrical Engineering and had a career in industry, the National Bureau of Standards, and a private company, Pragmatronics.

Two notorious Nazi extermination camps were located in Poland: Auschwitz-Birkenau, 38 miles west of Krakow in the town of Oswiecim, and Treblinka, northeast of Warsaw, on the Warsaw-Bialystock rail line. At the mouth of the Vistula River, 22 miles east of Danzig, a third concentration camp, Stutthof, was established in Poland.

The other major concentration camps which became well-known to the public were primarily in Germany: Buchenwald, with its sub-camp, Ohrdruf, in central Germany, 5 miles north of Weimer; Dachau, in southern eastern Germany, 14 miles northwest of Munich; and Ravensbrück, camp for women, on the Havel River, 56 miles north of Berlin. The other major concentration camp, also serving as a work camp, Mauthausen, was in the Daunbe Valley, 16 miles east of Linz, Austria. These camps were surrounded by dozens of sub-camps.

Also scattered across Germany were Bergen-Belsen, in lower Saxony near the town of Celle, north of Hanover; Nordhausen, in the Harz mountains, 3 miles fron Nordhausen in Saxony; Sachenhausen near Berlin in the outskirts of Oranienburg; and Neuengamme, on the outskirts of Hamburg.

Flossenburg was east of Prague in the Bavarian forest on the border between Germany and Czechoslovakia; while Theresienstadt was situated northeast of Prague.

Westerborg, northeast of Amsterdam near the town of Drenthe, was the transit camp for Dutch Jews; and Drancy, a northeast suburb of Paris, served as an assembly camp for French Jews.

The only concentration camp in France was Natzweiler-Struthof, 31 miles south of Strasbourg in the Vosges mountains.

Other Jews survived by being hidden through the heroic and unselfish efforts of individuals.

End Notes

155 Doris Kearns Goodwin, *No Ordinary Time*, New York: A Touchstone Book, Simon & Schuster, 1994, p. 102.
156 David Wyman, Ed., Charles H. Rosenzveig, Project Director, *The World Reacts to the Holocaust*, Baltimore, 1996, pp. 703-705.
157 Facsimile in David S. Wyman, *America and the Holocaust*, New York and London, 1990, Document 11, p. 19
158 Reported in *The New York Times*, pp. 1 and 10.
159 *The New York Times*, 2 March 1943, pp. 1 and 4.
160 Martin, Gilbert, *Atlas of the Holocaust,* Oxford: Pergamon Press, 1988, p. 245

CHAPTER 41

THE HOLOCAUST, PART II, RESCUERS AND RESCUED

Many individuals and organizations helped relocate Jews and found safe havens for them. Some underground rescue networks were private groups, others were organized by religious groups. The rescue efforts ranged from the extraordinary work of an entire village to an organization by a single individual. During the four years of the German occupation, for example, Le Chambon-sur-Lignon, France, an impoverished mountain village of 3,000, led by Pastor André Trocmé, saved the lives of about 5,000 refugees, mostly children. Nicholas Winton was a stockbroker by day with the London Stock Exchange. By night and on weekends, he organized six transports of Jewish children from Prague to England, saving almost 650 children before the last transport was cancelled because the war broke out.

Individuals took great personal risks to hide Jews in attics, barns, potato bins, or accepted Jewish children as part of their Gentile families.

The Hidden Children

The first international gathering of the "Secret Survivors of the Holocaust" was held in May 1991 in New York City. Otto Verdoner, one of children who survived because he was hidden, said they had expected 300 or 400, but 1,500 attended. "And it was the first time we all sort of came out of the closet." And we said, "Our experiences were awful."

"I have no personal memories of my own until the day I went into hiding. I was hidden by a Christian family. I was not hidden in the way in which the family of Anne Frank was hidden who were hidden out of sight. I was in hiding but not hidden. My identity was hidden. I was passed off as the nephew of the lady of the house where I was hidden. I was allowed to play outside. It was a large house in a small village, out in the Dutch countryside, next door to a farm, a milk-cow farmer. The story that was put out was that I was the lady's nephew. This woman was a widow, Dutch nobility, and had a lot of class. She had remarried a widower, a bank executive. There were her two children and his three children, a niece of theirs, so there were six young people; the youngest of them was twelve. His youngest daughter was twelve. The others went on up from there to eighteen. Plus the parents, there were eight people living in that house. And they took in a Jewish child at considerable risk to themselves.

The Dutch Underground
The Jewish Council

"The Dutch underground was quite active and established a veritable underground railway, having put the word out to pastors and ministers out in the countryside that families were needed to hide children, and who did they recommend. This woman had actually contacted a cousin of hers who she knew was most likely active. It was the sort of thing you didn't talk about unless you were working with it. But she indicated to him that if there was something she could do to help, he should not hesitate to ask her.

"My father had considerable contacts with the Dutch underground and considerable contacts throughout Holland so there is an interesting situation there. There were, at the time of the invasion, 30,000 German Jewish refugees in Holland. They had started coming across in 1933, so when the war hit Holland in 1940, there were 30,000. In the last year before the invasion, the trickle had become a flood and it was impossible to absorb them into the community as they came in. So a refugee camp had been built. This German-Jewish refugee camp then became a concentration camp, a transit camp after the invasion. That was Westerbork.

"The Nazis established Jewish Councils in every country that they took over. The Jewish Council was supposed to carry out their orders. And the Jewish Council figured they would be in there fighting the good fight, trying to do the best thing they could for the Jewish population. In the end, they fooled themselves and everybody was fooled.

"My father worked for the Jewish Council to supply Westerbork with food. The Jewish Council had been given the task of raising the money to feed all those Jews. They had to raise it from the Jewish community. My father, therefore, had considerable permissions to travel around Holland, buying food and getting it transported to that camp. That was his job with the Jewish Council. So he traveled around Holland and had incredible contacts and networks. There was a concerted, semi-organized underground railway that the Dutch Resistance organized and helped keep going to find Gentile homes for Jewish children."

My Identity Is Now Hidden

"My first memory is the day I arrived at that house. I have absolutely no memory from before that. It is quite reasonable that I wouldn't have any memory from before. My identity now is hidden; it was changed; I was no longer who I had been; I needed to be somebody different. I don't know what they used for a last name, but Otto is a common enough Dutch name that it didn't need to be changed.

"I remember arriving at that house, long after dark, so it was most likely about the middle of November. I don't know the exact date. I remember that it was a day of train rides and train stations and waiting with people. My family lived in the suburbs of Amsterdam. At a certain point during the Occupation, all Jews were ordered to move into Amsterdam. Our house in the countryside was commandeered. We moved in with my father's parents in the south district of Amsterdam. So I had been living there most recently, so there was one upheaval from the house where I was born, and lived the first year or two, to the next year with my grandparents. And that undoubtedly was already a very tense and scary time. Even a three-year old will pick up things like that. If it is something that can be explained to a child, an illness is unforgivable, but it is definable and understandable. What was being done to the Jews was, nobody knew what was going on, what the next thing would be. Everybody was sort of hunkering down, waiting for the invasion of the Allies, sure that the war was going to end in a few weeks or months. When the Frank family went into the attic, they fully expected the war to be over in three months. And it was three years. And they were there almost two years before they were found and deported.

"My oldest sister was four years older than me, and she was with the mayor of a small village; she was just known as the mayor's 'Yoka.' Yoka is the nickname a little Dutch girl gets if her name is Josefine. And no further questions were asked. As it happens, my sister is blonde and blue-eyed, so it was easier to pass off a Jewish girl than a Jewish boy, and a blonde and blue-eyed girl certainly. My sister, Fran, was with a childless couple, in the middle of Amsterdam, who were very active in the underground. They were known in the underground network and they took Fran in themselves.

"The tensions were horrible. Things were just weird, weird, weird. My sisters were sent into hiding in the summer of '42. They were two years and four years older than me. So the summer of '42, I was three, Fran was five and Yoka was seven, almost eight. It is very interesting that my sister, Fran, says that she has absolutely no memories before the day she went into hiding. She was five years old. But it is the same thing, her identity was, at that point, changed. It is like you slam a door, everything disappears, you are somebody else. And you have no history, no antecedents, no memories, everything is wiped out. Parents, grandparents, siblings.

"Three years ago, I asked my cousin who was eighteen in Holland, 'Were you around when I went into hiding?' 'Oh,' she says, 'I was at your grandparents' every day.' I said, 'Do you remember the day I went into hiding?' She said, 'Yes, I do.' I said, 'Tell me about it. What time of year was it? What day was it? What month?' She says, 'I don't know that.' She says, 'You were wearing a blue snowsuit.' So I said, 'What was said? What happened?' She said, 'These people came in through the garden to the kitchen and your parents were in there with you. And *those people left with you through the kitchen door and through the garden and that was it.' She says, 'I wasn't in the room. I don't know what they said to you.' She said, 'There wasn't another word spoken in that house that day.'*

"I played in and around the house [in the village]. *I don't remember being taken to church. I was young enough to be left home. Some of the boys were still around the house, but the oldest ones were already off at school elsewhere. And they were partly scared for their sons and daughters because the Germans were recruiting laborers. They were picking up, not just Jews, but anyone. If you were Jewish, you got 350 calories a day; and if you were not Jewish, you got 500 calories a day.*

"There were no significant incidents while I was with that family. They took good care of me; they were excellent people. I remember very early on after I got there. I was there in the countryside, and the Dutch really do use wooden shoes. The fields are muddy and dirty. So I had my first pair of wooden shoes which were undoubtedly hand-me-downs. It had snowed, not much, two or three inches of wet, sticky snow and I went out in my wooden shoes. The snow sticks to the bottom, and as you walk, you built up sort of stilts, pointy stilts under your feet. Pretty soon I fell over and was lying in the snow crying because this was a total mystery. A kid from the city had no concept of what should be done. And some of my foster-brothers noticed this and came out to me and kicked at the snow which immediately fell off the wooden shoes. And I felt foolish but also felt good that I had been rescued and had been saved from this particular bit of craziness. And it had been made rational and sane. So there was some rational sanity in the world, and there were people who would take care of you if you were stuck. And I didn't know how much I was being taken care of.*

"There was a lot of tension about that [my identity]. *I was not hidden in an attic, but one day, I remember this. Somebody comes walking up this long, gravel walk to the house, a substantial house on a substantial plot of land, in a uniform and nobody knows who that is or what that uniform is. Well, nobody could figure it out, 'Somebody get Otto up in the attic and keep him quiet.' There was that degree of nervousness at my being there. It wasn't that I was hidden; I was allowed to play outside, the farmer next door knew I was there. But this unidentified person in an unidentified uniform; it turned out to be a substitute postman. And besides which, he might have smelled a rat about me and said something.*

"I met my foster-mother again ten years ago when she came to visit her son who had immigrated to Canada and has raised his children there. She was visiting him in Vancouver. I thought it was important that I bring my children up to her, my wife, to meet her and her to meet them. That was something she had earned. And I wanted to do the 'mitzvah' and show her that her efforts had born success. When I saw her now as an adult (the last time I had seen her, it was as a six-year old). And now I was forty-seven. So I looked at this woman with my adult eyes and I saw stature. I saw bearing. I saw a definiteness of manner and purpose, a no-nonsense air, no lies, no deceptions and real character, real bearing. What the term 'nobility' should imply, a noble person.

"And I also then got to hear some stories, one of which was that, when I arrived, she took me to meet the farmer next door with whom they traded off the books, off the records. All the cows were counted and numbered by the German occupation forces, but nevertheless the farmers could always hide stuff. There was more food in the countryside. I was taken to meet the farmer next door and I remember seeing him, vaguely, at the fence. I remember being at that fence and being licked by a cow, thoroughly startled, a city kid. She tells me that she took me over to meet him and he said in this very, very flat Dutch accent which translates as, 'Yes Mrs. B that's obvious that's your family.' She had dark hair, dark brown hair and dark brown eyes, she wasn't one of your typical Dutch rosy-cheek blondes. And I had brown hair and I had brown eyes. He could have been a very simple Dutch farmer who was saying, 'Yeah, that kid really looks like you; you can see the family resemblance.' Or he could have been somebody who said, 'You can count on me to keep my mouth shut.'

"After the war there was a woman in that village who got treated as a collaborator; she and her husband had been collaborators. She got her head shaved and paraded down the streets, shamed and abused, not treated with respect and human dignity, which was the way we had been treated during the war. And it was repeating that behavior. But there was that much anger, hurt and vengeance. She came, with her shaved head, to my foster-mother and pleaded with her. She said, 'Can't you do something? Can't you make them stop? Can't you tell them to leave me alone?' She continued to be booed, hissed and tormented. And my foster-mother was a person with face, with presence. She was not a farmer-villager, but whose villa was at the edge of the village. So this woman came to her, 'Wouldn't you do something, tell them to stop and leave me alone. After all, I never said anything about Otto.'

"As my foster-mother's son-in-law said at the time, and he was already the daughter's boyfriend then, 'That was the worst and best kept secret in the village.' In other words, everybody in the village knew and nobody in the village said anything."

I Didn't Recognize My Father

"When the war ended, my father was still alive and he came to get me. I didn't know who he was. He showed up; I didn't recognize him. I had to be told that was your father. Wow, I had a father!! I was ecstatic, I was delirious, I dragged him around the village shouting to everybody, 'Look, look, this is my father!' I didn't ask him about my mother. Then he took me back to their house, in the suburbs of Amsterdam, and here come these two older girls. These are my sisters of whom I have no memory. So when I was three years old, the door slammed. Now when I am six years old, the next door slams, and the people I've lived with for the last three years disappear completely. I'm now living with my father, but my foster-mother and my foster- siblings are all gone and I don't see them again as far as I know.

"I was enrolled in school; that was a new experience. Being with other children was a new experience because, although I was allowed to play around outside the house, playing with other children in the village was undoubtedly too risky. Totally left out. I plunged right into first grade with a vengeance, Dutch first grade, someone who has not played with other children. I was only in Holland for one year before we immigrated to America which happened in '46, so that door slammed."

I Learned About My Mother

"After the war, when my father came back, we didn't talk about my mother. It never came up. But my father was the guy who brought all the food into the camp, where my mother was imprisoned. He could move anything he wanted to into or out of the camp. He smuggled all her letters out, and he smuggled letters into her. His letters to her are gone; her letters to him he saved. And I had them in my files. I looked at them once in a while, though it was too difficult to read that and I didn't know who anybody was. There were handwritten notes in the margins and I couldn't read the handwriting. So about eight years ago, my sister said, 'Give me all the letters, I'm going to translate them.' She did and I finally learned about my mother.

"My mother had been arrested in the spring of '43, shortly after I went into hiding. She was trapped by a guy who was running a scam. Scams abounded. This business of getting a stamp on your identity card saying you were exempt from this or that. My grandparents' visas for Palestine, which were bona fide, were very valuable. It meant they had a certain special status in the eyes of the Germans. They were still Jews who could be murdered for no reason at all, but they were a little more valuable than other Jews. This man was selling visas for Portugal. He claimed he could get visas for Portugal. He didn't have visas for Portugal. What he had was a good line and he convinced my mother that he could get her this and she gave him a lot of money for it. Then he turned her over to the Germans for trying to do something illegal. Of course, he got paid by the Germans for turning her in.

"She was sent to the transit camp, Westerbork. When she got there, she was somebody they knew. Westerbork was a peculiar situation. It had been a German-

Jewish refugee camp before the war and it was, therefore, internally administered by the German Jewish refugees. They had their administrative structure in this camp already in place. The Germans just came in and added a little layer at the top and some gun emplacements to enforce it.

"The day-to-day operations were carried out by this administration. A lot of them had known my mother's father because my grandfather had a theater in Amsterdam. He booked acts from all over Europe into his theater. After 1933 this trickle became a flood of German Jewish refugees... And one of the first things my grandfather did when the trickle became a stream was to buy a rooming house. So here are people who need a place to stay. He was a node in this network, trying the fit the German-Jewish refugees into the Dutch economy... so that when my mother arrived in this camp, on the train from Amsterdam, this was old man Schlauser's daughter. And this was Herr Verdoner's wife, the guy who brought so much food to the camp. She had what she called 'vitamin C', connections.

"When she arrived in camp, they gave her a job in the administration. My mother spoke French, Italian, German, English and Dutch. She was a champion fencer. This was a woman of considerable energy, force and talent. They gave her a job, secretary in the offices. She could take shorthand and type. She was employed by the German-Jewish administrators of the camp. One of the tasks this administration had to carry out every week was to post a list, on Monday night, of 1,000 names because, on Tuesday morning, there would be an empty train that needed to be loaded up, locked up, and would head east. People being relocated for labor in the east. That was the lie, the cover story that was constantly told. You knew it would be worse, but you knew you could survive if you could be tough enough.

"Who does this German administration put on the list first of all? The first thing they put on the list, the Dutch Jews. But my mother had a job in the administration, which was like one of these stamps, one of these exemptions. And they knew that there were some camps that the trains went to that were worse than other camps. They had heard enough rumors to know that, for instance, Bergen-Belsen was a better camp. Bergen-Belsen was not a death camp; it was a transit camp. That people died by the dozens, by droves, by the hundreds, of disease and malnutrition, mistreatment and abuse.

"Eventually they had to put their own names on the list. My mother didn't have her name put on the list for almost a whole year. She had access to paper and a typewriter, so she could go back into the office in the evenings and write long letters to my father. Of course, you were allowed one postcard with six lines every two weeks. My mother was in that camp for almost a whole year. She was let out at a certain point. Actually, she considered being in the camp easier than to be out in the streets of Amsterdam because they were constantly raiding the streets of

A Time to Speak

Amsterdam, picking people up. So you lived in constant fear and terror of being picked up and shipped out. Once you were in Westerbork, you were away from that hellish situation. The job was up; you were in the trap; and you didn't need to think about it anymore. You had been caught. She didn't even want to get out. She felt safe there with her position, with her connections, with her 'vitamin C.'

"What happened then, there were fewer and fewer Jews left in Amsterdam and finally, in September of '43, the last Jews were rounded up in Amsterdam. As it happened, my father that day, wasn't in Amsterdam. He was in Westerbork delivering food. And he heard that the last train with Jews had just left Amsterdam and was headed for Westerbork. This was the train with the Jewish Council on it.

"So my father rode out of the camp on the truck. When they got to the first good-sized village where he had connections, he said, 'Thank you very much,' to the truck driver, 'Thank you for being so helpful.' He got out of the truck, took off his star and went into hiding. For the next four or five months, from hiding, he continued to supply my mother with food and necessities. He delegated it to some other people, so my mother had a good supply of food and clothing while she was in that camp. Once he went into hiding, a friend was going to do that, keep packages coming to my mother, but he spaced it out. And my mother got sick, my mother got hepatitis. In January of '44, she was in the hospital in the camp. They had excellent doctors, excellent nurses, no supplies. My mother was recovering, getting much, much better.

"Before that time, up to December, my father arranged for her to escape from that camp. He did that more than once and she didn't come out, she refused. Because one of the rules of the camp was: if you escape, then the next Monday night everybody in your family is on the list. And since they knew that there were some camps that were better than others, some destinations that were better than others, you tried to get on a train when you knew the destination was going to one of the better places. The fact that there were death camps at the end of those destinations was not really understood. I think it is sort of clear from her letters.

"She refused to go because her parents were there, her favorite aunts and uncles were there. Her brother may still have been there at that time. She told my father, 'No.' The letters give hints of the fireworks between the two of them. There were apparently fireworks before the war. On February 7, 1944, the list went up and in order to come up with 1,000 names and, in order to create some room for people who were very sick and couldn't' get into the infirmary because it was too crowded, everybody who was in the infirmary, they put their names on the list. Everybody in the hospital suddenly found their name on the list. And my mother was still there, and my father's parents were still there. So my mother sent a note to her father, who was in the camp, saying, 'My name is on the list. Do what you can.

Try to pull strings, try to get somebody to take her name off the list.' No, they needed room in the hospital.

"So on February 8, everybody from the infirmary was carted down to the train, in the snow and the mud, got on the train and that train went to Auschwitz and it arrived there Thursday morning, across northern Europe in an unheated boxcar, a train full of people who were taken out of the infirmary. The trail does not go any further.

"I really only learned it when my sister translated the letters. They got the book published, Signs of Life. She sent me a copy; most likely she gave it to me in 1990. That was the beginning of the end of denial, being the first stage after loss. Then I had evidence that 'Yes, I had had a mother.' Something that had never been discussed. And yes she had lived and yes she had died.

"Survivors who had had an adolescence, who had reached adulthood, had a very different experience as a result of the war. The war had a very different impact on them as opposed to children. Mostly we survived by being hidden; we couldn't survive the camps. So everybody assumed that nothing happened to them. They weren't in the camps; they were hidden children, no great traumas." [161]

Hidden by a Farm Woman

Lisa (Dawidowicz) Murik and her family were given refuge by a Polish farm woman. In a videotaped and transcribed interview in the United States Holocaust Memorial Museum Archives, Lisa Murik recounted how her family was saved.

She was born in Ostrog, Poland (Ostroh, Ukraine), where she lived with her parents and two sisters. Her parents owned and operated a small grocery in the town. She went to public school until the outbreak of the war in 1939. Life in their town changed drastically when the Germans occupied Poland: first, registration at the *Judenrat* (office); the obligatory yellow star on the arm band and later, because the arm band was hard to see, a yellow circle in back and in front; forced labor; and finally placement in the ghetto created in their town. By 1942, the Jewish population of Ostrog realized what was happening and families built shelters in their basements or where-ever they could find a place to hide from the Nazis.

"And one morning when we woke up, we saw trucks right in front of the gate along the street, a lot of Germans, and we understood that something is going to happen. So we crawled into the shelter. And we could hear stomping around in the house, looking, and it was terrible that day. We sit quiet. We didn't have food in there. We didn't expect, you didn't know when they could do it, so you couldn't prepare yourself. So then, after a couple of days sitting in there, the water pipe broke, and the water started coming up, gushing out there, and was almost to our necks, and we had to get out. We couldn't stay no longer. So we came out during the

night, went into the house, we changed the clothes. We didn't think about nothing, just to get out.

"And right across the street from the ghetto, there was Gentile people which my mother knew and she secured, we had to run, they will keep us. So we ran from our house to the front house which was closer to the road, and we looked around, nobody was there, and we went across the street. And my mother knocked on the back door, and the man opened the door and he said if we not going to leave he is going to call the Germans. He no want to see us and he doesn't know us. So we had no place to go, so next door was another Gentile person who knew us. My mother went over there, and he says he can keep us overnight and during the day we will have to leave because it is right by the main road and he really don't have a place to keep us. So he had a big stack of hay in the middle of the yard. Anybody could walk over and punch the hay and find us. And we crawled in there. He brought us some food and we sat the next day, all day, and the evening he bought us some clothes so we be looking like Gentile people, and we started walking.

"Where we were going we didn't know ourselves. My mother had in mind there was a woman living on the outskirts of the city, maybe she will keep us. So we walked over to her place, and when we got to her place we heard German voices in the house. So we couldn't do nothing, so she had like a little shack which she used to keep a pig in there. We crawled in this little shack and we sat there and waited until the Germans left. When the Germans left, my mother knocked on the door, and the woman said she is very sorry, she couldn't keep us. She has no room and her daughter is dating those Germans. She says, 'You can stay tonight if you want, and tomorrow maybe. You have to go.' So we stayed overnight and the next morning, early morning, my mother got up, she got dressed, and she left us there, and she went to look for a place.

"She was gone all day, and in the evening she came, she says, 'I find a place.' She didn't know the person, the person didn't know her. She was a very nice Gentile woman. She believed in God. She said God sent us to her and she has to do it. She was a poor woman. And we came there, the next morning we came there. And the next morning she put us in the barn at first. She knew that we couldn't stay there because anybody who comes in the fields to work, because her husband was a forest man, and everybody had a piece of ground and worked in those fields. She was afraid anybody come to the field would see us.

"So we were there for awhile and in Europe, they really make a big ditch, big hole, and they put potatoes and they keep them over winter there. She had potatoes in there. So she took the potatoes out. She put some straw down and she put some boards over top. She put a pole in the middle to hold it on, and on top, she put in pumpkins, a whole bunch of pumpkins. And she just made a small hole so we could climb in there. And we went in there, it was in the fall. We went in there, and we sit there for sixteen months in that little hole, in that little place. You couldn't even stretch your feet out. And she brought us food once a day. We had one potato, each of us, a day, and a quart of water a day. She, herself, didn't have much food. She was glad to feed us with that, and we were happy to get this so long as we are safe.

"And some days when it was quiet she used to come take the pumpkin away so we can get some air. One day she took the pumpkin away. And we were sitting and talking between each other; and all of a sudden, a car came by and threw the pumpkin on the hole. So I said to my father, I said, 'Ah, I am going to open up. I will push it.' He said, 'No, leave it alone.' And right after that, two Germans passed by. It looked like the car knew...we...that we were there, and she has to save us. And we was there for quite awhile. And the woman knew what was going on, because if they caught people at Gentile's houses, they killed the Gentile and the Jews. She didn't care. She just want to save us.

"She had one little boy, she had three kids, and one little kid was four years old. He used to go in the field sometimes and get some carrots out of the ground and bring them down to us. He used to say, 'The Germans will not live too long enough to kill you.' He was very nice, the little kid.

"And we were there, and then one day, like she noticed it, she thought somebody saw us. It was wintertime. It was cold. She says we have to get out of there. And we went out of there, and we go into the forest. On ice! We laid on that, and we had hardly any clothes. We laid all night on that ice. Everybody, when I tell them, I tell them the story about this ice, they don't believe me and I didn't get pneumonia or something. It looks like our bodies were so strong, they took anything. And we stayed overnight and the next morning, we went back in, and we stayed there until 1944.

"In 1944, she, herself, used to go to the city and bring us newspapers so we could read to her because she couldn't read and write. So in the evenings she used to bring a candle with the paper, and my father used to read the news to her. And we told her if she goes into town, see what happens, if she talks to people, tell us what is happening. So in that year of '44, she came back and said the people were talking the Russians were coming back. So it was good news, already the Germans were leaving. So one day she came and she says, 'The Germans are out. There was bombing and all that, and the Germans are out, and the Russians are back in.'

"So my parents go out. And they left us still in that hole because they were not sure what was going on. They left to town. And we were sitting there; and my sisters were giving me a hard time because they were upset. I was upset myself. And we could do nothing about it. And she didn't know where they were either. So after

A Time to Speak

a couple of days, there was a big snow and they came back. They came back, and they couldn't find us because the snow covered the ground so bad. They knew where the place was, it was hard to find the opening. And we heard inside that somebody is walking around and like working with something. We were afraid to say anything, because we didn't know really who it was. So at that time I said to my sisters, 'I think maybe they came for us. Just don't cry, don't make noise.' And at that time, I heard my mother's voice in Jewish—'Kids, we are here.' Oh, when I heard that, I was in heaven! And they came with a wagon, with horses, some comforters, down comforters, and clothes for us. They threw down the clothes, and they pulled us out of there. We couldn't even stand up, so weak we were.

"And they put us right on that wagon. And a doctor, gynecologist, a woman doctor, she took us into her house. And my younger sister could hardly walk at all. Another doctor took her in and kept her for awhile, to put her back on her feet. And we really had a hard time getting back on our feet because whatever food we ate didn't stay with us because we were not used to all that stuff. And there was a lot of nice Gentile people who came and brought us food and brought us everything. And then we started looking around, looked for our own house. Our house was gone. So then we find another empty house, so we moved in there. And we stayed there for awhile.

"And then, in the fall, my mother adopted a boy who was left alone. The way she adopted him, this gentlemen had him and had another little girl with him. And he came to our house. He knew my parents. He came over and asked we take him in. My mother right away said, 'Fine. He is mine.' And we had a hard time with him, because he was so used to the Gentile person he didn't really want to stay with us. But after a while he stayed with us. And then from there we left to Lódz, and we were there for awhile. And from there, we went to Germany to a DP camp in Berlin. And we were there for awhile, and from there we went to another DP camp in Eschwege. And from there we left for the United States. In 1949, we came here." [162]

Martin Gilbert says there were "300,000 survivors of the concentration camps, and over a million and a half European Jews survived Hitler's efforts to destroy them." [163] They were waiting in concentration camps, hiding in potato bins, until Allied troops arrived to liberate them. What awaited the liberating troops was an unbelievable spectacle, one which has never been erased from their memories.

End Notes

161 As part of his process of healing, in February 1991, Verdoner had a memorial service for his mother and he shares his story at local schools.
162 United States Holocaust Memorial Museum Archives, Record Group 50, Oral History, United States Holocaust Memorial Museum collection. Extracts from interview with Lisa (Dawidowicz) Murik, RG-50.030*168, May 30, 1989.
163 *Atlas of the Holocaust*, p. 242

CHAPTER 42

THE HOLOCAUST, PART III, THE WITNESSES

The Nazis dismantled three of their extermination camps; Belzec, in the spring of 1943 and Treblinka, in the fall of 1943. These camps were plowed under, trees planted and seeds sown so the camps would look like farms. The camp Chelmno, in western Poland, was dismantled in late 1944 to eliminate evidence of mass murders.

Auschwitz-Birkenau had been liberated by the Russians on 26 January 1945. As Allied pushed forward into German territory, they encountered refugees on the road and rumors of the existence of more concentration camps.

Members of the American Fourth Armored Division overran Ohrdruf, a subcamp of Buchenwald, on 4 April. GIs were face to face with corpses, each with a bullet hole through the back of the skull and piles of corpses in a shed. They left the camp untouched and Generals Eisenhower, Bradley and Patton visited the camp a week after its liberation. Eisenhower said, "We are told that the American soldier does not know what he is fighting for. Now, at least, he will know what he is fighting *against*."

As Allied troops swept through the German lines, more and more camps were liberated and soldiers couldn't believe what they saw.

On 11 April, the 20,000 inmates in Buchenwald rose in revolt so the camp was already liberated when the U. S. Army arrived in the afternoon. The following day, with Allied forces approaching Westerbork, the camp was handed over to Kurt Schlesinger. (The right-hand man of the camp commandant and head of the principal subdivision, in charge of the main index for the compilation of lists of those to be deported.)

On 15 April, British troops of the 7th and 11th Armored Divisions entered Bergen-Belsen. Five days later, medical volunteers from London hospitals arrived to remove the dead and get the inmates to a wing of the German military hospital in Bergen. Also on 15 April, American troops entered Nordhausen. A unit of the American 51st Field Hospital was established near Nordhausen and prisoners were transferred to the 51st Field Hospital. In the latter half of April, officers of the British Grenadier Guards liberated the camp at Neuengamme.

Advance troops of the Soviet Army arrived at Stutthof on 22 April, and the same day soldiers from the Polish People's Army and from the Soviet Army liberated Sachsenhausen.

The American 7th Army arrived to liberate Dachau on 29 April. At Ravensbrück, women prisoners were handed over to the Danish and Swedish Red Cross on 28 April, and Soviet troops reached the camp on 29-30 April.

Also in April, Norwegian, Danish, Belgian and French prisoners at Mauthausen were released to the International Red Cross, and American troops entered the camp on 5 May. A day earlier, American troops had arrived at Flossenbürg.

On 3 May, prisoners at Theresienstadt were handed over to the Red Cross and the Red Army arrived on 8 May.

Although the press had reported the facts of Nazi genocide as early as 1941-1942, not until the soldiers reported what they saw and the public looked at pictures and films, did people recognize the enormity of the atrocities.

With choked voices and tears in their eyes at the memories of what they witnessed, the men who went in the camps said the camps were "unreal, a real shock, terrible, devastating."

Buchenwald

John Macinko, recently retired from the University of Colorado Language Laboratory Center, formerly served in the Signal Operations Battalion assigned to the Third Army. He was near Weimar in April 1945 when Buchenwald was liberated.

"I guess we can start with my experience at Buchenwald Concentration Camp. It is probably the single, most vivid impression I got out of the war. What happened was, we were on our way to the city of Weimar which is in central Germany. On the way, we noticed we were flagged over. A convoy went speeding by. These people were heavily armed, the likes of which we had never seen before because everyone in the convoy looked like they were rough combat veterans, heavily bearded, heavily armed, and the convoy seemed to be led by MPs which was unusual. And after they went by, we went on our way.

"Later that day, towards late afternoon, a fellow who was attached to our outfit, and whose job was to take photos of the most interesting things that were happening in the area. He came back to us and said, 'You fellows are going to have to get out and see that camp.' 'Well, what camp?' 'They just liberated a Concentration Camp this afternoon.' We had no idea what a concentration camp was. The United States Army had not come across any prior to this. So just out of curiosity, a group of us got into a couple of jeeps and headed out to the camp (he had given us a description, a little map of how to get there). And it was a real shock.

"We came to this large barbed wire, fenced in area and, as soon as we went through the open gates, all around us we saw these walking skeletons. These were grown men that probably didn't weigh more than sixty-five or seventy-five pounds.

We didn't see any women in the camp, a lot of men and some children. They all looked extremely emaciated. We hadn't seen anything like this before. It seemed like their eyes were deeply, just sunken, their cheeks were hollow, bones protruding, everything. Really, the first impression was a skeleton with skin stretched over it, and it drew their face back in such a way that they had a perpetual grin; their teeth were visible and bulging hollow eyes. It was just really strange.

"Then we wandered over to this area where we saw this large cart, a large four-wheel wagon, high, sort of like what one might use on a farm. It was loaded with bodies; they were stacked on this cart jut like cordwood. Again, all these bodies, just skin and bones. Then another pile of bodies were beside a building, just piled against the wall of the building.

"Then we found that the building these bodies were piled against turned out to be a crematorium. These large oven-like furnaces. We keep calling them ovens because that's what they looked like; they looked like large baker ovens, bakery ovens, but they are really furnaces and the prisoners in these camps had to take these dead bodies; they would put them in the front end of the furnace; the gas was turned on; the bodies were burned; and the ashes were raked out of the back end of the furnace and more bodies were put in front. And this went on continuously. These ovens had been shut down earlier in the day and there were still some half-burned bodies in the ovens at the time.

"So we walked around the camp after seeing these furnaces and really didn't have any place in particular to go. We just were dumbfounded by what we saw. I still remember one incident that was rather interesting. There was a little boy about ten years old and in my very limited GI German I asked him, 'Why are you here?' And in perfect German, he responded, 'Because my parents were Russian.' And that was it. It seemed to be that was sufficient reason for him to be in that camp. I have no idea what happened to his parents. He had no idea either.

"About that time, a prisoner walked up to us and, in fairly fluent English, he introduced himself. He was a Belgian and he said he would like to show us around the camp. This fellow was in very good physical condition and I commented to him about it and he said he had just been a prisoner for about two or three months at that camp. We asked him why he had been taken prisoner and he said he really didn't know. All he knew was that he was crossing the border from Germany back to Belgium, or heading back toward Belgium, and he was told his papers weren't in order. He said he had no idea what was wrong because they were the very same papers he had used at previous crossings. And he felt they just needed more slave labor, so they took him prisoner. At any rate, he was in fairly good health and offered to show us around. He said, 'You've got to see the lower camp.' We had no idea what he meant by this, so we went along.

"The camp was built on a slight hill, on a slight slope, I should say. At the lower end of the camp, there was an enclosure that, as far as I can recall, contained two barrack structures. Outside the barracks there was a deep pit and in this pit there were perhaps a hundred, two hundred bodies, just thrown in there at random, apparently the Germans had planned on bulldozing dirt over this pit before the Americans arrived, but with the rapid advance of the U. S. army, they were caught off guard.

"This guide, I'll call him, took us into the first barracks and we were greeted by a sight and a smell that was just unbelievable. The barracks was very dimly lit; on each side there were bunks stacked four high. The bunks consisted of nothing more than rough framework with rough boards laid across to form large shelves. And on these shelves the men slept with their heads toward the aisle, their feet toward the wall, and they were stacked in there very tightly, essentially no space between them and four rows high. And we saw quite a few young-looking people, maybe in their early teens, but also quite a few older people. It turns out this lower camp, these were people the camp commanders, for some reason or other, had given up on and they were just left to die. They had either tried to escape or they had perhaps stolen some food or for some reason, they had broken some of the rules of the camp and they were just thrown into the lower camp and left there to die. The stench in the place was the most difficult to contend with. I don't know whether they had any kind of bathing or toilet facilities in the place. I doubt it. No doubt they probably had some buckets scattered around and that was probably their toilet and somebody had the responsibility of carrying it out. I didn't see any. I can't recall seeing any signs of plumbing. There was a rather crude stove in the center of the barracks and one or two light bulbs, and otherwise, they had no other facilities. The stench was such that you felt you wanted to turn and run out again and yet the surroundings were so unreal you just couldn't. You just couldn't walk away. You wanted to see more, you wanted to experience more. The prisoners laying there were reaching out with their hands and in various foreign accents we could hear words like 'American.' They wanted to shake our hands. We sort of held back. It was sort of embarrassing, in a way, because you wanted to greet these people and yet you were almost afraid to touch them because you had the feeling that something was crawling all over your body. It was a very unreal experience.

"Then we walked out to the far end of the barracks and our guide showed us how these people ate. There were two troughs, not unlike troughs one would see on a farm for feeding livestock. And there was a chute coming down from the upper camp and apparently the leftovers from the mess hall of the main camp, or food that was considered too rotten or spoiled to feed the ones in the main camp, it was dumped into this chute and ran down into these troughs that formed like an inverted T. And this is where the prisoners in this lower camp ate. Those who were strong enough had first crack at whatever food came down, the weaker ones were pushed off to the ends, and the weakest ones just never even got out there. Periodically, I guess daily, they would check the various prisoners; the stronger ones would carry out the bodies of those who had died and try to clean up after them, because the place had a terrible stench because there was no way to wash or clean up. The bodies were carried out, and probably, in a day or so, other prisoners took their place.

"We finally left this lower camp. We just couldn't believe what we had seen. It was bad enough in the main camp because the main camp already had prisoners who were starving so one can imagine how much leftover food there was.

"At that point, our guide said there is one more thing you have to see. About this time, the soldiers and the MPs of the American Army, who had liberated this camp, came by and said 'Everybody has to leave.' It was starting to get dark. But this guide said, 'There is one more place you have to see.' So we followed him through a maze of alley-ways through the camp. As we were walking through, he would point to a building and would say, 'This building here is a typhus building where they experimented on prisoners.' They would perhaps somehow infect them and work with various kinds of treatment. And apparently there were several other buildings in the camp that were used similarly for diseases.

"We finally got to this building which looked like most of the others, walked in and found it wasn't a regular dormitory. It had been converted to, more like a first aid station or something of that sort. There were several different offices and he took us to this one office, or one room, and opened a drawer and said, 'Have you any idea what this is?' There were sheets of substance there that looked like parchment. We fingered these and everybody made their guesses as to what it was. We were quite surprised to find out it was human skin. What they had done in this camp was, and I guess it was done in other camps as well, take the prisoners who were young and healthy, with nice, smooth skin. First they were tattooed, fancy tattoos were placed on their upper body, and then they were killed. They were skinned, and the skin was treated in some way that made it feel like a parchment (it's the only thing I can think of because I had never felt anything like that before). He said these were considered special gifts to various people in the German hierarchy when they would have lamp shades or other types of decorations. I guess lamp shades was one of the more common uses, and they would use this skin to make the shade, with the tattoo, with the fancy colors and patterns.

"Well about that time we had to leave. It was starting to get dark.

"I think everybody was surprised at what they came across. Buchenwald was the first camp the Americans came to. The Russians had come across some of these camps earlier, coming through Poland, even before the American Army was engaged in France. And their descriptions of these camps were considered to be propaganda. There was a British correspondent who was traveling with the Russian Army who sent a description of the camps to the BBC and they refused to air them because they said it was propaganda.

"There are enough people who are survivors, likewise the captured German film which document many of the activities in the camps. It's all there. I know there will always be people who will say, 'We think those films were made up and so forth.'"

Dachau

Fraser Richards was in the Chemical Warfare Division, working covertly in Europe and ended up in Munich on 26 April with a huge column of tanks.

"And I have down here that Dachau was the twenty-seventh, and I remember that night my sergeant coming to me, 'Lieutenant, you've got to see this.' Here I am, an American officer, and I'm supposed to be apprised of everything that is going on. We knew nothing about this, nothing. And I went up there with several other infantry officers, and it had just been liberated a few hours before, went in, and that's a whole different story. I'm sure you've heard a lot about that, the stench, people, and the bodies. And I remember specifically going into a barracks, and I can picture it right now, the barracks, and the ovens way in back, the freight cars full of bodies was unbelievable. I walked into this barracks, and this old lady walked over to me, crawled over to me, and hugged my boots."

Nordhausen

The 68th Medical Groups arrived at Nordhausen to find themselves in a situation difficult to describe: 2,500 emaciated bodies strewn about the area; the living and the dead piled together for disposal in the crematories; 407 emaciated, louse-infested individuals who could be moved by ambulance or hand-carried to a field hospital. Gil Reimers, who served in the supply pool of one of the medical outfits and who has recently been honored for his community service in Boulder, Colorado, was there.

"Then we went on into, one was Nordhausen, just a few days after it was bombed real bad, and the stench of bodies was so bad you could hardly stand it. You see, Nordhausen was a town of two or three hundred thousand people and they practically bombed that thing flat and they went in with bulldozers and pushed enough stuff off to the side so you could drive through.

"After Nordhausen, we got into helping clean up some of the concentration camps. And we lost a bunch; they got held up somewhere along the way, our company of litter bearers. So all of us out of company headquarters had to carry litters *that night. What they did, they would try to pick out the ones they figured would live, and we'd take them on into a tent that was the hospital. A lot of the others were already dead, or near death. I've got a bunch of pictures. But it was devastating.*

"But that was pretty hard to do. But I think we worked, I don't remember, but I know we worked all night. And it was a good thing those people were, you know, thin, because your arms got so tired. Their arms were so thin, it was just skin against skin. All we could do was pick them up on a litter and carry them out of there. But I heard afterwards that a lot of them died through our kindness because we tried to feed them and their bodies were so torn up, they hadn't had food for so long, their bowels weren't working. I guess now, when they have something like that, they IV them first and then try to feed them. That was probably the worst part of the whole thing. They talk about the Jews, the Holocaust and all that. But there were a lot of other nationalities there. They picked up all kinds of people, the Poles, the Czechs and all of that. There was one old fellow there who died pushing a wheelbarrow. He just went right down over it. It was pretty devastating. The bodies were just stacked up on wood, the living and the dead together. And you would look at them, especially the children, and say, 'They were somebody's baby.'"

Looking at some of photographs of the concentration camp that he took, Reimers continued, *"It's hard to remember all that stuff. I've never talked very much about that because it is so farfetched, unless you were there, you didn't realize what it was. Now a lot of the young people are saying, 'There was no such a thing.' They look at you and say, 'What's the matter with you, old man? Ain't no such a thing happened.'"*

But it did happen! More than fifty years later, people are still trying to explain, to understand, to come to terms with what happened.

CHAPTER 43

IWO JIMA AND OKINAWA

Saipan, Tinian, Peleliu, and the Philippines were under American control by the end of October 1944. The islands of Iwo Jima and Okinawa remained to be captured.

IWO JIMA

D-Day morning on Iwo Jima was 19 February 1945 when the American Marines of the Fourth and Fifth Assault Divisions landed on a beach of black volcanic ash to face 21,000 stubborn fighters of the Japanese Imperial Forces. Iwo Jima is an island only four and a half miles long, two and a half miles at its widest point and one half mile at its narrowest point, with natural barriers of offshore rocks and a strong undertow.

American Marines faced an enemy that was persistent, resourceful and uncanny. Their weapons, with smokeless powder, were effective in preventing the Marines from seeing where the shots came from. Furthermore, in efforts to confuse the Americans, Japanese soldiers often wore the uniforms of Marines they had killed. They could provoke the Americans to reveal their position by calling out, in perfect English, "Corpsman, help me, I'm hit," and they would greet the Marine with cocked rifles.

At the time of the invasion of Iwo Jima, the Japanese had fortified the island with interconnecting caves and tunnels which made it difficult to see the enemy, two airfields, and an underground hangar below one of the airfields.

A month of vicious fighting followed the invasion, with heavy losses on both sides. Marines had to dig into soft volcanic ash which didn't provide the needed traction for motorized equipment. They could dig a fox hole in the volcanic ash with their hands, but the ground was too hot to remain inside for very long. The nights were cold and pungent sulphurous smoke eerily came out of the mines in Motoyama.

The Third Wave

Joe Malcolm, a Marine officer, was in the third wave of those landing on Iwo Jima.

"Then we come up to the next operation, after Saipan, Tinian, they called it

Workman Island. We knew the shape of the island and we were briefed on it very well, and then came Time Magazine with a picture, 'Iwo Jima next?' Jeez, what are these guys trying to do to us? Well, it was next.

"I was third wave on Blue Beach Two. They had an airfield there, the Japs did, and that was the main reason to take Iwo Jima was to get an airfield for our bombers to go over from Tinian to bomb Tokyo. They had to have someplace to land. So that's why we went in there to get that island, to make an airfield. The number of Marines killed to the number of pilots saved, I don't know that it would balance out. But it made the pilots feel better.

"Well, we were all veterans by this time and we had been shot at before. I think it was February nineteenth we went in there and I remember it was just a little bit chilly because we had been down south. And so I landed in the third wave, and the amtrac that I had, got hit, a shell came along. The door you let down, we got hit right on the corner there, so we let the infantry out and picked up some wounded on the beach and turned around like we were supposed to and went back to the ship to bring the cargo in.

"This damned thing was leaking on us all the time. We made the trip back to the ship and we had this thing tied up by rope, untied it, got a bunch of mortar ammunition and this, that, and the other thing, and went on back.

"I told my people, 'Now follow me.' I didn't know I had a brake about to go out. You guide it by brakes and that was what propelled us through the water. They had kind of gougers on them. I had a brake going out, so to make straight line, I had to circle. So here we were circling and we didn't want to float too far down because we could see all the shells landing and we didn't want to land down there, not again. And so we got in there all right, then the amtrac sank on us. We were all in there on the island, so we naturally set up a perimeter there and had our machine guns lined up. That was an easy place to get killed.

"We could get killed on the beach, or you could go in the infantry and get killed there. We worked bringing up ammunition, mortar, artillery shells. Our infantry is the one that really took it. They were just cut to ribbons. I walked back that first night, we had these amphibian trailers which weren't too successful, bringing water and stuff like that. One of my people was wounded in the hand. I said, 'Don't worry about this,' and I poured sulfa (we had sulpha which later on we found wasn't such a good idea).

"The next morning we went up and it was full of napalm, all kinds of shrapnel bouncing off, and we were happy behind this. But I walked back to where we were setting up a kind of headquarters on Blue Beach and I could have stepped on a dead marine all the way. Our people, of course, mortar shell landed all night long.

"Being an officer was a little better because we had to worry about troops and everything and we didn't have to worry about ourselves. Well, you get fatalistic. You think, well, if I'm going to take one, I'll take one, that's all I can do. And so then my CO called me down to his dugout and he says, 'We need some troops, we are going to take a company in to back up the infantry between amtracs and any other bandsmen. You're the CO.' So I go up and find out... so it wasn't bad. We're just backing up the infantry and throwing up defense because the Japs were slipping down at night, where we had the wounded, and they were bayoneting them.

"We never had a great love for the Japanese because they were just mean as hell. Of course, we always figured they were mean and every time we had a chance, we would kill one, you know. On Iwo, you always had to worry about anything lying on the ground, like a piece of tin, because they would dig underneath that. They would see you come by and then 'powwwww.' Take no chances.

"On Iwo there was a cave we were going to take. I crawled up there and I had a white phosphorous grenade. You know they burn very badly, so I get up next to that thing, pop it in and lean back, and that guy must have caught it like this, 'Here for you,' he said and threw it right on back. Jesus Christ, it rolled down this hill. That guy was a cool customer, I'll tell you that.

"One night, the area we were in, there was always some guy shooting at us from the cliffs. So I get my gunnery sergeant and said, 'Let's go up and kill that son of a bitch tonight.' He said, 'That's a good idea.' So we waited until it got dusk, so got out through the lines, we get in there and there is the flash of a rifle. At that time the Japs had rockets and we used to see them shoot over here and they'd go past us to somebody else's outfit so we weren't worried about it. This night, the gunny and I are lying out there waiting and caught this old Jap shooting on the beach down through our area. And all of a sudden I'd hear a 'put' and I'd look up and this damn rocket, something went wrong and it turned. He said, 'Jesus, it's going to land right here. Let's get the hell out of here.' And it did. And I'm looking over my shoulder, I think, I'll hit the deck, just as it gets close. I didn't have a chance to hit the deck. I ran right into an anti-aircraft replacement, guns ripped up, but they were still there, full tilt, I ran right into that, knocked my helmet off and then the thing went off behind. My God, that jarred everything, my ears were ringing, sand and all that. I feel around. I'm alive. Pretty soon the gunny says, 'Are you OK?' I says, 'I think so.' Anyhow, he reached down and put my helmet on my head.

"By the time we went to Iwo, it was well organized. There wasn't any sloppiness, certain ships designated as hospital ships. So we had learned the tricks of the trade by the end of the war pretty well.

"Our troops were real good, though, they watched out for one another in our squad. I'll tell you they watched each other and took care of you." [164]

Flag Raising on Iwo Jima

On 22 February, the third day of fighting, Marines raised the American flag on Mount Suribachi, 560 feet above the rest of the island, the highest point on the island. The sight of the Stars and Stripes waving on top of the heavily fortified Japanese volcano gave Marines an uplift, but Joe Malcolm remarked:

"I remember when they put the flag up on Suribachi, I had a pair of binoculars (some Navy gunfire officer had got his ticket and I thought I'd need those beautiful binoculars), so I put them up there and I could see the flag up there. Well, I said, 'We have a flag on Suribachi.' It didn't mean anything to us because we were worried about what was ahead of us."

Another Marine, Dewey Pickard, was waiting to land on Iwo Jima when he saw the flag raised and described what he saw:

"I saw the first flag raising from the deck of our LST. We were waiting for beach space to come ashore to unload our 155MM Howitzers, which we used on this island. It gave us good feelings to see Old Glory waving from the top of the extinct volcano. We cheered and cheered!!

"Incidentally, my cousin, Paul Terry, Jr was one of a group that carried the first flag up Mt. Suribachi and helped put it up. It was later replaced by a larger flag which became a world famous photograph and is an inspiration to us to the present time. He [Paul Terry, Jr.] went into the Marine Corps soon after the war started. He was an 81MM mortar man, with the 5th Marine Division. He went ashore at Iwo Jima first day (D-Day) and fought until killed in action on March 3, 1945." [165]

The Navajo Code Talkers On Iwo Jima

The Navajos, trained to send messages in the unbreakable voice code were also part of the invasion of Iwo Jima.

Teddy Draper was in the 28th Marines, Headquarter's H and S Headquarters Battalion, and witnessed the action on Iwo Jima.

"And we start studying it [Iwo Jima]. They have a plastic island just like you. And then how are we going to do it. At first we were going to land, it was marked for the landing from the north side. And then they changed it again, from the south side. And we were marked right next to Suribachi, on the green beach— 28th Marines. Twenty-eighth Marine Division will land here, and then the 4th Marine Division. And then the 3rd Marine Division.

". . .We know what to do, and they told us, 'You're going to take this island in three days. It's only two and a half miles, and four and a half miles long.' Oh, boy, this is going to be—Just take the airstrip. It's simple like that. We'll just take the airstrip and we're there. . .

"When we got there early in the morning, guess we were about ten miles off from there, we got our breakfast. We got a big steak. And eggs. We got a big breakfast. But some people don't eat...And then the laughing go down. Every time we move, we know we're approaching that bombardment...

"Everybody went quiet. So everything went silent—quiet, very quiet, and all you hear is the airplanes, and then bombardment. And I went on the top of the ship and looked from there. And you can just see the bombing—really a bombardment—just bombing and fire. It just seemed like the island was burning, early in the morning. We got closer then. All the equipment -inspect our equipment, inspect our rations, inspect our—everything had to be inspect [sic]. 'O.K. lay down below.' And we were pretty close. The first wave was just about going in. And the message says—we got a message in Navajo—that they sent some swimmer early this morning—to the beach. But it was a confidential message, you know. It's got to be Navajo. So we got that out. And, then another message from the Generals and their staff, the HR...They might withdraw and land other times, so—and the hour came, and then the message, and then they give the plan of the day in Navajo, a Navajo word, in Navajo words, too. Not in English, see. And what they're going to do, what they found, all the Navajos on that beach. So we are the guys that gets it first, all these confidential messages. We write them down. As soon as we write them down, the Lieutenant will pick it up, and that's the last time we saw it."

Draper was part of the tenth wave to land on shore amid artillery shelling and smoke bombs, dropped by the Japanese between the landing beach and Suribachi. By the end of day two, there were only two of his outfit left. His interview continued:

"The second day we got more men, but the second day in the morning time on the Suribachi, more people got killed in hand to hand fighting. Well, we were sitting right in the foxhole, and the rock extended on my left side towards the east, and there was something on the top of the hill. Every time I look there, it seems like it's moving. I look at it and then I look at it again. It's still moving. It is more like a helmet shape. That's the type was moving around. And I told him, Preston, 'I see a Binaa-a-dahl-ts'ozi (ones with narrow eyes) up there.' I guess it's, it wasn't too far off from us. Not that far, but it was a little farther than that. You know how you see it against the horizon. There really is somebody over there. And I said, 'Let's holler Jap' They almost brighten up over it. Say, 'Jap.' Tum, tum, tum. They go tum, tum. And there's many of them going down that way and this way and there were already some down here past us.. .. There's a Jap coming, and they shoot every place. And there's a rock here and then the other side's kind of this type, this shape, too. That's where we were sitting. So we were almost protected here. Almost like a boulder, type, setting over here. So we got a good position. Then all these Marine guns,

A Time to Speak

machine guns were lined up here and back there. Boy! All over. And that's where we had some hand-to-hand fighting, on the other side. With the rifle. With the bayonet. Everything. Battle does on for about twenty-five minutes, something like that, that we battle. And then the third day we were up. We didn't get any messages all through there. There's some messages coming but it's in the Morse Code. . . and the first day we cut off the neck between the Suribachi and the main body of the island. And the third day, Ira and his platoon put up the flag. A small one but they blast it out. Snipers. And they went back for another one, the bigger flag. They put it on. That's the one that they took the famous picture of. [A reference to Joe Rosenthal, the AP photographer who happened to be on top of Mount Suribachi, took the photo of Marines raising the American flag on Iwo Jima. Rosenthal's photograph is probably the best known war picture from the South Pacific. Based on his photo, Felix de Weldon sculpted the bronze monument which stands on a hillside overlooking the Potomac River and the capital.]

"I was, we were just about, close to a hundred feet away from the north side. And they were, I guess they were afraid to get up that pole again. They just laid down, and the Lieutenant was hollering over there. We can hear, 'Ira Hayes, Ira Hayes.' And then there's other guys. I know their faces, but I kind of mix up their names, and I can't see who they are. There was a lot, what I'm talking now, there's a lot of things happened here and here.

"And then we went back down below and our Sergeant, Ray, says Sergeant see right [sic] was the one that told us to go back down. So we went back there and then they told us to send them a message in Navajo that we took—they wrote it— took Suribachi, Mount Suribachi, hour and hour. That meant what time it was. And let it go into headquarters. Then we got another message that we have to move over more. Regroup your platoon and go on the north side. Then attack, the time. Some zero numbers." [166]

When the flag was hoisted on Mount Suribachi, the word went out in code, *"Naastosi Thanzie Dibeh Shida Dahnestsa Tkin Shush Wollachee Moasi Lin Achi."* Decoders translated the Navajo words, *"Mouse Turkey Sheep Uncle Ram Ice Bear Ant Cat Horse Intestines,"* and the word went out in English that the American flag flew over Mount Suribachi. [167]

OKINAWA

American troops landed on Okinawa, an island southwest of Japan, on Easter Day, 1 April 1945. The number of casualties in the battle for Okinawa was a sober reminder of the terrible cost of war: 127,000 Japanese soldiers, 80,000 Okinawan civilians, 7,613 Americans killed on land, 4,907 in air and kamikaze attacks.[168] Japanese officials say there were more than 234,000 killed; the Japanese dead are estimated from 72,907 to 107,539, including 20,000 Okinawan conscripts and 42,000 civilians, and 24,000 Japanese sealed in caves.[169] Whatever numbers are accurate, the battle for Okinawa was a grisly battle.

Ivan L. Hobson, who had already seen action on Peleliu, went into Okinawa.

"As my second operation, I landed on Okinawa. I fought there and was also wounded. That time it was a hand grenade that hit my leg. It was an 'opportunity' to get leave for the States.

"We were in the China Sea side of the island for the invasion. There were some Army units and two Marine divisions. There also was the 6th Marine Division on the Pacific side. They maneuvered as though that division was going to make the initial invasion. We knew this was happening. It was very logical that the invasion would come from the Pacific and, in addition, we weren't discovered by the Japanese in the China Sea. Submarines kept the waters cleared. There was no Japanese air contact. The Japanese drew more of their troops southward and eastward on the island on the Pacific side thinking that's where the invasion was taking place. We, in the actual landings, were to cut the island about one-third in the south, two-thirds of it in the north, the latter which had more of the mountains. The south was more level with a heavier population. The objective was to get, as much as possible, the Japanese down in the more level territory as much as possible. That worked.

"For this invasion, my unit was on the seventh wave. The amtracs, the amphibious tanks, came out to the ships to pick us up, and took us in as the next wave of troops. The crews of the amphibious tanks reported that there was no opposition. We landed, that first day, our company of 300 or so, and we had just one casualty as I remember. As we got going across the island, (it was supposed to take us three weeks to get across), actually we got across in three days as the Japanese troops had been pulled away from that area. As we turned southward, we met the enemy and got the dickens blown out of us.

"They were very dedicated. I'll tell you one of my horror stories. We came upon a little opening area down in the southern part of Okinawa. There were three or four dead US soldiers, who had been tied to bayonet posts. The Japanese had used them as target practice, with their bayonets. We had to cut them down. It was very dramatic and it made us madder, I guess. We were going to get even, that was our attitude toward them at that time.

"I've taken the attitude all these years that my combat experiences were a story-telling situation. I felt like, if I kept it within myself, it would eat me up mentally.

"I was certainly no hero. If anybody ever said, at least where I was, that they were never scared or frightened, I would say they were either lying or they were never in the front lines. I'll tell you, I was scared a number of times. I wasn't

A Time to Speak

Map of Okinawa and adjacent islands, showing landing points.

scared that I was going to be killed. I don't remember addressing that issue. When you saw movement of people in front of you, and sometimes they had these 'banzai' attacks in which the Japanese came on and came on and came on. They were just human targets, you had no problem killing them or they would have killed you, given the chance. The effort wasn't to kill everybody, but that's what happened.

"Most of the Japanese people in Okinawa weren't the ones we were fighting. They were innocent civilians. The Marines are not very well liked on Okinawa even to this day."

The Los Banos Rescue

With Manila under American control and after securing the island of Iwo Jima at the end of March 1945, there was a daring attempt to rescue prisoners of war held in the Los Banos prison camp, south of Manila.

After years of imprisonment, Sister Mary Louise Kroeger (from Chapter 24) recalled the rescue.

"This morning, 23 February, we went mad. . . and we heard planes overhead. We had been caught before, waving to the planes, and we were told if we did it again we would be dead, shot. So we learned not to show any emotion when the planes were over. This kept up and I couldn't figure out what was happening. And all of a sudden I could see this motion in the camp, and I looked up and there were the paratroopers coming from the planes. Of course, we didn't know what they were, we were so far gone. When they came, it was the signal to the guerrillas, who had come in from the mountains the night before to break into the camp; and as they came in, the amphibious tanks were also landing. . . Of course we went running up to them and threw our arms around them, but they knocked us away and we said, 'These American men are as mean as the Japanese.'. . They were thrusting us away as we were stopping them doing their job. . .

"Afterwards, when we saw them, the tears were rolling down their faces. They got us out right then, herded us out, tears and all because we had to get into the tanks, and the Japanese were already coming down. They got all 2,500 out. We lost an American and a Filipino." [170]

The Allied Armies were closing in on Germany and victory in Europe was close at hand, but a swift capitulation of Japanese forces was still not assured.

End Notes

164 Colonel Malcolm served in Vietnam and Korea, now retired he meets and talks about hunting and fishing with former members of the armed forces.
165 Pickard lives in Lakeland, Tennessee and volunteers at the local newspaper, making phone calls to boost circulation.
166 Excerpts from interview with Teddy Draper, Window Rock, Arizona, July 10, 1971, Doris Duke Number 1163, Doris Duke Interviews, MS 417, Manuscript Division, J. Willard Marriott Library, University of Utah, Salt Lake City, Utah.
167 Cited by Bruce Watson in his article, "Jaysho, moasi, dibeh, ayeshi, hasclishnih, beshlo, shush, gini", *The Smithsonian*, V. 24, August 1993, p. 34.
168 Martin Gilbert, *The Second World War*, p. 700.
169 *Leatherneck Magazine of the Marines*, October 1995, pp. 31-32.
170 Excerpts, interview, Imperial War Museum Sound Archive, Sister Mary Louise Kroeger, #5022

CHAPTER 44

APRIL, A MONTH OF DEATHS

The public, already shocked and numbed by the number of wartime deaths on the battlefields, from air-raids and in the concentration camps, now learned of the April death, execution, and suicide of three wartime leaders.

Death of President Roosevelt

On 12 April stunned Americans wept when they got the news that President Roosevelt died at his summer cottage in Warm Springs, Georgia. Mrs. Roosevelt, writing to her four sons, serving in the military, said, "He did his job to the end, as he would want to do." [171] On the same day, Vice-President Harry Truman took the oath of office. Roosevelt died before he could open the United Nations Conference on 25 April and less than a month before he could savor the Allied victory over Nazism.

The people's grief over the President's death went hand in hand with their uncertainty about the future outcome of the war under an untested President Truman.

Benito Mussolini

No one mourned the death of Mussolini. He had already been forced to resign on 25 July 1943 and he had set up a phantom Fascist government at Lake Garda, where he continued to read documents, receive visitors, and write articles about his betrayal by the Italians and the Germans.

Mussolini, like other Fascist leaders, met an ignoble death. on 28 April, when he, several of his friends and his mistress, Clara Petacci, were executed by a group of Italian partisans near the lakeside village of Dongo. His body, and that of his mistress, were taken to Milan where they hung upside down on 29 April. On the same day, the German troops in Italy signed the unconditional surrender of their troops.

Hitler's Suicide

Hitler's suicide/death led to speculation and to myths. On 30 April, as Russian soldiers entered Berlin and waved the Red Banner from the Reichstag, Hitler, in his bunker, shot himself.

He had chosen to stay in his bunker fifty feet below ground, together with

A Time to Speak

Goebbels, Bormann, his personal staff, and Eva Braun, with whom he had lived secretly since 1936 and whom he married a few hours before his suicide.

On 29 April, in his bunker, Hitler wrote his final will, and on 30 April, he shot himself with his Walther 7.65. Eva Braun, took poison. Their bodies were taken from the bunker, doused with gasoline, and set on fire. Admiral Donitz succeeded Hitler and vowed to continue the struggle against Bolshevism.

Since 1945 there have been myths surrounding the details of Hitler's death and Hitler's will. This was particularly true at the time of the 50th Anniversary of V-E Day, when letters to the editor of the *London Times* (15 May 1995) appeared. The first sentence of one letter, "Hitler's death," by Mr. R. W. Leon was intriguing. "Sir, As the first man on our side to learn the facts about Hitler's death (Mr. Hugh Thomas's letter, May 1) may I report what I heard in the first week of May 1945 from Hitler's press attaché, who had newly left the bunker bearing Hitler's will concealed on him. . . Later, as commander of an interrogation team, I had the facts corroborated from others who were present in the bunker."

Mr. Leon's book, *The Making of an INTELLIGENCE OFFICER* [172] elaborates on the information in his letter and the extracts are quoted with his permission.

Leon joined the Territorial Army, but when war came he was made a gunner in the Royal Artillery and was posted to the 145th Field Regiment serving with the 61st Division in Northern Ireland. Because he was fluent in German, he was transferred from Artillery to Intelligence. After the Normandy invasion, he was posted to Europe in a field security section to the American 9th Army, part of the 21st Army Group under Montgomery. Their job was to advance with the leading tanks, stop the enemy from destroying any papers, and to capture any personnel belonging to the organization RSHA (Reichssicherheits-hauptampt). When they reached Hanover, Leon was ordered to stay.

In Hanover, a young Luxembourger reporter, Jules Schaeffer, came to the intelligence officers with a newspaper scoop and a request for help getting back to his paper. It was an interesting story of the marriage of Hitler and Eva Braun and their suicide. The reporter claimed to have an informant who was one of the SS guards at Hitler's bunker. He carried no papers and no passport, but he had a wad of Reichsmarks, amounting to several thousand marks. It was Leon's task to interrogate him.

"I asked him how he acquired this money and he claimed it was his monthly wages saved up over a period of time. He lied further by saying, that when he took refuge in the cellar, he grabbed his savings but alas not his passport. His story was falling to pieces. I then pointed out that the money he was carrying was in high value notes all in numerical sequence, and thus had come

straight from the bank . . . Schaeffer looked troubled and I added to his troubles, by mentioning, that if it proved that he was a member of the German armed forces, the fact he was operating in civilian clothes would make him a spy or saboteur. If this was the case, he could be shot out of hand under the rules of the Geneva Convention. . . . Schaeffer collapsed and confessed all, or nearly all, for he held back the most important news."

His real name was Heinz Lorentz and he was one of Hitler's adjutants, for the Press liaising with Goebbels and the Ministry of Propaganda. Leon's interrogation continued:

". . .he told me of Hitler holding onto the reins of power to the last. The leader of the German Empire was in a terrible physical state, but his malevolent will never flagged. He looked twenty years older than he was, with trembling hands, for his nervous system was shot to pieces. His SS guards were loyal to him alone, and everyone in that bunker knew, that his life lay in Hitler's hands. They had to be loyal, or they would be shot.

"Lorentz was an important witness to events in Hitler's bunker and had given news, which we never heard from the Russians. I therefore sent him back to be interrogated thoroughly by experts.

". . .It was many weeks later that Lorentz, still held in camp 031, was given an order by one of the sergeants of the guard, which he did not hear or did not obey quickly enough. The sergeant took him by his shoulder and gave him a shove in the direction to which he should go. The sergeant felt something strange in the shoulder pad of the jacket. Lorentz had his jacket taken off, the shoulder ripped open, and there concealed within was Hitler's last will and testament. Now Lorentz had to undergo another interrogation by Bill Oughton, where the truth finally came out.

"Bill Oughton's interrogation of Lorentz revealed that Hitler had three secretaries constantly on duty, working on a shift basis, so whatever time of day or night he wished to dictate, one secretary was always there."

With the Russian Army so close to Berlin, and fearful that the Russians would not publish his will, Hitler chose three messengers to take copies of his will to the West, Heinz Lorentz, Colonel von Below, Hitler's Luftwaffe adjutant, and a third person whom Leon could not recall. All three managed to get to the West through Russian lines. One copy was recovered from Lorentz and the other two, although hidden, were also recovered.

In his book, Leon reports that the interrogation of former members of the *Sicherheitsdienst* and the *Gestapo* gave him additional information about Hitler, his thinking and his last days. The highest ranking officer to pass through Camp 030 was SS Major General Werner Best. Best was the German Reich's Plenipotentiary and head of the German civilian administration in Denmark. After the 1943

Danish August uprising, he assumed dictatorial power and vowed to govern the Danes with a heavy hand. Among other questions, Leon asked Best about Hitler's suicide:

"Why did Hitler leave his suicide so late? Every day he lived after it was clear, that your armies were beaten in the field, led to the loss of life, both on our side and yours, as well as many of those innocent victims held in concentration camps. If he had loved his country as he, pretended he would have had the courage to die sooner."

Best replied, *"The Führer would never surrender, and always intended to be victorious or die. He intended to fight to the last. This he did for history's sake. Future generations will applaud him and judge him as a man of iron resolve."*

In his political testament, Hitler claimed that his love for and loyalty to his people had guided all his thoughts and actions. *"After six years of war which, despite all setbacks, will one day go down in history as the most glorious and heroic manifestation of the struggle for existence of a nation, I cannot abandon the city which is the capital of this Reich."*

He claimed his work would continue, referring to "a seed has been sown in German history that will one day grow to usher in the glorious rebirth of the National Socialist movement in a truly united nation."

Hitler continued to blame Jewry and stated he never wanted war. The true culprit was the Jews who wanted and provoked war. The final sentence of his will affirmed his anti-semitism, "Above all, I enjoin the government and the people to uphold the race laws to the limit and to resist mercilessly the poisoner of all nations, international Jewry." [173]

A few minutes after the bodies of Hitler and Eva Braun were taken from the bunker, doused with gasoline and set on fire, the Red Banner was raised over the Reichstag. The unconditional surrender of Germany was becoming more and more likely, but the unknown and untested Harry Truman would still face the war in the Pacific. President Truman had to make the momentous decision to detonate the atomic bombs on Japanese cities.

End Notes

171   Colorado Springs *Gazette-Telegraph*, 12 April 1945.
172   R.W. Leon, *The Making of an Intelligence Officer*, London: Date Luce Press, 1995
173   Werner Maser, translated from the German by Arnold Pomerans, *Hitler's Letters and Notes*, New York: Harper & Row Publishers, 1974, pp. 346-365.

CHAPTER 45

COLLAPSE, SURRENDER, AND VICTORY IN EUROPE

At the beginning of May 1945, there was a sense that the European conflict was coming to an end. The specter of the Yalta agreements hung over the military operations as Allied units raced toward the east to meet the Red Army coming toward the west. American troops were forbidden to move farther east than the already-established demarcation line.

The rapidly moving American armies found bedraggled and sometimes sullen German soldiers, anxious to surrender to them rather than to the Russians. Prisoners of war were abandoned by their guards and left uncertain about what would happen next. Civilians wept with joy at being liberated, but looked with despair at their devastated farms and houses. To some soldiers, it seemed that society itself had collapsed.

The Last German-Held Corner in Czechoslovakia

It took Melvin Goldstein's Second Infantry Division a year to go from Normandy to Czechoslovakia. Once it crossed the Mulde River and moved through the Sudetenland, however, there was minor resistance. Everywhere there were signs of collapse and German troops were described by the official history of the Second Division as "Home Guard units, service troops, battle-exhausted units of one-time high quality branches of the Wehrmacht . . . surly looks and sullen faces as the Germans walked with eyes looking to the ground." Pilzen was officially taken by the Second Division on 7 May 1945, described by Goldstein:

"There was an armored division that preceded us by a day and we came in afterwards. Some went into Pilzen, others went down further into Klatovy, where I was. Others went into Rokycany, and others went further north. But generally, along that Pilzen line was as far as we could go. Because of the arrangements made at Yalta, the Russians were to take Prague.

"The reason we found that out was this. We got there about a week before the war was actually over, and the Germans were still in Prague. The Prague radio, the partisans were broadcasting all kinds of pleas for help because they knew we were this close. And they wanted us to come and drive the Germans out because Czechs were still being killed. But we had orders that we could not move any further, and we found out those orders came from up above because the Russians were

to take Prague. The Czechs wanted to get the Germans out; they wanted us to be there to prevent the Russians from coming in. That was the stalemate. But we couldn't move. That was as far as we got. As I say, the pleas over the radio were pretty pitiful, but unfortunately there was nothing we could do about it.

"The Germans pulled back, and at that point, we were taking thousands and thousands of German prisoners. Most of them knew the game was up and they were ready to surrender. The whole thing was collapsing around us. The 11th Panzer Division surrendered to us. The Panzer Division was in pretty good shape. They knew better than to go toward Prague. The Russians would be a lot tougher on them than we would be. They knew that a lot of their people were being sent back to Russia. With the exception of the Panzer Division, most of the prisoners were old men, young kids.

"The prisoners were taken, camps were set up, and they were kept in stockades. They were pushed back to the rear. All of them had equipment, actually, rolling equipment so we pushed them along in the conveyances they had.

"I made a point, any time we took prisoners, I let them know I was a Jew. I wanted them to know I wasn't going to take anything from them, that they had better watch out. I had compelling reasons to be a little tough on them.

"In addition to that, there were all sorts of civilian refugees pouring in this direction. It was quite a hubbub.

"We were welcomed, the Czechs were very happy to see us, took us into their homes. We had all kinds of parties, they composed songs for us. Our regimental commander was Colonel Philip Dewitt Ginder, they composed 'The Colonel Ginder March.'

"We stayed in that area for almost a month. And we got to know the people, and there were all kinds of soccer matches set up, all kinds of entertainment."

Goldstein, who today lives in Stanford, Connecticutt, revisited the Czech republic in 1996.

SURRENDER IN ITALY

The Italian campaign was coming to a close when the 10th Mountain Division took the German "Gothic Line," in the northern Italian Appenine mountains, and opened the way to the Po Valley. Max Peters, a member of the 10th Mountain Division clearly remembered:

"From then on, they just surrendered right and left. You'd go some place and there would be twenty or thirty of them waiting and begging to surrender. . .

"My battalion was supposed to leapfrog ahead the next day and go up to the Brenner Pass. This was on May fifth. Paul Turner and I were together, and we were just getting ready. In the morning, we were going to be the lead group to go into the Brenner Pass. Suddenly the word came back, the war in Europe is over.

A Time to Speak

They surrendered. And our guys just went crazy. They started shooting their rifles. I grabbed Paul and said, 'Let's get out of here.' So we went and hid in a ditch and we sat there and drank a Coke while all of these bullets were running over our heads. They were our own guys celebrating, but I said, 'Let's not get killed off right here at the very end.' Finally they calmed down and the next day we all went down to Lake Garda and had a bath."

To Berlin

Ken Bangs was secretary to the Adjutant General of the 78th Division and used a typewriter instead of a machine gun.

"We entered the actual combat during the Battle of the Bulge and we occupied Berlin after the Armistice was signed.

"During the Battle of the Bulge, we went up into the Ruhr pocket toward the end of the war. We were moving very rapidly at that point because the Germans were giving up. We went into Dusseldorf, Germany about one o'clock in the morning. Our front lines had taken Dusseldorf at midnight. We were there at one o'clock, and we occupied a boiler factory. So our headquarters was in the office of this boiler factory. It was more modern and up-to-date than anything I had ever seen at that point. The offices were all padded with leather doors so that they were soundproof. They had the most elaborate communication system in the building. Some of it I had never seen before. We set up our office about one or two o'clock in the morning and we were working at eight o'clock in the morning when the secretaries who worked in the factory came to work. They didn't even know we had occupied the town. They came to work and we were there. They went home. We were moving so fast that the civilians didn't know that the Army was retreating. We were picking up so many prisoners of war, we didn't know what to do with them. It was a problem.

"In Berlin, I guess we were the first group in there. And I had points to come home before we moved in, but I decided I would like to see Berlin, so I just stayed with them and I was with them for about three months. As it was always the case, we would move into a town or city, a group, I was usually a part of it, with a major. We would go in and find housing for all of us. And since I was in Division Headquarters, we always picked a nice place for us to live. Our Division Headquarters was in an apartment building where we had very nice housing, we even had maid service. The weird thing was that the Russians had been there ahead of us, and they had pulled all of the plumbing fixtures off the walls and taken them back to Russia. So we had no plumbing in these lovely apartments. Berlin had been bombed but there was still housing. We had to dig ditches or trenches out in the back yard, latrines.

"We were given orders never to be on the street by yourself, always at least two, because of the friction between the Russians and the Americans. You see, we were in West Berlin and they were in East Berlin. We didn't dare go into the area where they were. And if you happened to get in their section, they would attack. The United States could have gone in first, but it had been arranged that the others would go first, so we held back.

"So one evening, three of us went to the Berlin Symphony in this beautiful Opera House. Of course, there was no heat, and of course, this was in the middle of December and we sat there shivering, but I think it was the most beautiful music I ever heard. And the string instrument players sat there with gloves on and when they had to play, they would pull off their gloves and play. But it was a wonderful evening.

"When we occupied Berlin, we had the opportunity to visit Hitler's office. It was a huge building, more than a block square. His office was the whole first floor and you walked in, three or four chairs on each side, it was a block long. His desk was down at the end, and anyone who came into his office had to walk that block. He had an opportunity to analyze every individual. He had several minutes to see. It was an impressive place. Right back of his desk was a room that had a bed and a bathroom, and when he worked late at night, that's where he stayed. Also, we had an opportunity to see the war rooms, they didn't make the impression on me that the office did. You could just imagine walking across that floor, it would take you five minutes at least." [174]

CAPITULATION IN DENMARK

In Denmark, there were tears of joy, toasts with the champagne they had been saving for this moment. More than a million enemy troops in Holland, Denmark and northwest Germany surrendered to Field Marshal Montgomery's 21st Army Group. The Danes, who had formed a "Waiting Army," ready to obey General Eisenhower's command to start fighting, were spared a fight. The "Danish Brigade," a voluntary group formed in Sweden by escapees, however, did move into action at the time of the liberation. Gerd Schiotz, who with her husband Aksel, had been active in the Danish Resistance shared the excitement of the last days of the war and the news of victory.

"Everything was breaking down. It was chaos everywhere. We were listening to the BBC all the time, following the news, slowly, when they crossed the Rhine, coming up towards Denmark and the Russians were very close to us. We were absolutely lost. We did nothing but wait. Axsel had no concerts, there was no singing. We had to go to bed at eight o'clock. You couldn't be in the streets. Dark everywhere. It was officially forbidden to listen to the BBC, but we all had little things so it wouldn't show, but we kept ourselves informed. We received from the BBC all of the messages for the parachutists to come. They completed every broadcast, quoting lots of girls names, 'Gerda, Anna-Louisa' because that was code for where to dump the explosives and the arms. Lots of activities, lots of killing, lots of connections with Sweden. The Germans were desperate and they couldn't trust anybody, not themselves. It was an awful insecure period. Axsel had to go underground because he couldn't sleep at home.

"May 1, nothing happened. May 2, it was snowing, it was late spring out of the arctic winters. We didn't know what to do. We didn't know whether the Russians would come before the Allies. May 5, in the afternoon, we were listening to the BBC, the Danish speaker in London. He said, 'Just a moment, just a moment...they have capitulated.' Everybody was crying. Everybody became wild. We opened the doors and shouted all over the place. Our friends came to our house because we usually knew a little more. These refugees from the camps, French, Dutch, came, and in a half an hour, we had twenty or thirty people. We had saved some bottles and it was on the lawn. The loudspeaker was thundering. People kept coming. We had champagne. It was wonderful; we were absolutely wild. Now we were switching to the Danish radio, which was German controlled. It was taken over by the Danes, the Danish Resistance, and they started playing Axsel's records in between the news. Montgomery was coming up to Denmark. It was completely fantastic! We had powdered coffee from the Red Cross. At twelve o'clock noon on May 6, Aksel had to appear at the radio. He had not been in the German-controlled radio since August '43. First the king, then the Resistance temporary government, and Axsel. The king was congratulating the people.

"We tried to get to our apartment. We couldn't get in so we said, 'We live here, he's got to find his music.' In our apartment were mattresses, guns, hand grenades, helmets. They had been working all night, rounding up Nazis. The Resistance movement people took Aksel in a Resistance car to the radio station, Denmark Free Transmission.

"Afterwards came the shooting because the remaining Nazis were defending themselves on the roofs of houses. Quite a few people were shot. It was so sinister, people were killed in the street.

"At six or seven o'clock, Axsel went again to the radio station to sing. Then he met in the street some Allied pilots. They couldn't find a place, and he invited them up because we had Resistance movement mattresses. We had not any food. I ran to other houses and said, 'You are invited to look at some Allied pilots. I have to feed them but I have no food.' 'Oh, I have some jam, I have some ham,' and they carried what they had saved and we fed those Canadian, American and Australian pilots and we had them around the table and looked at them eating. They were *starved. We lit the fire in the fireplace and they took the kids on their lap. Then they slept on the Resistance movement mattresses.*

"Two or three days later, Axsel was ordered to go to Stockholm to celebrate the freedom festivities there. He came back with clothes. He took off his jacket and then his pants, then he appeared in a very nice blue nightgown. I was going to have that."

Ruth Woldike, who, with other Jews, had been smuggled out of Denmark in October 1943, was part of the "Danish Brigade."

"It was called the 'Danish Brigade.' When everybody could see that Germany had lost the war, they had what was called the 'Danish Brigade,' asking young people, men and women, to join and be trained. I don't know what they imagined. They thought they could protect people. They gave them thorough training.

"I was a kitchen worker and was supposed to learn how to cook for one hundred fifty people. I never learned it, but I did my best. We were also trained in defending ourselves, how to fire a rifle, first aid.

"I came back from Sweden on the fifth of May, Liberation Day. I remember when I marched into Denmark. We came over by Helsingor. I was sitting on a kitchen wagon, cooking for the company I was with, all the way to Copenhagen. When we came to Copenhagen, we were actually attacked by some snipers. Then I was sent to the German border with my company and stayed there for a month or six weeks. That was actually as a sort of police force. We were watching the Germans going home. They were miserable. There was no pity left, but actually they were miserable. And they had nothing to go back to.

"The Germans had to leave the country on foot. They had baby prams, wheelbarrows loaded with cheese and bread for their poor relatives who didn't have anything.

"And it was taken away from them on the border, most certainly. That was what we [the 'Danish Brigade'] were there for. They were not allowed to bring any watches or other things they might have. That may seem vengeful, but it is understandable."

PRISONER RELEASE
American

The Germans guarding war prisoners were fearful of the arrival of the Russian army and left their posts hastily.

Christian Chapman, who flew three missions on D-Day, continued to fly for the Royal Air Force until he was shot down in February 1945. He was taken prisoner, and with Australian and English soldiers, he walked east across the Rhine

A Time to Speak

and eventually arrived early in April at a camp for air force prisoners of war, located on the Baltic Sea between the Elbe and the Oder rivers.

"...and on May 1, the German guards told the Allied leaders (there were 30,000 prisoners there) that they were leaving, and they were just going west to give themselves up to the Allied forces. They didn't want to stay and face the Russians.

"There was a group of French officers who had been shot down earlier and had been in camps in the south and had promised the soldiers that they would return as soon as they could to help out. They asked me to join them. On May 1, we left the camp and just commandeered a truck and just drove south.

"The next two months for me were one of the most extraordinary periods of my life. We crossed the Soviet forces as they were moving up at the end of the war. The first element was a jeep with four soldiers and the one in the back had an enormous bandage around his head and they signaled us to follow them, so we made a U-turn and went back to a village we had just crossed. This was not a French village with little houses, but this is in Brandenberg, which is very rich and you had a sort of houses scattered around this main road going through the village. And the jeep stopped and from nowhere came these figures, silently marching, Russian prisoners of war who had been working the farms. They were assembled around this jeep, silently, and the soldier with the big bandage pulled out a balalaika and started playing it. And there were some women prisoners and they started dancing. And you had a poor bedraggled German soldier who had been taken up there and stood, sort of shaking his head, watched this and just walked away.

"We eventually left them and went back south, and crossed the first division (the jeep was just a forward element) and they came from Asia, I had never known if they were Kirgizs or Tadzhiks or where they came from, but they were Asians, and as soon as they saw us, they took guns and took our watches, pens, or whatever we had. That was our first experience with Asians. And later, when we had to deal with the Russian political commissars, they pointed to their fellow soldiers from Asia and said 'Be careful, they've got hot blood.' And it was very clear that the Russians, the greater Russians that is, from Moscow or Leningrad or Russia itself, felt much closer to us.

"We drove 100 kilometers to the south through village after village and all the houses had white sheets out. It was a terrorized area, even before the Soviet forces arrived. And when we got into the area which the Soviet forces had already overrun, you had these big, rich farm houses that looked as if a tornado had blown through them, all the furniture, all the papers, all the books had been thrown out in a circle around the houses. It was really terrifying. And we would walk into a farmhouse and say we would want to eat and drink. We weren't threatening. We just drove on, we didn't touch those German farmers or their wives or anything. But the record of the Soviet soldiers going through Poland and Germany was very bad. They had suffered a great deal, but it is also an experience that one is very rarely given is to be in a position in life, where you enter a city, where you could do anything you wanted to. And there is no retribution. You could kill people, you could steal, you could take women, you could do anything and there will be no consequence.

"When you are totally master of a situation, it leaves you shaken. Because then you realize that the only thing that guides you is some kind of compass up there. And if you don't have the compass...You sort of measure the degree to which one is kept morally close and straight and everything else by the fact that we are social animals and we live in a society. And we wouldn't think of stealing, we wouldn't think of harming somebody. But when you are put into a situation where all of society has collapsed and broken down, it is an extraordinary experience.

"The Soviet occupation for the Germans was a tremendous trauma, there is no question, and very quickly the political commissar began to take all of the troops in their hands and sort of establish themselves. The level of brutality...on the Allied side, there were rapes and drunkenness, but I've never heard of the level of violence that there was on the part of the Soviets.

"Finally, the Soviets came from an impoverished economy, the poverty of the Soviet Union and so they took everything, all the machinery, all the furniture, everything they could carry away. They took our watches.

"What a time of disorder!"

French Prisoners of War

Thin and hungry after their imprisonment, French prisoners wondered who would rescue them, the Russians, or the Americans?

French soldier, Louis Bedel, was arrested again in 1944 and was condemned in January, 1945, and sent to a disciplinary Kommando under the orders of the Red Cross, at Lubthen, north of Mecklenburg, where they worked on the construction of a road. Bedel wrote in his Journal:

"One question worries us. What are the Americans doing? We have heard the cannons from the west for several weeks. Now it is calm. Why don't they break through? The Rhine is more important. We don't go to work anymore. Everything is disorganized. Our overseer has been mobilized, near Wehrwolf, as a sort of volunteer.

"The guards are still here, almost invisible except for giving us our food. At night, one of them always makes the rounds. But a chap that woke up about 2 o'clock in the morning didn't hear anything. He listened. Nothing. He woke his neighbor. They called out, someone is sick, help. Always the same silence. They must have run away. We brought out two big iron bars, brought back from the work yard, attacked the door and the lock gave way quickly. A glance outside, not a man. The gate of the barbed wire cracked - It was liberty. What effervescence! We rushed toward the guard house. They had left, leaving their arms and munitions. They went to give themselves up to the Americans, fearing the revenge of the Russians. We organized for their improbable return. We went to the farm, waking up the conscripts who worked and announced their liberation. They received us deliriously. We kissed on the lips (what an idea), it seems it was their custom. They offered a Schnapps that they had made clandestinely with grain and beets. It was terrible. That day, we were the masters. What troops would come?

"We went to a village. The baker gave us a good ration. I found my good friend Daugon, nightmare ended. We pushed on toward the principal road. A mob of soldiers, their eyes without life, the last defenders of Berlin, walked without stopping. Some threw down their arms. The Russians are coming. It was a disorganized army which made me think of June '40. We decided to requisition their vehicles. With our arms pointed, the occupants got out protesting. They guessed our determination. We took their revolvers. The most unhappy were those that took off their boots in exchange for our shoes. Then we chased them away. We came back with six vehicles which would serve us to go back to France, we thought. The ones who knew how to drive verified the motor, the gas tank. As war booty, I had field glasses, a pair of boots, a little big but supple, an almost new pack. I didn't want any arms. For me, the war was over, really over.

"We sought one another's advice. Should we follow the convoy or should we stay here where the food supply is more certain? Two days passed. Then the first GIs with their astonishing jeeps, overflowing with joy. We gave them our bowls of ragout and they gave us their sophisticated rations, powdered coffee, cigarettes, chewing gum. Some comrades got in the jeep to test it. They had the jitters, drivers a bit mad, they dashed across the fields, feet on the ground, but the engine hugged the ground amazingly. We decided that two would leave on reconnaissance. If the crossing of the Elbe of 80 kilometers seemed easy, they would come back to get us. In the evening, they returned. Impossible to cross the river, a single bridge reserved for military traffic. The M.P. wanted to send us across the meadow where millions of people waited in precarious conditions.

"The next day we had contact with an officer who spoke French. He asked us to be patient. Only the military trucks could cross the bridge. Fruitless to try to return by our own means. Two days afterwards, the capitulation of Germany was announced and we left our cottage.

"We spent the first night in the vast courtyard of a factory. They distributed

American rations. It was a real Tower of Babel - all nationalities, all uniforms without counting civilians and deportees.

"The next day we left on a train which crossed Belgium, Brussels, where there was a delirious and comforting welcome. Finally, France, France. Hazebrouck, formalities and interrogation. Supplied with provisional papers, ration card for food, a little gratuity, dispatch of a telegram. We were disinfected by the Americans, the DDT killed all of the parasites. I was completely astonished not to scratch anymore. Again the train, taken to Paris, en route to Brittany. Oh, how the air is light and pure! Finished the stench of captivity. The heart beats. At each station, a group gets off, effusive good-byes, we will write, we will see one another again. Last embrace with Daugon who left at Rennes.

"It was 23 hours when I arrived at Saint Brieuc, 20 May, 1945, Impossible to get to Pleubian. The Red Cross lodged us in a barracks. In the morning, we were worried. How to complete the last journey? It is Sunday and no little train. Fortunately, volunteers came with trucks using gazogène. Two of them took charge of about twenty prisoners. More good-byes. I recognized the familiar countryside which had haunted my nights.

"Cécile comes down to the courtyard, her eyes sparkling with tears. I embrace my beloved Guy [his son] whom I scarcely recognize in spite of the photos. Friends, neighbors surround us. We invited them as well as the chauffeur and the comrades to have a drink. The kitchen is bursting. I feel a little lost. Finally, we are alone; everyone understands we need affection. . . Guy looks at us with big eyes. What can he understand of the drama and our bitter joy? We bend down to him, clasp him in our arms while a slight, nervous smile prevailed over us. It seems that dreamed of moment was not real. We separate, not as strangers, but as those, who after an interminable and cruel separation, want to read the traces left by such a nightmare, to better obliterate them. Finally, joy swelled our hearts. Our happiness was born again."

Guy Bedel, born in March 1939, was six months old when his father, Louis Bedel, was called up and left to serve in the army.

"In any case, the return of my father was something that remains engraved in my memory and I will never ever forget it. He arrived by truck in May '45 with perhaps a dozen men, returning from the war. I remember simply, I looked at him for a long time. He took me in his arms and when he put me down, I remember one thing, frozen in place, looking at him. He had a particularity, he was bald. As I said before, I didn't know many men, and never a bald man.

"I remember as well, the arrival of the Americans in the village. I don't know how to tell you, in the minds of the children that we were, what it represented, but we saw the population absolutely smiling, a gaiety at that moment after six

A Time to Speak

difficult years. Suddenly, the liberation of a country, the people who came to save us. It was formidable. And we children, we discovered one thing: chewing gum. I also learned about powdered coffee. The Americans arrived with their tanks, the American and French flags everywhere. It is an extraordinary souvenir. I have the impression of a merry-go-round turning in my head. Something extraordinary."

V-E DAY

After five years, eight months and six days of bloodshed, the war in Europe ended. The world was deliriously happy as they read the official news of Germany's unconditional surrender. On 7 May, General Jodl, the representative of the German High Command and Grand Admiral Donitz, the designated head of the German state, signed the act of unconditional surrender of German land, sea and air forces in Europe.

In accordance with arrangements between the three great powers, Great Britain, Russia, and the United States, the official proclamation of V-E Day came on 8 May 1945.

London

No country celebrated as jubilantly as Britain, which had endured six years of the conflict. Ellen Harris, who was a Reuter press reporter in the Houses of Parliament during the Second World War, gave an interview to the Imperial War Museum Sound Archive.

"And I say that the last day of the war with Europe was my outstanding day in the House of Commons. We knew that there was going to be a signature, bringing the war in Europe to an end. The Far East, of course, went on. It was coming to an end that day. Now the House of Commons, they were all sitting, but they got through the business. This was at the end of the week, early rising. The business was finished, which automatically the speaker calls for the 'rising' of the House. Those in favor, 'aye.' And the House rises and you are off. So somebody had to keep it going and it was one member after another who talked and talked, then somebody would butt in and say a little bit, and kept this going on, more or less, a lot of nonsense, to keep the House sitting. In the meantime, the word had gone through that Churchill was trying to get through from Number 10 and he couldn't get through the crowds. They had everybody, gradually, because we had our radios, they in turn knew there was going to be this big announcement from the 'mother of parliaments,' that was the great thing. And it took Churchill, well I don't know how long, he just couldn't get through, police everywhere, even at a walking pace, he couldn't get through. But now he arrives and a terrific cheer went up. The House was packed, you can imagine, not a space anywhere. All got their question papers and their parliamentary papers in their hand. Churchill walked in. A great cheer went up all the way around the House and the silence because he had reached his place. And he rose to say how happy he was to bring news that the war in Europe was now at an end. To my dying day, I shall never forget it. I couldn't move. I couldn't do anything. Whatever had happened, although we had known this was coming, the House itself just went into just one great roar of cheers. Papers went up in the air. I just sat and the tears were rolling down and there was nothing I could do about that. But it was relief, you see, after all this long time. This kept up, the roaring, and the cheering and the shouting for some time. And then the speaker dissolved the House. They were up entirely and everybody came out, and the House got up.

"I came home quite early in the day and said to my husband in the middle of the afternoon, 'What are we going to do?' He said, 'What do you mean, what are we going to do?' Well, I said, 'This is a most momentous day, we can't stay home.' 'Can't we?' he said, rather surprised. 'We must go up to the West End somewhere.' 'Well, he said, 'Where, it will be so crowded?' 'Never mind, let's be in the crowd.' This is how I was that day, you see. So we got up to Whitehall, Charing Cross, and we got through gradually and I was underneath the Treasury balcony, thousands upon thousands of people packed tight. You might have seen some of this in recent TV pictures, every now and again they show it. I was standing right underneath the balcony when they shouted and shouted for Churchill. Nobody was quite certain where he was. He came out on that balcony and it was an unrecorded speech. Nobody was there to do anything. I couldn't get through to report anything afterwards. He came out on the balcony and flung his arms out and he said, 'Londoners, I love you all,' and he said a few words. He praised them for their fortitude. 'They had won the war,' he said. He thanked them all. It was short and sweet, but lovely for the Londoners. And he finished up once more, 'Londoners, I love you all.' The cheers, it was a wonder the clouds didn't come down. It was really a most momentous occasion. And no photographers there at all. It was all unexpected. They didn't know where he was.

"How we, after that, managed to get through the short end toward the Houses of Parliament, then around and got home. But to me, that is my most outstanding day of myself in Parliament, starting with Churchill in the morning and then late at night." [175]

New York

Even though Americans realized the war was only half overr for the United States, it didn't diminish the celebration for victory in Europe. Pauline Parish, a WAVE, was in New York City when the end of the hostilities was announced.

"It was V-E Day and everybody poured out of these barracks, these old apartment buildings. They got into their cars, on the trolleys, they got into any kind of transportation they could. We had no more toilet paper left. All of the toilet paper was gone. So then a bunch of us, one of the officers had a convertible, so after everybody deserted us and went down to the center of New York City, Times Square was the place you should go. We got into this old Ford roadster and down we went into the middle of it. Here we were, six WAVE officers, riding around down there on the top of this car. We became kind of fair targets, you see, for all different service people. And all of a sudden, the navy sailors began to get on the fenders and they fended off all of these other guys who were attempting to attract our attention. We had a marvelous time in Times Square, enjoying the V-E celebration. It was an exciting, exciting period of time because it was almost the end of the war and there had been so much death..the whole place just erupted. I've never been in the middle of a celebration like that. Strangely enough, really very orderly. There was no breaking windows, there was none of that stuff. It was a mob, but it was a mob filled with joy and excitement that this thing was almost over. Yes, this war was almost over. And that was a very special night in my life when that happened. I'll never forget those sailors on the fenders being our big protectors. We probably needed a little of that."

To Japan

For many American soldiers, however, V-E Day was only a symbol. It was true that Germany was defeated; the war in Europe was over; but the war raged on in the South Pacific. American Marines did not secure the island of Okinawa until 21 June.

The American military was preparing the next steps to achieve victory; the invasion of Japan itself, Operation Downfall, scheduled for November 1945.

End Notes

174   Bangs took advantage of the GI Bill to finish his MA and get his PhD. He is retired as Professor of Business Administration.

175   Excerpts, Interview, Imperial War Museum Sound Archive, Ellen Harris, #9820.

CHAPTER 46
OPERATION DOWNFALL
THE MANHATTAN PROJECT

The Allies accepted the unconditional surrender of all of Germany's forces in Europe. Now, they demanded the same unconditional surrender of Japan's Army, or risk the complete destruction of their forces, as well as of the Japanese homeland. Meanwhile, there were other events that would bear on the ending of the war. On 16 July 1945, at Alamogordo, New Mexico, the United States successfully tested the first atomic bomb, which was the result of the research of the Manhattan Project, begun in August 1942, and carried out in a laboratory under the football field at the University of Chicago.

OPERATION DOWNFALL

The First Edition "Downfall" Strategic Plan, 28 May, 1945 was marked "Top Secret." The documents are now declassified and provide an interesting insight into the military plans for the invasion of Japan. The purpose of the operation was to force the unconditional surrender of Japan by seizure of vital objectives in the Japanese Archipelago.

The overall objectives were: (1) Lowering Japanese ability and will to resist, by establishing sea and air blockades, conducting intensive bombardments, and destroying Japanese air and naval strength; (2) Invading and seizing objectives in the industrial heart of Japan.

The assumptions were that the Japanese would continue the war to the utmost of their capacity and would prepare to defend the main islands of Japan with all means available. Furthermore, the operations would be opposed, not only by the available military forces of the Empire, but also by a fanatically hostile population.

It was estimated that there were three hostile divisions in southern Kyushu and three in northern Kyushu, with a total of eight to ten total hostile forces; and twenty-one hostile divisions on Honshu. There was the possibility of amassing 2,000 to 2,500 planes; the hostile fleet elements would be forced to withdraw to the Yellow Sea or the Western Sea of Japan but would be able to maintain suicide attacks against Kyushu landings.

In addition, with the continuation of Russian neutrality, the production capacity of hostile industries and raw materials in Manchuria, North China and Korea would remain relatively unimpaired.

To implement Operation Downfall the first phase on 1 November 1945 would require 766,700 troops; the second phase, 1 March 1946, 1,026,000 troops, including forces from the Sixth Army, Eight Army, Tenth Army, First Army, Far East Air Force, US Army Forces Middle Pacific, US Army Forces Western Pacific, Army Services Command "C", Naval Forces, US Pacific Fleet, and the 20th Air Force. [176]

In the light of such preparations and massive troop requirements, it is not surprising that American soldiers, poised to attack Japan, were apprehensive. Marine, Dewey Pickard, shared a map from the booklet, *Top Secret, The Story of the Invasion of Japan* (Ranger Publications) and marked, "Blue is where my outfit would have landed." It was the southern most island of Kyushu, the invasion scheduled for 1 November 1945.

The Manhattan Project

J. Robert Oppenheimer directed the group of American and European-refugee scientists of the Manhattan Project at the Los Alamos National Laboratory in New Mexico. In 1943, he personally recruited David Hawkins, an instructor in the philosophy department at the University of California at Berkeley, to assist with the top-secret project. Hawkins became the official historian of the project. Hawkins retired from the University of Colorado in 1981 after receiving one of the prestigious MacArthur Fellowships.

"*I went to Los Alamos after people moved in. The US Engineers had taken over that private school that was there at Los Alamos and were busy turning it into a place where a larger number of people would be housed.*

"*I was there as a non-physicist because I was a friend of Robert Oppenheimer. I was well enough educated in physics and related subjects so I could catch onto what was going on in the laboratory. I had been a rather good junior friend of Robert Oppenheimer, talking Sanskrit tradition, philosophy and Niels Bohr's ideas about physics and the universe. He was a great follower of Niels Bohr.* [Bohr, a Danish physicist, received the Nobel Prize in physics in 1922 for investigating atomic structure and radiation.] *Anyway I was invited to come and do administrative jobs. First, and this is very amusing, I was the liaison between the civilian and the military because they were fighting with each other over all sorts of petty issues. You can imagine the military, accustomed to be top dog at a military post and here was this group of arrogant civilians, academically arrogant civilians. That really wasn't a very important job, that was really superficial. I helped start a town council, a town radio, had meetings with people. And I was the go-between. But after two or three months that evaporated.*

"*Then I did odd jobs like deferring young men from the military, the draft.*

A Time to Speak

After about a year, I was given the job of writing the technical history of Los Alamos, which is the only record of what happened, and not a very good one, in one sense, because I didn't discuss personalities. So I stayed about a year after the war.

Moral Issues Discussed

"What's important to me now is that I got deeply involved with quite a sizeable group of young physicists who were concerned about the moral issues. They were creating the moral issues, in a sense, by working on the bomb. They were vastly concerned with the aftermath, the long term history. Unlike 99.99 percent of people who first heard about the bomb, they really understood its potentiality. They understood what a mega-ton explosive meant and what it would do to a city, and what it would do to warfare. We explored all these issues, a sizeable group of us did, not always as a group, but two or three people talking informally, the idea spread.

"Niels Bohr came to Los Alamos from Denmark as a refugee. When Hitler decided to execute the Jews in Denmark, they got almost all of them out. So Bohr was flown to England, where he met Churchill, with his message, which was the need for an international system. Basically, this weapon is too big for warfare. You can kill each other, but you mustn't destroy each other's societies. Clausewitz was the famous authority on the theory and history of warfare. He said the aim of war is to bring the enemy to do your will, not to destroy him. [Karl von Clausewitz, Prussian army officer and military theorist. His treatise, *On War* was published in 1833.] Genocide was out of the pale, and the recognition that this was a genocidal weapon was very, very slow to come. In fact, it really took fifty years, but anyway, we all knew that.

"And when Oppenheimer was confronted with the argument that we shouldn't use the bomb, he said, 'If it is not used in this war, it will not be known, and it will spread secretly in the arsenal of many nations, and that will be World War III. Better it be known now.' That's not a pacifist argument. That was his personal rationale [for using the bomb].

"You can say he had already agreed because he was head of the project to make the bomb. General Groves wanted to use it for a very simple reason. If it wasn't used, it would be his neck with Congress. They had spent two billion dollars. Groves was a narrow, competent administrator who saw his own job on the line. It [the bomb] had to be used. Oppenheimer had already agreed to go along, so, in a sense, he was a captive of Groves. But he did have a real argument, not just a rationalization. The price had been paid already in the bombing of civilians. That was not a new issue. If you were going to have LeMay in the Pacific theater with B-29s dropping napalm on cities, if you have LeMay dropping a couple of atomic bombs, it is not going to be a great novelty, politically, morally. [General Curtis LeMay, commander of the Twentieth Air Force in the Marianas, started fire-bombings against mainland Japan to destroy the industrial capacity.]

"The crucial turn came, maybe late 1943, General Groves came, and I was there when he explained that a spy had told him that the Germans were not developing the bomb. But, of course, that might be a double agent saying that to confuse us. He didn't want that to be true. But it was, in fact, true. When V-E Day came, and the war in Europe was over, some of the young physicists, young people in the laboratory, came to Oppenheimer and said, 'Why don't we just quit?' because the original justification for this weapon has evaporated which was the basis for the whole creation of the Manhattan Project.

"So anyway, that formed the nucleus of one of the groups that joined to make the Federation of American Scientists after the war, trying to persuade the government that international control of this new technology was the only solution. And we persuaded enough people, Oppenheimer in particular was very persuasive, that it became a serious proposal to the United Nations. It was serious, almost, because one of the provisions was that in all such matters, the veto power would be abolished, which would mean that Russia would always be four to one, voted down. Anyway the Russians wouldn't accept it. And I think that most people in the American government breathed a sigh of relief because they didn't want to do that anyway. They wanted to build up our military strength. And Oppenheimer, to the end, fought against this, building up the military, but at the same time, he was an adviser and had to contribute technical advice. So he was always in this ambivalent position.

Rationale For Continuing The Project

"There was a meeting of (I don't know how big a group in the laboratory), those who were interested, those who were concerned in which Oppenheimer spoke and gave this rationale for continuing. Groves would have said, 'Yes, we need it to end the war in the Pacific,' but Oppenheimer said, 'Perhaps that, but also the world needs to know about it.' 'Why can't it be used simply as a demonstration on an uninhabited island?' 'Well, technical objections, maybe it wouldn't work and that would be a catastrophe, a political catastrophe to have people from all countries there; and second, it must be known to the whole world in the most dramatic way, as something that will kill large numbers of people and will destroy a city. Otherwise, the lesson will not be learned. And if the world does learn this, then there is a fighting chance that we can prevent the use of nuclear weapons in any future warfare.' We can eliminate the existence of nuclear weapons and just have other forms of nuclear technology, power plants. It was all rather abstract then.

A Time to Speak

"The bombing of Nagasaki remains a second question, which was not one of broad policy that we ever heard of, and I don't think it was a question of broad policy. Three bombs had been made at that point. LeMay, I believe, wanted to use everything. He just liked bombing. I believe that the command that went to the Air Force 509th Unit that did this B-29 bombing, I believe the order was, 'Drop one bomb, and you have permission to use the second.' They only had two in the field at that point. The third one was still on its way. It was, in other words, a field decision; it was sanctioned ahead of time. And how that field decision was actually made, I don't know, but it was in the clear to use it. And there may be been questions of a personal nature involved. I don't think it was an erratic decision. I think it was a decision that had been previously sanctioned. And the fact that it was Nagasaki, as you probably know, was an accident of the weather, but it would have been some city.

"I could have gone to watch the test [of the bomb]. *I was, after all, the historian. I should have seen it with my own eyes. And I was afraid of it. And I didn't want to be away from home. It is funny. I had listened to stories about the early-understood possibility that the nuclear bomb might ignite the nitrogen in the atmosphere, destroy the planet. Very careful studies had been made which showed, if they were correct, it was utterly remote as a possibility. It would take vastly greater amounts of energy to do this and even so, it might not spread worldwide and blow a hole in the atmosphere. When I was writing the history, I had to give a reference to this. I had heard about it and hadn't given it too much attention. I heard about it with the assurance that this was long since impossible.*

"I interviewed Edward Teller [American physicist who helped develop the atomic bomb and who provided the theoretical framework of the hydrogen bomb] and other people about this and they gave me the detailed analysis. And I had a question. But suppose something is wrong with your calculations? Suppose there is some factor involved that we don't yet know about? And they would sort of look grave. From Edward Teller, I got a characteristic 'tellerian' answer, 'Oh well, worse things could happen,' which is what you call gallows humor. And I asked Robert Oppenheimer about it, and he gave me a very careful explanation of the most important fact which was that 'Big atoms repel each other with enormous repulsion, because they have a very high electrical charge at the same time, the nuclei.' Then I asked one of our visitors from Washington who listened to my concern and he said, 'Well it is too late now.' I remembered Pascal's great wager: if Christianity is false and you become converted, you have very little to lose; if it's true, you have eternity to gain. And I turned that argument upside down and I said, 'If this argument is correct, we gain very little; if it's false, we lose everything.' And how do you calculate probabilities for a wager of that kind?

"That was in the background of my mind, and I just didn't want to see it. And also I think I was a bit repelled by the enormous technical enthusiasm of people who wanted to see it because it was such 'a beautiful big bang' if it worked. And it was a powerful aesthetic experience, so powerful that even the generals were shaken. 'What have we done?' It didn't' change any policies. The policies were made by people who had this powerful experience. For the calculators, it was just a weapon. Anyway, many of us became 'nuclear pacifists.'

"It isn't genocidal; it isn't the destruction of the eco-system. A full-scale war, more and more people realize, a full-scale nuclear war wouldn't just annihilate large fractions of humanity and put its existence in question, but it would irreversibly damage the whole eco-system of the planet.

"We all sort of understood the baptism that we had, politically speaking. Understanding was something that would come slowly to the world."

President Truman made the decision to hasten the unconditional surrender of Japan by dropping the atomic bomb. His decision set off events which changed, not only the face of war, but gave birth to the nuclear age. The nuclear arms race began and the potential for nuclear war became part of political reality.

A Time to Speak

End Notes

176   Information cited from "Operation Downfall," Record Group Number 407, Record Identification, E427, Box 699, National Archives II, Washington, D. C.

CHAPTER 47

THE ATOMIC BOMB

*I*n recent years, historians and others have argued about whether dropping the atomic bombs were justified. The debate was particularly heated in August 1995 at the time of the Smithsonian Museum exhibit of the *Enola Gay* (the plane which dropped the bomb), set to coincide with the 50th anniversary of the dropping of the bomb. The curators at the Smithsonian Museum were blamed for a revisionist "blame America first" attitude, while the critics of the focus of the exhibit were accused of being "too patriotically correct."

Servicemen scheduled to invade Japan were unanimous in the opinion that they had no regrets about President Truman's decision to drop the bombs. Paul Murphy's comments are representative of their attitude:

"*The only thing I'm unhappy about is the Smithsonian Institute and the do-gooders that think that the atomic bomb should not have been dropped. It saved a lot of lives. I'm glad it happened, and I'd do it over again if I had a chance. And had not the war ended, my ship would have been the flagship of the invasion of Japan and Admiral Spruance* [Commander of the Fifth Fleet] *would have been in charge of it. We were the Fifth Fleet flagship. Admiral Spruance and his flag were on board our ship.*"

Others suggest that Japan was ready to surrender, that the United States could have demonstrated to the Emperor and the Japanese Army the power of the atomic bomb and its potential devastation by dropping it away from a city or into the sea.

The Fatal Voyage of the **Indianapolis**

Once Truman had made the decision to drop the atomic bomb, the bomb cores for the uranium bomb, for Hiroshima and for the plutonium bomb, for Nagasaki, had to be delivered to the scientists and the aircrew waiting on Tinian Island, in the Marianas.

The USS *Indianapolis* was chosen to carry the bomb cores, and the ship sailed from San Francisco. The fate of that cruiser was relegated to insignificant news coverage, in the light of the end of the war. In the newspapers for 15 August, proclaiming the end of the war, there was also a short story, at the bottom of page one, "Cruiser *Indianapolis* Sunk Off Leyte with Loss of 883 Lives."

A Time to Speak

For petty officer third class, Paul Murphy, the sinking of the *Indianapolis* was significant. After delivering the secret cargo, the *Indianapolis* sailed to its next assignment, but the ship came under attack. Murphy was one of 317 survivors of the 1197-man crew.

"We were called to make this last run with this article which we didn't know what it was. We made the steam record from San Francisco to Honolulu. We had the atomic bomb components on it and we didn't know that. After we dropped the bomb parts off in Tinian, which is part of the Marianas (the Marianas was my first operation when I went overseas); then we went to Guam, took on supplies and refueled. We received our orders to proceed to the Philippines and we were to meet the battleship Nevada a day and a half after we left there. And we were going to train at the same time. At that time, 25 percent of the people on that ship were 'first time at sea,' three weeks of sea duty, they got the Purple Heart and got sunk.

"Anyway, our orders were such that the Port Authorities at Guam indicated that we were to proceed and use a zigzag course at the Captain's discretion. They did not tell us that we were going to be in enemy waters where anything had happened the previous week. A destroyer was sunk the day before we left. They didn't tell us that.

"So the night that we were sunk [30 July], the Captain told the officer of the deck that it was pitch black, he could cease to zigzag. We could zigzag during the daytime in daylight hours, and in the evening, at his own discretion, he could cease it at night time. He said, 'If anything changes, call me.'

"A few minutes after midnight, the moon came up and we sailed between the moon and a Japanese submarine that surfaced, charging its batteries. We made a perfect silhouette. The submarine submerged, took his telescope and looked 360 degrees around because we should have been escorted. Major war vessels were supposed to be escorted during the war. We were not. If there were enemy in the area, we should have been. Destroyers and destroyer escorts are the ones that have radar to detect submarines. We don't.

"So all he had to do, he saw that we weren't escorted as far as he could tell, so he just wound up on our ship, and when we passed, he fired six torpedoes and two of them hit us. We think three, but they were saying two. We went down in twelve to fifteen minutes. It knocked out all power, no radio SOS went off, verbal 'Abandon ship' was given in the forward part of the ship. I was in the aftward part of the ship. I had just gotten off watch, I had 8:00 to 12:00 that night and retired in the after part of the ship. And when it hit, it knocked me out of the bunk. I had a rubber life belt on and I grabbed a kapok jacket and went to my general quarters station, which was the after control tower in the rear of the ship. The after control tower controls the fire of the 8-inch guns. When I got up there, I went into the control tower and my best buddy was sleeping soundly on the deck. He didn't wake up. I woke him up, gave him a life jacket. He got off the ship, but he only lived two days in the water.

"I stayed there until the ship rolled over to the starboard side. There were 5-inch guns on the deck below the one I was on, and those guns were under water when I stepped off. I didn't have to jump or anything. I stepped off and started swimming. And I got out into the oil-slick water. I had a life jacket on and I had gotten another life jacket, just in case somebody needed it. And I did run into one of my other friends who was swimming around without one.

"I turned around and the last thing I saw was the ship had gone completely over and the propellers were turning. They were the last thing in the water. I was afraid we would get sucked under or something, but that didn't happen to me. I was evidently far enough away that it didn't cause any suction. I did swallow, like many of the others, oil and salty water. The first night, we spent most of the night throwing up.

When The Ship Was Hit

"You didn't have much time to think. I think I was optimistic that we would be picked up. Then after time went by, I became exhausted. I passed out probably a couple of times. There is a Lord, and he answers your prayer. But other than that, I more or less just laid back and waited to be rescued. That was about the only way you could save yourself, not overexert yourself, don't drink salt water. Anybody that drank salt water was gone. The dehydration and the hallucination and the mental loss...the wildest drunk you've ever seen is a man who drank salt water. It can't get worse than that.

"There were at least 300 that went down with the ship. In the forward area, some say the bow was blown off. I can't say that because I didn't see that. Then one of the torpedoes exploded in a magazine compartment, which was dynamite, and that just blew everything up and set fires in the lower level. Anybody that was quartered in that forward area, if they did get off, they were burned pretty badly. Some of them did. Our medical officer, his hands were burned and he survived in the water and administered to survivors. He was a hero. Our chaplain was a Catholic priest, he died in the water. A lot of them died in the water. I'd said 500 to 550 died from exhaustion [1,197 man crew; 880 made it into the sea].

"There were 317 of us lucky enough to be pulled out of the water and survived. In fact, the ship that picked me up, one of the men died before they got him to the Philippines. So he got that close to being saved.

"You are like a cork, your legs are dangling. I had dungarees on. The constant rubbing of the cloth against your skin caused ulcers there. You couldn't stand

A Time to Speak

to have anybody come up near you or touch you. I had my shoes on. I'm sure nobody wanted me to touch them with my shoes.

"Yeah, we had schools of sharks. I never saw a large shark, I never saw a dorsal fin like some of them did. We saw schools, and during the daytime, because of our large group, we could splash and holler and raise cain and they would leave us alone. I don't think any of them attacked at night. I'm not sure about that. I've had them brush up against me. I've seen some of the fellows with knife cuts on their buttocks or on their heels if they didn't have shoes on or didn't have pants on. Some of the guys got off the ship with no clothes on. They were in the shower.

"During those four days, to keep up morale, we talked, and we prayed and we helped each other out. I have one friend up in North Dakota that found out later on that I went out to get him twice. He was with us in the cargo and he was ten years older than I, married, had two children, heard his wife was pregnant. He was in my division. One night, about the third night, I heard him hollering. He had left the group and went way off by himself. He wanted help. I swam out to where he was. I had to holler at him to get directions so I could find my way out there. Swimming with a life jacket is kind of tough. I got out to him and then I got behind him and I pushed him. He doesn't remember a lot of it, he was kind of delirious. I hollered back to the group and got directions and I pushed and I swam and I got him back to the cargo net. And I told him, 'Now Ralph, you hang on there.' And it wasn't very long, he was out there again. This time he wasn't very far, but I couldn't get anybody else to go get him. So I went out again: fortunately, he wasn't very far. This time I got him back. I untied the string off his vest and tied it around the cargo net and I scolded him good.

"We assumed we would be found the next day. That day came, planes flew over us. In the meantime, we were trying to gather into groups. Probably by the end of the next day, I probably ended up in one of the largest groups. I think it was probably around 150 or 200 men in the group that we gathered together. We stayed together. We had life jackets, no rafts and no lifeboats. We didn't get any of the lifeboats off. The rafts were washed off. There were cargo nets. If they are laid out flat, they were intentionally used for what we used them for. They had a cork disk on each side section, so it floated like a blanket. So if you could get your body in between a section to hold it together and also to give it extra buoyancy with your life jacket. So I probably spent 50 percent of my time in that cargo net with a life jacket and I would get out occasionally to get on the outer edge to help somebody.

"During the daytime, after the first day, I tore off a shirttail and put it over my face during the day because I was getting blistered and the salt water ulcers on my face. I was getting to the point where I couldn't stand the hot and blazing sun in the daytime. And it was cold at night."

"We weren't there"

"Getting back to where we were to meet the Nevada, the afternoon that we were to come in contact with an airplane, pulling or towing a sleeve for aerial practice, the plane was there. We weren't. They reported back to the base that we weren't there. And that evening we were to be met with a tug, pulling a surface target for surface practice. It was there, we weren't. They reported back that we didn't show up. We were due in to port that evening, and the port director took our plotting ship off of the plotting board and set it aside and assumed we'd probably be in the next day. And did nothing about it.

"Ironically, everything went wrong that could go wrong. My captain, Captain McVay, had a friend. He was to meet us at Leyte in the Philippines. And he was going to throw the largest Red Cross party that had ever been thrown in the Pacific for our group. And he was there and we weren't. The next day he reported to Admiral Kincaid's office and, while he was there, he saw a partially decoded Japanese submarine message to Tokyo and it said that a battleship of the Idaho class was sunk at the exact location we would have been that day. They didn't recognize that we were a heavy cruiser and not a battleship. So he said to Kincaid, 'That's what happened to Charlie's ship, what shall we do about it?'

"They sent one plane over to try and find us and they didn't find us. And nothing was done.

"On the fourth day...planes flew over us every day and some of the rafts had flares on them. At night they fired flares, but the planes didn't see them.

"Thursday afternoon, an Army pilot was making a routine search of the sea, and he had a radar device that was suspended out the belly of his plane that made a circle, and they could detect some of the objects that might be below. We saw this plane come in; it was making circles. Just before he got to our area, one of the cables broke off of this radar, and the crew called him back. He was on his belly and he was fishing this up and he saw an oil slick. So they followed this trail of oil slick, thinking it was probably a submarine that had been hit. And he wanted to find out and maybe get his first kill on a submarine. Well, as he progressed, it got thicker and thicker and then he saw heads bobbing around in the water, and he was down to about 3,000 feet. He saw there was a major disaster of some sort, but they didn't know whether they were Japs or Americans.

"So he wired back to his base in Peleliu and the co-commander of the base received the message and he sent one PBY plane out with supplies and food. This guy flew out there. He got out there and he circled around. We were scattered over about a 25-mile area and he saw the stragglers. Some of the boys had gone out by themselves to try and swim to shore. And he saw that they were being attacked by

A Time to Speak

sharks. So he wired back to the base and said, 'Hey there's a major sea disaster. Send all help.'

"That message went to the commander of the base. They sent one PBY out. So there were two of them flying around. They dropped lifeboats and life rafts and water and food. And that was the fourth day. Then the first pilot that was out there, who lives in Indiana (a great guy who comes to everyone of our meetings) he wired back to the base and said, 'I'm going to attempt an open sea landing. There are stragglers down there and I'm going to have to help them.' So he landed and taxied around and picked up 56 boys, put them on the wings, in the aisles, tied them on the wings with airplane cords, gave them all a drink of water. From our group, I got one guy on.

"He only picked the ones in serious condition and, of course, he couldn't take all of them. But that was the first time they knew that an American ship was sunk and that these were American survivors.

"When he flew out to meet us and make contact, he went over a destroyer that was commanded by Graham Claytor [Claytor was later Secretary of the Navy for President Carter and became president and CEO of Amtrack], *the USS Doyle, and he told the captain of that ship that he was heading in the direction of sea disaster. And the Doyle followed him. When the Doyle got out there, he had been told by radio, afterwards, that it was the Indianapolis (he was a relative of the captain, too). He shined his searchlights up in the air which could have drawn enemy if there were any around. But he did this intentionally to let the survivors know that help was coming. I don't know whether it was a good idea or not. It wasn't in the case of the group I was with. We overexerted ourselves trying to swim out to where the ship might come up to us.

"The next morning was when most of us got picked up. I got picked up by the Bassett. They picked up approximately 150 boys and took us to the Philippines and we went into a hospital at Samar. They laid us on rubber-sheeted beds and poured liquid penicillin over us to clear up our saltwater ulcers. We were there, I don't know, it is very vague to me how long we were there. Nobody has ever told me, it would be there seven to ten days. Then they flew us to Guam in a freighter and we went into a submarine rest camp there and we stayed probably about two weeks, getting our energy back. We had ice cream in gallon buckets, steaks every night and beer. The submariners had pretty good duty. And then we came back to the States.

"To manage with no food and water for four days, I think your body absorbs some moisture. The main thing to have control over is not to drink that salt water. I tasted it and it was good. You had to have control and discipline. It would be easy to fall off, and a lot of them hallucinated and would say they saw the ship coming up from the bottom and just below the surface. And you could down and get a drink of water or you could get some oranges or something. They would dive down and some of them never came back. And you couldn't keep them from doing that. But in my group, we had quite a few boys in my division, which was fire control, and I think we did an awful lot to help each other. And I think we had better survival, percentage wise, of any division.

"The Bassett was a fast attack transport so they had many ships that carried tanks for landing. They dropped vessels in the water to pick us up. They came alongside the ship and we climbed up ladders to get on board ship, if we could. I didn't think I'd have any trouble. I started up the ladder and fell off and they put me in a wire basket and took me up. Then they cut our clothes off, set us in showers and tried to wash off all that oil and gave us some nice oranges. They took pretty good care of us.

"I don't know whether you are aware of it or not, but the commander of that submarine that sunk us was named Hashimoto. My captain was court-martialed, erroneously. Somebody had to be the scapegoat and Admiral King made him the scapegoat despite everybody else telling him he shouldn't. Admiral King was a lieutenant in Asia when my captain's father (who was an admiral) reprimanded him for doing something wrong. At any rate, he was court-martialed, first time a navy officer in charge of a combat ship was ever court-martialed in any war. They brought the commander of the submarine over to testify at his court-martial. He did not affect the outcome of it.

"In fact, he told the court that no matter what, if McVay had been zigzagging, he still would have been sunk because he was in the right spot. Captain McVay committed suicide in 1968 because he was getting Christmas cards from wealthy families who had children aboard ship who were lost and they constantly sent him a Christmas card, saying, 'If it wasn't for you, my son would be here.' And that got the best of him. McVay's sentence was remitted, but he lost all possibility of ever holding a major job in the navy. His career, his dad and his grandfather were both admirals. He retired as a rear admiral, a courtesy." Paul Murphy, along with other survivors, testified recently at a hearing in Washington, D.C., hoping to overturn McVay's court martial. However, the ruling stands.

The Bombing of Hiroshima

The crew of the *Enola Gay* have no regrets that they dropped the bomb which ended World War II. Only one crew member of the Captain Robert Lewis, expressed remorse in his often quoted journal entry, "My God, what have we done?"

In interviews in the *New York Times International* (6 August 1995, p. 8) and in the short documentary made for the *Enola Gay* exhibit at the Smithsonian Institution (1995), former crew members stressed the context in which the decision

A Time to Speak

to drop the bombs was made. It had been a long war, a devastating war, in which the casualties increased as the Allies approached Japan. It had been a long war in which Americans, servicemen and servicewomen and those on the home front, were united in their patriotism. The object of fighting the war was to win, using whatever means were available to shorten the war, to end the war, and to save lives. [Paul Tibbets prefers to let the official comments speak for the crew.]

The facts are: the 509th Composite Group was activated 17 December 1944 to train at Wendover Army Air Field in Utah. Colonel Paul W. Tibbets organized and trained them to drop atomic bombs simultaneously in Europe and Japan. In May 1945, they were ready to go to war and moved overseas to Tinian.

On 6 August 1945, the *Enola Gay*, a B-29, named for Tibbets' mother, dropped the 8,000 pound uranium bomb, nicknamed "Little Boy," over Hiroshima at 8:15 a.m. It leveled the city.

The Devastation

It was not only the secrecy which amazed a Navy pilot, but also the total destruction he witnessed later as he flew over Hiroshima.

"I had been on Saipan for months, near Guam, and I had never heard of an atomic bomb. The secrecy was amazing. I was right in the middle of all of these people, the Air Force people, who were preparing for it. I had never even an inkling.

"When I saw it go off, I didn't know what it was. I turned to my copilot and said, 'Gosh, they must have hit an ammo dump.' We were flying about every three days over the Empire. I don't even know what I was doing up there at the time, I can't recall the mission.

"What I saw at Hiroshima, it's buried behind fifty years of memory. My reaction was one of almost horror. It was just leveled; it was gone. It just wasn't there. I had seen Hiroshima from the air when it was still a city and I could make a comparison. It was just devastated, of course, the whole city was gone. Some smoke. We didn't spend very much time there for a variety of reasons. We were under orders to do something else and we went back to Okinawa.

"Most of my impressions and thoughts came later. I don't remember when they came, I remember talking with my wife about it that I kind of regretted that the bomb was dropped because I had seen a great deal of the war. I knew that we were winning. It was obvious we could fly those big old slow planes right over the middle of the Empire. Nobody would come up and challenge us. And just a few weeks before, you would have had everybody on your tail.

"I think it was necessary. Iwo Jima took place just weeks before and Okinawa was a very vicious war. To us, it was a very serious war. Dropping the bomb was not necessarily the wrong thing to do. I didn't make a judgement like that. I just thought that someday what is happening would happen. It was such a devastating thing,

such a decisive thing. The Japanese simply wouldn't quit. They were very worthy adversaries. They were tough.

"The war was very real to the people who were fighting and lots of people were still getting killed every day, particularly at Iwo. That was terribly vicious. They were viciously fought wars and the Japanese showed no inclination to give up. I think it was in the best interest to stop it. I got to come home anyway.

"Thousands and thousands of people would be involved in the invasion of Japan. You have to have seen an invasion, and I saw a good many of them. It is almost unbelievable that you can condition men to do it. I've always marveled, and I've had that question in my own mind how they could ever train those Marines to do that. It is just so incredibly hazardous. And of course, they did lose thousands.

"I've always wondered why they had to drop the second one. I would say my opinion would differ radically from most people in my position. I recall the dropping of the bomb was really an anti-climax. I don't know that I had strong opinions at the time. The idea that we should use the bomb was not that wrong. We had to end the war; we had to stop it, and they showed no inclination to stop. We were sure glad when it did stop. Again there are questions, but there are not answers."

A Witness And Survivor

Nabuka lived in Hiroshima at the time of the bombing. Midori Johnson translated Nabuka's remarks:

"In the morning about 6 a.m. a mushroom cloud; then after it was like rain because of the wind. The windows were broken and the houses were not torn down but tilted. In the doorway, the glass door was broken. My older brother stayed overnight in his office which is the public service utility company in the center of Hiroshima. Fortunately, he was in the third story, a concrete building. But inside, the building was shattered and all died except my brother. But the other brother who had a job in the bank, 8:15 a.m., he was on his way to his job and he got hit and he barely made it home, but one month later he died.

"I was under a table, 'Hide under a table, they said, 'When bomb drop, hide under the table,' so that training really helped. Some people come to stay in my home. Lots of people, three or four days, they stay. People were dying every day, but those people who escaped, they had to step over the dead people and most of the skin was hanging from the body. There weren't enough doctors. They piled up the bodies. The place where they buried the dead is a very beautiful city street now."

A Time to Speak

Nagasaki

On 9 August, *Bock's Car*, named for Fred Bock, who was to be the pilot, [The pilot was Charles W. Sweeney] dropped the 10,000 pound plutonium bomb, "Fat Boy" on Nagasaki [the original second target was Kokura].

Fred Olivi, one of the crew of the *Bock's Car*, gave a detailed account of what it was like to be part of the crew: memorable, dramatic, hair-raising, and without regrets for having bombed Nagasaki.

"In World War II, I was the copilot that dropped the second atomic bomb on Nagasaki on the ninth of August, 1945. I belonged to the 393rd Bomb Squadron, the 509th composite group. We went overseas in June 1945 to accommodate dropping the two bombs on Japan.

"What really occurred, I was flying B-24s first, and all of a sudden I was at Lincoln, Nebraska where the pool was for all of the personnel that was supposed to be assigned to individual group squadrons. So, normally a shipping order would be about thirty or thirty-five pilots, navigators, bombardiers and all of a sudden, my name comes up on orders and there are only about ten of us. And I became curious right away because they were departing from the norm. And I said, 'I wonder what this is about?' I had a friend of mine who worked in headquarters and I got a hold of him and I said, 'Hey, I came in on orders and it's different from the rest. Instead of the normal thirty or thirty-five, there are only ten or eleven of us.' And he says, 'Where are you going?' and I said, 'I'd like to find out too.' So he says, 'Come along to the headquarters and we'll look it up.' So he looked it up and he said, 'Oh, yeah, you are going to Wendover, Utah.' And I said, 'What's that?' and he said, 'It is west of the Salt Flats, west of Salt Lake City, in the Salt Flats.' So I said, 'So I'll be flying B-24s' and he said, 'Yeah.' He said 'The last time I knew it was a B-24 RTU unit which means that was the last phase of training before going overseas and you're probably going to take over from a pilot who got hurt or got sick and you'll fly with them a little while and then you'll go over to Europe.'

"So that was fine with me because the 15th Air Force was full of B-24s and they were in Italy. And being Italian, I was looking forward to seeing my relatives. So the next day, I got on the troop train and got to Wendover, Utah. So when we got to Wendover, Utah, the first thing I saw was this big-tail B-29. I said, 'No, something is wrong. I don't belong here because I was a first pilot of B-24s. We were met at the station by the then, Colonel Tibbets. He took us immediately into a room and proceeded to tell us why we were there. He said we were investigated by the FBI and they talked to my neighbors, my school teachers back in Chicago and we had to be cleared for this highly secret project.

"So he told us what we were going to do and one of the things that kind of stuck in my craw was - he made the statement that you pilots would become copi-

lots. And right away that picked up my ears so I just couldn't wait to find out what he meant by that. So after he was all through explaining everything, he asked if there were any questions. I got up and I said, 'Yes, Colonel, I understood you to say that we were to be copilots on the B-29.' He said, 'That's right.' And I said, 'I don't exactly relish that because I am a B-24 first pilot in charge of the aircraft. Now you are putting me over to the right side in the right seat and I'm just a copilot.' Well, he looked me straight in the eye and he says, 'Lieutenant, if you want to be in this outfit, you'll be a copilot and like it. If you don't like it, the door is open anytime.' So, of course, I didn't go because it was the biggest aircraft we had in our inventory at the time. So I stayed and got checked out in the B-29 and in June 1945, we left the States for Tinian.

"The word 'atomic' was never used. They just said, 'We had a bomb that could destroy an entire city and that's what Tibbets told us when we were being briefed about what we were doing there, because again there were just ten or eleven of us.

"We had flown missions against the Japanese Empire, just to get acclimated, and trying to find out exactly what we were supposed to do. We were unique to the extent that we were bombing from 30,000 feet. The other B-29s weren't doing that because they had orders from LeMay to do whatever they had to do. They had their job and we had ours. So we practiced dropping bombs from 30,000 feet. We were different to the extent that we were stripped. We only had two twin-50 machine guns in the tail and that was our only defense against the Japanese fighters. The other was the high altitude and the fact that we were stripped of our other turrets other B-29s had. So we flew a couple of missions to get used to doing it and then, of course we were briefed for the two atomic missions and much to my surprise, I didn't go on the first one. Major Sweeney was my pilot and our job, our crew job, was to drop the instrumentation, the minute they dropped the atomic bomb, the instrument carrying ship would drop the instruments and record different things the scientists wanted to know about, what was needed to make it a successful bomb. So I was told I wasn't going to go because I was preempted by some observers and some people that they wanted to go on the aircraft.

"The first one had been dropped and ours came three days later. And of course, I talked to some of the personnel on the Enola Gay to get an idea, and of course, they showed us that first bomb blast at Trinity in New Mexico. Of course, that was on a tower; it wasn't dropped. But when they found out it was successful to explode an atomic bomb, we got the word, 'yes,' we were going to go over seas and we had our practice missions and we were briefed and I didn't go on the first one, but I thought OK, if I didn't go on the first one, I'll go on the second one. But somehow I guess Tibbets got a little reluctant. He said to me one day before the

A Time to Speak

mission, 'Would you like to go along?' And I said, 'Sure I'd like to go along.' So he says, 'Well, OK, you can go.' Just like that. That was the end of it.

"There were three pilots on board. Sweeney was the aircraft commander, Albury was the pilot and with myself as copilot. Normally, Sweeney would not fly with us because it was Albury and myself, pilot and copilot and Sweeney, being squadron commander, just flew whenever he wanted to. But as a result of that, there were three pilots on board the Nagasaki mission. That occurred because I was part of the original crew and Sweeney was actually the interloper. And of course, he was the one in charge of the aircraft and that's the way it went.

"I remembered that when we took off, normally we would go by way of Iwo Jima and that was the halfway point to the Japanese Empire. On our mission to Nagasaki that time, instead of going by way of Iwo Jima, we went by way of Okinawa, a little southwest and we had to do this because the weather was bad and they re-routed us that way and instead of flying at the normal 9,000 feet, we flew at 17,000 feet, to avoid some of the weather. We took off from Tinian at 3:48 in the morning and we headed for our rendezvous point which was Kagoshima at the southern tip of the Japanese mainland and, we rendezvoused there.

"We were the first one to get to the rendezvous point. A short time later, Captain Bock met us there. Now there was a little misinformation when the story of the Nagasaki mission was released. Unbeknownst to me (I was a second lieutenant), prior to takeoff, we had a problem with our booster pump to get the gasoline from the rear bomb bay up to our wing tanks and on up to the engines. It was discovered at the pre-flight check of the aircraft before takeoff. I knew nothing about it, but Sweeney and our engineer went to Tibbets and told him that we had a problem with our booster pump in the rear bomb bay and we couldn't get the gasoline up to the engines. And Tibbets said, 'That's all right, that's only ballast for the 10,000 pound bomb up in the front bomb bay.' He said, 'You won't need it.' So with that, Sweeney concurred and we took off. Again, I was in the dark about this. I knew nothing about it. I wasn't brought into the conversation.

"So we take off, we get to our rendezvous point. Prior to our rendezvous point, the bomb had to be armed by Commander Ashworth (he was a Navy man). He was the weaponeer on board and he had an assistant whose name was Phil Barnes. And Phil Barnes' job was to sit in the radio compartment with a little black box with a little flickering light. And I remember, during the flight, I was curious, I didn't know what was going on. Anything scientific we knew nothing about; they didn't get involved with us at all. So one time I said to him (Barnes), 'What's with the light, Phil, this flickering?' And he said, 'As long as it flickers slowly, that's fine, but if it starts flickering real fast, we are in trouble.' 'That means something is not happening correctly in the internal ingredients of the bomb.' And he says, 'It could explode.' If it had exploded, they would have found nothing of us. We would have been vaporized. There was nothing we could do about it.

"So we just went on about our mission, going to our rendezvous point and the bomb had to be armed by Commander Ashworth. So he went back and he armed the bomb, did what he was supposed to do. He had to change some kind of plugs and make the bomb 'live.' He did that, he came back and told Sweeney, 'We're all set.' From that time on, we were just a flying bomb, anything could have happened, like the flickering light.

"So we got to our rendezvous point and we were the first ones there. Captain Bock got there about five minutes later, and we had to wait for the third aircraft. Now in our briefing, they told us we could only wait fifteen minutes at the rendezvous point, then go on to our primary target which was Kokura, not Nagasaki. A lot of people don't know that our primary target was Kokura. So we waited the fifteen minutes, nothing happened. The third aircraft was the photographic airplane. Fifteen minutes went by, no airplane. For some reason Sweeney decided to wait another fifteen minutes, which was against orders. We waited the second fifteen minutes, nothing happened. And for some reason, Sweeney was the aircraft commander, he waited another fifteen minutes, so that was forty-five minutes that we wasted from being on our way to bombing our target.

"So finally Sweeney realized the third aircraft was not going to show, so he says, 'Let's go to Kokura.' So this we did and we immediately started for Kokura. Kokura was about an hour away and we were up at 30,000 feet, we were pulling all this power, and we were already about an hour behind our regular schedule because of the delay at the rendezvous point. When we got to Kokura, the cloud covers had changed. Now prior to takeoff from Tinian, two aircraft were sent to Kokura and Nagasaki. Their job was to radio the conditions of the weather as we were coming up to do our bombing. So they took off an hour ahead of us and they radioed the weather conditions at that time were clear.

"By the time we got over Kokura, the cloud cover had changed It was about seven-tenths to eight-tenths cloud coverage. We had orders to bomb visually only; we couldn't use any other methods. So when we got there, we could see we were in trouble. So to see if our bombardier, Captain Beahan could see the aiming point, we made three bomb runs in three different directions in hopes of seeing the aiming point and dropping it like we were supposed to do. Unfortunately, that didn't happen. So we were over that area for almost an hour trying to get this thing going and finding our target.

"So this is when Sweeney says, 'Well, let's go on to our secondary target, Nagasaki.' And this is when I discovered that we had the problem with our booster pump to get the gasoline from the rear bomb bay up to our wing tanks. And I was surprised as I thought everything was going fine. And I heard the conversation between Sweeney and Kuharek, 'We'd better figure our gasoline supply.' So our engineer did the job, figured it out and he said we had enough gasoline to make one bomb run on Nagasaki, then go into our emergency landing field at Yantang in Okinawa.

"So immediately we took off. Now going up there, I think it was about an hour, an hour and fifteen minutes from Kokura. Again, we were at 30,000 feet, using all this power and using all this gas. When we got there, the cloud cover was even more intense than the one that was over Kokura. So immediately the decision was made between Sweeney and the Commander Ashworth that we'd have to drop it by radar, which was against orders. This was one of the things that could have been a problem.

"We got to Nagasaki, and we started our bomb run by radar. Now when you make bomb run on radar, there is a radar man in the back [with a scope], our navigator has a scope and they were checking the image to make sure they were in agreement of what they were coming up to as far as the city was concerned and make sure they had the correct target. So we were about 98 percent complete on the radar bomb run when Captain Beahan, up in the nose hollered, 'I see it, I got it, I got it.'

"So when he said this, the radar bomb run was relinquished. And he took over the bomb run because that's the way the orders ran. So we had only about 35 to 45 seconds to set up the bomb site, to kill the drift, and make sure that he was somewhere in the area with dropping the bomb. As it turned out, we were about one mile and a half or two miles off the actual aiming point. The destructive power of the bomb wouldn't have made any difference anyway. Anyway, we were going according to the flight plan.

"So we dropped the bomb. The minute we dropped the bomb, Captain Bock, who was the only other aircraft accompanying us (the third aircraft never showed up), he dropped his instrumentation. Now both these bombs that were dropped over Hiroshima and over Nagasaki exploded about 1,500 feet above the ground and part of that was necessary because the blast effect was supposed to do a lot more damage. Unfortunately, in our situation, because of the topography of Nagasaki, there were mountains on one side, and when we exploded the bomb, it kind of restricted the blast effect. And in fact, some of the towns that were close to the mountain weren't damaged hardly at all. But the rest of the city was completely destroyed.

"When we dropped the bomb, we had to turn to a left bank of 60 degrees, and make a turn of 180 degrees and head in the opposite direction because if we had been going in a straight line, a bomb falling out of a trajectory like this, we would have been over the point of explosion. And the scientists said, 'We don't want that. Use this maneuver, and there will be no structural damage to the aircraft.' So this we did.

"As we were in the turn, I remember I had the special glasses on that we had to have to protect our eyes against the flash. We were in bright sunlight, and you know what bright sunlight is when there is no interference from the clouds. So I was looking out the window the minute the bomb exploded, and we were in bright sunlight before. It was about one hundred times brighter than the sunlight. I had never seen a light like that. And, of course, we knew the bomb had exploded and we continued on around. So we immediately looked down to see what we could see. We couldn't see anything because in the center of the city was the mushroom cloud that was coming up to our altitude and it took about 45 or 50 seconds to get to our altitude of 30,000 feet. And, of course, the telltale top in the mushroom top was all part of it. It got to our altitude and then continued on up. As it got to our altitude, of course, I was looking at the mushroom cloud. Inside it was this boiling cauldron of a salmon colored pink and some brown and different colors. And this was the result of what happened to the exploded bomb. So it got to our altitude and went on past to 50,000 or 60,000 feet.

"Now for some reason Sweeney said, 'Let's go back and see what we can see,' since we could see nothing the first time. In spite of our gasoline situation, he was the aircraft commander and that's the way it went. So we turned around and decided to take another look. Now all of us were concentrating down below and we weren't paying attention to the mushroom cloud. And all of a sudden, one of the crew men in the back hollered, 'The mushroom cloud is coming toward us.' Now this was another hazard that the scientists told us to stay away from because of its radioactivity. And we all looked up right away and we see this thing coming toward us. Immediately Sweeney put the aircraft in a dive down to the right, full power, and I was looking out the window to see, and it was on our left. For a while, I couldn't tell whether the cloud was gaining on us, or we were gaining on the cloud. And I thought, if this is the way it's going to be, I kept hoping, in the meantime though, that we were going to pull away. Eventually I could see that we were getting away from the radioactive cloud. And we did pull away and immediately started for Okinawa and our emergency landing.

"Now the minute the bomb exploded, they told us there were going to be shock waves. It hit us shortly after the bomb exploded. The first one was the worst one because it shook the aircraft up pretty thoroughly and all we could do was just look at each other and hope that nothing happened structurally to the aircraft because we were there and there was nothing we could do to prevent it. A short time later, we were hit by a second shock wave of lesser intensity and a short time after

A Time to Speak

that there was one of lesser intensity than the second one and there were just three of them. Some write-ups they had about this, they said there were five, but absolutely not, there were not five, there were three.

"That went by and our next problem was getting to Okinawa. And that wasn't too far away. Again we were nip and tuck. We didn't know exactly. Hopefully we were going to make it. So we get to Okinawa. This was our furthest base forward that they were using for the invasion of Japan. So we get there and make a radio call because of our gas situation, we want to get on the ground. No answer. We did this the second time. No answer. A third time. No answer. A fourth time. No answer. Finally Sweeney realized we can't just jet around there wasting time and gasoline and he said, 'I'm declaring a May Day. Fire all the flares we've got, and we are going to get on the ground.' So this he proceeded to do, but in doing so, he cut out three or four aircraft that were on the approach of the active runway. And we came in pretty hot because we wanted to get on the ground and we didn't know exactly what our situation was with t he gasoline.

"We hit the ground doing about 150 or 160 miles per hour. Now that was much too fast for the 29. Sweeney lost control and it started to veer to the left. Now when this occurred, we had reversible props on board. Immediately, when Sweeney saw we were going to start veering off the runway and heading toward a group of aircraft parked along the active runway, he activated the reversible props and brought the aircraft under control. If we hadn't had the reversible props, I wouldn't be here telling the story. That corrected the problem and we continued on down the active runway. And as we turned off the first taxi, and we had to park the aircraft and park it on the hard stand. Before we got out of the aircraft, we said, 'Let's not say anything about what we did; just tell them we are here for gasoline and we are going to go back to Tinian.'

"Well, it so happened that we were the first B-29 they ever saw. There were a lot of GIs around. They were curious to see a different aircraft, a bigger one than they were used to seeing. We got to the hard stand, we parked it and we got out. And, of course, they started asking all kinds of questions, 'Where did you come from? What kind of airplane is this? (they'd probably never seen one) How high does it fly? How fast?' We answered their questions very politely, whatever they wanted to know, we told them.

"So it was time to go and have something to eat while the airplane was being resupplied with gasoline. So we got on trucks and went to the mess hall. It so happened that I rode with a Captain Cheshire, who was a British war hero, he got the Victoria Cross for bombing the dams in Germany or in Holland. So he was a big hero there and I was walking with him and a professor Penney who had worked on the bomb. He was the British counterpart of our scientists. I remember Captain

Cheshire says he was amazed at the performance of our B-29s at high altitude because they had bombers that couldn't do that. They had bombers, the Lancasters and the Sterlings, and when they got up that high, they got a little sloppy and they didn't have good control of the aircraft. So, of course, that made me feel pretty good about the whole thing.

"So we proceeded to get in line to get our food. By this time, the word had gotten around that another bomb had been dropped on Japan. But again, the word 'atomic' was never used. It was still a secret that hadn't been revealed So we got in line and the word had gotten around. This GI, who was dishing out the food, was beside himself because he just knew this was the end of the war and he was going to go home and he was tickled pink. So as we came abreast of him, he said, 'You fellows hear about the bomb that was dropped on Japan?' And we said, 'No, we hadn't heard anything about it.' We just played dumb. 'Well, he said, 'That means I'm going to go home. They can't take any more of these bombs.' I don't know how much he knew about the strength of the bombs, but he was just thrilled because he was going home. And he says, 'I'll tell you something else, that airplane came from this base, it was a P-38 and the bomb was the size of a golf ball.' How this got around, I don't know, but this was something that was prevalent at the time. And of course we said, 'Oh, is that right?' like we didn't know anything about it. Here it took the biggest aircraft we had in our inventory and the bomb was 10,000 pounds. He just knew that that was it. After that we finished eating and got into our aircrafts and flew back to Tinian. And the whole mission took about seventeen hours. We got back to Tinian about 9:30 that night, and I was very happy to get home because it was a long day.

"The scientists told us if we were around this atomic material that we may become sterile. Of course, I wasn't married at the time so it didn't bother me so much, but the other fellows who were married, of course. So I thought, if that's the way it is, that's the way it is, but I was thinking about the fellows that were married, how they would take it. They just accepted it. But anyway, it turned out that Sweeney went home and he had ten kids. So that shot that theory all to pieces. And that's the way it was.

"We were scared, sure. There were thirteen of us on the aircraft and nobody even thought about it until we got back to Tinian. We started counting heads and we realized there were thirteen on board. And of course, if you are superstitious, you'd begin to wonder if thirteen was a lucky number or an unlucky number. We had the two extra weaponeers on board and we had a radar counter measure man who was keeping tabs on what was happening to the Japanese radar and things like that. He had an indication if they were coming up to meet us and battle with us. The thirteen men, it didn't even enter our mind when we took off. "We just

A Time to Speak

had some Japanese antiaircraft fire, but no fighters because they were coming up to meet us and this Jake Beser, the radar counter measure man, had said they had scrambled and were coming up to meet us, but when they saw the mushroom cloud develop, they stopped and they didn't follow us any more.

"No, I had no regrets that we dropped the atomic bomb, when I found out that we were going to invade the Japanese Empire in November 1945. The Japanese character being what it is, the way they defended the islands that we fought them for, it was with great ferocity. If they did that for the islands, which was far enough away from their homeland, you could imagine what they were going to do when we invaded the Japanese mainland, their homeland. We found out later that even the youngsters were told what to do and how to do the GIs in when they came for the invasion of the Japanese country. And they had places to go to, they had places assigned already on the beaches to fight the GIs who were coming for the invasion. So they were well prepared. They also had aircraft stashed aside so they could use the kamikazes. It would have been a battle. We would have lost one million people and the Japanese would have probably lost five million.

"But to me, the fact that we dropped the bomb that hastened the end of the war and made the Japanese realize that it was futile for them to go on. To me, it was worth it because it did save the American lives.

"I do recall just prior to the bomb being dropped, to letting the bomb go, I thought we are going to kill a lot of people and a lot of civilians because they weren't in combat. It is just something that went through my mind and I immediately forgot it because the beast being what it is, you kill a lot of people.

"I may add this. You know we've had this controversy with the Smithsonian, and the powers that be there said it was a 'cultural war,' that we wanted to destroy the Japanese race or help destroy it, and we wanted to destroy their way of life. What they don't realize is that in February or March of 1945, we were kept on base; they told us we couldn't leave for three days because they wanted to know what the results of the Battle of the Bulge was. The thinking was that if they had split the Allied forces and gone to the North Sea, we were going to go over there and drop the bomb on Germany. So that changes the whole theory that this was racist.

"I've had occasion, when I've given these speeches and I have a question and answer period. Invariably somebody gets up and says, 'Well, how does it feel to kill all these people?' I'm not a bloodthirsty killer and right away I get a little bit on the defensive and I say to the fellow, 'I just don't enjoy doing it.' 'Well, he says, 'you must have some feeling about killing all these people.' 'Yeah, I didn't think it was necessary, but if we had to end the war, people had to die, in wartime, people die.' It rankled me to have him ask me such a question, but he wanted to put me on the spot. After the question and answer period was over, I went over to where the *fellow was sitting and I said, 'I have some questions I'd like to ask you. To that person who asked that bothersome question, 'You, sir, may I ask you a question, and I'd say, 'Were you ever in service?' 'No'. 'Were you ever in combat?' 'No.' 'Then how can you sit here and try to ask me how I felt if you have never been in combat and you've never been in service.' I said, 'Talk to the Marines who were going to invade the Japanese empire in November 1945 and ask them if they felt we were right in dropping the bomb and ending the war.' Of course, to me, there is no comparison between the two. We did what was right to end the war and that was the name of the game: end the war."*

The death toll at Hiroshima was 140,000 out of a total population of 327,457; at Nagasaki, 70,000 out of a total population of 286,702. These figures do not take into account the unknown number of people who have died later from radiation poisoning. [177]

End Notes

177   *The Boulder Daily Camera*, 6 August 1994, p. 7D

CHAPTER 48

SURRENDER
V-J DAY

Through Army intelligence, it was known that Japan had sent feelers, asking the Soviet Union to mediate a peace settlement which would have allowed Japan to keep its political system and pre-war empire. However, the Soviet Union declared war on Japan on 8 August and invaded Manchuria.

But it was also known, through the same decoded messages, that Japan would conclude a peace but would not consider unconditional surrender to be an acceptable alternative to continued resistance. Japanese newspapers ran editorials, critical of the Potsdam Declaration which called for unconditional surrender and suggested the government ignore it and reject it. [178]

Even after the bomb was dropped on Nagasaki, the Japanese Supreme War Council was divided about whether to accept unconditional surrender. Three generals favored surrender, and three favored continuing the war, believing the Japanese Army would inflict terrible loses on the Americans when they invaded the home island of Japan. [179] The debate continued through the evening of 9 August, when the Emperor appeared. Premier Suzuki pleaded for Hirohito's intervention to end the war. Hirohito broadcast the surrender message to his nation.

Young officers, who did not want to acknowledge the surrender, tried to seal off the Imperial Palace and tried to find Hirohito's recorded message in order to destroy it. Their coup ended when the commander of the Eastern Army refused their request and ordered them out of the palace.

Midori Johnson, a young Japanese, heard Emperor Hirohito's broadcast of the surrender message to his nation. In her opinion, the Emperor deserves the credit for ending the war.

"There was a big conference. At that conference, the Army was still insisting we should fight until the very last person. Then there was the Emperor at that conference and an Army minister asked the Emperor to make a decision. We listened to that special announcement and the Emperor said, 'Let's quit fighting and do anything for the country of Japan to survive.' He said he would do anything to stop the war. He said he wouldn't mind being captured and surrender to the United States, or the Allied Force, which was the most disgraceful thing. Japanese honor demands no surrender to or capture by the enemy. That means he would be killed.

A Time to Speak

He would do it, but he wanted to save the Japanese people. That decided everything."

Japan accepted the surrender terms and V-Day was proclaimed on 15 August 1945. The official surrender took place on the battleship *Missouri*, in Tokyo Bay, on 2 September with General MacArthur signing for the Allies, and Admiral Nimitz for the United States. A representative from each of the Allied powers also signed. Foreign Minister Shigemitsu signed for the Japanese.

With the news of peace, Americans let their emotions go with spontaneous eruptions of joy. Sirens and car horns blared; torn paper littered the streets, girls kissed soldiers and sailors; conga lines paraded through streets; and church bells pealed.

On hearing the news of the victory, a navy pilot wept. *"I recall the day the war ended. My roommate aboard ship was a flight surgeon, the squadron doctor. I was down in the little small room we had, quarters; my nickname was "Tulagi." I had lived on the island of Tulagi. 'Tulagi, Tulagi, the goddamn war is over.' We went up on deck and cried like babies. It was a very emotional moment."*

"Dutch" Westerberg was scheduled to go into Japan, but V-J Day was declared and his division came home on the Queen Mary.

"But when that old 30th Infantry Division sailed into New York, we were the first division home after V-J Day. They had a sheet across that ship '30th Infantry Division, Old Hickory, 117th Breakthrough Regiment.' And they are very proud of that. And we came sailing into New York about 9:30 at night. Every bell, every light, everything that would make any noise, people were just ecstatic. There wasn't a dry eye on that ship and we had almost 40,000 men on that boat. We went by the Statue of Liberty and they were crying their eyes out, so happy when we hit ground. They were down on their knees kissing that. It was really a sight to behold. That was certainly a welcome, my God, they blew their top getting us home, it was the first outfit that came from the European Theater Operation. It was a wonderful experience."

Japanese Soldiers

Hirakubo, a Japanese supply officer, reacted with resignation to news of Japan's defeat. At the same time, he looked toward a brighter future for Japan. In a taped interview for the Imperial War Museum Sound Archive, he said:

"I was in the 31st Mountain Regiment. In rainy season, I was to get food for recovery of soldiers. Orders to split, one to defend Burma-Thailand border and one to go to Malaya Peninsula to defend landing of British forces. The evening of 15th August, usually I was going to division headquarters to give money, almost

every week, one day going and one day returning. And I heard about the broadcasting of the Emperor to surrender. So I went back to take back my battalion.

"Not surprise, but just sort of feeling of having lost everything. We didn't believe, although we were making preparations for next battle, that Japan itself had decided to finish. Just simply, we found ourselves crying.

"Many things happened in the units in Burma. I made a very preaching to the soldiers, what we should be behavior from now.

"Some platoons escaped in the mountains with provisions and munitions. They said they would continue to fight and wait until the next war came out, five years later.

"I said, 'We lost the war, our generation lost the war, we spoiled all the country of Japan, so we cannot pass it on to the next generation unless we recover it. Our aim is to go back to Japan and work more, including for the people who died in the war, we must work triple or more to make Japan recover. So until we go back to Japan, we must sustain and keep ourselves pride, no good making other things..." [180]

The peak strength of the armed forces during World War II was 72,835,500. The total number of battle deaths was 14,904,000; battle wounded, 25,218,000 and civilian deaths, 38,573,000. Many more were wounded or missing in action.[181]

The figures are stupefying. The cost in human life and suffering, the persecution of ethnic groups, the destruction of cities and farm lands made World War II the most devastating war in history.

End Notes

178 Harry A. Gailey, *The War in the Pacific*, Chapter 16, "Unconditional Surrender", pp. 486-487.
179 Martin Gilbert, *The Second World War*, p. 716
180 Excerpts, Interview, Imperial War Museum Sound Archive, Hirakubo, #11516
181 *Fact Sheet World War II*, 50th Anniversary of World War II Commemoration Committee.

CHAPTER 49

RETRIBUTION AND RESTORATION

The world could not return to a prewar state of affairs. Too many events had occurred which had changed individuals, countries, and the balance of world power.

The estimated economic costs World War II were enormous: $1,600,000,000,000! [182] Resources, both governmental and volunteer were necessary to re-establish economic stability in a war-torn world.

Difficult tasks faced the Allies and the Axis powers. The Allies had to honor their commitment, made at the Yalta Conference in February 1945, to bring war criminals to justice and punish them. The Europeans and the Japanese had to cope with the enormous task of rebuilding cities, where, for many citizens, conditions were as difficult as they were in 1939. Humanitarian aid through governments, volunteer organizations and individual initiative helped create the postwar world.

RETRIBUTION

There remained a period of unfinished business, during which some people felt a need to "settle accounts." There were incidents of local retribution against collaborators with the Nazis.

Individual Retaliation

Mme Dravalen in Lorient described one situation in which the French took vengeance into their own hands.

"*There was a family who had a big house and German officials were imposed on them. The daughter had her communion while they were there. He* [one German] *was at the communion. At the liberation, when the accounts were settled, the woman, who was a very fine lady, she had her head shaved because she had a German in her house and he was at her daughter's communion. She invited him and he was at the dinner.*" [After the war, Europeans retaliated against women who were guilty of what was often called "horizontal collaboration." Their punishment: to have their heads shaved and then to be paraded through the streets.]

Trials Of Maréchal Pétain And Pierre Laval

On an official level, the French tried and convicted Maréchal Pétain and

Pierre Laval. On 23 July 1945, the French high court convened to judge Pétain, maréchal of France and former head of the French State at Vichy. He had become a symbol of France's defeat and collaboration. In particular his anti-Jewish legislation, which deprived Jews of their rights and sent then to concentration camps, was odious. Pétain was condemned to death. However because of his age, his sentence was commuted to a life sentence on the Ile d'Yeu.

Pierre Laval as Minister of State was the heir presumptive to Pétain. In general, while he tried to protect France's interests, he was head of the government during two years of Vichy actions which left a bitter taste. No one was willing to forget his statement in June 1942, *Je souhaite la victoire de l'Allemagne, car sans elle, le Communisme s'installerait partout en Europe*. (I hope for Germany's victory, because without it, Communism would install itself everywhere in Europe).

Laval's trial took place before a hostile court, with so much heckling, the defense was cut off. He was condemned to death on 9 October 1945 and executed on 15 October 1945.

Trials Against War Criminals

Two declarations set the stage for bringing war criminals to justice. In December 1942, Great Britain, the United States, the Soviet Union and eight other countries vowed that those responsible for the extermination of Jews would not escape retribution. In July 1945, at the Potsdam Conference, the Allies demanded the surrender of the Japanese armed forces, the Allied occupation of Japan, and the trial of Japanese war criminals.

The Nuremberg Trial

For the first time in history, war crime trials were held. In August 1945, a week after the Potsdam Conference, the London Conference drafted a charter of the International Military Tribunal for crimes against peace, war crimes, and crimes against humanity. [The Kellogg-Briand Pact of 1928 had previously outlawed wars of aggression.]

In September, the International Court, with Telford Taylor, as the Chief Prosecutor for the Nuremberg Trials, charged the Nazi government and leaders with conspiracy to commit murder, terrorism and destruction of peaceful populations. In October 1946, the Tribunal handed down its judgement: twenty-two Nazi leaders were indicted and condemned for war crimes and crimes against peace.

One young French woman worked for the Allies at the Nuremberg trials:

"*When I arrived in Germany at the end of the war, fraternization was forbidden and they gave us the leaflets which imagined New York destroyed, with the Germans as sentinels before the sky scrapers. And we always said, 'We didn't know*

America like that.' Therefore we didn't fraternize. Two years later, it was finished and it was the super-fraternization with those in American uniforms.

"I stayed in Paris until the end of '45. At the end of '45, I left for Germany for three years. And after that I came back to Paris. One of my employers at Nuremberg was Marshall [General George C. Marshall]. He returned to Paris as there were no more crimes to judge. Then I went to the American Embassy for the American government.

"When I arrived in the city of Nuremberg, it was completely destroyed. It was a city that suffered three large bombings, the first two did not cause too much damage. But the bombing of January sixth, 1945 completed destroyed the city. It was a religious holiday and people had gone to church and restaurants. Close to the Church was the Rathaus, a restaurant where we ate as they did before the war. There was a set of very lovely china and glass and beautiful silverware. They tell the story that the day of the bombing on January sixth, everyone had eaten a big lunch and afterwards, they gave the personnel a holiday, 'Leave everything on the table and tomorrow we wash the dishes.' The next day the city was completely bombed. When the personnel went back to the restaurant, in all of the rubble they found the dishes intact and nothing broken. And they washed the dishes!

"When I arrived in Nuremberg, it smelled terrible because there were cadavers everywhere. They needed to vaccinate people for typhoid and you couldn't get paid unless you had a medical certificate of your vaccination.

"I was present at the great trial of Nuremberg. I was chosen for the Grande Commission des Recours en Grace, (called in English, Allied Control Council), presided over by a French general. There was a French secretary, a Russian secretary, an English secretary. The Germans were apart.

"The night before the executions, one had to type the judgement notification of the deceased and leave the hour blank. I was twenty-two years old and I typed the judgements of all these men. I had to redo the one for Göring because he committed suicide.

"The next day, one had to make an inventory of their personal items, box them up, and send them to the family. We lived so much in the horror of it. At one time, I was inundated and overwhelmed by the documentation. In the office next door, there were all of the boxes of proof: the peoples' shoes, the cans of asphyxiating gas, the remains of human bones. We saw them every day.

"Several years ago, there appeared a German film about the war crimes at Nuremberg. It began by showing a hanging and ending by showing another hanging. I had a rendezvous with a friend after the movie and, I think if my friend had not been there, I think I would have thrown myself into the Seine, because I couldn't endure that any more."

A Time to Speak

The Nuremberg Trials accomplished their objectives, to bring those responsible for war crimes to justice. Critics question whether the Soviet Union should have participated in the Trials since the Red Army participated in seizing Poland and also invaded Finland. Many Germans argue that the Allied air raids over Germany, especially the destruction of Dresden, was a war crime.

In Germany, a Denazification Policy Review Board established tribunals, giving the Germans control over certain sanctions; disqualification from various levels of employment, incarceration in labor camps, and confiscation of property. Nazi organization members were dealt with in German administrative proceedings.

International Military Tribunal For The Far East

Less well-known is the International Military Tribunal for the Far East, placed in the hands of General MacArthur, the Supreme Commander for the Allied Powers. On 30 November 1945, President Truman appointed Joseph Berry Keenan as the chief prosecutor of Japanese war criminals. The Class A war-criminal suspects were tried in Tokyo, charged with crimes against peace, violations of the customs of war, and crimes against humanity. Not until three years later, in November 1948, were the verdicts rendered: of the twenty-eight tried, seven were sentenced to death; sixteen to life imprisonment; two to shorter terms of imprisonment; two died during the trial and one was sent to a psychiatric ward.

Japanese critics have said the trial was unfair because Japan was not allowed to raise the issue of the bombing of Hiroshima and Nagasaki.

Class B and C suspects were tried by U. S. military tribunals in Yokohama, the headquarters of the Eighth Army, and other trials were held by the U. S. Military, located at sites on Pacific island battlegrounds.

T. Saito, a Japanese Army Guard who from 1941-1945 worked in POW camps in Malaya, Thailand, including the Burma-Thailand railway camp. When the war was over, he found himself a prisoner and on trial. He received a fair trial from a military court.

During the trial, Brigadier Toosi, a former war prisoner, wrote that Sergeant Saito *"was a very strict sergeant. He gave us few concessions, but was honest and just in his dealings with us."*

Later on, when the work was very heavy and needed to be done properly and quickly, Toosi asked him for three things: more food, regular working hours and one holiday per week. The prisoners got what they requested! And this was at a time when thousands of troops died in prison camps in Thailand. Nobody died in the prison in which Saito was in charge. Brigadier Toosi testified that Saito had tried his best and had done his duty. But Saito also knew that Toosi gave evidence that caused other people to be executed. Saito told the interviewer that he was very glad that nobody died in his prison. Saito was not executed. [183]

Critics of both the Nuremberg Trials and the Tokyo War Crimes Trial maintain that these trials were a victor's justice.

Occupation Troops

American soldiers were deployed as occupation troops. George Watts, owner of George Watts & Sons in Milwaukee, was a Marine and went into Japan as part of the American forces of occupation, and found Japan still ready to fight but also ready to rebuild.

"*I went into the occupation of Japan, stopped at Wake Island, Johnson Island, Guam and then flew into Tokyo harbor and then flew down to Kyushu. We ended up in the occupation there.*

"*We walked through the area where the bomb had been dropped in Nagasaki. They had blown up one whole valley and the valley adjacent to it was still like old Japan. It was fascinating. We'd go over there and drink a beer or something and you'd feel like you were in old Japan. The Japanese were polite. Aside from the fact that some of our Marines killed Japanese policemen, murdered them, it was a very pleasant occupation. They resented the fact that the Japanese policemen were so autocratic, not to them, but to their citizens and somehow that caused a few of them to die.*

"*One of my best friends was a guy, so smart that he learned Japanese in a very short period of time, but he also did their calligraphy. He was very quick, very bright, very much of a communist. He heard, through various informers, that the Japanese villages on Kyushu were just loaded with weapons. He spoke to them on radio, saying that this had come to their attention and they should turn in all of their weapons at the armories right away. And so the Japanese obediently did. You have never seen so many weapons. There were whole gymnasiums stacked with weapons right to the wall, right to the ceiling. Most of the weapons were rather primitive, swords, but there were mortars, machine guns, artillery. So the Japanese were prepared to fight.*

"*They had nothing at all, I can remember going in to a middle class Japanese family home and the only heat they had were three little lumps of charcoal. In the wintertime it is in the twenties and the wind blows right through the house and these dear people were sitting next to these three lumps of charcoal.*

"*But it is very evident that what MacArthur had given them was the hope that their hard work would be rewarded. And did they work. All of Tokyo, when I flew over it, was orange, orange. And that's because all the buildings had burned down, big and little ones, and tiles were orange. And the tiles went right to the ground. It was much worse than the atomic bomb, more vast, square miles after* square miles just burned to the ground. And they burned them up in great fire storms, I don't know, thousands of civilians must have died. But within a few weeks, you could see this regeneration of the Japanese."

Many veterans in Europe agreed with Ken Bangs who stayed on in Paris after the war ended. Bangs called it *"an anti-climatic existence, a clean-up time waiting until we could get home. Soldiers wanted to get married or see their families, get jobs or go back to school."* Bangs' job was to prepare documents for the discharge of Army personnel and arrange their transfer to shipping points to return to the United States.

Other occupying troops acted as city managers in small towns until the local government could be restored. Officers volunteered in educational reconstruction and in military governments in Germany, facilitating a return to democracy.

While waiting for demobilization, soldiers like Fraser Richards volunteered to help the refugees.

"After V-E Day, we were sort of in limbo, actually in Munich at that point. We were ordered to head back to Charleville in northern France, so we worked our way back and we came to a little town just north of Munich, just off the Autobahn and here was a group of about four hundred Yugoslav peasants, a sort of an encampment, primarily older people and young kids. So we were ordered to stay there for a while. We stayed in the school building and since I had a lot of school teachers in my outfit, we started taking all of the kids, teaching them English.

"The morning we were to leave, very hush, hush. We got all packed up and as we left, the whole little road was lined with all of these people, 400 people saying good by to us. They sang this song and it was very touching. I have never been able to find this little town, maybe it has been renamed."

Bob Bradfield went to Korea to provide an American presence.

"They hadn't planned to occupy Korea and suddenly the Russians were down across the 38th Parallel and into Seoul itself. And the decision was made in Washington to get somebody up there fast. So my unit, along with others, were suddenly thrown into the 24th Corps and it was sent to Korea. It had three divisions and auxiliary units that eventually got there. But talk about being at the long end of a non-existent supply line, that was it. For months and months we lived on field rations simply because they couldn't get anything else to us. The three little divisions were terribly under strength, but it was enough to make the Russians pull back. It sure wasn't evident up there, very hostile, that we were Allies. They cut the power off, every night or so. Initially, the five of us were the only troops in this town, about 150 miles south of Seoul and there was a railroad headquarter division there. Eventually a military government came in and the canon company of the 20th Infantry came in, and we finally lived with them.

"Actually we were charged, first of all, with sending the Japanese Kwantung Army (the Army which garrisoned Manchuria) to Japan. We saw lots of Japanese there and of course they were extremely cooperative. If just gave you a funny feeling to have one of two of you and a whole Japanese battalion standing out there looking at you.

"What you did, you could sit there and drink yourself blind, you entered into the life of the community. We went to the fights on Saturday night, there were no movies, we went to the girls' high school graduation, anything to get some entertainment. Nobody spoke Korean, I think there were three Korean-speaking men in the entire 24th Corps. What we did was look for the nearest six-year old kid who had been around the troops for a while, he already knew enough English to help you. We did wind up in some places where we were reduced to drawing pictures on little pieces of paper. You could write numbers and they could understand your arabic numbers.

"I was in Korea about eight months and then back to the States. We might not have had to fight the Korean War if we had stayed longer.

"We had very little patience with all of the riots that occurred down in Manila, all of these people saying 'We want to go home,' What they were doing was sending these long-service guys back first."

Postwar Conditions

For many average citizens, life was almost as difficult as it was during the war. For the average Briton, the rationing of food, clothing, gasoline and electricity continued for many years after the war. "*England was a country of strikes, industrial unrest, of shortages of everything,*" said Jack Elford. Bine Hirsch added, "*The trains didn't run, the buses didn't run, There wasn't electricity, it was off for hours each day. Gas was available at certain times, coal was still rationed. England was bankrupt. There was a sense of hope; a sense of fairness, a sense of equalizing, the sense of privilege was changed all of a sudden.*"

In a letter written to an American cousin, Suzanne (Suzel) Sigwalt wrote:

"*The consequences of the world war were disastrous for France; beyond the destructions of the towns, villages, roads, rails, harbours, brought about by the war, there was the systematic plundering of the national thrift, organised by the nazis, who were masters in that destruction kind, and the taking to pieces of the factories during 4 years.*"

The repatriation of German prisoners of war began in 1946. The POWs who worked for Morris Long in Fraser, Colorado wrote letters describing the German situation after the war.

In a letter, 11 April, 1946, from Werner Moeckel who, with Martin Friedl,

A Time to Speak

did the Army accounting for the camp wrote from Westphalia:

"... *Living here is a hell of a thing, cities are in rubble, you cannot imagine the destruction. I did not think myself that it is that bad. A lot of people are still homeless and live in cellars and holes like savages. The food situation is as poor as it can be. Remember when we were over there, always said we were hungry. I don't say it any more, but this is not only here that way. It is all over Europe... There is practically nothing to buy, no matches, no toilet paper, no clothes, no spices, no hotel rooms, no nothing. Rebuilding work is going very, very slow because industry, the small part that is left, cannot produce the requested quantities. I guess it needs about 10 to 15 years of hard work to bring the country up to pre-war standards... I am sure happy that I had a chance to spend my prison time in the States and in such a fine place as Fraser was where I found such a lot of good and understanding people and where I learned such a lot about your wonderful free country. I shall always remember it. While hoping to hear from you soon, sincerely yours, Werner Moeckel.*"

Rudolf Prause, the camp interpreter wrote on 16 February, 1948 to thank the Longs for a CARE package.

"*Dear Mr. Long,*

"*Today it was like Christmas. I got a parcel containing two blankets, two (illegible) soles, two cakes of soap and more thread. Be embraced, Mr. Long, and thanks so much. I dare say you will never realize what it meant to us. We'll get the two blankets colored and with some difficulty to make two overcoats out of them and then by gosh, next winter, we will walk about in overcoats, a pleasure we consider it enjoyable...Life here in Germany is all messed up. Too sad to be detailed... I'm not exaggerating, I wished I were back in Fraser as a POW. People here are selfish, callous, the trouble is you've got to act the same way, less you want to go to the dogs. It is too hard to write a cheerful letter from this country, so I'd better wind up by saying again, thanks for having been kind three years ago and today let me hear about you. My best wishes to you, your wife.*

Sincerely yours,
Rudi"

RESTORATION

To alleviate the suffering, the crippled economies needed to be restored to help citizens to return to a productive life. Perhaps the greatest contribution to post-war recovery was the many-faceted humanitarian and economic aid programs, set up through non-profit and government agencies.

The Marshall Plan

The most extensive and far-reaching aid was through the Marshall Plan. In April 1948, President Harry Truman said, "In all the history of the world, we are the first great nation to feed and support the conquered." He was referring to the Marshall Plan which, after being approved by Congress, sent more than $13 billion dollars in reconstruction aid and technical assistance to sixteen European countries, including the former enemy, Germany.

The plan was born after a trip in postwar 1945 by former general and Secretary of State, George C. Marshall, and others, when they surveyed the destruction in Europe: German cities reduced to rubble, deplorable living conditions, civilians looking for scraps from discarded GI rations.

On 12 July 12 1947, sixteen nations, Iceland, Ireland, Great Britain, France, Portugal, Norway, Netherlands, Belgium-Luxembourg, Italy, Sweden, Denmark, West Germany, Austria, Greece and Turkey met in the French Foreign Ministry as the Committee for European Economic Cooperation. The Soviet Union walked out of preliminary talks and did not allow Poland or Czechoslovakia to participate.

The immediate impact of the Marshall Plan, for civilians, was as simple as the availability of white bread, canned American soup and orange juice. For European industry, the Plan put small and large companies back on their feet with the backing of American dollars. From 1948 to 1951, industrial production in Europe increased 36 percent. Its legacy was the creation of the mechanism for currency exchange among the European nations, the forerunner of the European Union. The importance of economic aid and individual initiative is evident in another part of Suzanne (Suzell) Sigwalt's 1947 letter.

"In 1945, we had to begin from the real beginning about everything. Within two years the whole of the French workmen have furnished a tremendous work. The roads and the rails have been built again, as good as the bridges. The harbours and the rails have been cleared up, and are used again. In the towns and the villages, the ruins have been cleared up, and prefabricated houses provided for the sufferers. The electric, telephone and telegraphic lines have been laid again. The whole of the agricultural ground has been cleared off the mines - millions of mines have been found and destroyed - the fields ploughed and cultivated, unfortunately all the mines could not be found, and teams still frequently explode, either by ploughing deeply or by carrying wood in the forests. . .But the reconstruction of a whole country cannot be done in two years. Much has been done, but there is still an immense work to do."

Humanitarian Aid

Non-profit agencies undertook missions to help individuals adjust to the postwar world. One Quaker explained:

"After the end of the war in '45, there grew a considerable amount of public questioning as to what was happening with the German civilians. How were they being treated? And a number of German cultural groups and human rights groups wanted to know. General Clay, who was in charge of the Occupation, took the position that they were being treated all right. And finally, there was enough pressure from the American Council of Voluntary Agencies which represented all of the social work groups to oblige Clay to say he would let a delegation come in. The Council could pick out a group of people to come in and look around and wherever we wanted to go and talk to whomever we wanted and make a report. And we did. There was a Catholic priest, a Lutheran minister...and we went in and did that. We then talked to Clay. But he hadn't read our report, we told him our views. After he read our report, he was absolutely incensed. . . he was just really put off by the criticism. . . We submitted our report. And on the basis of the report of conditions in Germany, provisions were made for a number of welfare agencies to go in and work, including Quakers, Lutherans, Presbyterians. Some of the operations in Vichy France, at the end of the war, found themselves doing just the opposite of what they had been doing before. They were now taking care of Germans and collaborators, or alleged collaborators who were at a disadvantage."

The YWCA

A YWCA worker, who had worked with the women in the Japanese internment camps in the United States, found herself in Japan after the war with a different YWCA program, this time geared to helping the youth adjust to a democratic society.

"MacArthur decided that if we were going to democratize Japan, we had to start with the youth, so he asked all of the youth-serving agencies in the United States to select one worker to make a team that would go to Japan and spend nine months. The YWCA sent somebody; we had the Catholic Youth and the Camp Fire Girls.

"Institutes set up to courses in young women: how to hold a meeting; call a meeting to order, who is responsible, how to carry out responsibility given to you by the group itself; how to write up minutes and keep records; how to get young people interested; and what type of program do you want to plan for young people."

The United Nations

The UN Charter was drawn up at a conference in San Francisco in 1945. Its aims were to maintain international peace and security, and to achieve cooperation in solving international economic, social, cultural. and humanitarian problems. United Nations agencies became involved in post-war relief programs, for example UNICEF, the Children's Emergency Fund and UNRA, the United Nations Relief

Agency.

Ethel B. was in Greece from 1945 to 1948 where she worked to start a rehabilitation center for adults, her salary paid by UNRA.

"*Most of our adult patients were amputees. The Italians had laid mines all around the countryside and they stepped on the mines and they lost maybe one arm and a leg, or two legs. It was terrible. We had a lot of people of the outlying districts in Athens because that's where the mines were laid and then they would bring those people in.*

"*And we had some good orthopedic doctors that were trained in England. One thing that was interesting, we tried to sell them the idea of having a hook instead of having an artificial arm or hand that would do nothing. No way would they have anything like that. 'In the United States, they don't get those things,' and we tried to tell them that they really did. People get a job. You can't hold a job with a hand that doesn't do anything. They said, 'It didn't look nice,' and we couldn't convince them that they would work very well.*"

The Berlin Airlift

Another humanitarian effort to aid Germany was the Berlin Airlift. At the end of the war, the United States, France, Great Britain and the Soviet Union carved Berlin into four sectors. Berlin was in the Soviet sector, but the four powers were to be allowed free movement within Berlin.

The Soviet Union wanted the other Allies out of Berlin. They blocked rail and road traffic, also traffic by water into the Western sector of the city; they cut off electricity except for two hours a day, between 11 p.m. and 1 a.m. Finally, on 23 June, the lights in Berlin went out. Josef Stalin had ordered the shutdown of the only power plant.

To sustain Berliners, Operation Vittles began on 26 June and lasted for eleven months. U.S. and British pilots delivered supplies: 2 million tons of supplies in more than 250,000 flights.

The United States

There was a dissimilarity between the hardships in postwar Europe and Japan, and those in the United States. The United States, untouched by bombs, faced an easier task: to re-tool factories to produce commercial goods; and to reintegrate veterans, through the GI Bill, into productive careers.

Some of the women interviewed recalled that their concerns often centered around the difficulty of obtaining appliances to set up housekeeping, trying to find a bathtub, a heating stove, or a refrigerator was not easy.

With the new appliances to make life easier, most women according to

A Time to Speak

Jewell Wolcott left their wartime jobs.

"*The women were encouraged to go back home and let the men, the returning soldier, this hero, was entitled to this job. He had to support a family. A woman did not have to support a family. A man did, so was entitled to a job. They filled a niche, then there was no longer that niche.*"

Soldiers returning from the battlefields took advantage of the GI Bill, the Servicemen's Readjustment Act of 1944. It provided special job placement benefits from the US Employment Service; up to four years of educational and vocational training, with the government paying up to $500 a year, books and fees, plus a living allowance; up to fifty-two weeks unemployment insurance at $20 a week; and guaranteed loans to guy a home, a farm or a business. In December 1945, 40,000 married veterans took their wives and children with them and went to college. During 1946 and 1947, more than 2.5 million veterans were students.

After V-J Day, President Truman warned of the tasks ahead, necessary for the return to a peacetime routine. We needed time to heal from physical and psychological wounds. We encountered persons of different races and cultures, whether friend or foe. World War II was the defining event of the 20th century and changed the world forever as the atomic age was launched. We learned we are all part of a global community. As one former Marine put it so succinctly, "*We look at things differently now.*"

End Notes

182   *Fact Sheet World War II*, 50th Anniversary of World War II Commemoration Committee.
183   Excerpts, taped interview, translated from the Japanese, Imperial War Museum, Sound Archive, T. Saito #12771

A Time to Speak

POSTSCRIPT

I wish I could have included every single story I heard. I have stayed in touch with many that were interviewed, both in the United States and abroad. By telephone, by letter or Christmas card, I hear about what they are doing. I am sad when I learn that one of these friends has died.

We were young. Visits to the German and American cemeteries in Normandy remind us that soldiers died at ages eighteen or nineteen. Women just out of high school took wartime jobs or secretly worked in Resistance movements. I've often asked myself if I could have done it, but one French woman told me, *"There wasn't any choice."*

Although the World War II generation was untried, they responded to events with courage. They were not heroes or heroines, but ordinary people thrust into extraordinary circumstances. Everybody, regardless of nationality, ally or enemy, was in the same boat. They had a job to do and they did it.

Women who entered military service or took jobs for the first time acquired personal and financial independence and broke down the preconceptions of what women were capable of doing.

Pessimism still exists and some think we haven't learned from the example of World War II. A French woman commented, *"The lessons haven't been completely assimilated and unfortunately, we continue to act toward Yugoslavia exactly as we did in Munich in '38. Why?"*

This translates into a fear of a third world war, the menace of the atomic bomb. For one man, it would represent "the end of the human species." The Japanese students confirmed this fear of a third world war. To them it is a greater concern than unemployment. *"Yes, people are still afraid of atom bomb. People believe that World War III will come. Many countries have atomic bombs, so if countries present crazy, war will happen. I worry, I am afraid of World War III."*

A more optimistic note was expressed by one American Quaker, *"There was a major change in the point of view of looking at the problems of peoples in other cultures and trying to shoulder some responsibility for helping them. From that standpoint, I think we made some advances in understanding."*

The circumstances of the war raised our collective conscience to turn us away from isolationism. We must adopt a world view. We must stay involved in the world, remain vigilant, and willing to help to avoid future tragedies.

There is the hope that we learned the horror, futility, and waste that comes from war. People have a common longing for compassion, understanding and tolerance.

Werner Moeckal, a former POW in Fraser, Colorado, wrote from Germany, (7 March 1947), *"I want peace, work, and food. If a man has that, he must be satisfied if he is not crazy . . ."*

Gaston Vandermeerssche, the captured and tortured spy, imprisoned for two years by the Germans, said, *"We have to learn to respect each other and like each other, not only for national ground areas, but we should be citizens of the world, all children of God. He made us different because He likes differences. The differences, that's beautiful."*

Fraser Richards found himself with a downed German pilot who had been an exchange student in Connecticut. They visited a family near Munich who prepared a dinner for them.

"Here I am an American officer and we've just taken over Munich and this poor old family with this young daughter and I have this German pilot who could have turned a gun on me right then, but didn't. The German family was quite nervous about it. I told them I went to school with him, he was a buddy of mine, I skied with him, and they couldn't believe it. And I've always thought, I wonder what happened to all of them. I was in my late twenties and I thought 'What is happening here? Why can't we be friends?' That's what they wanted, that's what those older troops wanted. They just wanted to go home."

Ludger Hartmer, a German soldier who saw action in Stalingrad and was later a prisoner of war in Russia, offered this advice for world peace: *"We are learning how to avoid wars, and the only way for us to continue to learn is through contacts with people, getting to know one another, and not through contacts among our political leaders."*

One of the most touching interviews was with Gilles Mahé, a Resistance member whose injuries during his years in German concentration camps left him disabled for the rest of his life.

At the end of our conversation about the atrocities of war and the need to be ever alert to impending tragedies, Gilles offered some refreshment. He limped to the kitchen and returned, carefully balancing a tray with a bottle of champagne and four glasses. He poured the champagne, and we raised our glasses for the toast. Gilles made the toast, saying quietly, *"To Peace,"* and we drank silently.

A Time to Speak

To every thing there is a season, and a time to every purpose
under the heaven,
A time to love, and a time to hate; a time of war,
and a time of peace.
(Ecclesiastes 3:1,8)

ACKNOWLEDGMENTS

I want to thank Bill Schiller, my editor at Turner Publishing Company, who believed in the book from the moment he read a few sample chapters and who deftly and gently encouraged me to make the painstaking cuts of material I didn't want to leave out.

And special thanks:

to the staff at Turner Publishing who took care to see the book was beautifully and carefully produced;

to Rosemary Tudge and her staff at the Imperial War Museum Sound Archive; and to Paul, Tony and the Boys (the security staff) who let me in each morning and suggested the local corner pub, "The Two Eagles" as an inexpensive and congenial place to have my noon meal. At that time (1994, the 50th Anniversary of V-E Day), the pub was decorated with flags and posters of World War II, and in the background, tapes played familiar songs, "Lili Marlene" and "The White Cliffs of Dover;"

to Brewster Chamberlin and Travis A. Roxlau who arranged for me to work in the United States Holocaust Memorial Museum Archives, and to Amy Rubin who searched for just the right video interviews necessary to complete my research;

to Stan Larson of the Manuscripts Division of the Marriott Library, University of Utah, who provided me with transcripts from the oral interviews in the Navajo Code Talkers collections.

to P. Jane Fox, administrator coordinator of *Legion* (the Canadian servicemen's magazine), who inserted a request to hear from Canadian servicemen;

to Kevin Simpson, staff writer at the *Denver Post*, who shared all of the information he gathered covering the 50th Anniversary celebration of D-Day; and who introduced me to prospective interviewees in the United States and Germany;

to Dave Trexler, a retired glider pilot, who made of list of prospective interviewees from various branches of military service,lent videos, and provided information about the Glider Museum in Terrel, Texas;

to Louis Bedel in Dinan who met me at the Montparnasse train station with a newspaper tucked under his arm for identification and who later introduced me to former French solders, prisoners, and resistance members.

to Kaye Bache-Snyder who read the first complete draft and offered helpful suggestions;

to Alice Price Knight who corrected my punctuation and suggested rearranging chapters to make the book easier to read;

to Sybil Downing who gave me a lot of practical advice;

to all those who offered helpful suggestions: Lucia and Charles Baker, Sally Griffin, Bill Hosokawa, Marian Kreith, Tom Masamori, Ellen Nagy, Randy Roark, Sabine Schaffner, Marianne and Fred Schwab, Jorg Waltje.

SELECT BIBLIOGRAPHY

I list here only those books and documents which have been of particular use to me in writing the background information. It is not a complete list of all of the works and sources I have consulted.

Books

Two books in particular provided historical information and battle statistics.

Gilbert, Martin, *The Second World War*, New York: Henry Holt and Company, 1989, p. 178; p. 217, p. 242; p. 246; p. 300; p. 318; p. 330; p. 377; pp. 391-392; pp. 397-398; pp. 419-420; p. 476; p. 508; p. 539; p. 541; p. 559; p. 592; p. 593; p. 620; p. 624; 642-643; p. 649; p. 661; p. 666; pp. 662-681; p. 669; pp. 700-701; p. 716; pp. 704-719.

Shirer, William L. *The Rise and Fall of the Third Reich*, New York: Simon and Schuster, 1960, p. 40-41; pp. 241-248; pp. 248-256; pp. 270-272; pp. 322-356; p. 667; p. 839; pp. 974-979; p. 842; pp. 1018-1022; pp. 1044-1069; p. 1082.

Amouroux, Henri, *La vie des Français sous l'Occupation*, Paris: Librairie Arthème Fayard, 1961

Beasley, W. G. *Japanese Imperialism, 1894-1945*, Oxford: Clarendon Press, 1987, p. 102, p. 142, pp. 156-158, p. 211

Bolloré, Gwenn-Aël, *J'ai Débarqué le 6 juin 1944*, Paris: le cherche midi éditeur, 1994.

Brackman, Arnold C., *The Other Nuremberg, The Untold Story of the Tokyo War Crimes Trials*, New York: William Morrow and Company, Inc., 1987, pp. 17-30; pp. 45-53; pp. 406-413

Brown, Jimmy, *Harry Tate's Navy*, Inverurie, Scotland: self-published, 1994.

Bruce, George, *The Warsaw Uprising, 1 August - 2 October 1944*, London: Hart-Davis, 1972, p. 206.

Caidin, Martin, *Black Thursday (Schweinfurt raid)*, New York: Bantam War Book Series, E. P. Dutton edition, October 1960; Bantam Edition, February, 1981, pp. 69-79; pp. 150-151; pp. 158-16.

Chambrun, René de, *Ma Croisade Pour l'Angleterre, Juin, 1940*, Paris: Librairie Académique Perrin, 1992, p. 29

Chambrun, René de, *Pierre Laval Devant l'Histoire*, Paris: Editions France-Empire, 1983

Chamberlin, Brewster and Marcia Feldman, editors., *The Liberation of the Nazi Concentration Camps 1945*, Washington, D. C.: United States Holocaust Memorial Council, 1987

Ciechanowski, Jan M., *The Warsaw Rising of 1944*, Cambridge: University Press, 1974, pp. 312-315.

Collins, Larry and Dominique Lapierre, *Is Paris Burning?*, New York: Simon and Schuster, 1965

Cohen, Stan, *V for Victory, America's Home Front During World War II*, Missoula, Montana: Pictorial Histories Publishing Company

Cook, Haruko Taya & Theodore F. Cook, *Japan at War, An Oral History*, New York: The New Press, 1992, p. 49.

Cruickshank, Charles, *The German Occupation of the Channel Islands*, London: Oxford University Press, 1975, Alan Sutton Publishing Inc, Wolfeboro Falls, New Hampshire, 1991, pp. 127-133; 262-278; 280-291.

David, Kathia and Thomas Sertillanges, conception et réalisation, *la Mémoire de Paris 1919-1939*, Paris: livre et exposition de la Mairie de Paris, 1993.

Debon, André, *La Mission Helmsman*, Paris: Edition L'Harmattan, 1997

Dossogne, Victor, S. J., *Victor*, privately published by friends and colleagues and cited with permission from Michael J. Sheeran, S. J., President of Regis University, Denver.

Durand, Yves, *La France dans la Deuxième Guerre Mondiale 1939-1945*, Paris: Armand Colin, 1989.

Durand, Yves, *Les Causes de la Deuxième Guerre Mondiale*, Paris: Armand Colin, Paris, 1992, Chapter 5, pp. 79-83.

Dziewanowski, M. K., *A History of Soviet Russia*, Englewood Cliffs, New Jersey: Prentice Hall, 1989, p. 99, p. 202, pp. 126-127, p. 130.

Enever, Ted, *Britain's Best Kept Secret, Ultra's Base at Bletchley Park*, United Kingdom: Alan Sutton Publishing Limited, 1994

Foot, M. R. D., *An Outline History of the Special Operations Executive (S.O.E.)*, London: British Broadcasting Corporation, 1984, p. 129

Fournier, Paul, *Rawa-Ruska, 1942-1992, Cinquantième Anniversaire*, Toulouse: 1000 & 1 Feuilles, 1992

Gailey, Harry A., *The War in the Pacific*, Novato, California: Presidio Press, 1995, Chapter 16, "Unconditional Surrender", pp. 486-487

Gilbert, Martin, *Atlas of the Holocaust*, Oxford: Pergamon Press, 1988, p. 242, p. 245.

Gluck, Sherna B., *Rosie the Riveter Revisited, Women, the War and Social Change*, Boston: Twayne Publishers, 1987, page 8

Goodwin, Doris Kearns, *No Ordinary Time*, New York: A Touchstone Book, Simon & Schuster, 1994, p. 102.

Gutman, Israel, Editor in chief, *Encyclopedia of the Holocaust*, New York: Macmillan Publishing Co., 1990

Hallie, Philip, *Lest Innocent Blood Be Shed*, New York: Harper Perennial, HarperCollins Publishers, Inc., 1979.

Hargrove, Hondon B., *Buffalo Soldiers in Italy, Black Americans in World War II*, Jefferson North Carolina: McFarland & Company, Inc., Publishers, 1985, p. 153

Hatamiya, Leslie T., *Righting a Wrong, Japanese Americans and the Passage of the Civil Liberties Act of 1988*, Stanford, California: Stanford University Press, 1993

Hickman, Tom, *What did you do in the War, Auntie?*, London: 1995, BBC Books, p. 32, p. 37

Hitler, Adolf, *Mein Kampf*, translated by Ralph Manhcim, Boston: Houghton Mifflin Company, 1971, Volume I, Chapter II, Chapter XI, Nation and Race; Chapter XIV, "Eastern Orientation or Eastern Policy", p. 652; p. 654.

Hosoya, A., N. Ando, Y. Onuma, R. Minear, editors, *The Tokyo War Crimes Trial, An International Symposium*, Kodansha Ltd., distributed through Harper & Row, Publishers, New York, 1986, pp. 15-27; p. 45; p. 194

Humphrey, George, *Wartime Eastbourne*, Beckett Features, 1989

Hunt, Ray C., and Bernard Norling, *Behind Japanese Lines, An American Guerrilla in the Philippines*, The University Press of Kentucky, 1986, p. 159; pp. 161-162; pp. 213-216

Keegan, John, *The Battle for History, Refighting World War II*, New York: Vintage Books, 1996

Kitchen, Martin, *Europe Between Wars*, London and New York: Longman, 1988, pp. 76-77

Koch, H. W, *The Hitler Youth, Origins and Development 1922-1945*, New York: Dorset Press, 1975

Kurzman, Dan, *Fatal Voyage, The Sinking of the USS Indianapolis*, New York: Pocket Books, a Division of Simon and Schuster, Inc., 1999

Le Journal de l'Ouest, *Les Années 40, du pain noir... à la renaissance, la vie quotidienne de 1940 à 1949*, Responsable de l'Edition, Daniel Yonnet, Rédacteur en chef, Pierre Berruer, p. 7

Le Monde Edition, *La Deuxième Guerre Mondiale 1939-1945*, Paris: 1994

MacGregor-Hastie, *The Day of the Lion, Fascism in Italy 1922-1945*, New York: Coward-McCann, Inc., 1963, p. 187, p. 191, pp. 209-210, p. 217, p. 223-, pp. 240-242

Manson, Jean, *De la résistance à la déportation/Le système concentrationnaire nazi*, édité pour, Oeuvres Sociales de l'U.N.A.D.I.F., Supplément au Numéro 336 du Journal "Le Déporté - Pour la Liberté", Imprimeries A. Humblot et Cie., Nancy, 1980

Maser, Werner, *Hitler's Letters and Notes*, translated from the German by Arnold Pomerans, New York: Harper & Row Publishers, 1974, Chapter Eight, "The Political Testament of 1945."

Mayer, Allan, *Gaston's War*, Novato, California: Presidio Press, 1988, p. 153

Morison, Eliot and Henry Steele Commager, *The Growth of the American Republic*, New York: Oxford University Press, 1942, pp. 494-495; p. 515

Moulin, Pierre, *U. S. Samurais in Bruyères, People of France and Japanese Americans: Incredible story*, 1988, p. 200. Book out of print, lent by Tom Masamori.

Nagata, Donna K. Nagata, *Legacy of Injustice*, New York and London: Plenum Press, 1993, p. 191

Nouchi, André, Agulhon, *La France de 1914 à 1940*, Paris: Collections Nathan-Université, 1974, Chapitre , pp. 53-71.

Parker, R. A. C., *Europe 1915-45*, New York: Delacorte Press, 1967, p.2, p. 7, p. 160.

Porche, Douglas, *The French Secret Service, From the Dreyfus Affair to the Gulf War*, New York: Farrar, Straus and Giroux, 1995

Riasanovsk, Nicholas, *A History of Russia*, New York, Oxford: 1993, p. 254, p. 263

Richardson, Horst Fuchs and Dennis Showalter, editors, *Sieg Heil! War Letters of Tank Gunner, Karl Fuchs, 1937-1941*, Hamden, Connecticut: Archon Books, 1987, pp. 68-69; p. 45

Sakowska, Ruta, *The Warsaw Ghetto, 1940-1945*, published privately in Warsaw, Poland, 1996.

Salonne, M. P. *Fends la Bise, Scènes du Maquis Breton*, France: Editions Bloud & Gay, 1945

Scholl, Inge, *La Rose Blanche*, traduit de l'allemand par Jacques Delpeyrou, Paris: Les Editions de Minuit, 1953

Schultz, Duane, *The Doolittle Raid*, New York: St. Martin's Press, 1988

Schumann, Willy, *Being Present, Growing Up in Hitler's Germany*, Kent, Ohio: Kent State University Press, 1991

Schweitzer, Pam, Lorraine Hilton, Jane Moss, editors., *What Did You Do In The War, Mum?*, England: Age Exchange Theatre Trust, 1985.

Servagnat, Capitaine, Commandant des F.F.I. des l'arrondissement d'Epernay, *La Résistance et les Forces Françaises de l'Intérieur dans l'Arrondissement d'Epernay*, Presses de l'Imprimerie de Montligeon, La Chapelle-Montligeon (Orne), 20 September, 1946

Sibley, Milford Q., and Philip E. Jacob, *Conscription of Conscience: The American State and the Conscientious Objector, 1940-1947*, Ithaca, New York: Cornell University Press, 1952, pp. 10-11; p. 50, and pp. 61-62

Steinhoff, Johannes, Peter Pechel, Dennis Showalter, *Voices from the Third Reich, An Oral History*, Washington, D.C.: Regnery Gateway, distributed to the trade by Kampmann, 1989, xxxiii-xxxiv, pp. 172-173.

Stevenson, John, *British Society 1914-1945*, London: Allen Lane, 1984, p. 266

Taylor, Telford, *The Anatomy of the Nuremberg Trials, A Personal Memoir*, New York: Alfred A. Knopf, 1992, Chapter 22, "Nuremberg in History", pp. 341-369.

Tee, Tan Chong, *Force 136*, Singapore: Asiapac Books, 1995

tenBroek, Jacobus, Edward N. Barnhart, Floyd W. Matson, *Prejudice, War and the Constitution, Japanese American Evacuation and Resettlement*, Berkely and Los Angeles: University of California Press, 1954

Verlag, Econ, *Nuremberg, A Nation on Trial*, translated from the German by Richard Barry, New York: Charles Scribner's Sons, 1979, p. 279

Werth, Alexander, *Russia at War 1941-1945*, New York: E. P. Dutton & Co., Inc., 1964

World Book Encyclopedia, 1996, Vol. 8, p. 340

Wyman, David S., editor, *America and the Holocaust*, New York and London: Garland Publishing Co., 1990, Volume I, Document 11, p. 19

Wyman, David S., Ed., Charles H. Rosenzveig, Project Director, *The World Reacts to the Holocaust*, Baltimore: Johns Hopkins University Press, 1996, pp. 703-705.

4th Special Battalion, publication, November 7, 1944, prepared under the direction of Lieutenant Commander M. C. Juge; and edited by Chief Yeoman, D. C. Boudreau and G. G. Pannebaker, SK1c, funded by the 4th Special C. B. Welfare Fund.

Periodicals

Glines, C. V., "An American Hero," *Air Force Magazine*, November 1993

Friedrich, Otto, "Pearl Harbor, Day of Infamy," *Time Magazine*, 50th Anniversary Special, 2 December 1991, p. 33.

Leatherneck Magazine of the Marines, October 1995, pp. 31-32

Moussié, Pierre and Suzanne Moussié, *Histoires Paralleles, 1939-1944*, No. 102bis de la revue Archistra, 1992, pp. 17-18; pp. 22-26; p. 108. Citations with permission from Pierre Moussié

Watson, Bruce, "Jaysho, moasi, dibeh, ayeshi, hasclishnih, beshlo, shush, gini", *The Smithsonian*, V. 24, August 1993, p. 34

Archives

A video interview telling about Nicholas Winton's work is found in the United States Holocaust Memorial Museum Archives, Record Group 50, Oral History, United States Holocaust Memorial Museum collection. Nicholas Winton, RG50.393*.0002)

All references to other archival material from the United States Holocaust Museum collection are cited as requested.

References to extracts from oral history recordings from the Imperial War Museum Sound Archive, London are cited in the End Notes as requested by the Imperial War Museum.

The transcribed manuscripts from the Manuscript Division of the J. Willard Marriott Library, University of Utah, Salt Lake City are cited as requested, either from the Navajo Code Talkers (Ms 504) or the Doris Duke interviews (Ms 417).

Grand County Historical Association collection of letters from former German POWs, written to Morris Long, cited with their permission.

From the archives of Auguste Le Carpentier, copies of tracts, translated by the author and cited with Le Carpentier's permission.

Brochures and Pamphlets

68th Medical Groups by Colonel Francis P. Kintz, M.C. and Major John Edgar, M.S.C., Res. Pamphlet reprinted from *The Military Surgeon*, Vol. 106, Nos. 1, 2, 3, January, February, March, 1950

Great Lakes Bulletin (Vol. XIX No.12)

Bible Meditation League (now Bible Literature International),"From Pearl Harbor to Calvary," 1950

Drea, Edward J., "Recognizing the Liberators, U.S. Army Divisions Enter the

Concentration Camps," Army History, The Professional Bulletin of Army History, Washington, D.C., Fall 1992

Karnik, Zdenek, *Lidice*, translated by Frido Bunzi, published in 1982 by the State Centre for the Preservation of Historical Relics and Protection of Nature, district of Central Bohemia.

Magrid, Ken, *Women of Courage*, aired on Channel Six, Denver, 27 May 1994, *Women of Courage, The Women Airforce Service Pilots of World War II*, 1993, cited with Magrid's permission.

Piper, Franciszek, *Auschwitz, How Many Perished, Jews, Poles, Gypsies*...Krakow, 1994

Pokoyny, Jiri, *The Czech Lands 1918-1994*, translated from the Czech by Anna Bryson, brochure published by Prah-Martin Vopenka, 1994

Auschwitz-Birkenau Guide Book, State Museum, Oswiecim, 1996

Panorama Denmark, From Occupied to Ally: Danish Resistance Movement 1940-45, brochure published by Frihedsmuseets Venners Forlagsfond, 1992

October 1943, The Rescue of the Danish Jews from Annihilation, text, Therkel Straede, translator, Teresa Mesquit, Royal Danish Ministry of Foreign Affairs, Denmark, 1993

Brochures and pamphlets collected by author in Normandy, June 1995

Information from author's tour of Musée des troupes aéroportées, Sainte-Mère-Eglise, 7 June 1995; Auschwitz-Bierkenau State Museum, October 1996; Bletchley Park, 7 May, 1995; Silosa Island, Singapore, April 1995.

Unpublished Memoirs

Schwab, Fred E., "Timetable, Persecution of Jews in Germany, Laws, Ordinances, and Action," 1992

Bedel, Louis, diary, "Guerre et Captivité"

Chapman, Christian Addison, "D-Day - A Memoir"

Cherry, Robert C., "Love Affairs, The Story of a Happy Life as Lived by Robert C. Cherry"

Childs, Everett L., "Year to Remember," 1989

Fisher, James B., "A Look Back," manuscript prepared by Mrs. Jean Hahn, oral historian, from tapes and interviews made during July and August 1990.

Gockel, Franz, "Normandie," translated from the German by Derek S. Zumbro, May 1994

Lopez, Carmel, diary, "Motorless Morons," copy given to author by his son, Christopher Lopez

Poirier, Emmanuel, "Témoignage de M. Emmanuel Poirier"

Adrienne (Farrell) Jackson and Morag (Maclennan) Beattie, editors, "Hut 4 Naval Section, Bletchley Park 1941-1945," London, 1995

Leclerc, Marcel, "Souvenirs de ma Déportation en Allemagne, 1943-1945,"

Paris, Raymond, January 1989

Letters

Brown, Brian, to author, 22 January 1995, Chesham, Bucks, England.

de Shazer, Jacob, to author, 26 February 1996, Salem, Oregon.

E. P., letter to "Dear Friend," sent to author by Lois G. Melvoin

Furmanczyk, Wieslaw, to author, 10 December 1996 and 11 May 1997, Warsaw.

Hartmer, Ludger, to author, 12 September 1997, Hamm, Germany

Harvey, Frank, to author, 15 March 1995 and 18 January 1996, Castlegar, British Columbia.

Knowles, Valerie Fiddelaar, to author, 16 August 1995, Clwyd, North Wales.

Mother, letter to "Dear Son", early 1941, found and given to author.

Pickard, Dewey, to author, 5 April 1996; 18 May 1996, Lakeland, Tennesee

Rendall, Bill, to author, 7 September 1996, Kinderhook, New York

Rouleau, Joseph G., to author, from Englewood, Colorado

Servagnat, Pierre, to Bill Rendall, 5 janvier, 23 février, 23 mars, 14 avril, 1992, copies to author

Sigwalt, Suzanne (Suzel), to "Marian," Strasbourg, 1947; letter giving author permission to quote extracts, 5 March, 1995, Romanswiller, Alsace.

Young, John L., to author, 27 November 1994, Bolton, Ontario, Canada

Interviews

All interviews are by the author and tape recorded unless otherwise noted.

Jesse Arbor, telephone interview, Chicago, 18 March 1997

Betty and Ken Bangs, 19 July 1994

Vincent Beach, Boulder, 8 September 1994

Guy Bedel, Quimper, France, 22 July 1996

Louis Bedel, Toulouse, France, 19-21 January 1995

Gwenn Aël Bolloré, Paris, 17 October 1995

William Bower, Boulder, 29 July 1994

Bob Bradfield, Boulder, 7 October 1996

Brennen, George F., videocassette (raw footage of the ceremonies 11-11-89 at the former

A Time to Speak

Laurinburg Maxton Air Base in honor of WWII glider pilots and George F. Brennan and Thornton Schofield, Market Garden experiences, 1944), lent by Dave Trexler. Author's transcription reviewed by George Brennan, October 1996.

Yves Briand, Dinan, France, 22 January 1995

Mary C., Seaford, England, 30 April 1995

Christian Chapman, Washington D. C., 15 January 1995

Robert Cherry, Denver, telephone interview, 7 October 1996

Everett Childs, Boulder, 31 August 1994

Ruth Correll, Boulder, 9 September 1994

Jean Cotten, Quimper, France, 22 October 1996

Charles Coulombel, Dinan, 26 September 1995

Leeta Crook, Fort Collins, Colorado, 8 March 1996

Jean-Pierre Crouzeau, Village l'Aunerie, Le Lorey, 12 October 1995

Louis Dalibot, Dinan, 26 September 1995

René de Chambrun, Paris, 5 October 1994

Dolores Divine, Boulder, 20 March 1996

Maria Domas, telephone interview, Huntington Beach, California, 29 April 1997

Mme Marguerite Dravalen, "Le Guermeur", Ploemeur, 25 July 1996

Margaret Duncan, Boulder, 29 August 1994

Roger Dutertre, Hudimesnil, France, 23 June, 1994

Jack Elford, Boulder, 15 July 1994

Jim and Allison Fisher, Boulder, 5 September 1995

Thelma Foster, Boulder, 13 July 1994

Wieslaw Furmanczyk, Warsaw, 31 October 1996

Elfriede Gamow, Boulder, 2 March 1995

Franz Gockel, Hamm-Rhynern, Germany, 17 July 1997

Melvin Goldstein, telephone interview, Stamford, Connecticut, 19 February 1997

Sally Griffin, 14 July 1994, Boulder

Antide Guesner, 22 January 1995, Dinan

Joyce H., Seaford, England, 30 April, 1995

Ludger Hartmer, Hamm-Rhynern, Germany, 17 July 1997

Frank Harvey, interview taped for his sister and copy sent to author, February 1995, Castlegar, British Columbia

James H. Harvey III, Denver, 13 March 1996

David Hawkins, Boulder, 8 September 1997

Stanley Hendrickson, Boulder, 20 April 1996

Marie-Madeleine Herbelin, Boulogne-Billancourt, France, 16 June 1994

Bill Herron, Boulder, 24 August 1994

Sue Hirokama, Denver, 26 June 1997

Bine Hirsch, Boulder, 15 February 1995

Ivan L. Hobson, telephone interview, Salt Lake City, 6 March 1996

Don Inselman, Commerce City, CO., 13 November 1995

Adolphe Jaede, Ile de Groix, France, 17 July 1995

Bernice Janssen, 6 January 1995, Milwaukee

Joe, Japanese soldier, Denver, 26 June 1997, interview translated by Midori Johnson

Midori Johnson, Castle Rock, Colorado, 11 September 1995

Kathryn Kawakami, Denver, 26 June 1997

Georges Kieffer, Dinan, France, 22 January 1995

Marian Kreith, Boulder, 27 March 1995.

Thérèse Lamotte, Léhon, France, 27 September 1995

Marie and Robert LeBerre, Quimper, France, 22 October 1994

Jean LeBranchu, Dinan, September 1995

Mme Lebranchu, Dinan, 26 September 1995

Auguste Le Carpentier, Quettreville-sur-Siene, France, 21 June, 1994

Marcel Lherbette, Dinan, France, January 23 1995

Yvonne Lenoir, Boulogne-Billancourt, France, 16 June 1994

Bob Levine, telephone interview, Princeton, New Jersey, 4 March 1997

Elizabeth Lipstreu, Boulder, 21 November 1994

Don Look, Boulder, 19 July 1994

Morris Long, Denver, 14 September 1994

John Macinko, Boulder, 21 September 1994

Aïde Mahé, Dinan, France, 27 September 1995

Gilles Mahé, Dinan, France, 22 January, 1995

Joe Malcolm, Boulder, 31 August 1994

Dorothy Martin, Boulder, 11 May, 1994

Tom Masamori, Denver, 13 February 1996

Friede Metzger, Denver, 15 April 1997

Bernice Mittag, 6 January 1995, Milwaukee

Albert and Geneviève Moline, Levallois-Perret, France, 28 October 1994

Mary Mulhollen, Milwaukee, 6 January 1995

Paul Murphy, Broomfield, Colorado, 25 October 1995

Nabuka, Denver, 26 June 1997, interview translated by Midori Johnson

Fred Olivi, Chicago, 11 November 1994

Gil Pannebaker, Boulder, 9 October 1996

Raymond Paris, Sainte-Mère-Eglise, 12 October 1994,

Polly Parish, Boulder, 19 July 1994

Marie Perréal, Paris, 26 October, 1994

Max Peters, Boulder, 19 September 1994

Turza Pflug, Colorado Springs, 20 October 1995

Walter Plywaski, Boulder, 24 September 1997

Mr. and Mrs. Paul Postivit, Boulder, 1 December 1994

A Time to Speak

Charlie Poston, Boulder, 13 December 1994

Gil Reimers, Boulder, 16 September 1994

Fraser Richards, Boulder, 22 April 1996

Marianne Schwab, nee Rothschild, June 21, 1992. Interviewer, Angilika Rieber with Bruni Hoffmann, videotape, Gisa Hillesheimer, Germany, translation, Marianne Schwab

Gerd Schiotz, Copenhagen, 19-21 September 1995

John Sedillo, Denver, 31 January 1996

Pierre Servagnat, Epernay, France, 18 April 1995

Colonel Clifford G. Simenson, Boulder, 14 June 1995

Sister Damian Mary Simmons, 25 August 1994, Denver

Sister Jeanne d'Arc, Denver, 25 August 1944

Oddvar Solstad, telephone interview, 23 March 1999, Marblehead, Massachusetts

Mr. and Mrs. Zesa Starr, Denver, 22 June 1995

Howard Teague, Lafayette, Colorado, 7 September 1995

Rigomar Thurmer, Boulder, 11 July 1995

Dave Trexler, Boulder, 22 July 1994

Roberta Trexler, Boulder, 21 November 1994

Gaston Vandermeersche, Milwaukee, 5 January 1995

Otto Verdoner, Boulder, 20 May 1997

Mal Walker, Estes Park, Colorado, 20 September 1996

Martha and George Watts, Milwaukee, 6 January 1995

Katherine Welch, Boulder, 22 September 1994

"Dutch" Westerberg, Boulder, 18 May 1994

Christa Willen-Henrichsen, Nederland, Colorado, April 1997

Ruth Woldike, Copenhagen, 21 September, 1995

Roland and Jewell Wolcott, Boulder, 30 August 1994

Dorothy Young, Grand Lake, Colorado, 10 September 1996

Interviews with those who wish to remain anonymous

Mrs. A. H., Prague, 25 October 1996

B. L., Boulder, 10 June 1998

E. B. former YWCA staff worker, Boulder, 29 August 1994

E. B. former UNRA staff worker, Boulder, 29 August 1994

F. L., Paris, 12 April 1995

M. D., Boulder, 10 March, 1995

Hungarian woman, Boulder, 22 March, 1995

Navy Pilot, Boulder, 22 May 1997

Former Muscovite woman, Boulder, 21 April 1997

Two Russian physicians, Boulder, 7 May 1997

A Time to Speak

Seaford Ladies, (A.H., J.P., B.L., A.P., I.J.), Seaford, England, 28 April 1995;

Woman from Dresden, Colorado Springs, (Interview, transcription of notes taken, 19 October 1995)

Responses to a letter to John Lehndorf, the Food Editor of the Boulder, Colorado *Daily Camera* (30 April 1997) asking for wartime recipes: Edna Benson, Betty Bradfield, Marilyn Decker, Dorothy, Julia Frey, Gennie Gablehouse, Rose Miller, Opal Pastore, Marjorie Phillips, Bernadette Reed.

(From the original back cover flap)

    Jeanne Manning was born in Kansas City, Kansas in 1926, but has spent most of her life in Colorado. She graduated from Colorado Springs High School in 1943 and from Colorado College in 1946.

    She received the M.S.J. in 1948 from the Medill School of Journalism, Northwestern University and pursued a career in advertising. Later she received the M.A. in French from the University of Colorado in 1968 and a PhD in French from Yale University in 1981. She taught college French until she retired in 1992, then taught a pilot course in French on the Internet for the Annenberg/CPB Project in Washington, D.C. until 1997.

    Currently, she is the chairperson of the Graduate School Advisory Council of the University of Colorado at Boulder and a member of the Board of Stewards of the Episcopal Ministries to the University of Colorado, Boulder.

    She married Ted Manning in Colorado Springs in 1950; they live in Boulder and have three children and eight grandchildren.